D0142272

Psychological Foundations of Sport

Edited by

John M. Silva III

The University of North Carolina at Chapel Hill

Diane E. Stevens

Brock University

Allyn and Bacon

Boston • London • Toronto • Sydney • Tokyo • Singapore

Vice President, Editor in Chief: Paul A. Smith
Series Editorial Assistant: Annemarie Kennedy
Marketing Managers: Mandee Eckersley
Production Editor: Annette Pagliaro
Editorial Production Service: Innovation Publication Services
Composition Buyer: Linda Cox
Manufacturing Buyer: Suzanne Lareau
Cover Administrator: Linda Knowles
Electronic Composition: Omegatype Typography, Inc.

Copyright © 2002 by Allyn & Bacon
A Pearson Education Company
75 Arlington St.
Boston, MA 02116

Internet: www.ablongman.com

All rights reserved. No part of the material protected by this copyright notice may be reproduced or utilized in any form or by any means, electronic or mechanical, including photocopying, recording, or by any information storage and retrieval system, without written permission from the copyright owner.

Library of Congress Cataloging-in-Publication Data

Psychological foundations of sport / edited by John M. Silva, Diane E. Stevens.
    p. cm.
  Includes bibliographical references and index.
  ISBN 0-205-33144-0
    1. Sports—Psychological aspects.   I. Silva, John M.   II. Stevens, Diane E.
GV706.4 .P673   2002
796'.01–dc21

                               00-052200

Printed in the United States of America

10 9 8 7 6 5 4 3 2 1   05 04 03 02 01

All my work is dedicated to my parents, Jennie and John Silva, whom I can never thank enough for providing me with the greatest family environment full of love, guidance, and support. I also dedicate this text to the Silva and Maki families, especially my father-in-law Vilho Maki, who passed away recently, and to Dr. Burris Husman and Dr. Thomas Sheehan for the intellectual stimulation and the intangibles. Finally, I dedicate this text to all the graduate and undergraduate students whom I have taught and who in some way found that sport psychology enhanced their life in a positive way. And of course Taylor, Tally, and Buddie.

JMS

To my parents, Alex and Shirley Mack: your love and support has allowed me to fly.

DS

Contents

Preface

I have been down this road before. What do you say about your own text? And who really reads the preface anyway? Just kidding.

Everybody talks about the importance of "psychological factors in performance," but exactly what does that mean? Coaches always say, "Concentrate," or "You are making too many mental mistakes." How do athletes develop the ability to concentrate in the heat of competition or when things are going poorly and their game is breaking down? What specific psychological factors influence performance? Can sport psychology really help me perform better or understand why so many youths drop out of sports? Can I use this information to help me in my sport, with my schoolwork, or if someday I coach or have a child who participates in sports?

What do you want out of a sport psychology textbook? The answer depends on who the reader is, of course. If you are an undergraduate student, you want answers to questions. Why do undergraduates enroll in a sport psychology course? Many are curious and have questions based on their experiences, because just about everybody has participated in or played sports at some time during their youth or adolescence. An undergraduate student wants interesting, clearly written, cohesive information that is not laborious to wade through. You want to see the relevance of the research, the theories, and the applications to your own life, whether in sports or in your personal or academic life. You want to read a chapter and be stimulated, not bored. You want to put the book down and say, "You know, that makes sense" or "I've done that in competition—wow, that's me!" You really want to learn something and not have to struggle to remember it because the writing is so layered with academic jargon or intellectual exercises that impress only the author. You want it to be an interesting, challenging, and thought-provoking book. You want a text that covers the material taught in the class and has references that you can use not only in this course but also in papers you may have to write in other classes. You want "a keeper." Contrary to popular belief, even undergraduate students want to build a library.

This text is targeted primarily toward the undergraduate student enrolled in a sport psychology course. The authors have tried to write to stimulate and challenge the student, and to provide a comprehensive analysis of sport psychology from theory to research to practice. The text is a blend of sound information from both basic and applied sources, from sport psychology and psychology. The authors all teach sport psychology and are experts in the areas in which they have contributed. They understand what the undergraduate student wants from a chapter, and they have delivered. We think you will get answers to many of your questions, and we hope the readings generate many more questions that one day you may answer yourself.

If you are a graduate student or fellow professional, you will find this text attractive simply by viewing the lineup of contributors in the table of contents. You will recognize the names as regular participants and contributors to the field of sport psychology. This text combines the work of well-established and -respected sport psychologists along with that of "rising stars" and young professionals just starting to make their mark in the sport psychology literature. This blend of the old and the new provides the perspective and broad view needed in a text and combines that perspective with the fresh insights and up-to-date literature that distinguish this book from some of the cookie-cutter texts that have flooded the market recently. Graduate students and fellow professionals will enjoy not only the stimulating reading offered in the chapters but also the comprehensive references available to support their personal research as well as supplemental reading recommendations. For the graduate student and professional, this text will be an indispensable reference source and will take an easily identifiable spot on the bookshelf. We hope that it will be the type of text that both teachers and students will enjoy using.

For many of us in the field of sport psychology, that first undergraduate course in sport psychology turned on the light and provided the inspiration for us to learn more about sport psychology and about how to become a sport psychologist. We hope this text inspires another generation of sport psychologists who are as excited as we are about advancing the field and about giving themselves full-time to the best job in the world—teaching, researching, and practicing sport psychology.

Acknowledgments

I gratefully acknowledge Diane Stevens for agreeing to co-edit this text with me and for being a good friend and colleague before, during, and after this project. The contributors to this text deserve a special thank-you—their efforts have produced a comprehensive and up-to-date view of the field that is without rival. I have enjoyed getting to know old friends better and establishing new friendships through this combined effort.

I thank Mark Funkhouser, who interested me in writing my first sport psychology text and who put the bug in me to write this one. Joe Burns, thanks for your support and your behind-the-scenes work on my behalf. Morten Andersen, thanks for the great foreword and for all the applications of sport psychology you have provided firsthand throughout the years. Kelly McMahon, many thanks for the tremendous amount of help you gave me on this project.

All students play a special role in my life—like an extended family of sorts. However, I would be remiss if I did not mention and acknowledge the significant role that David Conroy, Heather Deaner, Erik Dunlap, Elizabeth Freeland, Jon Metzler, and Mike Navarre played in my personal and professional life while I was working on this text. I am grateful for all you have done to inspire me and support me, for making it easy for me to smile and laugh, for giving me many memories, and for helping me to always keep the big picture in mind, through the good times and the bad, as your former mentor and as your friend—thank you.

In addition, Diane Stevens and I would like to thank the following reviewers of the text whose comments contributed to the book's development: John Caruso, University of

Massachusetts, Dartmouth; David Furst, San Jose State University; Patricia Laguna, California State University, Fullerton; and Ben Ogles, Ohio University.

John M. Silva III
Chapel Hill, North Carolina

A project this size cannot be undertaken alone. I gratefully acknowledge the chapter authors, who contributed their insights, thoughts, and imagination to this book. The strength of this endeavor lies with you. I also thank my mentors, Albert Carron, Craig Hall, and John Partington, whose unending support and willingness to share their experiences are invaluable to me. Special thanks to Jonathan Metzler for going above and beyond...yet again, and to my husband, Scott: many thanks for your unwavering support of this project, despite many late nights.

I express my sincere thanks to my co-editor John Silva for so selflessly allowing me the opportunity to take part in this project. His professional dedication and commitment to friendship will remain with me forever.

Diane E. Stevens

Foreword

One last deep breath on the sideline of the Minneopolis Metrodome. Then the usual, deliberate trot to midfield. As I face the goalposts far away at the end of the field, like a good friend they are there waiting for me, as always patient, bright, and filled with promise of a good time, no matter what. Of course, I scarcely notice. I have work to do. Some unfinished business to attend to.

I know that it is loud here. Not so much because I hear it, but because the ground is shaking. The stadium is shaking. The noise 70,000 screaming fans can produce is amazing.

I come closer…to destiny…to utopia…to a professional highlight. Actually, I come closer to the line of scrimmage and Dan Stryzinski, who is ready, giving me the spot. I am behind it now. Walking toward an index finger pointed at the inside front corner of the left hash on the 28-yard line in overtime of the 1998 NFC Championship game. I feel good. Another deep breath. A verbal cue, three steps back. I look up and have my target. Another breath, two steps to the right. Last deep breath. I narrow my focus. I have the spot. I hold it. Still. On automatic. The moment of truth. One moment of many. But this one is special. This one took 17 years to show up. I feel warm and comfortable, and I have this incredible sense of knowing. The snap from Adam Schreiber hits Dan's hands perfectly. Dan lowers the ball into position. No need to turn the laces. They are already facing my yellow friends 38 yards away. I glide to the ball smoothly, effortlessly. I see it clearly. The ball looks huge. As my left leg makes contact with the ball, I already know. It is good. As the ball splits the uprights, I am already running toward midfield where I am met by many happy, ecstatic teammates. Underneath a pile of 300-pound linemen is not a good place to be, so I decide to keep running. As I start to look around, I notice something very strange. Silence in the Metrodome. Deafening silence.

My father is a retired child psychologist. When my twin brother, Jakob, and I were much younger, we participated in a study done in Copenhagen, Denmark, on twins and their similarities, differences, and so on. I don't remember much of the study or the resulting conclusions from the experts. Since then, I have had very little experience with any type of psychology. Of course, as an athlete, I always heard about different players working with a "guy" and always wondered why they would need that. I figured that if they had made it to the professional level, they were already in good shape physically and mentally. Was I wrong!

I met John Silva in the late 1980s through Tommy Barnhardt, a teammate of mine with the New Orleans Saints. Tommy had worked with John for some time and suggested that I meet him. I am glad that I did. 1989 was not my best year kicking. I suppose by most standards it was O.K., but my standards were higher. I soon found out that my expectations were a little too unrealistic and somewhat self-destructive. Through methodical sessions of interviews, talks, and tests, John and I came up with a game plan that I follow to this day. It includes an honest look at where I was as an athlete and where I wanted to go.

There are many roads we can take in life, but without some idea of where we want to end up, it becomes very difficult to get there. To me it became very obvious quickly that I needed to drop some of my absolute goals and my perception that perfection was the only way. It is fun to strive for, but unrealistic to expect. Sport psychology has helped me set windows for goals and made me understand that goals should be specific, realistic, motivational, and never threatening. I also learned that it takes discipline to become mentally trained. It takes an investment of time and of will. To get to a point at which you are able to perform at the highest level possible in perceived pressure situations, you must have, in addition to your natural-born talents, an abundance of mental strength that you can draw on to accomplish your goals and perform freely. It is a fun journey down a path that sometimes is bumpy, but never boring.

I think what I have enjoyed the most about sport psychology has been the process of getting ready every year: the excitement and the anticipation of the upcoming season and the knowledge that I have a plan that works for me whether I miss a 26-yard field goal in the Superbowl or make a 38-yarder to win the NFC Championship game. I know that no matter what I choose to do in my life, great satisfaction comes from knowing that I am mentally strong and disciplined and that I am able to meet any situation with a sense of purpose and freedom. I trust my hopes, not my fears. The advantage in professional sports goes to the athletes who are willing to mentally train themselves with the same vigor and commitment that they have done physically. I hope that your journey will be as rewarding as mine and that you find your own special pot of gold at the end of your rainbow.

Morten Andersen
New Orleans Saints 1982–1995
Atlanta Falcons 1995–present
Eight-Time NFL Pro Bowl Player

Contributors

Brock University
    John Hay
    Diane E. Stevens

Lafayette College
    Luis Manzo

McGill University
    Gordon Bloom

Queen's University
    Jean Côté

Springfield College
    Allen Cornelius

University of Idaho
    Damon Burton
    Sarah Naylor

The University of North Carolina at Chapel Hill
    Barbara Bickford
    Diane E. Stevens
    Heather Deaner
    Jamie Robbins
    John M. Silva
    Jonathan Metzler
    Julie Partridge
    Stacey Rosenfeld

University of Saskatchewan
    Peter R. E. Crocker
    Thomas R. Graham
    Kent C. Kowalski
    Nanette P. Kowalski

University of Waterloo
    Steven R. Bray
    Kim D. Dorsch
    E. J. McGuire
    W. Neil Widmeyer

Western Illinois University
    Laura Finch

About the Editors

Dr. John M. Silva is a Professor of Sport Psychology in the Department of Exercise and Sport Science at the University of North Carolina at Chapel Hill. He received his Ph.D. from the University of Maryland and his MS and BS from The University of Connecticut. Dr. Silva is the founding president of the Association for the Advancement of Applied Sport Psychology (AAASP), the largest scholarly sport psychology association in the world, with an international membership of more than 1000 sport psychologists. He served as the inaugural editor of the *Journal of Applied Sport Psychology,* the first nonproprietary sport psychology journal in the United States.

Dr. Silva has spoken and conducted workshops regionally, nationally, and internationally on various sport psychology topics and has presented invited addresses in Denmark, Norway, Sweden, Greece, Spain, Germany, the Soviet Union, South Korea, Japan, and the United States. In 1991, he was awarded the first Distinguished Graduate Alumni Award from the College of Health and Human Performance at the University of Maryland. Dr. Silva has served as a sport psychology consultant for athletes and teams for more than twenty years. He has provided onsite services to athletes at national, international, and world competitions and has served on the Sports Medicine Committee for the United States Team Handball Federation since 1987. From 1995 to 1999, he chaired the federation's Sport Science and Technology Committee, which oversees sport science service provision for their national and Olympic teams.

Dr. Silva's research interests include psychometrics in sport, performance enhancement, cognitive intervention, psychology of the elite athlete, and training stress. He is a fellow in AAASP, a certified AAASP consultant, a member of the USOC Sport Psychology Registry, a Research Consortium Fellow, and a member of the American Psychological Association.

As a participant, Dr. Silva has run five marathons and played on the Carolina Team Handball Club that won a Bronze Medal at the National Championships in 1991. He has coached several Carolina players selected to the U.S. National Team and has coached the Women's South Team in the 1993 Olympic Festival as well as the Men's South Team, which won the Gold Medal in the 1995 Olympic Festival. He also coached two Carolina alumni who were selected to compete for the United States in Team Handball in the 1996 Olympic Games.

Diane E. Stevens, Ph.D., is an assistant professor of sport psychology at Brock University. She completed her doctoral degree in kinesiology in 1996 at the University of Western Ontario. On graduation, Dr. Stevens accepted a position at the University of North Carolina, which she held until 1999. Her current research interests include group dynamics/team building and the self-presentational implications of sport participation. A former competitive athlete, her current recreational interests include tennis and other outdoor activities.

1

The Evolution of Sport Psychology

John M. Silva III

University of North Carolina at Chapel Hill

- Sport psychology is both a science and a profession. Sport psychology research continues to be produced, and the practice or application of sport psychology principles has increased dramatically over the past twenty-five years in North America.
- Sport psychology originated in the former Soviet Union. The Soviet system of integrating elite and Olympic sport teams with highly trained sport scientists provided a science-practice model that was very successful for more than three decades.
- Since the early 1900s, sport psychology has developed academically and professionally worldwide. Sport psychology is now taught and practiced on every continent of the world.
- The United States is a leader in sport psychology research and technology but has lagged behind other countries in addressing professional and service provision issues. This has resulted in ethical dilemmas that relate to professional training, use of title, and the right to practice and apply sport psychology with athletes.
- Sport psychology currently is at a critical juncture in the United States because the resolution of professional issues, accreditation of graduate programs, and the marketing of certified consultants will influence the effectiveness and persuasiveness of the field for at least the next decade.

Sport Psychology Is a Dynamic and Emerging Field

Sport psychology has many different connotations and definitions. The definition of *sport psychology* may vary depending on many factors, such as to whom you are speaking, what type of training that person received, and even in what part of the world the individual was

The role of sport psychology in optimizing elite athlete performance continues to evolve.

educated. One unmistakable aspect of sport psychology is the rich variety of perspectives that have influenced its evolution. These perspectives include motor learning, psychology, psychophysiology, and counseling. These diverse influences add a complexity and context to sport psychology that make the field attractive to many individuals. Sport psychology is focused on using knowledge and theory from these perspectives in an attempt to understand, explain, and predict behavior in the social context of sport and exercise. This is a challenge that should not be underestimated. Sport is a unique institutionalized social setting that is unlike most other social settings. Sport is a subculture, with each sport generating its own system of norms, rules, language, value systems, racial and gender issues, and organizational hierarchy. As scientists have become more aware of the uniqueness of sport and the challenges sport places on those who become socialized in and through this complex social setting, the study of sport psychology has become more specialized and formalized. Sport psychology is a dynamic field of study that is constantly evolving as both a discipline and a profession. This chapter examines this evolution from the past to the present and projects into the future of a field that has unlimited potential to provide research and applied services to sport participants and individuals engaged in exercise.

Sport Psychology: A Global Sketch

Before examining the evolution of sport psychology in North America, let's take a brief look at sport psychology around the world. Because sport psychology initially developed in the Soviet Union, this global sketch provides a balance to our perspective on sport psychology and demonstrates the international interest in research and the application of sport psychology principles.

I recently asked students in an undergraduate sport psychology class, "Where do you think sport psychology, as we know it today, originated?" This is always a risky, open-ended question to ask creative undergraduates. The responses always vary, and on this day one student replied, "With the Greeks, in ancient times." I am sure athletes have used sport psychology principles throughout the ages, and the Greek ethic of "strong body, strong mind" is certainly a philosophy both built on and ignored through the centuries. It is somewhat surprising, however, that the systematic, scientific study of psychological principles applied to sport and athletic performance was generally ignored until the early 1900s. Sport was considered more of a spectacle or a recreative pastime and generally not deemed worthy of the serious attention of scientists. A broad historical perspective easily demonstrates that sport has experienced periods of great interest and periods during which it was virtually banned from public display. It was only after industry and technology began to ease the hardships of everyday life that sport began its rise toward institutionalization, international popularity, and global participation. With the specter of sport taking on global connotations, including competitions between countries, hemispheres, the modern Olympics, and world competitions, it was inevitable that science would enter the quest toward achieving competitive excellence.

Origins of Sport Psychology: The Soviet Union

One of the first countries documented as a leader in the formalized study of sport psychology was the Soviet Union. As this country grew into a world power, the relation among government, military, and sport grew into close alignment. In 1917, Lenin signed a decree for the establishment of regular physical activity and training in the school system. Shortly after, in April 1918, he established an organization known as "Vsevobuch" to safeguard the gains made by the Revolution. This organization trained individuals in several military disciplines and in physical training and education (Shteinbakh, 1987). The Soviets were very assertive in their search for excellence in government, in the military, and in sport. In the area of sport psychology, departments were established for the systematic study of sport from a scientific perspective in the Institutes for the Study of Sport and Physical Culture in St. Petersburg (Leningrad) in October 1919, and shortly thereafter in Moscow. The Soviet perspective, or "system," was unique and became a topic of great interest to the sporting world for several generations as Soviet sport gradually developed world recognition. The development of the Soviet system was interrupted by the two world wars, but the commitment of the Soviets to sport psychology as a central element in the understanding and development of elite performance became a model that was to be emulated, questioned, and even condemned. There is, however, little question that the advancement of sport psychology was a major factor in the rise of the Soviet Union in world competition.

How did the Soviets bring sport psychology into their sport system, and what factors led to the important role sport psychology played in the rise of the Soviets as the dominant country in Olympic and world competition for more than twenty-five years? In 1989, a small group of North American sport psychologists were invited to tour and speak at the Institutes for Sport and Physical Culture in East Germany and the Soviet Union. As a member of that delegation, I was given an unusual opportunity to learn how the Soviets established sport psychology in their sport organizations and to explore the unique relationship established among sport psychology, science, and athletics in two countries that dominated Olympic sport for three decades.

Soviet Sport Psychology Integrated Sport Systems.   An important aspect of the Soviet approach is how sport psychology became instantly integrated into the *Soviet sport system.* Psychologists assigned to the Soviet sport psychology program were selected for their expertise in human performance. They were dedicated to the scientific study of sport psychology and were also interested in understanding the practical application of psychology to sport performance. From the outset the focus of the system was on understanding and developing psychological principles of performance that were then "tested" or applied with athletes competing in national training programs at the Institutes for Sport and Physical Culture. At the height of Soviet sport dominance (1960–1980), research was being conducted on sport- and sports medicine–related issues at more than 130 institutes. Over 87 million individuals participated in organized sport at over 7,000 sport and sport–technical clubs. In the early 1980s it was estimated that more than 350,000 individuals were employed full-time in physical culture as coaches, instructors, researchers, and other positions related to sports medicine (Shteinbakh, 1987). The Soviet government expended billions of rubles to develop and promote the Soviet sport system as another example of the success of the "Socialist Approach." To assist in the generation of the money needed for such a massive program, the government initiated a state lottery in 1970. "Sport-loto" and "Sprint" generated billions of dollars for the Soviet sport machine, whose production of success was considered as compulsory as industrial production. And what a machine it was. In the 1980 Olympics held in Moscow, the Soviet squad won eighty Gold, sixty-nine Silver, and forty-six Bronze Medals!

Info Box

The Soviet Union used the sport sciences very effectively in developing elite athlete talent. Sport psychology was a major part of the sport science delivery system. As a result of its success in international sports competition, the Soviet system drew the interest of sport psychologists worldwide.

The Soviet System.   What made the Soviet sport system so good? Although sport historians will debate that question for decades, there is no doubt that the sport sciences and the applied research conducted at the Institutes for Sport and Physical Culture played a major role not only in how the athletes in the Soviet program were trained but also in how future coaches were trained. Young children were constantly tested in their physical education programs for skill development and sport-related decision-making capacity. Those with extraordinary potential were often provided opportunities to continue their education at an Institute for Sport and Physical Culture. At the institutes, children received training in a wide array of motor and sport skills. This approach was believed to provide a solid motor-and-skill foundation for the sport in which the athlete would eventually specialize. These government-sponsored schools "took responsibility for sports promotion effectively free of charge" (Shteinbakh, 1987). The top athletes at these schools received expert training as well as an education tailored to individual programs of interests and considerate of interruptions resulting from training and competitions. These schools provided an optimal training environment that fully integrated sport sciences such as psychology, physiology, and biomechanics into the daily training regimen, and they nurtured the academic development of many top athletes in the advanced study of the sport sciences.

What a brilliant idea! Can you imagine being trained by a two-time Olympic medal winner who also has an advanced degree in sport psychology or exercise physiology? What athlete would not pay attention and be eager to learn from someone who has been there and experienced success and can share academic expertise? Victor Chukarin is one excellent example of this *closed-loop system.* Chukarin graduated as a Merited Master of Sport from the Lvov Institute of Physical Culture. He was the All-Around Gymnastics Champion of the USSR from 1949 to 1951, the 1954 World Champion, and the Olympic champion at the 1952 Helsinki and 1956 Melbourne games. Chukarin then became the head of the gymnastics department at the Lvov Institute after he retired from competition. The benefits of this system should be obvious—top athletes are selected at a young age, provided a high level of training and coaching at no expense, and are able to pursue their education in the sport sciences. After the athletes retire from international competition, they are reintegrated into the Soviet system as highly trained coaches, often with advanced degrees. Not only did this model provide expert coaching by highly trained former athletes, but also it produced coaches who had gone through a system that integrated the sport sciences (including sport psychology) into the training regimen. Thus, many Soviet coaches understood the potential beneficial role of sport psychology and did not fear the intervention of sport science "outsiders." Unfortunately, no such model currently exists in the United States, and many athletes receive no early training from coaches who have formal expertise. Athletes who do receive high-level training at a young age must pay a lot of money for this benefit.

Furthermore, because most coaches in the United States are not trained in a competitive or educational system that emphasizes and integrates the sport sciences, they are often reluctant to allow someone else to have this influential role with "their" athletes.

Current Developments in the Soviet Union.   From the 1950s through Gorbachev's fall in 1991, leaders of the Soviet Union attempted to create a sense of unity among the multitude of ethnic groups that made up the Soviet Union by promising economic growth, full employment, educational opportunities, and social welfare. The former Soviet Union comprised a multitude of ethnicities as a result of its extensive colonization. Ethnic groups included the Russians, Poles, Buriats, Yakuts, and Chechens, to name but a few. These ethnic groups brought with them their own national identities, cultural distinctions, religious beliefs, and traditional kinship ties (Gatrell, 1995). However, social, political, and cultural aspects of life in the former Soviet Union have changed drastically since the 1991 breakup of the country, and as a result the future of sport psychology in the region is in question (Melnikov, 1992). From 1985 through 1991, under the leadership of Mikhail Gorbachev, fundamental social, political, and economic changes took place under the policies of *perestroika* and *glasnost*. Perestroika, in theory, was to provide more for the Soviet people, and it embraced some of Western philosophies, such as fundamental human rights and checks on state power (Kullberg, 1994). Under glasnost, the easing of tensions, the Soviet people were urged to become more politically active and to express their views without fear of persecution (Reisinger, Miller, & Hesli, 1995). However, Gorbachev's plan of perestroika and glasnost proved to be too little and too late. The ethnic minorities were tired of being exploited by the Russian supremacy, and they formed their own allegiances and rebelled against the old Soviet regime through a coup attempt involving a three-day mass demonstration in 1989 (Gatrell, 1995). The ethnic uprisings and revolts against the old Soviet regime eventually resulted in the disbanding of the Soviet Union and the creation of the *Commonwealth of Independent States (CIS)*. The CIS comprises fifteen independent states: Armenia, Azerbaijan, Belarus, Estonia, Georgia, Kazakhstan, Kyrgyzstan, Latvia, Lithuania, Moldova, Russia, Tajikistan, Turkmenistan, Ukraine, and Usbekistan.

Although the problems associated with ethnic minority exploitation were alleviated, the new independent states have encountered a host of new and serious problems. Food, housing, and personal safety are serious concerns (Sloutsky & Searle-White, 1993). Most of the newly formed states are lacking in resources, and some of the smaller ones have been hit particularly hard. The establishment of effective governments has been a problem as well. Even in the Russian republic, the government is currently unstable, and its economy is wounded by a disorganized military, obsolete technology, a lack of raw materials, a decline in agriculture, inflation, few investments, corruption and crime, and economic disparity between the classes (Birman, 1996; Frank, 1992).

The Soviet breakup had widespread effects on the daily social functioning of former Soviet citizens, so it is no surprise that other areas of social life, such as sport, were affected as well. Before the breakup, Melnikov (1992) estimated that 200 sport psychologists were actively working in the Soviet Union. Soviet sport psychologists were widely accepted and were regarded as valuable assets in the performance enhancement of elite athletes. With the breakup, coaches, sport psychologists, technical support personnel, facilities, and other resources were disbanded, but not in a systematic or equitable manner. In addition, the athletes who once competed under the Soviet flag were scattered among the various states to which they decided to pledge allegiance.

Info Box

Political turmoil and the breakup of the Soviet Union resulted in a dramatic reduction of money and services provided to Soviet Olympic sports. The dynasty of Soviet sport ended in the 1980s, and now the independent state of Russia is slowly rebuilding the sport science system that was so effective in developing elite-level talent.

The status of sport psychology in the former Soviet Union today and the direction it will take in the future remain unclear. Current research in the republic of Russia is centered around theoretical and applied issues in high-performance sport and the psychological issues of group involvement in recreational sport activities (Kantor & Ryzonkin, 1993). Nevertheless, as evidenced in the 1998 Winter Olympic Games in Nagano, Japan, the republic of Russia has rebounded and reestablished itself as a world contender in winter sports. Whether other republics are interested in or able to invest the resources required to rebuild their sport science delivery programs and their Olympic sport programs remains to be determined. One important fact cannot be overlooked: the Soviet Union effectively integrated high-level sport with the systematic application of the sport sciences, including sport psychology. In most countries of the world, this achievement has not been replicated at the level of proficiency demonstrated by the Soviets.

European Countries Develop Sport Psychology

The practice of sport psychology in Europe was initially influenced by the *Sovietization* of top-level sport in Eastern European countries. The Soviet model emphasized the political institutionalization of sport and the sport sciences. Thus, countries such as East Germany, Bulgaria, and Czechoslovakia were exposed to the sport sciences in the early and mid-1900s. By the early 1970s, North American and European professionals with different ideologies started to interact and formally share information. Europe played a significant role in the formalization of sport psychology through the research institutes established in Eastern Europe and through the efforts of Italy's Ferrucio Antonelli. In April 1965, Antonelli organized the first International Congress in sport psychology in Rome. It was at this historic meeting, attended by more than 400 experts representing 27 countries, that the *International Society of Sport Psychology (ISSP)* was established (Antonelli, 1989). In 1969, European sport psychologists further promoted the communication process with the founding of the Federation Europeane de Psychologie des Sports et des Activities Corporelles *(FEPSAC—European Federation of Sport Psychology)* in Vittel, France. A brief overview of sport psychology's development in both Western and Eastern European countries demonstrates the broad perspective and appeal sport psychology enjoys in Europe today.

Western Europe

Italy.   According to the 1992 edition of the *World Sport Psychology Sourcebook,* Italy has the most sport psychologists (350) of any European country (Salmela, 1992). Italy has also served as the home to both the International Society of Sport Psychology (ISSP) and the *International Journal of Sport Psychology* (IJSP). Italy has played a prominent role in the formalization of sport psychology organizations, but it still lacks specific and extensive training in sport psychology graduate education. The medical profession in Italy established the first scientific support system for sport, and many medical doctors involved in sport psychology regarded it as a secondary interest (Salmela, 1992). No universities in Italy during the late 1950s and 1960s had a faculty in psychology, so it was inevitable that the first practitioners of sport psychology would be medical personnel (Antonelli, 1989).

Today, a second group of sport psychologists is emerging. This group comprises people with diverse backgrounds, including philosophy, sociology, psychology, and physical education. Perhaps the best preparation currently available in Italy is provided by the *Italian Association of Sport Psychology* (Associazionne Italiana di Psicologia dello Sport, AIPS). Founded in 1974, AIPS seeks to facilitate the acceptance and development of sport psychology in Italy (Antonelli, 1989). Membership in AIPS is not by itself a measure of competence. To qualify for certification, AIPS members must pass the examination for admission to the National List of Italian Sport Psychologists (Antonelli, 1989). Since 1982, AIPS has offered an intensive training program that includes 240 hours of theory and practice and a final practical exam before an expert panel (Salmela, 1992). Approximately forty to forty-five candidates have passed each year and earned the privilege of being called sport psychologists (Salmela, 1992). Finally, AIPS maintains a sport psychology registry similar to that maintained by the United States Olympic Committee (USOC).

Germany.   R. W. Schulte and H. Sippel are often cited as the fathers of sport psychology in Germany. During the 1920s, Schulte developed methods and equipment for testing physical and motor skills (e.g., reaction time, concentration, physical strength, speed of movements), and Sippel became the director of the first sport psychology laboratory in Germany. Sippel investigated the influence of physical exercise on mental performance and wrote several books on the psychology of the physical sciences (Geron, 1982). The growth of sport psychology stagnated as Germany entered World War II, and eventually Germany was torn apart by Eastern and Western European ideologies. However, the reunification of Germany has provided a unique climate for the growth of sport psychology. According to Hackfort (1993), sport psychologists in Germany have been unified in the *German Association for Sport Psychology (ASP)* since 1990. Of the 220 members attending the ASP's annual conference in 1991, approximately 75 percent were working at colleges and universities, and most were engaged in research (Hackfort, 1993). Although Germany continues to address social and cultural issues related to reunification, sport psychology in western Germany is more advanced than in many Western European countries. Academic initiatives have integrated sport psychology into both sport and mainstream psychology (Salmela, 1992). The early 1970s saw the creation of more than thirty sport science institutes across Germany, and the 1980s was a period of rapid growth in sport psychology. Germany offers an interesting combination of Eastern and Western European ideology, and it appears to have successfully orchestrated a diverse, yet unified approach to the advancement of sport psychology. In addressing the future of sport psychology in Europe, Paul Kunath (1995), a German sport psychologist and a leader in developing the ISSP, states that exercise and sport psychology should be a specific discipline with defined qualifications resulting in sport psychologists earning a specific license.

Info Box

Sport psychology is fairly well developed in Western Europe with university programs, active professional organizations, and scholarly and applied journal publications. Some countries have certification requirements for the practice of sport psychology. The expansion of research and applied services should continue in Western Europe.

Britain.   Sport and exercise science in Britain was fragmented from its earliest days, with separate organizations for biomechanics, physiology, psychology, and sports medicine. In 1985, however, the *British Association of Sport Science (BASS)* was formed as an amalgamation of the Biomechanics Study Group, the British Society of Sport Psychology, and the Society of Sport Sciences (Biddle, 1989). Within BASS is the Sport Psychology Section (SPS), a clearly defined subcommittee that also maintains representation in FEPSAC. As a separate entity, the National Coaching Foundation (NCF) oversees coach education and is the organization through which sport psychology is passed to coaches, teachers, and sport organizations (Biddle, 1989).

There is no formalized graduate training in sport psychology, but it is possible for students to receive specialized training in certain areas of sport psychology up to the doctoral level (Salmela, 1992). Reliant on personnel trained and educated in physical education, rather than in psychology, relatively few members of BASS qualify for full membership in the British Psychological Society (BSP). However, Biddle (1989) noted that interest in sport psychology continues to grow and that more formalized training will speed the legitimization of the field in Britain.

France.   In 1913, Frenchman Baron Pierre de Coubertin initiated one of sport psychology's earliest events—an international congress of psychology and physiology directed toward sport in Lausanne, Switzerland (Hackfort, 1993). You may recognize his name as the founder of the modern Olympic Games. Unfortunately, the study and practice of sport psychology in France lagged behind the insight of Pierre de Coubertin, and before the 1980s research in sport psychology was very modest. In the early 1980s, however, a research department and a sport psychology laboratory were developed at the Institut National du Sport et de l'Education Physique of Paris (INSEP), and a specialization was created in Science and Technique in Physical and Sport Activities (Ripoll & Thill, 1993).

Sport psychology researchers currently are represented by the *Société Française de Psychologie du Sport (SFPS),* which is associated with FEPSAC and ISSP (Ripoll & Thill, 1993). Additionally, INSEP has employed some sport psychologists to research talent identification and development (Salmela, 1992). Sport psychology in France lacks a specialized journal for the publication of relevant research, but it continues to build an institutionalized base within the university system and develop as an academic discipline.

Eastern Europe

Bulgaria.   Of the Eastern European countries, Bulgaria is perhaps the remaining example of the classic Soviet Union model, which focused directly on performance enhancement in the elite athlete. Laboratories were established in 1966 in institutes across the country to monitor elite athletes and conduct research. By the 1980s, research involving the psychological preparation of athletes for competition and the effect of sport training on the athlete's psychological development dominated research. The overall emphasis of sport psychology (as in other socialist countries) is focused on talent identification and the systematic use of the sport sciences in training. According to Salmela (1992) Bulgaria's 127 sport psychologists are the largest contingent of sport psychologists in any of the Eastern European countries. The Bulgarian overall method of preparation has been noteworthy in the success of their athletes in world competitions in wrestling and weight lifting.

Czechoslovakia.   Unlike other countries, interest in sport psychology in the former country of Czechoslovakia evolved through individual writings, rather than through the development of institutes and laboratories. In 1928, Peclat submitted one of the first theses in sport psychology, entitled "The Psychology of Physical Sciences," at Charles University in Prague. In 1932, Chudoba's "The Psychology of Training" was published as a sport psychology manuscript, and in the early 1950s an institute for physical education and sport was established at the University of Prague (Geron, 1982). The breakup of Czechoslovakia into the Czech Republic and Slovakia and the ensuing civil unrest resulted in disruption of the sport science delivery system. As with other countries in transition, sport psychology and the sport sciences in general require rebuilding.

Info Box

Many Eastern European countries were strongly influenced by the Soviet system of research and service provision. Today, many Eastern European countries face political and economic hardships that affect the educational, research, and service provision opportunities in sport psychology.

Poland.   Like other socialist countries, major academies and institutes of physical education provide the background for organized athletics and consequently the dissemination of sport psychology services and research. Specifically, the *Polish Scientific Society of Physical Culture (PTNKF)* houses a Sport Psychology Section (SPS) that acts as the primary sport psychology organization in Poland (Salmela, 1992). The official objectives of the SPS are to acknowledge the achievements of sport psychology theory and practice, initiate cooperative research in Poland and internationally, and organize forums for the exchange of information. No organized or formalized training in sport psychology currently exists in Poland; however, sport psychology courses are offered through the eight physical education institutes (Salmela, 1992). Additionally, no sport psychology journal exists, but researchers can publish their work in institutional journals offered at each of the institutes.

Hungary.   Sport psychology in Hungary is unique among European countries because it is firmly rooted in controlled laboratory research rather than in applied experiences with athletes. No refereed journal exists for sport psychology, but many articles have been published in the *Hungarian School of Physical Education Quarterly* and *Hungarian Psychology.* The primary sport psychology organization is the Sport Psychology Section (SPS) of the Hungarian Psychological Society (Salmela, 1992).

Asia.   Sport psychology in Asian countries is predominantly centered in Japan and China. Hong Kong, lacking a higher institutionalized degree program in physical education, has not offered opportunities for teaching or research in sport psychology. The teaching and application of sport psychology in Singapore remains in an embryonic development stage; however, Singapore has shown marked interest in the development of sport psychology (Salmela, 1992). India is developing a specialized publication for the research and practice of sport psychology, and there is no doubt that sport psychology will continue to expand in Asian countries. For now, however, Japan and China are the focal points for sport psychology practice and research in Asia.

Japan.   Sport psychology in Japan began in the early 1920s. The National Research Institute of Physical Education was founded in 1924, and psychology was introduced in the late 1920s. The institute edited a journal that included articles on various sport science topics, including psychology. *Matsui,* considered the father of sport psychology in Japan (Geron, 1982), was a professor of psychology at the Tokyo University. He participated in the evolution of the National Research Institute of Physical Education, wrote and translated the first sport psychology articles published in Japan, and prepared students in the area of sport psychology. However, as in the European countries, it was not until after Japan successfully overcame the devastation brought about by World War II and its subsequent social restructuring that sport psychology began to develop.

The Japanese Society of Physical Education (JSPE) was formed in 1950 to help promote research activities. The JSPE publishes the *Japan Journal of Physical Education (JJPE),* which serves as an important source of research information in sport psychology (Fujita & Ichimura, 1993). The Sport Sciences Committee of distinguished researchers was formed in 1961 within the Japan Olympic Committee (JOC) as part of the Japan Amateur Sports Association (JASA) to apply sport sciences to elite athletes. A subcommittee representing sport psychology was formed within the JOC, marking the first time that sport psychology was incorporated into organized athletics (Fujita & Ichimura, 1993). Consistent with developments worldwide, interest in elite sport has increased significantly in Japan since the 1960s. After the 1964 Olympic Games in Tokyo, sport psychology research began to develop as a science independent of physical education (Fujita & Ichimura, 1993). Interest in sport psychology continued to grow, and in 1973 the *Japanese Society of Sport Psychology (JSSP)* was created as a separate society from the JSPE to oversee the direction and promotion of sport psychology in Japan (Fujita & Ichimura, 1993). The *Japanese Journal of Sport Psychology (JJSP)* was also established in 1973 and serves as an important outlet for the development and promotion of sport psychology in Japan. Research was effectively applied to the 1986 Asian Games National Team and the 1988 Olympic Team (Fujita & Ichimura, 1993).

Salmela (1992) estimated that 250 sport psychologists, 30 universities, and 5 colleges have physical education programs in which sport psychology is a compulsory subject. With a solid base in colleges and universities, the application of sport psychology in competitive sport has been increasing, and Japanese sport psychologists have recognized the need to address the issue of training counselors to practice applied sport psychology. Japan is well positioned to continue the growth and development of sport psychology as both a discipline and a profession.

China.   Since the Cultural Revolution of 1966–1976, both psychology and sport psychology have undergone a transformation. The Cultural Revolution produced a resurgence of interest in science, and the Research Institute of Psychology was restored in June 1977. The institutions in China are based on the former Soviet Union's structure and include institutes of physical education and culture, whose focus is training coaches and physical educators for China's sport schools (Salmela, 1992). The psychologists and researchers in sport psychology work in close collaboration with coaches and teachers, thereby increasing their own knowledge of the field and its application.

Although the early 1960s saw a development of scientific research in sport, lack of a unified and clear research orientation limited sport psychology research until 1978 when the *Physical Education and Sport Psychology Commission* was established. Between 1979 and 1985, approximately 200 sport psychology papers were presented at the meetings of the National Society of Sport Psychology. Although sport psychology was taught as a compulsory course in the institutes of physical education and physical culture, the field was considered a bourgeois pseudoscience and was banished from all sport programs until 1976. However, since 1984, a limited number of master's programs have been offered at various institutes of physical education, such as the Wuhan Institute, where a doctoral program is planned to be established. Interestingly, psychology departments are found in only five of China's approximately 1,100 tertiary educational institutions (Kirby & Lui, 1994). Although sport psychology is not taught in any of the psychology departments, it is taught within at least 50 departments of physical education (Kirby & Lui, 1994).

Today, sport psychology in China plays an active role in education, research, and coaching and mixes traditional methods from the East with the newest information from the West (Salmela, 1992). China is second only to Japan in the number of sport psychologists in Asian countries, and Salmela estimated in 1992 that there were 200 sport psychologists in China.

Info Box

The science of sport psychology is growing rapidly in Asia, where interest in research and practice is very strong. Japan is a leader in the research and application of sport psychology principles, and several Japanese Olympic teams have utilized the services of sport psychologists. Several other Asian countries are positioned to expand research and applied aspects of sport psychology.

India.   The first major effort to study and apply the sport sciences in India was started at the *Netaji Subhas National Institute of Sports (NIS)* in Patiala (Bhattacharya, 1987). The government established this institute in 1961, and it has since become one of Asia's premier sport institutes. At the seventh annual conference of the Indian Association of Sports Medicine (IASM) in Varanasi in 1977, delegates with an interest in the psychological aspects of sport formed the Indian Association of Sport Psychology and established an official journal for the association (Bhattacharya, 1987). Later, in 1985, Dr. Kamlesh of the College of Physical Education, Patiala, formed the Sport Psychology Association of India. Since 1980, sport psychology courses have been taught at the NIS to develop and upgrade elite coaches and prepare teams for international competitions (Salmela, 1992). Most recently, sport psychology has been introduced as an option for study within the psychology departments of Punjab University, Chandigarh University, Pataila, Varanasi, and Kashi Vidya Peeth. Despite the growing interest in sport psychology, no formal graduate programs specialize in sport psychology in India. Given the interest in sport psychology at the institutional and governmental levels, India should make notable developmental and research advancements within the next decade.

The Development of Sport Psychology in Australia

Significant developments in Australian sport psychology were initiated in the 1960s, and numerous advancements in the areas of training, scholarly publications, professional organizations, and professional practice have been achieved in the past three decades. These advancements have received increasing acceptance within the Australian sport community, the profession of psychology, and in the public sector. The future growth of sport psychology in Australia appears very promising at the Olympic level as well as in the public sector.

Originally, Australia's colleges were modeled after the British education system, and many of the colleges' positions were filled by British professors (Abernethy, Bond, Glencross, & Grove, 1992). In addition to the British, North Americans influenced the development of Australian sport psychology. In the late 1960s and early 1970s, several Australians who had attended Ph.D. programs in the United States and Canada returned to Australia with knowledge in motor-skill acquisition and various areas of sport psychology. On their return, these individuals filled teaching positions at the Institutes of Technology, Colleges of Advanced Education, and universities across Australia in the departments of physical education and sport science (Abernethy et al., 1992). In the late 1970s, psychology departments at the graduate level began to interface with exercise science programs offering graduate education and training in sport psychology. Prospective sport psychologists are encouraged to do undergraduate work in both human movement science and psychology and then specialize in sport psychology at the graduate level (Abernethy et al., 1992).

The first professional organization to acknowledge sport psychology in Australia was the Australian Council for Health, Physical Education, and Recreation (ACHPER) in 1975. A special interest group within ACHPER was formed to promote sport psychology; unfortunately, this group was somewhat unstructured and no longer exists today (Abernethy et al., 1992). Shortly after the demise of ACHPER, the *Australian Applied Sport Psychology Association (AASPA)* was established in 1986. This organization originally was considered controversial because of its restrictive membership criteria, which excluded sport psychologists focusing on education and research. The development of the *Sport Psychology Association of Australia and New Zealand (SPAANZ)* in 1989 helped to reduce the controversy. SPAANZ brought AASPA, the sport science group, and ACHPER together to discuss important issues in the field (Abernethy et al., 1992). This was a great advancement in opening lines of communication among and between the groups. In addition to those organizations, Australia established the *Asian and South Pacific Association for Sport Psychology (ASPASP)*, which held its inaugural congress in 1991. This organization allows for international dialogue between countries in Asian and South Pacific regions and will further develop sport psychology. In addition to these professional organizations in sport psychology, other professional organizations have demonstrated their support for the field. Sport psychologists are employed through the *Australian Institute of Sport (AIS)* located in Canberra. The Australian Olympic Federation (AOF) enhanced its support of sport psychology in the 1984 Los Angeles Olympic Games. At the Los Angeles Games in 1984, the AOF employed one sport psychologist, and at the 1988 games in Seoul the number of sport psychologists increased to four (Bond, 1989). Advancements have been made in the area of interorganizational cooperation since the Australian Psychological Society (APS) endorsed the AASPA and demonstrated an interest and acceptance of sport psychology as a field of study and application (Bond, 1989). In addition, the practice of sport psychology has been promoted with governmental regulation of coaching accreditation.

Sport Psychology in North America

The history of sport psychology in North America presents an interesting portrait, interfacing highlights of insight and advancement with periods of conflict and stagnation. Although less than 100 years old, the history of sport psychology in North America reflects the diversity of an interdisciplinary field rich in traditions that have both facilitated and impaired the focus and development of a promising field. This section provides an overview of the major historical developments in North American sport psychology and offers a contemporary comment on recent developments that have future significance.

The Early Years

Although many historical accounts of sport psychology are provided in the literature, perhaps Wiggins (1984) offers the most comprehensive. Sport psychology is akin to many disciplines because several of the early writings on the topic of psychology and sport were philosophical, theoretical, or avocational. These professionals did not conceive their writings as part of any "sport psychology movement" but rather were proponents of exercise, espousing the psychological benefits of regular physical activity. The individuals who wrote some of the early works were often well known and highly respected in the academic and scientific communities. From the 1890s to the 1920s, a remarkable number of essays were published in physical education and psychology journals detailing the psychological benefits of exercise, the social and psychological nature of competition, and spectator attraction to live sporting events (Patrick, 1903; Scripture, 1899; Triplett, 1897). These writings stimulated interest on the topic of psychology and physical activity, but few, if any, developed into a sustained line of writing or research. It was not until *Coleman Roberts Griffith,* a University of Illinois professor, became the director of the Athletic Research Laboratory in 1925 that sport psychology as we know it today gained impetus and momentum. Griffith is recognized as the "father of North American sport psychology," and rightfully so. In addition to the laboratory he established, Griffith was an active writer, researcher, and consultant. He is an outstanding model for aspiring sport psychologists today because he embodied the science–practice model, not only in principle but also in behavior. For example, he researched personality and performance and psychomotor skill learning; he designed psychological and psychomotor tests; and he conducted qualitative research through interviews with football legends like Red Grange and Knute Rockne. He was hired by Philip K. Wrigley of the Chicago Cubs in 1938 to work as the team's sport psychologist. Griffith published over twenty-five articles specifically on sport psychology from 1919 to 1931. He published two books on the psychology of sport and athletics (Griffith, 1926, 1928) and began a book on the psychology of football that he never finished (Kroll & Lewis, 1970). Clearly, Griffith was a man ahead of his time. Unfortunately, when his laboratory was closed in 1932 for lack of financial support, no graduate students emerged to carry on his groundbreaking work. Griffith retired in 1953 as the provost of the University of Illinois.

During the 1920s through the early 1970s, the fields of motor learning and sport psychology were closely intertwined because many of the individuals conducting research examined topics that often were related to the psychology of motor learning. Griffith conducted motor learning research as well as work that clearly would be labeled sport psychology research by contemporary standards. Much of the work that followed Griffith leaned more toward the motor learning genre, and thus sport psychology entered into a period of relative dormancy in North America for several decades. During this time, however, motor learning laboratories were established at Pennsylvania State University by *John Lawther* and at the University of Wisconsin by *Clarence Ragsdale* in the 1930s. *Franklin Henry* instituted a course in the psychology of physical activity at the University of California at Berkeley in 1935, but it was not until the late 1940s and the 1950s that sport psychology research was reignited. University of Maryland professor *Warren Johnson* published a series of studies on various aspects of personality and performance that were to signal the reemergence of sport psychology in the post–World War II era (Johnson & Hutton, 1955; Johnson, Hutton, & Johnson, 1954). What transpired from the 1960s to the present in North America will be noted by future historians as the most critical growth and development period the field has known.

Sport Psychology Explodes in the 1960s

The 1960s will be remembered for many reasons. The cultural, sexual, racial, and musical revolutions of that decade influence us in our everyday life today. The 1960s were a "happening" decade for sport psychology as well. Publications on topics such as audience effects, personality, aggression, anxiety, motivation, leadership, and the dynamics of coaching were becoming popular and were appearing in notable physical education journals such as the *Research Quarterly*. In 1965, concurrent with the *First International Congress of Sport Psychology* held in Rome, Italy, Warren Johnson of the University of Maryland recommended a meeting of several Canadian and U.S. faculties who were active in sport psychology research and teaching. The group met in Chicago in the spring of 1966, and from this meeting two landmark events transpired. As representatives of the group, Johnson and Arthur Slater-Hammel of Indiana University successfully petitioned the International Society for Sport Psychology (ISSP) to host the second International Congress in Washington, D.C., in the fall of 1968. As a prelude to this international event, the first annual meeting of the newly formed *North American Society for the Psychology of Sport and Physical Activity (NASPSPA)* was held in 1967 before the annual meeting of the American Alliance for Health, Physical Education, Recreation, and, Dance (AAHPERD) in Las Vegas, Nevada. From 1967 to 1973, the NASPSPA meetings were held in conjunction with the AAHPERD meetings. As NASPSPA grew and became more focused on motor learning, motor development, and sport psychology, it became obvious that the society was ready to hold its own separate conference. This occurred in 1973 at the University of Illinois. In many ways this separation marked the start of a specialization trend in sport psychology that would become far more pronounced and significant in the 1980s.

The developments of sport psychology in the United States were paralleled in Canada, where in 1977 several faculty, some of whom had studied with Franklin Henry at Berkeley, established a separate society for motor learning and sport psychology called the *Canadian Society for Psychomotor Learning and Sport Psychology (CSPLSP)*. Scientific conferences are held annually, and occasionally the CSPLSP and NASPSPA hold joint conferences along with other international congresses, such as the ISSP and the United States Olympic Scientific Congress. The stimulus created by these organizations resulted in a dramatic increase in research and in the founding of several refereed scientific journals that provided a written outlet for the research being produced (see information box for a list of journals in sport psychology). Many colleges and universities in the United States and Canada initiated formal undergraduate and graduate courses in sport psychology during the 1970s, which resulted in increased visibility for sport psychology in the academic setting. Interest in graduate training in sport psychology began to increase in the 1970s as many undergraduate students majoring in exercise and sport science sought to specialize their training in the emerging subdisciplines of that field. The growth of sport psychology in the 1960s and 1970s was primarily in the academic arena, and this focus initiated the recognition of academic integrity with physical educators, sport scientists, psychologists, athletes, and coaches.

Info Box

Major Sport Psychology Journals
Canadian Journal of Applied Sport Sciences
International Journal of Sport Psychology
Journal of Applied Sport Psychology
Journal of Sport Behavior
Journal of Sport and Exercise Psychology
The Sport Psychologist

Specialization Denotes Change for Contemporary Sport Psychology

If the 1960s and 1970s are recognized as periods of rapid growth and development for the field of sport psychology, the 1980s and 1990s will surely be noted as periods of specialization and change. As the visibility of sport psychology increased in academic settings, it was simply a matter of time before individuals from psychology, the media, and the public became more interested in this discipline and in the application of sport psychology information. Although some pioneering work was being conducted in applied aspects of sport psychology by individuals such as Warren Johnson, *Bryant Cratty,* and *Bruce Ogilvie,* mainstream sport psychology was well entrenched in the academic and scientific aspects of sport psychology. This singularity of focus would prove troublesome for sport psychology, because many "academic" sport psychologists were not closely attuned to developments taking place in the applied aspects of sport psychology. With each passing year during the 1980s, more and more individuals began to label themselves "sport psychologists" and offer their services to professional and Olympic programs as providers of applied sport psychology. The field was expanding at a rapid rate, and sport psychology was no longer solely an academic entity.

In 1980, the *United States Olympic Committee (USOC)* established a Sport Psychology Advisory Board that attempted to initiate some level of service provision for the 1984 Los Angeles Olympic Games. This board eventually facilitated the hiring of *Shane Murphy* in 1985 as the first full-time sport psychologist whose role was to provide service to national teams at the Colorado Springs Olympic Training Center.

The professionalization of the field was occurring at a rate few professionals anticipated and some wished to ignore. Although the expansion of applied and professional aspects of sport psychology was accelerated by the media attention afforded to all the sport sciences during the 1984 Los Angeles Games, this was clearly a problematic event for sport psychology. With no control over entry into the field, the 1980s will perhaps be best remembered as "the best of times and the worst of times." Since before the 1984 games to the present, sport psychology has struggled with issues that relate to regulation of entry into the field, graduate training and preparation, certification, and accreditation of graduate programs (Andersen, & Williams-Rice, 1996; Conroy, 1996; Murphy, 1988; Silva, 1984, 1989a, 1992, 1996a, 1996b, 1997, 1997 August; Taylor, 1991).

Info Box

Sport psychology in North America began with the science–practice model implemented by Coleman Griffith. Through the 1960s and 1970s, the emphasis was on research and scholarship. The 1980s witnessed a rapid expansion of applied sport psychology, and today North America confronts important training and professional issues that will shape the future development of sport psychology in North America.

Advancing Applied Sport Psychology

During the 1980s, many individuals gravitated to sport psychology without proper training, and in some instances with no formal exposure to or training in sport psychology. This migration created ethical and professional issues that required careful professional and organizational attention. For approximately the three-year period of 1982–1985, NASPSPA was petitioned informally and formally to take action that would provide some regulation and direction to those in the field of sport psychology and to those wishing to enter sport psychology from related disciplines. After much dialogue and debate, NASPSPA voted in the spring of 1984 not to become involved in addressing the professionalization of sport psychology (Magill, 1984). The NASPSPA vote was a historic decision that resulted in the formation of a new organization called the *Association for the Advancement of Applied Sport Psychology (AAASP)*, which the author founded to focus exclusively on the field of sport psychology and the many challenges confronting sport psychology in the applied and professional domains (Silva, 1989b). Although divisions or subgroups of other organizations focused on motor learning, motor development, and sport psychology, AAASP addressed *only* sport psychology from the perspectives of intervention/performance enhancement, social psychology of sport, and health psychology. AAASP was designed to be interdisciplinary, balancing the importance of both psychology and sport psychology, and it was the first organization to have a student member elected to its executive board with full voting privileges. The first AAASP conference was held in Jekyl Island, Georgia, October 9–12, 1986, and was attended by more than 300 sport psychologists from all over the world. In 1989, the *Journal of Applied Sport Psychology (JASP)* was published as the association's official journal and was the first nonproprietary journal in the field of sport psychology. On September 5–6, 1989, in Seattle, Washington (AAASP, 1990), the *AAASP certification* committee, led by Daniel Kirschenbaum of Northwestern University, presented the AAASP fellows with a document outlining the criteria necessary for AAASP certification as an applied consultant (current AAASP certification criteria can be obtained from www.aaasp.online.org). AAASP began certifying qualified members in 1992, and as of December 2000 there were 150 AAASP-certified consultants.

Shortly after the formation of AAASP, a special-interest group that had formed within the *American Psychological Association (APA)* applied for and earned divisional status. In 1987, the APA recognized Sport Psychology as the forty-seventh division in the world's largest psychological association. *APA Division 47* and AAASP have many common interests, and many active professionals are members of both organizations. Division 47 and AAASP have jointly developed informational brochures that provide career guidance to aspiring young sport psychologists and to individuals interested in education in this specialization.

Members of organizations such as Division 47 and AAASP have done much positive and innovative work to advance the field of sport psychology, but several unresolved issues remain from the period of rapid expansion in the 1980s. These issues include effective graduate training models, gaining entrance to the field, the use of the title "sport psychologist," and the regulation of the field by organizations or state law. Such ongoing matters must be resolved in the next decade if sport psychology is to prosper and develop as a reputable profession. Concurrent with these concerns, considerable attention needs to be directed to the nature and quality of graduate training in applied sport psychology. These matters and other important issues confronting sport psychology are addressed next.

Major Issues Confronting Contemporary Sport Psychology in North America

Graduate Education and Training.   It is fitting to start this discussion with the topic of graduate education and training. Graduate students represent the future in any field of study, and the type and quality of training they receive provides the professional foundation upon which they will build. When sport psychology was primarily an academically oriented discipline, there was little discussion about the nature or quality of education and training taking place in sport psychology graduate programs. Most students followed a predictable program of study that emphasized mostly social psychological theory and research applied to sport. Students learned research skills by assisting with and eventually conducting studies that were often part of the research program being conducted by faculty at the institution the students attended. Generally, graduate students finished their programs prepared to teach and conduct research in sport psychology. This model worked well during the 1960s and 1970s, but it became less than satisfactory during the 1980s, when the interest and demand for applied sport psychology services began to increase. With many programs and faculty well entrenched in their model of graduate education, a great lag became apparent between the type of training that was needed to function as a contemporary sport psychologist and the type of training students actually received in their graduate program. Most programs remained "research-only" programs, and today many are focused exclusively on theory and research. Many professionals, however, were being asked to provide applied services, or they were interested in seeking situations in which they could apply sport psychology principles and knowledge with individual athletes or teams. Thus, the opportunity for service provision jumped ahead of the nature of the training experiences that most graduate students were receiving. To further complicate the matter, some individuals with an advanced degree in psychology or counseling but with little or no background in sport psychology began to offer their services as "sport psychologists." Research training continues to be accessible in sport psychology graduate programs, while applied training and supervised applied experiences remain underdeveloped in most contemporary graduate programs (Andersen, Williams, Aldridge, & Taylor, 1997; Silva, 1996b, 1997).

The issue of training, which remains unresolved today, is harmful to the integrity and professionalism of the field. Undergraduate and graduate students often ask, "Why is it taking so long for people to fix the situation?" I always respond that there are many difficult aspects to any form of change; however, a change in the way graduate students are trained will take time, resources, and, most important, effort by faculty. That is why it is extremely important that these deficiencies in training be addressed immediately. For graduate education and training to accommodate the need for applied services, sport psychology program directors and faculty need to do the following: (1) establish a formal and recognizable program identity, (2) establish graduate programs in sport psychology that have a core of faculty specifically trained in sport psychology, and (3) develop supervised practicum experiences for graduate students. Let's briefly examine each of these areas and why they are important to the change process.

Too many programs in sport psychology have attempted to be all things to all students. Some programs try to be research *and* applied science practice programs and ultimately do neither particularly well. There is a place in sport psychology for *both* research-based programs and science–practice programs. Faculty, however, must recognize their own preferences, expertise, and motivations. If a program is research based, it should promote itself as that and provide students interested in a research perspective with an outstanding graduate experience. If a program has a *science–practice* orientation, a different set of experiences must be afforded to the student, including clinical, counseling, and hands-on supervised practicum experiences with athletes. It should also be made clear to prospective graduate students that a research-based program will not prepare them for consulting with athletes and that a science–practice program will not provide the same level of research opportunity that a research-only program offers. Because many students are interested in AAASP certification, every program, regardless of orientation, should advise students whether they will be AAASP certifiable at completion of their graduate program.

The second issue is establishing a core of faculty trained specifically in sport psychology. The number of students a program admits should define a core faculty and the nature of the experience that students will receive in the program. Far too many one-person programs have defined sport psychology graduate programs. One faculty member cannot possibly provide the breadth and diversity of training necessary for advanced degree training. If a program admits a small number of students each year (say, two or three), obviously fewer core faculty are necessary; however, organizational guidance from AAASP or APA Division 47 is needed on this matter.

The last area that can facilitate change in graduate education and training is the provision of formal *supervised practicum experiences,* which involve face-to-face consulting with athletes and teams. These experiences should be part of every graduate student's formal course of study in any science–practice program. The supervisor should be AAASP certified, and the supervision should be provided "in session" to maximize the learning experience for the graduate student. It is unfortunate that many students continue to learn intervention and performance enhancement through trial and error simply because they have not had the opportunity to be mentored by an experienced sport psychologist. It is equally or even more unfortunate when graduate students from related fields attempt to generalize their expertise to sport psychology with little course work and no supervised experiences with athletes. As sport psychology continues to evolve professionally, graduate program training will become more specialized and focused, and programs will have to meet standards similar to those of graduate programs in other allied health fields. This process of program development and quality control is called *accreditation.* A major issue confronting the field of sport psychology is that no accreditation of graduate programs currently exists.

Accreditation of Graduate Programs.   If you are an undergraduate student in psychology and are currently considering applying to a particular graduate school in psychology, some of the first questions you may ask are: Who is on faculty? What type of research is conducted by the faculty at the school? and Is this program APA accredited? The APA is a major accrediting organization in the field of psychology, providing programs with guidance and making site visits to evaluate program quality for accreditation or reaccredidation. In 1945, APA President Carl Rogers realized that failure to regulate the training of clinical psychologists would be an abuse of public trust in the profession of psychology, and he formed a committee to establish accreditation criteria for graduate programs in clinical psychology (Routh, 1994). The first year programs were approved, in 1946, only eighteen met the criteria set forth by the committee. This bold move, however, put into place the first set of standards toward which graduate programs in psychology could aspire by providing recommendations for curriculum design and development. Many programs eventually made the changes recommended as necessary for accreditation, and the standard of education and training had been successfully established in the field of psychology.

Now, all psychology students contemplating graduate school want to know whether the program they are interested in is APA accredited.

What about sport psychology? Does sport psychology have an accreditation program? This topic has been widely discussed at professional conferences and in sport psychology journals (e.g., Conroy, 1996; McGowan, 1996; Murphy, 1996; Silva, 1989, 1996a, 1996b, 1997; Silva et al., 1999), but to date very little movement has been made toward accreditation by sport psychology organizations. Some of the common arguments offered against accreditation for sport psychology programs are the same ones that were used unsuccessfully to stop accreditation in psychology over fifty years ago. They include: (1) cost, (2) the potential elimination of programs that are not accredited, (3) a stifling of program creativity, and (4) unrealistic standards set by the accreditation committee. These arguments proved to be false fears in psychology. Today accreditation is an important element in the institutional and public acceptance of training standards in psychology (Selden & Porter, 1977). Silva and colleagues (1999) provide a detailed account of how accreditation can serve sport psychology and its development, as well as factual information that counters the arguments against accreditation in sport psychology. The evolution of sport psychology will continue in the direction of establishing and enhancing standards of training for graduate programs, and the leadership of an organization like AAASP or Division 47 of APA will initiate program registration and eventually accreditation. The *AAASP Graduate Training Committee,* established by President Robin Vealey in September 1998, is currently studying this prospect. Program accreditation will provide a great service to future graduate students, and this enhancement will be reflected in better-trained and better-prepared professional sport psychologists in the future.

Info Box

Sport psychology is in a crucial period of its development. The field is confronted with major challenges in the areas of graduate training and program accreditation, the use of title and the right to practice, the marketing and promotion of certified consultants, and the ability to effectively integrate sport organization at the professional and collegiate levels. The positive resolution of these issues will have a dramatic effect on the role sport psychology plays in the area of service provision to athletic teams in the next decade.

Integrating Sport Organizations.   If the United States has failed to effectively develop any area of sport psychology, it is the integration of sport organizations. The very organizations we should be serving know very little about sport psychology, who is a sport psychologist, or where to find a sport psychologist. Ask any coach or athletic director to name five *certified sport psychologists,* and you will immediately discover that the very people involved in hiring sport psychologists do not know any! Whose fault is this lack of awareness and recognition? Not the coach's or the athletic director's. It is the responsibility of the organizations in sport psychology to educate sport administrators about where to look and what to look for when considering the services of a sport psychologist. An educational outreach process is needed to inform collegiate, Olympic, national, and professional organizations about the qualifications of a sport psychologist. Such an effort would stimulate the development of greater career opportunities for sport psychologists, particularly those who have been trained properly and have received certification status. Potential outreach efforts should be directed at, but not limited to, athletes, coaches, athletic directors, National Collegiate Athletic Association (NCAA), professional organizations, and the public. The educational process should involve promoting AAASP certification standards as the minimum criteria for practice. Certification should be promoted and used as a tool to educate those in positions to hire sport psychologists. Many individuals in administrative positions continue to hire practitioners who are not specifically trained in sport psychology, preferring to base their decisions on personal networks and referrals from associates. This practice too often results in the hiring of former athletes or clinical psychologists with no formal training in sport psychology. Enhancing awareness of the minimum standards for sport psychology service provision also will enhance understanding of the nature of applied sport psychology.

Job Opportunities.   Misconceptions persist regarding employment in the field of applied sport psychology. Students interested in specializing in applied sport psychology are often misinformed concerning job availability and are continually discouraged by the myth that no jobs are available in sport psychology. The reality is that the ratio of jobs to new Ph.D.'s with specialized training in sport psychology compares favorably with that of other academic disciplines in the social sciences. The number of new Ph.D.'s in applied sport psychology is very limited (thirty new Ph.D.'s each year according to Andersen et al., 1997), and the number of available sport psychology jobs is quite small. The relative placement rate for sport psychologists is favorable as shown by the results of the AAASP Graduate Tracking Committee (Andersen et al., 1997). This study indicated that the vast majority of sport psychology doctoral graduates who were interested in academic careers were placed in academic jobs with an emphasis on sport psychology.

The reality of the job market is that well over 90 percent of university positions in the United States are in Exercise and Sport Science (ESS) departments. These departments have traditionally hired Ph.D.'s from ESS programs with specializations in sport psychology and interdisciplinary training in clinical, counseling, or social psychology. Individuals with only clinical, counseling, or social psychology training are at a competitive disadvantage for these positions. This situation will continue until either psychology departments hire sport psychologists or a standard training model is developed for sport psychologists that enables students trained in either psychology or ESS to compete for academic positions in ESS departments.

Ethical Issues: Title and Practice within Competency Areas.   All professional fields move to protect themselves from individuals who are not competent or properly trained to practice in that specialization. From law to medicine to psychology, all types of professions and trades attempt to regulate entrance and practice through education, training experiences (*apprenticeships*), certifications, and licensure. Sport psychology has been rather slow in determining the set of experiences necessary for *title* and *practice privileges.* Certification by AAASP has been in place since 1992, but this procedure alone has not eradicated the inappropriate use of title or practice. Many psychologists with little or no background or training in sport psychology continue to call themselves "sport psychologists" simply because they are licensed as psychologists. The term *sport* is equally important as the term *psychologist,* but because "sport psychologist" is not a protected title, it is up to the ethical standards of practitioners to follow AAASP, APA, and other organizations' guidelines about practicing within their competencies. No organization or state agency currently monitors the title "sport psychologist." This is obviously a serious concern because many athletic directors and coaches do not know where to look for a sport psychologist. Often a friend of the team physician or a friend of someone in the organization who is a psychologist may be asked to serve as the "sport psychologist." Without proper training and experience with athletes and athletic groups, individuals practicing outside their area of competency could deter the coach and athletes from sport psychology without their ever having experienced the services of a properly trained sport psychologist.

The title issue in sport psychology can be resolved by state licensure similar to that for psychology or by accrediting graduate programs that prepare individuals to sit for certification examination. Without graduating from an accredited graduate program, an individual would not be eligible to gain certification (similar to athletic training certification). Some have even suggested the creation of a new title that could be held only by individuals who graduate from accredited programs and successfully pass specialization certification examinations. Titles such as "sports counselor" or "performance enhancement consultant" have been discussed at recent conferences. Although some may consider squabbles over title to be rather boorish, the reputation of a field often rests on the perception of title and what that title connotes to the consumer and the public. As sport psychology matures and more systematically addresses the issues of training and accreditation, the issue of title should be effectively resolved to the satisfaction of both the discipline of psychology and the discipline of exercise and sport science.

The Future of Sport Psychology

Occasionally, students in my undergraduate sport psychology course ask, "Is there a future in sport psychology?" With all the issues to be addressed and all the unfulfilled potential in the applied area, such a question is certainly worth asking. The future is often on the minds of students, and an action in the present will determine the advancements that will be made in sport psychology. The next decade may be the most important in the brief history of sport psychology in the United States. If significant advancements are initiated in the training of sport psychologists and the marketing of sport psychology, a boom in the interest for applied services by competent practitioners could result. Consider the possibilities if every NCAA athletic department were as interested in hiring a certified sport psychologist as they are in hiring certified athletic trainers or strength and conditioning coaches. The number of competently trained sport psychologists currently being trained could never fill that need alone. With proper education about and exposure to sport psychology, many professional sports teams—the NFL, say, or the NBA, the WNBA, the NHL, and others—would generate scores of jobs for sport psychologists. Why doesn't this need exist today? The need itself does exist, but the marketing of the field has been virtually nonexistent. Because certified consultants are not promoted to sport organizations, many organizations do not actively seek sport psychology support services from individuals with specialized training. As the quality of service provision continues to increase and as organizations have more positive experiences with qualified consultants, the prospects for employment with sport teams will increase.

Sport psychology is clearly at a crossroads as we enter the new century. If sport psychology continues to evolve professionally, graduate programs will become accredited; training and educational models will become highly developed, including supervised practicum experiences and rotations for graduate students; the field will move more strongly through state licensure to protect itself from those not qualified to practice; and a significant educational and marketing effort will be put forth by AAASP and APA Division 47 to help administrators, coaches, and athletes to identify qualified and certified sport psychology consultants. If such developments do not occur in the next decade, student interest in sport psychology as a career option, which is currently extremely high, will begin to decline as students seek specializations that offer greater personal development and financial opportunities. Sport psychology will return to the position it held in the 1960s and 1970s: that of a little-known and seldom-practiced subdiscipline of physical education exercise and sport science.

Evolution is a process of change. As a prospective sport psychology student, a graduate student in sport psychology, or a professional, you can be a productive part of the advancement of sport psychology.

Key Terms (in order of appearance)

Soviet sport system
closed-loop system
perestroika
glasnost
Commonwealth of Independent
    States (CIS)
Sovietization
European Federation of Sport
    Psychology (FEPSAC)
International Society of Sport
    Psychology (ISSP)
Italian Association of Sport
    Psychology (AIPS)
German Association for Sport
    Psychology (ASP)
British Association of Sport
    Science (BASS)
Société Française de Psychologie
    du Sport (SFPS)
Polish Scientific Society
    of Physical Culture (PTNKF)
Matsui
Japanese Society of Sport
    Psychology (JSSP)

Physical Education and Sport
    Psychology Commission
Netaji Subhas National Institute
    of Sports (NIS)
Australian Applied Sport
    Psychology Association
    (AASPA)
Sport Psychology Association
    of Australia and New Zealand
    (SPAANZ)
Asian and South Pacific
    Association for Sport
    Psychology (ASPASP)
Australian Institute
    of Sport (AIS)
Coleman Roberts Griffith
John Lawther
Clarence Ragsdale
Franklin Henry
Warren Johnson
First International Congress
    of Sport Psychology
International Society for Sport
    Psychology (ISSP)

North American Society for
    the Psychology of Sport and
    Physical Activity (NASPSPA)
Canadian Society for
    Psychomotor Learning
    and Sport Psychology
    (CSPLSP)
Bryant Cratty
Bruce Ogilvie
United States Olympic
    Committee (USOC)
Association for the Advancement
    of Applied Sport Psychology
    (AAASP)
*Journal of Applied Sport
    Psychology* (JASP)
AAASP certification
American Psychological
    Association (APA),
    Division 47
science–practice
core
supervised practicum
    experiences

accreditation
AAASP Graduate Training
   Committee

certified sport psychologist
apprenticeship
title

practice privileges
evolution

References

AAASP (1990, Winter). AAASP passes certification criteria. *AAASP Newsletter, 5,* 3–8.

Abernethy, B., Bond, J., Glencross, D. J., & Grove, R. J. (1992). Oceania-Australia. In J. H. Salmela (Ed.), *The World Sport Psychology Sourcebook* (pp. 8–14). Ithaca, NY: Mouvement Publications.

Andersen, M. B., Williams, J. M., Aldridge, T., & Taylor, J. (1997). Tracking the training and careers of advanced degree programs in sport psychology, 1989 to 1994. *The Sport Psychologist, 11,* 326–344.

Andersen, M. B., & Williams-Rice, B. T. (1996). Supervision in the education and training of sport psychology service providers. *The Sport Psychologist, 10,* 278–290.

Antonelli, F. (1989). Applied sport psychology in Italy. *Journal of Applied Sport Psychology, 1,* 45–51.

Bhattacharya, B. B. (1987). Sport psychology in India: Current status and future directions. *The Sport Psychologist, 1,* 161–165.

Biddle, S. (1989). Applied sport psychology: A view from Britain. *Journal of Applied Sport Psychology, 1,* 23–34.

Birman, I. (1996). Gloomy prospects for the Russian economy. *Europe-Asia Studies (Great Britain), 48,* 735–750.

Bond, J. W. (1989). Applied sport psychology in Australia: History, current status and future issues. *Journal of Applied Sport Psychology, 1,* 8–22.

Conroy, D. E. (1996). Science-practice and accreditation in applied sport psychology. *Journal of Applied Sport Psychology,8,* S51.

Frank, P. (1992). Power struggle in post-soviet Russia. *World Today, 48,* 155–158.

Fujita, A. H., & Ichimura, S. (1993). Contemporary areas of research in sport psychology in Japan. In R. N. Singer (Ed.), *Handbook of research on sport psychology* (pp. 52–57). New York: Macmillan.

Gatrell, P. (1995). Ethnicity and empire in Russia's borderland history. *Historical Journal (Great Britain), 38,* 715–727.

Geron, E. (1982). History and recent position of sport psychology. In E. Geron (Ed.), *Handbook of sport psychology, Volume I: Introduction to sport psychology* (pp. 25–44). Jerusalem, Israel: Wingate Institute for Physical Education and Sport.

Griffith, C. R. (1926). *Psychology of coaching.* New York: Scribners.

Griffith, C. R. (1928). *Psychology of athletics.* New York: Scribners.

Hackfort, D. (1993). Contemporary areas of research in sport psychology in Germany. In R. N. Singer, M. Murphey, & K. L. Tenant (Eds.), *Handbook of research on sport psychology* (pp. 40–43). New York: Macmillan.

Johnson, W. R., & Hutton, D. H. (1955). Effects of a combative sport upon personality dynamics as measured by a projective test. *Research Quarterly, 26,* 49–53.

Johnson, W. R., Hutton, D. H., & Johnson, G. B. (1954). Personality traits of some champion athletes as measured by two projective tests: The Rorschach and H-T-P. *Research Quarterly, 25,* 484–485.

Kantor, E. & Ryzonkin, J. (1993). Sport psychology in the former U.S.S.R. In R. N. Singer (Ed.), *Handbook of research on sport psychology* (pp. 76–79). New York: Macmillan.

Kirby, R. J., & Lui, J. (1994). Sport psychology in China. *Perceptual and Motor Skills, 79,* 760–62.

Kroll, W., & Lewis, G. (1970). America's first sport psychologist. *Quest, 13,* 1–4.

Kullberg, J. S. (1994). The ideological roots of elite political conflict in post-soviet Russia. *Europe-Asia Studies, 46,* 929–953.

Kunath, P. (1995). Future directions in exercise and sport psychology. In S. J. H. Biddle (Ed.), *European perspectives on exercise and sport psychology,* (pp. 324–331). Champaign IL: Human Kinetics.

Magill, R. (1984, Fall). President's message. *North American Society for the Psychology of Sport and Physical Activity Newsletter,* p. 1.

McGowan, R. W. (1996). Eclecticism: An anti-egocentric model of performance. *Journal of Applied Sport Psychology, 8,* S50.

Melnikov, V. M. (1992). Soviet Union. In J. H. Salmela (Ed.), *The world sport psychology sourcebook* (pp. 119–121). Ithaca, NY: Mouvement Publication.

Murphy, S. M. (1988). The on-site provision of sport psychology services at the 1987 U.S. Olympic Festival. *The Sport Psychologist, 2,* 337–350.

Murphy, S. (1996). Wither certification? *Journal of Applied Sport Psychology, 8,* S52.

Nitsch, J. (1992). Sport psychology: Fundamental aspects. In H. Haag, O. Grupe, & A. Kirsch (Eds.), *Sport science in Germany: An interdisciplinary anthology* (pp. 263–296). Springer-Verlag.

Patrick, G. T. W. (1903). The psychology of football. *American Journal of Psychology, 14,* 104–117.

Reisinger, W. M., Miller, A. H., & Hesli, V. L. (1995). Public behavior and political change in post-soviet states. *Journal of Politics, 57,* 941–970.

Ripoll, H., & Thill, E. (1993). Contemporary areas of research in sport psychology in France: Overview and perspectives. In R. N. Singer, M. Murphey, & K. L. Tennant (Eds.), *Handbook of research on sport psychology* (pp. 34–39). New York: Macmillan.

Routh, D. K. (1994). *Clinical psychology since 1917: Science, practice and organization.* New York: Plenum.

Salmela, J. H. (1992). *The world sport psychology sourcebook.* Champaign, IL: Human Kinetics.

Scripture, E. W. (1899). Cross-education. *Popular Science Monthly, 56,* 589–596.

Selden, W. K., & Porter, H. V. (1977). *Accreditation: Its purposes and uses.* Washington, D.C.: Council on Postsecondary Accreditation.

Shteinbakh, V. (1987). *Soviet sport: The success story.* Moscow: Raduga Publishers.

Silva, J. M. (1984). The emergence of applied sport psychology: Contemporary trends—future issues. *International Journal of Sport Psychology, 15,* 40–51.

Silva, J. M. (1989a). Establishing professional standards and advancing applied sport psychology research. *Journal of Applied Sport Psychology, 1,* 160–165.

Silva, J. M. (1989b). The evolution of the Association for the Advancement of Applied Sport Psychology and the Journal of Applied Sport Psychology. *Journal of Applied Sport Psychology, 1,* 1–3.

Silva, J. M. (1992). On advancement: An editorial. *Journal of Applied Sport Psychology, 4,* 1–9.

Silva, J. M. (1996a). Current issues confronting the advancement of applied sport psychology. *Journal of Applied Sport Psychology, 8,* S50-S52.

Silva, J. M. (1996b). A second move: Confronting persistent issues that challenge the advancement of applied sport psychology. *Journal of Applied Sport Psychology, 8,* S52.

Silva, J. M. (1997). Initiating program accreditation in sport psychology. *Journal of Applied Sport Psychology, 9,* S47–S49.

Silva, J. M. (1997, August). Advancing progressive training models in applied sport psychology. In C. M. Janelle (Chair), *Training, employment, and accreditation issues in sport psychology—student perspectives.* Symposium conducted at the meeting of the American Psychological Association, Chicago.

Silva, J. M., Conroy, D. E., & Zizzi, S. J. (1999). Critical issues confronting the advancement of applied sport psychology. *Journal of Applied Sport Psychology, 11,* 163–197.

Sloutsky, V. M., & Searle-White, J. (1993). Psychological responses of Russians to rapid social change in the former U.S.S.R. *Political Psychology, 14,* 511–526.

Taylor, J. (1991). Career direction, development, and opportunities in applied sport psychology. *The Sport Psychologist, 5,* 266–280.

Triplett, N. (1897). The dynamogenic factors in pacemaking and competition. *American Journal of Psychology, 9,* 507–553.

Wiggins, D. K. (1984). The history of sport psychology in North America. In J. M. Silva & R. S. Weinberg (Eds.), *Psychological foundations of sport.* Champaign, IL: Human Kinetics.

2

Psychology of Personality

Stacey M. Rosenfeld
The University of North Carolina at Chapel Hill

- Although scholars have debated a concrete definition of personality, it can be conceptualized as the interrelation among a person's psychological core, typical responses, and role related behaviors, all of which are unique to that person and remain consistent over time.
- Several theoretical perspectives explain the relationship between personality and behavior including Freudian Theory, Drive Theory, Trait Theories, Social Learning Theory, Observational Learning, and the Interactional Approach.
- To evaluate personality theories, researchers have established many assessment techniques to measure both personality traits and mood states.
- Personality assessment techniques are beneficial also in applied settings. The specific personality assessment techniques that are typically used in the field of sport psychology are emphasized.

Consider you are the coach of a women's volleyball team, and, as coach, you are involved in team selection. You have decided that athletes with particular qualities will make the team. These qualities include height, skill, physical ability, experience, leadership potential, and confidence. The latter two variables are psychosocial characteristics that are considered part of one's personality. What other personality variables would be valuable for an athlete on your team? While some coaches feel strongly about the physical and motoric qualities necessary for success in sports, would there be consensus regarding psychological characteristics?

In order to gauge the impact of personality on sport performance, a basic understanding of the construct is essential. Particular attention should be directed toward questions such as what constitutes personality, what is the relationship between personality and behavior, how do various theories of personality help us understand behavior, and how does one measure personality. The following chapter will address these personality-related concerns. The discussion begins with an analysis of the elements of personality.

An athlete's personality can play an important role in high level performance.

What Constitutes Personality?

Have you ever tried to describe someone to a friend? What types of adjectives did you employ in your description? What kinds of traits or behaviors did you focus on when you developed the description? Maybe you said this person has a good personality. Just what is personality?

Although a definition of **personality** is debated, the construct has been discussed as "consistent behavior patterns originating within the individual" (Burger, 1986, 5). Based on this definition, personality is described as *consistent,* as it is relatively stable over time and across situations; *within* the individual, as it is not solely dependent on situational forces; and *individual,* to connote the vast differences in behavioral responses among individuals when faced with similar situational challenges.

Rather than formulating a definition, Hollander (1976) proposed a model to account for personality. In this way, personality can be separated into three interrelated, hierarchical levels (see Fig. 2.1).

1. A psychological core
2. Typical responses
3. Role-related behavior

Psychological Core

The **psychological core** is the nucleus of the personality structure and represents the most fundamental level of personality. Developed primarily from early interaction with the social environment, the psychological core reflects most accurately who a person really is. Your fundamental likes and dislikes, values, attitudes, memories from past experiences, and expectations for the future are located in the psychological core. NBA (National Basketball Association) prospects described as having good work ethics, for instance, may have elements in their psychological cores that value effort, persistence, and determination. In general, your core includes what you normally think and feel about yourself, others, and the world around you. For example, you may be a confident, self-assured individual. This would mean that even in a threatening, potentially humiliating situation, you

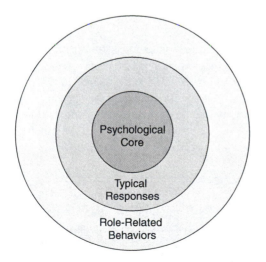

FIGURE 2.1 *Hollander's Model of Personality.*

would remain calm, positive, and certain in your abilities. If you were to remove the behaviors you exhibit so others may view you in a positive light, what would remain is your psychological core, the personality level that is commensurate with who you really are. Because of its centrality to your character, the psychological core is the most difficult level of personality to change.

Typical Responses

Typical responses represent the manner in which you usually react and respond to the external world. You may, for example, describe yourself as assertive, conscientious, and serious based on how you normally behave. Because typical responses develop from the psychological core, they are often indicative of underlying tendencies. For instance, if you are typically extroverted, this may suggest that your psychological core includes an outgoing, unreserved personality structure. Nevertheless, one must be extremely cautious in generalizing others' behavior to psychological core characteristics. If, for instance, gymnasts appear generally extroverted, we cannot necessarily conclude that they think they are extroverted, that they value this type of behavior, or that they would act the same way in all situations. Perhaps they are, at the core, shy individuals who realized they must develop a more outgoing personality to be successful in their sport. Maybe they typically act this way while involved in sport so that their fans will like and support them. Therefore, assuming that behavior always translates to psychological core characteristics is presumptuous and often erroneous because we must examine behavior across time and in different situations.

Role-Related Behavior

The peripheral circle of the personality structure reflects how you act based on your immediate social situation, considering the expectations surrounding that role. Because individuals encounter infinite situations and assume a myriad of roles, **role-related behaviors** represent the most superficial, changeable level of personality. Therefore, role-related behaviors are generally not assumed to be valid indicators of the psychological core. You may be a quiet, unassuming student in class one day and a point guard leading your team in front of 20,000 spectators that evening. How you behave in each of these situations is in part a function of the behavioral requirements for that role. As our environment changes oftentimes, so do our behaviors. It is generally expected that "student" behaviors include attention and diligent note taking. The role of a point guard, on the other hand, requires complex motions, decision making, and cognitive functions under highly observable conditions. Thus, the same person may behave in drastically different ways based on different role requirements.

Some psychologists question the influence of underlying personality structures because people do act so differently in various situations. If, for example, student–athletes can behave so distinctly depending on the situations they encounter, do their personalities really affect their behaviors? Or is it that the demands of the situations they face determine how they behave? Psychologists have formulated a variety of different theories in an attempt to answer these questions and explain how personality is related to behavior.

Info Box

All people have psychological cores at the hearts of their personalities that can predispose them to have typical responses. However, given the variety of situations that they may encounter, these typical responses may differ across situations as well as over time. People may assume roles in certain situations and exhibit behaviors that coincide with those roles, behaviors that may not be congruent with their psychological cores or typical responses.

Theories of Personality

Attempts to describe and understand personality date back thousands of years. In 400 B.C., Hippocrates labeled four personality types based on the four bodily humors: black bile, yellow bile, blood, and phlegm. These fluids, present in various amounts in all individuals, were proposed to contain the universal elements (air, fire, earth, and water). The four personality types included the depressed, "melancholic" personality (resulting from an excess of black bile); the irritable, "choleric" personality (excess of yellow bile); the optimistic, "sanguine" personality (excess of blood); and the calm, "phlegmatic" personality (excess of phlegm) (Atkinson et al., 1993). Other early attempts at understanding human behavior included phrenology, the science that dictated that skull and brain shape determined development and behavior, and physiognomy, which posited that people behaved in a manner consistent with the animal their faces most closely resembled.

In general, personality theories have gravitated from static, rigid conceptions of character to more dynamic, or flexible, interpretations. Although early theoretical approaches focused more on physiological and psychological traits, recent trends point toward a more comprehensive perspective that examines how individual behavior varies across time and situations. The early theories presented by Freud, Hull (Drive Theory), and the Trait Approach all contain a static interpretation of the human psyche. The more dynamic learning theories, including the work of Rotter, Bandura, and the Interactional Approach, are generally accepted as the most appropriate models for discourses involving the personality–performance relationship.

Early Theoretical Approaches

Freudian Theory.   Despite the early attempts at personality speculation described in the previous section, Sigmund Freud, the first acknowledged personality theorist, did not emerge until the end of the nineteenth century (Burger, 1986). Freud is considered the father of psychoanalysis and is credited for revolutionizing the study of psychology and associated disciplines (Feldman, 1992). He studied personality and behavior through a unique approach referred to as a psychodynamic perspective. Psychodynamic theorists contend that the study of personality should include a detailed analysis of the underlying psychological forces that influence who we are and how we act (Gleitman, 1992).

Freud, the most prominent psychodynamic theorist, began his career as a physician but soon became interested in early forms of hypnosis. Observing his mentors hypnotize their patients, Freud developed an appreciation for the patients' relaxation during hypnosis and realized that this state appeared to be a prerequisite to any psychological disclosure by his patients. Building on the work of his predecessors, Freud developed his own technique, instigating a pivotal change in physician–patient interactions. Instead of speaking to his patients, Freud let his patients speak freely to him. His role became primarily facilitative because he let his patients relax and talk about anything that came to mind. This process became labeled "free association." Freud maintained that patients would eventually reveal their problems and the underlying forces that had triggered and sustained them. Based on his clinical work, Freud developed his own theory to explain personality through the existence of three distinct parts: the id, the ego, and the superego. Freud (1961) argued that these parts interact to influence personality and behavior.

Freud (1961) contended that the most basic personality structure, the only one present at birth, is the *id*. The id is irrational and operates according to the "pleasure principle." It is concerned solely with seeking pleasure and avoiding pain. The id usually directs behaviors geared toward satisfying sexual and aggressive tendencies at an unconscious level.

During a child's first couple of years, the second personality structure, the *ego,* begins to develop (Freud, 1961). The ego's maturation is precipitated by the child's inability to operate exclusively by the "pleasure principle." After all, it is not too long before children realize that they don't get everything they want and that they can't always act out their sexual or aggressive urges. So, the ego develops and provides the individual with a more realistic framework. The rational, conscious ego functions according to the "reality principle," posing and answering the question, "How can I manage reality most effectively?" The ego exists not to thwart the id but to keep its instincts satisfied within the confines of objective reality.

The third and final personality structure, the *superego,* is formed by the time a child is five to six years old. Also irrational, the superego develops out of parental and societal expectations, rules, and norms and operates according to the "morality principle," a code detailing what society deems right versus wrong (Freud, 1961). One part of the superego corresponds to what is traditionally called the "conscience" or the internal actor that punishes individuals with guilt following moral transgressions. Another part, labeled the "ego ideal," hosts internal representations of the parent-approved, morally correct you; in other words, your ego ideal contains images of how you would like to be.

Because the id, ego, and superego represent opposing needs and desires, conflict frequently develops. The ego mediates conflict between the pleasure-seeking id and morally bound superego, yielding in the end to the more powerful of the two forces. For example, Freud would argue that the id, hosting an individual's aggressive tendencies, successfully vies for expression when that individual participates in a contact or collision sport. In these sports, the superego restraints are relaxed (because of the acceptance of aggression in these sports), and the ego subsequently yields to the id.

Sometimes, even when unconscious urges housed in the id are repressed by a powerful superego, the urges find substitute outlets for expression. These covert manifestations of id activity are referred to as "ego defense mechanisms" and allow the ego to maintain its integrity in potentially compromising situations. Ego defenses temporarily insulate the ego and are adaptive if used only occasionally. Examples of such defense mechanisms include repression or the subconscious burying of difficult material (e.g., a soccer goalie who "forgets" how the opposing team scored the game winner last year), and rationalization, a more acceptable interpretation of an individual's emotions or behaviors and often referred to as a "sour grapes" excuse (e.g., a benched athlete who believes the coach has something against him). Other common defenses are projection, attributing one's shortcomings or difficulties to others (e.g., a lacrosse attacker who misses a shot on goal and blames a teammate for a poor pass), and displacement, the release of negative energies in an inappropriate direction (e.g., a defeated tennis player who expresses frustration by yelling at his or her little sister at home later that evening). All of these defenses serve as protective, coping mechanisms for the conflict-ridden ego; however, ego defense mechanisms mask, but never resolve, the underlying problem. Therefore, the problem remains a concern until the individual has dealt with it appropriately on a conscious level. Furthermore, the overuse of defense mechanisms may result in a distorted reality. In this way, individuals who frequently employ such protective mechanisms may shield themselves to such a degree that they can no longer perceive objective reality.

While Freudian theory has spanned an entire century, the public and the scientific community did not approve of Freud's writings, and his work still lacks credibility in many academic circles. During his lifetime, psychological societies considered him too radical, and he was ostracized. The unaccountability of his theory was one of the most prominent criticisms of Freud's work. Examining and interpreting unconscious activity is an arduous task, and without measurement it is impossible to predict an individual's behavior based on deep-seated, unconscious tendencies. Thus, the scientific community responded by moving toward the more concrete, quantifiable science of behaviorism.

Drive Theory. Unlike other theories of personality, behavioral theories often focus on "behavior for its own sake" (Liebert & Spiegler, 1990). Theorists are interested in what motivates different behaviors and how to predict behavior across a wide range of situations. While behavior does not always correlate directly with personality, attention to behaviorism may help with understanding personality manifestation. After all, behavior theories can explain how certain habits develop, and it is these habits that, if sustained across situation and time, may become indicative of underlying personality features. For instance, if a springboard diver is repeatedly reinforced (by coaches/teammates/spectators, or by solid performance) for remaining composed under pressure, he or she may make a habit of maintaining emotional control, even in high-intensity situations. This learned composure, after enough practice, may essentially become a feature of the athletes' personalities, as woven into their psychological makeup as any other trait.

Behaviorism has its roots in Clark Hull's drive theory (1943, 1952), which was an initial attempt to understand behavior through a more direct, accountable approach. Hullian drive theory assumes that behavior (B) is a function of habit strength (HS) multiplied by drive (D), yielding the formula $B = HS \times D$. **Habit strength** refers to conditioning a high probability of a dominant response; **drive** represents a physiological tension, representing primary needs (e.g., food), that motivates an individual to act a certain way (Hull, 1943). In simpler terms, how people act is a direct consequence of the motivation for a behavior that a particular situation evokes (drive) and what they have best learned to do in this type of situation (habit strength). The higher their drive, or motivational level, the more apt they are to elicit their dominant response. Furthermore, only one response can be dominant. The response that has the greatest habit strength (conditioning) has the highest likelihood of expression in a high-drive situation. In the last example, the diver demonstrates a highly conditioned response of emotional stability that will, fortunately, be expressed in high-drive (or high-pressure) situations.

It is important to note, though, that the dominant response is not always the correct response. A sport-specific example helps clarify this point: Suppose a tennis player often tosses the ball too low in preparation for her serve. She works for two weeks on higher tosses in practice (a low-drive situation). During practice she may be able to evoke her nondominant (less conditioned) response, in this case, the correct, higher toss. However, in a close game situation (when drive is high), she will more likely revert to her dominant response, a lower serve toss. In this case, the athlete has been conditioned to internalize the low-toss response, and in high-drive situations, this dominant response will be elicited even though she has practiced the correct, high toss for two weeks. With continued practice in varied situations, the tennis player *may* be able to condition the correct, high service toss to dominance. Then when placed in a high-drive situation, the correct response (high toss) will be exhibited since it is now dominant over the incorrect (low toss) response.

Fitts and Posner (1967) described a three-step learning process that can help develop a habit strength for a correct, dominant response in sport. The **cognitive stage** of skill learning is the first stage a learner experiences. The athlete walks his or her way through a skill, attempting to determine the important cues surrounding its performance, thereby creating a mental schema for its enactment. For example, during the cognitive stage of learning to execute a handspring vault, the gymnast would imagine herself, and talk herself through, performing each stage of the skill. She would picture her initial foot placement at the start of the runway, her stride to the springboard, her takeoff and contact with the springboard, her arms' reach for the horse, followed by her forward rotation over the apparatus, and finally her solid landing on the other side. This cognitive stage of learning requires a great deal of mental processing.

In the **associative stage,** the athlete learns to associate a particular set of movements with the desired outcome or success. Here, the gymnast learns that only if she takes off before the springboard on her right foot, maintains a straight body line, and quickly pops her hands off the horse will she be in a position to stick her vault. In this stage, she engages in a great deal of repetition of the required movements and learn to adjust for errors (e.g., adds a hop at the end of her landing after she over rotates). Through practice trial and error, she develops an understanding of what she needs to do to master the skill.

In the final, **autonomous stage,** the response becomes dominant and automatic. In this phase, cognitive interference during skill performance is minimal because the performer's energy is directed more toward perceptual processing. Although the gymnast still concentrates on her approach, bodyline, and dismount, she has mastered the skill and can, with less conscious processing, perform it correctly in a host of situations. She does not need to devote so much conscious attention to the skill, because she has reached the stage at which she can execute the vault automatically.

It is important to recognize that not all learners make it to the autonomous stage with every skill. Even after years of practicing, second baseman may still have to talk himself through a double play pivot at the bag. Thus, the autonomous phase of learning is a desired, but not always attainable, stage.

The principles of Hullian drive theory and motor learning are particularly relevant when examining coaches' implementation of practice drills. Coaches intentionally use repetition during practice in order to develop a strong habit strength or dominant response surrounding a correct behavior. Once a correct response is taught and elicited, it is conditioned repetitively in varying gamelike situations to ensure that it dominates all competing responses. It is important in sport, then, to develop a response that is not only dominant but also correct. Consider the age-old adage, "Practice makes perfect." With a firm understanding of Hullian drive theory, it is apparent that only "perfect" practice makes perfect because the repetition of an incorrect habit only strengthens that maladaptive response.

It is evident, then, that if an athlete has a dominant response that is correct, he or she can maintain consistent performance even in high drive situations. This is particularly important in sport, where situations are often laden with pressure for both athletes and coaches. Athletes who have correct, dominant responses can perform consistently in these instances, thereby increasing the likelihood of success for themselves and their teams.

Info Box

Athletes must condition themselves to exhibit the correct dominant response despite their levels of drive. Elite athletes have conditioned themselves to perform correctly under both high- and low-pressure situations. In fact, elite athletes are conditioned so well that the correct dominant response is performed automatically, without any thought process at all, allowing for consistent elite performances.

Trait Theories. In contrast to Freudian theory and Hullian drive theory, trait approaches are less concerned with understanding individual behavior and more focused on how people with varying degrees of particular traits tend to behave (Burger, 1986). **Traits,** defined as relatively stable characteristics exhibited over time and across situations, are considered generalizable and are used to understand behavior in a variety of environments. Accordingly, an individual who possesses the trait of shyness may act timidly from one day to the next across a wide range of situations. For instance, a shy hockey player may keep to himself during team trips and also may respond to the media quite timidly. Thus, it is important to observe a person's behavior in different environments over a period time in order to make informed hypotheses about that individual's traits. If an individual's behavior is not observed comprehensively enough, it is possible that the behaviors noted might be manifestations of **states,** feelings and thoughts related to a particular time and/or situation. If, however, we see convergence in behavior across time and situation, we can reasonably assume that these behaviors are manifestations of a particular trait. We then can gauge the strength of the trait by how frequently it generalizes from one situation to another.

Trait theory has generated much of the available personality research, particularly in sport (Gill, 1986). Part of this results from the ease with which traits can be assessed through self-report behavioral measures. One of the most influential trait theorists Gordon Allport (1937, 1961) believed traits to be the fundamental features of personality. His primary assertions, accepted by most trait psychologists, include:

1. Traits are fundamental features of personality and may direct and sustain behavior. That is, the traits that we possess motivate us to act in a certain way.
2. Traits are more generalizable (apt to be exhibited in many types of situations) than habits or attitudes.
3. Traits describe the frequency, intensity, and generalizability of behaviors. The more frequent, intense, and generalizable the behavior, the stronger evidence that an underlying trait is directing it.
4. Traits are distinct entities, independent of other traits. One athlete may be conscientious and tough-minded, while another may be conscientious but more tender-minded.
5. Traits may be measured empirically (through the use of inventories) and are normally distributed in the population. For example, if you were to measure how generally relaxed versus tense people are, you would find that most individuals fall toward the center of that continuum, with smaller percentages exhibiting primarily relaxed or tense personalities.
6. Behaviors that are inconsistent with a trait do not deny the trait's existence. Just because you observe a normally emotionally controlled rugby player lose his temper during a game does not mean the athlete lacks a controlled disposition. It is possible that something about that particular game (e.g., opponents' unusually physical play) triggered this atypical response.

Like Allport, Raymond Cattell (1979) believes traits to be important in any study of personality. Cattell used a statistical procedure called factor analysis to isolate sixteen personality traits from the hundreds suggested to determine character, and he developed the 16 PF, an objective personality test. Nevertheless, Cattell (1965) does understand the influence of the environment and developed the formula $R = f(S, P)$ to account for human behavior. In this formula, a person's response (R) is a function (f) of the situation (S) and the individual's personality (P). The construction of sport-specific tests in sport psychology is largely reflective of Cattell's comprehensive work in personality (Cratty, 1989).

Finally, Hans Eysenck, also through the use of factor analysis, collapsed recognizable traits into personality factors: introversion, extroversion, neuroticism, and psychoticism. These factors, which appear to be universal personality constituents, or "source traits" (Eysenck & Eysenck, 1985), are bipolar dimensions (e.g., extroversion–introversion) along which all individuals fall. Eysenck contends that an individual's placement on each of these three continuums (e.g., levels of introversion/extroversion, neuroticism, psychoticism) is largely determined by hereditary factors (Eysenck, 1975).

Though widely researched, trait theory has generated considerable criticism. Serious challenges arose from Walter Mischel (1968), who argued that people do not behave as consistently or predictably as trait theorists purport. Mischel contends that individuals are not simply a collection of traits and that behavior depends largely on situational restrictions and implications. Thus, a swimmer may act confidently during swim meets, but less so in social situations outside the team. However, trait theorists, to explain the discrepancy in behavior, would argue that the swimmer does not possess a *strong* trait of confidence. According to this viewpoint, it is not the situation that is determining the swimmer's behavior but rather the operation of a moderately developed trait that should demonstrate only moderate situational generalizability.

Thus, although it has been suggested that situations do indeed affect behavior, it is not necessary to abandon the trait perspective altogether (Carron, 1980). After all, traits *do* play some role in determining individual behavior. Moreover, traits predispose us to states, how we feel at a given point in time. Take the example of the "confident" swimmer: If this athlete has high trait confidence, he or she is more likely to feel confident in a wide range of situations. For instance, the swimmer will probably be inclined to eagerly anticipate an approaching meet as a chance to showcase his or her talents and compete against other proficient athletes. The swimmer will likely feel calm, yet energized, entering competition. Since successful sport performance is related to affect, or a state profile, the trait–state relationship deserves attention in personality analyses regarding sport.

Although sport psychologists should recognize the limitations of trait theories, this perspective should not be discounted completely. Attention to trait approaches may help clarify the underlying relationships between personality and behavioral responses. Other personality theories, called learning theories, offer a more situational approach to human behavior. Considering elements from trait theories and learning theories together may provide the most comprehensive perspective on the personality–sport performance relationship. The following section discusses two prominent learning theories, social learning theory and observational learning.

Info Box

Personality traits predispose us to behave in certain general ways over time and across situations. However, we are not always in the same emotional state or mood all the time. In general, our personality traits will be exhibited in behavior, but the behavior is also influenced by our emotional state at that moment.

Learning Theories

Learning theories attempt to explain how situational influences may affect human behavior. This effect may be transient, or limited in expression to replications of the original situation, or a more global, static phenomenon, depending on the strength of the situational influence and the susceptibility of the learner. For example, a little boy who idolizes a professional football player and avidly follows this athlete's professional and personal affairs may begin to imitate his dress, speech, and behaviors to such an extent that some of the mannerisms become his own. Thus, if exposed to a powerful enough influence, an individual's behavior may change and, particularly if the individual is young and impressionable, this exposure may influence personality development and a whole class of future behaviors.

Learning theorists have typically conducted research in two fashions. The first line of research examines the relationship between behavior, expectations, reinforcement, and punishment. The second examines the impact of observational learning. Social learning theory addresses the first consideration.

Social Learning Theory.   Julian Rotter's (1954) theoretical approach marked a key transition from early theories of personality to learning theories, and personality researchers began to pay more attention to the influence of learning on behavior and subsequent personality development. Rotter's early work has been so influential that he is considered the "Father of Social Learning Theory." In contrast to the earlier notion of radical behaviorism, which suggested that behavior is simply a response to the environment, Rotter posited that humans have the capacity to choose to react to stimuli in a variety of ways. Thus, Rotter added the intervening variable of the organism to Watson's (1914) stimulus–response model.

Watson: stimulus → response
Rotter: stimulus → organism → response

In this way, an individual does not respond just to environmental cues but can actively choose how he or she will respond to such stimuli.

Rotter contends that three major factors influence behavior. These factors reflect the complexity of behavior and include situational expectancies, generalized expectancies, and reward/punishment values.

Expectancies refer to the "probability held by the individual that a particular reinforcement will occur as a function of a specific behavior on his part in a specific situation or situations" (Rotter, 1982, 50). When the probability of positive reinforcement is salient, we are apt to engage in that behavior; however, if punishment seems imminent (especially if the punishment is salient), there will be more of an inclination to refrain from exhibiting that particular behavior.

Situational expectancies describe calculations of reinforcement probabilities in individual scenarios. For example, a baseball player who feels ill before practice will have to decide if missing practice will result in punishment, in the form of his coach's disapproval. In this way, the athlete examines a particular situation and his potential behavioral responses and gauges the effects of probable responses. Perhaps the team has a game scheduled the coming weekend, and the player suspects that if he skips practice, the coach may bench him during competition. Based on the assessment of probable punishment (the coach depriving the athlete of valuable playing time), the athlete may decide to attend practice despite his discomfort. If, on the other hand, he worries that attending practice will worsen his condition or if he does not believe his coach will punish him, the athlete may choose to skip practice that day.

Through the feedback received from learning experiences, **generalized expectancies** are developed over time. Thus, if the ballplayer in this scenario has missed practice before (and has been punished by a suspension) or has seen his teammates benched following absences from practice, he may have internalized the punishment probabilities of this particular behavior. Realizing the similarity between the present situation and his past experiences, the athlete may decide to attend practice based on the generalized expectancy regarding attendance transgressions.

Although situational expectancies often lead to the development of generalized expectancies, in some situations the two can represent conflicting concerns. In sport, often the athlete must weigh the situational expectancies versus the generalized expectancies present in a given scenario. For instance, 80 percent free-throw shooter in basketball has a generalized expectancy that he will usually score from the free-throw line. However, suppose the athlete approaches the foul line at the end of a game, when the team is down by one point, with only three seconds remaining. Situational expectancies may overpower the generalized expectancy, because concerns about the consequences of a miss may inhibit performance. In this situation, the athlete is more concerned with the environmental constraints, even though it would be in his best interest to focus on the generalized expectancy for successful free-throw shooting.

Situational expectancies, therefore, may overpower generalized expectancies, sometimes leading to negative consequences. In other circumstances, however, it may be important to prioritize the situational expectancy above the generalized expectancy. For example, a basketball player who typically fouls opponents (generalized expectancy) may have to refrain if the athlete is about to foul out with considerable time remaining in the game. Thus, in sport, as in other social settings, it is important to consider both situational and generalized expectancies and prioritize the expectancy more conducive to success in a given situation.

According to Rotter (1982, p. 51), **reinforcement value** refers to the "degree of preference for any reinforcement to occur if the possibilities of their occurring were all equal." At issue here is the value a particular reinforcement holds to the individual, independent of expectations about the probability of that reinforcement occurring. The reward that holds the most value to the individual has the greatest chance of eliciting the particular behavior to which it is tied. Recall the baseball player who was contemplating missing practice: Even if he perceives there to be only a small chance of his coach benching him, if he highly values playing, he will attend practice to avoid this slightly probable, yet significantly undesirable, consequence.

Thus, if situational and generalized expectancies for reinforcement are high, and the reinforcement value perceived in the situation is worthy, it is probable that a particular behavior will be elicited. If, on the other hand, the situational expectancy and generalized expectancies do not suggest a high probability of reinforcement, and if the individual is particularly concerned with avoiding an undesirable punishment, the probability of the behavior occurring is significantly decreased. Rotter contends that in each situation experienced, individuals weigh these three concerns and then act according to the perceived probabilities of each. Obviously, as a person develops a "learning history" over time, these evaluations can be made instantaneously.

Observational Learning.   Albert Bandura's social learning theory (Bandura & Walters, 1963) focuses primarily on observational learning. Through observational, or "no-trial learning," it is possible to learn vicariously through simple exposure to others' behavior. This process requires: (1) an observer (the learner), (2) an actor who serves as the observer's model for behavior, and (3) and modeling cues, or the components of the model's behavior. For example, a little girl who watches figure skating on television might ask her parents if she can take lessons herself and might, after several weeks of practice, actually attempt some of the elements of the routines she has observed.

For observational learning to occur, the observer must be exposed to the cues (via television in the example), acquire the cues (by paying attention to the skaters' routines), and accept the cues as a guide for future behavior (incorporate the moves into her early attempts at skating). If the salience of the environmental situation is strong enough, the influence of personality traits upon behavior should be minimal. Therefore, although the little girl generally may be a cautious, apprehensive individual who is slow to attempt physically risky activities, observing the talented, glamorous skater may have been powerful enough for her to elicit the behaviors herself.

Bandura's (1965) classic "Bobo Doll Study" illustrates the concept of observational learning. In this experiment, nursery school children served as observers and watched a 5-minute film in which an adult, male model beat, yelled at, and struck with a mallet a plastic Bobo doll. The researcher then manipulated the visible reinforcement for these behaviors. While one group's film concluded with another adult rewarding the model with candy and soda and commending the aggressive behavior (the model-rewarded condition), the other group of children saw this adult punish the model by shaking a finger, spanking, and threatening the actor not to behave that way again (the model-punished condition).

After viewing the film, each child was placed in a room with a Bobo doll, three balls, a mallet, a pegboard, plastic farm animals, and other assorted playthings. Subjects had the option of engaging in imitative (e.g., playing with the Bobo doll and mallet) or nonimitative behavior (e.g., play with the plastic animals). The children were left alone for 10 minutes, were positively reinforced for correctly modeled behaviors, and were assessed on their ability to recreate the modeled behavior. Results indicated that the children generally were proficient at acquiring the behavior but that performance of the observed behavior depended on whether the children were in the model-rewarded versus model-punished group. Reproduction of the aggressive behavior was more prevalent among the children in the model-rewarded condition than children in the model-punished condition.

The previous experiment demonstrates the power of observational learning, not just of select behaviors but of the reinforcements they elicit. Through others, we are able to learn vicariously about the rewards and punishments, and subsequent expectancies, connected to different behaviors. If we value the reward we have watched another receive, we are likely to imitate the behavior that elicited it. Contrarily, when we witness another's punishment, we are apt to counterimitate, or act oppositely, of the modeled behavior.

Instances of observational learning are abundant in sport, particularly in youth sport. Observational learning may affect even a child's motivation to participate in sport. If a youngster sees an older sibling or friend rewarded for little league participation (e.g., parental approval and reinforcement), he or she may want to join a team to experience similar rewards. Then, once the child is involved in sport, observational learning may continue to affect his or her behavior. For example, a youth athlete who witnesses his/her teammate slack on his drills (without punishment) may slack off as well, to escape the physical fatigue that the exercises instill. However, if the coach punishes the model with additional conditioning following practice, the observer may put forth his/her maximum effort during drills in order to avoid similar punishment. The athlete has learned, through observation of a teammate, that skimping on drills results in an undesirable consequence, so he or she will act to avoid such punishment.

Learning theories suggest, then, that individuals often exhibit behaviors based on situations they encounter and people they observe. Athletes, for instance, may act differently with teammates versus their peers or coaches. Consequently, it is important to examine the social and situational influences that affect individuals in sport. Learning theories, nevertheless, fail to account for individual differences. For example, soccer forwards in the same situation (e.g., against an opposing team's talented defenders) may respond in different ways. One forward may get frustrated after several failed attempts to move the ball toward the goal and may begin to diminish his or her effort, but the other forward may persist, perhaps displaying even more effort in order to get the ball past the opponent's defenders. Although the forwards face the same situation, they respond quite differently, perhaps due to varying levels of an underlying trait (e.g., persistence). Furthermore, learning theories do not account for the fact that many individuals exhibit similar behaviors across various situations. A rugby player who is self-reliant in most situations (e.g., practices, team trips, family matters) may be high in trait self-reliance. Attention to both personality and situational influences, the interactional model, may yield the most comprehensive understanding of human behavior.

Interactional Approach

The **interactional approach** draws from both the early theoretical approaches and the social learning theories to yield a model that considers the person and the situation to account for human behavior. Sport psychologists who advocate this comprehensive approach understand that an athlete's personality interacts with each environment he or she encounters. In sport, select personality characteristics may be displayed in some situations but suppressed in others. A hockey player, for example, may check his opponent assertively but not initiate physical encounters when off the ice. This athlete discriminates between situations and decides when assertive behavior is appropriate. On the other hand, the same situation may evoke different responses from two individuals (e.g., one doubles tennis player is calm approaching a semifinals match, but the other is quite anxious), suggesting that traits are operating to some extent.

The interactional model also stresses the significance of behavior expectancies (as discussed by social learning theorists) but incorporates individual differences through the notion of reinforcement value (Rotter, 1982). Thus, while two people may perceive the same impending reward if they display a certain behavior, they may value this reward differently. For instance, the coach of a high school softball team may have conveyed her respect for hard work to her athletes. One pitcher on the team may consequently stay after practice each day to work on her technique, thereby impressing the coach with her extra effort. Another pitcher on the team may recognize the potential reward for staying after practice (e.g., the coach's approval) but may not value this reward as much and may therefore choose to leave after the regularly scheduled practice. The two pitchers in this example have different reinforcement values for the coach's approval. The individual differences in reinforcement value are an example of the individual uniqueness, in additional to situational requirements, considered in interactionalism.

Sport psychologists who support an interactional approach to behavior recognize the potential influences of personality and situation. Examining both variables together often leads to a better understanding of an athlete's behavior. Because personality is an important element in the interactional model, researchers have attempted to quantify personality traits through various types of assessment. Personality measures help sport psychologists understand the underlying traits that may influence athletes' behavior in different situations.

Measuring Personality

Personality assessment occurs in both research environments and clinical settings. Research and clinical sport psychologists commonly administer objective, self-report tests and engage in interview processes in order to gather information. Sport psychologists may learn about an athlete's behavior and personality three different ways, yielding a **triangulation of information.** First, the clinician may listen to what the athlete says during the sessions they have together. An athlete, for example, may tell a sport psychologist that he is generally a confident individual. Second, the sport psychologist can observe the client in different situations. Does the athlete act confidently before and during practices and games? Finally, the sport psychologist may choose to administer objective instruments that measure select personality characteristics. Having an athlete complete a confidence inventory may provide additional information about how confident this athlete is. Ideally, the triangulation of information is congruent. That is, the three forms of assessment provide similar information about the athlete's personality. In this example, the athlete would describe himself as a confident person during a counseling session, would exhibit confident behavior in various situations that the sport psychologist observes, and would score high on a confidence inventory. Congruence among these sources suggests that the athlete has a good understanding of himself, a necessary prerequisite for any type of intervention that may occur. A lack of congruence between these sources may suggest the athlete does not fully understand himself. Close examination of the information from these sources may help athletes better understand their psychological strengths and weaknesses and how these factors may impact their sport performance.

Through assessment, then, it is possible to gain a better understanding of the motives and forces underlying an individual's behavior, and, in applied frameworks, clinicians can structure an intervention to redirect behavior through attention to these causal factors. According to Singer (1988), psychological testing in sport can be employed for the following purposes:

1. *Description:* Test results can have educational value, providing athletes with information concerning personality characteristics that may relate to performance.
2. *Diagnosis and Intervention:* Information can be used to design intervention programs to help athletes modify certain personality characteristics that tend to influence athletic performance.
3. *Prediction and Selection:* Tests have been used to predict an athlete's probability for success in sport. This was particularly true in the former Soviet Union system of selection.

Before personality inventories can be employed for any of these purposes, careful attention must to be given to the psychometric properties of testing instruments. There are two major requirements for the construction of sound psychological tests: reliability and validity.

Reliability refers to a test's ability to produce consistent results and is typically assessed by giving the same subject a test twice (test–retest) or by statistically correlating a subject's responses to items that address the same construct (internal consistency). Validity measurements attempt to assess whether the test actually measures what it purports to measure. There are several measures of validity, including construct validity, face validity, empirical validity, factor validity, and concomitant validity. Construct validity, the most important in personality research, describes the degree to which a test assesses a hypothetical construct and is usually determined through the correlation of test results with actual behavior (Thomas & Nelson, 1996). For example, if a field hockey player completes a new precompetitive anxiety inventory and the results suggest that this athlete is highly anxious, sport psychologists who observe and/or speak with her before various competitive situations should identify signs of anxious behavior. This correlation between the test and the observed behavior indicates that the test may have an acceptable degree of construct validity and, with more rigorous examination, may be a worthy candidate to assess precompetitive anxiety in the future.

Several types of assessment have been developed in the history of personality measurement. These tests typically have taken the form of projective, observational, or objective tests. Projective tests, including the Rorschach Test (Rorschach, 1924) and Thematic Apperception Test (Morgan & Murray, 1935), provide the subject with an ambiguous picture. Based on the subject's response, the researcher draws conclusions about what the subject is "projecting" about his or her personality. These tests, which attempt to uncover a person's innermost feelings, are used principally by psychologists who follow psychodynamic perspectives (Atkinson et al., 1993) but are not often used in sport settings. The subjectivity involved in response evaluation raises serious doubts as to the validity of projective techniques (Kleinmuntz, 1982).

Social learning theorists, with their focus on behavior and situational requirements, often use observational techniques to understand personality. Observers have a checklist of possible behaviors and then code subject behavior into distinct categories. The resulting profile can provide valuable information concerning the subject's behavioral patterns. Observational methods are occasionally used in sport. For example, the Coaching Behavior Assessment System (Smith, Smoll, & Hunt, 1977) allows researchers to code coaches' behavior to better understand their leadership styles. Furthermore, as discussed before, sport psychologists may observe athletes at practices and/or competitions to gather information about the athletes' behaviors that may facilitate the intervention process. Similar to projective techniques, however, observational methods are susceptible to the subjective biases of the observer, and their validity is therefore questionable.

Finally, objective inventories, which elicit structured responses from subjects, are the most popular techniques employed in personality research. In addition to their greater reliability and validity than projective or observational tests, objective measures are simple to administer and easy to score. Sport psychologists may administer these inventories during an intervention process to help athletes understand the psychological forces that relate to sport performance and to objectify any changes that the athletes have experienced due to the intervention. Objective personality tests have been designed to measure traits (general behavioral tendencies), states (how the subject feels at that moment), and more recently, sport-specific variables. Objective inventories typically require test takers to choose a response that best describes their behavior, thoughts, and/or feelings on a number of easily scored questions. Trait and state measures will be discussed in the following sections, and sport-specific inventories will be addressed in Chapter 3.

Info Box

In the field of sport psychology, objective and observational assessments are the primary forms of measuring an athlete's personality. Sport psychology consultants may observe an athlete in practice, in a game, or may simply ask about typical responses in an interview. An objective test such as the 16 PF or POMS may provide another source of information that can educate the consultant and help to structure an intervention.

Trait Measures

Trait measures attempt to assess stable personality characteristics through self-report questionnaires. These tests generally instruct subjects to respond to items based on how they usually act. One of the most popular trait inventories is the Minnesota Multiphasic Personality Inventory (MMPI; Hathaway & McKinley, 1940). Originally constructed to measure psychopathologies such as depression, hysteria, and schizophrenia, later it was generalized to normal subject groups. The MMPI is a 566-item test consisting of 10 scales that assess constructs such as masculinity–femininity, introversion–extroversion, and depression. The California Psychological Inventory (CPI; Gough, 1960), developed strictly for use with normal groups, particularly high school and college students, contains 480 questions. The instrument addresses 18 personality variables, including responsibility, sociability, and intellectual efficiency.

Cattell's aforementioned focus on trait psychology precipitated his development of the *16 Personality Factor Test* (16 PF; Cattell, Eber, & Tatsuoka, 1970), largely employed for personality assessment purposes. The 187-item, self-report test measures 16 personality factors that are scored along a continuum. Examples of these factors include reserved versus outgoing, tough-minded versus tender-minded, and relaxed versus tense. An individual who takes this test receives a profile that plots his or her scores against established population norms. Thus, it is possible to determine where subjects stand on personality traits compared to their target, age and gender adjusted, populations.

The recommended use of trait measures in sport psychology research is to help athletes identify their psychological strengths and weaknesses. A host of investigations have attempted to determine elite athlete profiles (Silva et al., 1985, 1981), and interventions with other athletes often are targeted at working toward enhancing their profiles and adaptive factors related to elite performance. Through the 16 PF, it has been suggested that certain personality characteristics are predictive of elite athletic performance (Silva et al., 1985, 1981). These traits include emotional stability, conscientiousness, tough-mindedness, placidity, self-sufficiency, self-control, and relaxation. Elite athletes are more likely to exhibit this cluster of "core" characteristics than their nonelite counterparts. A sport psychologist may choose to use information from an athlete's 16 PF profile to help structure an appropriate intervention. Thus, a clinician working with a distance runner whose 16 PF results indicate that he or she is, for example, tense and apprehensive may develop an intervention geared toward alleviating the runner's anxiety.

State Measures

State inventories, in contrast to trait measures, attempt to assess more transient emotions and behaviors instead of relatively stable characteristics. Test directions usually instruct the subject to answer "according to how you feel right now." An instrument often used to measure state or affect in sport psychology is the **Profile of Mood States** (POMS; McNair, Lorr, & Droppleman, 1971). The POMS assesses six affects, including tension, depression, anger, vigor, fatigue, and confusion.

State measures are typically used in sport psychology to determine the components of an athlete's mood at a given point in time. Specifically, sport psychologists may want to assess athletes' affects during the precompetitive period, or the 24-hour period preceding competition (Silva & Hardy, 1984). For instance, a sport psychologist may have an athlete complete a POMS test within a half-hour period prior to competition. The sport psychologist then may compare the athlete's measures of tension, depression, anger, vigor, fatigue, and confusion to the profile established for elite performers. Elite athletes typically exhibit an **Iceberg Profile** with lower than average levels of tension, depression, anger, fatigue, and confusion and a higher than average level of vigor (Morgan, 1980).

State measures such as the POMS, in addition to trait measures, provide the sport psychologist and athlete with information that may help direct the course of an intervention. While there are numerous general and sport-specific trait and state measures, sport psychologists must pay careful attention to the psychometric properties and assessment purposes of any psychological test given to an athlete or team for diagnostic or intervention purposes. Chapter 10 will provide a more detailed description of the use of assessment in intervention.

Conclusion

Various theories of personality have been proposed to explain behavior. The interactional mode of behavior, which considers personality characteristics and environmental demands, appears to have the most practical applications in the study of sport psychology. All theories, however, may provide insights about the numerous factors influencing sport behavior and performance. Through the use of personality measures, sport psychologists may better understand the individual variables affecting athletic performance, allowing them to structure interventions with their clients more effectively.

Key Terms (in order of appearance) _____

personality	cognitive stage	reinforcement value
psychological core	associative stage	Observational Learning
typical response	autonomous stage	Interactional Approach
role related behavior	traits	triangulation of information
Freudian Theory	states	16 Personality Factor Test
Drive Theory	Social Learning Theory	(16 PF)
habit strength	situational expectancy	Profile of Mood States (POMS)
drive	general expectancy	Iceberg Profile

References

Allport, G. W. (1937). *Personality: A psychological interpretation.* New York: Henry Holt.

Allport, G. W. (1961). *Pattern and growth in personality.* New York: Holt, Rinehart and Winston.

Atkinson, R. L., Atkinson, R. C., Smith, E. E., & Bem, D. J. (1993). *Introduction to psychology,* 11th ed. New York: Harcourt Brace Jovanovich.

Bandura, A. (1965). Influence of models' reinforcement contingencies on the acquisition of imitative responses. *Journal of Personality and Social Psychology, 1,* 589–595.

Bandura, A., & Walters, R. H. (1963). *Social learning and personality development.* New York: Holt, Rinehart and Winston.

Burger, J. (1986). *Personality: Theory and research.* Belmont, CA: Wadsworth.

Carron, B. (1980). *Social psychology of sport.* Ithaca, NY: Mouvement.

Cattell, R. B. (1965). *The scientific analysis of personality.* Baltimore: Penguin.

Cattell, R. B. (1979). *Personality and learning theory: The structure of personality in its environment,* Vol. 1. New York: Springer.

Cattell, R. B., Eber, H. W., & Tatsuoka, M. M. (1970). *The 16 factor personality questionnaire.* Champaign, IL: Institute for Ability and Personality Testing.

Cratty, B. J. (1989). *Psychology in contemporary sport,* 3rd ed. Englewood Cliffs, NJ: Prentice Hall.

Eysenck, H. J. (1975). *The inequality of man.* San Diego: EdITS.

Eysenck, H. J., & Eysenck, M. W. (1985). *Personality and individual differences: A natural science approach.* New York: Plenum.

Feldman, R. S. (1992). *Elements of psychology.* New York: McGraw-Hill.

Fitts, P. M., & Posner, M. I. (1967). *Human performance.* Belmont, CA: Brooks/Cole.

Freud, S. (1961). The ego and the id and other works. In J. Strachey (Ed. and Trans.), *The standard edition of the complete psychological works of Sigmund Freud,* Vol. 19 (pp. 3–66). London: Hogarth. (Original work published 1923)

Gill, D. (1986). *Psychological dynamics of sport.* Champaign, IL: Human Kinetics.

Gleitman, H. (1992). *Basic psychology,* 3rd ed. New York: W.W. Norton.

Gough, H. G. (1960). *Manual for the California Psychological Inventory,* rev. ed. Palo Alto, CA: Consulting Psychologists.

Hathaway, S. R., & McKinley, J. C. (1940). A Multiphasic Personality Schedule (Minnesota): I. Construction of the schedule. *Journal of Psychology, 10,* 249–254.

Hollander, E. P. (1976). *Principles and methods of social psychology,* 3rd ed. New York: Oxford Univ. Press.

Hull, C. L. (1943). *Principles of behavior: An introduction to behavior theory.* New York: D. Appleton-Century.

Hull, C. L. (1952). *A behavior system: An introduction to behavior theory concerning the individual organism.* New Haven, CT: Yale Univ. Press.

Kleinmuntz, B. (1982). *Personality and psychological assessment.* New York: St. Martin's.

Liebert, R. M., & Spiegler, M. D. (1990). *Personality: Strategies and issues,* 6th ed. Pacific Grove, CA: Brooks/Cole.

McNair, D. M., Lorr, M., & Droppleman, L. F. (1971). *EDITS manual for POMS.* San Diego, CA: Educational and Industrial Testing Service.

Mischel, W. (1968). *Personality and assessment.* New York: Wiley.

Morgan, W. P. (1980). Test of champions. *Psychology Today, 14*(2), 92–93, 102, 108.

Morgan, C. D., & Murray, H. A. (1935). A method for investigating fantasies: The thematic apperception test. *Archives of Neurological Psychiatry, 34,* 289–306.

Rorschach, H. (1924). *Psychodiagnosis: A diagnostic test based on perception.* New York: Grune and Stratton.

Rotter, J. B. (1954). *Social learning and clinical psychology.* Englewood Cliffs, NJ: Prentice Hall.

Rotter, J. B. (1982). *The development and application of social learning theory.* New York: Praeger.

Silva, J. M., & Hardy, C. J. (1984). Precompetitive affect and athletic performance. In W. F. Straub & J. M. Williams (Eds.), *Cognitive Sport Psychology.* Lansing, NY: Sport Science Associates.

Silva, J. M., Schultz, B. B., Haslam, R. W., Martin, T. P., & Murray, D. F. (1985). Discriminating characteristics of contestants at the United States Olympic Wrestling Trials. *International Journal of Sport Psychology, 16,* 79–102.

Silva, J. M., Shultz, B. B., Haslam, R. W., & Murray, D. F. (1981). Psychophysiological assessment of elite wrestlers. *Research Quarterly for Exercise and Sport, 52,* 348–358.

Singer, R. N. (1988). Psychological testing: What value to coaches and athletes? *International Journal of Sport Psychology, 19,* 87–106.

Smith, R. E., Smoll, F. L., & Hunt, E. (1977). A system for the behavioral assessment of athletic coaches. *Research Quarterly, 48,* 401–407.

Thomas, J. R., & Nelson, J. K. (1996). *Research methods in physical activity.* Champaign, IL: Human Kinetics.

Watson, J. B. (1914). *Behavior: An introduction to comparative psychology.* New York: Henry Holt.

3

Personality and Sport Performance

Heather Deaner and John M. Silva III

The University of North Carolina at Chapel Hill

- This chapter expands on the definition provided previously and discusses the relationship between personality and performance in athletics.
- The skeptical theorists argue that there is no relationship between personality and sport performance. The credulous theorists argue the contrary from two perspectives: the Gravitational Model and the Personality and Performance Pyramid.
- Athletes who have personality characteristics such as positive precompetitive affect, emotional control and stability, self-discipline, low-trait anxiety, and high organizational ability are more likely to exhibit better performances.
- Factors such as sport type and gender also are related to the personality and sport performance relationship.
- There are several implications and applications of the relationship between personality and athletic performance. Knowing the psychological strengths and weaknesses of athletes can help to inform themselves as well as coaches and sport psychologists.

Personality: A Complex Concept

In the previous chapter, theorists defined personality as "consistent behavior patterns originating within the individual" (Burger, 1986, 5) and explained it in terms of three interrelated levels: a psychological core, typical responses, and role-related behaviors (Hollander, 1976). Personality comprises the forces and factors that influence how an individual behaves, as well as the traits and states exhibited by an individual through behavior in various situations (Silva, 1984). Carron (1980) summarizes personality by focusing on a balanced definition that includes the commonality as well as the uniqueness of traits, the stability as well as the adjustment of the organization of traits, and the physical as well as the psychological manifestations of traits (i.e., how traits are translated into behavior).

The first dimension of personality is the commonality and the uniqueness of traits. Compare your personality to that of a sibling or friend. In some regards, your personalities may be quite similar. Perhaps you are both extroverted and high achievers. In other facets, you are unique in comparison to your sibling or friend. Perhaps you are low-trait anxious while your sibling or friend is high-trait anxious. Kluckhohn and Murray (1948) summarized this dimension of personality by stating that each individual is like all others, like some others, like no other. Simply stated, individual personalities can be similar, but no two personalities are exactly the same.

The second dimension of personality is stability. Personalities are comprised of relatively stable, enduring characteristics exhibited over time and across situations (Silva, 1984). In fact, personality characteristics often are difficult to change or modify once they are well engrained. Have you ever tried to stop an unwanted habit such as throwing your bat or racket? Can you recall how difficult it was to change a habit or behavioral tendency once it was well engrained as a response? Perhaps you have yet to overcome some bad habits. Habits are difficult to change because they are conditioned responses; they result from numerous repetitions of the same behavior with rewards or punishments associated with the behavior. The response or behavior exhibited is a product of the habit strength and the drive (i.e., the level of desire and intensity). For example, a basketball player who continuously displays poor free-throw form and poor performance (i.e., habit strength) and is very anxious about shooting free throws in games (i.e., high drive) is likely to exhibit his or her dominant response (i.e., poor form/performance) in game situations. Although relatively enduring characteristics are difficult to change, adjustments can be made. For instance, an athlete who lacks emotional control has the power to take the necessary steps to gain emotional control and respond differently to situations that result in emotional responses. Although this change would be very beneficial for the athlete, it would also be very challenging because the response pattern may have years of learning history behind it resulting in a well-conditioned response.

Last, personality is a combination of both the psychological and the physical manifestations of traits. Traits such as anxiety, vigor, need-achievement, and intelligence are psychological characteristics. These psychological characteristics predispose an individual to affective states that accompany actual behaviors. For example, high-trait anxious athletes may avoid high anxiety situations, but when they cannot, their high-trait anxiety may predispose them to an affective state that results in behaviors such as sweating palms and rapid shifts of attention. These behaviors in turn affect their personalities so that a cycle is formed. For example, a wrestler (Scott) attempts a takedown in the final seconds of a tied match. Scott's opponent counters the move and gains the takedown resulting in Scott losing the match. If Scott is characterized as high-trait anxious, his unsuccessful attempt at a late match takedown serves to reinforce his high-trait anxiety. It may manifest itself in avoidance or hesitant behavior when Scott is placed in a similar match situation. On the other hand, if Scott was successful in his takedown attempt, the reward of winning may reinforce his assertive behavior providing him with added confidence in similar situations. Obviously, a takedown late in the match resulting in a win is not going to change Scott from a high-trait anxious person to a low-trait anxious person. However, if Scott has similar positive experiences over a long period of time, his expectancies can change and he may become less anxious in end of match situations.

Personality often is misunderstood in sport psychology, and a psychological dimension as powerful as personality requires careful examination. The important concept to remember is that while each individual may be predisposed toward certain characteristics, it is the interaction of these dispositions with actual environmental experiences that determines how one's personality is formed, how one actually behaves, and how one's personality may be modified over time. Because personality can influence behavior, and feedback about behavior (i.e., rewards and punishments) can influence subsequent dispositions to act, early researchers were very interested in the question of whether personality "drew" a participant to a particular sport or sport type. Recently, many sport psychologists also have addressed the relationship between personality and high-level performance. Let's examine the potential influence of personality factors upon performance in competitive sport environments.

Influence of Personality on Sport Performance

The influence of personality on sport performance has been a highly debated issue resulting in the formation of two divergent perspectives: the credulous and the skeptics. The skeptics believe there is no relationship between personality and sport performance (Kroll, 1976; Rushall, 1970). The credulous camp believes personality is related to participation and success in sport (Newcombe & Boyle, 1995). However, even within the credulous camp a division exists as to how strong the personality–performance relationship is. The debate that has ensued between the skeptical and credulous camps has produced three positions purported to explain the relationship between personality and sport performance. The first position states that there is no relationship between personality and sport performance (Fisher, Ryan, & Martens, 1976). The second position states that some individuals are born with certain psychological characteristics that enhance sport performance and therefore predispose them to success (Morgan, 1974). The final position is based on the Personality Performance Pyramid (Silva, 1984). It states that when participants initially enter the field of sport, personality may play a minor role. However, participants who advance to elite levels of sport tend to demonstrate a cluster of adaptive or desirable psychological characteristics.

Is Personality Unrelated to Performance?

The position that no relationship exists between personality and sport performance is supported by the skeptics who question whether athletic participation can be predicted from psychological data (Rushall, 1970). The skeptics' arguments are based on three criteria: the lack of generalizability in the available research, limitations in the research designs in sport personality research, and theoretical issues such as the meaning of personality and the interpretation of behavior in sport personality research. In short, the skeptics argue that the research in the area of personality and sport performance is flawed in many respects, such as sampling, testing, and interpretation procedures, and that even the nature of personality and its assessment cannot be agreed on within the sport psychology field. The particular definition of personality and the measurement technique one researcher uses often is quite different from the definition and measurement technique another researcher uses. Because of these methodological and theoretical limitations, the skeptics argue that studies showing a significant relationship between personality and sport performance cannot be considered reliable. However, several studies have shown a relationship between personality and sport performance (Mahoney & Avener, 1977; Morgan, 1979; Silva et al., 1984), and more researchers, particularly in the fields of psychology and forensics, are adopting a credulous viewpoint (Digman, 1990).

The Gravitational Model

The idea that certain individuals are born with psychological characteristics that predispose them to select into certain sports is called the **Gravitational Model** (Morgan, 1974). The Gravitational Model assumes that various sports require certain psychological characteristics; therefore, individuals are drawn toward or "gravitate" toward the sports that are best suited to their psychological makeup. For example, individuals who are more "aggressive" would gravitate toward collision sports, such as football or hockey, as opposed to precise or controlled sports, such as baseball or figure skating. This model was very attractive because it had an intuitive appeal. The psychological makeup you possess "matches" you to the characteristics of certain sports. Is this really the case, or does the sport environment and family environment influence your personality development and sport selection process?

The Gravitational Model is no longer widely accepted for a variety of reasons. In all probability, you were not drawn to your sport as the Gravitational Model indicates. Can you recall the first time you played peewee football, little league baseball, soccer, or some other sport? How did you become involved and at what age? Chances are you were four or five years old, and your parents or a relative signed you up to participate. At such a young age, children have little control over their lives and the decision-making process. Parents or other socializing agents often consciously influence sport socialization because of their prestige, proximity, and power to distribute love, rewards, and punishment (McPherson, 1981). Perhaps you know people who were not interested in participating in a particular sport, but they were forced to participate by a parent. The Gravitational Model also fails to explain the attrition that occurs in sport, particularly at the younger age levels. Many kids drop out because they do not enjoy the sport or because they do not enjoy the competitive environment. Perhaps you remember the neighborhood kid who played youth football yet hated contact and was not a very assertive person. Did you have any friends who competed in gymnastics because their parents required it, yet they were not coordinated or graceful? Vast differences in personality exist in sport at the younger age levels (Silva, 1984). A whole range of personalities can be seen on one team, yet, according to the Gravitational Model, these personalities should be quite similar. Are athletes born with psychological characteristics that predispose them to self-select into particular sports? The evidence suggests this is not the case.

Personality and Performance Pyramid

The third perspective on the influence of personality on sport performance suggests that most participants enter sports at an early age with different ability levels and personality characteristics. As participants are socialized into and through the sport subculture, certain personality characteristics and psychological adjustments can enhance advancement to higher levels of competition (Silva, 1984). Examining the personality performance relationship within various levels of competition can assist in understanding the characteristics of athletes. While there is no ideal profile for all athletes, there is a model that can explain some of the commonality as well as the uniqueness of the personalities of athletes. The **Personality and Performance Pyramid** (Silva, 1984; see Fig. 3.1) proposes that at entrance and lower levels of competition, personality is very heterogeneous and does not predict performance very accurately. Generally, participants are at younger age levels, and their personalities are still developing. In addition, the psychological demands of sport are not communicated with clarity until the late childhood and early teen years when competition often takes on a serious demeanor. At these lower levels of competition, physical skills best predict performance because there is a wide range of abilities and maturational rates among participants. However, as participants move to higher levels of competition, some homogeneity in certain "adaptive" personality characteristics increases the probability of continued involvement at these advanced levels. Given that physical abilities are more evenly matched at the higher competitive levels, it is the psychological characteristics that best predict performance at these levels. Athletes who have developed the adaptive psychological characteristics will increase their probability of success at higher levels of competition.

As an athlete advances up the competitive pyramid to the elite level, one of the following situations occurs. First, an athlete possesses the physical talent to compete at the higher level but fails to make the necessary psychological adjustments and drops out or is cut from the team. This is seen most often when athletes attempt to go from the high school level to the collegiate level or from the collegiate level to the professional level. Many athletes are unable to make a smooth transition to the next level because of impatience, poor emotional control, or loss of confidence. For example, an athlete who questions his or her

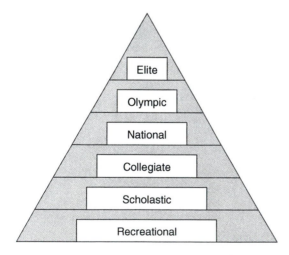

FIGURE 3.1 *Personality and Performance Pyramid.*

belief in oneself and adopts a pessimistic view is decreasing the probability for a successful transition despite possessing the necessary physical talent. Second, athletes make desirable and adaptive psychological adjustments, thus increasing the probability for advancement to the higher levels. Many elite athletes, such as Michael Jordan, Dan Marino, and Jackie Joyner-Kersee, have adjusted to the demands of competitive sport and have performed at a high level over a period of time although they often may have experienced failures or setbacks at lower competitive levels. Third, athletes fail to make the psychological adjustments but succeed in spite of themselves. John McEnroe and Dennis Rodman are two examples of such athletes. Both have displayed quick tempers, erratic behaviors, and lack of emotional control within their sports. Yet even with the limitations generated by these characteristics, these athletes have achieved success in the sports of tennis and basketball, respectively. However, John McEnroe and Dennis Rodman are exceptions to the rule. Many athletes who fail to make positive psychological adjustments do not succeed at higher levels of competition. Those who do succeed with psychological characteristics that conflict with the demands of high level competition often have shorter careers, are forced into retirement, or have many interpersonal conflicts with teammates and coaches.

Info Box

Elite athletes tend to have similar body structures and physical abilities, such as height, weight, speed, or strength, that seem to be adaptive physical characteristics; if they don't have them, the likelihood of advancing in a particular sport is small. Similarly, sport psychology has found some very similar personality characteristics of elite athletes that may be conceptualized as adaptive.

Personality Characteristics of Elite Athletes

Although it is difficult to predict performance with psychological variables at lower competitive levels, psychological variables have been found to relate to performance at higher competitive levels. In a study conducted by Morgan (1979), 10 out of 16 finalists for the 1974 United States Heavyweight Rowing Team were identified correctly following psychological evaluation. These correct predictions were due in part to the differing psychological profiles that have been found to exist between mentally healthy, elite athletes and less successful, mentally unhealthy athletes (Morgan, 1979). These distinguishing profiles characterize the basis of the *Mental Health Model*. It states that elite athletes generally experience greater positive mental health than do their less successful counterparts (Cox, 1994). According to the Mental Health Model, athletes with greater positive mental health will be more likely to achieve athletic success and advance to or remain at high levels of competition (Gill, 1986; Weinberg & Gould, 1995). Support for the idea that adaptive characteristics may be related to higher levels of performance has been found in a series of experiments conducted with Olympic and national level teams (Mahoney & Avener, 1977; Silva et al., 1984). Silva and colleagues (1984) found several psychological factors predicted performance and allowed for the correct classification of Olympic trial participants into qualifier and nonqualifier categories. The psychological variables that increase the probability of reaching higher levels of the competitive pyramid are unique because they all represent a positive competitive adaptation by the athlete. Closer examination of these predictors will demonstrate how valuable it is for an athlete to possess or develop these qualities in the stressful competitive environment.

Positive Precompetitive Affect

How do you feel as game time approaches? Excited, nervous, energized, tense? All of these responses are examples of affect. Silva and Hardy (1984) defined **affect** as the feelings and cognitions that together provide a particular mind-set. This mind-set is dynamic; it changes according to personal and/or situational variables. For example, an unranked tennis player who is matched against a ranked tennis player may feel excited the night before the match. However, as the match approaches and the fans fill the stands, the unranked tennis player now may feel nervous and tense. This tennis player's affect changed during the precompetitive period. The **precompetitive period** is defined as the interval 24 hours or less prior to the initiation of competition. The change in affect this tennis player experienced was in a negative direction that can be detrimental to performance. On the other hand, **positive precompetitive affect** can facilitate performance (Silva & Hardy, 1984). Athletes who can successfully monitor and control their precompetitive affects have clear advantages because they will have optimal mind-sets prior to entering competition.

The **Profile of Mood States (POMS)** was developed to measure athletes' precompetitive affects (McNair, Lorr, & Droppleman, 1971). This measurement examines the psychological mood states of tension, depression, anger, vigor, fatigue, and confusion. The POMS can distinguish a positive affective state from a negative one. Specifically, athletes who score low on tension, depression, anger, fatigue, and confusion and high on vigor are characterized as possessing positive affects. In addition, through administering this test, it has been found that many successful elite athletes possess positive affects prior to competition (Cox, 1994). Morgan dubbed the successful athlete's pattern on the POMS the **Iceberg Profile** because it resembles an iceberg (see Fig. 3.2). Scores at the 50th percentile represent the population norm or the "surface" of the waterline. Successful elite athletes score below the norm on the negative traits and above the norm on the positive trait of vigor creating a pattern that resembles an iceberg. In contrast, those elite athletes who are less successful may show various profiles. They are less likely to demonstrate the classic Iceberg Profile.

The precompetitive period is extremely important for athletes because no matter how hard or how long they train, poor precompetitive affect can undermine the preparation. Athletes who fail to demonstrate the classic Iceberg Profile may be plagued by **tension,** thus increasing the probability for poor performance. The affective state of tension can increase anxiety and cloud the athletes' minds with negative cognitions; they either think about irrelevant information or are so tense they have tunnel vision and hardly think at all. **Depression** also can hinder performance. Have you ever entered competition fearing the possibility of failing and disappointing teammates, family members, your coach, or yourself? How did you play? Depressive feelings and cognitions often negatively impact performance because your mind is distracted by extenuating circumstances and not focused on the task at hand or because your energy level is low. **Anger** also can have a negative impact on performance because it has a negative correlation with concentration (Silva,

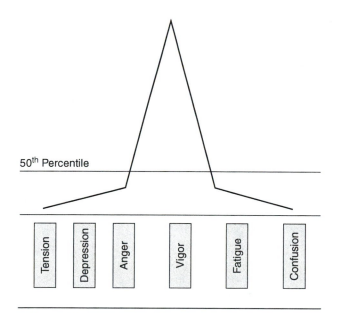

50th Percentile

Tension   Depression   Anger   Vigor   Fatigue   Confusion

FIGURE 3.2   *Iceberg Profile.*

1979). Instead of focusing on the moment, athletes who are angry focus on the source of that anger and may respond inappropriately. After a mistake, an athlete characterized by high anger is more likely to become frustrated instead of coping. Anger focuses the athlete's attention on the past, but sport demands a present and future orientation to respond quickly and anticipate play. High levels of mental **fatigue** also reduce the ability of athletes to perform up to their potential. Just as physical fatigue drains athletes of energy, so does mental fatigue. Mental fatigue strips athletes of the mental energy they need to compete successfully, and it slows and hinders decision-making processes and response times. **Confusion** results in athletes who are not clear-headed about task requirements, personal objectives needed to be successful, or their ability to implement a game plan. Instead of making firm decisions in the heat of the competitive environment, athletes high in confusion will be more likely to question themselves and be tentative and hesitant in their performance. They may be awed by the venue, location, or competition. Last, athletes low in **vigor** lack the mental energy they need to compete. These athletes are not "pumped" or "psyched" to compete. Instead of looking forward to competing, athletes low in vigor mentally pull away from competition. They wish the competition were two hours away, tomorrow, or the next day instead of right now.

Athletes who demonstrate the Iceberg Profile during the precompetitive period have more positive and adaptive mind-sets just prior to competition. These athletes are low in tension and anxiety; therefore, they maintain their competitive focus. Their minds are clear and focused on positive thoughts. They score low on depression and approach success instead of trying to avoid failure. Their focus is on the task at hand as opposed to worrying about outside factors. They have low levels of anger; therefore, they are able to concentrate on task-relevant variables (i.e., components of the game) as opposed to outside variables. They are focused on the present as well as anticipating future events. Athletes who exhibit the Iceberg Profile are also low on fatigue; therefore, they possess the necessary mental energy required to compete. This allows them to remain mentally strong and to quickly make smart decisions. These athletes also score low on confusion, which enables them to make clear judgments and have a sense of where they are and what they are about. They are certain of the requirements, their objectives, and how they will go about achieving those objectives. Last, these athletes score high in vigor. They are ready to compete and possess the mental energy needed to do so. They mentally move toward the competition and are excited for the opportunity to compete.

Research in a variety of sports has supported the positive influence of precompetitive affect on performance. Silva and colleagues (1984, 1981), Highlen and Bennett (1979), and Gould, Weiss, and Weinberg (1981) all have demonstrated the relationship between positive precompetitive affect and performance in the sport of wrestling. Mahoney and Avener (1977) found that successful gymnasts had more positive affects just prior to competition than less successful gymnasts. In addition, Gibson (1990), when studying collegiate gymnasts, found performance increased as positive precompetitive affect increased. This relationship also has been demonstrated in elite level male distance runners (Morgan et al., 1988). Thus, the relationship between precompetitive affect and performance is an important consideration for performers, particularly at higher levels of competition where even the smallest psychological advantage may mean the difference between success and setback. Athletes who consistently possess a positive precompetitive affect, so that it becomes an enduring characteristic, are increasing their probability for successful performance and are at a clear advantage over those athletes whose precompetitive affect is negative or inconsistent.

Info Box

The six factors measured by the POMS are interrelated. Athletes who are successful in reducing their levels of tension also will observe a reduction in fatigue and an increase in vigor. Similarly, a reduction in anger could affect tension or fatigue.

Emotional Control

Have you ever missed an outside shot in basketball, hit a backhand into the net during a tennis match, false started in track, or shot wide of the goal in lacrosse? How did you respond to your missed opportunity? Perhaps you got upset, gave up, swore, or blamed your teammates; or maybe you said, "I'll be ready next time," and recovered quickly. Everyone makes mistakes now and then. The key is how you respond to those mistakes. Do your emotions get the best of you, or do you manage and control your emotions effectively? **Emotional control** is the second predictor of elite performance. Elite athletes who successfully control their emotions are often more successful than those athletes who allow their emotions to control them. During the course of a game, athletes may face numerous adverse situations, such as a referee's bad call, poor team or individual performance, or even heckling fans. Athletes low in emotional control often get upset and frustrated by these situations and lose focus. They may exhibit undesirable behaviors, such as yelling at teammates or the coach, or drawing a technical or personal foul. On the other hand, athletes high in emotional control handle these adverse situations more favorably. As a result, they often refocus their attention to task relevant information and continue to perform effectively. That is not to say these athletes never get upset or frustrated. They do. However, these athletes keep their emotions under control allowing them to quickly refocus their attention and effort toward the task at hand.

Emotional Stability

Emotional stability is the athlete's ability to recover from success or failure quickly. At the collegiate and professional levels of sport, success and failure are hot topics for the media driven society in which we live. Headlines boldly sum up the successes and failures

Emotional control can be an important psychological factor when the game is on the line.

of today's elite athletes as do radio stations, local and national news centers, and electronic sources. No doubt they also will have a picture to capture the joy of success or agony of defeat that the athlete displays. Sports are emotional, and no one experiences the wide range of emotions more than the athletes themselves. However, athletes are not defined by a single moment, whether it be a success or a failure, as the media tends to portray them. Instead, athletes are defined by their cumulative experiences, which include both successes and failures. That is why emotional stability is so important. Elite athletes compete with all their resources until they are physically, mentally, and emotionally drained. However, while athletes can control how they compete, they cannot control the outcome. Sometimes they are successful, and other times they fail. Although successful experiences should be enjoyed by the athlete, success must be kept in perspective. Likewise, while it hurts to lose, especially after extending so much effort, failures must be kept in perspective as well.

Keeping successes and failures in perspective allows the athlete to prepare for the next competition. This is extremely important because most athletic teams have long competitive seasons. The NFL comprises a 17-week regular season (16 games), the NHL regular season comprises approximately 80 games, MLB has approximately 160 regular season games, and the NBA has approximately 80 regular season games. These numbers obviously do not include preseason and postseason competition. Imagine if Michael Jordan got so upset after a regular season loss that he could not get psychologically ready for his next game, or he got so excited after a win that he was emotionally flying high and could not bring his emotions back to a normal level. This is what happens to athletes who are emotionally unstable. They ride an "emotional roller coaster," experiencing extreme highs after successes and extreme lows after failures. These extreme emotional swings can be psychologically and physically exhausting and, therefore, a hindrance to performance. Successful elite athletes are characterized by emotional stability. Their emotional highs and lows are not often extreme, and they tend to return to a normal emotional level quickly. They expect success and, of course, enjoy it, but they are mature enough to understand that more challenges lie ahead, sometimes as soon as tomorrow in professional sports. Failure, although disappointing, simply increases the interest and challenge level for an elite athlete.

Self-Discipline

When you were young, did your parents ever tell you to clean your room, feed the dog or cat, or do your homework? Your parents were trying to instill a sense of discipline. However, this form of discipline is different from self-discipline. How do they differ? Discipline is placed on an individual from outside sources (e.g., by parents, coaches, teachers), but **self-discipline** originates within the individual. Athletes at almost every competitive level from high school to college are disciplined. Coaches tell athletes what to do and how and when to do it. As a result of these instructions, athletes' lives are very structured. However, as an athlete moves up the competitive ladder to elite competition, it is self-discipline that becomes more important. Self-discipline is the ability to structure one's environment and to give up immediate rewards to strive for future rewards and goals of a greater magnitude. Self-discipline is not easy. There are no guarantees in life, and there is certainly no guarantee that athletes will achieve future rewards or goals simply because they give up immediate rewards to work toward those future goals. For instance, a soccer player may give up time that could be spent with friends in order to get extra practice on the weekends in the hope of making the starting lineup. However, there is no guarantee that she will achieve her goal even though she made that sacrifice. Self-discipline is often characteristic of successful elite athletes. For them, the price associated with making sacrifices is far out-weighed by the potential future gains. The possibility of their future successes serves to maintain their motivation while they are relinquishing immediate personal satisfaction or gratification. The important point is that athletes exhibit these behaviors in the absence of any obvious immediate reward, and the behaviors are self-initiated, meaning that no one tells them what, when, or how long they should exhibit the behavior. Self-disciplined athletes will work long and hard for the goals they have set for themselves. Obviously, this characteristic can be a great facilitator of athlete development and performance.

Low-Trait Anxiety

Many sport psychologists believe that anxiety is the single most powerful debilitator of performance. Athletes who have high-trait anxiety focus on the possibility of failure, but athletes who have *low-trait anxiety* view competition as a challenge. High-trait anxious athletes often avoid new opportunities because they may not succeed. Just the opposite is true of low-trait anxious athletes. They seek out new opportunities to approach success.

High-trait anxious athletes view competition as threatening; they often perceive situations as more threatening or dangerous than is actually the case. For example, if a team's luggage were late in arriving for an away game or match, athletes characterized as high-trait anxious would be more likely to let this mishap affect them. They would be likely to focus on the mishap and worry that their routines were not going as planned, instead of adapting and focusing on what they can control. In addition, high-trait anxious athletes often have difficulty in playoff games because their perspective becomes one of "do or die" instead of treating the "big" game as any other game or as an extension of practice. Under pressure situations or following mistakes, their high-trait anxiety serves to debilitate their performance. They focus on the mistake or the consequences of the situation instead of recovery. Their minds wander or focus on their past failures, the current threatening circumstances, and the potential negative consequences of the future. For example, a gymnast characterized by high-trait anxiety who has just fallen off the balance beam will be likely to focus on that mistake throughout the rest of the routine and perhaps carry it over to the remaining events. She may recall past falls off the beam, focus on the low score she will receive, and/or focus on the effect her fall could have on the team's overall score. Her self-confidence and self-efficacy may waiver. This obviously can be detrimental to performance, especially in a sport requiring such high levels of concentration and physical steadiness as does gymnastics.

Low-trait anxious athletes respond much more effectively to mistakes and high-pressure situations than do their high-trait anxious counterparts. They recognize their mistakes, but, unlike high-trait anxious athletes, they are able to move past them and mentally to recover quickly. Thus, they are focused on what is taking place in the present in the game or match as opposed to their recent mistakes. Low-trait anxious athletes are able mentally to recover quicker because they are not as devastated by their mistakes as are high-trait anxious athletes. In fact, low-trait anxious athletes are challenged and motivated by their mistakes to work even harder. As a result of their approach, low-trait anxious athletes have lower **critical response times** (CRT) than do high-trait anxious athletes (Cratty, 1989). The CRT is the amount of time it takes for an athlete to mentally and physically recover from a mistake and get back into the game. Because mistakes are viewed as less devastating for low-trait anxious athletes, they experience smaller performance decrements after mistakes are made and generally have much shorter CRTs than do high-trait anxious athletes. High trait-anxious athletes view their mistakes as threatening and, therefore, often experience large performance decrements and have slower CRTs. In fact, athletes characterized as high-trait anxious may never return to previous performance levels following a mistake and may avoid similar situations in the future.

Doing it right! Practice provides opportunity for psychological as well as physical conditioning.

High Organizational Ability

Have you ever felt that there were too few hours in a day? How do you juggle your responsibilities associated with school, sports, work, family, and friends? High-level athletes deal with this question too. Not only must they juggle those responsibilities, but also their athletic responsibilities often place abnormal time and fatigue constraints on them. Elite athletes spend hours in practice, training, and competition. It is crucial that their lives are structured. If athletes fail to manage their time properly, conflict will arise as competing demands are placed on them. For example, if collegiate athletes fail to schedule adequate time for studying, and their grades fall, they may be facing academic ineligibility and be forced to the sidelines. Because of the complexity of their lives, it is essential that elite athletes have **high organizational ability** so that they may balance all aspects of their lives. However, it also is important that elite athletes possess the self-discipline to match the high organization because the two go hand in hand. If an athlete does not have the self-discipline to complete a particular task, high organization will not be as beneficial. In addition, if an athlete is self-disciplined but is low in organizational ability, the self-discipline will not be maximized to its fullest. This relationship is supported by the fact that athletes high in self-discipline also tend to be highly organized.

Not only is each predictor (i.e., positive precompetitive affect, emotional control, emotional stability, self-discipline, low-trait anxiety, and high organizational ability) important, but even more important is the sum of these predictors. Taken together, these predictors are very adaptive in bringing out an athlete's physical talent level. Without even one predictor, it is less likely that an athlete will be able to perform to the level of their physical abilities.

Info Box

It is important to remember that although these personality traits are very difficult to change, they can be changed. For example, athletes that lack self-discipline are not destined to fail but must work hard to strengthen this weakness so that they can succeed in sport.

Other Variables Related to Personality and Sport Performance

Can athletes of one sport be distinguished from athletes of another sport on the basis of personality? Are football players different from wrestlers? Are soccer players different from gymnasts? Do female athletes differ from male athletes on personality characteristics as they do on certain physical characteristics such as strength and speed? These types of questions have attracted some attention within sport personality research. Specifically, researchers have examined the variables of sport type and gender and their influence upon personality. However, much of the research has been inconclusive. While some studies do show personality differences based on sport type and gender (Kroll & Crenshaw, 1970; Newcombe & Boyle, 1995; Schurr, Ashley, & Joy, 1977; Singer, 1969; Williams, 1980), many of these studies are old and focus only on a few select sports or a few select characteristics. As a result, it is difficult to ascertain the potential influence of sport type and gender on personality and sport performance at this time.

Implications and Applications for the Field of Sport Psychology

What do the findings reviewed in this chapter mean, and how can the information be utilized by athletes, coaches, and sport psychologists? If it is known that certain psychological characteristics are adaptive and enhance the probability of climbing the competitive ladder, how can this information be applied to the field setting?

Athletes

The implications and applications for the athletes are tremendous. Athletes who want to advance and be successful at high levels of competition can benefit from learning to take personal inventory. Athletes are very skilled at taking inventory on their physical attributes. Ask a football player for a list of his strengths and weaknesses, and you are likely to get a detailed list. A running back may say, "I run the forty in 4.3 seconds, have soft hands, and move well laterally, but I need to make my moves crisper and improve my run blocking technique." Ask that same athlete for a list of his psychological strengths and weaknesses, and you are likely to get a delayed, fragmented response. Many athletes neither take inventory of their psychological characteristics nor pay close attention to these characteristics until they are confronted with adversity, challenge, or failure. Throughout this chapter, it was highlighted that at elite levels of competition, it is the psychological characteristics as opposed to the physical characteristics that separate the successful athletes from the less successful. Athletes who are aware of their mental strengths and weaknesses can make the necessary adjustments, whereas athletes who are unaware of their psychological strengths and weaknesses will not know what adjustments are needed. In short, Athletes who are serious in their pursuit of athletic excellence need to address both the physical and the psychological components. To address the psychological components of sport, athletes may wish to seek the services of an AAASP (Association for the Advancement of Applied Sport Psychology) certified sport psychologist who has the necessary training to help athletes assess their psychological strengths and weaknesses. Together, the athlete and the sport psychologist can identify areas of strengths and weaknesses through psychological assessment and then devise a game plan for maintaining the strengths and improving the weaknesses. Unfortunately, the probability of an athlete being able to work with a sport psychologist is at times dependent on the coach and his or her acceptance of and belief in the value of sport psychology.

Coaches

Coaches often interact with their individual players in different ways. A softball coach may challenge or yell at one of her pitchers who is struggling but may encourage or console another pitcher in the same situation. Whether consciously or unconsciously, the coach has taken some form of inventory on her players and has made personality judgments. Perhaps she categorized one pitcher as mentally tough and therefore strong enough to endure the criticism, but another pitcher was categorized as sensitive, emotional, and therefore susceptible to criticism and pressure. Many coaches make these judgments, and in doing so, they are suggesting that personalities affect sport behaviors. In fact, the traditional half time speech has been a tool used by coaches to psychologically motivate their players. Coaches need to be further educated about the personality/sport relationship so that they recognize the importance of the mental side of sport. However, most coaches are overwhelmed by their various responsibilities to their individual players, team, school, and athletic director; have limited time available; and are uneducated about psychological principles and concepts. Because of these constraints, coaches are not well-suited or trained to develop the mental side of their athletes. However, coaches can recognize the importance of the mental side of sports and work to understand the individual differences in their players. After doing so, coaches can attempt to develop desirable psychological responses and mental sets in their athletes through various practice structures and feedback provided to their athletes. Coaches also need to utilize the services of sport psychologists as tools through which the mental side can be tapped. In addition, coaches need to educate their athletes on the relationship between personality and sport performance and foster in them the desire to improve their mental game.

Sport Psychologists

What do the findings about the relationship between personality and sport performance mean for sport psychologists? First, they indicate that further research is required on the relationship between personality and performance. The majority of studies indicate a moderate relationship between the two, but the field needs to continue this line of research and improve the methodological and theoretical limitations that plagued past studies. Thus, more conclusive results can be obtained, and a consensus on the personality/sport relationship can be reached. Second, new lines of research need to be developed. The number of females participating in sports has increased dramatically over the last few decades. This will continue with the emergence of women's professional basketball and the popularity and success of women's sports at the 1996 Olympic Games and the 1998 Olympic Winter Games. The research on gender has not increased sufficiently to parallel women's involvement. In addition, the variable of race needs to be examined with respect to personality characteristics and sport performance as it has been examined with respect to social psychological variables. Considering the number of African Americans competing in collegiate and professional sports, this seems to be a logical step. Third, many of the findings are concrete enough that sport psychologists should be incorporating them into their practices. As stated earlier, personalities are stable, yet through a conscious effort maintained over time, individuals have the capacity to make adjustments in behavior choices and responses to coaches, teammates, officials, and game situations. The sport psychologist is the facilitator in this process of change. The sport psychologist has the working knowledge of both psychology and sport that is necessary to help athletes help themselves. With help, athletes may adapt or modify personality characteristics that detract from their probability of advancing to higher levels of competition. Last, it is crucial that individuals within the sport psychology field educate those within the sport subculture about what the field has to offer.

Specifically, sport psychologists need to educate coaches, athletes, athletic trainers, and the others who make up the "athletic team" about the benefits of using sport psychology services. Without the vehicles to apply the findings, the research conducted in sport psychology will be to no avail. There is much work to do in examining the personality and sport performance relationship. This work should include research as well as application and involve sport psychologists as well as athletes and coaches.

Key Terms (in order of appearance)

Gravitational Model	Profile of Mood States (POMS)	vigor
Personality and Performance Pyramid	Iceberg Profile	emotional control
	tension	emotional stability
Mental Health Model	depression	self-discipline
affect	anger	low-trait anxiety
precompetitive period	fatigue	critical response time
positive precompetitive affect	confusion	high organizational ability

References

Burger, J. (1986). *Personality: Theory and research.* Belmont, CA: Wadsworth.

Carron, A. V. (1980). *Social psychology of sport.* Ithaca, NY: Mouvement.

Cox, R. H. (1994). *Sport psychology: Concepts and applications,* 3rd ed. Dubuque, IA: Brown and Benchmark.

Cratty, B. J. (1989). *Psychology in contemporary sport,* 3rd ed. Englewood Cliffs, NJ: Prentice Hall.

Digman, J. M. (1990). Personality structure: Emergence of the five-factor model. *Annual Reviews Psychology, 41,* 417–440.

Fisher, A. C., Ryan, E. D., & Martens, R. (1976). Current status and future directions of personality research related to motor behavior and sport: Three panelists' views. In A. C. Fisher (Ed.), *Psychology of sport* (pp. 400–431). Palo Alto, CA: Mayfield.

Gibson, J. L. "The relationship between precompetitive affect and collegiate gymnastic performance." Master's thesis, University of North Carolina, Chapel Hill, 1990.

Gill, D. (1986). *Psychological dynamics of sport.* Champaign, IL: Human Kinetics.

Gould, D., Weiss, M., & Weinberg, R. (1981). Psychological characteristics of successful and nonsuccessful Big Ten wrestlers. *Journal of Sport Psychology, 3,* 68–81.

Highlen, P. S., & Bennett, B. B. (1979). Psychological characteristics of successful and nonsuccessful elite wrestlers: An exploratory study. *Journal of Sport Psychology, 1,* 123–137.

Hollander, E. P. (1976). *Principles and methods of social psychology,* 3rd ed. New York: Oxford University Press.

Kluckhohn, C., & Murray, H. A. (1949). *Personality in nature, society and culture.* New York: Knopf.

Kroll, W. (1976). Reaction to Morgan's paper: Psychological consequences of vigorous physical activity and sport. In M. G. Scott (Ed.), *The academy papers.* Iowa City: American Academy of Physical Education.

Kroll, W., & Crenshaw, W. (1970). Multivariate personality profile analysis of four athletic groups. In G. S. Kenyon (Ed.), *Contemporary psychology of sport, proceedings of the second international congress of sport psychology.* Chicago: Athletic Institute.

Mahoney, M. J., & Avener, M. (1977). Psychology of the elite athlete: An exploratory study. *Cognitive Therapy and Research, 1,* 135–141.

McNair, D. M., Lorr, M., & Droppleman, L. F. (1971). *Profile of mood states manual.* San Diego: Educational and Industrial Testing Services.

McPherson, B. D. (1981). Socialization into and through sport involvement. In G. Lueschen & G. Sage (Eds.), *Handbook of social science of sport* (pp. 246–273). Champaign, IL: Stipes.

Morgan, W. P. (1974). Selected psychological considerations in sport. *Research Quarterly, 45,* 374–390.

Morgan, W. P. (1979). Prediction of performance in athletics. In P. Klavora & J. V. Daniel (Eds.), *Coach, athlete, and the sport psychologist* (pp. 173–186). Champaign, IL: Human Kinetics.

Morgan, W. P., O'Connor, P. J., Ellickson, K. A., & Bradley, P. W. (1988). Personality structure, mood states, and performance in elite male distance runners. *International Journal of Sport Psychology, 19,* 247–263.

Newcombe, P. A., & Boyle, G. J. (1995). High school students' sports personalities: Variations across participation level, gender, type of sport, and success. *International Journal of Sport Psychology, 19,* 247–263.

Rushall, B. S. (1970). An evaluation of the relationship between personality and physical performance categories. In G. S. Kenyon (Ed.), *Contemporary psychology of sport.* Chicago: Athletic Institute.

Schurr, K. T., Ashley, M. A., & Joy, K. L. (1977). A multivariate analysis of male athlete personality characteristics: Sport type and success. *Multivariate Experimental Clinical Research, 3,* 53–68.

Silva, J. M. (1979). Behavioral and situational factors affecting concentration and skill performance. *Journal of Sport Psychology, 1,* 221–227.

Silva, J. M. (1984). Personality and sport performance: Controversy and challenge. In J. M. Silva & R. S. Weinberg (Eds.), *Psychological foundations of sport* (pp. 59–69). Champaign, IL: Human Kinetics.

Silva, J. M., & Hardy, C. J. (1984). Precompetitive affect and athletic performance. In W. F. Straub & J. H. Williams (Eds.), *Cognitive sport psychology* (pp. 79–88). Lansing, NY: Sport Science Associates.

Silva, J. M., Schultz, B. B., Haslam, R. W., Martin, T. P., & Murray, D. F. (1984). Discriminating characteristics of contestants at the United States Olympic Wrestling Trials. *International Journal of Sport Psychology, 16,* 79–102.

Silva, J. M., Schultz, B. B., Haslam, R. W., & Murray, D. (1981). A psychophysiological assessment of elite wrestlers. *Research Quarterly for Exercise and Sport, 52,* 348–358.

Singer, R. N. (1969). Personality differences between and within baseball and tennis players. *The Research Quarterly, 40,* 582–588.

Weinberg, R. S., & Gould, D. (1995). *Foundations of sport and exercise psychology.* Champaign, IL: Human Kinetics.

Williams, J. M. (1980). Personality characteristics of the successful female athlete. In W. F. Straub (Ed.), *Sport psychology: An analysis of athlete behavior.* Ithaca, NY: Mouvement.

4

Understanding Individual Motivation in Sport

Laura Finch

Western Illinois University

- The concept of motivation is complex; however, it has been simplified to include the direction and intensity of behavior.
- Instinct Theory, Drive Theory, Need Achievement Theory, Attribution Theory, Goal Orientation Theory, and Cognitive Evaluation Theory provide explanations of motivation and behavior.

Why Study Motivation and Sport?

The sports pages gives us many examples, ranging from the bizarre to the familiar, of coaches and athletes attempting to increase their motivation. In a high-school cafeteria in suburban Chicago, a coach used fake blood and a starter's pistol to pretend he had been shot in an attempt to increase his players' motivation. In the southeastern United States, a Division I college football coach made his players watch a bull get castrated. He explained his actions by saying he hoped it would motivate the team for an important game. Many sports fans are familiar with Knute Rockne's famous "Win one for the Gipper" line, designed to inspire his Notre Dame football team to victory. In the gyms, pools, tracks, and stadiums across the world, many athletes listen to their favorite music before competitions to increase their motivation.

But motivation is not as simple as witnessing a spectacular pregame event, hearing a coach's catchy motivational slogan or inspirational speech, or listening to your favorite song. Motivation is a complex interaction of cultures, environments, and personal characteristics that inspire those in sport to reach their best performance. It is about the strivings of athletes and coaches—their wants, desires, and aspirations for their athletic performances. In short, motivation helps explain who we are and why we do what we do.

Defining Motivation

Motivation is one of the most misunderstood aspects of sport psychology. In fact, a leading expert in sport motivation said that motivation is less well understood in sports than in any other arena (Roberts, 1992). A primary reason for this lack of understanding is the plethora of definitions for the term. Motivation has been defined as many different things by the athletes and coaches who take part in sport and exercise. These definitions range from internal characteristics and external influences to consequences and explanations of behavior (Weinberg & Gould, 1995).

Some define motivation as an internal personality characteristic that an athlete possesses. That is, motivation is an attribute that some athletes have more of than others. For example, some athletes are thought to be highly motivated, but others are labeled as "unmotivated" or lazy. Defining motivation as simply an innate ability has led some coaches to give up prematurely on athletes rather than to help them understand and optimize their motivation.

Motivation is often characterized by long hours of individualized practice.

Others view motivation as an external influence, such as a reward. In other words, some athletes and coaches believe motivated behavior results from rewards in the environment, such as trophies or praise. The problem with defining motivation from this stimulus–response perspective is that not every athlete responds to the same reward in the same manner. Rewards that motivate some athletes to work harder may have the opposite effect (or no effect) on other athletes. The differential impact of rewards will be explained later in the chapter under Cognitive Evaluation Theory.

Finally, some athletes and coaches describe motivation as an explanation for the air behavior. They attribute their performance to their level of motivation. For example, it is common to hear coaches and athletes say they won a game because they "wanted it more" than the other team, implying that the victors had more motivation than their opponents did. In these cases, athletes and coaches relate motivation to competitiveness.

As these examples demonstrate, motivation can be viewed from many perspectives. Taken individually, each of these perspectives limits our understanding of motivation. Athletes can alter their levels and types of motivation through the successful application of sport psychology principles. Athletes are not "stuck" with one type of motivation or another. Taken collectively, these viewpoints expand our understanding of motivation. They offer an interactional perspective of motivation that can assist athletes to identify and reach their optimal level of motivation.

The study of motivation can be divided into three fundamental questions. The first question is, "What causes or initiates behavior?" Making sense of behavior's initiation, goal directedness, persistence, change, and cessation are important aspects of understanding what causes behavior. For example, to understand an athlete's motivation, it is just as important to know why an athlete participates in sport to begin with (the behavior's initiation) as it is to know why he or she chooses particular types of goals while participating in sport (goal directedness). It is equally important to understand the factors that help to sustain motivated behavior. Anyone who has started an exercise program only to stop after a few weeks knows quite well the difficult aspect of sustaining motivation to exercise.

The second fundamental question concerns behavior intensity: "Why do athletes work hard some days and put forth less effort on other days?" Or, "Why do some athletes have no trouble motivating themselves for competitions but get restless during practice drills?"

The third fundamental question involves individual differences in motivated behavior. "Why are some athletes quick to tackle challenging tasks whereas others engage in endeavors that are only minimally challenging?" Understanding individual differences in motivational factors, such as goal orientations and persistence levels, helps sport psychologists to be more effective in optimizing athletes' motivational levels.

Info Box

A succinct definition of motivation is elusive; however, the broad concept of motivation can help to explain behavior in sport. Motivation can give insight into the initiation, direction and intensity, and the sustainment of behaviors.

What Is Motivation?

Just what is motivation? It is more than positive thinking or trying harder. It is a dynamic process that involves people's incentives for activity and their drive toward particular behaviors in practice and competition. Specifically, and simply, motivation is the direction and intensity of behavior (Roberts, 1992; Weinberg & Gould, 1995). Understanding the direction of behavior is not enough (Roberts, 1992, 1993). Success in applying sport psychology principles to improve sport performance means understanding the intensity or energy level of behavior as well.

Some have suggested that this definition (motivation = the direction and intensity of behavior) appears too simplistic to adequately describe the wide range of motivated behaviors in sport (see, e.g., Weiss & Chaumeton, 1992). Also, this definition does not address how motivated behavior is sustained over time. However, this definition's simplicity is its strength. If coaches and sport psychologists can understand the direction and intensity of sport-related behavior, then they can more effectively help athletes optimize their motivation, which often leads to sustained behavior.

To understand the **direction** of motivation, the situations that attract a person must be analyzed. In other words, what situations does the athlete approach and what situations does the athlete avoid? **Intensity** can be interpreted as how much effort an athlete puts forth in particular situations. **Sustaining behavior** involves the motive structures and incentives that maintain goal-oriented behavior over time.

Certainly, the dimensions of drive and intensity are interrelated. In most cases, if an athlete is highly attracted or directed toward a particular activity, then he or she is typically intense in that situation. If a softball player is highly attracted to her sport, she is likely to work hard (or be "intense"). But this is not always the case, and this is why understanding motivation is so complex. For example, an athlete can be highly attracted to a situation (e.g., the sport of soccer) but may not be demonstrating intensity and is thought to be "unmotivated." Perhaps different situations would increase this athlete's motivation in, for example: a different level of soccer, playing for a different type of coach, or altering his or her intensity through goal setting. As these examples indicate, simplifying the definition of motivation as the direction and intensity of behavior helps sport psychologists more readily identify the components related to motivation deficits.

Motivation, however, does not occur in a vacuum. Sport psychologists must understand the athletic environment in which motivated behavior is expected to occur as well. Cultural factors, such as the emphasis on winning that is prevalent in the United States, and coaching philosophies also influence athletes' motivation. These outside influences may impact an athlete's ability to maintain optimal motivation over time. Thus, to fully understand motivation, the sport psychologist must consider both the athlete and his or her unique characteristics as well as the particular environment in which that athlete performs.

Differentiating Motivation from Other Psychological Processes

Those new to the field of sport psychology often mistakenly equate motivation with arousal. They perceive that the more "pumped up" athletes are before a competition, the more motivated they will be to perform well. Many coaches deliver emotional pregame, half-time, or timeout speeches, often involving theatrics such as throwing chairs or breaking chalk boards, to "motivate" their athletes. In fact, Woody Hayes, long-time Ohio State football coach, was reputed to "prebreak" his chalkboards or "pretear" his ball cap to make his dramatic points a bit more vividly. Although these pep talks are likely to increase the arousal of the athletes, whether they influence motivation is debatable. These melodramatic behaviors, in fact, may do more to increase athletes' anxiety than to optimize the intensity and direction of athletes' behavior.

Another misperception about motivation is that it is synonymous with trying harder or persisting. Some athletes may be trying hard (thus, thought to be motivated), but they may be trying hard at the wrong things or trying too hard. Persistence and trying hard are important parts of motivation. However, if taken to an extreme, they can be predictors of motivational problems such as burnout, overuse injuries, or inappropriate goal orientations.

Themes in the Study of Motivation

The study of motivation in sport includes a variety of definitions, assumptions, research, and theories. This variety, which seems contradictory at times, can be confusing for sport psychology practitioners. However, a number of unifying themes connect these areas. As theoretical perspectives on motivation are introduced, focusing on these themes can reduce confusion. Common themes noted by Reeve (1997) include:

• *Motivation is a dynamic process:* Motivation is a fluid process, rather than a particular event or condition. It varies according to individuals, situations, and time. Certain theoretical predictions, however, can be made about motivated behavior to help us understand its dynamic nature.

• *Motivation is more than personal willpower:* Motivation is not as simple as "trying harder" than your opponent or having a stronger will to win. Motivation must begin long before the game starts. Trying harder (or effort) is an expression of motivation; it is not the cause of it (Reeve, 1997).

• *Motivation includes both approach and avoidance tendencies:* A thorough understanding of motivation involves knowing not only what the athlete enjoys doing (approaches) but also what the athlete avoids. Learning about both sides of the motivational coin provides a more complete picture of the athlete's motivational orientation.

1. *Motivation varies not only in intensity but also in type:* In sport, we are accustomed to thinking about the intensity component of motivation (i.e., if you're not motivated, you just have to try harder). However, careful observation of motivated behavior should have you asking *why* the behavior is occurring. For example, is the athlete self-motivated or motivated by external sources? Does the athlete select challenging tasks or easy ones? The answers to these types of questions provide valuable clues about the athlete's motivational style.

2. *Motivation is influenced by both the self and the environment:* Some coaches believe they cannot influence an athlete's motivation. Some athletes believe they are solely

responsible for their motivation. Both parties are wrong—optimal motivation is an interactional process that requires an effective blend between the self-regulation of the athlete and the development of an optimal environment in which the athlete lives, trains, and competes.

3. *Motivation changes over time and across situations:* Motivation is rarely stagnant. The athlete who is a whirlwind in practice one day may be lethargic the next. Some athletes are highly motivated by rewards such as trophies and praise, whereas others are more internally motivated.

4. *Theories of motivation based on sound motivational principles can be applied to practical sport psychology interventions:* Good sport psychology practitioners base their interventions on sound theoretical underpinnings. Rather than viewing theories as abstract vestiges of research, practitioners should view them as roadmaps to successful intervention. Theories are practical, useful tools for explaining and solving the problems we encounter in sport psychology. To know the theories that explain motivation is to know motivation (Reeve, 1997).

Info Box

The broad conceptualization of motivation has allowed researchers to study a variety of themes in sport psychology. As with other psychological constructs, the study of motivation has precipitated the formation of many theories that attempt to explain motivation and how it relates to sport behavior.

Theoretical Perspectives on Motivation

The different interpretations and definitions of motivation and the misperceptions surrounding it make clear that a deeper understanding is needed. To develop an understanding of motivation and its application to sport psychology, a theoretical framework is necessary. The application of theoretical perspectives to sport provides ways of describing, evaluating, and analyzing athletes' motivation. Theories propose ideas, assumptions, and arguments that help to clarify the underlying reasons for motivation. These theories help explain why people act as they do regarding motivation and sport. In short, they help us to develop general explanations and to synthesize the research findings with the practical knowledge we have about sport motivation. Thus, theories play a useful role in helping us to understand motivation.

Early Theories of Motivation

Instinct Theory.   All theories of motivation are guided by the paradigm of the time. In the early 20th century, cognitive theories had not influenced psychology, and behaviorism was not in vogue either. Thus, the thoughts and behaviors of individuals were not thought to be major influences on motivation. Instead, major theorists of the time (e.g., James, Freud) thought behavior was driven by instincts. These theories do not hold much weight in modern sport psychology because instincts are difficult to define and measure and because psychologists now understand how thoughts and the environment can influence behavior.

Drive Theory. Similar to the relationship between arousal and performance, **Drive Theory** (Hull, 1943) also was used to explain motivated behavior. Hull was a behaviorist who studied animals and their needs. His theory suggested that motivation is related to desires to satisfy needs. Unsatisfied needs help stimulate or motivate behaviors. Thus, performance was thought to result from the drive (or motivation) an individual has to satisfy a certain need. Simply put, the more "motivated" athletes were, the better they were thought to perform. However, as we learned about arousal, higher levels of motivation do not always relate to better performance. Another weakness of this theory is that it does not account for varying levels of motivation across tasks and individuals.

Need Achievement Theory. Another theory is based on individual needs, particularly on the need to achieve. Motivation in sport is often interpreted as striving to excel or needing to accomplish. Murray (1938) labeled this desire to excel, relative to a standard of excellence, the need for achievement. This approach was used by other researchers (e.g., Atkinson, 1958, 1974; McClelland, 1961) to understand achievement-related behavior in competitive settings, and it has been influential in developing our understanding of sport motivation.

The need achievement theory helps us understand achievement motivation (Atkinson, 1964; Atkinson & Feather, 1966; McClelland, 1961). Need achievement is a personality trait thought to remain relatively stable across situations. This theory is based on the assumption that achievement behavior is inspired by two different motives: the motive to achieve success and the motive to avoid failure. The **motive to achieve success** (Ms) is the personal characteristic of seeking out achievement situations; the **motive to avoid failure** (Maf) relates to the escape from or avoidance of achievement situations where failure is a realistic possibility.

The motive to achieve success and the motive to avoid failure evolve from a variety of influences. Need for achievement is a multifaceted process that is manifested in high- versus low-achieving personalities. Reeve (1997) suggests that social, cognitive, and developmental processes influence the need for achievement. Parenting styles and other socializing agents, such as teachers and coaches, can influence the atmosphere in which an athlete develops a strong need for achievement. Cognitive processes, such as ways of thinking or perceptions of ability, certainly influence need achievement in athletes. For example, athletes who perceive their abilities to be high are more likely to seek out situations in which they have a chance for success, rather than avoid challenging situations. Last, developmental processes can influence how need achievement may change over time. For example, young children are less able to accurately estimate their abilities than older children (Nicholls, 1979).

The theory suggests that need for achievement is additive; it is a function of the interaction between the motive to achieve success and the motive to avoid failure. Thus, when the motive to achieve success is greater than the motive to avoid failure, an individual typically seeks out achievement-oriented situations. Conversely, when the motive to avoid failure is greater than the motive to achieve success, the person typically avoids achievement situations.

Info Box

When faced with a difficult task, such as competing against a higher-ranked opponent, an athlete with a motive to achieve success perceives the task as a challenge and approaches the situation believing in the opportunity for success. Conversely, an athlete with a motive to avoid failure perceives the situation as threatening and can actually engage in behaviors that increase the likelihood of failure.

Problems with Early Theories of Motivation.   The concept of achievement motivation is fundamental to the continued understanding of motivation. The cornerstone provided by all the theoretical constructs (instinct, drive, and need achievement) continues to influence our understanding of motivation in sport psychology today.

However, theories such as instinct, drive, and need achievement lack an understanding of the energy or intensity of behavior. They look at the supposed cause or direction of behavior without explaining its intensity component. Adequate theories of motivation must address both the intensity and direction of behavior (Roberts, 1993). In addition, the early theories of motivation were mechanistic, suggesting that people are passive and motivated simply by psychological drives or instincts rather than by their cognitions or their interpretations of their social environment (Roberts, 1992).

Roberts (1993) suggests that adequate theoretical explanations of motivation also must more thoroughly explain achievement-related behaviors. Achievement behaviors are behavioral intensity (trying hard), persistence (continuing to try hard), choice of activity (e.g., playing soccer rather than softball), and performance (outcomes). Coaches typically use these types of behaviors to assess athletes' motivation. Because motivation is an internal characteristic, external markers such as these achievement behaviors must be used to make hypotheses about the existence, type, and degree of motivation.

Finally, the weaknesses of the early theories have been magnified by the current paradigm in psychology, which has a cognitive–behavioristic framework. The new cognitive theories of motivation view humans as active rather than passive. They suggest that people subjectively interpret their thoughts and environment rather than simply being acted upon unconsciously by instincts. Examples of these cognitive theories of motivation include attribution theory, achievement goal orientation theory, and cognitive evaluation theory.

Attribution Theory.   Need achievement theory focuses on the personality characteristics of motive to approach success and motive to avoid failure. However, behaviors also can be understood according to people's perceptions and descriptions of their social environments (Biddle, 1993). This approach to understanding achievement motivation centers on the attributions individuals make for their performance in sport and how these attributions influence their motivation. **Attributions** are our explanations for our behaviors as well as for the behaviors of others. They are the factors we perceive to be responsible for the outcome of our behaviors.

Think about the many ways in which athletes describe their performance. Some may say they had good or bad luck, and some may say they had easy or hard opponents. Some athletes may say they tried hard or did not put forth much effort. Others may say they played great or did not play so well. These examples illustrate the numerous descriptions of athletes' performance. The descriptions often contain attributions—perceived reasons for an athlete's success or failure. Some of these reasons are controlled by the athletes, such as their ability and their effort. Other reasons are not within the athletes' control, such as an opponent's ability and luck.

These attributions can tell us a great deal about athletes' motivation. These perceived causes of athletic success or failure influence athletes' expectancies for future success, their emotional responses, and their future behaviors. For example, if a wrestler usually perceives winning matches as "getting lucky," he will probably react to these victories with less pride than an athlete who attributes his win to superior talent or preparation. The "lucky" wrestler will generally approach his next practice with less persistence and expect less opportunity for success in the future than a wrestler who attributes his victory to hard work and ability. This example does not imply that an occasional attribution to luck is always equated with a perception of less ability, but it demonstrates the potential differences in attributions.

These differences in perceived causes of success and failure can be better understood by examining the central tenets of **attribution theory.** It was popularized by the work of Heider (1958) and Weiner (1972, 1979, 1985, 1986) and has been applied to understanding motivation in sport. As the previous example demonstrates, athletes can give numerous reasons why they succeeded or failed in a particular event. These reasons, or attributions, then influence the athletes' subsequent motivation for a particular event.

Heider (1958) organized these attributions into four factors: ability, effort, task difficulty, and luck. Crediting a victory in a sprint race to your amazing speed is an example of an ability attribute. Blaming a loss on not working hard enough is an effort attribute. Explaining a victory with the opinion that your opponent is not as talented as you are is a task difficulty attribute. Finally, saying you lost a game because of a bad call by an official is an example of a luck attribute. Thus, making attributions involves both personal (internal) and situational (external) factors (Biddle, 1993).

Weiner (1972, 1979, 1985, 1986), whose research originated in the study of academic success and failure, further categorized these attributes into a framework using the dimensions of causality. Using Heider's framework as his base and borrowing from Rotter's (1966) work on locus of control, he developed a two-dimensional model of attributions. Weiner (1979) later added a third dimension assessing controllability (see Fig. 4.1). As the

FIGURE 4.1   *Weiner's Three Dimensional Locus of Causality Model (Weiner, 1985).*

	INTERNAL	EXTERNAL
Stable	Ability (Uncontrollable)	Task difficulty (Uncontrollable)
Unstable	Effort (Controllable)	Luck (Uncontrollable)

figure suggests, attributions can be divided according to their stability, their causality, and their controllability.

Future motivation can be predicted by the attributions athletes make for their performance and by the stability, causality, and controllability of those attributions. Consider Kate, a basketball player, who attributes her poor performance to a lack of effort, an internal and unstable factor over which she has control. Kate's motivation will likely be higher in the future because she can control her effort and put forth more intensity in future situations. On the other hand, Kate's teammate Jen attributes her performance to poor ability. According to attribution theory, Jen is less likely to have higher motivation in the future than Kate will. Also, Jen is likely to perceive a decreased probability of future success. Thus, attributions influence athletes' expectations for future success. This in turn influences whether athletes choose to participate in similar tasks in the future (Weiner, 1985). Athletes who make unstable and external attributions for their success are less likely to have optimal achievement motivation than are those athletes who make stable, internal attributions.

Info Box

Attribution theory suggests that achievement motivation is higher in athletes who make attributions that are stable, controllable, and internal.

Achievement Goal Orientation Theory. In a simplified comparison, attribution theory examines motivation based on attributions made about performance, but **achievement goal orientation theory** examines motivation based on goals set for performance. Attribution theory explains changes in behavior that result from perceptions of which goals are most appropriate in given situations, not from high or low motivation levels (Roberts, 1993). The goals athletes adopt are related to their perceptions of success and subsequent behavior. Some athletes may set goals to beat opponents, while other athletes may set goals to improve upon their personal performance. These athletes define success differently. One group of athletes is not more motivated than the other, but they vary in their motivation levels.

Several psychologists have been prominent in developing achievement goal approaches (e.g., Dweck, 1986; Maehr & Nicholls, 1980; Nicholls, 1984, 1992), and their concepts have been applied in sport psychology literature (e.g., Duda, 1989, 1992, 1993; Roberts, 1992, 1993). Achievement goal approaches assume that people define success according to two types of goals: task involvement and ego involvement (Nicholls, 1989). Task-involved goals are related to self-mastery and skill improvement; success is defined relative to the self. Ego-involved goals emphasize success relative to others. Defining success according to exceeding the performance of others is an example of an **ego orientation.** If swimmers define success solely as winning the race, regardless of performance, an ego orientation is being employed. Conversely, swimmers who define success around setting new personal records are using a **task orientation.**

Although some researchers (e.g., Dweck, 1986) have argued that task and ego orientations exist as a dichotomy (that is, you are either one or the other, not both), sport psychology research literature generally has supported the notion that these orientations are not independent constructs (e.g., Duda, 1989, 1993; Nicholls, 1989). In other words, an athlete can be high on both ego and task orientations, low on one and high on the other, or low on both.

Two misperceptions are commonly held about the differences between task and ego orientations (Duda, 1993). The first is that task-oriented athletes are not interested in winning (they only want to improve); the second is that ego-oriented athletes do not care about playing well (they only want to win). These perceptions are inaccurate. Athletes who adopt a task-oriented style are still interested in winning, and ego-oriented athletes do want to play well. But the two groups differ in how they define success and interpret losing (or performing poorly). It is these perceptual differences that have an important impact on motivation.

The choice of goal orientation has an important influence on the achievement related behavior of the athlete. Achievement-related behaviors lead to understanding the athlete's motivation. Athletes who use a task orientation are thought to persist longer in the face of failure, choose more challenging goals, and work harder. Because of these behaviors, athletes who have a task orientation generally perform better in evaluative situations. These task-oriented athletes select tasks that challenge them, and they are persistent—behaviors that bode well for strong performances. On the other hand, ego-oriented athletes are thought to have less persistence, choose extreme goals (either very easy or extremely difficult), and have weaker work ethics. These attributes are particularly apparent in ego-oriented athletes who have low perceived competence. Because ego-oriented athletes typically do not challenge themselves in practice situations, they are more likely to perform poorly in evaluative situations or to make excuses for their poor performance.

Cognitive Evaluation Theory.   The last theory of motivation presented in this chapter describes the influence of rewards on behavior and performance. The previous theories focused on individual characteristics that influence motivation, such as attributions and goals. As previously discussed, motivation can be influenced by forces within the individual or from the environment. **Intrinsic motivation** involves internal motives for participation, such as challenge, skill improvement, fun, and personal mastery of a task. **Extrinsic motivation** involves external motives for participation, such as material rewards (e.g., trophies, ribbons, medals), social status, and social approval from coaches, peers, and others.

The primary motives most athletes, especially younger or beginning athletes, cite for participating in sport are intrinsic, such as having fun and learning and perfecting new skills, rather than extrinsic rewards such as money. **Cognitive evaluation theory** (Deci & Ryan, 1985) helps us to understand the relationship between intrinsic and extrinsic motivation and the effects of external rewards on our motivation. This theory helps to explain why the "common sense" philosophy that more rewards result in greater performance is often wrong.

Cognitive evaluation theory is based on the assumption that individuals have two innate needs: to feel competent and to feel self-determining in initiating their activities (Deci & Ryan, 1985; Vallerand, Deci, & Ryan, 1987). Individuals have a natural desire to feel proficient and have free will in deciding their actions. Based on these needs, cognitive evaluation theory makes predictions about how to enhance athletes' perceptions of their personal competence and self-determination. According to this theory, any event that influences these two needs impacts athletes' intrinsic motivation. These events may range from reward distribution to amount and type of feedback and reinforcement to the structure of situations.

Cognitive evaluation theory further contends that there are two processes by which situations can influence intrinsic motivation: a controlling aspect and an informational aspect (Deci & Ryan; 1985; Vallerand, Deci, & Ryan, 1987). The controlling aspect refers to the individual's locus of causality. If the situation is perceived as controlling the athlete's behavior, an external locus of causality is developed. For example, if athletes feel events are forced on them or that their activities are initiated by someone other than themselves (e.g., an excessively demanding parent or coach), they have an **external locus of causality.** An **internal locus of causality** occurs when athletes feel they have initiated their actions.

If the controlling aspect of an event is high (an external locus of causality), the event or reward is perceived as controlling the athlete's behavior. For example, when an athlete feels controlled by a reward (e.g., playing for money), the motivation for his or her behavior is extrinsic. This controlling aspect of the reward conflicts with the athlete's innate need for self-determination. This low level of self-determination could lead to a decrease in intrinsic motivation. On the other hand, if the controlling aspect of the reward is low (an internal locus of causality), the reward is not seen as controlling behavior, and intrinsic motivation is typically increased.

The second aspect of the event's influence on intrinsic motivation is the informational one (Deci & Ryan, 1985; Vallerand, Deci, & Ryan, 1987). The informational aspect influences intrinsic motivation by altering the athletes' feelings of competence. Events provide athletes with information. Events that provide positive information are rewarding and provide athletes with an increased sense of perceived competence. This increased sense of perceived competence then leads to an increase in intrinsic motivation. Events that provide athletes with negative information about their abilities typically lower perceived competence and therefore reduce intrinsic motivation.

It is important to remember that the influence of rewards on intrinsic motivation depends on the meaning of the reward to the athlete. Also, all extrinsic rewards do not automatically undermine intrinsic motivation. If the reward is based on actual achievement, positive information about competence is provided and intrinsic motivation is increased. Conversely, if the information received is negative or interpreted as such, the athlete's feelings of competence are decreased and intrinsic motivation is undermined. Consider runners in a 10K race who receive a cash prize for placing in the top five. Runners setting personal records who receive a prize may interpret the reward quite differently from runners who have just run the worst race of their careers. Thus, the same reward means very different things to athletes depending on their interpretation of the reward and its controlling and informational impact on their intrinsic motivation.

Info Box

Athletes are more motivated if they feel competent in their sport skills and if they feel they are self-driven, not controlled or manipulated by external factors.

Conclusion

Motivation is a complex psychological construct that is often simplified into terms of direction and intensity of behavior. Understanding the reasons an athlete initiates and sustains behavior can help coaches and sport psychology consultants grasp what motivates the athlete. Several theories were advanced to facilitate understanding motivation, including instinct theory, need achievement theory, attribution theory, achievement goal orientation theory, and cognitive evaluation theory. The next chapter expands on the motivational principles offered by these theories. If developed properly, these principles can result in sustained intrinsic motivation.

Key Terms (in order of appearance)

motivation	motive to achieve success	task orientation
direction	motive to avoid failure	intrinsic motivation
intensity	attribution	extrinsic motivation
sustaining behavior	Attribution Theory	Cognitive Evaluation Theory
Instinct Theory	Achievement Goal Orientation	external locus of causality
Drive Theory	Theory	internal locus of causality
Need Achievement Theory	ego orientation	

References

Atkinson, J. W. (Ed.). (1958). *Motives in fantasy and action and society.* Princeton, NJ: Van Nostrand.

Atkinson, J. W. (1964). *An introduction to motivation.* Princeton, NJ: Van Nostrand.

Atkinson, J. W. (1974). The mainstream of achievement-oriented activity. In J. W. Atkinson & J. O. Raynor (Eds.), *Motivation and achievement* (pp. 13–41). New York: Halstead.

Atkinson, J. W., & Feather, N. T. (1966). *A theory of achievement motivation.* New York: Wiley.

Biddle, S. (1993). Attribution research and sport psychology. In R. N. Singer, M. Murphey & L. K. Tennant (Eds.), *Handbook of Research on Sport Psychology* (pp. 437–464). New York: Macmillan.

Deci, E. L., & Ryan, R. M. (1985). *Intrinsic motivation and self-determinism in human behavior.* New York: Plenum.

Duda, J. L. (1989). Goal perspectives and behavior in sport and exercise settings. In C. Ames & M. Maehr (Eds.), *Advances in motivation and achievement,* Vol. 6 (pp. 81–115). Greenwich, CT: JAI.

Duda, J. L. (1992). Motivation in sport settings: A goal perspective analysis. In G. C. Roberts (Ed.), *Understanding motivation in sport and exercise* (pp. 57–91). Champaign, IL: Human Kinetics.

Duda, J. L. (1993). Goals: A study of social-cognitive approach to the study of achievement motivation in sport. In R. N. Singer, M. Murphey & L. K. Tennant (Eds.), *Handbook of Research on Sport Psychology* (pp. 421–436). New York: Macmillan.

Dweck, C. S. (1986). Motivational processes affecting learning. *American Psychologist, 41.* 1040–1048.

Hardy, L., Jones, G., & Gould, D. (1996). *Understanding psychological preparation for sport: Theory and practice of elite performers.* Chichester, UK: Wiley.

Heider, F. (1958). *The psychology of interpersonal relations.* New York: Wiley.

Hull, C. (1943). *Principles of behavior.* New York: Appleton-Century-Crofts.

Maehr, M. L. & Nicholls, J. G. (1980). Cultural and achievement motivation: A second look. In N. Warren (Ed.), *Studies in cross-cultural psychology* (pp. 221–267). New York: Academic.

McClelland, D. C. (1961). *The achieving society.* New York: Free.

Murray, H. A. (1938). *Explorations in personality.* New York: Oxford.

Nicholls, J. G. (1979). Development of perception of own attainment and causal attributions for success and failure in reading. *Journal of Educational Psychology, 71,* 94–99.

Nicholls, J. G. (1984). Achievement motivation: Conceptions of ability, subjective experience, task choice, and performance. *Psychological Review, 91,* 328–346.

Nicholls, J. G. (1989). *The competitive ethos and democratic education.* Cambridge, MA: Harvard Univ. Press.

Nicholls, J. G. (1992). The general and the specific in the development and expression of achievement motivation. In G. C. Roberts (Ed.), *Understanding motivation in sport and exercise* (pp. 31–56). Champaign, IL: Human Kinetics.

Reeve, J. (1997). *Understanding motivation and emotion,* 2nd ed. Orlando, FL: Harcourt, Brace.

Roberts, G. C. (1992). Motivation in sport and exercise: Conceptual constraints and convergence. In G. C. Roberts (Ed.), *Motivation in sport and exercise.* Champaign, IL: Human Kinetics.

Roberts, G. C. (1993). Motivation in sport: Understanding and enhancing the motivation and achievement of children. In R. N. Singer, M. Murphey & L. K. Tennant (Eds.), *Handbook of Research on Sport Psychology* (pp. 405–420). New York: Macmillan.

Rotter, J. B. (1966). Generalized expectancies for internal versus external control of reinforcement. *Psychological Monographs, 80* (Whole No. 609), 1–28.

Vallerand, R. J., Deci, E. L., & Ryan, R. M. (1987). Intrinsic motivation in sport. In K. B. Pandolf (Ed.), *Exercise and sport science reviews* (pp. 389–425). New York: Macmillan.

Weinberg, R. S. & Gould, D. (1995). *Foundations of sport and exercise psychology.* Champaign, IL: Human Kinetics.

Weiner, B. (1972). *Theories of motivation: From mechanics to cognition.* Chicago: Markham.

Weiner, B. (1979). A theory of motivation for some classroom experiences. *Journal of Educational Psychology, 71,* 3–25.

Weiner, B. (1985). An attributional theory of achievement motivation and emotion. *Psychological Review, 92,* 548–573.

Weiner, B. (1986). *An attributional theory of motivation and emotion.* New York: Springer-Verlag.

Weiss, M. R., & Chaumeton, N. (1992). Motivational orientations in sport. In T. S. Horn (Ed.), *Advances in sport psychology* (pp. 61–99). Champaign, IL: Human Kinetics.

5

Applying Motivational Principles to Individual Athletes

Jonathan Metzler

The University of North Carolina at Chapel Hill

- Seven fundamental motivational principles are related to performance.
- Adhering to motivational principles can reduce the probability of performance decrements.
- Several techniques can enhance the motivation of an individual athlete.

> *"While I do compete to win, I want to be the best, mentally and physically. I want to be an asset, not a detriment to the team."*
>
> —A. C. Green (personal communication, August 16, 1999)

These words by A. C. Green, a 15-year-plus veteran of the National Basketball Association, illustrate the internal motivation that has helped him become a highly successful elite athlete. He exhibits his motivation through his behaviors. He strives to improve himself physically by running, biking, swimming, and monitoring his diet. He spends time in the gym taking jump shot after jump shot, working to refine his shooting technique. Given his level of internal motivation and the resultant behavior, it is not surprising that Green, at the start of the 2000 NBA season held the NBA record for most consecutive games played (1,133). He is an athlete on a mission to be the best player he can possibly be and to contribute the most he can to his team in every game. Furthermore, he has a high level of self-confidence in his ability to reach his potential and perform successfully.

There are many other examples of athletes who demonstrate this high level of internal motivation and self-confidence; however, many athletes are motivated primarily by external factors. They may be motivated by winning a trophy, obtaining a scholarship, gaining recognition, upholding an image, gaining friends, or pleasing others. Although it is important to understand motivation in the context of motor learning, skill development, and exercise adherence, this chapter examines motivation as it pertains to athletic performance. In essence, this chapter is an attempt to answer the question: "What are some motivational principles that often affect performance?"

To enhance the motivation of an athlete, one must first understand the sources of motivation that drive the athlete's behavior. To understanding an athlete's source of motivation, consider the athlete's personality, the situational factors (incentives) present in the environment, and how these factors influence and interact with each other. Specifically, assessing the athlete's attributional style, levels of intrinsic and/or extrinsic motivation, self-confidence, self-efficacy, and optimism can provide insight into the individual motivation of that athlete.

Fundamental Motivational Principles

Each athlete is a unique individual and is motivated in a unique way. Although it is impossible to suggest a universal technique to enhance the motivation of all athletes, there are several fundamental principles of motivation in sport that are related to performance. This section will identify and describe these principles to set a foundation for techniques that will enhance motivation and performance in sport.

Attributional Style

As noted, in Chapter 4, it is natural for athletes to examine their performances for the causes of their successes and failures. Athletes may attribute success or failure to many factors, such as ability ("we had more talent"), effort ("we played with more heart"), or task difficulty ("they have superior athletes"). Athletes also may attribute success or failure to such things as officiating, weather, or luck. According to **attribution theory** (Weiner, 1979, 1985, 1986), all attributions that athletes use to explain success or failure can be placed into three attribution categories: stability (stable versus unstable), causality (internal versus external), and controllability (controllable versus uncontrollable). For example, after winning a match, a wrestler states, "I knew going in that I had the talent to win. I also studied my opponent and developed a sound strategy that worked well. Even with my ability and good strategy it took 100 percent effort to finally get the victory." The wrestler attributed success to a stable factor (ability), a controllable factor (strategy), as well as an internal factor (effort). A different wrestler faced with the same success may make significantly different attributions: "I was lucky. My opponent has had to deal with an injury, and the referee gave me a couple huge breaks right at the end." This athlete attributed his success to external factors (luck, opponent's injury, officiating). In addition, he has made attributions to factors that are unstable (luck) and uncontrollable (opponent's injury, luck, and officiating). It is evident that the evaluation of performance made by a particular athlete is dependent on the athlete's attributional style.

Understanding an athlete's attributional style is important for understanding the motivation of that athlete. The **attributional style** of an athlete is the general pattern of attributions an athlete tends to make (Weiner, 1986). For instance, Sara is a tennis player who frequently attributes her success or failure to the ability of her opponents. When Sara loses, she explains that she faced a tough competitor. Conversely, when she wins, she states that her opponent lacked the ability to compete with her. Similarly, when Sara receives a good grade on a test, she attributes her success to the lack of difficulty of the exam. She attributes a low grade on an exam to the increased difficulty of the exam. Her attributional style predisposes her to attribute success or failure to external and uncontrollable factors. Unfortunately, Sara's attributional style may actually cause her to lose motivation because she believes that her success is a result of factors outside her personal control. Whether Sara exerts effort (motivation) or not, she may perceive that effort will not affect her success or failure. If Sara were to attribute her success in a tennis match to her strategy and effort, she would expect to achieve success again if she prepares another good strategy and exerts a similar amount of effort. In the same manner, by attributing her good exam score to her effort in studying, Sara will develop an expectation to do well again if she studies diligently.

Info Box

Principle #1: Athletes who make internal and controllable attributions will expect to achieve successful performances and will practice persistently to increase the likelihood of future successful performances.

Singer and Orbach (1999) introduced a conceptual model of attribution and its effect on motivation. After athletes perform, they naturally evaluate the performance. The evaluation process includes determining whether the performance was a success or failure and developing an attribution to explain these results. The type of attribution made by an athlete will influence his or her motivation. Singer and Orbach (1999) suggest that athletes who expect future success are more motivated than those who do not. Athletes who attribute success to an internal, controllable, and unstable (adaptable) factor, such as effort, will increase their expectations for success because they believe their efforts had a strong influence on the performance. If athletes increase their expectations for success, they will exhibit persistence in practice. They believe that exerting effort in practice will result in the increased likelihood of future successful performances. Athletes who make external, uncontrollable, and stable attributions, such as to the opponent's ability, will not increase their expectations for success. They believe their efforts had a limited effect on the performance. These athletes believe that the opponent's ability plays a greater role in performance than their own effort. Thus, they may lack the motivation to exert effort in practice. Obviously, athletes who believe their efforts will lead to successful performances are more motivated to exert effort. Therefore, athletes who attribute their success to internal and controllable factors, such as effort, are more motivated to sustain a high level of effort in practice and in competition.

Singer and Orbach (1999) suggest that athletes who attribute success or failure to ability (categorized as internal, uncontrollable, and stable) also will be less motivated. These authors assert that athletes who make ability attributions are less motivated to improve their skills because they believe their ability is constant. A common misconception is that ability cannot be changed. However, ability *is* changeable, although it is not as transient as effort may be. Although effort may fluctuate from one performance to the next, ability remains fairly constant. Ability can be developed, however. Athletes spend many hours developing their speed, agility, and jumping ability. Elite athletes are able to make the honest attribution to ability and use it as motivation to work on their weaknesses. For instance, when Michael Jordan entered the National Basketball Association, he was able to penetrate and create his own shot close to the basket. However, he did not have the ability to consistently shoot well from outside, especially from the three-point range. By the end of Michael Jordan's professional career, he had developed his shooting ability so that he was a threat even from beyond the three-point circle. Jordan's outside shooting ability improved over years of practice. Athletes who attribute failure to lack of effort believe that if they exert greater effort, they can develop skills necessary for success. Similarly, athletes who attribute failure to lack of ability but believe, like Jordan, that they can improve their ability may also develop the skills needed for future success. Whether athletes attribute success to effort or ability, they should make internal and controllable attributions. Athletes who takes responsibility for their performance by making effort and ability attributions are willing to do what it takes to improve, exhibiting high levels of internal motivation.

Intrinsic Versus Extrinsic Motivation

As a coach develops a general understanding of an athlete's motivational orientation, he or she may notice that the athlete is influenced more by internal motives or external motives. The preceding chapter explained that **intrinsic motivation** involves internal motives for participation, such as challenge, skill improvement, fun, and personal mastery of tasks. Conversely, **extrinsic motivation** involves external motives for participation, such as material rewards (e.g., trophies, ribbons, medals), social status, and social approval from coaches, peers, and others.

As coaches attempt to enhance motivation, they must understand where athletes fall on the intrinsic-to-extrinsic motivation continuum. Most people initiate participation in sport due to intrinsic motives. Gould and Petlichkoff (1988) cited major motives for youth sport participation as: having fun, being with friends, improving skills, experiencing excitement, achieving success, and developing fitness. For those of us who are inundated with stories about how this team hasn't gone to the playoffs in years and this player signed for $12 million, both external motives, it is refreshing to watch a second grade soccer game. Picture 16 to 20 kids clustered around the soccer ball, kicking away and laughing. To the right is a goalie trying to catch a butterfly, and to the left is another goalie picking dandelions. Somehow the ball squirts out and eventually rolls into the goal. The parents cheer, and the children realize that something good happened and they join in. After the game is over, the kids come running to the sideline asking questions such as, "What was the score?" and "When are we going for ice cream?" The absence of extrinsic motives demonstrated by these young players exemplifies intrinsic motivation in its purest form.

Unfortunately, not long after their initiation into sport participation, children learn that there also are extrinsic rewards in sport. The focus shifts from being out on the grass in the sunshine with friends having fun to checking the boxscore, increasing playing time, and getting awards. Do these extrinsic rewards actually undermine intrinsic motivation? According to **Cognitive Evaluation Theory** (Deci & Ryan, 1985; see Chapter 4), extrinsic rewards can improve or reduce intrinsic motivation depending on locus of causality and how information is provided to the athlete. If the **locus of causality** (what controls behavior) is shifted away from the athletes, they are more extrinsically motivated. For example, the soccer players who used to play for fun, to improve skills, and to be with friends now compete to receive prestige from their peer groups. Simply put, the children used to play soccer for the fun of it (internal control); now they play to feel important (external control), and this need is what controls their behavior. Although the behavior may be maintained, if the extrinsic motivator is taken away, the behavior may be reduced or even halted. The intrinsic motivation has been replaced by primarily extrinsic motives, and the intrinsic motives may have lost value or importance to the athletes.

Info Box

Principle #2: Athletes who are intrinsically motivated will perform and persist at a task regardless of whether external rewards are present.

A classic example of the controlling effect of extrinsic rewards is found in the story of the boys throwing rocks at a man's house (Siedentop & Ramey, 1977). One afternoon, some boys decided that it would be fun to throw rocks at this old man's house. Obviously irritated, the man responded by yelling at the boys to get off his lawn and stop throwing rocks at his house. This just added more excitement to the boys' endeavor, so the next day they returned to have more fun. Meanwhile, the old man had devised a new strategy to reduce their behavior. When the boys showed up, the man came out of the house and offered them 25 cents each to throw rocks at his house the next day. The boys were delighted and agreed. The next day, sure enough, the boys threw rocks at the house, and the man paid them each a quarter. He told them to come the next day and receive the same amount. Once again the boys showed up and threw rocks, and the man paid them each a quarter. He told them to come again the next day; however, he could only offer them 15 cents to throw rocks. The boys agreed somewhat reluctantly but did return the following day. Then the man paid them each 15 cents and told the boys that from now on he could only afford to give each of them a nickel to throw rocks at his house. The boys were noticeably upset and, in fact, did not come back the next day.

In this example, the extrinsic reward (money) became the controlling factor. When it was removed, the intrinsic motive (enjoyment) no longer existed. This concept is often illustrated in sport when a child goes from playing for the fun of the game to playing for an external reward, such as parental or peer approval, social acceptance, or a trophy or award. In fact, Ryan (1977) found that collegiate athletes receiving athletic scholarships were less intrinsically motivated than those who did not receive scholarships. From this study, it can be suggested that the motive to maintain the extrinsic reward actually decreased the intrinsic motive to compete for fun.

Info Box

Principle #3: Extrinsic motivation has the capacity to undermine intrinsic motivation.

In a later study, Ryan (1980) found scholarship football players to be less intrinsically motivated than their nonscholarship counterparts. However, he found that female athletes and male wrestlers who received athletic scholarships reported greater intrinsic motivation than those that were not on athletic scholarship. Ryan concluded that the scholarships provided to female athletes and wrestlers were not controlling factors but provided competence information. Athletes who received scholarships evaluated the extrinsic award as information about their athletic ability. This positive information, although extrinsic, actually enhanced intrinsic motivation. Ryan suggested that, in football, scholarships are less informative and more controlling because many football players receive scholarships but only a few female athletes and wrestlers are rewarded.

If extrinsic motivators are perceived as information and are appropriate for the behavior displayed, the athlete gains a feeling of personal competence. As the feeling of personal competence strengthens, the feeling of self-confidence also strengthens. Understanding an athlete's level of self-confidence also can provide insight into the level of motivation of the athlete.

Absolute Versus Relative Standards

Another psychological factor that influences athletes' motivation is their goal orientation. Athletes tend to be task-oriented or ego-oriented (Nicholls, 1984; Duda, 1987). Task-oriented athletes judge success by **absolute standards,** personal standards that are not compared to or affected by the standards of those around them. For instance, track athletes in the 100-meter sprint who are task-oriented will focus on their personal time in the race. If an athlete has a personal best of 10.3 seconds, the athlete will focus on matching that time or consistently running near that time. The time of the opponent is mostly irrelevant to the task-oriented athlete. In fact, a task-oriented athlete who wins a race with a poor time will not find the win to be extremely rewarding. The athlete will be disappointed in the time and will be motivated to improve. A task-oriented athlete who loses a race but runs a very fast time or even a personal best will see the competition as a success and will be motivated to continue training hard. Athletes who are task-oriented focus on performing up to their capability level; the outcome is simply a motivational consequence.

Info Box

Principle #4: Athletes who judge themselves by absolute standards will exhibit more consistency in their motivation and thus increase the likelihood of performing consistently regardless of the level of competition.

Task-oriented athletes are motivated by the task itself rather than by their competition.

The ego-oriented athlete judges success by **relative standards.** Thus, an ego-oriented athlete in the 100-meter race will tend to focus on the times of the competitors. If the most competent competitor in a race has a personal best of 10.8 seconds in the 100-meter sprint, the ego-oriented athlete will focus on beating 10.8 seconds. Instead of being motivated to run the fastest race possible and continuing to work on maximizing capabilities, the ego-oriented athlete is motivated to run better than the opponent. In this example, the ego-oriented athlete may run significantly below his or her capability but may actually be pleased because he or she won the race. By focusing on absolute standards (what can I do in competition), athletes who are task-oriented are more likely to perform at a consistently high level. The performance of ego-oriented athletes is actually a function of the competition they are facing. This orientation allows for a wide fluctuation of performance that is counterproductive to consistency and excellence in sport and may hinder athletic skill development and performance capabilities. Thus, coaches must gain an understanding of the goal orientation of athletes to help facilitate growth towards task-orientation rather than ego-orientation.

Task-oriented athletes tend to focus on the process of competing. The focus of individuals who are task-oriented is on improving over time, regardless of their current ability level (Elliott & Dweck, 1988). The goal for these athletes is self-mastery and development of their skills. Thus, these athletes can be very motivated in practice because they view practice as part of the process of development and self-mastery. On the contrary, ego-oriented athletes focus on how they compare to the athletes around them. After practicing with the same players, it can become boring to ego-oriented athletes to compare themselves to teammates against whom they are consistently successful. It may become difficult for ego-oriented athletes to maintain a high level of motivation in practice. In addition, ego-oriented athletes often focus on the outcome of the competition as their measure of success. Athletes who tend to focus on the outcome may get discouraged and actually lose motivation if they do not achieve the desired result, regardless of how they performed. In contrast, process-oriented athletes are able to acknowledge their level of performance, regardless of the final outcome. Process-oriented athletes may actually be excited to get back to practice after a failure to begin working on aspects of their game that need improvement.

Info Box

Principle #5: Athletes who focus on the process of competition rather than the outcome will have more control over success and failure. This will stimulate higher levels of persistence.

UCLA's legendary basketball coach John Wooden (1997, p. 55) wrote the following in his book *Wooden: A Lifetime of Observations and Reflections on and off the Court:* "I told my players many times, 'Failing to prepare is preparing to fail.' If you prepare properly, you may be outscored but *you will never lose.* I wanted our players to believe that to their very souls because I know it is the truth. You always win when you make the full effort to do the best of which you're capable."

Motive to Approach Success Versus Motive to Avoid Failure

Chapter 4 identified theories of motivation that provide insight into understanding the motivation of athletes. For instance, according to the **Need Achievement Theory** (Atkinson, 1964; Atkinson & Feather, 1966; McClelland, 1961), each athlete's personality predisposes him or her to approach success or to avoid failure. Individuals who have greater motives to achieve success than to avoid failure will seek out achievement situations (Silva & Weinberg, 1984). Conversely, those who have a greater motive to avoid failure will frequently avoid achievement situations. In sport competition, athletes are constantly confronted with achievement situations. Consequently, it is desirable for athletes to have a motive to approach success and thus seek out achievement situations. Athletes who are motivated to approach success view situations in sport as opportunities to succeed and do not overconcern themselves with fear of failure. On the contrary, athletes who are motivated to avoid failure view situations in sport as opportunities to fail. They do not focus on the abilities they must bring to the task to increase the probability of success. Athletes who fear failure will attempt to avoid situations in which they believe they may fail. In the next section, these motives are considered in greater detail within the context of self-confidence, another characteristic of personality.

Info Box

Principle #6: Motivation and performance will be optimized by athletes who are motivated to approach success.

Self-Confidence, Optimism, and Self-Efficacy

This section investigates the effects of self-confidence, self-efficacy, and optimism on motivation. (For an extensive look at the theoretical aspects of these concepts, please refer to Chapter 12.) Self-confidence is defined as the strength of the general belief in one's ability. Self-confidence is often used in very general terms. If people are self-confident, they believe that if they apply ability to a task, they can complete it. For athletes to be self-confident, they must have a tendency to be optimistic. Optimism is defined as "a tendency to look on the more favorable side or to expect the most favorable outcome of events or conditions" (Manzo, Silva, & Mink, 1998). Simply stated, optimistic athletes have positive and persistent attitudes. Optimistic athletes always see the opportunity for success, even in moments when failure seems inevitable. In addition, fully self-confident athletes must be optimistic about their level of competence in their sport (Manzo, Silva, & Mink, 1998). Athletes who have high levels of self-competence will believe in their ability to meet the performance demands of their sport. Without high self-competence in an activity, athletes cannot exhibit self-confidence in the activity. For instance, a football player that puts on a pair of ice skates for the first time probably will not seem very self-confident while attempting to skate around the rink. Conversely, he may feel very competent on the football field and thus exhibits a high level of self-confidence. Related to the self-competence component of self-confidence is the concept of self-efficacy (Bandura, 1977). Self-efficacy in athletics is the belief that one can execute a specific skill and that this skill will result in a successful outcome. The concept of self-efficacy can be thought of as a specific form of self-confidence that is focused on specific skills or techniques. Soccer players may have high self-efficacy in their ability to kick penalty shots, a specific soccer skill.

The following example reveals how these unique concepts of self-confidence are related. If a basketball team is down by 15 points with 4 minutes left in the game, the optimistic athletes see the possibility of climbing back in the game and winning it. Self-confident athletes believe that the team has the ability to come back from that deficit. Self-competent athletes believe in their ability level in the specific sport of basketball. Athletes also may have strong self-efficacy in their own personal ability to hit clutch three-pointers down the stretch to bring the team back. Clearly, these concepts are unique yet highly interrelated.

Info Box

Principle #7: Athletes with high levels of self-confidence, self-efficacy, and optimism will exhibit greater motivation to perform and to persist in challenging situations.

An athlete who is self-confident, has high self-efficacy, and is optimistic will exhibit higher levels of motivation than another athlete who lacks these qualities. The *Need Achievement Theory* (Atkinson, 1964; Atkinson & Feather, 1966; McClelland, 1961) discussed in the previous chapter helps to explain the relationship among self-confidence, self-efficacy, optimism, and motivation. One underlying premise of this theory is that people strive to accomplish; they have a need for achievement. Consequently, if athletes need to achieve and are self-confident (believe in ability to achieve), they will most likely attempt to achieve, generally. Similarly, assuming that athletes are motivated to achieve, if they have high levels of self-efficacy in their ability to score a penalty kick in a soccer game, they will be motivated to take that shot when the situation arises.

Self-confident athletes often are defined by their desire to have the outcome of a competition rest in their hands. In sport psychology, this is known as the **motive to approach success.** There are numerous examples of athletes who have such high levels of self-confidence, self-efficacy, and optimism that they are highly motivated to actually take a game over with their behaviors. In football, John Elway and Dan Marino consistently drove their respective offenses down the field to score game-winning touchdowns. Likewise in basketball, Larry Bird and Michael Jordan had the ability and motivation to overcome a deficit in the final quarter, sometimes even the final play, of the game. A powerful example occurred when Michael Jordan stole the basketball from Karl Malone in Game 6 of the 1998 NBA finals. Down by one point, Jordan believed that if he took a shot, the Bulls would win the game. Do you think this affected his motivation? Jordan got the ball and appeared to be possessed. Fans who have observed Jordan over time saw that familiar look in his eyes, as if he were saying, "I'm gonna win this game right now." The belief that your actions will result in a favorable outcome allows you to have a motive to approach success.

On the other hand, athletes that have self-doubt often exhibit considerably lower levels of motivation. Self-doubting athletes may wonder whether their ability will allow for achievement. Think about a time when you tried something very novel to you. Maybe you were in a class in which a requirement was to deliver a 20-minute speech on the ecology of grasslands in Alaska. Many people are filled with self-doubt in a situation such as this, and instead of being motivated to do the speech, many are motivated to avoid the situation altogether. In fact, in this example it may be common to observe that students call in sick on the day they are supposed to deliver the speech. This is an example of the **motive to avoid failure.** This motive is exhibited in sport as well. A tennis player has a match against a higher ranked opponent. She is filled with self-doubt about her ability to compete at this high level. She sees that the probability is high that she will fail. If she is motivated to avoid failure, the resulting behavior may be to give a weak effort. By giving a weak effort, the athlete can attribute failure to effort; however, if she gives 100 percent and loses it is conclusive evidence of personal inadequacy (an internal and stable attribution). If she expends little effort, then she can attribute her loss to something other than a lack of ability, such as external attributes such as luck or even lack of effort (internal and unstable attribution). If Michael Jordan had a motive to avoid failure in the situation described previously, he may have passed off early in his drive up-court to a teammate who would have taken the final shot. Then he would not have had to explain why he missed the game-winning shot to the media and millions of fans watching worldwide. He didn't fail; someone else did. However, if Jordan had been motivated to avoid failure, he would not have provided himself an opportunity to succeed by being in the mix of the action to determine the result of a world championship game.

In summary, athletes who are self-confident, have a high level of self-efficacy in a certain task, and are generally optimistic will tend to be motivated to approach success. Those athletes who doubt their abilities or who are pessimistic will tend to be motivated to avoid failure. In essence, the positive attitude exhibited by self-confident, optimistic athletes allows them to shrug off failure and think that next time they will be successful. They remain motivated even in novel tasks or in the performance of tasks that they need to improve on. Both Magic Johnson and Michael Jordan did not have three-point range when they entered the NBA; however, their self-confidence motivated them to practice and develop this skill. By the time they retired, they were threats from behind the three-point arc. Athletes hindered with self-doubt and pessimism may lack motivation or may be motivated to sabotage any chance of being successful.

Situational Factors

Situational factors can be very powerful motivators. The excitement of playing in front of a large audience, in a new stadium, or on national television may increase the motivation level of many athletes. In addition, the media may actually "hype" the game to increase public curiosity. For instance, during college football season, every Saturday is labeled "Game Day" by ESPN. They send a small army of a television production crew to a university to promote what they believe is the game of the week in college football. Athletes may be motivated to live up to the media billing or to silence media criticism. In fact, the media provides an unbelievable number of statistics that can be motivational devices if the athletes do not filter them. The media will tell the audience that Duke has lost only one nonconference basketball game at home in the month of November since 1994. If the Duke players hear the statistics, they may be motivated to keep the streak alive by beating their next nonconference opponent at home. Similarly, coaches often will increase the importance of a competition to motivate athletes. They may emphatically point out to the players that the upcoming opponent is the rival school, and it would be embarrassing if they lose. The coaches may explain that once they lose a game in the postseason tournament, their season is over; they plead with the players to be "ready to go" for competition. Coaches also may show film of the last time the team faced a particular opponent and point out how the opponents taunted the players once they established a comfortable lead.

Obviously, the motivational impact of a situation may be very intense. However, the motivational impact of a situation may be subtle as well. Athletes may be motivated simply by obtaining new uniforms or by having a college or professional scout in the audience. For instance, for the majority of the season a basketball player may exhibit a motive to achieve success by consistently taking the open shot; however, once a scout is in the audience, the player consistently hesitates and passes off the open shot, exhibiting a motive to avoid failure. A coach may observe similar behavior from a player whose parents are at the game.

Athletes are affected in many ways by the demands of the situation. Although it is understandable that various situations affect athletes in different ways, athletes who can maintain a constant high level of motivation across a variety of situations will observe a greater consistency in their performances. Thus, coaches, educators, parents, and sport psychology consultants must consider the athlete's personality, the situation the athlete is in, and how these factors interact to begin to understand the athlete's motivation. The athletes, however, cannot allow other people or situations to dictate their motivation. If athletes become dependent on the situation, they will likely observe fluctuations in their motivation evidenced by the amount of effort they expend in each competition. As effort fluctuates, athletes may observe decrements in performance. Thus, athletes must build a foundation based on intrinsic motivation that can limit the effects of situational factors. Athletes must respect the motivational impacts of situations that may confront them but also should work to maintain a consistent level of intrinsic motivation.

Fundamental Motivational Principles: A Summary

Motivation is a very complex psychological construct. However, it can be defined as several fundamental principles that can affect sport performance:

1. Athletes who make internal, controllable, and flexible attributions will expect to achieve successful performances and will practice persistently to increase the likelihood of future successful performances.
2. Athletes who are intrinsically motivated will perform and persist regardless of the external rewards that are present, not present, or presented and then removed.
3. Extrinsic motivation has the capacity to undermine intrinsic motivation.
4. Athletes who judge themselves by absolute standards will exhibit more desire to excel and thus increase the likelihood of performing consistently, regardless of the level of competition.
5. Athletes who focus on the process of competition rather than the outcome will have more control over success and failure. This will stimulate higher levels of persistence.
6. Athletes who are motivated to approach success will optimize motivation and performance.
7. Athletes with high levels of self-confidence, self-efficacy, and optimism will exhibit greater motivation to perform and to persist in challenging situations.

Performance Problems Related to Motivation

Understanding the motives that influence athletes to behave is essential for maintaining proper performance levels. Motivation, in its simplest form, is the initiation, direction, and sustaining of behavior. In sport, many problems related to motivation arise when the direction of the behavior is inappropriate for the situation or does not facilitate athletic performance, the intensity of the behavior is above or below an optimal range, or the direction and intensity do not remain stable and thus the behavior is not sustained. Each of these problems will be discussed as the consequences of improper motivation are examined.

Decreased Performance

All athletes experience games or competitions in which they have poor performance. Elite athletes attempt to condition themselves physically and mentally to decrease the likelihood of a poor performance. One of the benchmarks of an elite athlete is the ability to perform

Athletes are often motivated by their success, but the real test of motivation is to persist when confronting failure.

at a high level consistently. However, even some elite athletes experience fluctuations in performance. Tiger Woods, one of the world's great golfers, scores an 8 now and again on the golf course. In contrast to one bad performance, a decrease in performance is considered a significant change that has endured through a few performances. In sports, the term **slump** is often used to describe this phenomenon (Henschen, 1998). Decreased performance or slumps can be related to the motivation of the athlete. It is easy to get frustrated when a slump occurs and start questioning whether the effort expended is related to the performance. Slumps have the capacity to discourage an athlete from trying in practice or even in games. In essence, slumps can undermine an athlete's intrinsic motivation. The following is an example of how a decrease in performance can affect an athlete.

Michael, a college swimmer, began the season with solid times and improved quickly but the times reached a plateau after several weeks of training and competition. Race after race, he kept getting consistent times, but he saw no improvement. After a few weeks, Michael's performance began to suffer. At the start of the season, he had been the first swimmer to every practice and was usually the last to leave, but he now arrives late to practice, goes through the motions, and leaves just as practice ends.

Several possible causes for the change in Michael's behavior are related to motivation. It is possible that the direction of his motivation has changed. He may be very motivated to succeed at school and finds that swimming conflicts with his academic motivation and goals. He may have developed a significant relationship, motivating him to devote time and energy to his significant other and decreasing his motivation to swim. He may be more motivated to direct his energy to his family because his mom has been diagnosed with breast cancer. The motive to swim may be unimportant to Michael when compared to the motive to care for his mom. In each of these scenarios, the direction of the athlete's motivation is altered resulting in behavior changes that draw the athlete's energies away from sport. However, a directional change in motivation is only one explanation for Michael's decrease in training output and performance.

Another explanation of the change in Michael's behavior may be that he lacks motivation. A lack of motivation in this explanation refers to the intensity component of the motivation definition. Michael's practice behaviors may not be as intense because he believes that his prior efforts did not produce results. He may have lost motivation because his self-confidence in his ability to experience improvement in his performances has decreased. Michael may be discouraged with the results of his training. This can decrease his motivation to continue training intensely. Michael may think, "Why should I work out so hard when I haven't been able to see any gains in weeks?" The lack of improvement, despite his constant training and intense motivation, may have caused Michael to shift his locus of control from internal to external. He now believes that his training does not affect his competitive performances.

So far, the examples have illustrated how a lack of motivation or conflicting motivations can decrease training and performance. It is important to note that a decrease in performance or a slump that is unrelated to motivation also can affect athletes' levels of motivation. Decreases in performance provide information to athletes that they are not as competent as they thought. According to Harter (1978), people need to feel competent to be motivated in an activity. Inconsistent performance, lack of improvement, or a slump can reduce athletes' feelings of competence, thus reducing motivation. The reduction of motivation then can reduce the behaviors needed to improve performance. For instance, Erika is a teammate of Michael's on the swim team. Erika consistently obtains good times, but she is focused on the outcome of each competition. At the beginning of the season, she faced weaker competition and won every race. Now, as she competes against tough competition, each failure to win adds to her frustration, and she develops the belief that her training behaviors will not impact the outcome of her races. Thus, Erika decides that if her behaviors do not effect the desired outcome, there is no reason to waste extra energy training. Erika feels that she works too hard to always finish in second place or lower. As she becomes more frustrated because of her decrease in performance (defined as whether she won or lost), she may lose her motivation to train, just as Michael did. Of course, if she does not continue training at a high level, she is likely to obtain even slower times. This will only facilitate a continuation of her slump.

Not Performing to Potential

Some athletes may get stuck in a slump in which they experience a decrease in performance. Other athletes may never reach the level of performance that they are capable of achieving. Not performing to potential is defined as a lesser performance than is expected from an athlete. For instance, we expect United States sprinter Maurice Green to run the 100-meter dash in less than 10 seconds every time. He probably holds an expectation of himself to run 9.9 seconds or less. If Maurice Green ran the 100-meters in 11 or 12 seconds, there would be speculation that something is wrong. Sometimes, if a healthy athlete does not perform to his or her potential, it is related to a decrease in motivation or, more specifically, the intensity of motivation. For example, when Maurice Green steps into the blocks, he usually has elite sprinters around him. If he is not motivated to run his race the fastest that he can, he not only might lose the race but also might finish last. If his source of motivation is intrinsic, he will run the fastest possible whether he is alone or with other sprinters. However, he may use the competition as motivation, a form of extrinsic motivation. If Maurice becomes more motivated competing against high-caliber sprinters, what would happen if he ran against an unknown college sprinter in an open meet? He may give a lackluster performance because he knows that running at only 75 percent of his capacity will most likely win him the race. If he compares himself to his competition, his motivation may vary for each race, and his performance will not be consistent.

The behavior pattern of performing below potential is easy to observe. An athlete who performs well against tough competition but performs significantly worse against weaker opponents may require external motivation to perform at a high level. This is especially true in closed skill sports, such as track, swimming, or gymnastics, where scores are individualized, and there is no direct interaction between opponents. In open sports, such as basketball, soccer, and football, where there is an opponent attempting to limit the performance of the opposite athletes, the relationship is more complex. For instance, a softball player may see her batting average decrease against a strong pitcher in the league. However, it may be that this pitcher is performing extremely well and that the player's batting performance decreased due to excellent pitching, not due to a decrease in motivation.

Performing below potential can happen in high-school athletics. Often, there is one athlete on a high-school team who is significantly more talented than the rest of the team members and possibly the rest of the league. These athletes usually have received many letters from colleges and universities asking them to consider their school for further education. They may have played in front of college scouts many times. In some sports, such as men's basketball, the athlete may consider going directly into the professional ranks from high school. Although these athletes may be extremely talented, they frequently do not perform to their potential. High-school star athletes often are extremely successful without expending 100 percent effort. This is called the **fat cat syndrome.** However, this ability to perform with little motivation can undermine the ability to succeed at a high level of competition. Because of the success that has come so easily to these athletes, they frequently have not developed all their skills and abilities at the high-school level. Once they arrive at college, the competition is increased, and many athletes may not make the starting lineup for the first time in their athletic careers. In addition, weaknesses that were not evident in high school will be exposed because of the increase in the level of play. The fallacy of relative standards will become very apparent to these athletes. High-school superstar athletes may not have intrinsic motives to improve based on absolute standards. When they face stiff competition in college that is far more challenging, they experience frustration and may lose motivation to participate.

Burnout and Dropout

An excessive desire to be successful can cause athletes to increase their training to levels that are too intense or even unhealthy. Inexperienced athletes may believe that if they train every day, sometimes two sessions a day, they will see greater gains and improvements. Coaches also may think that the more training athletes receive, the better they will perform. Thus, pressure is put on the athletes by themselves and/or their coaches to visit the weight room frequently, attend 3–4 hours of practice each day, spend time refining technique outside of practice, and study film of the upcoming opponent. While physical injury can be debilitating to athletes, the psychological and emotional equivalent of physical injury is burnout.

Silva (1990) developed the **training stress syndrome,** a conceptual model, to explain the process that leads to burnout in sport. The amount of training activity imposed on athletes' bodies and minds is referred to as **training stress.** The results of training stress can be either positive or negative adaptation. Training results that are positive are called **training gains.** Athletes who have training stress greater than their ability to adapt to that stress may experience a plateau or a decrease in performance. For instance, many athletes use weights in their strength-training regimens. Weights allow athletes to easily measure strength-training gains. One week, a lacrosse player may bench-press 235 pounds; three weeks later, he may bench-press 245 pounds, obviously a gain in strength. Initially, athletes also may observe increases in self-confidence and motivation to train; this may catalyze further increases in training stress imposed by the athletes themselves (e.g., adding more weight or lifting weights more often). However, if the training stress becomes too great, athletes may see their bench presses level off. The failure to experience training gains combined with a drop in motivation has been termed **staleness** by Silva (1990). Staleness should not be confused with being in a slump, a decrease in skill-specific performance (Henschen, 1998). In contrast to an athlete in a slump, who observes a consistent decline in performance, an athlete experiencing staleness observes a performance plateau during which there is neither a decrease nor an increase in performance and motivation clearly drops. If athletes do not make positive adaptations to overcome staleness, they may experience **overtraining.** Overtrained athletes experience psychophysiological malfunctions such as extreme fatigue, chronic illness, and excessive use of defense mechanisms (Silva, 1990). If overtraining is not overcome, athletes may enter burnout, the final stage in the syndrome. **Burnout** is an undesirable state in which athletes are psychologically and physically exhausted by the constant failure to match the training stress imposed. Burnout has significant negative psychological and physical responses, and athletes are likely to consider quitting.

Burnout is not caused solely by increases in physical training, such as running, swimming, or weight training. An increase in training stress may be increased practice time, frequency, intensity, or stress imposed by the coach and/or teammates. For example, Coach Yates may feel an urgency to be fully prepared for the first volleyball game of the season. To meet her objectives the week before the first game, she believes she must have her athletes in the gym for 3 hours a day instead of 2. The coach also believes that she must repeat a drill several times to be confident that her athletes will be able to execute it correctly. However, after many repetitions, the athletes may believe that they are not accomplishing anything with further repetitions. They may begin to feel that they are reaching staleness. If the pattern continues throughout the season and is accompanied by constant psychological pressures and the liberal use of punishments, the players actually may become physically and mentally exhausted by practice. They may begin to lack the motivation to go to practice (avoidance). In fact, they may actually dread going to practice. Raglin and Morgan (1989) identified the five most common causes of burnout in college athletes as severe practice conditions, boredom, extreme physical fatigue, lack of recovery time, and physical and emotional exhaustion.

From a motivational standpoint, burnout is very detrimental, thus coaches and athletes always should take preventive measures to avoid its occurrence. Athletes who are experiencing burnout have failed to observe their efforts resulting in a "payoff." Athletes may ask the questions, "Why am I working so hard?" or "Is this really worth the work?" Burnout can lead to **dropout,** a complete withdrawal from the activity. Schmidt and Stein (1991) suggested that an athlete experiencing burnout considers personal investment and alternatives in deciding whether to remain committed to the sport or to drop out. Athletes consider the time they have invested in training for their sport, the enjoyment of being part of a team, and the possibility of rewards. These are contrasted with the alternatives of not participating in sport. If the alternatives are less desirable or the personal investment is high, it is likely that the athlete will be motivated to persist. When the opposite is true, the athlete will likely be motivated to drop out of sport and engage in another activity.

Many negative consequences in sport performance are related to motivation. In some instances, an athlete's lack of motivation or decrease in motivation causes performance problems. In other cases, performance problems occur, and the motivation of an athlete is negatively affected. Athletes who do not exhibit the qualities outlined in the fundamental motivational principles discussed earlier in this chapter may not be able to maintain a consistent level of motivation; thus, they may not be able to perform at consistently high levels. The next section will discuss techniques that can be used by coaches, sport psychologists, parents, or athletes to enhance motivation and thus overcome performance problems or limit potential performance problems.

Techniques for Enhancing Individual Motivation

Coaches use many techniques to motivate athletes. Many coaches yell and scream at athletes to achieve higher levels of effort in practice or competition. Some coaches place increased importance on certain games, hoping to generate a sense of urgency that will motivate team members to play their best. Coaches often use rewards such as game balls or increased praise for those athletes who perform extremely well in a competition. They may punish athletes who do not perform well by forcing them to complete extra running drills at 6 A.M. Coaches attempt to shape athletes' behaviors by using motivational techniques; however, the examples focused on punishment and rewards may not be successful in sustaining motivation. To observe consistently high levels of performance, the athletes' motivation must be maintained at a high level. Several techniques based on fundamental principles of motivation will not only initiate and direct behavior but also *sustain* it at a high level.

Info Box

Technique #1: Promote intrinsic motivation by defining success appropriately and focusing on absolute standards.

Define Success Appropriately

Success frequently is defined in terms of winning. In professional and major college athletics, athletes and coaches often are criticized for being unsuccessful because of average or below average winning percentages. Dan Marino, a veteran quarterback for the Miami Dolphins who currently holds most of the National Football League's records for his position, is an example of an athlete who consistently has performed at an extremely high level but is considered unsuccessful by some of the media because he has not been able to win a Super Bowl. Similarly, Frank Solich, head coach of the University of Nebraska football team, has been heavily criticized for not living up to the previous success of coach Tom Osborne, who won three national championships in 4 years. Many followers of college football actually deemed Solich unsuccessful in his first season with the Cornhuskers, despite their finishing with a 9–4 win-loss record.

Defining success in terms of winning creates an outcome-orientation, and, thus losing is interpreted as failure. Alternatively, defining success as performing up to the level of personal capability will facilitate development of a task-orientation. After a competition, athletes can evaluate whether they played up to their ability levels. After the competition, athletes can ask themselves, "How did I perform compared to what I am capable of performing?" If the answer to the question is, "I performed well offensively but I was slow defensively," the athlete likely will be motivated to improve the areas (defense) that were lacking in the performance completed. If athletes perform up to their full capabilities they can be proud of achieving success no matter what the score. The athlete who judges success by absolute standards is intrinsically motivated.

Obviously, outcomes of competitions are important, and athletes should not be satisfied with losing. However, athletes must place the outcomes of competitions in context with their performances during competitions. Essentially, there are four possible scenarios regarding competition outcome and performance. First, athletes may achieve a victory but admit that they played poorly. Although the athletes are successful in winning, they are unsuccessful in terms of performance. Athletes who are task-oriented will accept the win but will not be fully satisfied with their performance; they will be motivated to improve their performance.

Conversely, athletes who are outcome-oriented will focus on the win and may not perceive a need to improve their performance. They may be content with the win alone. The second scenario occurs when athletes win and play up to their capabilities. These athletes should be happy not only with obtaining a victory but also with performing well. Athletes who acknowledge their successful performance will work to replicate this performance in future competitions. They may realize that the successful performance put them in a position to win. Once again, a narrow focus on outcome alone may hinder some athletes from examining successful performance and how to sustain that level of performance. They are content and do not look for performance areas to improve or replicate.

A third scenario may occur when athletes lose and play poorly. Outcome-oriented athletes may become frustrated with losing and may overlook the part their performance played in the outcome. Outcome-oriented athletes may be unable to focus on their unsuccessful performance and on techniques to improve their play. Instead, they may dwell on the outcome and feel sorry for themselves. On the other hand, task-oriented athletes will see that they did not perform well, which is one possible reason for their losing the game. They will be motivated to improve their performance to increase the likelihood of a successful performance in the future and possibly getting a win as well.

Finally, a team may perform extremely well but still lose the competition. The outcome-oriented athletes, again, may become frustrated and may not realize that performing well is a success in itself, or they may become discouraged because they played well and did not obtain the desired outcome. Outcome-oriented athletes might say, "Well, we performed that well and still lost, so why practice?" Frustration and discouragement can be very debilitating to motivation. Task-oriented athletes will not be happy with the loss but will regard their performance as a success and attempt to build on it for future successes. Furthermore, they will continue to believe that successful performances will eventually lead to successful outcomes. They are not discouraged by the loss because they were able to accomplish good things in their performance. It is evident that an outcome-orientation, which is characterized by judging by relative standards, will result in decrements in motivation regardless of the outcome. They may win and not attend to evaluating the performance, or they may lose and become discouraged. Regardless of whether they win or lose, task-oriented athletes, those who judge by absolute standards, will focus on achieving a successful performance in the future. All athletes are upset with losing and happy with winning, but task-oriented athletes will be motivated to improve or replicate their performance despite the outcome.

Of course, athletes who consistently succeed in terms of absolute standards but never achieve their desired outcome (e.g., wins and losses, playing time) may eventually lose their motivation. For instance, a team handball player who has been a substitute for 3 years and has not had much playing time may not be content with continuing as a practice player. Defining success in terms of absolute standards can help to maintain the motivation of athletes, but the power of outcomes cannot be overlooked.

Info Box

Technique #2: Help athletes to take control of success by making internal attributions, specifically to effort.

Assess and Modify Attributional Style

When success is defined by absolute standards ("How did I perform in relation to my own capability?"), athletes will feel a greater sense of control over success or failure. They are more apt to attribute success or failure to internal and controllable sources, such as effort and performance. For example, athletes on a basketball team easily can attribute success to their ability, preparation, and effort because they executed well and played hard in a competition. If they failed to achieve success, they could again attribute the outcome (failure) to effort or their own preparation. In essence, the athletes could take responsibility for their successes and failures.

Athletes frequently will adhere to a faulty attributional style. Some athletes may talk about how they were able to execute the offense well because the opposition was not at full strength (because of injury or because they had played the night before). By attributing their performance to outside factors, the athletes are negating any preparation time and effort that they put into the competition. In essence, these athletes have relinquished any responsibility for the performance they exhibited. If these athletes believe that they are not factors in the performance, they may have no motivation to prepare or exert effort for the next contest.

Coaches must assess the attributional style of each athlete and modify it if it is faulty. To begin restructuring faulty attributions, have the athlete consider whether he or she is in control of his or her effort. In fact, Dweck (1975) found that by attributing failure to lack of effort instead of lack of ability, performance actually was enhanced more than when the participants actually succeeded at the task. Once the athlete realizes that no one else controls his or her effort, the coach or sport psychology consultant can move to link effort to performance and emphasize that both are linked to outcome.

Info Box

Technique #3: Teach athletes that they can control their effort and, consequently, their performance.

Emphasize the Effort–Performance–Outcome Relationship

Many athletes believe that the harder they try, the more likely they are to win or succeed. If these athletes exert as much effort as they possibly can and do not observe the desired outcome, they may become frustrated and decrease the amount of effort exerted, thinking that effort plays no role in the outcome. When they exert effort and do not achieve the desired outcome, they could blame lack of ability. It is very difficult for them to accept that they do not possess enough ability to obtain an outcome. Instead of accepting that they do not have ability, many athletes will develop a motive to avoid failure. They avoid challenging situations or do not exert effort in situations. They frequently will seek out opportunities in which the chance of failure is so minimal that they are almost guaranteed the desired outcome. They need to observe an immediate payoff for the effort exerted.

A flaw in this approach is that athletes link effort directly to outcome, rather than to performance. Coaches and sport psychology consultants must emphasize to athletes that effort affects performance and that performance affects outcome. A high amount of exerted effort refers to the energy put into preparing to compete as well as into competing. Athletes who expend 100 percent effort probably will observe a performance that is consistent with their ability level. However, neither the performance nor the outcome is guaranteed. A softball player may have a very effortful game and may drive the ball well, but she goes 0 for 3 at the plate. The boxscore displaying a 0 for 3 game for the hitter does not give an accurate assessment of the effort exerted in preparation for competition or for the actual performance. On the other hand, if the batter did not exert effort, she may not have even hit the ball hard enough to challenge the defense. The exertion of effort can increase the likelihood of a desired performance. Similarly, consistently good performances can only increase the likelihood of a desired outcome. However, if athletes do not perform well, they may not be in a position to experience a desirable outcome such as winning.

Coaches can motivate athletes by teaching them that effort leads to performance and that performance has a limited effect on outcome. Thus, the goal for each athlete should be to give consistent effort across all competitions to observe consistently high-level performance (relative to the athlete's ability), which will put the athlete in a position to achieve the desired outcome. Athletes who understand this concept, realize that they control their own efforts, and define success in terms of performing to their ability will be highly motivated intrinsically.

Info Box

Technique #4: Use content feedback to provide athletes with knowledge of their performance.

Influence of Feedback on Motivation

Feedback can play a major role in facilitating or debilitating the motivation of an athlete. It comes from many sources, including oneself, coaches, teammates, and significant others. It is essentially an objective or subjective evaluation of the performance of the athlete. For instance, a coach can provide feedback by telling a swimmer that she had a good stroke during a race. In this example, the swimmer gains an understanding that she executed her stroke well and had "easy speed." Knowing that she demonstrated good technique may motivate her to continue her rigorous training and work on technique improvement.

According to Smith (1998), feedback can motivate in three ways. First, objective feedback (e.g., statistics, boxscores) can correct distorted perceptions that athletes have about themselves. For instance, a point guard in basketball may feel that she played a great game; however, the final statistics indicate that she committed more turnovers than assists. On receiving the feedback from the statistics, the athlete can determine how to reduce the number of turnovers she commits in a game. Without the feedback, she may not work on making better decisions with the ball. Second, feedback can generate feelings within the athlete. The thumbs-up given to a tennis player after hustling for point may invoke positive feelings in him, which may serve as an acknowledgment that his effort has paid off. Finally, feedback allows for goals to be evaluated. If objective goals are set (e.g., run the 110-hurdles in 13.8 seconds), athletes can gain objective feedback directly from the results of the competition. Subjective goals (e.g., get out fast, attack each hurdle) can be evaluated by athletes themselves or by coaches. A coach's perspective can help the player evaluate whether or not a goal was actually obtained. For instance, an athlete may feel that he did get out fast and attacked each hurdle; however, his coach may observe the athlete hesitating at hurdles 6, 7, and 8. Feedback can be helpful to athletes. Some feedback may be task irrelevant, however, and athletes must identify the feedback that is most useful to them.

Feedback obviously plays an important role in motivation and subsequent performance. Two common forms are content feedback and emotive feedback. The goal of **content feedback** is to give the athlete knowledge of performance. After an athlete performs, the coach gives content feedback, such as which techniques were done correctly or which may need improvement. An example of content feedback is when a coach tells a volleyball player, "Your serve was good. It was low and hard. You are not bending your knees enough on your digs, though." Content feedback provides an athlete with information that increases perceived competence or establishes areas that may need some adjustment. **Emotive feedback** is a very different form of feedback. Although some content feedback may be imbedded in the emotive feedback, the communication is generally highly charged, negative, and critical. For example, a college coach may yell to a player, "What the heck are you doing out there? That was so pathetic, a junior high-school player can do better. Get out of there and let a real player take a rep."

Emotive feedback can have a powerful influence on behavior, but it can also turn players off or make them doubt themselves and doubt the confidence the coach has in their abilities. Extensive use of emotive feedback may result in athletes playing to gain the coach's approval or to make sure the coach doesn't get upset. These are extrinsic factors that have the capacity to undermine any intrinsic motivation athletes may possess. Athletes, like all people, can read body language to gauge whether statements are sincere. For instance, an athlete makes a turnover at a critical point in the game. If the coach kicks the bench and starts hollering swear words while sending in a substitute, the athlete may not respond well to content feedback as he or she sits down on the bench. To maintain high levels of intrinsic motivation, coaches must control their own emotions and provide athletes with appropriate content feedback. It is important for coaches to use emotive feedback only when appropriate, when it is clear that the athletes need something to spark their efforts. When a coach has patiently provided content feedback to an athlete but has not observed the athlete implementing the feedback, the coach may need to resort to some emotive feedback to arouse the athlete to attend to the content feedback. Coaches also must balance their content feedback with their verbal and nonverbal emotive behaviors. A technique that can facilitate the use of content feedback is setting goals with the athlete.

Goal Setting

According to Botterill (1978), setting goals can influence motivation in athletic performance. Locke and colleagues (1981, p. 145) reviewed the effectiveness of goal setting in work psychology. They explained that "the beneficial effect of goal setting on task performance is one of the most robust and replicable findings in the psychological literature." They found that goal setting stimulates effort and increases persistence to achieve the goal. The setting of goals actually provides athletes with motivation to achieve the goals, thus facilitating performance.

Info Box

Technique #5: Set specific, challenging yet realistically attainable goals.

Characteristics of Good Goals. Locke and Latham (1985) suggested that goals may have the most beneficial effects when they are specific rather than general. A softball player should set a goal to improve her batting percentage from .275 to .300 over a season rather that setting a general goal to hit for a higher average. In addition, many researchers suggest that short-term goals be set so that athletes will be able to evaluate progress and enhance motivation (Bar-Eli, Hartman & Levy-Kolker, 1994; Bell, 1983; Carron, 1984;

Gould, 1983; Harris & Harris, 1984). For instance, the softball player could set a goal to see her batting average improve from .275 to .280 after 2 weeks. Short-term goals can be used as stepping-stones on the path to attaining a long-term goal. It has also been recommended that goals be set high enough to be difficult to achieve (Locke et al., 1981). Kyllo and Landers (1995), in a meta-analysis of goal-setting research, found that challenging goals that are realistically attainable are superior to extremely difficult goals. Thus, a high jumper who consistently jumps six feet would not want to set a goal of jumping eight feet. Burton (1984, 1989) and Martens (1987) found that performance goals were more effective than outcome goals because outcomes are not within the control of the athlete. Winning the meet would not be a good goal for the high jumper to set; however, setting a goal to jump above 6 feet would be within his control and would facilitate motivation. Finally, good goals are set in positive terms rather than negative terms (Gould, 1998). An athlete who sets a goal positively ("I am going to make accurate chest-high passes today") is approaching success. An athlete who states the goal negatively ("I don't want to make bad passes today") is in an avoidance state of mind, attempting to avoid failure. In summary, good goal setting includes goals that are specific, short-term as well as long-term, challenging yet realistically attainable, performance oriented, and stated positively.

Info Box

Technique #6: Performance windows provide an excellent means of evaluating objectively measurable goals and thus sustaining motivation.

Performance Windows.   A goal is not complete without evaluating the progress made toward it. To evaluate goals, they must be measurable in behavioral terms (Cox, 1998; Gould, 1998). A goal with great specificity will be measured accurately. For instance, a basketball player could set a goal to shoot the ball well in the next competition. How does the athlete know whether the goal was attained? "Shooting the ball well" must be defined before it can be measured. A more specific goal would be to make 50 percent of the field goals and 78 percent of the free throws taken in the game. After the game, the athlete can examine the official box score to see if the goal was attained. How does the athlete, however, interpret a field goal percentage of 48 percent? If the athlete observes a 48 percent field goal percentage, did the athlete fail? Although goals should be specific and measurable, setting a single point may not facilitate a realistic evaluation of performance. A single point may not take into account all of the situational factors that may affect the performance measure. In dynamic sports, such as basketball, ice hockey, or soccer, the opponent may adjust the defensive strategy to affect many performance measures set as goals by the offensive players. Playing well but failing to reach these goals may be discouraging, especially if it occurs regularly. Goals that are too limited can "inhibit extremely high levels of performance" (O'Block & Evans, 1984, p. 190). In essence, a single finite point may actually be too limiting to allow for some expected variation in the performance, either above or below the goal set.

A goal range can be set to allow the athlete freedom to have slight fluctuations in performance but still attain the goal range set. O'Block and Evans (1984) developed **interval goal setting;** goal intervals were obtained using previous performance measures to predict future performance. Interval goal setting establishes the goal interval by using the averages of prior performances and the best of prior performances to calculate an upper boundary, midpoint, and lower boundary. The goal interval allows for variability in performance.

At the Sport Psychology Clinic at the University of North Carolina, the work of O'Block and Evans has been adapted into a highly practical system of interval goal setting. The athlete and sport psychology consultant discuss past and current personal performance standards to establish a **performance window.** Similar to goal intervals, performance windows have upper and lower boundaries as well as midpoints; however, these numbers are obtained through a discussion with the athlete in an attempt to provide a sense of ownership in the goal-setting process. First, the athlete is asked to estimate an average measure for himself or herself on the task. Eddie, a 100-meter sprinter, may frequently run near a 10.5-second time in the event. Consequently, he may decide to set his midpoint at 10.5 seconds. Second, he is asked to identify his slowest time in the past season that would still be acceptable. Eddie may choose 10.8 seconds as his upper boundary, setting up the top window at 10.8 to 10.5 seconds. Finally, Eddie is asked to identify a challenging yet realistic lower boundary to represent his previous personal best or a time slightly lower then his previous best. Eddie decides to set his lower boundary at 10.1 seconds, understanding that it will take an exceptionally fast performance to obtain that time. Eddie has now established a lower window of 10.5 to 10.1 seconds. The result of this process is the establishment of a goal interval in the form of a range that allows the athlete to monitor his performance and worry less about who is in the race with him today.

Each athlete must feel a sense of ownership in his or her goals. By working with the athlete, the sport psychology consultant or coach can direct the athlete to set his or her own goals. Additionally, the athlete should be asked to type out his or her goals. If he or she cannot make this minimal effort, the goals the sport psychology consultant or coach *gives* to the athlete will not be internalized and meaningful. The athlete should have ownership of the goals to maximize motivational benefits and performance enhancements.

Many motivational benefits result from setting goals as performance windows. First, performance windows are based on task-orientation rather than outcome-orientation. They are effective in motivating athletes to perform consistently within the ranges set. At the same time, the windows provide standards of excellence that are realistic to motivate athletes to improve. Windows also allow for variability in performance that is not permitted by a single, specifically defined point. Finally, athletes who perform within their windows enhance the strength of their perceived self-competence, which is related to their self-confidence (Chapter 12 provides additional information on goal setting, self-confidence, and performance).

Techniques for Enhancing Motivation: A Summary

There are several techniques that can be used to enhance and maintain a high level of motivation in athletes. Coaches can be instrumental in developing and utilizing the following techniques with their athletes:

1. Promote intrinsic motivation by defining success as effort and performance and by encouraging athletes to set absolute standards.
2. Help athletes take control of their motivation by making internal attributions (effort and ability).

3. Teach athletes that they can control their effort, enhance their ability level, and consequently increase the likelihood of enhanced performance.
4. Use content feedback to provide athletes with knowledge of performance and of how this performance relates to positive and negative outcomes.
5. Set specific and challenging, yet realistically attainable goals, and be sure the athlete is actively involved in this process.
6. Consider athletes' recent past and projected performances when developing performance windows.
7. Provide performance windows to evaluate objectively measurable goals and thus sustain motivation.

Conclusion

Motivational principles can have many beneficial effects on athletes' performance. Coaches and sport psychology consultants can help athletes learn these principles to develop a foundation of intrinsic motivation. Athletes who can adhere to these principles will develop an internal desire to sustain training and will continuously examine ways to improve. Unfortunately, if the motivational principles are applied improperly by a coach, sport psychology consultant, parent, or the athletes themselves, they can cause a decrement in motivation and performance and may even result in dropping out from sport. The techniques outlined in this chapter provide guidelines for developing a sound motivational base that results in consistent motivation across situations, performance enhancement, and performance consistency.

Key Terms (in order of appearance)

Attribution Theory	motive to approach success	burnout
attributional style	motive to avoid failure	dropout
intrinsic motivation	slump	feedback
extrinsic motivation	fat cat syndrome	content feedback
Cognitive Evaluation Theory	training stress syndrome	emotive feedback
locus of causality	training stress	interval goal setting
absolute standards	training gains	performance window
relative standards	staleness	
Need Achievement Theory	overtraining	

References

Atkinson, J. W. (1964). *An introduction to motivation.* Princeton, NJ: Van Nostrand.
Atkinson, J. W., & Feather, N. T. (1966). *A theory of achievement motivation.* New York: Wiley.
Bandura, A. (1977). Self-efficacy: Toward a unifying theory. *Psychological Review, 84,* 191–215.
Bar-Eli, M., Hartman, I., & Levy-Kolker, N. (1994). Using goal setting to improve physical performance of adolescents with behavior disorders: The effect of goal proximity. *Adapted Physical Activity Quarterly, 11,* 86–97.

Bell, K. F. (1983). *Championship thinking: The athlete's guide to winning performance in all sports.* Englewood Cliffs, NJ: Prentice Hall.

Botterill, C. (1978). The psychology of coaching. *Coaching Review, 1,* 1–8.

Burton, D. (1984). Goal setting: A secret to success. *Swimming World,* Feb. (pp. 25–29).

Burton, D. (1989). Winning isn't everything: Examining the impact of performance goals on collegiate swimmers' cognitions and performance. *The Sport Psychologist, 3,* 105–132.

Carron, A. V. (1984). *Motivation: Implications for coaching and teaching.* London, Ontario: Sports Dynamics.

Cox, R. H. (1998). *Sport psychology: Concepts and applications.* Boston: McGraw-Hill.

Deci, E. L., & Ryan, R. M. (1985). *Intrinsic motivation and self-determination in human behavior.* New York: Plenum.

Duda, J. L. (1987). Toward a developmental model of children's motivation in sport. *Journal of Sport Psychology, 9,* 130–145.

Dweck, C. S. (1975). The role of expectations and attributions in the alleviation of learned helplessness. *Journal of Personality and Social Psychology, 31,* 674–685.

Elliott, E. S., & Dweck, C. S. (1988). Goals: An approach to motivation and achievement. *Journal of Personality and Social Psychology, 54,* 5–12.

Gould, D. (1983). Developing psychological skills in young athletes. In N. L. Wood (Ed.), *Coaching science update.* Ottawa, Ontario: Coaching Association of Canada.

Gould, D. (1998). Goal setting for peak performance. In J. M. Williams (Ed.), *Applied sport psychology: Personal growth to peak performance.* Mountain View, CA: Mayfield.

Gould, D., & Petlichkoff, L. (1988). Psychological stress and the age-group wrestler. In E. W. Brown, C. F. Branta, et al. (Eds.), *Competitive sports for children and youth: An overview of research and issues. Big Ten body of knowledge symposium series, Vol. 16* (pp. 63–73). Champaign, IL: Human Kinetics.

Harris, D. V., & Harris, B. L. (1984). *The athlete's guide to sports psychology: Mental skills for physical people.* New York: Leisure.

Harter, S. (1978). Effectance motivation reconsidered: Towards a developmental model. *Human Development, 21,* 34–64.

Henschen, K. P. (1998). Athletic staleness and burnout: Diagnosis, prevention, and treatment. In J. M. Williams (Ed.), *Applied sport psychology: Personal growth to peak performance.* Mountain View, CA: Mayfield.

Locke, E. A., & Latham, G. P. (1985). The application of goal setting to sports. *Journal of Sport Psychology, 7,* 205–222.

Locke, E. A., Shaw, K. N., Saari, L. M., & Latham, G. P. (1981). Goal setting and task performance. *Psychological Bulletin, 90,* 125–152.

Kyllo, L. B. & Landers, D. M. (1995). Goal setting in sport and exercise: A research synthesis to resolve the controversy. *Journal of Sport and Exercise Psychology, 17,* 117–137.

Manzo, L. G., Silva, J. M., & Mink, R. (1998). "Sport confidence: A theory generated measure" (manuscript). The University of North Carolina at Chapel Hill, 1998.

Martens, R. (1987). *Coaches guide to sport psychology.* Champaign, IL: Human Kinetics.

McClelland, D. C. (1961). *The achieving society.* New York: Free Press.

Nicholls, J. G. (1984). Conceptions of ability and achievement motivation. In R. Ames & C. Ames (Eds.), *Research on motivation in education: Student motivation,* Vol. 1. New York: Academic.

O'Block, F. R., & Evans, F. H. (1984). Goal setting as a motivational technique. In J. M. Silva & R. S. Weinberg (Eds.), *Psychological foundations of sport.* Champaign, IL: Human Kinetics.

Raglin, J. S., & Morgan, W. P. (1989). Development of a scale to measure training induced distress. *Medicine and Science in Sport and Exercise, 21,* 60.

Ryan, E. D. (1977). Attribution, intrinsic motivation, and athletics. In L. I. Gedvilas & M. E. Kneer (Eds.), *Proceedings of the NAPECW/NCPEAM National Conference.* Chicago: Office of Publications Services, University of Illinois at Chicago Circle.

Ryan, E. D. (1980). Attribution, intrinsic motivation, and athletics: A replication and extension. In C. H. Nadeau, W. R. Halliwell, K. M. Newell, & G. C. Roberts (Eds.), *Psychology of motor behavior and sport–1979.* Champaign, IL: Human Kinetics.

Schmidt, G. W., & Stein, G. L. (1991). Sport commitment: A model integrating enjoyment, dropout, and burnout. *Journal of Sport and Exercise Psychology, 13*(3), 254–265.

Siedentop, D. & Ramey, G. (1977). Extrinsic rewards and intrinsic motivation. *Motor Skills: Theory into Practice, 2,* 49–62.

Silva, J. M. & Weinberg, R. S. (1984). *Psychological foundations of sport.* Champaign, IL: Human Kinetics.

Silva, J. M. (1990). An analysis of the training stress syndrome in competitive athletics. *Journal of Applied Sport Psychology, 2,* 5–20.

Singer, R. N., & Orbach, I. (1999). Persistence, excellence, and fulfillment. In R. Lidor & M. Bar-Eli (Eds.), *Sports psychology: Linking theory and practice* (pp. 167–190). Morgantown, WV: Fitness Information Technology.

Smith, R. E. (1998). A positive approach to sport performance enhancement: Principles of reinforcement and performance feedback. In J. M. Williams (Ed.), *Applied sport psychology: Personal growth to peak performance* (3rd ed.) (pp. 28–40). Mountain View, CA: Mayfield Publishing.

Weinberg, R. S. & Gould, D. (1995). *Foundations of sport and exercise psychology.* Champaign, IL: Human Kinetics.

Weiner, B. (1979). A theory of motivation for some classroom experiences. *Journal of Educational Psychology, 71,* 3–25.

Weiner, B. (1985). An attributional theory of achievement motivation and emotion. *Psychological Review, 92,* 548–573.

Weiner, B. (1986). *An attributional theory of motivation and emotion.* New York: Springer-Verlag.

Wooden, J. R. (1997). *Wooden: A lifetime of observations and reflections on and off the court.* Chicago: Contemporary Books.

6

Emotion in Sport

Peter R. E. Crocker, Kent C. Kowalski, Thomas R. Graham, and Nanette P. Kowalski

University of Saskatchewan

- When reading about emotion in sport, confusion often exists because key terms are often used interchangeably and without substantive definitions. Words like *emotion, emotionality, affect,* and *mood* have qualitative definitions, and each term has specific and distinct meaning within the realm of emotion in sport.
- Conceptual views of emotion include the evolutionary perspective, emotion and physiology, social construction, and cognitive views.
- Cognitive theories of emotion include Attribution Theory and Cognitive–Motivational–Relational Theory.
- Given the complexity of these specific cognitive theories of emotion, applying the philosophies of theory often involves creating sport-specific models such as Action Theory and Individual Zones of Optimal Functioning.

> *To be leading the team for such a long time, then watch someone else unable to do the job, repeatedly, was really frustrating. The most threat was that I was being told that I was no longer good enough.... I got so angry and vented my feelings to try to change the situation.... After the championships I was so depressed that I withdrew and stayed away from basketball and drank heavily for a few months.*
>
> —Wheelchair basketball athlete

Most athletes can easily recall experiencing diverse emotions such as joy, anxiety, anger, pride, and sadness before, during, and after a sporting event. Emotional states can shift rapidly, varying from joy to despair in a matter of moments. Think of a critical turnover, an opponent mistake, or an official's call that changes certain defeat into a stunning victory. The victors' faces are aglow with joy. The losers' expressions are often of stunned silence or open expressions of profound sadness and dismay. But emotion in sport is more than just a reactive expression to victory or defeat. Sport scientists have argued that precompetitive and competitive emotional states can influence the athlete's ability to perform (Hackfort, 1991; Hanin, 1997; Hardy, Jones & Gould, 1996). Further, the athlete's ability to control emotional states like anger can not only affect performance but also influence the public's perception of athletes and sport.

Emotion and sport are inseparable. The key is how the athlete regulates and directs emotion.

Since emotions are so prevalent in sport, athletes and coaches need to understand what factors produce emotions, the various functions and consequences of emotions, and the mechanisms of regulating or controlling emotions. This chapter is designed to provide an overview of emotion in sport, starting with definitions of several key emotion terms. Next is a brief history of the conceptualization of emotion with emphasis on various views that have influenced how sport scientists and practitioners look into emotions. This conceptualization section will lead into cognitively based models of the production of emotions. Finally, recent sport-specific models will illustrate how emotions and performance can affect each other. Overall, this chapter is designed to provide a theoretical understanding of emotions operating in sport. It will serve as a solid foundation for the following chapters on anxiety and sport performance and emotional control in sport.

Definitions and Basic Concepts

Defining *emotion* is not easy or without controversy. Vallerand (1983, 1984) noted that finding a definition of *emotion* that would satisfy all researchers is almost impossible. Yet having a descriptive definition of key emotional terms is necessary to understand the contributing factors (antecedents) and the consequences of emotions in sport. Students are often confused when reading sport research on emotion because writers have used terms such as *emotions, emotionality, affect, feeling states, arousal,* and *moods* interchangeably. This lack of clarity makes it difficult to explain how emotions affect sport performance and vice versa. To help the student, we provide descriptive definitions of *emotion, moods, affect,* and *temperament.* Although the focus of this chapter is emotions in sport, it is necessary to consider other emotional states when explaining various sport models and findings.

Emotion

Emotions are complex psychophysiological states of limited duration that have adaptive functions (Lazarus, 1991). Although theorists disagree about all the characteristics of emotions, the following are common: quick onset, short duration, common perceptual or cognitive appraisal antecedents, distinctive physiological or neurological patterns, distinctive subjective feeling (commonly referred to as *affect*), and distinctive facial or bodily expression (Cornelius, 1996; Ekman, 1994; Lazarus, 1991). Emotions include happiness, pride, surprise, sadness, disgust, anger, anxiety, shame, guilt, and fear. There is major disagreement among emotion theorists about which emotions should be considered basic or primary. Some theorists list only six or seven emotions, although others include up to fifteen distinct emotions (Ekman, 1994; Izard, 1971, 1994; Lazarus, 1991).

Mood

Mood is a diffused, global, subjective feeling state. Unlike emotions, mood involves more durable feeling states. Many theorists agree that mood states involve a subjective experience like emotions, but in moods emotion-defining attributes such as facial expressions, specific physiological patterns, and specific cognitive appraisals are absent (Davidson, 1994). Frijda (1994) proposed that moods, unlike emotions, do not involve relationships between a person and a particular object. For example, when a gymnast is afraid while on the balance beam, she is afraid of something. When in a bad mood, however, the gymnast's emotional state is not directed toward a particular person or thing. It is thought that moods bias thoughts, behavior, and subsequent discrete emotions in the same direction as the positive or negative mood state (Davidson, 1994). For example, an athlete in a negative mood is likely to recall previous negative memories, see the negative side of a situation, behave in a negative manner, and experience negative emotions like anger. The investigation of mood states and performance has a long history in sport research (Morgan & Pollock, 1977; Rowley et al., 1995).

Affect

One of the most difficult emotional terms to define is **affect.** In sport research, this word has often been used interchangeably with *emotion* (e.g., Hanin, 1997). Affect is a subjective feeling state that can be pleasant or unpleasant, varies in intensity, and is often associated with preceding thoughts and subsequent actions (Weiner, 1986). Affects can range in duration from temporary states to more trait-like dispositions that can last days, months, or even years (Watson & Clark, 1994). Terms used to describe affective states in sport settings include *pure emotions* (e.g., anger, anxiety, happiness), *mood states* (e.g., vigorous, calm, pleased, annoyed), and *cognitive-behavioral states* (e.g., competence, confidence, motivated, laziness) (Hanin & Syrja, 1997; Silva & Hardy, 1984; Vallerand, 1987). *Affect* definitions often do not include physiological arousal or facial/bodily expression (Weiner, 1986). When seeing the term *affect*, students must carefully examine how the writer is using the term.

Temperament

Temperament refers to stable individual differences in how people experience and express emotions (Goldsmith, 1994). The term *temperament* is often seen in developmental research with children but is not a frequently used term in sport research. Most sport researchers prefer to use the term *trait* or *disposition* to describe stable emotional states. These characteristic ways of emoting can remain relatively stable for months to years. An athlete with an angry temperament is more likely to experience and express anger, and possibly corresponding aggressive behavior, in sporting situations compared to an athlete with a happy temperament. A commonly cited trait emotion in sport research is competitive trait anxiety. It is defined as the tendency to perceive competitive situations as threatening and to respond to these situations with anxiety states (Martens, Vealey, & Burton, 1990).

Info Box

Emotion, mood, affect, and temperament are related terms that are often used interchangeably. Because each of these terms has its own unique substantive definition however, it is important to understand the proper context and to use the terms appropriately.

Conceptual Views of Emotion:
A Brief Historical Review

The Evolutionary Perspective

An evolutionary view holds that emotions are universal (the same across cultures) and have specific adaptive functions that enable people to deal with situations that occur repeatedly in evolutionary history (Cornelius, 1996). A key idea is that distinctive facial expressions are associated with specific emotions (e.g., happiness, sadness, fear, disgust, anger) and are recognized across cultures (Darwin, 1872/1965; Ekman, 1994). The facial expression is part of a distinct pattern of autonomic nervous system activity that organizes facial expressions, thoughts, and behaviors. One criticism of the evolutionary view is that there are cultural differences in how emotions are expressed. To account for these cultural variations, Ekman suggests that people learn **displays rules** that govern how emotions should be expressed in specific situations. Through the socialization process, parents, teachers, and coaches teach children appropriate ways to express emotions. Think about the ways that you have been taught how to manage anger in sporting situations.

From an evolutionary perspective, the function of emotion is to allow people to deal with situations in ways that may have been adaptive in our evolutionary past. Emotion allows us to act quickly and without a lot of thinking and planning. The distinct physiological pattern prepares the body for specific types of action. The facial expression serves to send information to others about our emotion. Dieter Hackfort, a German sport psychologist, has incorporated the expressive role of emotion as a central piece of Action Theory (Hackfort, 1991, 1993). We discuss his theory in more detail later in the chapter.

Info Box

The evolutionary concept of emotion states that emotions are universal, adapt over time, are somewhat individualized by cultures, and have important functional value.

Anger is a common emotion that is experienced and expressed in sport. According to the evolutionary view, anger occurs when a person automatically perceives another person threatening his or her well-being. Anger arises very rapidly and is associated with a specific physiological pattern, such as increased arousal. The athlete exhibits the characteristic facial expression with eyebrows furrowed towards the nose, lips pulled back, and teeth bared. The athlete also experiences an impulse to attack the offending person physically or verbally. Whether the athlete continues to express the emotion or act on the impulse to attack will be determined, to a large extent, on learned behavior.

Emotion and Physiology

Physiological processes dominate explanations about how emotions arise and their effects on sport performance. Physiological explanations of emotion focus on how bodily and brain processes influence emotional experiences and behavior (Cannon, 1927; LeDoux, 1995). Physiological explanations dominate for several reasons. First, from a subjective experiential perspective, many strong emotions, such as anger, seem to involve physiological activation. Second, early "emotion" theorists such as William James and James Cannon were trained in physiology and anatomy and were influenced by the thinking of evolutionary theory. Third, physiological processes can be assessed by objective measures such as heart rate, blood pressure, blood flow, skin temperature, eye pupil dilation, and sweating. Fourth, the psychology field was dominated in the middle of the twentieth century by behavioral perspectives that discouraged the use of "mentalistic" concepts and encouraged objective measures. Employing objective measures of physical reactions created a belief that this type of research on emotion was more scientific compared to measures of subjectively experienced mental states (Watson, 1971). These social and research forces pushed physiological investigations of emotion to the forefront.

Info Box

The emotion and physiology conceptual view argues that emotion directly affects physiological systems. In addition, it argues that physiological activation has the potential to invoke emotional responses.

Within the sport psychology field, emotion research emphasizing the influence of physiological systems on sport performance has primarily focused on arousal mechanisms. Sport researchers have attempted to determine how physiological activation affects performance though impairment of underlying mechanisms such as attention, decision making, memory, and neuromuscular control (see Hardy, Jones & Gould, 1996; Landers & Boutcher, 1993). There is a danger, however, in equating emotion with physiological states. Emotions like anxiety are often confused with arousal. Although high-anxiety states are associated with physiological activation, high arousal may not necessarily be linked to anxiety. Further, diverse positive and negative emotions, such as fear, anger, and joy, may also be linked to high arousal. Therefore, trying to explain emotion–performance relationships through only arousal mechanisms may be misleading.

Social Construction: The Role of Culture

Social construction theorists argue that social institutions such as education and sport play a major role in influencing how athletes experience and express emotion. Instead of focusing on physiological changes, emotional expression, subjective feeling, or even specific thoughts, social constructionists are more interested in how emotions become part of the culture's social practices (Averill, 1980, 1993; Cornelius, 1996; Ellsworth, 1994). Averill (1993, 1995) uses the term **emotional syndrome** to refer to social rules that people learn to determine when certain emotion states and responses are appropriate. A major focus of the social construction perspective is to determine how societal rules "help constitute (not simply regulate) the way we think, feel, and act during an emotional episode. [And that]...

a primary goal of research should be to specify such rules for a variety of different emotions, both within and across cultures" (Averill, 1995, 205).

Info Box

The social construction conceptual theory reasons that organized cultural institutions, such as education and sport, play a major role in influencing how athletes experience and express emotion.

Consider the emotion of anger in sport. Anger occurs when an athlete believes someone else has committed a wrongful act, such as trying to intimidate a skilled teammate or breaking the rules to gain an unfair advantage. The socialization process directed by authority figures (parents, teachers, coaches, etc.) will determine whether the act is wrongful. Athletes learn the appropriate circumstances and reactions for anger. For example, Canadian ice hockey players generally learn that skilled teammates must be protected from physical intimidation. Through the encouragement of parents, commentary of hockey analysts, coaching instruction, and the structure of the rules, older youth players learn that it is acceptable to get angry when an opponent makes a hard check on your skilled player and that appropriate expression can involve physical retaliation (Smith, 1983). A key implication of the social construction position is that cultural differences will lead to differences in the experience and expression of emotion. Differences in the teaching of acceptable or unacceptable behavior will lead to cultural differences in how athletes evaluate and respond to specific situations.

Cognitive Views

During the 1960s, there was an increased scientific recognition that people's interpretions of situations and physiological processes are critical to emotion (Arnold, 1960; Lazarus, 1966; Schachter & Singer, 1962). The cognitive view focuses on the role of perceptual and thinking processes in emotion generation and regulation. An athlete's emotional experience, expression, and control depend on how a situation affects personal goals and well-being. Because athletes bring different experiences and goals to any situation, individual differences in emotional experiences and reactions are not uncommon. Cognitive theories attempt to explain individual differences in terms of factors like personal well-being, self-esteem, personal identity, goals, future expectancies, and coping (see Lazarus, 1991; Crocker & Graham, 1995a). These concepts are explained in later sections that detail specific cognitive theories of emotion.

Many cognitive theorists, although emphasizing the central role of cognition, also recognize that physiological processes are involved in emotion (Lazarus, 1991). This physiological involvement is captured by the idea that some emotions produce an impulse to action or readiness to action. For example, joy involves a sense of pleasure combined with the urge toward exuberance and contact seeking (Frijda, 1994). On the other hand, an athlete will have an urge to strike when angry. The athlete may not strike because of the perceived consequences of retaliating, but the urge to strike is present.

Given the central role that cognitive-based emotion models have played in contemporary sport psychology, the next section reviews two theories that have shaped recent thinking. Key concepts in both Attribution Theory (Weiner, 1985) and Cognitive–Motivational–Relational Theory (Lazarus, 1991) are central to several sport-specific emotion–performance models (e.g., Hackfort, 1993; Hanin, 1997) as well as to a profusion of sport research studies.

Cognitive Theories of Emotion

Attribution Theory

Attribution theory (Weiner, 1982, 1985, 1986) has been a prominent cognitive model in the study of sport-related emotion. A primary reason for its popularity is that it attempts to explain emotion in achievement settings, and what better arena in which to study achievement than sport? Various physical activity settings and populations have been investigated, including gymnastics (McAuley & Duncan, 1990), team sports (Robinson & Howe, 1989), distance runners (Santamaria & Furst, 1993), softball (White, 1993), exercise settings (McAuley, 1991; McAuley & Duncan, 1989), and children in sport (Vlachopoulos, Biddle, & Fox, 1996, 1997). These studies and others have provided important insights into the relationships between the reasons that people believe outcomes occur and their emotional experiences.

Weiner's view of emotion is very general and includes emotions (e.g., anger, pride, sadness) and affective feeling states (e.g., content, confident, competent, stupid). Weiner's thinking has been influenced by the social constructionists' view of emotion. He defines emotion as "a complex syndrome or composite of many interacting factors. Emotions are presumed to have (1) positive or negative qualities of (2) a certain intensity that (3) frequently are preceded by an appraisal of a situation and (4) give rise to a variety of actions" (Weiner, 1986, p. 119).

Weiner argued that in achievement situations people try to determine why an outcome happened. These reasons of perceived causality, called **attributions,** influence future expectations, behavior, and emotion. In sport, four common reasons given for achievement outcomes are ability/skill, effort, luck, and task difficulty. Other reasons may include teamwork, teammates, mood, fatigue, weather, facilities, practice, officials, and coaches (see Biddle, 1993; Hardy, Jones & Gould, 1996; Gill, 1986). Take the following statement from a 10-year-old soccer player who was crying after a 5–0 loss, the team's third straight loss. "We just suck! We can't stop the other team; we cannot even kick the ball straight! We all just stood around and let the other team run all over us." This young girl ascribed the loss to a couple of causal factors including the ability of the other team, but mostly to the lack of her team's ability.

Weiner initially suggested that attributions (like opponent's ability, referee's decisions, and personal ability) could be classified into two dimensions: locus of causality and stability. **Locus of causality** refers to whether the outcome could be attributed to oneself or to external factors such as officials or weather conditions. The **stability** dimension refers to the degree that the cause is expected to remain stable over time. In the above example, the young soccer player's emotion and motivational behavior might be different if she believed the outcome would be different in future games. These dimensions are shown in Figure 6.1. A third dimension, called **controllability,** was added later to indicate whether the athlete has intentional control over an outcome. For example, illness and lack of effort are both internal and unstable. However, lack of effort is under an athlete's volitional control. Believing an important match was lost because of a lack of effort will likely lead to quite different emotions (e.g., guilt or anger) compared to emotions experienced if the loss was attributed to illness such as the flu (e.g., sadness or sympathy).

The question arises whether emotions are a result of the outcome of a sporting event or of the attributions that follow success or failure. For example, was the young soccer player upset because the team lost or for the attributions she gave for the loss. Weiner theory states that both the type of outcome and the attributions must be considered. He argued that emotions arise from two types of cognitive evaluations (appraisals) in achievement settings: outcome and attribution. In outcome appraisal, performance is evaluated automatically in terms of subjective success and failure. Based on this performance appraisal, general positive and negative outcome-dependent emotions occur. These emotions include feeling happy following success and feeling sad following failure. Athletes tend to be happy following a victory, whether the win was due to superior ability, great effort, or good luck. Emotions generated by outcome appraisals are labeled **outcome dependent–attribution independent.**

Weiner believed, however, that more specific emotions such as pride and guilt are determined by a reflective appraisal process in which athletes search for reasons for the outcome. This evaluation process occurs most readily in response to important outcomes and to unexpected or negative outcomes (Weiner, 1986). Knowing that the opponents won the match because they cheated will lead to different emotions than believing they were a superior team in skills and tactics. Attributions given for an athletic outcome can be classified into specific causal dimensions that are uniquely related to a set of emotions (see Table 6.1 on page 116). Locus of causality is primarily responsible for the development of emotions like pride or feelings of self-esteem. The stability dimension is concerned with future

FIGURE 6.1 *Two Causal Dimensions Used to Classify Specific Causal Ascriptions for Achievement Outcomes.*

		Stability	
		Stable	Unstable
Locus	Internal	Ability Aptitude Intelligence	Health/illness Effort Practice
	External	Task difficulty Teammate's ability Coach's ability	Officials Luck Weather

TABLE 6.1 *Appraisal–Emotion Process for Four Different Outcome–Attribution Situations.*

Perceived Athletic Outcome	Outcome-dependent Emotion	Causal Ascription	Causal Dimensions	Attribution-dependent Emotion
Failure	Feel bad	Lack of effort	Internal locus Unstable Controllable	Guilty
Failure	Feel bad	Official's judgment	External locus Unstable Controllable	Angry
Success	Feel good	Ability	Internal locus Stable Controllable	Proud
Success	Feel good	Luck	External locus Unstable Uncontrollable	Relief

expectancy and has been associated with the time-related emotions of hope and hopeless-ness. If athletes are defeated in a competition and believe the cause was sickness, they are likely to expect different results in future competitions and to experience some sense of hope. The controllability dimension is strongly associated with social emotions including gratitude, sympathy/pity, shame, guilt, and anger. An athlete who makes a critical mistake or loses an important match because of perceived lack of effort will often experience guilt and be the target of anger expressed by teammates and coaches.

Weiner's theory has great intuitive appeal, but its ability to predict emotion in sport settings has been mixed. Although several sport attribution studies have indicated that ap-praisal is moderately to strongly associated with emotional experience, the relationship be-tween specific types of appraisals (outcome versus causal attributes) and emotions are not consistent with the model (McAuley & Duncan, 1990; Robinson & Howe, 1989; Valle-rand, 1987). Contrary to Weiner's (1985) position, each study indicated that outcome ap-praisal was the dominant predictor of both outcome-dependent and attribution-dependent emotions in this domain. People involved in athletic situations experienced positive emo-tions when they succeeded and experienced negative emotions when they failed. It will be instructive to consider these studies.

McAuley and Duncan (1990) examined the appraisal–emotion relationship in gym-nastics participants and found that both outcome (success or failure) and attribution ap-praisals were significant predictors of general or outcome-dependent affect (a measure including pleased, satisfied, happy, depressed). Further, only outcome appraisal predicted self-related affects thought to be tied to attributions (a measure including competent, proud, shame, guilt, and disappointment). The attribution appraisal of stability was the only significant predictor of social or other related affects (gratitude and anger). McAuley and Duncan also found that outcome and attribution appraisals shared variance with the various affective states; that is, both types of appraisals were correlated with each other along with their association with the various affects. What their research showed, however, is that if you knew the type of perceived outcome (success or failure), attributions added very little to the understanding of general and self-related affects.

Robinson and Howe (1989) examined the relationship between appraisal and emotion in a large sample of high-school students involved in a competitive team sport program. Emotional states include general affects, self-related affects, and other-related affects. The findings showed that outcome and attribution appraisals had important roles in predicting all types of affective states. These results run contrary to Weiner's (1985) contention that general emotions are totally outcome-dependent. Second, outcome appraisal was found to have the greatest predictive power for not only general affective states but also attribution-dependent, self-related affects as well. Again, this is not consistent with Weiner's (1985) theory.

Vallerand (1987) employed a sample of high-school basketball players to investigate emotional experience. Immediately after a game in a basketball tournament, the athletes were asked to complete a questionnaire to indicate whether they had a good or bad game, which factors had caused their performance, and how they were feeling emotionally. Only self-related and general affects were assessed. Two important results were found in common with the previously mentioned studies. First, outcome appraisal predicted both general and self-related affects. Second, although attribution appraisal was significantly related to general and self-related affects in success conditions, its influence was limited in comparison to outcome appraisal.

In summary, sport research suggests that outcome appraisals are an important determinant of emotional states and that causal attributions play a smaller role. Some major challenges, however, face researchers in understanding these processes. First, it is often difficult to separate outcome and attribution processes. Most studies use some form of retrospective method; that is, they ask athletes to recall their appraisals and emotions some time after an event. Given this delay, it may be difficult for some athletes to remember what attributions they used to explain the outcome. Second, the experience of specific emotions may cause them to selectively remember or even falsely reconstruct their appraisals. Third, emotional experience does not occur only after a game or match. Emotions are experienced as the athlete reacts to many situations throughout a competition. It might be useful for researchers to ask athletes to recall specific emotions experienced during the competition and then to identify how the situation was evaluated in outcome and attributions. Despite the challenges identified here, attribution research and theory has highlighted the central role of cognitive appraisals of emotional experience in sport.

Cognitive–Motivational–Relational Theory

Richard Lazarus, a prominent stress and emotion theorist, has had a major impact on stress and coping research in sport (e.g., Crocker & Graham, 1995b; Gould, Finch, & Jackson, 1993). In the last decade Lazarus has argued that psychological stress should be considered a subset of the emotions (Lazarus, 1991, 1993a). He suggested that recognizing approximately fifteen specific emotions is informative in understanding how people attempt to adapt and cope with their environment. His ideas are influencing sport researchers' investigations about how emotion is generated and how emotion affects performance (e.g., Hanin, 1997; Graham & Crocker, 1997).

Info Box

Cognitive–Motivational–Relational Theory explains how thoughts and motivations interact with the environment to produce performance-affecting emotions.

Lazarus (1991) argued that emotions arise as a joint product of personality and environment. Motives and cognition are critical because people evaluate the significance of encounters in terms of the their own motives and beliefs. The evaluation or appraisal process involves making a number of decisions, many of which occur automatically, about how the encounter will maintain, enhance, or harm one's well-being. **Primary appraisal** is a motivationally oriented appraisal that consists of determining whether the situation is important, whether personal goals are being attained or threatened, and the type of ego-involvement (Lazarus, 1991, 1993b). **Secondary appraisal** includes an evaluation of blame and credit and who is responsible (agency), future expectancies, and coping options (Lazarus, 1991). Coping plays a significant role in that it can change the encounter and influence the appraisal process. To clarify how the emotion process occurs in athletic situations, seven key psychological factors are discussed. These factors are self- or ego-involvement, fate of personal goals, appraisal, personal meaning, provocation, action tendencies, and coping (Lazarus & Lazarus, 1994).

Self- or Ego-Involvement.   **Ego-involvement** consists of diverse types of self-identities, such as moral values, ego ideals, life goals, other people and their well-being, and self-esteem and social esteem. Ego-involvement develops over time and is heavily influenced by the prevalent cultural beliefs that drive how parents, coaches, and significant others encourage or discourage the behaviors of athletes. Let's consider the ego-involvement in the development of athletic identity. For many competitive athletes, being an athlete is a key aspect of how they view themselves and how they respond to situations that threaten or enhance this self-identity. A person with a strong athletic identity will experience strong positive emotions such as joy or pride when success is achieved. Conversely, negative emotions are likely to follow failure, especially if the failure is perceived to be the result of not living up to athletic ideals.

Recall the quote at the beginning of the chapter from the wheelchair basketball athlete. Interviews with this athlete clearly indicated that being an athlete, despite his disability, was a key aspect of who he was. Indeed, he used athletics to gain social acceptance and approval to prove to others that he wasn't so different. Being unable to show his ability and being relegated to the bench during the championships, however, was a major threat to his sense of self. Both ego ideal and self-esteem were at stake. The athlete reported that he did not work hard during training because he didn't think it would make a difference. This produced a sense of guilt for letting himself and others down. Further, not playing threatened his social status within the team and the wheelchair basketball community and among his peers. The end result was myriad negative emotions and behaviors, both during and after the championships.

Fate of Personal Goals.   An athlete's personal goals must be involved for emotions to occur. The important goals that an athlete brings to a situation (reflecting the athlete's values and beliefs) can be achieved (resulting in benefit) or frustrated (resulting in harm).

Take a swimmer competing in national championships. If the athlete achieves a personal goal (a personal best or a particular placing) then she will experience positive emotions. Failure to achieve the goal will result in negative emotions. A second factor to consider is the size of the positive or negative discrepancy. Larger discrepancies between goals and performance will result in more intense positive or negative emotions. For example, exceeding one's personal-best performance by 10 percent in a major championship will result in stronger positive emotions than simply matching one's personal best.

Appraisal.   How an athlete evaluates the importance, meaning, consequences, and options for dealing with a situation is paramount to emotion. The more important the situation, the more intense the subsequent emotion will be. If a situation has no relevance to an individual's well-being, then no emotion will occur, regardless of the outcome (Lazarus, 1991). For a seasoned performer, there is a lot more at stake in a playoff game than in an exhibition. This is one reason that exhibition or preseason games are often devoid of intense emotions for highly experienced players. On the other hand, a rookie trying to crack the lineup is likely to perceive these competitions as critical to achieving long sought after personal goals. Not surprisingly, these athletes experience much different and stronger emotions than the veteran athletes.

The emotion process is also influenced by other evaluations, such as determining who is responsible (blame/credit), future expectancies, and coping options. Knowing or believing who is responsible, when either a positive or negative event has occurred, will have a direct effect on emotion. **Expectancies** involve knowing if things are going to get better, worse, or stay the same. Coping options or coping potential involves determining what can be done in stressful situations and the consequences of those actions. To understand how these three appraisal processes influence emotion, let's consider a basketball player who was just injured during a collision. Initially she is very angry if she believes that the other person was responsible. This anger may transform into unhappiness as she realizes that her season may be over. After evaluating that the injury is minor, however, and that excellent treatment is available, her expectancies are that the situation will get better. She also believes she can manage the treatment of the injury and continue to pursue her athletic goals. This will change the emotional state of unhappiness into a different emotional state, such as relief.

Personal Meaning.   The end product of the appraisal process is personal meaning (Lazarus & Lazarus, 1994). Each athlete will derive slightly different personal meaning from any particular sport setting because of individual differences in personal goals, values, future expectancies, and other appraisal variables.

Provocation.   When an encounter is evaluated as important, there are four types of provocation that will produce either positive or negative emotions, depending on the perception of harm or benefit (Lazarus & Lazarus, 1994). The first type of provocation involves a real event that produces personal harm or benefit. For example, a football player may be promoted to the starting lineup (benefit) or, conversely, may be demoted to a nonplaying role (harm). The second type of provocation is an encounter that doesn't remove a harm and doesn't maintain a benefit. For example, the football player demoted to the bench is unable to change his status even after working hard in practice. The third type of provocation involves anticipating a harm or benefit in future contests. If our demoted player thinks he will not do well in future practices, he is likely to experience feelings of anxiety. The last provocation type is the non-occurrence of an expected event, such as a significant other failing to do or say something. For example, the demoted football player works hard in practice over several days, noting to himself significant improvement in skill. He is convinced that the coach will acknowledge his toil and improvement. The head coach, however, walks by and says nothing. The lack of positive feedback when it was expected (and wanted) triggers a negative emotional response by the athlete.

Action Tendency.   Lazarus (1991) suggested that many emotions, such as happiness, anger, and fear, are associated with **action tendencies** that mobilize the body to respond. These urges to respond are automatic and occur without conscious thought. A gymnast who is experiencing fear before a complex move on the balance beam will exhibit a host of physiological responses such as trembling, excessive sweating, and glassy eyes (large pupils). She will also experience an urge to flee or to get away from the beam. Another example of an action tendency is the urge to strike when angry. Athletes have to learn to control these action tendencies and channel the impulse into a more culturally appropriate response.

Coping.   Athletes need to manage the high level of stress that occurs in competitive sport. **Coping** refers to a deliberate and planned process involving thoughts and actions

The ability to cope and recover quickly is crucial for all athletes particularly those in central positions.

used to handle specific stressful demands (Lazarus, 1991; Lazarus & Lazarus, 1994). Coping can also be used in advance of an anticipated stressful event so that the athlete has a planned response to meet the situational demands. Coping can alter a stressful situation in two ways. First, **problem-focused coping** is aimed at actively changing the situation. Strategies may include planning, information seeking, problem solving, increasing effort, and the acquisition of new skills. Our football athlete tried to change his negative emotion–eliciting situation by increasing effort in practice. A second class of coping skills is termed **emotion-focused coping.** This involves managing the emotion itself and includes strategies such as mental and behavioral withdrawal, denial, distancing, and relaxation.

It is often necessary to use emotion-focused coping when first experiencing emotions, especially negative emotions, before effective problem-focused strategies can be used. For example, a hockey player may experience anger after being checked headfirst into the boards. His initial impulse is to attack the opponent. He uses emotion-focused strategies such as self-talk ("Don't lose your cool!" or "Control yourself.") to suppress the action tendency. He then uses problem-focused strategies (e.g., increased effort, planning and initiating a hard check) to change the situation and the emotional state.

Summary of Cognitive–Motivational–Relational Theory

Lazarus's emotion theory tries to explain the dynamic, unfolding nature of emotion. Students need to understand that the relationship between appraisal, coping, and emotion is bidirectional (see Fig. 6.2 on page 122). This is a critical point because emotion in sport is not a static process but is constantly changing. The process of emotion begins with an encounter that is appraised in terms of meaning. The appraisal process generates an emotion, with its associated characteristics of cognition, subjective feeling, physiological changes, and "action tendencies." Now the athlete has to manage or cope with the emotional state (and the constantly changing person–situation that triggered the emotion). Coping has several functions. First, it may alter the person–environment situation. The altered situation is then reappraised, and this may lead to a change in the type or intensity of the emotion (Lazarus, 1991). Second, coping may facilitate or suppress the tendencies of the athlete to act in a certain manner. However, appraisal of the short- and long-term interpersonal and social consequences of specific expressions and behavior may lead to coping efforts that result in quite different actual behavior. This can only happen if the individual perceives these coping options (and possible consequences) and has the coping skills necessary to produce the desired actions. Further, athletes can use anticipatory coping before the person–situation relation becomes troubled. If an athlete knows something emotional may occur, she can prepare to modify, avoid, or deal with it more effectively.

There has been little systematic investigation of Lazarus's emotion theory in the sport field. Dissertation research by Graham (1999) investigated how goal importance and the size of the goal discrepancy (either positive or negative) can predict discrete emotions in addition to casual attribution dimensions advocated by Weiner's attribution model. One study examined emotional responses in high-performance adolescent soccer players following a fitness test evaluation. For athletes failing to reach self-selected fitness goals, both causal attributions and goal characteristics predicted sadness. For athletes who attained or exceeded fitness goals, only the size of the goal discrepancy affected happiness. The more

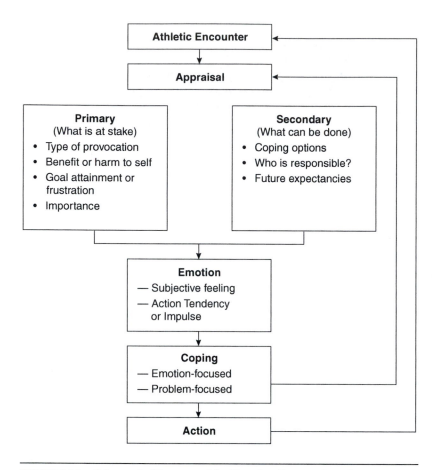

FIGURE 6.2 *Schematic Diagram of the Emotion Process Based on Cognitive–Motivational Relational Model.*

the self-selected fitness score goal was exceeded, the higher was the happiness score. A second study examined swimming and track-and-field adolescent athletes in actual competition settings. For both positive and negative emotions, subjective evaluation of performance (exceeding or failing to achieve performance goals) was the primary predictor. Goal importance and causal attributions made no or small contributions to explaining emotions. Goal importance wasn't a factor because the great majority of athletes rated the importance of the competition to be very high.

Given the complexity of Lazarus's theory, it may be several years before researchers will be able to determine the validity of all its components in sport settings. Nevertheless, some sport psychologists have incorporated Lazarus's ideas about cognitive appraisal into their sport-specific models of emotion and performance relationships (e.g., Hackfort, 1989; Hanin, 1997). These models will be considered next.

Emotion–Performance Relationships: Sport-Specific Models

Action Theory

Dieter Hackfort, a German sport psychologist, advocated a theory of emotion that is based on the premise that emotions are developed, actualized, and modified by actions (Hackfort, 1989, 1991). **Action Theory** holds that actions and emotions influence each other in a reciprocal manner. First, actions can influence the regulation of emotions. Actions can cause new emotions or they can cause a change in the intensity or quality of previously experienced emotions. For example, a field hockey player who scores an important goal may experience an increase in joy or happiness. Second, emotions can influence the regulation of actions. A soccer player who is angry at her teammates for their poor performance may channel the high arousal of the angry state into playing with more physical intensity.

Info Box

Action Theory maintains that emotions are directly influenced by actions and that actions, in turn, affect emotions. According to this theory, emotions are created, actualized, and modified by actions.

Rather than labeling emotions as dichotomous states such as positive/negative or bad/good, Action Theory emphasizes that emotions should be regarded as having benefits (positive functions) and costs (negative functions) in regulating action (Hackfort, 1989). The benefit or cost of an emotion depends on the actions that are required in the specific situation. For example, in some situations cognitive anxiety can signal impending danger to an athlete and cause him or her to initiate safety strategies before further action (if enough time is available). A rock climber may experience a heightened level of anxiety when climbing a difficult rock face. This emotional state may signal her to reconsider her actions or to initiate actions such as tightening, checking, and possibly adding more pitons and karabiners. The anxiety benefits the climber by regulating her actions toward taking realistic precautions and protecting herself (Hackfort, 1989). In other situations, anxiety may influence an individual's actions in a negative way. A gymnast may experience anxiety before a competition routine, resulting in poor concentration and increased muscle tension. These symptoms of anxiety maybe costly to the gymnast because she may be not perform as well as she usually does.

Fundamental to Action Theory is the assumption that actions and emotions are functions of the interactions between a person and the environment. Actions and emotions are determined by the way an individual interprets the person–environment situation. For example, a tennis player may play the same opponent in two different situations, a tournament final and a practice. In a tournament, the amount of media attention, the number of fans, or the importance that the player places on winning the tournament are all factors that may influence the player's actions and emotions. Perhaps he tenses up and experiences a great deal of anxiety in this situation, causing him to play a poor match. Alternatively, in the practice situation there may be no fans and nothing is really at stake. Although the opponent is the same, the player may interpret the practice match as quite different from the tournament. This change in perception may cause him to experience little anxiety and to play a much better match. The changes that occurred in the tennis player's actions and in his level of anxiety were directly related to how he interpreted the different person–environment situations.

Athletes' interpretations (appraisals) of specific person–environment situations depend on their previous experiences in similar situations and their expectations about the current situation (Hackfort, 1986). In addition, emotions are influenced by athletes' perceptions about their personal resources for handling the situation and the importance they place on the outcome of their actions (Hackfort, 1989). These concepts of appraisal and coping are similar to those in Lazarus's (1991) emotion theory.

One of the major contributions of Action Theory is the emphasis on understanding the function of emotion in sport. To understand more about the functional meaning of emotions in specific situations and to gain insight into the techniques people use to control their emotions, Hackfort and Schlattmann (as cited in Hackfort, 1993) developed a procedure called "video-stimulated self-commentary." The first step in the procedure involved athletes observing themselves on videotape in sport situations. Second, the athletes watched the videotape a second time while commenting on their behaviour and feelings in specific situations. The athletes commented about the quality of the experienced emotions, the intensity and consequences of the emotions, and any emotional reactions that had been hidden or faked (Hackfort, 1993). Third, athletes were interviewed about the videotaped situations and their comments about their behaviours and feelings in the situations. The final step in the procedure was analysis of the functional role (benefits and costs) of the emotions that athletes experienced in the different situations.

Data from the video-stimulated self-commentaries provided evidence that emotions can have stimulating and restricting effects on athletic performance for both athletes and interacting others (i.e., opponents). Specifically, the date showed that athletes use emotional expression in three ways. First, athletes can present experienced emotions. Second, athletes can fake emotional experiences and express nonexperienced emotions. Third, athletes can attempt to hide experienced emotions (see Fig. 6.3). Action Theory suggests that the presentation of emotions (or lack of presentation) can have two functional meanings: self-regulative or social-regulative (Hackfort, 1993).

When emotions are presented or not presented for the purpose of controlling one's emotions, they are considered to have a **self-regulative functional meaning** (Hackfort, 1993). For example, an athlete may present an emotional reaction for the purpose of reducing his activation/arousal, reducing the intensity of his emotion, or changing the quality of the emotional experience. A football player may yell loudly and angrily after a play with the intention of releasing and reducing the anger he is experiencing. On the other hand, an athlete may present a different emotional reaction from the one that is actually being experienced in an attempt to overcome the experienced emotion. A rugby player may yell loudly and angrily with the intention of increasing her level of activation and overcoming her feelings of lethargy. Conversely, an athlete may not present an emotional reaction at all, even though emotions are being experienced, in an attempt to protect himself (i.e., self-

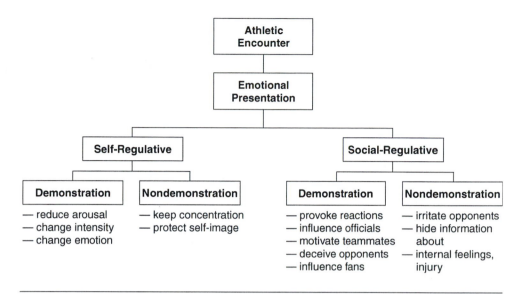

FIGURE 6.3   *Self-Regulative and Social-Regulative Functions of Presenting Emotions in Sport (Modified from Hackfort, 1993).*

image). For example, if a player values portraying emotional control, she may suppress showing obvious signs of anger even though she is experiencing the emotion.

When emotions are shown or hidden for the purpose of influencing other people's emotions, they are considered to have a **social-regulative functional meaning** (Hackfort, 1993). For example, an athlete may show emotions in an attempt to motivate teammates or frustrate or intimidate opponents. A volleyball player might yell enthusiastically after she makes a great block on the opposing team's best hitter to both motivate her teammates and frustrate her opponents. Alternatively, an athlete may present certain emotional reactions that are not actually experienced to gain emotional support from teammates or deceive the opponents. A hockey player may laugh off a very hard check, even though he is hurt, so that his checker will think that he was uninjured by the check. Finally, an athlete may not present his or her emotions to either irritate or hide information from the opponent. A hockey player may skate off the rink with no emotional reaction at all after a hard check to hide that she was injured.

Hackfort presented many interesting ideas concerning the roles of action and emotion in sport. Rather than advocating simple cause–effect relationships between emotion and sport (i.e., anxiety causes a decrease in performance), the theory proposes that actions and emotions influence each other in a reciprocal manner and that each influences the regulation of the other. It also proposes that emotions should be regarded as having benefits (positive functions) and costs (negative functions) and not be labeled as strictly positive or negative. The benefits or costs of an emotion are determined by the actions that are required in each specific situation. A concept fundamental to the theory is that a person's interpretation of a situation determines what actions and emotions are experienced. Clearly, Action Theory recognizes the influence of cognitive appraisal on the meaning of the sporting situation as well as the role of social rules of the athletic community concerning when emotions should be displayed and appropriate ways to show emotional responses. Nevertheless, it is not clear what conditions are necessary to produce different self-regulative or social-regulative functional meaning. Despite these limitations, Action Theory presents interesting and provocative ideas about the study the athlete and social roles of emotion in sport.

Individual Zones of Optimal Functioning

Yuri Hanin (1989, 1997) is a European sport psychologist who developed a sport-specific emotions–performance model. Based on more than 25 years of research and observations with elite athletes, Hanin argued that each athlete's best performance occurs in a personally optimal emotional zone. His model, called the **Individual Zone of Optimal Functioning** (IZOF) Model, focuses on an individualized approach to emotion. For each athlete, optimal performance occurs when individually meaningful emotional states are in specific zones. The emotional states and the optimal zones are often very different for various athletes (Hanin, 1997).

The IZOF model relies on athletes identifying the types and intensities of positive and negative affective states associated with good and bad performances. Hanin (1997), like Weiner (1986), considers emotion and affect synonymous. Positive affect states include terms such as *motivated, self-confident, vigorous, daring, happy, eager,* and *good.* Negative terms include *aggressive, dissatisfied, angry, worried, exhausted, afraid,* and *lazy* (see Hanin & Syrja, 1995, for a list of affective terms). Although some emotion theorists argue that Hanin is confusing emotions (e.g., happy, angry) with behaviors (e.g., aggressive, lazy) and motivated cognitive states (e.g., confidence), Hanin asserts that his model has ecological validity because affective states are selected by athletes and are predictive of performance.

When the IZOF model is applied to emotions, both content and intensity need to be considered. First, content is composed of two related but independent factors: optimal–dysfunctional and positive–negative valance. These two factors combine to form four categories: (1) P+: positive, pleasant, facilitating emotions; (2) N+: negative, unpleasant, facilitating emotions; (3) P–: positive, pleasant, debilitating emotions; (4) N–: negative, unpleasant, debilitating emotions (see Fig. 6.4). The affective terms selected for these four categories vary across athletes.

For each *facilitating* emotion, there is an individual zone of *optimal* intensity associated with high performance. For each *debilitating* emotion, there is an intensity zone identified as being *dysfunctional* and associated with poor performance. The IZOF model holds that performance is related to the combined influences of optimal and dysfunctional emotions. Best performances should occur when facilitating emotions are in the optimal zone, and dysfunctional emotions arise from the debilitating zone.

A description of the IZOF methodology will help clarify the content and intensity concepts of the IZOF model. Each athlete is required to recall previously successful and poor performances. Athletes then go through a series of steps to determine their Positive–Negative Affect (PNA) profile (Hanin, 1997). First, the athlete identifies optimal PNA patterns by selecting up to five positive and then five negative content terms that describe his or her affective states during successful performances. Next, dysfunctional PNA patterns are identified

FIGURE 6.4 *Example of How an Athlete May Categorize Positive and Negative Affective States Related to Optimal and Dysfunctional Effects on Performance.*

Optimal

P+	N+
Confident	Aggressive
Determine	Intense
Vigorous	Nervous
Cheerful	Attacking

Positive ———————————————————— Negative

P–	N–
Carefree	Dissatisfied
Easygoing	Lazy
Relaxed	Depressed
Satisfied	Sad

Dysfunctional

in a similar fashion, but the athlete focuses on poor performances. Finally, the athlete determines a zone of intensity in which (a) the optimal affective states are helpful during good performances and (b) the dysfunctional states are harmful during poor performances. Hanin advocates the use of a ten-point intensity scale. The resulting PNA profile can be compared to affective states experienced during subsequent successful and poor performances.

Research evidence for emotion–performance relationships is limited because the model is relatively new. Hanin (1997), in a review of his colleagues' work, argued that some basic tenets of the model have been supported. Syrja, Hanin, and Personen (1995) found a relationship between performance and zones of optimal and dysfunctional emotions in junior soccer players. Players who rated their competition performances as successful were more likely to be closer to their optimal facilitating zones and outside their dysfunction zones. Hanin (1997) reported a study with squash and badminton players that produced similar results (Syrja, Hanin & Tarvonen, 1995). Hanin and Syrja (1995) also found that specific positive and negative emotions can be facilitating for some athletes and debilitating for others. Junior hockey players from Finland found many emotions had both facilitating and debilitating performance effects. For a particular athlete, a high level of intensity for a specific emotion could be debilitating although a low level of intensity could be facilitating. Furthermore, Hanin and Syrja found evidence of what they termed reversal effects. Some positive affective states (e.g., carefree, overjoyed) were identified only as debilitating, whereas some specific negative states (e.g., aggressive, attacking, intense) had only facilitating effects on performance.

The IZOF model is unique in the sport psychology field. Rather than preclassifiying emotions as positive or negative, Hanin argues that affective states can have both facilitating and debilitating effects on performance that are specific to each athlete. Although the

IZOF model provides researchers with a new paradigm for investigating emotions in sport, there still are several unresolved theoretical questions that have major implications for practical interventions. First, it is not clear how specific affective states are produced in athletes. Hanin (1997) utilizes Lazarus's (1991) proposal that appraisal and relational meaning give rise to emotion. Lazarus's theory, however, is based on distinct emotions and not on global cognitive–affective states. Second, even if appraisal processes were involved, why would the same emotional state produce individual differences in performance? It is not clear what underlying mechanisms produce performance changes or what other factors combine in systematic ways with emotions to produce specific performance levels. Third, the IZOF model was based on elite performers with extensive performance histories. No evidence exists that even the basic tenets of the model apply to younger or less experienced performers. The model's validity with different sport populations needs to be established. Last, the inclusion of cognitive–motivational terms, moods and discreet emotions in the definition of emotions creates conceptual confusion. Understanding the underlying mechanisms governing performance may require a clearer separation of cognitive–motivational states (e.g., feeling motivated, confident) from affective and emotion states.

Conclusion

This chapter addressed the complex nature of emotions in sport. Emotions involve distinct subjective feeling states (affect), bodily expressions, and physiological changes. Understanding how emotions influence performance and other social roles in sport is difficult because researchers have used terms such as *emotion, mood,* and *affect* interchangeably. The use of various terms and the relative emphasis of different emotion components (e.g., physiological, expressive, affect) are the result of historical developments and the theoretical assumptions and biases of researchers from various disciplines. An evolutionary perspective seeks to determine whether emotional expression is relatively invariant across cultures and emphasizes how emotional expression conveys information to others. Physiologically oriented researchers focus on how changes in central and peripheral systems contribute to emotional experience and regulation. Social constructionists argue that understanding emotional experience and expression requires a detailed understanding of the rules for emotions in a particular culture. Cognitive researchers recognize the involvement of physiology but concentrate on cognitive evaluation of situations in terms of constructs such as personal meaning, threats and benefits to self-identity, causal attributions, expectancies, and coping.

The cognitive perspective dominates contemporary sport psychology research and intervention. Two sport-specific emotion–performance models are Action Theory (Hackfort, 1989) and Individual Zones of Optimal Functioning (Hanin, 1997). Action Theory focuses on the costs and benefits of emotions in regulating action. It also addresses how expressing emotions can serve self and social functioning. Self-regulation can include reducing arousal or changing the intensity and type of emotion being experienced. Social-regulation could involve motivating teammates, influencing officials, and frustrating or deceiving opponents. The IZOF model focuses on how different affective states can be either functional or dysfunctional. Top performances are thought to be associated with keeping specific affects in optimal zones and other affects out of dysfunctional zones. Optimal and dysfunctional affects and their corresponding zones are unique to each athlete.

Researchers are working hard to determine how personal factors and situational demands interact to produce emotions. A thorough understanding of emotion in sport demands a consideration of various theoretical perspectives. Humans are biological animals with an evolutionary history living in ever-changing social–cultural settings. Neglecting any of these realities results in a less than satisfactory explanation of emotion. Key steps in sport research include determining how different emotions influence performance and identifying how they affect the underlying cognitive and physiological mechanisms related to performance. Much sport research has been directed toward answering these questions on a critical sport emotion—anxiety. The next chapter will explore theory and research related to anxiety and sport performance.

Acknowledgements.   The writing of this chapter was supported in part by a Social Sciences and Humanities Research Council of Canada grant to the first author.

Key Terms *(in order of appearance)*

emotions	controllability	problem- focused coping
mod	outcome dependent—attribution	emotion-focused coping
affect	independent affect	Action Theory
temperament	primary appraisal	self-regulative functional
displays rules	secondary appraisal	meaning
emotional syndrome	ego involvement	social-regulative functional
attributions	expectancies	meaning
locus of causality	action tendency	Individual Zone of Optimal
stability	coping	Functioning

References

Arnold, M. B. (1960). *Emotion and personality,* Vol. 1 & 2. New York: Columbia Univ. Press.

Averill, J. R. (1980). A construction view of emotion. In R. Plutchik & H. Kellerman (Eds.), *Emotion: Theory, research, and experience,* Vol. 1 (pp. 23–43). New York: Academic.

Averill, J. R. (1993). Illusions of anger. In R. B. Felson & J. T. Tedeschi (Eds.), *Aggression and violence: Social interactionist perspectives.* Washington, DC: American Psychological Association.

Averill, J. R. (1995). Passerby [a commentary on Lazarus, 1995]. *Psychological Inquiry, 6,* 204–208.

Biddle, S. J. H. (1993). Attribution research and sport psychology. In R. N. Singer, M. Murphy & L. K. Tennant (Eds.), *Handbook of research on sport psychology* (pp. 437–464). New York: MacMillan.

Cannon, W. B. (1927). The James Lange theory of emotions: A critical examination and an alternative theory. *American Journal of Psychology, 39,* 106–124.

Cornelius, R. R. (1996). *The science of emotion: Research and tradition in the psychology of emotion.* Upper Saddle River, NJ: Prentice Hall.

Crocker, P. R. E., & Graham, T. R. (1995a). The generation of emotion in sport and physical activity: The importance of perceived individual goals. *International Journal of Sport Psychology, 26,* 117–137.

Crocker, P. R. E., & Graham, T. R. (1995b). Coping by competitive athletes with performance stress: Gender differences and relationships with affect. *The Sport Psychologist, 9,* 325–338.

Darwin, C. (1872/1965). *The expression of the emotions in man and animals.* Chicago: Univ. of Chicago Press.

Davidson, R. J. (1994). On emotion, mood, and related constructs. In P. Ekman & R. J. Davidson (Eds.), *The nature of emotion: Fundamental questions* (pp. 51–55). New York: Oxford Univ. Press.

Ekman, P. (1994). All emotions are basic. In P. Ekman & R. J. Davidson (Eds.), *The nature of emotion: Fundamental questions* (pp. 15–19). New York: Oxford Univ. Press.

Ellsworth, P. C. (1994). Sense, culture, and sensibility. In S. Kitayama & H. R. Markus (Eds.), *Emotion and culture: Empirical studies of mutual influence* (pp. 23–50). Washington, D.C.: American Psychological Association.

Frijda, N. H. (1994). Varieties of affect: Emotions and episodes, moods, and sentiments. In P. Ekman & R. J. Davidson (Eds.), *The nature of emotion: Fundamental questions* (pp. 59–67). New York: Oxford Univ. Press.

Gill, D. L. (1986). *Psychological dynamics of sport.* Champaign, IL: Human Kinetics.

Goldsmith, H. H. (1994). Parsing the emotional domain from a developmental perspective. In P. Ekman & R. J. Davidson (Eds.), *The nature of emotion: Fundamental questions* (pp. 68–73). New York: Oxford Univ. Press.

Gould, D., Finch, L. M., & Jackson, S. A. (1993). Coping strategies used by national figure skaters. *Research Quarterly for Exercise and Sport, 64,* 453–468.

Graham, T. R. "The contribution of goal characteristics and causal attributions to emotional experience in youth sport participants." Ph.D. diss., University of Saskatchewan, 1999.

Graham, T., & Crocker, P. R. E. (1997). The contribution of goal characteristics and casual attributions to emotions in youth sport participants. *Journal of Sport and Exercise Psychology, 19,* S57.

Hackfort, D. (1986). Theoretical conception and assessment of sport-related anxiety. In C. D. Spielberger & R. Diaz-Guerrero (Eds.), *Cross-cultural anxiety* (pp. 79–91). New York: Hemisphere.

Hackfort, D. (1989). *Emotion and emotion control in sports: Benefits and costs.* First IOC World Congress on Sport Sciences, Oct. 28–Nov. 3.

Hackfort, D. (1991). Emotion in sports: an action theoretical analysis. In C. D. Spielberger, J. G. Sarason, W. L. Van Heck (Eds.), *Stress and emotions,* Vol.14 (pp. 56–73). New York: Hemisphere.

Hackfort, D. (1993). Functional attributions to emotions in sport. In J. R. Nitsch & R. Seiler (Eds.), *Movement in sport: Psychological foundations and effects. Proceedings of the VIIIth European Congress of Sport Psychology,* Vol.1 (pp. 143–149). Sankt Augustin, Germany: Academia Verlag.

Hardy, L., Jones, G., & Gould, D. (1996). *Understanding psychological preparation for sport: Theory and practice of elite performers.* New York: Wiley.

Hanin, Y. L. (1989). Interpersonal and intragroup anxiety in sport. In D. Hackfort & C. D. Spielberger (Eds.), *Anxiety in sports: An international perspective* (pp. 19–28). New York: Hemisphere.

Hanin, Y. L. (1997). Emotions and athletic performance: Individual zones of optimal functioning model. In R. Seiler (Ed.), *European yearbook of sport psychology* (pp. 29–72). Sankt Augustin, Germany: Academia Verlag.

Hanin, Y. L., & Syrja, P. (1995). Performance affect in junior ice hockey players: An application of the individual zones of optimal functioning model. *The Sport Psychologist, 9,* 169–187.

Hanin, Y. L., & Syrja, P. (1997). Optimal emotions in elite cross-country skiers. In E. Muller, H. Schwameder, E. Kornexl & C. Raschner (Eds.) *Science and skiing* (pp. 408–419). London: Spon.

Izard, C. (1971). *The face of emotion.* New York: Appleton-Century.

Izard, C. (1994). Innate and universal facial expressions: Evidence from developmental and cross-cultural research. *Psychological Bulletin, 115,* 288–299.

James, W. (1890). The principles of psychology. In R. M. Hutchins (Ed), *Great Books of the Western World.* Chicago: Encyclopaedia Britannica, 1952, LIII, 348.

Landers, D. M., & Boutcher, S. H. (1993). Arousal-performance relationships. In J. M. Williams (Ed.), *Applied sport psychology,* 2nd ed., (pp. 170–184). Mountain View, CA.: Mayfield.

Lazarus, R. S. (1966). *Psychological stress and the coping process.* New York: McGraw-Hill.

Lazarus, R. S. (1991). *Emotion and adaptation.* New York: Oxford Univ. Press.

Lazarus, R. S. (1993a). Why should we think of stress as a subset of emotion. In L. Goldberger & S. Breznitz (Eds.), *Handbook of stress: Theoretical and clinical aspects* (pp. 21–39). New York: Free Press.

Lazarus, R. S. (1993b). From psychological stress to the emotions: A history of changing outlooks. *Annual Reviews of Psychology, 44,* 1–21.

Lazarus, R. S., & Lazarus, B. (1994) *Passion and reason: Making sense of our emotions.* New York: Oxford Univ. Press.

LeDoux, J. E. (1995). Emotion: Clues from the brain. *Annual Review of Psychology, 46,* 209–235.

Martens, R., Vealey, R. S., & Burton, D. (1990). *Competitive anxiety in sport.* Champaign, IL: Human Kinetics.

McAuley, E. (1991). Efficacy, attributional and affective responses to exercise participation. *Journal of Sport and Exercise Psychology, 13,* 282–294.

McAuley, E., & Duncan, T. E. (1989). Causal attributions and affective reactions to disconfirming outcomes in motor performance. *Journal of Sport and Exercise Psychology, 11,* 187–200.

McAuley, E., & Duncan, T. E. (1990). Cognitive appraisal and affective reactions following physical achievement outcomes. *Journal of Sport and Exercise Psychology, 12,* 415–426.

Morgan, W. P., & Pollock, M. L. (1977). Psychologic characterization of the elite distance runner. *Annals of the New York Academy of Sciences, 301,* 383–403.

Robinson, D. W., & Howe, B. L. (1989). Appraisal variable/affect relationships in youth sport: A test of Weiner's attributional model. *Journal of Sport and Exercise Psychology, 11,* 431–444.

Rowley, A. J., Landers, D. M., Kyllo, L. B., & Ethnier, J. L. (1995). Does the iceberg profile discriminate between successful and less successful athletes? A meta-analysis. *Journal of Sport and Exercise Psychology, 17,* 185–199.

Santamaria, V. L., & Furst, D. M. (1993). Distance runners' causal attributions for most successful and least successful races. *Journal of Sport Behavior, 17,* 43–51.

Schachter, S., & Singer, J. (1962). Cognitive, social, and physiological determinants of emotional states. *Psychological Review, 69,* 378–399.

Silva, J. M., & Hardy, C. J. (1984). Precompetitive affect and athletic performance. In W. F. Straub & J. M. Williams (Eds.), *Cognitive sport psychology* (pp. 79–88). Lansing, NY: Sport Science Associates.

Smith, M. (1983). *Violence and sport.* Toronto: Butterworths.

Syrja, P., Hanin, Y. L., & Personen, T. (1995). Emotion and performance relationship in soccer players. In R. Vanfraechem-Raway & Y. Vanden Auweele (Eds.), *Proceedings of the IXth European Congress on Sport Psychology: Integrating laboratory and field studies.* Part I, (pp. 191–197). Brussels: FEPSAC/Belgian Federation of Sport Psychology.

Syrja, P., Hanin, Y. L., & Tarvonen, S. (1995). Emotion and performance relationship in squash and badminton players. In R. Vanfraechem-Raway & Y. Vanden Auweele (Eds.), *Proceedings of the IXth European Congress on Sport Psychology: Integrating laboratory and field studies.* Part I, (pp. 183–190). Brussels: FEPSAC/Belgian Federation of Sport Psychology.

Vallerand, R. J. (1983). On emotion in sport: Theoretical and social psychological perspectives. *Journal of Sport Psychology, 5,* 197–215.

Vallerand, R. J. (1984). Emotion in sport: Definitional, historical, and social psychological perspectives. In W. F. Straub & J. M. Williams (Eds.), *Cognitive sport psychology* (pp. 65–78). Lansing, NY: Sport Science Associates.

Vallerand, R. J. (1987). Antecedents of self-rated affects in sport: Preliminary evidence on the intuitive–reflective appraisal model. *Journal of Sport Psychology, 9,* 161–182.

Vlachopoulos, S., Biddle, S., & Fox, K. (1996). A social-cognitive investigation into the mechanisms of affect generation in children's physical activity. *Journal of Sport and Exercise Psychology, 18,* 174–193.

Vlachopoulos, S., Biddle, S., & Fox, K. (1997). Determinants of emotion in children's physical activity: A test of goal perspectives and attribution theories. *Pediatric Exercise Science, 9,* 65–79.

Watson, D., & Clark, L. A. (1994). Emotions, moods, traits, and temperaments: Conceptual distinctions and empirical findings. In P. Ekman & R. J. Davidson (Eds.), *The nature of emotion: Fundamental questions* (pp. 89–93). New York: Oxford Univ. Press.

Watson, R. I. (1971). *The great psychologists,* 3rd ed. Toronto: J. B. Lippincott.

Weiner, B. (1982). An attribution theory of motivation and emotion. In H. Krohne & L. Laux (Eds.), *Achievement, stress and anxiety* (pp. 223–245). Washington, D.C.: Hemisphere.

Weiner, B. (1985). An attribution theory of achievement motivation and emotion. *Psychological Review, 92,* 548–573.

Weiner, B. (1986). *An attributional theory of motivation and emotion.* New York: Springer-Verlag.

White, S. A. (1993). The effect of gender and age on causal attributions in softball. *International Journal of Sport Psychology, 24,* 49–58.

7

Competitive Anxiety and Sport Performance

Sarah Naylor and Damon Burton
University of Idaho

Peter R. E. Crocker
University of Saskatchewan

- Anxiety is a multidimensional construct that can influence any performance situation, particularly athletic performances within competition.
- Performance anxiety can have both state and trait characteristics and can be exhibited as somatic and cognitive anxiety.
- Cognitive, personal, and situational factors may contribute to competitive anxiety.
- Four major models attempt to illustrate the relationship between competitive anxiety and sport performance: the inverted-U model, the zones of optimal functioning model, the catastrophe model, and the reverse model.

We have all watched sporting events in which a talented athlete just didn't get the job done under pressure—a major league pitcher who gives up a game-winning home run in the bottom of the ninth, or a quarterback who seldom performs well in playoff games. Regardless of the sport, the position, or the competitive level, almost all athletes have been victims of "competitive anxiety" at some time during their careers. The concept of competitive anxiety intrigues sport researchers, coaches, and athletes. Anxiety is an important basic emotion that influences sporting performance.

This chapter provides an overview of competitive anxiety, beginning with how our understanding of anxiety has changed over the past 90 years. Next, we cover the measurement of anxiety in sport. Third, the chapter addresses some of the antecedents of competitive anxiety, to illustrate that anxiety can be affected by personal and situational variables. Fourth, we discuss anxiety–performance relationships in the context of sport performance, and theoretical models are introduced that attempt to explain this relationship. Finally, we examine how anxiety may affect underlying mechanisms that govern performance and whether anxiety can benefit sport performance under some conditions.

Definitions and Basic Concepts

Before discussing the ways in which competitive anxiety can affect our thoughts, feelings, and behaviors, we will outline some basic concepts. This section addresses how anxiety has been conceptualized and provides working definitions for key anxiety terms such as *state* and *trait anxiety, cognitive anxiety,* and *somatic anxiety.*

Anxiety Defined

Whether it was an athletic competition, a math test, or a graduation speech, most people have experienced some level of worry about their performance. The concept of anxiety,

Anxiety: Is competition a threat or a challenge?

consequently, has been important to researchers across all areas of psychology, and especially in sport (Hackfort & Schwenkmezger, 1993; Hardy, 1997; Martens, Vealey, & Burton, 1990; Parfitt, Jones, & Hardy, 1990; Smith, Smoll, & Schutz, 1990). **Anxiety** refers to cognitive concerns and autonomic responses that accompany a stressful situation, particularly when the perceived situational demand exceeds the individual's ability to meet that demand in personally meaningful situations (Lazarus, 1991; McGrath, 1970; Spielberger, 1966). Not surprisingly, researchers have found that some people experience anxiety to a much greater degree than others (Spielberger, 1966). Some people seem to worry about almost everything, while others worry only about important sport competitions or school tests.

Trait and State Anxiety

Before 1970, most researchers subscribed to a trait, or disposition, approach to personality (Spielberger, 1966; Vealey, 1992). Traits are relatively stable characteristics; that is, they refer to a general predisposition to manifest a cluster of behaviors across situations. Traits were conceptualized to be normally distributed (i.e., bell curve distribution) in the general population. This means that most people would be classified as moderately trait anxious, and only a small percentage of the population would exhibit either high or low amounts of trait anxiety. **Trait anxiety** refers to a general disposition to respond to a variety of situations with feelings of concern or worry as well as perceptions of heightened arousal. **State anxiety** refers to the anxiety experienced at a particular moment. High competitive trait anxious athletes are likely to experience high state anxiety in competitive situations, regardless of situational variables. In contrast, an athlete with low competitive trait anxiety generally experiences low state anxiety across most competitive settings.

Although trait theories were extremely popular for several decades, research conducted using this paradigm confirmed that traits did not predict behavior accurately (Martens, Vealey, & Burton, 1990). Contemporary sport researchers (Vealey, 1992) have advocated an interaction paradigm that views behavior as a product of both personality and situational factors. The interaction approach promotes the notion that personality and environment act together to determine individual behavior, with neither one being more important or influential overall (Spielberger, 1966). Contemporary anxiety research employs the interaction paradigm (Martens et al., 1990). When anxiety is measured, athletes are asked how they "normally feel" (i.e., trait anxiety) and how they feel "in this competitive situation" (i.e., state anxiety). Research supports the idea that individuals high in trait anxiety tend to have higher, possibly excessive, state anxiety reactions and to perceive a wider variety of situations as threatening than teammates with low trait anxiety (Martens et al., 1990; Spielberger, 1966).

Info Box

Anxiety is a function of both personality and environment, and some athletes experience anxiety to a greater degree than others. High trait anxious athletes are likely to experience high state anxiety in highly competitive situations, but low trait anxious athletes are more likely to experience low state anxiety in the same situations.

Multidimensional Nature of Anxiety

Although anxiety was viewed as a unidimensional construct, recent conceptions hypothesize it to be a multidimensional emotion with both mental and physiological components (Borkovec, 1976; Davidson & Schwartz, 1976; Liebert & Morris, 1967). Individuals do not react to stressful situations identically. Some individuals report that they feel "butterflies in their stomachs," while others see "images of disaster." The first reaction is an example of **somatic anxiety,** "the physiological and affective elements of the anxiety experience that develop directly from autonomic arousal" (Martens et al., 1990, p. 6). Other somatic anxiety responses include muscular tension, shortness of breath, sweating, "cotton mouth," frequent urination, and increased heart rate. Conversely, for the person who sees images of disaster, **cognitive anxiety** is the problem. Cognitive anxiety is defined as negative expectations or evaluations of success that athletes have about the situation, their response potential, and the subsequent consequences (Morris, Davis, & Hutchings, 1981). Cognitive anxiety symptoms include self-doubt, concerns over not doing well, and an inability to concentrate.

Although cognitive anxiety and somatic anxiety are considered conceptually independent, results reveal that they moderately interrelated (i.e., correlations between .35–.65; Martens et al., 1990; Morris, Davis, & Hutchings, 1981). This is not surprising because most emotion theorists argue that emotions like anxiety are characterized by cognitive and affective feelings and physiological activation (Izard, 1994; Lazarus, 1991) The moderate interrelationships between somatic and cognitive anxiety may occur for several reasons. Somatic anxiety taps an individual's subjective perception of autonomic functioning. Individuals may vary both in their perception of this functioning and in their physiological response to the same level of cognitive anxiety. Second, high levels of physiological activation, which may be reported as somatic anxiety, may be associated with other emotions such as fear and anger. Third, athletes may have different abilities to manage cognitive and somatic anxiety. One athlete may be able to control somatic anxiety through relaxation techniques, which greatly reduce somatic anxiety but may only moderately reduce cognitive anxiety. Another athlete may reduce cognitive anxiety by replacing negative thoughts with positive thoughts, only partially decreasing somatic anxiety. Fourth, the moderate relationship can also be the result of measurement error in assessing both somatic and cognitive anxiety.

The "conceptual independence" of cognitive and somatic anxiety signifies that although they may act in concert to affect performance, they may also act separately and quite differently. Based on this fact, researchers developed three specific predictions about multidimensional anxiety in sport (Martens et al., 1990). First, the temporal patterning principle predicts that somatic anxiety remains low until several hours before competition, rises sharply until the onset of competition, and then declines and levels off once competition begins. In contrast, cognitive anxiety may be elevated several days before competition but remains stable as the time to compete nears unless expectations of success change. Second, the anxiety–performance hypothesis postulates that cognitive anxiety should be more consistently and strongly related to performance than somatic anxiety. Third, the anxiety–performance relationship trends principle predicts that over time cognitive anxiety and performance should demonstrate a negative linear relationship, but somatic anxiety and performance should exhibit an inverted-U relationship. These predictions will be revisited in the section on anxiety–performance relationships.

Info Box

Anxiety can be manifested in physical symptoms or psychological symptoms, referred to as somatic or cognitive anxiety, respectively. Somatic and cognitive anxiety may also interact with each other and cause a variety of effects on athletic performance.

Measuring Anxiety

This section briefly describes the best and most commonly used measures of trait and state competitive anxiety. The instruments include the Sport Competition Anxiety Test (SCAT; Martens, 1977), the Sport Anxiety Scale (SAS; Smith, Smoll, & Schutz, 1990), the Competitive State Anxiety Inventory-2 (CSAI-2; Martens et al., 1990), and the Mental Readiness Form-2 (MRF-2; Krane, 1994).

Sport Competition Anxiety Test (SCAT)

Sport anxiety research before the late 1970s employed general anxiety instruments, such as the State–Trait Anxiety Instrument (Spielberger, Gorsuch, & Lushene, 1970) and the Taylor Manifest Anxiety Scale (Taylor, 1953). Martens (1977) argued that sport-specific instruments should have better predictive power in sport than general instruments. He developed a unidimensional sport-specific trait anxiety scale called the Sport Competition Anxiety Test (SCAT). The SCAT consists of ten anxiety statements and five additional spurious items. The following are examples of SCAT statements:

Before I compete, I feel uneasy.
Before I compete, I get a queasy feeling in may stomach.
Before I compete, I am nervous.

Each SCAT item is scored on a three-point scale: 1 = Hardly ever, 2 = Sometimes, 3 = Often.
In a series of studies, Martens (1977) found the SCAT to be a better predictor of state anxiety in both controlled and field settings than more general measures of trait anxiety (Gill, 1985; Martens, 1977). It has acceptable psychometric properties, with internal consistency values of .95 to .97 and test–retest reliability of .85 in adults (Martens, 1977). The strength of the SCAT is reflected in its wide use in sport research (Burton, 1997), but one weakness is that it does not separate the cognitive and somatic effects of trait anxiety.

Sport Anxiety Scale (SAS)

Smith and colleagues (1990) developed the Sport Anxiety Scale (SAS) as a multidimensional measure of an athletes' predisposition to become anxious in competitive situations (competitive trait anxiety). The Sport Anxiety Scale comprises three subscales: a seven-item worry subscale, a five-item concentration disruption subscale, and a nine-item somatic anxiety subscale. Sample items from each of the three subscales are: "I feel my stomach sinking" (somatic); "I'm concerned about performing poorly" (worry); "My mind wanders during sport competition" (concentration disruption). Individual items are rated on a 4-point Likert scale, from 1 = not at all to 4 = very much so. The psychometric properties of SAS are acceptable, with a 7-day test–retest reliability greater than .85 and subscale internal consistency values of .88 (somatic), .82 (worry), and .74 (concentration disruption). The SAS subscales are generally intercorrelated between r = .5 and r = .6. Smith and colleagues (1990) also provide concurrent and construct validity evidence that SAS is a valid measure of competitive trait anxiety.

Competitive State Anxiety Inventory-2 (CSAI-2)

Martens and colleagues (1990) developed a sport-specific measure that assesses the multidimensional nature of competitive sport anxiety. The Competitive State Anxiety Inventory-2 (CSAI-2) has three 9-item subscales, measuring cognitive state anxiety, somatic state anxiety, and state self-confidence. Sample items for each of the three CSAI-2 subscales are: "I am concerned about this competition" (cognitive anxiety); "I feel jittery" (somatic anxiety); "I feel self-confident" (self-confidence). Individual items are rated on a 4-point Likert scale from 1 = not at all to 4 = very much so. Seventeen studies during the development of the CSAI-2 and forty-six subsequent independent investigations provided substantial evidence of the instrument's psychometric properties, and particularly its reliability and validity (Burton, 1997). Scale reliabilities range from .79 to .83 (cognitive), .82 to .83 (somatic), and .87 to .90 (self-confidence).

Mental Readiness Form (MRF)

Sport anxiety researchers (Krane, 1994; Martens et al., 1990; Murphy et al., 1989) found that many anxiety instruments, such as the CSAI-2, were too long to be used in some field-testing situations. In response to this limitation, Murphy and colleagues (1989) developed a three-item version of the CSAI-2 to measure cognitive and somatic state anxiety and state self-confidence. This short form, labeled the Mental Readiness Form (MRF), asked subjects to mark a spot on a 10-cm line bounded by the descriptors of *calm* and *worried* for cognitive state anxiety, *relaxed* and *tense* for somatic state anxiety, and *confident* and *scared* for state self confidence. The MRF proved to be quicker and easier to use in field research, and correlations were moderate with components of the original CSAI-2. Subsequently, Krane developed the revised version of the MRF (MRF-2), which had an 11-point Likert scale. A third version (MRF-3) employed slightly modified anchor terms, including *worried–not worried* for cognitive anxiety, *tense–not tense* for somatic anxiety, and *confident–not confident* for self-confidence. Only one item is used to determine each corresponding scale in the CSAI-2, so there is no reliability evidence for the MRF scales. Krane (1994) found that the three items in the revised versions of the MRF demonstrated higher correlations with CSAI-2 subscale scores (r = .54 to r = .79) than did the original MRF. Moreover, Krane, Joyce, and Rayfield (1994) provided initial construct validity for the MRF-2 by demonstrating support for the three predicted relationships between cognitive and somatic anxiety and performance (described in the section on Multidimensional Nature of Anxiety).

Antecedents of Competitive Anxiety

Now that some groundwork has been established that allows a basic conceptual and measurement understanding of competitive anxiety, we will explore the antecedents, or causes, of anxiety in sport. Although athletes experience anxiety in different forms and at different times, researchers have identified some basic principles that underlie anxiety reactions. Even though athletes demonstrate highly individualistic anxiety responses, there is a great deal of commonality in the development of those responses (Burton, 1997).

A Cognitive Framework for Studying Competitive Anxiety Antecedents: Lazarus's Model of Emotion

It may seem that anxiety is something that happens to an athlete, but Lazarus and colleagues (Lazarus, 1991; Lazarus & Folkman, 1984) argue that anxiety results from an athlete's cognitive evaluation of a situation and how it affect his or her well-being. In the previous chapter, Lazarus's model was covered in detail. Therefore, only the key processes and how they influence anxiety in particular are reviewed here. Lazarus's model holds that the stress and emotion an athlete experiences in a competitive situation involve primary appraisal, secondary appraisal, and coping strategies.

In primary appraisal, athletes evaluate the degree of personal significance, or importance, of an upcoming competition. Lazarus identified three different appraisals that typically occur: challenge, threat, and harm/loss. If individuals perceive a situation as challenging, little anxiety should occur. In this case, athletes have put a "positive spin" on the competition and are motivated by the challenge. If athletes attach either threat or harm/loss appraisals to competitive situations, anxiety is more likely to be experienced. Lazarus contends that primary appraisal is affected by three factors: (1) goal importance, or how the situation will impact valuable personal goals; (2) ego involvement, or how the athlete identifies with or is committed to the goal; and (3) degree of goal attainment, or how the situation may help or hurt personal goal achievement. To put this into perspective, let's look at a specific case study:

Case Study: Touchdown Tommy—High School Quarterback

Tommy is a high school senior and the starting quarterback on the football team. As the team reaches the halfway point in its season, its standing is 4–1, with its toughest games yet to come. So far, the victories were fairly easy, but the loss occurred on the last play of that game. The team is tied for first place, and is favored to win the league championship if they continue to play well. Throughout the season, Tommy's coach has had the team set both individual and team goals, and Tommy believes in those goals completely. The team's most important goal is to play well enough to advance to the city championships, although Tommy's biggest individual goal is to improve his touchdown-to-interception ratio, which has been steadily improving over the past 4 years. This week's game is against the other first-place team. The statistics show that they're a big and physical team and that their pass defense is their key to success. The city paper has already printed an article proclaiming this the most important game of the year for both teams.

As Tommy prepares for the "big game," he begins to think about what is at stake. Because Tommy views the upcoming game as important to achieving his personal and team goals for the season, to which he has made a strong personal commitment, he has appraised the situation as having the potential to benefit self- and social-esteem. This leads to high levels of motivation to prepare well. On the other hand, if Tommy were concerned that Friday's game would lead to defeat and hurt his touchdown-to-interception ratio rather than help it, he would likely perceive the situation as *threatening* to self- and social-esteem and experience anxiety. Lazarus and colleagues suggest that two other personality factors may influence the relationship between situational factors and individual appraisal, namely, trait anxiety and self-confidence. If Tommy has a high level of trait anxiety, therefore, he is more likely to perceive the upcoming game as threatening, whereas high levels of trait self-confidence should prompt more challenge appraisals.

Regardless of the primary appraisals that athletes make, they also engage in secondary appraisals to assess how well they can manage the situation (Folkman, 1992). In this stage, individuals ask themselves, "What can I do?" Thus, during secondary appraisal, people evaluate how much personal control they have over preventing or overcoming harm and maximizing their chances for achieving positive outcomes from the situation. Two interrelated elements of secondary appraisal are perceived control and coping potential. **Perceived control** assesses whether personal coping efforts can reduce or eliminate the source of threat in the situation (e.g., "How much control do I have over changing the situation?"). **Coping potential** evaluates an individual's coping resources (e.g., "Do I have the tools to manage the situation?" and "Can I make them work in this situation?"). Lazarus's model holds that the amount and intensity of anxiety responses increases when athletes perceive little personal control or reduced coping potential.

Primary and secondary appraisal processes often operate simultaneously. During secondary appraisal, Tommy will assess how much control he has over reducing or eliminating any threat to self-identity (Lazarus, 1991). Even if Tommy determines that he can control a number of performance factors, the key is whether he believes that his efforts will affect the course of the game. If Tommy has initially perceived the situation as beneficial to self-identity, he will most likely assume control over his practice efforts. However, if he doesn't believe his efforts can make a difference, his response will be much less constructive. The biggest problem will occur if Tommy initially perceives the situation as threatening and also views any effort he puts forth as futile. In this case, Tommy is almost certainly destined to experience anxiety of greater and greater levels as game time approaches.

The final component of the emotional evaluation is coping. Coping strategies are the actual cognitive and behavioral techniques that athletes employ to deal with problems and to improve emotional well-being. Although there are numerous coping strategies that athletes may use (see Gould, Finch, & Jackson, 1993), Lazarus and Folkman (1984) defined two major categories of coping strategies that they call problem-focused coping and emotion-focused coping. Problem-focused coping can include both cognitive and behavioral strategies that focus on changing the source of stress. For Tommy, a problem-focused strategy for dealing with the upcoming game may be to increase the intensity and duration of effort he exerts during practices. He might also work with his coach to refine existing plays and strategies designed to confuse the opposing defense. In contrast, emotion-focused coping strategies are cognitive or behavioral strategies designed to decrease emotional distress, even if the situational threat remains unchanged. If Tommy were using emotion-focused coping strategies, he might try to garner emotional support from his parents and friends and to reinterpret the situation in a more positive light, such as "The game will be a good learning experience."

(continued)

Case Study   *(continued)*

Just as with primary appraisal, trait anxiety and self-confidence levels probably make a difference in the coping strategies used. If Tommy is high in trait anxiety and low in trait self-confidence, he will likely question his ability to reduce the source of threat and spend his time trying to manage his feelings with emotion-focused coping strategies. On the other hand, if he has high trait self-confidence and low trait anxiety, he will probably problem-solve and increase his practice efforts. It is important to note that coping is a dynamic process that involves continuous appraisal and reappraisal (Folkman, 1992). Thus, Tommy may engage in primary appraisal, secondary appraisal, and coping strategies many times during the week before the game. Even if his first impression of the upcoming game were threatening, he might reappraise the situation as challenging if his team's practices are going well and his receivers are performing beyond original expectations. In the same way, with a more positive feeling about the team Tommy may engage in more problem-focused coping strategies, rather than relying on primarily an emotion-focused approach.

Info Box

The amount of anxiety experienced in a given situation depends heavily on the athlete's evaluation of the situation, the degree of significance placed on the event, the athlete's perceived control over the situation, and the coping strategies the athlete possesses.

Personal Antecedents of Competitive Anxiety

The Lazarus model of emotion provides a framework for understanding the cognitive process that individuals go through when experiencing specific emotions. Athletes appraise a situation as benefiting, threatening, or harming self-identity and manage it accordingly. The same situation may be viewed in many different ways, however, depending on the personal characteristics of the athlete. For example, Tommy may see Friday's game as challenging, whereas the opposing quarterback may assess it as threatening, suggesting that individuals bring different personality characteristics and experiences into every appraisal, including those that lead to competitive anxiety. Not surprisingly, anxiety researchers have attempted to identify the most important antecedents of competitive anxiety (Martens et al., 1990; Parfitt, Jones, & Hardy, 1990; Hardy, Jones, & Gould, 1996). Results have demonstrated at least five important personal antecedents, including (1) trait anxiety, (2) self-confidence/self-efficacy, (3) goals/expectancies, (4) age/experience/skill level, and (5) gender.

In general, research confirms that trait anxiety affects competitive state anxiety reactions consistent with conceptual predictions. As levels of trait anxiety rise, athletes are more likely to experience higher state anxiety in a number of evaluative situations (Crocker, Alderman, & Smith, 1988; Gould, Petlichkoff, & Weinberg, 1984; Karteroliotis & Gill, 1987; Maynard & Howe, 1987). Available results, however, have failed to identify whether trait anxiety affects cognitive or somatic anxiety to a greater extent. As with levels of trait anxiety, the research on self-confidence (Vealey, 1986; Yan Lan & Gill, 1984) has moderately supported its predicted antecedent relationship with competitive state anxiety. Vealey (1986) demonstrated that as the level of sport confidence increases, the level of competitive state anxiety decreases. On the other hand, Yan Lan & Gill (1984) revealed only minimal confidence–state anxiety relationships. These equivocal results may be the result of different measurement tools, but variables in addition to self-confidence may play an important role in competitive anxiety responses.

Research supports the role of goals and expectancies as antecedents of competitive state anxiety (Jones, Swain, & Cale, 1990; Krane, Williams, & Feltz, 1992; Lane, Terry, & Karageoghis, 1995). These studies demonstrate that when athletes have set goals and developed positive competitive expectancies, levels of competitive state anxiety decrease. In addition, this research links goals and expectancies with cognitive, rather than somatic, anxiety.

Research also supports the role of age/experience/skill level as antecedents of competitive anxiety (Gould et al., 1984; Hammermeister & Burton, 1995; Krane & Williams, 1994). In general, as age, experience, and skill level increase, levels of competitive anxiety decrease. All three studies found that age, experience, and skill level were more strongly related to cognitive than to somatic state anxiety. The findings are congruent with conceptual predictions because as athletes become increasingly familiar with competitive situations, they know what to expect and have fewer "threats" to worry about and more positive expectations of success. These athletes have also had more practice in managing competitive situations. An alternative possibility is that athletes who experience high anxiety levels may have dropped out at younger ages.

Finally, studies provide support for the role of gender in competitive state anxiety. Krane and Williams (1994) found that females reported higher levels of somatic anxiety than did their male teammates, and Jones and Cale (1989a) found that temporal patterning differed based on gender. Jones and Cale's results reveal that males experience constant levels of cognitive anxiety before competition and large increases in somatic anxiety immediately before competition. In contrast, females seem to experience more gradual increases in both cognitive and somatic anxiety before competition.

Situational Antecedents of Competitive Anxiety

Elements within the competitive situation can also be anxiety provoking (Burton, 1997). These situational factors operate to facilitate or threaten personal well-being. Examples of situational antecedents of anxiety include game location, the opponent, time of day, weather conditions, and size of the audience. Although these situational factors may be important, most research has focused on two other situational antecedents: temporal patterning and sport type.

Temporal patterning, or changes in state anxiety as time to competition nears, is one of the most studied situational antecedents of competitive anxiety. A number of studies have demonstrated different patterns of change for cognitive and somatic anxiety as the time to compete approaches (Caruso et al., 1990; Gould et al., 1984; Jones & Cale, 1989a; Jones, Swain & Cale, 1991; Karteroliotis & Gill, 1987; Krane & Williams, 1987; Swain & Jones, 1992). These studies typically administered a state anxiety measure several times prior to competition (e.g., 2 weeks, 1 week, 2 days, 1 day, 2 hours, and 30 minutes) and identified differences in athletes' state anxiety as competition approached. Multidimensional anxiety theory predicts that cognitive anxiety remains constant before and during competition unless expectations of success change, whereas somatic anxiety is predicted to remain low until right before competition, increasing rapidly until the onset of competition before declining somewhat and stabilizing (Martens et al., 1990). Research on temporal patterning has provided solid support for these predictions. It seems likely that once athletes begin competing, their energies are occupied with the task at hand and they become less aware of their somatic anxiety symptoms (Morris, Davis, & Hutchings, 1981).

In addition to temporal patterning, sport type is an important antecedent of competitive anxiety (Krane & Williams, 1987; Hammermeister & Burton, 1995). Research shows that athletes from individual sports experience higher levels of both cognitive and somatic state anxiety than do team sport participants, primarily because of the higher threat of personal evaluation (Griffin, 1972; Simon & Martens, 1979; Martens et al., 1990). In addition, athletes from subjectively scored sports (e.g., gymnastics, diving) tend to experience greater levels of cognitive and somatic state anxiety than do performers from objectively scored sports (i.e., swimming, track; Martens et al., 1990). Personal control is hypothesized to mediate this sport-type difference in anxiety, with subjectively scored sport athletes perceiving less control over success and greater anxiety than do objectively scored sport athletes. Finally, athletes from contact sports (e.g., football, wrestling) tend to experience higher cognitive and somatic anxiety than do those from noncontact sports (e.g., tennis, running; Simon & Martens, 1979; Martens et al., 1990). One reason for the higher anxiety in contact sport is its increased risk to physical well-being.

Info Box

Although situational factors, such as timing of an event or sport type, may affect competitive anxiety, athletes with higher levels of self-confidence or who use goals routinely may reduce the effect these situational factors have on anxiety.

Consequences of Competitive Anxiety: Anxiety and Performance Relationships

Researchers and practitioners are not only interested in the personal and environmental antecedents of competitive anxiety, but they also want to understand how competitive anxiety affects other variables, particularly performance. Variables such as appraisal, self-confidence, level of trait anxiety, time to competition, sport type, and skill level play a major role in the intensity and duration of athletes' anxiety reactions, but is competitive anxiety really detrimental to performance, or are athletes able to manage it without negative consequences? Think back to the last competitive situation you were really worried about—an athletic competition or some other performance situation. Were you too anxious to perform at your best? Sport research has generally found that high levels of competitive anxiety negatively affect myriad psychological variables as well as performance (Bird & Horn,

1990; Edwards & Hardy, 1996; Gould et al., 1993; Hardy, Parfitt, & Pates, 1994; Kenow & Williams, 1992; Krane, 1993; Prapavessis & Carron, 1996). Although competitive anxiety has been documented to have detrimental effects on psychological variables such as cohesion, leadership, and self-confidence, the consequent variable that is of greatest interest to sport researchers and practitioners is performance.

Multidimensional anxiety theory (Martens et al., 1990; Morris, Davis, & Hutchings, 1981) predicts that high levels of both cognitive and somatic anxiety should impair performance, and that cognitive anxiety will have a greater debilitating effect on performance than will somatic anxiety because of the extensive disruption of attention to the task (Wine, 1980). The overall results of the research assessing the relative effects of cognitive and somatic state anxiety on performance have been equivocal. For example, five recent studies have demonstrated that performance is more strongly related to cognitive than somatic anxiety (Burton, 1988; Edwards & Hardy, 1996; Gould et al., 1993; Hardy, Parfitt, & Pates, 1994; Krane, 1993). In contrast, a number of studies have found that somatic anxiety is more strongly related to performance than is cognitive anxiety (Barnes et al., 1986; Gould et al., 1987; Jones & Cale, 1989b; Krane, Williams, & Feltz, 1992; Maynard & Cotton, 1993). A few studies found no relationship between competitive anxiety and sport performance (Hammermeister & Burton, 1995; Martin & Gill, 1991; Maynard, Smith, & Warwick-Evans, 1995). Although these results concerning the exact nature of the anxiety–performance relationship may appear confusing at times, the bulk of the evidence suggests that cognitive and somatic anxiety can predict performance (Burton, 1997). Many of the difficulties in understanding anxiety–performance relationships may be explained by the different conceptions of that relationship (Hardy, 1997). The next section provides an overview of conceptual models developed to explain the anxiety–performance relationship. Most sport-specific anxiety–performance research has been conducted using the inverted-U model, but three other models—zones of optimal functioning, catastrophe, and reversal theories—are also briefly discussed.

Anxiety–Performance Models

The Inverted-U Hypothesis. The bulk of anxiety–performance research has focused on testing the **inverted-U hypothesis** (Yerkes & Dodson, 1908), one of the most studied topics in anxiety research. The inverted-U hypothesis states that arousal, measured as a single dimension, aids performance up to an optimal range, after which further arousal prompts performance to decline (see Fig. 7.1 on page 144). The inverted-U hypothesis holds that the optimal arousal level for maximum performance varies as a function of task complexity (Jones, 1995); as the number of required decisions and potential responses to the environment increase, the athletes' optimal arousal level decreases. For example, kicking a field goal requires the place kicker to determine the direction and strength of the wind, the leg force needed to cover the distance between the ball and the uprights, and to maintain concentration by blocking out crowd noise. In contrast, executing a block in football requires the athlete to set his feet and exert maximum forward force in concert with the rest of the offensive or defensive line. Clearly, the place kicker has many more things to consider and more potential changes to make in his form to execute the kick correctly. Therefore, his optimal arousal level will be lower than the offensive lineman's to ensure that he

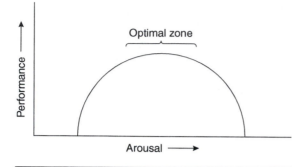

FIGURE 7.1   *Inverted-U Model Predicting the Relationship Between Arousal and Performance for an Individual.*

will be able to address each facet of the kick. The lineman's optimal arousal level will be higher, due to more physical, less analytical elements of his task.

Although historically the inverted-U hypothesis was instrumental in providing a conceptual framework for investigating the anxiety–performance relationship, it has fallen out of favor with anxiety researchers because of several major concerns (Jones, 1995; Hardy & Fazey, 1987). First, the inverted-U is a model based on historical conceptions that equate arousal states with anxiety. The model does not consider the subjective or cognitive aspects of anxiety. Implying that anxiety is synonymous with arousal is a grave error (Jones, 1995). Although arousal states are often associated with anxiety, heightened arousal can occur without anxiety. A second criticism is that the inverted-U relationship is oversimplistic. Hardy (1990) suggested that the optimal level of arousal may not occur at an intermediate point on the performance curve but rather that arousal may aid performance until some critical point at which performance drops off dramatically. Third, the inverted-U hypothesis does not explain why performance is poorer below or beyond the optimal level (Jones, 1995). That is, does optimal arousal influence information processing efficiency, or neuromuscular coordination, or some other system or combination of systems underlying performance? Fourth, research supporting the inverted-U hypothesis has been criticized on methodological grounds, such as for inconsistent measurement of performance and poor statistical techniques (Hardy & Fazey, 1987; Weinberg, 1990).

The inverted-U hypothesis does not account for the multidimensional nature of anxiety. Multidimensional anxiety theory (Morris, Davis, & Hutchings, 1981; Martens et al., 1990) predicts different relationships with performance for cognitive and somatic anxiety, with somatic anxiety demonstrating an inverted-U relationship with performance, and cognitive anxiety and performance exhibiting a negative linear relationship. Results testing these predictions have been equivocal (Burton, 1988; Caruso et al., 1990; Edwards & Hardy, 1996; Gould, Petlichkoff, & Weinberg, 1984; Hardy, 1990; Hardy, Parfitt, & Pates, 1994; Martin & Gill, 1991; McAuley, 1985). Researchers testing a variety of theories have confirmed that somatic anxiety enhances performance up to an optimal point, after which further anxiety increases prompt a gradual decrease in performance (Burton, 1988; Edwards

& Hardy, 1996; Hardy, 1990; Hardy, Parfitt, & Pates, 1994). Other research (Caruso et al., 1990; Gould, Petlichkoff, & Weinberg, 1984; Martin & Gill, 1991; McAuley, 1985) has failed to support such a relationship between somatic anxiety and performance. Findings from the same studies have found equivocal relationships between cognitive anxiety and performance, with the predicted negative linear relationship being both supported (Burton, 1988; Edwards & Hardy, 1996; Hardy, 1990; Hardy, Parfitt, & Pates, 1994) and refuted (Caruso et al., 1990; Gould, Petlichkoff, & Weinberg, 1984; Martin & Gill, 1991; McAuley, 1985). Some experts believe that to completely understand the anxiety–performance relationship, more complex models are needed that specify the joint impact of cognitive and somatic anxiety on performance, such as catastrophe theory and reversal theory.

Individual Zones of Optimal Functioning. In Chapter 6, we reviewed how individual zones of optimal functioning (IZOF) were applied to the study of general cognitive–emotional states. Originally, Hanin (1980, 1986) applied the IZOF idea to predicting how anxiety influenced performance. Hanin argued that each elite athlete performs best when precompetitive anxiety is in an individually determined optimal zone. The IZOF model differs from the inverted-U in three significant ways. First, each athlete has an individual zone of optimal functioning. Rather than peak performance occurring at some intermediate anxiety level, some athletes perform best at high anxiety levels and other athletes perform best at moderate or low anxiety levels (Gould & Tuffy, 1996). Second, Hanin (1978, 1986) argued that there is a bandwidth of optimal functioning. Anxiety levels that exceed or fall short of this bandwidth are associated with poorer performance (see Fig. 7.2). Third, situational or personal factors, such as task type or athletic experience, cannot predict an athlete's optimal zone (Hardy, Jones, & Gould, 1996). It should be noted that Hanin's writings (1978, 1986) were unclear about whether his model was addressing cognitive anxiety or physiological arousal.

The IZOF model requires special measurement and data analysis considerations. The model is based on intraindividual analysis rather than group comparison. Each athlete's performance is compared to his or her own optimal zone of functioning. To determine an athlete's IZOF, Hanin (1989, 1995) suggests two different measurement protocols. One method involves repeatedly assessing precompetitive anxiety and the associated performance. A second method is to ask each athlete to recall precompetitive anxiety associated with previous peak performances. This latter technique, although less demanding than

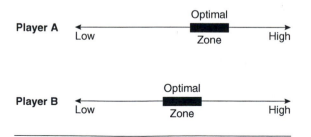

FIGURE 7.2 *Individual Differences in Optimal Anxiety Zones for Best Performance for a Skill.*

repeated measurements, is more prone to measurement error due to memory recall and bias (Gould & Tuffy, 1996).

Research has generally supported the IZOF model (Gould & Tuffy, 1996: Hanin, 1995). The IZOF model appears to be a better predictor of sport performance than the inverted-U hypothesis. There have been, however, several criticisms of the model. First, much of the earlier research was based on an unidimensional model of anxiety. Many of the instruments that were used did not separate somatic effects from cognitive effects. Nevertheless, recent research using multidimensional anxiety measures has provided partial support for the IZOF model (Krane, 1993; Gould et al., 1993). Second, there has been no explanation about how IZOF develops. Third, it is unclear why best performances are more likely to occur in the identified optimal zone (Gould & Tuffy, 1996). Although Gould and Tuffy suggest that cognitive and neuromuscular mechanisms may be involved, there has been no systematic evaluation of these mechanisms in IZOF research. This also leads to a problem with relating precompetitive anxiety to performance. As discussed in Chapter 6, athletes can use coping strategies to modify emotional states. It doesn't follow that an athlete who experiences high precompetitive anxiety (somatic or cognitive) experiences that emotional state during performance. By definition, anxiety is a dynamic construct.

Catastrophe Theory.   Hardy (1990) pioneered sport research using **catastrophe theory,** hypothesizing that the relationship between anxiety and performance will differ significantly depending on the interaction between cognitive and somatic anxiety. Catastrophe theory makes two important predictions. First, it hypothesizes that when cognitive anxiety is low, somatic anxiety and performance will demonstrate the traditional inverted-U relationship. Second, when cognitive anxiety is high, somatic anxiety and performance are predicted to follow an inverted-U relationship to a certain point, beyond which athletes should demonstrate a "catastrophic" drop in performance of such magnitude that they will likely not be able to recover during that competition. Again, there is a marked decrease in the attention directed to the task with high levels of cognitive anxiety. With already high cognitive anxiety, high somatic anxiety is likely to attract more, and more disruptive, attention than if cognitive anxiety were low. With so much outside distraction, few, if any, resources are left to devote to the task at hand, causing the performance catastrophe.

Research testing these predictions has lent support to the theory, demonstrating that cognitive anxiety affects the nature of the somatic anxiety–performance relationship (Fazey & Hardy, 1988; Hardy & Parfitt, 1991). When cognitive anxiety is low, the somatic anxiety–performance relationship assumes the traditional inverted-U shape. When cognitive anxiety increases to high levels, however, a catastrophe occurs. Testing catastrophe theory is extremely demanding because of the differential predictions and consequent measurement issues, but it remains a promising area for future research and may help to unravel how cognitive and somatic anxiety jointly influence performance.

Reversal Theory.   **Reversal theory** was developed by Apter (1982) and was adapted to sport by Kerr (1989, 1993) to explain how differential levels of anxiety are experienced. Reversal theory postulates that motivation levels are characterized by interactions between arousal and the appraisal of arousal to produce qualitatively different types of emotional states. The interpretation of arousal states is affected by metamotivational states. Kerr has focused on the telic and paratelic metamotivational states. The **telic motivational state** is characterized as more serious and goal-oriented, whereas the **paratelic motivational state** is a playful and activity-seeking state. Reversal theory hypothesizes that high arousal in a telic state will be labeled as unpleasant and experienced as anxiety (and potentially debilitating to performance), whereas the same level of arousal in the paratelic state will be labeled as positive and experienced as excitement (potentially enhancing performance). Conversely, low arousal levels in the telic state will be experienced positively as relaxation, whereas low arousal will be viewed negatively as boredom in the paratelic state (see Fig. 7.3).

Reversal theory, like catastrophe theory, suggests that high levels of both cognitive and somatic anxiety will lead to poor performance, but low cognitive and high somatic anxiety will enhance performance (Burton, 1997). Research supporting reversal theory's predictions (Svebak, 1982; Svebak, 1983; Svebak & Murgatroyd, 1985) has found that telic-dominant individuals reported higher levels of muscular tension and increased heart rates (somatic anxiety) than individuals who are paratelic-dominant.

Catastrophe and reversal theories present a much more complex picture of the anxiety–performance relationship than does the original inverted-U hypothesis. Although the predictions made by each theory may be more abstract and more time-consuming to measure, it is clear that the multidimensional nature of anxiety combined with athletes' individual differences justifies addressing the potential measurement difficulties confronted when testing these theories.

Mechanisms Underlying Anxiety–Performance Relationships

The four models that attempt to predict how performance will change as a function of anxiety have fostered much sport research. The models, however, have a major weakness in that they do not explain why specific intensities of cognitive and somatic anxiety affect performance.

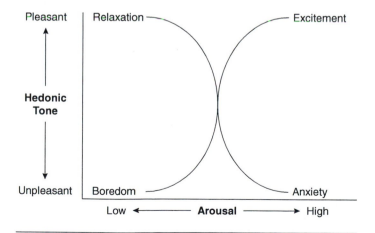

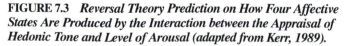

FIGURE 7.3   *Reversal Theory Prediction on How Four Affective States Are Produced by the Interaction between the Appraisal of Hedonic Tone and Level of Arousal (adapted from Kerr, 1989).*

Determining how somatic and cognitive anxiety impact on underlying mechanisms governing performance may aid in understanding anxiety–performance relationships. These mechanisms include both cognitive information processing and neuromuscular control systems (Landers & Boutcher, 1993; Jones, 1990; Parfitt & Hardy, 1993; Parfitt, Jones, & Hardy, 1990).

Anxiety can affect information processing such as perception, decision making, memory, and response selection (Parfitt, Jones, & Hardy, 1990; Jones, 1990; Usher & Hardy, 1986). The ability to selectively attend to the right information may be reduced under high levels of anxiety (Easterbrook, 1959). Another perceptual effect may be **hyperdistractibility,** the inability to focus or concentrate on specific information (Jones, 1990; Parfitt, Jones, & Hardy, 1990; Wine, 1980). This perceptual limitation leads to errors such as not seeing opponents in passing lanes or being distracted by fans' comments. Anxiety can also impair information processing by limiting conscious attentional capacity or resources. (Jones, 1990; Hardy, Jones, & Gould, 1996). Athletes can handle only a limited amount of information at one time. Being preoccupied with worry or concern will result in fewer attentional resources available for decision making and response selection. Examples of attentional errors are throwing a ball to the wrong base, slow decision making when there are several choices, or not remembering team tactics under high competitive stress.

Somatic anxiety can also impact performance through disruption of the neuromuscular systems. Heightened physiological arousal may impair manual dexterity and fine motor control (Parfitt, Jones, & Hardy, 1990). Performance errors would include lack of spatial–temporal coordination such as in making a finesse pass or a delicate touch shot. High somatic anxiety may lead to error in sports requiring steady muscular control, such as rifle and pistol shooting (Gould et al., 1987).

One major limitation in sport anxiety research is that investigators have generally focused on global performance rather than on subcomponents that underlie performance (Parfitt, Jones, & Hardy, 1990; Parfitt, Hardy, & Pates, 1995). Intuitively, cognitive anxiety should affect cognitive information processing types of tasks, as in the case of our place kicker, whereas somatic anxiety should have more impact on physiologically based activities, as with our offensive lineman. Unfortunately, Parfitt, Jones, & Hardy (1990) report that the results are not so straightforward. Laboratory studies have found that both cognitive and somatic anxiety affect cognitively and physiologically based tasks. Furthermore, it is difficult in real sport settings to determine whether performance is deteriorating because of specific types of information-processing difficulties or neuromuscular coordination breakdown. This difficulty, combined with the fact that anxiety can change throughout a competition, makes determining the exact nature of how cognitive and somatic anxiety affect performance a challenge.

Info Box

Research indicates that anxiety has debilitating cognitive effects on performance, including an inability to selectively attend to correct information or to make good decisions, as well as physical effects, including impairment of manual dexterity and fine motor control and reduced spatial–temporal coordination.

Can High Levels of Anxiety Ever Benefit Performance?

There has been recent controversy about whether competitive anxiety always harms performance (Burton & Naylor, 1997; Hanin, 1997; Hardy, 1997; Jones, 1995). In general, anxiety is viewed negatively because anxiety symptoms should impair performance. Research (Hanin, 1997; Hardy, 1997; Jones & Hanton, 1996), however, has not necessarily supported this idea. Jones, based on earlier work in test anxiety, suggested that anxiety varies in both intensity and direction. Most anxiety research assesses the intensity of somatic and cognitive anxiety. Jones argued, however, that how athletes label or interpret these symptoms might be more important than their intensity. For example, some athletes report that feeling nervous and experiencing muscular tension is a signal that they are sufficiently prepared and ready to perform well, whereas other athletes focus on these same feelings as indicative of a lack of preparation that may produce poor performance (Jones, 1995). In other words, even though two athletes may report high intensity levels of somatic symptoms thought to be indicative of anxiety, one athlete's performance may suffer while the other's is unaffected or even enhanced. These results have prompted the idea that some levels of competitive anxiety can be both debilitating (i.e., harmful) and facilitating (i.e., helpful) to performance (Hardy, 1997; Jones, 1995).

To explain how anxiety can be both helpful and detrimental to performance, Hardy (1997) uses Carver and Scheier's (1988) control theory of anxiety. This theory holds that the **facilitative** and **debilitative** perceptions of anxiety will be determined by perceived control, of being able to cope with performance demands, and by the expectancy that personal goals will be attained. If athletes feel in control of their coping responses and able to attain their goals, then anxiety will facilitate performance. In contrast, if athletes lack a feeling of control over threat, then anxiety will hurt their performance. These ideas are similar to Lazarus's ideas about appraisal processes reviewed early in this and in Chapter 6. However, it is not clear why athletes who perceive they have control would experience high levels of cognitive anxiety. In addition to perceived control and confidence, Jones (1995) suggested that "trait affectivity," or an individual's predominant style of interpreting the world, might moderate individual differences in facilitative/debilitative interpretation of anxiety intensity. Athletes high in trait negative affect are more likely to perceive anxiety symptoms as debilitative. In contrast, athletes high in trait positive affect are more likely to label some levels of anxiety as facilitative.

Using Lazarus's (1991) model of emotion, Burton and Naylor (1997) contend that both an imprecise definition of anxiety and limitations of current measurement technology have led researchers to label nonstressful arousal states as facilitative anxiety. In short, both positive and negative emotions can elicit symptoms that are similar to anxiety. Athletes may perceive symptoms such as "concern about performing well" or "butterflies in the stomach" as challenging or exciting rather than threatening. Although strong evidence links these symptoms to anxiety, we have largely failed to investigate whether these symptoms may also be indicative of other, more positive affective or emotional states. Indeed, athletes who interpret concern about performance, elevated heart rate, or muscle tension as evidence of excitement or readiness will likely experience those symptoms positively as challenge appraisal, which may actually enhance performance. Thus, Burton and Naylor (1997) believe that it is this measurement misinterpretation that has led to the flawed notion of "facilitative anxiety." They believe athletes are not experiencing anxiety at all but rather the positive, facilitating affective states of excitement and challenge. Central to resolving this problem is the measurement of athletes' *perceptions* of the situation, although we currently have no instrument that accurately distinguishes between positive and negative emotions elicited by the same symptoms. Nevertheless, the idea that the positive and negative effects of anxiety on performance are moderated by other appraisal, motivational, and personality variables such as confidence, perceived control, and trait affect is likely to intrigue researchers over the next decade.

Conclusion

Competitive sport can engender high levels of anxiety in athletes at all levels. Anxiety is best conceptualized as multidimensional, consisting of cognitive and somatic components. Further, there are individual differences in how athletes experience competitive anxiety. Competitive trait anxiety is a predisposition to experience state anxiety in competitive situations. Research indicates that a number of personal and situational variables are related to anxiety. Cognitive–motivational relational theory (Lazarus, 1991), however, stresses that the appraisal of potential threat or benefit to self-identity (personal well-being) and appraisal of coping options and perceived control will be critical determinants of anxiety.

This chapter reviewed four models that attempt to represent how performance changes with different levels and types of anxiety. There is a consensus that models like the inverted-U are too simplistic. Complex models that consider the joint contributions of cognitive anxiety and arousal, like catastrophe theory, offer more promise of explaining how anxiety affects performance under various competitive conditions. The deterioration of performance under high anxiety conditions is probably the result of information-processing inefficiency or neuromuscular disruption. Anxiety can lead to perceptual narrowing, attention and memory limitation, and movement selection problems. Heightened somatic anxiety is associated with muscular tension and movement control difficulties.

There are still many challenges in understanding the complex relationships between anxiety and sport performance. First, one danger of the multidimensional anxiety view is that researchers may consider only the independent effects of somatic and cognitive anxiety on performance. Researchers need to consider the joint effects, that is, how cognitive and somatic anxiety combine to affect performance. Heightened somatic anxiety may simply reflect the perception of high arousal—a state associated with many strong emotions or vigorous physical activity. Second, to clarify how anxiety affects performance, it is necessary to control other variables related to performance, including skill level, tactical knowledge, physical strength, and fitness. It is possible that anxiety is experienced differently when athletes have more experience with a task or are in better physical condition. Intraindividual analysis, using many repeated observations of a single athlete, is a preferred method to control these variables, rather than comparing athletes to one another. Third, researchers need to determine how appraisal and coping are related to the development, modification, and control of anxiety. Understanding the appraisal–anxiety process may shed light on whether anxiety can be modified or reinterpreted to facilitate performance under specific conditions. How emotions, like anxiety, can be controlled is the focus of the next chapter.

Key Terms (in order of appearance)

anxiety
trait anxiety
state anxiety
somatic anxiety
cognitive anxiety
perceived control

coping potential
temporal patterning
multidimensional anxiety theory
inverted-U hypothesis
catastrophe theory
reversal theory

telic motivational state
paratelic motivational state
hyper-distractibility
facilitative anxiety
debilitative anxiety

References

Apter, M. J. (1982). *The experience of motivation: The theory of psychological reversals.* New York: Academic.

Barnes, M. W., Sime, W., Dienstbier, R., & Plake, B. (1986). A test of construct validity of the CSAI-2 questionnaire on male elite college swimmers. *International Journal of Sport Psychology, 17,* 364–374.

Bird, A. M., & Horn, M. A. (1990). Cognitive anxiety and mental errors in sport. *Journal of Sport and Exercise Psychology, 12,* 217–222.

Borkovec, T. D. (1976). Physiological and cognitive processes in the regulation of anxiety. In G. Schwartz & D. Shapiro (Eds.), *Consciousness and self-regulation: Advances in research,* Vol. 1 (pp. 261–312). New York: Plenum Press.

Burton, D. (1988). Do anxious swimmers swim slower? Reexamining the elusive anxiety–performance relationship. *Journal of Sport and Exercise Psychology, 10,* 45–61.

Burton, D. (1997). Measuring competitive state anxiety. In J. L. Duda (Ed.), *Advancements in sport and exercise psychology measurement.* Morgantown, WV: Fitness Information Technology, Inc.

Burton, D., & Naylor, S. (1997). Is anxiety really facilitative? Reaction to the myth that cognitive anxiety always impairs sport performance. *Journal of Applied Sport Psychology, 9,* 295–302.

Caruso, C. M., Gill, D. L., Dzewaltowski, D. A., & McElroy, M. A. (1990). Psychological and physiological changes in competitive state anxiety during noncompetition and competitive success and failure. *Journal of Sport and Exercise Psychology, 12,* 6–20.

Carver, C. S., & Scheier, M. F. (1988). A control-process perspective on anxiety. *Anxiety Research, 1,* 17–22.

Crocker, P. R. E., Alderman, R. B., & Smith, F. M. R. (1988). Cognitive–affective stress management training with high performance youth volleyball players: Effects on affect, cognition and performance. *Journal of Sport and Exercise Psychology, 10,* 448–460.

Davidson, R. J., & Schwartz, G. E. (1976). The psychobiology of relaxation and related states: A multiprocess theory. In D. Mostofsky (Ed.), *Behavioral control and modification of physiological activity,* 399–442. Englewood Cliffs, NJ: Prentice Hall.

Easterbrook, J. A. (1959). The effects of emotion on the utilisation and organisation of behaviour. *Psychological Review, 66,* 183–201.

Edwards, T., & Hardy, L. (1996). The interactive effects of intensity and direction of cognitive and somatic anxiety and self-confidence upon performance. *Journal of Sport and Exercise Psychology, 18,* 296–312.

Fazey, J. A., & Hardy, L. (1988). The inverted-U hypothesis: Catastrophe for sport psychology. *British Association of Sports Sciences Monograph No 1.* Leeds, UK: The National Coaching Foundation.

Folkman, S. (1992). Making a case for coping. In B. N. Carpenter (Ed.), *Personal coping: Theory, research and application* (pp. 31–46). Westport, CN: Praeger.

Gill, D. L. (1985). *Psychological dynamics of sport.* Champaign, IL: Human Kinetics.

Gould, D., Finch, L. M., & Jackson, S. A. (1993). Coping strategies used by national champion figure skaters. *Research Quarterly for Exercise and Sport, 64,* 453–374.

Gould, D., Petlichkoff, L., Simons, J., & Vevera, M. (1987). Relationship between Competitive State Anxiety Inventory-2 subscale scores and pistol shooting performance. *Journal of Sport Psychology, 9,* 33–42.

Gould, D., Petlichkoff, L., & Weinberg, R. S. (1984). Antecedents of temporal changes in, and relationships between CSAI-2 subcomponents. *Journal of Sport Psychology, 6,* 289–304.

Gould, D., & Tuffey, S. (1996). Zones of optimal functioning research: A review and critique. *Anxiety, Stress, and Coping, 9,* 53–68.

Gould, D., Tuffey, S., Hardy, L., & Lochbaum, M (1993). Multidimensional state anxiety and middle distance running performance: An exploratory examination of Hanin's (1980) zones of optimal functioning hypothesis. *Journal of Applied Sport Psychology, 5,* 85–95.

Griffin, M. R. (1972). An analysis of state and trait anxiety experienced in sports competition at different age levels. *Foil* (Spring), 58–64.

Hackfort, D., & Schwenkmezger, P. (1993). Anxiety. In R. N. Singer, M. Murphey & L. K. Tennant (Eds.), *Handbook of research on sport psychology* (pp. 328–364). New York: MacMillan.

Hammermeister, J., & Burton, D. (1995). Anxiety and the Ironman: Investigating the antecedents and consequences of endurance athletes' state anxiety. *The Sport Psychologist, 9,* 29–40.

Hanin, Y. L. (1980). A study of anxiety in sport. In W. F. Straub (Ed.), *Sport Psychology: An analysis of athlete behavior* (pp. 236–249). Ithaca, NY: Mouvement.

Hanin, Y. L. (1986). State trait anxiety research on sports in the USSR. In C. D. Spielberger & R. Diaz Guerrero (Eds.), *Cross cultural anxiety,* Vol. 3 (pp. 45–64). Washington, DC: Hemisphere.

Hanin, Y. L. (1989). Interpersonal and intragroup anxiety in sport. In D. Hackfort & C. D. Spielberger (Eds.), *Anxiety in sports: An international perspective* (pp. 19–28). New York: Hemisphere.

Hanin, Y. L. (1995). Individual zones of optimal functioning (IZOF) model: An idiographic approach to performance anxiety. In K. P. Henschen & W. F. Straub (Eds.), *Sport Psychology: An analysis of athlete behavior,* 3rd ed. (pp. 103–119). Ithaca, NY: Mouvement.

Hanin, Y. L. (1997). Emotions and athletic performance: Individual zones of optimal functioning model. In R. Seiler (Ed.), *European yearbook of sport psychology* (pp. 29–72). Sankl Augustin, Germany: Academia Verlag.

Hardy, L. (1990). A catastrophe model of performance in sport. In J. G. Jones & L. Hardy (Eds.), *Stress and performance in sport* (pp. 81–106). Chichester, UK: Wiley.

Hardy, L. (1997). Three myths about applied constancy work. *Journal of Applied Sport Psychology, 9,* 277–294.

Hardy, L., & Fazey, J. (1987). "The inverted-U hypothesis: A catastrophe for sport psychology." Paper presented at the Annual Conference of the North American Society for the Psychology of Sport and Physical Activity, June, Vancouver.

Hardy, L., Jones, G., & Gould, D. (1996). *Understanding psychological preparation for sport: Theory and practice of elite performers.* New York: Wiley.

Hardy, L., & Parfitt, G. (1991). A catastrophe model of anxiety and performance. *British Journal of Psychology, 82,* 163–178.

Hardy, L., Parfitt, G., & Pates, J. (1994). Performance catastrophes in sport: A test of the hysteresis hypothesis. *Journal of Sport Sciences, 12,* 327–334.

Izard, C. (1994). Innate and universal facial expressions: Evidence from developmental and cross-cultural research. *Psychological Bulletin, 115,* 288–299.

Jones, J. G. (1990). A cognitive perspective on the processes underlying the relationship between stress and performance in sport. In J. G. Jones and L. Hardy (Eds.), *Stress and performance in sport* (pp. 17–42). New York: Wiley.

Jones, J. G. (1995). More than just a game: Research developments and issues in competitive anxiety in sport. *British Journal of Psychology, 86,* 449–478.

Jones, J. G., & Cale, A. (1989a). Precompetition temporal patterning of anxiety and self-confidence in males and females. *Journal of Sport Behavior, 12,* 183–195.

Jones, J. G., & Cale, A. (1989b). Relationships between multidimensional competitive state anxiety and cognitive and motor subcomponents of performance. *Journal of Sport Sciences, 7,* 163–173.

Jones, J. G., & Hanton, S. (1996). Interpretation of competitive anxiety symptoms and goal attainment expectancies. *Journal of Sport and Exercise Psychology, 18,* 144–157.

Jones, J. G., Swain, A., & Cale, A. (1990). Antecedents of multidimensional competitive state anxiety and self-confidence in elite intercollegiate middle-distance runners. *The Sport Psychologist, 4,* 107–118.

Jones, J. G., Swain, A., & Cale, A. (1991). Gender differences in precompetition temporal patterning and antecedents of anxiety and self-confidence. *Journal of Sport and Exercise Psychology, 13,* 1–15.

Jones, J. G., Swain, A., & Hardy, L. (1993). Intensity and direction dimensions of competitive state anxiety and relationships with performance. *Journal of Sport Sciences, 11,* 525–532.

Karteroliotis, C., & Gill, D. L. (1987). Temporal changes in psychological and physiological components of state anxiety. *Journal of Sport Psychology, 9,* 261–274.

Kenow, L. J., & Williams, J. M. (1992). Relationship between anxiety, self-confidence, and evaluation of coaching behaviors. *The Sport Psychologist, 6,* 344–357.

Kerr, J. H. (1989). Anxiety, arousal, and sport performance: An application of reversal theory. In D. Hackfort & C. D. Spielberger (Eds.), *Anxiety in sports: An international perspective* (pp. 137–151). New York: Hemisphere Publishing.

Kerr, J. H. (1993). An eclectic approach to psychological interventions in sport: Reversal theory. *The Sport Psychologist, 7,* 400–418.

Krane, V. (1993). A practical application of the anxiety–athletic performance relationship: The zone of optimal functioning hypothesis. *The Sport Psychologist, 7,* 113–126.

Krane, V. (1994). The mental readiness form as a measure of competitive state anxiety. *The Sport Psychologist, 8,* 189–202.

Krane, V., Joyce, D., & Rafeld, J. (1994). Anxiety, situation criticality, and collegiate softball performance. *The Sport Psychologist, 8,* 58–72.

Krane, V., & Williams, J. M. (1987). Performance and somatic anxiety, cognitive anxiety, and confidence changes prior to competition. *Journal of Sport Behavior, 10,* 47–56.

Krane, V., & Williams, J. (1994). Cognitive anxiety, somatic anxiety, and confidence in track and field athletes: The impact of gender, competitive level and task characteristics. *International Journal of Sport Psychology, 25,* 205–217.

Krane, V., Williams, J., & Feltz, D. (1992). Path analysis examining relationships among cognitive anxiety, somatic anxiety, state confidence, performance expectations, and golf performance. *Journal of Sport Behavior, 15,* 279–295.

Landers, D. M. & Boutcher, S. H. (1993). Arousal–performance relationships. In J. M. Williams (2nd Ed.), *Applied sport psychology* (pp. 170–184). Palo Alto, CA: Mayfield.

Lane, A., Terry, P., & Karageoghis, C. (1995). Antecedents of multidimensional competitive state anxiety and self-confidence in athletes. *Perceptual and Motor Skills, 80,* 911–919.

Lazarus, R. (1991). *Emotion and adaptation.* New York: Oxford Univ. Press.

Lazarus, R., & Folkman, S. (1984). *Stress, appraisal and coping.* New York: Springer.

Liebert, R. M., & Morris, L. W. (1967). Cognitive and emotional components of test anxiety: A distinction and some initial data. *Psychological Reports, 20,* 975–978.

Martens, R. (1977). *Sport Competition Anxiety Test.* Champaign, IL: Human Kinetics.

Martens, R., Burton, D., Vealey, R. S., Bump, L. A., & Smith, D. E. (1990). Development and validation of the Competitive State Anxiety Inventory-2 (CSAI-2). In R. Martens, R. S. Vealey, & D. Burton (Eds.), *Competitive anxiety in sport* (pp. 117–190). Champaign, IL: Human Kinetics.

Martens, R., Vealey, R. S., & Burton, D. (1990). *Competitive anxiety in sport.* Champaign, IL: Human Kinetics.

Martin, J. J., & Gill, D. L. (1991). The relationships among competitive orientation, sport-confidence, self-efficacy, anxiety and performance. *Journal of Sport and Exercise Psychology, 13,* 149–159.

Maynard, I. W., & Cotton, P. C. J. (1993). An investigation of two stress-management techniques in a field setting. *The Sport Psychologist, 7,* 375–387.

Maynard, I. W., & Howe, B. L. (1987). Interrelations of trait and state anxiety with game performance of rugby players. *Perceptual and Motor Skills, 64,* 599–602.

Maynard, I. W., Smith, M. J., & Warwick-Evans, L. (1995). The effects of a cognitive intervention strategy on competitive state anxiety and performance in semiprofessional soccer players. *Journal of Sport and Exercise Psychology, 17,* 428–446.

McAuley, E. (1985). State anxiety: Antecedent or result of sport performance. *Journal of Sport Behavior, 8,* 71–77.

McGrath, J. E. (1970). *Social and psychological factors in stress.* New York: Holt, Rinehart and Winston.

Morris, L. W., Davis, D., & Hutchings, C. (1981). Cognitive and emotional components of anxiety: Literature review and revised worry-emotionality scale. *Journal of Educational Psychology, 73,* 541–555.

Murphy, S. M., Greenspan, M., Jowdy, D., & Tammen, V. (1989). "Development of a brief rating instrument of competitive anxiety: Comparison with the Competitive State Anxiety Inventory-2 (CSAI-2)." Paper presented at the meeting of the Association for the Advancement of Applied Sport Psychology, September, Seattle, WA.

Parfitt, C. G., & Hardy, L. (1987). Further evidence for the differential effects of competitive anxiety upon a number of cognitive and motor sub-systems. *Journal of Sport Sciences, 5,* 62–63.

Parfitt, C. G., & Hardy, L. (1993). The effects of competitive anxiety on memory span and rebound shooting tasks in basketball players. *Journal of Sport Sciences, 11,* 517–524.

Parfitt, C. G., Hardy, L., & Pates, J. (1995). Somatic anxiety and physiological arousal: Their effects upon a high anaerobic, low memory demand task. *International Journal of Sport Psychology, 26,* 196–213.

Parfitt, C. G., Jones, J. G., & Hardy, L. (1990). Multidimensional anxiety and performance. In J. G. Jones and L. Hardy (Eds.), *Stress and performance in sport* (pp. 43–80). New York: Wiley.

Prapavessis, H., & Carron, A. V. (1996). The effect of group cohesion on competitive state anxiety. *Journal of Sport and Exercise Psychology, 18,* 64–74.

Simon, J. A., & Martens, R. (1979). Children's anxiety in sport and nonsport evaluative activities. *Journal of Sport Psychology, 1,* 160–169.

Smith, R. E., Smoll, F. L., & Schutz, R. W. (1990). Measurement correlates of sport-specific cognitive and somatic trait anxiety: The Sport Anxiety Scale. *Anxiety Research, 2,* 263–280.

Spielberger, C. D. (1966). Theory and research on anxiety. In C. D. Spielberger (Ed.), *Anxiety and behavior* (pp. 3–20). New York: Academic.

Spielberger, C. D., Gorsuch, R. I., & Lushene, R. L. (1970). *Manual for the State–Trait Anxiety Inventory.* Palo Alto, CA: Consulting Psychologists.

Svebak, S. "The significance of motivation for task-induced tonic physiological changes." Ph.D. diss., University of Bergen, Norway, 1982.

Svebak, S. (1983). The effect of information load, emotional load, and motivational state upon tonic physiological activation. In H. Ursin & R. Murison (Eds.), *Biological and psychological basis of psychosomatic disease: Advances in the biosciences,* Vol. 42 (pp. 61–73). Oxford: Pergamon.

Svebak, S., & Murgatroyd, S. (1985). The effect of a threatening context on metamotivational dominance: A multimethod validation of reversal theory constructs. *Journal of Personality and Social Psychology, 48,* 107–116.

Swain, A., & Jones, J. G. (1992). Relationships between sport achievement orientation and competitive state anxiety. *The Sport Psychologist, 6,* 42–54.

Taylor, J. A. (1953) A personality scale of manifest anxiety. *Journal of Abnormal and Social Psychology, 48,* 285–290.

Usher, M. H., and Hardy, L. (1986). The effects of competitive anxiety on a number of cognitive and motor sub-systems. *Journal of Sport Sciences, 4,* 232–233.

Vealey, R. S. (1986). Conceptualization of sport-confidence and competitive orientation: Preliminary investigation and instrument development. *Journal of Sport Psychology, 8,* 221–246.

Vealey, R. S. (1992). Personality and sport: A comprehensive view. In T. Horn (Ed.), *Advances in sport psychology* (pp. 25–59). Champaign, IL: Human Kinetics.

Weinberg, R. S. (1990). Anxiety and motor performance: Where to from here? *Anxiety Research, 2,* 227–242.

Wine, J. D., (1971). Test anxiety and direction of attention. *Psychological Bulletin, 76,* 92–104.

Wine, J. D., (1980). Cognitive-attentional theory of test anxiety. In I. G. Sarason (Ed.), *Test anxiety: Theory, research and applications* (pp. 349–385). Hillsdale, NJ: Erlbaum.

Yan Lan, L., & Gill, D. L. (1984). The relationship among self-efficacy, stress responses and a cognitive feedback manipulation. *Journal of Sport Psychology, 6,* 227–238.

Yerkes, R. M., & Dodson, J. D. (1908). The relation of strength of stimulus to rapidity of habit-formation. *Journal of Comparative Neurology and Psychology, 18,* 459–482.

8

Emotional Control and Intervention

Peter R. E. Crocker, Kent C. Kowalski, and Thomas R. Graham

The University of North Carolina at Chapel Hill

- Several intervention strategies designed to establish or maintain emotional control are based on the Cognitive–Motivational–Relational Theory.
- Intervention strategies related to emotional regulation are grouped into four major categories: physiological arousal management, cognitive interventions, goal-setting interventions, and environmental factors.
- Athletes are affected by positive and negative emotions that must be controlled to ensure success. Coping strategies are used to manage or actively change emotion.
- A case study of stress and emotion control is provided at the end of the chapter to illustrate intervention strategies for emotion management.

Competitive sport places athletes under tremendous pressure to perform, often under public scrutiny. As coaches, fellow athletes, or spectators, many of us have seen athletes express their emotions in many ways. The popular press feverishly exploits instances of athletes losing emotional control. Recently, reports of athletes attacking coaches, officials, photographers, fans, and other opponents seem more commonplace. The ability to effectively regulate emotions also affects individual performance as well as the performance and emotions of others. Teaching athletes emotional control skills can help them enhance performance, improve social relations, and enjoy sport competition (Hardy, Jones, & Gould, 1996; Williams, 1998).

Chapters 6 and 7 discussed how emotions are generated and how emotional states might affect performance and other behaviors in sport. At least four areas are central to emotional regulation: subjective experience, physiological regulation, observable (expressive) behavior, and the consequences of emotional regulation (Walden & Smith, 1997). But how do we help athletes manage emotions? A central purpose of this chapter is to review a select number of cognitive-behavioral techniques that athletes can learn to control emotions. First, we provide a conceptual framework based on a cognitive-motivational-relational model of emotion to guide interventions. Next, based on the conceptual model, we review general categories of interventions. Specific techniques will be discussed that target appraisal processes, arousal control, and environmental management. The next section focuses on coping skills training programs that provide a set of general principles and intervention procedures for managing stress and emotion. Last, we review a real example of an athlete struggling to control competitive stress. This example shows how various emotional control strategies can be combined using a coping skills training program to help an athlete gain emotional control.

A Cognitive–Motivational–Relational Framework to Guide Intervention

Because intervention can be targeted toward subjective, physiological, expressive, and consequences of emotions, a key question is: What techniques should be applied to help athletes regulate emotional experience and consequences? A large number of applied sport psychology textbooks describe various techniques and how these techniques can be acquired (e.g., Hardy, Jones, & Gould, 1996; Harris & Harris, 1984; Murphy, 1995; Orlick, 1986; Williams, 1998). These books address interventions such as relaxation, energizing, biofeedback, goal setting, imagery, self-talk, cognitive restructuring, problem solving, time management, refocusing, attention control, concentration, environmental engineering, and many others. Discussing all these techniques, plus theoretical and application issues, is beyond the scope of this chapter. Nevertheless, this chapter outlines basic cognitive–behavioral applications that can be used to regulate emotions. To clarify how these interventions might control emotions, a conceptual framework based on cognitive theories of emotion is presented (see Fig. 8.1).

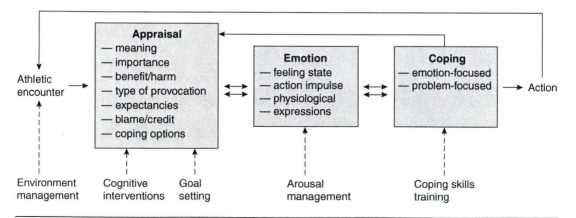

FIGURE 8.1   *A Conceptual Model of the Emotion Process and Associated Interventions to Control Emotion in Sport.*

The conceptual framework is based on the basic tenets of the cognitive approach to emotion discussed in Chapter 6. Several cognitive theorists (e.g., Lazarus, 1991; Weiner, 1985) identified key processes that are associated with the generation and regulation of emotional experience. Stress and emotion occur not solely as a result of the environment or because of the athlete's personality but because of the particular relationship between the person and the environment (Lazarus, 1991; Meichenbaum, 1993). Processes such as cognitive appraisal, physiological arousal, action tendencies or impulses, and coping strategies are critical in regulating emotions and their consequences. Figure 8.1 outlines the constantly changing process of emotion based on Lazarus's model. Interventions can be targeted to affect specific components of the model. These components include the environment, appraisal processes, physiological changes and action impulses, and coping strategies. Some intervention strategies may primarily affect only one component (e.g., progressive relaxation), whereas other strategies may directly or indirectly affect several components (e.g., goal setting, coping skills training). The following sections consider how various interventions can assist in emotional control in sport.

Physiological Arousal Management

Athletes often experience heightened levels of stress in competitive sport (Jones & Hardy, 1990). The effective management of physiological systems is a central feature of most sport psychology intervention programs (Hardy, Jones, & Gould, 1996; Vealey, 1988). Because changes in central and peripheral systems are thought to be strongly associated with key emotions like fear, anxiety, and anger (Lazarus, 1991), developing skills to self-regulate these systems is critical for effective emotional control. Most interventions are directed toward reducing arousal. Nevertheless, being able to increase arousal to produce performance-facilitating emotions is also important (Hanin, 1997). This section briefly reviews some arousal management techniques, with emphasis on how the techniques can assist in emotional control. A detailed description of how to use the techniques is beyond the scope of this chapter.

Relaxation techniques are often utilized in sport psychology interventions because they can have a direct impact on physiological arousal (Gill, 1985). These techniques can be divided into two general categories, physical and cognitive (Williams & Harris, 1998; Hardy, Jones, & Gould, 1996). Physical techniques include progressive relaxation, breathing control, and biofeedback. Cognitive techniques include meditation, imagery, and autogenic training. Like all skills, relaxation techniques require systematic practice before they can effectively reduce heightened arousal in competitive settings.

Progressive Relaxation

Progressive relaxation (PR) is a popular technique taught by sport psychologists (Williams & Harris, 1998). It essentially consists of contracting a muscle group, holding the contraction, and then relaxing. For example, an athlete would squeeze his or her fists for 10 seconds and then release this contraction, focusing on the difference between tension and relaxation of the muscles. The athlete then progresses to a new muscle group and repeats

In the heat of competition, successful athletes often balance emotional intensity with physical relaxation.

the tension–relaxation cycle. Although progressive relaxation was originally developed by Jacobson in 1930, many variations of this technique exist (Hardy, Jones, & Gould, 1996). Teaching athletes PR is thought to increase awareness of muscular tension and will allow them to regulate potentially dysfunctional arousal. The basic assumption of progressive relaxation is that a relaxed body will lead to a relaxed mind (Williams & Harris, 1998). That is, reducing muscular tension will have a direct effect on the athletes' emotional state. Some evidence indicates that PR can reduce state anxiety in athletes (see Hardy, Jones, & Gould, 1996).

Info Box

Progressive relaxation (PR) is one of the most popular intervention techniques taught by sport psychologists and involves the systematic clenching and releasing of muscle groups. This progressive exercise relaxes one muscle group after another until the entire body achieves a state of physical and psychological relaxation.

The full-fledged PR technique has some practical limitations in sport settings. It is often not feasible to find quiet, comfortable settings where athletes can spend 20–40 minutes progressively relaxing muscles. Because of the dynamic nature of emotions in sport, athletes need techniques that can be used quickly. Ost (1988) developed an applied relaxation training program that can be modified for sport settings (Hardy, Jones, & Gould, 1996). The program, learned over ten to twelve sessions, starts with progressive relaxation and proceeds though several stages to a rapid relaxation procedure. Individuals can achieve a relaxed state in this late stage in 20 to 30 seconds.

Biofeedback

Technological advances have allowed athletes to directly monitor physiological systems such as the cardiovascular system, cerebral activity, muscular activity, and skin temperature. **Biofeedback** involves receiving feedback, either visual or auditory, from these systems. Athletes can learn to control the activation levels of various systems through systematic training. Athletes can also learn that specific emotional states are associated with changes in these physiological systems (Cratty, 1989).

A primary assumption of using biofeedback to control emotion is that modifying existing physiological states changes the emotion type or intensity. There is little evidence in the sport field that biofeedback is an effective technique to control emotion. Most sport biofeedback research has focused on enhancing performance and, therefore, has not measured emotions directly (e.g., Cratty & Hanin, 1980; Daniels & Landers, 1981). Despite the potential of biofeedback, its use as an emotional control intervention is not widespread in sport.

Meditation

Meditation is a relaxation technique that is rooted in Eastern spirituality and was popularized in Western culture during the 1960s and 1970s (Benson, 1984). Meditation requires the athlete to assume a comfortable position in a quiet environment. The athlete focuses on controlled breathing and repeats a word (mantra) or focuses on a fixed object (Berger, 1994; Cratty, 1989). Using meditation as an emotional control technique assumes that it is capable of altering arousal states. There is evidence that meditation can reduce cardiovascular factors such as oxygen consumption, respiration, blood pressure, and heart rate. Given its potential to change physiological states associated with stress and emotion, some sport psychologists have incorporated meditation into cognitive behavioral interventions to help athletes control stress and enhance performance (Jones, 1993; Smith, 1980). Nevertheless, the utility of meditation as an emotion-arousal control technique in dynamic sport situations is still not well known.

Matching Hypothesis: Using Physical or Cognitive Relaxation Techniques

Many sport interventions have been directed toward managing cognitive and somatic anxiety. Some researchers have suggested that types of relaxation techniques should be matched with specific types of anxiety (Burton, 1990; Davidson & Schwartz, 1976). The **matching hypothesis** holds that cognitively based interventions, such as meditation, should be used to control cognitive anxiety. In contrast, physical or somatic techniques are best for somatic anxiety. In general, there is equivocal support for the matching hypothesis (Hardy, Jones, & Gould, 1996; Maynard & Cotton, 1993). One problem is that specific interventions tend to affect both somatic and cognitive anxiety. Physiological and cognitive systems do not appear to be functionally independent.

Limitations of Arousal Control Strategies

Relaxation techniques can be effective in reducing heightened physiological arousal associated with strong emotions like fear, anger, and anxiety (Novaco, 1980; Williams & Harris, 1998). Nevertheless, there are some potential dangers. First, relaxation techniques are primarily arousal reducing techniques. Both strong positive and negative emotions are associated with increased arousal. Reducing arousal states, especially in precompetitive periods, may impair the attainment of specific positive emotions necessary for good performances (Burton, 1990). Second, relaxation techniques do not directly affect the appraisal processes that are primarily responsible for emotions (Lazarus, 1991). Third, various levels of arousal are required for peak performance. Without a clear understanding of "optimal" arousal under various performance conditions (Landers, 1994; Hardy, Jones, & Gould, 1996), an athlete could reduce arousal below optimal levels. In some cases, arousal enhancing techniques, such as emotive imagery and energizing verbal cues, may be necessary (Williams & Harris, 1998). Fourth, Hanin (1997) has argued that specific affective states are required for individually optimal performance. His research suggests that for some athletes even negative emotional states associated with increased arousal can have beneficial performance effects. Although some researchers suggest that a relaxed state is often a feature of high performance (Jackson, 1992; Orlick, 1986), many researchers believe that the relationship among arousal, emotion, cognition, and performance is more complex (Hanin, 1997; Jones, 1995).

Cognitive Interventions

A common feature of sport psychology interventions is teaching athletes to control or modify thoughts (Hardy, Jones, & Gould, 1996; Vealey, 1988). An assumption of cognitive interventions is that cognitive processes play a critical role in emotion, behavior, and other cognitive–motivational states (Hackfort & Schwenkmezger, 1993; Zinsser, Bunker, & Williams, 1998). In terms of controlling emotion, **cognitive interventions** are designed to modify appraisal processes (Beck, 1993). Athletes can learn various cognitive skills to help form cognitive sets to appraise situations as less threatening, to actively change interpretation of the situation and their abilities to manage the situation, and to control response impulses.

Sport psychologists have used a variety of cognitive interventions including thought-stopping, cognitive restructuring, countering, reframing, and self-instructional training (see Bell, 1983; Ellis, 1982; Gauron, 1984; Meichenbaum, 1993; Zinsser, Bunker, & Williams, 1998). Although the specific procedures and intentions of these interventions may be different, the general purposes of the interventions are similar. Athletes learn that cognitive sets are influenced by their thoughts and that these cognitive sets will affect ongoing appraisals. These appraisals will, in turn, be largely responsible for emotions and subsequent behavior (Beck, 1993; Zinsser, Bunker, & Williams, 1998). Cognitive interventions assist athletes to recognize and correct dysfunctional thought patterns. Learning to control and shift cognition helps to control the cognitive functioning required for optimal functioning (Beck, 1993). A selected number of these techniques are described next.

Cognitive Restructuring

Cognitive restructuring is a psychotherapeutic technique, developed primarily for clinical populations, that has been used in some sport psychology interventions (Ellis, 1982; Cratty, 1989). A well-known cognitive restructuring intervention is Rationale Emotive Therapy (Ellis, 1982). This approach assumes that athletes create unpleasant emotional states, such as anxiety and anger, through thinking patterns that are based on irrational beliefs. Typical irrational beliefs are a need for personal perfection, a need for situations to be perfect, a belief that others must always treat you fairly and respectfully, an essential need for social approval, and a belief that self-worth depends on achievement (Cratty, 1989; Ellis, 1982; Zinsser, Bunker, & Williams, 1998). Holding these types of irrational beliefs makes athletes more vulnerable to dysfunctional emotions that can impair performance and reduce sport satisfaction.

Cognitive restructuring holds that to change thought patterns that lead to emotional control problems, the athlete needs to modify irrational beliefs. There are three basic steps in cognitive restructuring (Cratty, 1989). First, the athlete must understand that irrational beliefs lead to distorted thinking and prevent the athlete from controlling emotions and behavior. Second, distorted thoughts must be changed or restructured. Third, the athlete must substitute functional thoughts for distorted thoughts. Although the procedures sound straightforward, cognitive restructuring of irrational beliefs and thoughts is a very involved process and requires extensive clinical training.

Changing Negative Thoughts: Using Self-Talk to Control Emotions

A number of thought modification techniques advocated by sport psychologists can be generally classified as **self-talk.** Self-talk techniques can assist in controlling strong emotions like anxiety and anger (Meichenbaum, 1977, 1985; Smith, 1980; Zinsser, Bunker, & Williams, 1998). These techniques are similar to cognitive restructuring but do not assume that self-defeating thoughts are based on irrational beliefs. Rather, techniques like replacing negative thoughts with positive statements, reframing, and self-instructional training are designed to teach athletes skills to appraise athletic situations differently, create positive cognitive sets, and guide behavior in stressful situations.

Info Box

Self-talk is a technique used to replace negative, irrational, and distracting thoughts that sometimes lead to poor performance with positive, logical, and task-related thoughts.

A key step in using self-talk to control emotions is for the athlete to identify negative statements that are associated with negative emotions or contribute to the continuation of emotional episodes. Next, the athlete develops positive statements to replace the negative statements (Zinsser, Bunker, & Williams, 1998). For example, the statement, "This is too hard—I can't do it" is replaced with, "I've learned hard skills before—it just takes practice—work though it." Other examples of replacing self-defeating negative statements with more functional positive statements are shown in Table 8.1. The athlete can learn to replace statements though imagery and behavioral rehearsal procedures (Meichenbaum, 1993).

Self-instructional training is a specific form of self-talk (Meichenbaum, 1977, 1985). As the term implies, this technique teaches athletes to control emotions by learning and applying problem-solving talk to guide behavior in stressful situations. Take the example of the 3,000-meter runner who experiences fatigue-generated pain in the last 400 meters of the race. Rather than focus on the physical and emotional distress, the athlete can use skill specific self-talk. This self-talk could focus on technique and body posture. Self-instructional training techniques are powerful because they might not only shift appraisal processes but can also guide behavior to actively change situations threatening self-identify (Meichenbaum, 1985).

Limitations of Cognitive Interventions

Extensive research supports the idea that cognitive interventions can help athletes control emotional experience (Hardy, Jones, & Gould, 1996; Kerr & Leith, 1993; Smith, 1980). Like all intervention techniques, however, cognitive interventions have limitations. These techniques are based on controlling thoughts or self-statements and assume that these statements influence appraisal processes. Emotion theorists have recognized, however, that many cognitive activities are automatic and occur very rapidly (Arnold, 1960; Lazarus, 1991; Weiner, 1985). These automatic appraisal processes may be very difficult to control without directly influencing the underlying value structure of the athlete. Changing self-statements is likely to be more effective in creating positive cognitive sets that may bias cognitive appraisal (Beck, 1993) or controlling reflective appraisal processes that can contribute to ongoing

TABLE 8.1   *Examples of Replacing Potentially Self-Defeating Negative Statements with Positive Statements.*

Negative Statement	Replaced by	Positive Statement
The referee is out to get me. I'm so mad!		I can't control the referee. I need to focus on what I can do: play smart and hard.
I need to score well to win. The pressure is all on me to come through or the team loses. What happens if I *blow* it?! I'm losing control!		The score will take care of itself. I just need to try my best. Focus on my preparation plan. Just relax and use my skills. I've trained hard and things will be all right.
This is getting too hard. I want to get out of here!		I've learned lots of hard skills. Just work through it.
I'm not going to let that player embarrass me in front of my friends. I'm going to get her good!		Keep control. Don't get suckered in to retaliate. Use my skills and be smart.

emotional experience. Any effective use of cognitive intervention to control emotion requires extensive practice and consistent application (Meichenbaum, 1993).

Goal-Setting Interventions

> *To keep pushing through all that training, what works for me is setting small goals for myself.... I concentrate on improving in small ways, rather than improving by large amounts. After attaining each goal, I feel totally satisfied and I can go on to another goal.*
>
> —Alex Baumann, Olympic champion, swimming (quoted in Spink, 1995, 28)

The motivational benefits of goal setting in sport have been well documented (Burton, 1992; Gould, 1998; Weinberg, 1992). Performance-related benefits of goal setting include focusing attention, problem solving, and increasing effort and persistence (Locke & Latham, 1985; Weinberg, Burke, & Jackson, 1997). Emotion-related benefits, however, have received less attention (Hardy, Maiden, & Sherry, 1986). Competitive situations are often emotion engendering because of the potential to enhance, maintain, or threaten an athlete's sense of self-identity. Goal setting influences emotional experience indirectly by increasing the athlete's perceptions of control and improving ability to manage competitive demands that affect appraisal and coping processes.

In Chapter 6, both goal importance and goal–performance congruency were identified as critical factors in the emotion process. Goal importance affects emotional intensity. The more important the goal, the more intense is the subsequent emotion. If a situation has no importance, then no emotion is expected. The difference between goals and performance outcome (as perceived by the athlete) is a major factor in self-evaluation and emotion as well. The important goals that an athlete brings to a competition setting may be achieved (resulting in benefit) or frustrated (resulting in harm). Effective goal-setting practices can influence performance and emotions by having the athlete identify controllable specific goals and by helping achieve desired athletic goals through directing effort and persistence to these specific goals (Locke & Latham, 1990).

Individuals generally prefer goals that match their abilities (Burton, 1992; Deci & Ryan, 1985; Locke & Latham, 1990). Easy goals often lead to boredom because they offer little challenge and the benefits of attaining them are often considered relatively unimportant. Goals that are too difficult, on the other hand, result in goal frustration and negative emotions. Goals should be challenging enough that effort is required and the goal has value. Goals should also be realistic, so that regular success is experienced. Thus, realistic, challenging goals should help satisfy both the importance and discrepancy conditions for positive emotion.

Long-term or end goals provide overall direction in achievement settings. However, a danger exists in setting only long-term goals. Emmons (1992) reported that using only long-term goals might be associated with emotional distress for two reasons. First, the distant nature of end goals makes progress appear slower than it actually is. Second, it is more difficult to track progress toward end goals. To overcome this potential problem, athletes can set short-term goals that afford regular feedback on the size and direction of goal–performance discrepancies. In addition to providing regular feedback, short-term goals have emotional value because they can help athletes attain long-term goals (Locke, Cartledge, & Knerr, 1970). Obviously, it is important to set realistic short-term goals. Unrealistic goals lead to both short-term goal failure and a lack of progress toward the end goal—contributing to negative emotional experience. Second, goal specificity increases with regulation to short-term goals (Carver & Scheier, 1990). Differences between goals and performance are less ambiguous when goals are specific and measurable. Having specific goals also allows the athlete to focus on attainable goals rather than on less controllable competition outcomes such as winning or medals. As discussed in Chapter 7, increasing perceptions of control can assist in managing excessive competitive anxiety.

Environmental Factors

Often, the environment can be changed in a number of ways to make emotional control easier for athletes (Smith, 1980). First, the environment can be made less demanding so that athletes probably will not appraise the environmental demands as exceeding their personal resources. In youth basketball, for example, using a smaller ball than is used at the senior level makes ball control easier for young athletes. Other factors such as field size, height of goals, and playing surface can be altered to reduce the sport demands. Second, more resources can be made available to an athlete when a situation is potentially distressing. The presence of a supportive coach or parent, for example, gives an athlete a potential coping option if he or she feels their resources are being taxed. Educational training for coaches and parents can make life more enjoyable for athletes (Smoll, 1986; Smoll et al., 1993). A factor such as the availability of medical supplies (e.g., tape for injured limbs) and washroom facilities also can make the situation less prone to be a negative experience. Third, the training environment can be set up to enable the athlete to increase skill level and thus make the demands of competition less threatening. Clearly, the environment is closely tied to cognitive appraisal and behavior. Although athletes can be taught strategies for self-regulation and personal control, the environment can also be structured in ways that enhance the athletes' options and abilities to exert personal control over emotions.

Info Box

It is frequently not possible to change environmental factors in an attempt to gain emotional control; thus, proper psychological preparation is advantageous for regulating the emotions themselves.

Coping Skills Training

Sport psychologists have recognized that athletes use a variety of cognitive and behavioral skills to manage stress and emotion (Anshel, 1990; Crocker, 1992; Crocker & Graham, 1995; Gould, Eklund, & Jackson, 1993; Smoll, 1986). Within cognitive models of emotions, coping strategies are seen as a primary means to change a stressful athlete–environment relationship or to manage the affective and physiological experiences associated with emotion (Crocker,

Kowalski, & Graham, 1998; Lazarus, 1991). Based on the intervention model (see Fig. 8.1 on page 156), coping can influence emotional experiences by changing appraisals, controlling arousal and action impulses, and changing the environment to produce different appraisals.

Most coping models feature two basic types of coping dimensions based on the intention and function of coping efforts: problem-focused and emotion-focused (Compas, Malcarne, & Banez, 1992; Lazarus & Folkman, 1984; Crocker, Kowalski, & Graham, 1998). Problem-focused coping refers to cognitive and behavioral efforts used to change the troubled person–environment relation causing the distress. Emotion-focused coping involves strategies that help control emotional experiences. Microlevel analyses have suggested that the two basic coping function dimensions can be further divided based on specific coping strategies. For example, problem-focused coping can be subdivided into categories such as problem solving, planning, information seeking, precompetition and competition plans, self-talk, suppression of competing behavior, and increasing efforts. Emotion focused coping can be separated into such categories as mental and behavioral withdrawal, ignoring, isolation and deflecting, positive focus, relaxation, reappraisal, self-blame, acceptance, and wishful thinking. Many of the emotional control interventions that were discussed earlier fall under the categories of problem-focused and emotion-focused coping.

Research has consistently shown that competitive athletes use a number of coping strategies to manage stressful situations (Crocker & Graham, 1995; Crocker & Isaak, 1997; Gould, Finch, & Jackson, 1993; Gould et al., 1996). In many cases, athletes manage emotions using both problem- and emotion-focused coping. Emotion control is required not only in competition and training but also in many other situations, such as dealing with the expectations of the media and significant others, financial matters, interpersonal relationships, and injury. Given these multiple stressors, there is a consensus that no single type of coping strategy or intervention procedure is effective in all athletic settings (Hardy, Jones, & Gould, 1996; Meichenbaum, 1993). It is recommended, therefore, that athletes learn a diverse set of problem- and emotion-focused coping strategies to prepare them to manage emotions effectively in numerous, and sometimes novel, stress situations.

Many intervention programs teach athletes coping skills to effectively manage stress and emotion. Stress Inoculation Training (SIT; Meichenbaum, 1985) and Stress Management Training (SMT; Smith, 1980) are two coping skills training programs that have been used with sport populations to help athletes manage stress and emotion. SMT and SIT were developed as cognitive–behavioral intervention programs based primarily on the transactional framework of stress and coping. A key feature of these programs is that they help athletes develop a number of different coping skills to manage either the troubled athlete–situation relation or the emotional experiences associated with such relations. These coping skills training programs help athletes control dysfunctional emotions by producing more adaptive appraisals, improving coping responses, and increasing confidence to use their coping skills to manage numerous sources of athletic stress (Meichenbaum, 1993). Both SIT and SMT are described next, followed by a discussion of various issues related to their application and effectiveness.

Stress Inoculation Training (SIT)

The purpose of **Stress Inoculation Training** (SIT) is to provide athletes with a variety of coping responses that can be used to change the environment and control personal reactions in a given person–environment transaction (Meichenbaum, 1985, 1993). Athletes are taught cognitive, behavioral, and physiological coping skills. These skills may include arousal control, coping imagery, self-instructional training (task-specific self-talk), thought stopping, identifying controllable and uncontrollable stressors, cognitive restructuring (changing irrational beliefs), behavioral changes, and others (Kerr & Goss, 1996; Meichenbaum, 1985). Stress inoculation programs are dynamic because the needs of the athlete determine which intervention skills are taught.

The SIT intervention consists of three phases: (1) conceptualization, (2) skill acquisition and rehearsal, and (3) application and follow-through. The conceptualization phase helps athletes better understand, from a transactional model of stress and coping, the nature of their stress and how their appraisals influence emotion and performance. The role of coping and the need for effective coping skills are explained to provide a rationale for the SIT intervention program. To make the SIT intervention effective, it is important for the athlete and sport psychologist to develop a collaborative relationship. The goal of the skill acquisition and rehearsal phase is to help athletes develop and rehearse a wide variety of coping skills or to help them better use the coping skills they already possess. In the application and follow-through phase, athletes are given opportunities to practice their coping skills, starting with small manageable doses of stress and progressing to more stress-inducing settings (hence the label "stress inoculation"). Athletes develop a sense of "learned resourcefulness" by successfully coping with stressors through a variety of techniques including imagery, role-playing, modeling, and homework assignments (Meichenbaum, 1985; Kerr & Goss, 1996; Kerr & Leith, 1993).

Meichenbaum (1985) suggested that people can learn to manage stress and associated emotional experiences by learning to break down stress situations into four stages: (1) preparing for the stressor, (2) controlling and handling the stressor, (3) coping with feelings of being overwhelmed, and (4) evaluating coping efforts and self-rewards. Although the coping skills that are taught in SIT vary to meet the needs of individual athletes, techniques such as muscle relaxation, self-statements, and problem solving are used to teach athletes to cope with the four stages of stress. Using the four-stage approach, Crocker and Gordon (1986) provided examples of coping self-statements that soccer players can use to manage emotional experiences when playing in matches (see Table 8.2).

The SIT program is taught over numerous sessions and can be tailored to the needs of various sporting groups or individuals. For example, Kerr and Goss (1996) evaluated the effectiveness of SIT on reducing injuries and stress levels in female and male gymnasts competing nationally or internationally. The sixteen sessions consisted of the following: (1) obtain background information and introduce the stress management program, (2) discuss the importance of thought processes, (3) examine negative thought and irrational beliefs, (4) thought stopping, (5) replace negative thoughts with positive ones, (6) identify things we can and cannot control, letting go of things we cannot control, (7) positive self-statements, (8) dealing with distractions/refocusing, (9) relaxation/breathing, (10) imagery, (11) cue plans for skills and routines, (12) competitive plans, (13) simulations in imagery (performance and coping images), (14) actual simulations, (15) evaluation and revisions of plans, and (16) summary and review. Once a skill was taught, it was discussed in subsequent sessions. Athletes were responsible for completing training logs that contained homework assignments.

TABLE 8.2   *Coping Self-Statements for Each Stage of Stress for Use during Physical Soccer Matches (Adapted from Crocker & Gordon, 1986).*

Stage	Purpose	Examples
Stage 1: Preparing for the stressor	Focus on preparation of match demands. Combat negative thinking and prematch anxiety.	This could be rough, but you can handle it. Remember: don't react, focus on your role. It is going to be rough; keep your cool. Make a plan for how to deal with it effectively.
Stage 2: Handling the stressor	Control stress and emotional reaction. Focus on match demands and player role.	Psych yourself up—I can meet this challenge. Keep your cool. He's losing his; don't react. Use these feelings in a positive way. Man, that was a hard tackle! Get back in the game right away.
Stage 3: Coping with feelings of being overwhelmed	Learn to have control even if the worst happens. Set up contingency plans.	Get control, slow things down. Things are getting rough, try to manage it. Keep focused: what do I have to do? Work through it. Don't give in.
Stage 4: Evaluation of coping efforts	Evaluate coping attempts—what worked and what didn't. Recognize small gains—don't expect perfection.	You handled yourself well. I lost control in some situations—what could I do better? I'm getting better each time—keep working hard.

Cognitive–Affective Stress Management Training (SMT)

The goal of **Stress Management Training** (SMT) intervention is to have athletes develop an "integrated coping response" that enables them to better manage stressful situations (Smith, 1980). The integrated coping response, which includes both somatic and cognitive components, can be used across a wide variety of sporting situations. SMT is based on the transactional model and emphasizes four components: (1) the external situation, (2) cognitive appraisal, (3) physiological responses, and (4) behavior. A basic premise of the SMT model is that a change in any one or more of the four components has an effect on all other components in the system. The focus in developing an integrated coping response for athletes is primarily on the cognitive and physiological components.

SMT consists of five phases: (1) pretreatment assessment, (2) treatment rationale, (3) skill acquisition, (4) skill rehearsal, and (5) posttreatment evaluation (Smith, 1980). The pretreatment assessment assesses athletes' behavioral and cognitive coping skills and deficits. In the treatment rationale phase, athletes are asked to describe personally relevant stressful situations and corresponding stress responses. The integrated coping response is developed in the skill acquisition phase. Muscular relaxation is learned and combined with self-statements designed to reduce stress and improve performance. Athletes develop new self-statements to replace dysfunctional ones. Meichenbaum's (1985) self-instructional training is also taught during the third phase, which allows athletes to use specific cognitive strategies at various phases of their stress response.

An important difference between SIT and SMT occurs in the skill rehearsal phase of treatment. The SIT program is based on individuals practicing their coping skills with small, manageable units of stress that gradually increase in stressfulness over time The SMT program, on the other hand, uses a procedure called induced affect to generate high levels of emotional arousal in athletes, which they must "turn off" with their coping response. Induced affect requires that the athlete imagine high levels of affective or emotional arousal through suggestion and encouragement by the trainer (Smith & Ascough, 1985). An assumption of SMT is that if an athlete can learn to master high levels of emotional arousal, lower levels of emotion can also be controlled, but the opposite is not necessarily true (Smith, 1984). The fifth phase of SMT, evaluation, assesses the long-term effects of the training program.

The five phases of SMT can be taught over several sessions. For example, Crocker and colleagues (1988) developed a SMT program for high-performance youth volleyball players that consisted of eight 1-hour modules. These modules were: (1) conceptualization and introduction to relaxation training, (2) role of cognitive distortions and irrational beliefs, (3) controllable and uncontrollable stressors, (4) relaxation and induced affect, (5) self-instructional training, (6) self-instructional training and induced affect, (7) integrated coping response, and (8) meditation. The players were given homework assignments after each session that were reviewed before the next session. The purpose of the homework was to allow athletes to record their progress through the program, to identify successes and problems, and to increase program compliance.

Research Support for Coping Skills Training

Several sport studies have evaluated the effectiveness of SIT and SMT interventions in both adults and youth. Because stress can have effects across various athletic modalities, researchers have examined the effects of SIT or SMT on performance (Crocker, Alderman, & Smith, 1988; Crocker, 1989; Kerr & Leith, 1993; Mace & Carroll, 1985, 1989; Smith, 1980; Ziegler, Klinzing, & Williamson, 1982), rehabilitation from injury (Ross & Berger, 1996), injury occurrence (Kerr & Goss, 1996), pain tolerance (Whitmarsh & Alderman, 1993), and global stress and anxiety (Crocker, Alderman, & Smith, 1988; Mace & Carroll, 1985, 1989; Kerr & Leith, 1993; Larsson, Cook, & Starrin, 1988). Overall, the studies have supported the effectiveness of both coping skills training programs for controlling stress and emotion and enhancing performance.

A Case Study of Stress and Emotion Control: Jill's Story

This chapter has provided basic information on how athletes can regulate emotions. There is consensus that a diverse coping repertoire facilitates changing or managing the subjective experiences, physiological changes, expressive behavior, and behavioral consequences associated with emotion. It is critical for the reader to understand, however, that stress and emotion in athletic situations can be very complicated (Crocker & Graham, 1995; Gould et al., 1993; Gould et al., 1996). Because of the complex nature of the environment and the athlete's active role in that environment, interventions can be difficult and need to take into account an athlete's multiple goals. To illustrate this complexity, we provide details from a series of interviews with an athlete that clearly demonstrate that: (1) emotional experiences constantly change in a complex athlete–environment context over time and (2) regulating emotional experience is often bewildering to the athlete as he or she tries to achieve multiple goals. The following describes the experiences of Jill, a 22-year-old female participating in an elite team sport. To facilitate understanding her emotion and coping processes during the athletic season, we apply a cognitive–motivational–relational framework (Fig. 8.2 on page 172). The description of Jill's experiences is followed by a discussion of interventions that may have helped her more effectively manage stress and emotion.

Jill's final season was her last chance to achieve her athletic goals. She had been named team captain and was expected to lead the team in offensive production as well as provide general leadership. However, a number of interrelated stressors contributed considerable emotional distress. First, there was a troubled athlete–coach relationship. Second, there was role conflict in being named team captain. Third, early season performance success created the potential for Jill's achievement of cherished performance and personal goals. The pressure created by these situations, combined with a poor coping repertoire, set in motion a season of emotional experiences that Jill had never experienced or anticipated. Figure 8.2 on page 172 diagrams the entire athlete–environment transaction.

Let's consider how Jill appraised the athletic situations in terms of personal well-being. Jill's athletic self-identity and social identity were reflected in her desire to be perceived as a top player and to retain social status among her peers. Personal goals were to be the league scoring leader and to make the all-star team. She was strongly committed to her goals, making her vulnerable to negative emotions and distress. Her self-identity was further threatened by pressure from the media, from other teams that prepared to neutralize her skill, and from the other teams' coaches, who eventually voted for the all-star team. She also experienced pressures from significant others, such as her father and teammates.

Jill was confused about potential coping options and their perceived consequences. Inhibiting factors about what she believed would be appropriate or acceptable coping strategies complicated what she believed she could do to manage the demands. She had not anticipated having early success (league leading scorer) or feeling the pressure to perform, and thus she did not have a chance to prepare a coping repertoire. She desired emotional support from a significant other, but her boyfriend, whom she felt was the only person she could really share her emotional experiences with, was away at a different school. The coach was not an option since Jill believed the coach was focused on her own personal concerns. Nor could Jill approach teammates because they were perceived as too young and inexperienced.

The interviews with Jill revealed she had a very limited coping repertoire to manage her athletic stress and emotion. Jill did not know how to cope with the environment. She summed it up best by stating, "I guess for lack of maybe knowing any better, I don't know how, I didn't know what to do, really. I didn't know how to get it out or anything." Her coping repertoire for competitions consisted of prematch rituals such as putting on her shoes the same way before each match and increasing effort during the games. "I would try to come out really, really, really fast, and really, really hard, and play really, really good and establish myself early. And that way…it seemed like the pressure was off to do something…." A primary coping strategy Jill used between matches was to think about the situation as little as possible. She would try to block out her thoughts regarding her sport.

(continued)

Case Study   *(continued)*

In addition to the pressure to perform, distress was associated with Jill's role as team captain. This role was stressful because she felt it was thrust upon her and she never felt she was a true team captain. Given the social status of captain, Jill felt it was important to play well. Jill placed pressure on herself to achieve her performance goals, but the captaincy role also dictated that she should do well, thereby increasing the demands and stress to reach her performance goals. Further, the role conflict as captain was made more difficult because of a troubled athlete–coach relationship. That relationship was the most complex stressor to manage, because not only did it have to be managed, but also it had an influence at other stages in the coping process described earlier. Jill thought that the coach's goals were being achieved at the expense of Jill's and the team's goals.

Jill felt she had limited coping options to manage the athlete–coach relationship because she did not feel the coach would listen to her. She chose to avoid and not talk to the coach if possible. The numerous run-ins with the coach were probably the result of this coping strategy. The troubled athlete–coach relationship influenced other demands in Jill's athletic life. It increased the stress of being the captain. It limited possible coping options to deal with the pressure to perform, such as being able to use the coach for social support or technical and tactical advice.

Emotional Control Strategies for Jill

Jill has several interwoven perceived problems related to performance pressure, role confusion, and coach–athlete conflict. Applying the cognitive–behavioral perspective emphasized in this chapter, we will design a basic coping skill program for Jill. Before we start, we need to make a few assumptions. Jill's season is over, and many of the stressors simply do not exist anymore. Her limited coping repertoire, however, will make her vulnerable to any future stressors appraised in a similar fashion. Let's assume that Jill presented these problems early in the season and has asked for help in developing an intervention to improve her emotional control. Given the complexity of Jill's situation, the intervention outline below is fairly basic. The intervention program to teach Jill effective coping skills follows the basic framework of Meichenbaum's (1985) Stress Inoculation Training.

The comprehensive interviews over several sessions revealed many important features about the nature and severity of Jill's problems. Her description revealed how the athletic setting facilitated or threatened her self-identity. Information about social influences (media, significant others), personal influences (beliefs and behaviors), and the social and personal consequences (conflict with coach, interactions with other players, game and between-game behavior, emotional experience) are known. Further, we have a better understanding of how Jill coped with various perceived demands. Identifying why she chose not to use specific coping options may be as important as knowing what coping strategies she did use.

The first stage of intervention, after the assessment, is to educate Jill about the transactional nature of stress and emotion. Having her learn about how thoughts and emotions are interrelated will allow her to reconceptualize her stress/emotion reaction (Meichenbaum, 1985). This process will help her to:

1. increase her awareness about how evaluation of the situation, consequences, and coping options influence her behavior and emotion;
2. understand how stress can be divided into stages—anticipation, confrontation, possibly being overwhelmed, and evaluation; and
3. redefine stress and emotion in terms that can be managed.

The second stage of the SIT program will involve Jill in developing and rehearsing coping skills. Given the number of stressors in Jill's athletic life, we must be careful not to overwhelm her with too many coping options. Jill may identify which stressors she wishes to address first—this will clarify which athlete–situation relationships are important to her. Specific skills could be developed for the four stages of the stress process (anticipation, confrontation, possibly being overwhelmed, and evaluation of coping). Jill could learn a number of skills, including reappraisal skills (seeing situations differently), arousal control, anger control, communication skills, self-talk, and precompetition and competition preparation plans.

In the second stage, Jill could begin to understand and develop effective goal setting to direct performance and control emotion. To maintain or enhance Jill's ego ideal of being a top athlete, she has adopted outcome goals (being the top league scorer, league all-star) that are largely uncontrollable. She can redefine her outcome goals to process goals—that is, behaviors that will allow her to maintain her ego ideal. Adopting process goals and other effective goal setting will provide Jill with a sense of greater control and a better focus for her performance and emotional efforts. She needs to understand, however, that redefining her goals will be difficult because social influences (media, significant others) often focus on outcome to assess performance. Nevertheless, learning about effective goal setting may help her to educate others about the process of performance. This education process may change the environment, resulting in less performance pressure.

The third stage is the application of coping skills through paced mastery (success in small units). Various methods, such as imagery rehearsal, behavioral rehearsal, modeling, and role-playing, can help Jill apply the coping skills she developed in the second stage. The use of imagery rehearsal involves generating a hierarchy of stressful scenarios ranging from least to most stressful. For example, Jill could envision conversations with the coach progressing from simple greetings to pleasant conversations to discussions about soccer in general to evaluation of team practice sessions. In imagery rehearsal, Jill would be asked to see herself using learned coping skills (e.g., arousal control, self-talk, effective communication skills) in progressively more threatening situations. Coping imagery can also be employed. Jill would first imagine losing emotional control, along with the associated thoughts, feelings, and physiological reactions. Once in this state, she would see herself managing the situation by using the developed coping skills.

The last step is to graduate to real athletic situations. This step can be difficult because the competitive demands require athletes to deal with high-pressure situations. Because many of Jill's stressors occurred away from the many situations, however, they could be controlled. Again addressing the coach–athlete relation, Jill could learn to communicate with the coach in nonthreatening settings, such as simple greetings at the beginning of practice. Over time, this could progress to the scenarios outlined in her imagery rehearsal. Jill needs to understand that some emotional distress may occur, but she now has the skills to manage the emotional experiences. Furthermore, dealing with troubled coach–athlete relations will reduce long-term negative consequences.

In conclusion, the suggested intervention would allow Jill to learn coping skills to manage some of the demands in her athletic life. It is unlikely that any intervention would remove all the distress, because many of the situations are embedded in a complex social context. Nevertheless, developing and applying coping skills will increase Jill's confidence not only to manage the pressures of athletic competition but also to generalize to other aspects of her life (Smith, 1980).

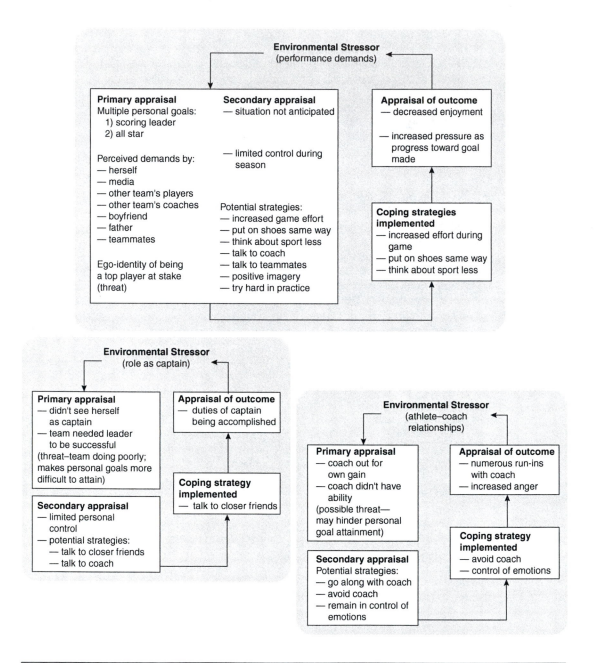

FIGURE 8.2   *Jill's Athletic Stress Incorporated into the Transactional Model of Emotion.*

Conclusion

In this chapter we examined how athletes can learn to self-regulate emotions in sport. A conceptual model based on cognitive–motivational–relational theory (Lazarus, 1991) was presented to organize how intervention strategies could impact environmental, appraisal, physiological, and coping components of stress and emotion. Based on the model, various cognitive–behavioral techniques were briefly reviewed. Arousal management skills, such as progressive relaxation, meditation, and biofeedback, can help athletes to reduce unwanted heightened physiological arousal. Cognitive interventions, such as cognitive restructuring, self-talk, and self-instructional training, work to modify or shift the appraisal processes that are so critical to emotional states. Goal setting was discussed as a means to help athletes gain better control over behavior and to increase the likelihood of their attaining important performance goals. Coping skill training programs, such as Stress Inoculation Training (SIT) and Cognitive–Affective Stress Management Training (SMT), provide a set of guiding principles and procedures for athletes to effectively learn and apply coping skills to control emotion. These coping skills can either change troubling or challenging situations or help athletes manage the emotional experiences. To tie together many of the ideas presented in this chapter, we presented a case study of a high-performance female athlete. Her athletic stress demonstrated the complexity of stress and emotion present in so many athletic settings. Suggestions to help this athlete develop a more effective coping repertoire were presented based on the SIT framework. In closing, although emotional regulation is complex and there are many unresolved issues (Underwood, 1997), research clearly indicates that athletes can learn to control emotions to enhance athletic experience.

Acknowledgments. The writing of this chapter was supported in part by a Social Sciences and Humanities Research Council of Canada grant to the first author.

Key Terms (in order of appearance)

physiological arousal management	matching hypothesis	coping skills training
progressive relaxation	cognitive interventions	Stress Inoculation Training
biofeedback	cognitive restructuring	Stress Management Training
meditation	self-talk	
	self-instructional training	

References

Anshel, M. H. (1990). Toward a validation of a model for coping with acute stress in sport. *International Journal of Sport Psychology, 21,* 58–83.

Arnold, M. B. (1960). *Emotion and personality,* Vol. 1 & 2. New York: Columbia Univ. Press.

Beck, A. T. (1993). Cognitive approaches to stress. In P. M. Lehrer & R. L. Woolfolk (Eds.), *Principles and practices of stress management,* 2nd ed., (pp. 333–372). New York: Guildford.

Bell, K. F. (1983). *Championship thinking: The athlete's guide to winning performance in all sports.* Englewood, Cliffs, NJ: Prentice Hall.

Benson, H. (1984). *Beyond the relaxation response.* New York: Berkley.

Berger, B. G. (1994). Coping with stress: The effectiveness of exercise and other techniques. *Quest, 46,* 100–119.

Burton, D. (1990). Multimodal stress management in sport: Current status and future directions. In G. Jones & L. Hardy (Eds.), *Stress & performance in sport* (pp. 247–277). Chichester, UK: Wiley.

Burton, D. (1992). The Jekyl/Hyde nature of goals: Reconceptualizing goal setting in sport. In T. S. Horn (Ed.), *Advances in sport psychology* (pp. 267–297). Champaign, IL: Human Kinetics.

Carver, C. S., & Scheier, M. F. (1990). Origins and functions of positive and negative affect: A control process view. *Psychological Review, 97,* 19–35.

Compas, B. N., Malcarne, V. L., & Banez, G. A. (1992). Coping with psychosocial stress: A developmental perspective. In B. N. Carpenter (Ed.), *Personal coping: Theory, research, and application* (pp. 47–63). London: Praeger.

Cratty, B. J. (1989). *Psychology in contemporary sport,* 3rd ed. Englewood Cliffs, NJ: Prentice Hall.

Cratty, B. J., & Hanin, Y. (1980). *The athlete and the sports team.* Denver: Love.

Crocker, P. R. E. (1989). A follow-up of cognitive–affective stress management training. *Journal of Sport & Exercise Psychology, 11,* 236–242.

Crocker, P. R. E. (1992). Managing stress by competitive athletes: Ways of coping. *International Journal of Sport Psychology, 23,* 161–175.

Crocker, P. R. E., Alderman, R. B., & Smith, F. M. R. (1988). Cognitive affective stress management training with high performance youth volleyball players: Effects on affect, cognition, and performance. *Journal of Sport and Exercise Psychology, 10,* 448–460.

Crocker, P. R. E., & Isaak, K. (1997). Coping during competitions and training sessions: Are youth swimmers consistent? *International Journal of Sport Psychology, 28,* 355–369.

Crocker, P. R. E., & Gordon, S. (1986). Emotional control training for soccer players. In J. Watkins, T. Reilly, & L. Burwitz (Eds.), *Sport Science* (pp. 187–191). New York: Spon.

Crocker, P. R. E., & Graham, T. R. (1995). Coping by competitive athletes with performance stress: Gender differences and relationships with affect. *The Sport Psychologist, 9,* 325–338.

Crocker, P. R. E., Kowalski, K. C., & Graham, T. R. (1998). Measurement of coping strategies in sport. In J. L. Duda (Ed.), *Advances in sport and exercise psychology measurement* (pp. 149–161). Morgantown, WV: Fitness Information Technology.

Daniels, F. S., & Landers, D. M. (1981). Biofeedback and shooting performance: A test of disregulation and systems theory. *Journal of Sport Psychology, 3,* 271–282.

Davidson, R. J., & Schwartz, G. E. (1976). The psychobiology of relaxation and related states: A multiprocess theory. In D. Mostofsky (Ed.), *Behavioral control and modification of physiological activity* (pp. 399–442). Englewood Cliffs, NJ: Prentice Hall.

Deci, E. L., & Ryan, R. M (1985). *Intrinsic motivation and self-determination in human behavior.* New York: Plenum.

Ellis, A. (1982). Self-direction in sport and life. In T. Orlick, J. Partington, & J. Salmela (Eds.), *Mental training for coaches and athletes* (pp. 10–17). Ottawa, ONT: Coaching Association of Canada.

Emmons, R. A. (1992). Abstract versus concrete goals: Personal striving level, physical illness and psychological well-being. *Journal of Personality and Social Psychology, 62,* 292–340.

Gauron, E. F. (1984). *Mental training for peak performance.* Sport Science International, Lansing, NJ.

Gill, D. L. (1985). *Psychological dynamics of sport.* Champaign, IL: Human Kinetics.

Gould, D. (1998). Goal setting for peak performance. In J. M. Williams (Ed.), *Applied sport psychology: Personal growth to peak performance* (pp. 182–196). Palo Alto, CA: Mayfield.

Gould, D., Eklund, R. C., & Jackson, S. A. (1993) Coping strategies used by more or less successful U.S. Olympic wrestlers. *Research Quarterly for Exercise and Sport, 64,* 83–93.

Gould, D., Finch, L., & Jackson, S. (1993). Coping strategies utilized by national championship figure skaters. *Research Quarterly for Exercise and Sport, 64,* 453–468.

Gould, D., Udry, E., Tuffey, S., & Loehr, J. (1996). Burn-out in competitive junior tennis players: I. A quantitative psychological assessment. *The Sport Psychologist, 10,* 322–340.

Hackfort, D., & Schwenkmezger, P. (1993). Anxiety. In R. N. Singer, M. Murphey, & L. K. Tennant (Eds.), *Handbook of research on sport psychology* (pp. 328–364). New York: MacMillan.

Hanin, Y. L. (1997). Emotions and athletic performance: Individual zones of optimal functioning model. In R. Seiler (Ed.), *European yearbook of sport psychology* (pp. 29–72). Sankl Augustin, Germany: Academia Verlag.

Hardy, L., Maiden, D. S., & Sherry, K. (1986). Goalsetting and performance anxiety. *Journal of Sports Sciences, 4,* 233–234.

Hardy, L., Jones, G., & Gould, D. (1996). *Understanding psychological preparation for sport: Theory and practice of elite performers.* London: Wiley.

Harris, D. V., & Harris, B. L. (1984). *The athlete's guide to sport psychology: Manual skills for physical people.* Champaign, IL: Leisure.

Jacobson, E. (1930). *Progressive relaxation.* Chicago: University of Chicago Press.

Jackson, S. A. (1992). Athletes in flow: A qualitative investigation of flow states in elite figure skaters. *Journal of Applied Sport Psychology, 4,* 161–180.

Jones, J. G. (1993). The role of performance profiling in cognitive behavioral interventions in sport. *The Sport Psychologist, 7,* 160–172.

Jones, J. G. (1995). More than just a game: Research developments and issues in competitive anxiety in sport. *British Journal of Psychology, 86,* 449–478.

Jones, G., & Hardy, L. (1990). Stress in sport: Experiences of some elite performers. In G. Jones & L. Hardy (Eds.), *Stress & performance in sport* (pp. 247–277) Chichester, UK: Wiley.

Kerr, G., & Goss, J. (1996). The effects of a stress management program on injuries and stress levels. *Journal of Applied Sport Psychology, 8,* 109–117.

Kerr, G., & Leith, L. (1993). Stress management and athletic performance. *The Sport Psychologist, 7,* 221–231.

Landers, D. M. (1994). Performance, stress, and health: Overall reaction. *Quest, 46,* 123–135.

Larsson, G., Cook, C., & Starrin, B. (1988). A time and cost efficient stress inoculation training program for athletes: A study of junior golfers. *Scandinavian Journal of Sports Sciences, 10,* 23–28.

Lazarus, R. S. (1991). *Adaptation and emotion.* New York: Oxford Univ. Press.

Lazarus, R. S., & Folkman, S. (1984). *Stress, appraisal, and coping.* New York: Springer.

Locke, E. A., & Latham, G. P. (1985). The application of goal-setting to sport. *Journal of Sport Psychology, 7,* 205–222.

Locke, E. A., & Latham, G. P. (1990). *A theory of goal setting and task performance.* Englewood Cliffs, NJ: Prentice Hall.

Locke, E. A., Cartledge, N., & Knerr, C. (1970). Studies on the relationship between satisfaction, goal setting and performance. *Motivation and Emotion, 15,* 9–28.

Mace, R. D., & Carroll, D. (1985). The control of anxiety in sport: Stress inoculation training prior to abseiling. *International Journal of Sport Psychology, 16,* 165–175.

Mace, R. D., & Carroll, D. (1989). The effect of stress inoculation training on self-reported stress, observer's rating of stress, heart rate and gymnastics performance. *Journal of Sports Sciences, 7,* 257–266.

Maynard, I. W., & Cotton, P. C. J. (1993). An investigation of two stress management techniques in a field setting. *The Sport Psychologist, 9,* 51–64.

Meichenbaum, D. (1977). *Cognitive behaviour modification: An integrative approach.* New York: Plenum.

Meichenbaum, D. (1985). *Stress inoculation training.* New York: Pergamon.

Meichenbaum, D. (1993). Stress inoculation training: A 20-year update. In P. M. Lehrer & R. L. Woolfolk (Eds.), *Principles and practices of stress management,* 2nd ed. (pp. 373–406). New York: Guildford.

Murphy, S. M. (1995). *Sport psychology interventions.* Champaign, IL: Human Kinetics.

Novaco, R. N. (1980). Anger and coping with stress: Cognitive–behavioral interventions. In J. P. Foreyt & D. P. Rathjen (Eds.), *Cognitive behavioral therapy: Research and applications.* New York: Plenum.

Orlick, T. (1986). *Psyching for sport.* Champaign, IL: Human Kinetics.

Ost, L. G. (1988). Applied relaxation: Description of an effective coping technique. *Scandinavian Journal of Behaviour Therapy, 17,* 83–96.

Ross, M. J., & Berger, R. S. (1996). Effects of stress inoculation training on athletes' postsurgical pain and rehabilitation after orthopedic injury. *Journal of Consulting and Clinical Psychology, 64,* 406–410.

Smith, R. E. (1980). A cognitive–affective approach to stress management training for athletes. In C. Nadeau, W. Halliwell, K. Newell & G. Roberts (Eds.), *Psychology of motor behavior and sport— 1979* (pp. 54–73). Champaign, IL: Human Kinetics.

Smith, R. E. (1984). Theoretical and treatment approaches to anxiety reduction. In J. M. Silva & R. S. Weinberg (Eds.), *Psychological foundations of sport* (pp. 157–170). Champaign, IL: Human Kinetics.

Smith, R. E., & Ascough, J. C. (1985). Induced affect in stress management training. In S. R. Burchfield (Ed.), *Stress: Psychological and physiological interaction.* New York: Hemisphere.

Smoll, F. L. (1986). Stress reduction strategies in youth sport. In M. R. Weiss and D. Gould (Eds.), *Sport for children and youths.* Champaign, IL: Human Kinetics.

Smoll, F. L., Smith, R. E., Barnett, N. P., & Everett, J. J. (1993). Enhancement of children's self-esteem through social support training for youth sport coaches. *Journal of Applied Psychology, 78,* 602–610.

Spink, K. S. (1995). *Mental training manual: Saskatchewan Sport Science Program.* Saskatoon, SK: University of Saskatchewan Printing Services.

Underwood, M. K. (1997). Top ten pressing questions about the development of emotion regulation. *Motivation and Emotion, 21,* 127–146.

Vealey, R. (1988). Future directions in psychological skills training. *The Sport Psychologist, 8,* 221–246.

Walden, T. A., & Smith, M. C. (1997). Emotion regulation. *Motivation and Emotion, 21,* 7–25.

Weinberg, R. S. (1992). Goal-setting and motor performance: A review and critique. In G. C. Roberts (Ed.), *Motivation in sport and exercise* (pp. 177–197). Champaign, IL: Human Kinetics.

Weinberg, R. S., Burke, K. L., & Jackson, A. (1997). Coaches' and players' perceptions of goal setting in junior tennis: An exploratory investigation. *The Sport Psychologist, 11,* 426–439.

Weiner, B. (1985). An attributional theory of achievement motivation and emotion. *Psychological Review, 92,* 548–573.

Whitmarsh, B. G., & Alderman, R. B. (1993). Role of psychological skills training in increasing athletic pain tolerance. *The Sport Psychologist, 7,* 388–399.

Williams, J. M. (1998). *Applied Sport psychology: Personal growth to peak performance,* 3rd ed. Mountain View, CA: Mayfield.

Williams, J. M., & Harris, D. V. (1998). Relaxation and energizing techniques for regulation of arousal. In J. M. Williams (Ed.), *Applied Sport psychology: Personal growth to peak performance* (pp. 294–236). Mountain View, CA: Mayfield.

Ziegler, S. G., Klinzing, J., & Williamson, K. (1982). The effects of two stress management training programs on cardiorespiratory efficiency. *Journal of Sport Psychology, 4,* 280–289.

Zinsser, N., Bunker, L., & Williams, J. M. (1998). Cognitive techniques for building confidence and enhancing performance. In J. M. Williams (Ed.), *Applied Sport psychology: Personal growth to peak performance* (pp. 270–295). Mountain View, CA: Mayfield.

9

Introduction of Sport Psychology Interventions

Allen Cornelius
Springfield College

- Intervention in sport psychology is a four-phase process. Assessment is the initial step and may take the form of structured interviews, objective tests, or performance profiling. Education, practice, and evaluation and modification follow assessment.
- The education phase of intervention is based on three theoretical foundations: psychophysiological, behavioral, and cognitive–behavioral.
- Research both supports and refutes the theoretical perspectives used in intervention. In general, however, sport psychology intervention is described as effective thus athletes may wish to seek sport psychology services.
- Sport psychology services are most effective if they are obtained from properly trained consultants. Those seeking sport psychology services should verify credentials such as certification by the Association for the Advancement of Applied Sport Psychology.

The field of sport psychology has accumulated substantial knowledge on the psychological aspects of sport, from how psychological characteristics can affect sport performance to how participating in sport can affect psychological characteristics. Sport psychologists are often asked to apply this knowledge to assist athletes with their performance. Both research on intervention techniques and professional experiences with athletes help sport psychologists understand which techniques work and which techniques do not work to enhance performance.

Though the interventions have been limited only by the creativity of the sport psychologist, effective interventions have common characteristics and are grounded in sound psychological principles. This chapter presents the basic structure of the intervention process and the underlying theories governing most interventions. The latter part of the chapter outlines the process of finding and evaluating a sport psychology consultant and discusses the effectiveness of self-help materials for conducting interventions.

Coach, athlete, and the sport psychologist each play a role in intervention.

What Is Intervention?

Athletes are very interested in learning how to enhance their performance. Whether they are interested in overcoming performance problems or simply interested in improving performance, athletes look for assistance. For example, athletes will seek advice from strength and conditioning trainers about how to improve themselves physically to enhance their performance. Similarly, athletes may look for psychological assistance from sport psychology consultants. These consultants examine the psychological processes of athletes and provide techniques to improve mental conditioning that will, in turn, better facilitate performance. This general process of evaluating and adapting the psychological processes of an athlete is known as **intervention.**

When athletes seek out a sport psychologist for assistance with their performance, what can they expect? Although each athlete and each sport psychologist has unique skills and talents that influence the process, a sequence of activities is common to most interventions. An intervention program, sometimes called psychological skills training, can be broken down into four phases: assessment, education, practice, and evaluation and modification.

Assessment Phase

Before beginning an intervention program to improve performance, it is vital to know in some detail about an athlete's skills, resources, past experiences, and problem areas. Without this knowledge, interventions cannot be effectively targeted to the areas most in need of attention. This assessment is similar to a physical exam. During a physical exam, a doctor often takes a medical history, asks questions about physical health and symptoms, and may request laboratory tests for a more detailed analysis of the patient's physical health. An assessment done by a sport psychologist inquires about athletic history and psychological health and symptoms and may include psychological tests for a more detailed analysis of the athlete's psychological health. From this knowledge, the sport psychologist and the athlete can arrive at an understanding of the areas needing improvement, and they can develop interventions to address these concerns. Sport psychologists use several techniques to conduct thorough assessments, including structured interviews, objective tests, and performance profiling.

Structured Interviews.   The most common assessment technique used by sport psychologists is the **structured** or semistructured **interview.** The purpose of this interview is for the sport psychologist to gather information about the athlete's sports experiences, about the athlete as a person, and about the athlete's current objectives. The formality and structure of the interview will vary with the personal style of the sport psychologist. The sport psychologist may use a very structured set of questions or may conduct a relaxed discussion about the athlete's experiences. Whatever the style, the focus of the interview is usually on the reason the athlete sought out the consultant, information about athletic history, family background, health status, and any recent significant changes in the athlete's life or athletic participation. Typical content of a structured interview is shown in Figure 9.1 on page 180. It should be emphasized that the content in this example may not reflect the actual flow or feel of the interview, and the interviewer's style and personality will affect how the interview is actually conducted.

An assessment interview is thorough and typically lasts an hour or more. At the conclusion of the interview, the athlete and the consultant should have a clear understanding of the concerns and the specific areas on which the athlete would like to focus. However, it may be useful to supplement the information gained from the interview with results of objective tests. Descriptions of some tests that sport psychologists use are included in the next section.

FIGURE 9.1 *Content of a Structured Interview.*

The following topics and questions are commonly covered by sport psychologists in an initial interview. This type of assessment gathers background information and helps determine those areas the athlete would like to address with the sport psychologist.

A. Description of the problem.
   1. What is the problem?
   2. How often does it occur?
   3. When did it begin?
   4. How long has it lasted?
   5. Where does it occur?
   6. What do you think is causing it?
B. Description of athletic experience.
   1. How did you get involved in your sport?
   2. How did you progress to your current level?
   3. What were the high points of your career?
   4. What were the low points of your career?
   5. Who have been the most significant influences in your athletic life?
   6. What are your present goals in your sport?
C. Family and Social Support.
   1. What is the composition and history of your family?
   2. What is your educational background?
   3. Do you or your family have any history of psychiatric problems?
   4. What is your family's history of sport involvement?
   5. What are your friendships like within sport?
   6. What are your friendships like outside sport?
   7. Describe your relationship with your coach.
   8. Describe your relationship with your teammates.
   9. What are other sources of social support?
   10. Are you satisfied with your social support system?
D. Health Status.
   1. What is your current state of health?
   2. What injuries have you had in the past?
   3. Do you have any current injuries?
   4. How are you sleeping lately?
   5. What are your eating habits?
   6. Do you drink alcohol or use drugs?
   7. What were the results of your last physical examination?
E. Changes Prior to the Onset of the Current Problem.
   1. Any recent physical changes (weight, strength, etc.)?
   2. Any mental changes (anxiety, motivation, etc.)?
   3. Any changes in competitive situations (competitive level, stage in season, etc.)?
   4. Any equipment changes?
   5. Any changes in relationships (social, teammate, coaches, etc.)?
   6. Any changes in thoughts, emotions, or behavior?

Adapted from Taylor and Schneider, 1992.

Objective Tests. Psychologists have used objective, paper and pencil tests for many years to measure a broad range of psychological constructs. Personality tests, anxiety measures, depression scales, relationship satisfaction scales, and so forth have been developed, validated, and widely used for assessment purposes. These tests can provide rapid, reliable, and cost-effective assessments of complex psychological characteristics. Sport psychologists have only recently attempted to identify and assess the psychological skills needed for exceptional athletic performance.

One of the first attempts to systematically measure the psychological skills of athletes was the Psychological Skills Inventory for Sport (PSIS; Mahoney, Gabriel, & Perkins, 1987). This inventory measures six cognitive abilities related to sport performance: anxiety control, concentration, confidence, mental preparation, motivation, and team focus. These constructs were based on the test developers' work with Olympic and collegiate athletes and were intended to measure the mental skills that distinguished elite performers from less skilled athletes. The original version contained 51 true/false items and was later revised to a 45-item, 5-point Likert response format (Mahoney, 1989).

Sport psychologists can use the PSIS to quickly assess athletes' ability levels on six psychological skills that are related to performing well. These skills are also teachable, and therefore, the PSIS can provide a guide for targeted interventions to address the skills in which the athlete needs improvement. Unfortunately, the PSIS has been shown to have shortcomings. Its ability to reliably and validly measure the six skills has been called into question (Chartrand, Jowdy, & Danish, 1992). We urge caution in administering and interpreting this assessment tool, and we suggest that other instruments are needed to more accurately assess athletes' psychological skills.

Another tool for assessing psychological skills is the Test of Performance Strategies (TOPS; Thomas, Hardy, & Murphy, 1996). This instrument is the culmination of 4 years of research based on the relevant research literature and the test developers' experiences as performance enhancement consultants with athletes. The TOPS consists of sixty-four items that measure the frequency of particular behaviors exhibited by an athlete in practice and in competition. These sixty-four items assess eight strategies used by exceptional athletes: goal setting, imagery, self-talk, relaxation, emotional control, attentional control, self-confidence, and automaticity. Although developed only recently, the care with which this instrument was constructed and the initial indications of its validity and reliability suggest it will be a useful assessment tool. With further support of its validity, sport psychologists will be able to use the TOPS to accurately assess athletes' psychological skills and to design intervention programs to address areas in need of improvement.

Depending on the situation, other objective tests may be useful as part of the assessment process. If anxiety is identified as a concern, the Sport Competition Anxiety Test (SCAT; Martens, 1977) could be used to measure the level of competitive anxiety. The SCAT is a fifteen-item test that measures the tendency to become anxious in competitive situations. If confidence is a concern, the Trait Sport Confidence Inventory (TSCI; Vealey, 1986) could be used to assess confidence levels. The TSCI is a sixteen-item inventory that measures athletes' beliefs that they are able to be successful in their sport. If trouble focusing and concentrating is identified as an issue, the Test of Attentional and Interpersonal Style (TAIS; Nideffer, 1976) may be a useful assessment tool. This inventory has scales that measure attention based on a model that divides attentional focus into two dimensions:

width and direction. Width of attention refers to the number of stimuli on which an individual is focusing. This ranges from narrow focus (focusing on only one or a few stimuli) to broad focus (paying attention to many cues at the same time). Direction of attention refers to the origin of the stimuli, ranging from internal (e.g., thoughts, feelings, bodily sensations) to external (e.g., crowd noise, teammates, flight of the ball). The TAIS has six scales that measure both effective and ineffective attentional styles. Although the validity of these scales recently has been called into question (Ford & Summers, 1992), the TAIS has been used widely to measure athletes' ability to focus appropriately.

Many other tests can be used by sport psychologists as assessment tools, depending on the specific concerns of the athlete. A directory of psychological tests used in sport psychology (Ostrow, 1990) provides a comprehensive listing and evaluation of tests used in research and applied settings. These tests can provide assessments of the skills and characteristics that are important to sport performance. Another assessment method, however, does not rely on objective assessment but rather on the athlete's own subjective evaluation. This method, called performance profiling, is covered in the next section.

Performance Profiling.   There is a unique interaction between the demands placed on an athlete by his or her sport and his or her ability to meet these demands. Standardized assessment tools such as those described above can generate an understanding of an athlete's skills, strengths, and weaknesses, but there may be unique characteristics and situations to which these instruments cannot be sensitive. **Performance profiling** is a technique that assesses the particular skills that an athlete deems important to his or her sport. Performance profiling is derived from **Personal Construct Theory** (Butler & Hardy, 1992; Kelly, 1955). This theory is based on the premise that people continually detect themes that help them make sense of the events in their lives. These themes, called constructs, compose a personal theory about an individual and his or her situation. For athletes, there will be personal constructs concerning their physical, technical, tactical, and psychological abilities in sports. Performance profiles can uncover an athlete's individual constructs related to sports performance.

When used as an assessment technique, there are three steps to constructing a performance profile (Butler & Hardy, 1992). The first step is an explanation of performance profiling as a technique to determine the characteristics that athletes believe are important to success in their sports. Completed profiles are often used as examples to help athletes understand the procedure (see Fig. 9.2). The second step is the development of a list of qualities, characteristics, or skills that athletes believe are necessary for elite performance. If done in a group format, this assessment can be done by brainstorming in small groups. If done one-on-one with a consultant, athletes are urged to write down as many qualities as they can think of, with the consultant helping to make the list comprehensive. These constructs should be as specific as possible and adequately cover all aspects of performance (strength, technique, mental skills, teamwork, etc.). From this list, athletes select those constructs that are most important. Twelve to fifteen constructs are probably the most that can be profiled effectively.

The final step in using performance profiling is that athletes rate their ability levels on each construct, usually on a scale from one to ten (one as low or poor, ten as good or exceptional). These ratings are then charted as in the example in Figure 9.2. This visual representation gives athletes clear indications of their strengths and weaknesses on the

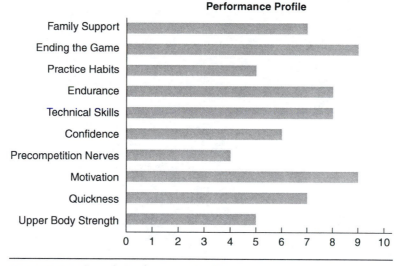

FIGURE 9.2   *Sample Performance Profile.*

characteristics identified as important. The strengths of this procedure are that the athletes determine the characteristics that are important and those in need of attention. A potential weakness is that athletes' perceptions of themselves and the areas identified as needing work may be inaccurate. It is, therefore, often desirable to have a coach or other expert also supply a rating on the constructs in the profile. This will help athletes arrive at realistic evaluations of their strengths and weaknesses.

Performance profiling is a flexible technique with a wide variety of applications. In addition to its utility as an assessment procedure, it can be used as an aid to goal setting, a way of monitoring progress, and as a tool in establishing good communication between coach and teammates (Butler & Hardy, 1992; Butler, Smith, & Irwin, 1993; Doyle & Parfitt, 1997; Jones, 1993; Dale & Wrisberg, 1996). It also is not limited to assessment of individual athletes but is useful for assessing team characteristics and qualities of effective coaching (Dale & Wrisberg, 1996).

Assessment, whether through an interview, objective tests, or performance profiling, is the first step in developing an intervention program. After the areas in need of improvement have been determined, athletes need to learn the skills necessary to address these concerns.

Info Box

To design an intervention strategy, sport psychologists must first gather data to provide general pictures of the athletes and their performance. Information that is triangulated by including structured interviews, objective tests, and performance profiling provide sport psychologists with the clearest pictures of the athletes.

Observing an athlete's actual game performance contributes to a sport psychologist achieving triangulation.

Education Phase

The next step in the intervention process is the education phase. This involves learning the skills needed to address the issues identified in the assessment phase. For example, if high anxiety during competition has been identified as a problem, an athlete may have to learn relaxation techniques or cognitive strategies to reduce anxiety. If motivation is a problem, perhaps effective goal setting is a skill that needs to be learned. Specific intervention techniques are covered in depth in Chapter 10, but whatever interventions are chosen, they each require education about their use and application. In this phase of the intervention process, a sport psychologist is most like a teacher helping the athlete learn the skills needed to enhance performance.

Interventions are based on a variety of underlying psychological principles. Depending on the particular area targeted for improvement, interventions can be derived from psychophysiological, behavioral, or cognitive–behavioral foundations. The foundation driving the intervention determines the skills that need to be taught during the educational phase of the intervention.

Psychophysiological Foundation.   Interventions grounded in a **psychophysiological** foundation are based on the belief that physiological processes of the brain and the body have a significant influence on performance. If athletes can learn to have greater control of their physiological processes, they will be able to have greater control over performance. One example of this type of intervention is **biofeedback.** It is a technique in which various physiological processes are monitored, and this information is "fed-back" to the individual. Through the use of this feedback, subjects learn to gain some control of their physiology. Biofeedback training to reduce heart rate, for example, has been shown to have a significant positive effect for golf putting (Boutcher & Zinsser, 1990). Other physiological parameters, such as respiration, blood pressure, muscle tension, and brain activity, also have been studied for their relationship to performance (Petruzzello, Landers, & Salazar, 1991).

Another example of a psychophysiological intervention is the use of relaxation techniques. Achieving and maintaining an appropriate level of physiological arousal for performance can be enhanced through the use of relaxation strategies. The education phase of a psychophysiological intervention involves instruction in the technique to be used (e.g., heart-rate biofeedback) and how it can be used to affect performance.

Behavioral Foundation.   Unlike psychophysiologically based interventions, **behavioral interventions** rely on an understanding and manipulation of the external environment. There is little or no attention to internal processes, either physiological or psychological. The primary modes of changing performance through behavioral methods are the concepts of reinforcement and punishment from the field of operant conditioning in psychology. A **reinforcer** is an event that follows a behavior that increases the likelihood of that behavior in the future. A **punishment** is an event that follows a behavior that decreases the likelihood of that behavior in the future. Through the effective use of reinforcement and punishment, behaviors can be modified toward more effective performance.

Behavioral techniques are common among coaches; they use verbal praise as a reinforcer for good performance and verbal criticism as a punisher for poor performance. The use of helmet stickers for good plays or games by football players is another example of using positive reinforcers to improve performance. A more sophisticated reinforcement strategy was implemented by a football coach who wanted to increase hustle and devotion during practice, reduce the number of penalties during games, and reduce the number of school-related behavioral problems (Siedentop, 1980). This coach established a point system for each of the targeted behaviors. The players who earned all the possible points for the week were rewarded with a helmet decal and placed in the pool of potential starters for the next game. This reinforcement system was quite successful in bringing about change in the targeted behaviors (Siedentop, 1980).

The previous examples highlight an important characteristic of many behavioral interventions. The interventions described above include the coach as the person who is in charge of the reinforcement and punishment. People in the athlete's environment who are in a position to reinforce or punish particular behaviors often must be included in this type of intervention. Coaches are an obvious source of reinforcement and punishment, but trainers, family members, and other significant people in the athlete's life also may be included as part of a behaviorally based intervention. Professional teams often supplement player's contracts with financial incentives for good performances (e.g., bonuses for a certain number of 100-yard games for a running back, a certain number of home runs for a baseball hitter). These also are based on operant conditioning principles of reinforcement. It is possible for an athlete to use a system of self-reinforcement for improved performance. Favorite meals, vacations, or major purchases can be used as rewards for particular accomplishments ("If I practice hard for three days this week, I will go out to an expensive restaurant this weekend," or "If I win this championship, I will reward myself with a trip to Disneyworld!"). Self-reinforcement takes a high degree of self-discipline but can be used as an intervention to bring about changes in performance. The education phase of a behavioral intervention involves teaching an athlete or coach about the basics of operant conditioning and constructing a system of reinforcers and punishers that will bring about the desired changes in performance.

Cognitive–Behavioral Foundation. Both psychophysiological and behavioral approaches to interventions ignore the internal, cognitive world of the athlete. What athletes believe and how they think are important determinants of their behavior, and **cognitive–behavioral interventions** address this important domain. These interventions are based on the belief that it is not the situation or the environment that determines behavior, but rather it is the interpretation of events that determines how people feel and behave (Beck, 1976; Ellis & Harper, 1975; Meichenbaum, 1977). Cognitive–behavioral interventions involve a process of discovery and exploration of current patterns of thinking, followed by a restructuring of these patterns to more appropriate and facilitative thoughts and beliefs.

For example, a cognitive–behavioral intervention was conducted for a hockey player who was incurring too many unnecessary penalties (Silva, 1982). This player believed he had to retaliate against opposing players who took the puck away from him. This retaliatory behavior was his means of regaining a sense of competency and social prestige. His retaliation often resulted in penalties, which hurt his and his team's performance. Once this retaliatory mind-set was uncovered, it was emphasized to the athlete that *not* retaliating would benefit his performance and his team's performance. Through continual reminders of this difference in mind-set, and through self-talk and imagery, the athlete was able to modify his retaliatory beliefs to a more performance-enhancing cognitive set. This change in beliefs about retaliation was accompanied by a significant reduction in penalties and an increased amount of playing time (Silva, 1982).

Sport psychologists commonly use positive self-talk and imagery to modify underlying beliefs of athletes to a more realistic, performance-focused orientation. The educational phase of cognitive–behavioral interventions involves learning techniques, such as imagery or self-talk monitoring, that then are used to modify the underlying beliefs related to the area being addressed.

Info Box

The education phase of intervention is based on one of three foundations: psychophysiological, behavioral, or cognitive–behavioral. Each foundation offers a unique perspective of the mind–body connection, providing unique skills that can be used to improve performance. Whatever theoretical foundation the skills are based upon, the skills must be repeated in order to be most effective.

Practice Phase

After skills have been learned in the education phase, whether psychophysiological, behavioral, or cognitive–behavioral in nature, they must be integrated as part of a regular training regimen. Remember, athletic skills are not acquired overnight, and psychological skills must be viewed in the same way. Skills like relaxation, goal setting, and positive self-talk seem easy to learn, but to implement them consistently takes practice, practice, and more practice. It takes some time to see any consistent benefit from some interventions. Consider relaxation as a skill, for example. Learning to relax is not a difficult task for most people. Being able to relax in the sport psychologist's office or in a quiet room, however, is very different from being able to relax in the heat of competition. Relaxation must be practiced on a regular basis to be used effectively in pressure situations. Most psychological skills require persistence and practice. As proficiency in these skills increases, there should be improvement in the issues identified in the original assessment.

Evaluation and Modification Phase

After assessment, education, and practice, there remains a final question to be answered in a comprehensive intervention process: Is the intervention working? This step is often ignored but should be an essential component. Ideally, evaluation should be an ongoing part of the intervention, so that modifications can be made to increase effectiveness. Evaluations vary in their sophistication from subjective assessments concerning progress to complex charting of improvement. Returning to the example of needing to decrease competitive anxiety, the consultant could simply ask the athletes if they feel less nervous during competition. An alternative would be to administer one of the objective measures concerning competitive anxiety (e.g., the PSIS, TOPS, or SCAT). If these measures were used during the initial assessment, comparisons to initial values can indicate clearly if improvements have been made. Whatever method of evaluation is used, this aspect of the intervention should not be overlooked. Careful and accurate evaluation can help build athletes' confidence that they are developing their mental skills and can identify those areas that are more resistant to change and may need more attention.

Effectiveness of Sport Psychology Interventions

Just as evaluation is an integral component of an effective intervention program, the field of sport psychology evaluates the effectiveness of interventions. In a review of 23 different interventions geared toward performance enhancement of athletes in competitive situations, most resulted in improvements in performance (Greenspan & Feltz, 1989). In general, educational, relaxation-based, and remedial-cognitive-restructuring-based interventions were found to be effective. In a follow-up of this review, twelve further interventions were examined with nine of these showing positive effects on performance (Vealey, 1994). These reviews show support for the use of psychological-based interventions to enhance performance, but the evidence is far from overwhelming. One reason for this is that conducting quality, controlled research on athletes in competitive settings is not a simple matter, and a relatively low number of studies of a sophisticated nature have been conducted (only thirty-five total interventions from the reviews cited above).

Many challenges face researchers studying performance enhancement interventions with competitive athletes (Vealey, 1994). One is the need for adequate control groups against which a comparison of any performance effect can be made. Athletes concerned with improving their performance may be hesitant to be placed in a control group while others are receiving potentially performance enhancing treatment. Another challenge is the need for data on the long-term effectiveness of interventions. Because psychological skills may take many months to show a significant effect on performance, it is vital to have follow-up assessments many months after the intervention is started. Such longitudinal research is costly to conduct, and it is difficult to control for extraneous variables over a long period of time. A further challenge is the need for extensive manipulation checks to insure that the intervention was perceived as intended. An example of a manipulation check would be an investigation of the effect of "success" imagery on performance. If the intervention had athletes imagine their most successful performances, a check is needed to insure that athletes actually did imagine their best performances and were able to do this vividly and accurately. Without such assurance, any effect of the imagery intervention is questionable. A final challenge is the documentation of the specifics of the intervention through a detailed protocol. Even relatively simple interventions can have many variations. The details of an intervention need to be documented carefully so that researchers can evaluate rigorously which specific components are the important ones.

The research evidence supporting sport psychology interventions is mounting, and the anecdotal evidence from practicing sport psychologists and athletes supports their efficacy. But if athletes are interested in seeking out sport psychologists to assist with the psychological components of their games, what would be involved? Finding and working with a sport psychologist is discussed in the next section.

Selecting a Sport Psychologist

The first step, and often the first hurdle, in trying to improve the mental side of performance is finding the appropriate help and expertise. This section discusses the important issues of finding and evaluating a sport psychology consultant and answers the following questions: (1) How do I find an applied sport psychologist? (2) What training does a sport psychologist have? and (3) What can I expect when consulting with a sport psychologist? To better understand the issues involved in finding a sport psychologist, this section is written from the perspective that you are seeking help for your own performance.

How Do I Find an Applied Sport Psychologist?

When Do I Seek a Consultant?   Many athletes seek out sport psychologists when something has gone wrong with their performance. They may be experiencing a slump or are having trouble making it to the next level of competition. Unfortunately, seeking out a sport psychology consultant rarely results in a quick fix to a problem. Like learning new physical skills, learning new psychological skills and applying them effectively in competition takes time and effort. This does not mean it is too late to seek out help if you are having a slump or some barrier to improving your performance. Realize that seeing results of an intervention, however, may take some time. Some sport psychologists recommend starting a psychological training program during the off-season when the time demands of practice and competition may not be so great (Weinberg & Gould, 1995). Whenever it is that you decide to seek out help with the psychological aspects of your game, you need to find a qualified professional with the appropriate skills and training. This may not be an easy task.

Where Do I Find a Sport Psychologist?   The field of applied sport psychology is a relatively young field, and it is unlikely that there are a large number of qualified sport psychologists in every community. The most common route to finding a consultant is through word of mouth. Other athletes, coaches, and trainers may have worked with sport psychologists in the past and can recommend someone to you. Another resource is the governing body of your sport because it may know a consultant who has worked with athletes in your sport and in your region. Local university exercise science and athletic departments also may be able to provide you with names of consultants in the area because sport psychologists often work with university teams. There also are several national organizations dedicated to sport psychology, and they may be able to provide you with names of consultants in your area (see Fig. 9.3 on page 190).

What Training Does a Sport Psychologist Have?

It is important to be an informed consumer when seeking the assistance of an applied sport psychologist. Simply because someone has been a successful athlete, coach, or sport personality does not mean they qualify to be a sport psychologist. This does not mean that athletes, coaches, and sport professionals cannot help you with the mental side of your performance; it means simply that they may not have the same training and expertise as sport psychologists.

Sport psychology is an interdisciplinary field combining aspects of psychology and sport science, and professionals offering consultative services to athletes for performance enhancement must have a unique blend of training and experience. It is important for you to evaluate the qualifications of a sport psychologist prior to any performance enhancement

FIGURE 9.3   *Resources for Finding a Sport Psychology Consultant.*

The following organizations have members who are actively interested in sport psychology. These organizations may be of assistance in finding a competent sport psychologist in your community.

- American Psychological Association
  Division 47—Exercise and Sport Psychology
  750 First Street NE
  Washington DC 20002-4242
  (202) 336-5500
  http://www.psyc.unt.edu/apadiv47

- Association for the Advancement of Applied Sport Psychology
  Contact the current president through the web at:
  http://www.aaasponline.org

  Note: AAASP provides certification for individuals who meet minimum educational and experience requirements in applied sport psychology.

- United States Olympic Committee
  USOC Sport Science and Technology
  1 Olympic Plaza
  Colorado Springs CO 80909

  Note: The USOC has a Sport Psychology Registry for individuals who are AAASP Certified and members of the American Psychological Association, and who meet minimum criteria established by the USOC.

---

training you receive. The following questions are a guide to evaluate the education, experience, and qualifications of a sport psychology consultant.

What Is Your Educational Background?   A sport psychology consultant should have at minimum a master's degree but preferably a doctorate. The particular field of study probably should be psychology or sport sciences, but degrees from other fields are possible. Regardless of the field of study, a consultant's education should include a strong background in psychology, sport sciences, and specific sport psychology courses.

What Is Your Experience Working with Athletes?   You want to know how much experience the consultant has working with athletes. You want to find out at what level of competition the sport psychologist has worked (recreational, collegiate, Olympic, professional, etc.) and with which sports. You also may want to know the names of specific individuals or teams with which they have worked, but this can be a tricky question. Consultants should be able to provide you with general information regarding types of clients with whom they have worked, but the relationship between athletes and their sport psychologists are confidential. An ethical sport psychologist will not reveal the identity of clients without their permission (American Psychological Association [APA] 1990; Whelan, 1996). Possibly the consultant has asked a few clients for permission to reveal their names as references. You could then seek out these athletes for information about how the consultant helped them. If consultants casually reveal the identities of athletes or teams with whom they have worked, this may be unethical, breaching the confidentiality between the consultants and the athletes. You might consider that if you work with these consultants, they may use your name as freely.

Do You Have Any Certification as a Sport Psychologist?   There are several types of credentialing that will document the education and experience of sport psychologists. The Association for the Advancement of Applied Sport Psychology (AAASP) has developed criteria for awarding status as a **Certified Consultant,** AAASP (AAASP, 1990). This certification requires completion of a doctorate degree with specific courses, training, and experience in psychology and the sport sciences (See Fig. 9.4 on page 192). Professionals in the field of sport psychology established these certification criteria to establish the minimum knowledge recommended for a professional to provide services to athletes.

Another credential a sport psychologist may have is **licensure** as a psychologist. Individual state governments provide licensure, and criteria for licensing vary somewhat from state to state. Requirements typically include a doctoral degree in clinical or counseling psychology, two years of supervised experience, and passing scores on national and state licensing exams (APA, 1987). Licensure as a psychologist insures training and background in psychology but does not indicate any specialization with athletes or in sport psychology. There are currently no specialty areas of psychology licensure, so there is no credentialing as a "licensed sport psychologist." If consultants are licensed psychologists, you should inquire about their training and background in sport psychology and with athletes.

A further source of evaluating a consultant's background and training in sport psychology is through the U.S. Olympic Committee (USOC). The USOC maintains a **registry of sport psychologists** determined as qualified to provide services to the USOC and the National Governing Bodies (NGBs) of each Olympic sport (US Olympic Committee, 1983). The USOC has recently adopted AAASP certification as part of the guidelines for acceptance in this registry, so there is likely to be much overlap in the qualifications.

The credentials discussed above are not endorsements of skill or expertise, and none of these credentials insure the competence of the person. The credentials do indicate that a certain minimum level of education and experience has been obtained, and this should increase the probability of a positive experience. If the consultants you are considering do not have any of these credentials, carefully inquire about their education and experience to insure that they have specific training for performance enhancement with athletes.

What Can I Expect When Consulting with a Sport Psychologist?

Licensing as a psychologist, certification by AAASP, or being listed on the USOC's registry gives documentation of consultants' training but no information on how they actually work with athletes. Sport psychologists vary greatly in how they work with athletes, and it is important to know what you can expect before you agree to work with a particular sport psychologist. Scheduling, length, and frequency of appointments, structure of interventions, policy and philosophy on attending practices and competitions, fee structure, and other details concerning how they work with clients are important considerations to discuss prior to entering into a working relationship with a sport psychologist. Many times it is advisable to have a written contract outlining the details of the consultation arrangement so that both parties know what is expected.

The previous questions outline the information needed to find and evaluate sport psychologists. Sport psychologists' education, experience, relevant credentials, and how they actually work with athletes are important factors to consider prior to agreeing to work with consultants on your performance enhancement issues. But what if you want to learn some psychological skills on your own? The next section briefly discusses the use of self-help materials to learn mental skills training.

FIGURE 9.4   *A Synopsis of Criteria for Certified Consultant Association for the Advancement of Applied Sport Psychology (AAASP, 1994).*

The following qualifications are the requirements for obtaining the credential of Certified Consultant, Association for the Advancement of Applied Sport Psychology:

1. Doctoral degree.
2. Knowledge of scientific and professional ethics and standards.
3. Knowledge of sport psychology subdisciplines of intervention/performance enhancement, health/exercise physiology, and social psychology.
4. Knowledge of biomechanical and/or physiological bases of sport.
5. Knowledge of historical, philosophical, social, or motor behavior bases of sport.
6. Knowledge of psychopathology and its assessment.
7. Training in basic counseling skills.
8. Knowledge of skills and techniques within sport or exercise.
9. Knowledge and skills in research design, statistics, and psychological assessment.
10. Knowledge in at least two of the following four areas: biological bases of behavior, cognitive–affective bases of behavior, social bases of behavior, and individual behavior.
11. Four hundred hours of supervised practical experiences in applied sport psychology.
12. Continuing professional education and contributions to the field of applied sport psychology.

For complete information on certification contact: Damon Burton, Ph.D.
(as of 2001)   AAASP Certification Committee Chair
                                                       Division of HPERD
                                                       107 PEB
                                                       University of Idaho
                                                       Moscow ID 83844-2401

Info Box

The most effective sport psychologist will have an extensive educational background in psychology, exercise and sport sciences, and sport psychology. The athlete may benefit most by working with an AAASP Certified Consultant. However, the sport psychologist's prior experience and personality also are important factors to consider.

Self-Help as a Mental Training Method

Athletes (e.g., Greer & Mills, 1990; Jenner & Seal, 1997; Jordan, 1994; Lynberg, 1993), coaches (e.g., Jackson & Delehanty, 1995; Riley, 1993), and sport psychologists (e.g., Loehr, 1990, 1994; Murphy, 1996; Nideffer, 1985, 1992; Orlick, 1986, 1990) have written extensively about the mental aspects of sports performance. Some of these books are biographical in nature, but others are intended as self-help books with instructions, exercises, and techniques for improving your mental game. The directory of sport psychology graduate programs compiled by AAASP contains a comprehensive bibliography of over 100 publications focused on sport psychology interventions (Sachs & Kornspan, 1996). The majority of these books describe the skills that are common to sport psychology interventions—goal setting, relaxation, imagery, arousal control, attentional focus, and so on. By reading and following the programs outlined in many of these books, you would be introduced to most of the mental training techniques commonly endorsed and used by sport psychologists. Why, then, should you seek out the assistance of a sport psychologist when all the information you need is available at your local bookstore? There is some support from the research that self-help materials geared toward psychological change are effective (Scogin et al., 1990). This research, however, can be misleading because few of the self-help materials available in bookstores have been studied. There is no research that evaluates the success or failure of sport psychology self-help books to bring about significant changes. Some of these books may help athletes with their psychological skills, but there is no research documenting their effectiveness. Extensive research has shown that interventions conducted by well-trained sport psychologists, when applied in consultative relationships, are effective in helping athletes (Greenspan & Feltz, 1989; Vealey, 1994). Even though most of the interventions used by sport psychologists are presented in these self-help books, simply reading a book and practicing what is prescribed in the pages has not been researched or proven effective.

There are several additional reasons to be skeptical that a self-help book on sport psychology will serve as an adequate replacement for consultation with a professional. Potential pitfalls that make success less certain are: (1) limitations on accurate self-diagnosis of the problem, (2) lack of monitoring for compliance with the techniques, (3) instructions may be confusing and misinterpreted, (4) interventions are not adapted for individual idiosyncrasies, and (5) the techniques may be misapplied (Ellis, 1993; Rosen, 1993). These factors detract from the idea that self-help materials can significantly improve sport-related mental techniques. It is appealing to believe the claims made on the covers of sport psychology self-help books, and these books certainly may help some individuals improve their mental games. However, consultation with a sport psychologist is what has been shown to be effective in enhancing the performance of athletes.

Conclusion

This chapter discussed the basic format of intervention programs used by sport psychologists to help athletes with their performance. The process starts with an in-depth assessment of the athlete's skills and problem areas. Assessment is followed by education in the skills needed to address the athlete's concerns, based on psychophysiological, behavioral, or cognitive–behavioral foundations. After education, it is practice, practice, practice until the skills become an integrated part of the athlete's routines. The final phase is evaluation and modification, in which the effectiveness of the intervention is examined and any changes needed are implemented.

Sport psychology interventions have received support from research on their effectiveness, but learning from them may not be an easy process. First, an athlete must find a consultant with the proper training and expertise. This is not always an easy task. There are self-help materials available, but it is questionable whether these self-help resources are effective in helping athletes. However, the benefits of training in psychological skills have been borne out by research and the voluminous anecdotal reports from athletes, coaches, and sport psychology practitioners. This overwhelming support highly recommends the use of sport psychology interventions in athletes' quests for successful performance.

Key Terms (in order of appearance) _____

intervention	biofeedback	Certified Consultant
structured interview	behavioral intervention	licensure
performance profiling	reinforcer	registry of sport psychologists
Personal Construct Theory	punishment	
psychophysiological intervention	cognitive–behavioral intervention	

References _____

AAASP passes certification criteria (1990). *AAASP Newsletter, 5*(1), 3, 8.

AAASP (1994). *Criteria for standard AAASP certification.* Logan, UT: Author.

American Psychological Association (1987). Model act for state licensure of psychologists. *American Psychologist, 42,* 696–703.

American Psychological Association (1990). Ethical principles of psychologists and code of conduct. *American Psychologist. 47,* 1597–1611.

Beck, A. T. (1976). *Cognitive therapy and the emotional disorders.* New York: International Universities Press.

Boutcher, S. H., & Zinsser, N. W. (1990). Cardiac deceleration of elite and beginning golfers during putting. *Journal of Sport & Exercise Psychology, 12,* 37–47.

Butler, R. J., & Hardy, L. (1992). The performance profile: Theory and application. *The Sport Psychologist, 6,* 253–264.

Butler, R. J., Smith, M., & Irwin, I. (1993). The performance profile in practice. *Journal of Applied Sport Psychology, 5,* 48–63.

Chartrand, J. M., Jowdy, D. P., & Danish, S. J. (1992). The Psychological Skills Inventory for Sports: Psychometric characteristics and applied implications. *Journal of Sport & Exercise Psychology, 14,* 405–413.

Dale, G. A., & Wrisberg, C. A. (1996). The use of a performance profiling technique in a team setting: Getting the athletes and coach on the "same page." *The Sport Psychologist, 10,* 261–277.

Doyle, J., & Parfitt, G. (1997). Performance profiling and construct validity. *The Sport Psychologist, 11,* 411–425.

Ellis, A. (1993). The advantages and disadvantages of self-help therapy materials. *Professional Psychology: Research and Practice, 24,* 335–339.

Ellis, A. E., & Harper, R. A. (1975). *A new guide to rational living.* Englewood Cliffs, NJ: Prentice Hall.

Ford, S. K., & Summers, J. J. (1992). The factorial validity of the TAIS attentional-style subscales. *Journal of Sport & Exercise Psychology, 14,* 283–297.

Greenspan, M. J., & Feltz, D. L. (1989). Psychological interventions with athletes in competitive situations: A review. *The Sport Psychologist, 3,* 219–236.

Greer, R., & Mills, K. (1990). *Winning.* New York: Regal Books.

Jackson, P., & Delehanty, H. (1995). *Sacred hoops. Spiritual lessons of a hardwood warrior.* New York: Hyperion.

Jenner, B., & Seal, M. (1997). *Finding the champion within: A step-by-step plan for reaching your full potential.* New York: Simon & Schuster.

Jones, G. (1993). The role of performance profiling in cognitive behavioral interventions in sport. *The Sport Psychologist, 7,* 160–172.

Jordan, M. (1994). *I can't accept not trying: Michael Jordan on the pursuit of excellence.* New York: Harper Collins.

Kelly, G. A. (1955). *The psychology of personal constructs,* Vol. 1 & 2. New York: W. W. Norton.

Loehr, J. E. (1990). *The mental game.* New York: The Stephen Greene Press/Pelham Books.

Loehr, J. E. (1994). *The new toughness training for sports: Achieving athletic excellence.* New York: Dutton.

Lynberg, M. (Ed.). (1993). *Winning! Great coaches and athletes share their secrets of success.* New York: Doubleday.

Mahoney, M. J. (1989). Psychological predictors of elite and non-elite performance in Olympic weightlifting. *International Journal of Sport Psychology, 20,* 1–12.

Mahoney, M. J., Gabriel, T. J., & Perkins, T. S. (1987). Psychological skills and exceptional performance. *The Sport Psychologist, 1,* 181–199.

Martens, R. (1977). *Sport competition anxiety test.* Champaign, IL: Human Kinetics.

Meichenbaum, D. (1977). *Cognitive–behavior modification.* New York: Plenum.

Murphy, S. (1996). *The achievement zone.* New York: Putnam.

Nideffer, R. M. (1976). Test of Attentional and Interpersonal Style. *Journal of Personality and Social Psychology, 34,* 394–404.

Nideffer, R. M. (1985). *Athletes' guide to mental training.* Champaign, IL: Human Kinetics.

Nideffer, R. M. (1992). *Psyched to win.* Champaign, IL: Human Kinetics.

Orlick, T. (1986). *Psyching for sport: Mental training for athletes.* Champaign, IL: Leisure.

Orlick, T. (1990). *In pursuit of excellence: How to win in sport and life through mental training,* 2nd ed. Champaign, IL: Human Kinetics.

Ostrow, A. C. (1990). *Directory of psychological tests in the sport and exercise sciences.* Morgantown, WV: Fitness Information Technologies.

Petruzzello, S. J., Landers, D. M., & Salazar, W. (1991). Biofeedback and sport/exercise performance: Applications and limitations. *Behavior Therapy, 22,* 379–392.

Riley, P. (1993). *The winner within. A life plan for team players.* New York: Putnum.

Rosen, G. M. (1993). Self-help or hype? Comments on psychology's failure to advance self-care. *Professional Psychology: Research and Practice, 24,* 340–343.

Sachs, M. L., & Kornspan, A. (1996). Reading list in applied sport psychology: Psychological skills training. In M. Sachs, K. Burke, & L. Butcher (Eds.), *Directory of graduate programs in sport psychology,* 4th ed. (pp. 216–227). Morgantown, WV: Fitness Information Technologies.

Scogin, F., Bynum, J., Stephens, G., & Calhoon, S. (1990). Efficacy of self-administered treatment programs: Meta-analytic review. *Professional Psychology: Research and Practice, 21,* 42–47.

Siedentop, D. (1980). The management of practice behavior. In W. Straub (Ed.), *Sport psychology: An analysis of athlete behavior,* 2nd ed. (pp. 49–55). Ithaca, NY: Mouvement.

Silva, J. M., III, (1982). Competitive sport environments: Performance enhancement through cognitive intervention. *Behavior Modification, 6,* 443–463.

Taylor, J., & Schneider, B. A. (1992). The sport-clinical intake protocol: A comprehensive interviewing instrument for applied sport psychology. *Professional Psychology: Research and Practice, 23,* 318–325.

Thomas, P. R., Hardy, L., & Murphy, S. (1996) "Development of a comprehensive test of psychological skills for practice and performance." Paper presented at the meeting of the Association for the Advancement of Applied Sport Psychology, October, Williamsburg, VA.

U.S. Olympic Committee establishes guidelines for sport psychology services. (1983). *Journal of Sport Psychology, 5,* 4–7.

Vealey, R. S. (1986). Conceptualization of sport confidence and competitive orientation: Preliminary investigation and instrument development. *Journal of Sport Psychology, 8,* 221–246.

Vealey, R. S. (1994). Current status and prominent issues in sport psychology interventions. *Medicine and Science in Sport and Exercise, 26,* 495–502.

Weinberg, R. S., & Gould, D. (1995). *Foundations of sport and exercise psychology.* Champaign, IL: Human Kinetics.

Whelan, J. (1996). Ethical principles for the advancement of applied sport psychology. *AAASP Newsletter, 11*(2), 50–51.

10

Intervention Techniques in Sport Psychology

Allen Cornelius
Springfield College

- Goal setting, arousal control, imagery, cognitive restructuring, and the use of preperformance routines are intervention techniques that are effective in enhancing performance.
- Challenging, realistic, specific, performance-related goals help to provide motivation, reduce arousal, and increase self-confidence in athletes.
- Using control techniques including biofeedback, relaxation, cognitive–behavioral interventions, and mental preparation routines can increase or decrease arousal levels.
- Imagery is a psychological skill with many components that must be practiced in order to be effective for an athlete.
- Distortions in thinking can negatively affect performance. Sport psychologists can teach athletes cognitive restructuring using thought stopping and self-talk to redirect them toward beneficial cognition.

Athletes trying to excel at their sport encounter a variety of hurdles. Performances may suffer from weaknesses in technical skills, lack of experience, need for more physical conditioning, or poor psychological skills. Coaches and instructors, playing time, and fitness training, respectively, can help address the first three areas, and applied sport psychology can help address a deficit in psychological skills. Sport psychologists have been studying sport performance for decades and have developed sophisticated interventions to help athletes achieve excellence.

As discussed in the previous chapter, the intervention process typically involves four phases: assessment, education, practice, and evaluation and modification. Sport psychologists have researched and applied numerous techniques that can comprise an intervention program, and these skills are typically taught during the education phase and then become well-learned during the practice phase. Goal setting, arousal regulation, imagery, and cognitive techniques

Intervention techniques can help every athlete maximize individual capabilities.

are the interventions with the most theoretical rationale and research support. A well-planned sport psychology intervention will contain components of any or all of these techniques. This chapter provides information on the theoretical bases, empirical support, and implications for intervention for each of these techniques.

To help bring the ideas and concepts in this chapter to life, you are encouraged to try out and practice the techniques described in this chapter. This will help you to experience what interventions are really like.

Goal Setting

Goal setting is a common activity in sport and in life. Winning a championship, defeating an opponent, improving your game, or not losing the next point are all goals toward which athletes routinely strive. Coaches and athletes spend considerable effort determining goals for the season, goals for specific practices, and goals for particular events. Simply stated, a **goal** is what an individual is trying to accomplish. Goals may be specific ("I want to raise my batting average by 25 points"), general ("I want to be faster"), long-term ("I want to qualify for the Olympics in 4 years"), short-term ("I want to practice for 3 hours today"), self-focused ("I want to bench press 300 pounds"), or other-focused ("We want to beat Duke").

The rationale for setting goals is the belief that it influences and directs behavior toward accomplishing the goal. Setting goals may keep people task-focused or give them a means for monitoring their progress. However, goals also can be frustrating and potentially counterproductive if they are unrealistic or if little progress is made toward their accomplishment. The goal setting behavior of athletes has received considerable attention from sport psychologists (Burton, 1989, 1992; Weinberg, 1994, 1995; Weinberg & Weigand, 1993). They have investigated how goal setting works in sports and what characteristics differentiate effective goal setting from ineffective goal setting. This information has made goal setting an essential intervention for sport psychologists, and this section of the chapter reviews the theory, research, and practical implications of goal setting in sport.

Theoretical Bases of Goal Setting

There are several theoretical explanations of how goals function to affect performance. These theories are derived from investigations of different aspects of goal setting, and are not necessarily competing or inconsistent with one another. Each contributes knowledge to the effectiveness and understanding of goal-setting applications.

Motivational Interpretation. A **motivational explanation of goal setting** has been developed from examining the extensive literature on goal setting in industrial/organizational settings (Locke et al., 1981). This theory states that goal setting directly influences motivation through three process: (1) directing attention, (2) increasing effort, and (3) increasing persistence. A fourth process, developing strategies, is an indirect mechanism for affecting performance.

This theory asserts that goals affect motivation by directing an individual's attention to the task on which energy needs to be focused. For example, if you practice with no goal in mind, you may slowly improve your skills, but there is no guide for directing your attention. If you have specific goals like, "Hit 20 forehands in a row without missing," or "Sink 20 out of 25 free throws," you know where to focus your attention. By directing your attention to specific elements of your performance, goals motivate you to work on specific skills, and the quality of these skills is likely to improve more quickly.

The **motivational explanation of goal setting** also states that goals influence the effort expended on tasks by providing measurement standards and feedback about progress toward the goal. If your goal is to run a 4-minute mile, and you currently are running a mile in 5 minutes, you have a clear indication of your current ability in relation to your goal. If you are committed to your goal, knowing you have not yet reached this level will motivate you to expend effort toward accomplishing this goal. The third mechanism, persistence, is a combination of directed attention and effort over time. In order to reach a goal, you will direct attention to the tasks related to the goal, you will expend effort on the tasks defined in the goal, and you will continue to expend effort until the goal is reached. Without a goal, tasks will be undefined, effort will be unfocused, and persistence will disappear rapidly. These motivational factors are the keys to why goal setting has a positive influence on performance. The development of strategies is a fourth mechanism that indirectly influences performance. Goals help direct attention and marshal effort, but they also help develop plans. If your goal is to lower your golf score by five strokes, you may direct more attention toward certain aspects of your game and increase your effort in particular areas. You are also likely to change your practice habits by increasing your time on the driving range, seeking out help from an instructor, developing different tactics for particular situations, and so on. Developing plans or strategies for attaining goals is an indirect, but important, component in the effectiveness of goal setting for improving performance.

The motivational explanation of goal setting suggests several characteristics that differentiate effective from ineffective goals (Locke et al., 1981). One characteristic is that goals should be specific. A specific goal gives a clear indication of where attention should be directed, how effort should be expended, and what strategies should be adopted. A goal stating, "Improve first serve percentage from 50 percent to 65 percent by practicing 30 additional minutes per day, focusing on a consistent high toss, and stepping into the court" gives clear guidance for directing attention and expending effort and has a clear strategy for accomplishing the goal. A second implication from the motivational explanation is that goals should be challenging, yet realistic. Challenging goals will maximize the expenditure of effort toward the goal, as an easy goal will require minimal effort. A third characteristic is that both long-term and short-term goals should be set. Long-term goals may appear too difficult and far-off to have much motivational power for directing attention and effort in the present. However, they can guide the development of appropriate short-term goals to accomplish the long-term goals. Wanting to complete a marathon is a long-term goal that may have motivational impact, but it may be too vague and intimidating for a novice runner. Short-term goals such as running a mile a day and increasing to greater endurance and distance are probably necessary for goal setting to have a positive motivating force.

The motivational theory has received a great deal of investigation and research support (Locke & Latham, 1990). However, other explanations for goal setting have been proposed that examine the more cognitive and affective components of the goal setting process.

Cognitive Explanations of Goal Setting.   An additional explanation for the effectiveness of goal setting is that goals affect psychological states such as anxiety and self-confidence (Burton, 1989, 1992). This explanation emphasizes and examines a distinction between outcome-oriented goals and performance-oriented goals. **Outcome goals** are based on winning and losing. Examples are winning the regional championship or defeating a particular opponent. **Performance goals** are based on task-related characteristics and are focused on an individual's own performance. Examples are improving time in a particular event or increasing proficiency at a specific skill. These different types of goals will have different effects on a performer's cognitive state. Athletes focused on outcome goals based on winning and losing may experience more anxiety and less confidence because their goals are not entirely under their control (Burton, 1989, 1992). For example, if you are in a contest against your arch rival, whom you have never defeated, and you are focused on winning, you are liable to be anxious and not very confident. However, given the same scenario, if you are focused on aspects of your own performance, you will have lower anxiety and increased confidence because your performance is more under your control, and you increase the probability that you will perform well (though you still may not win).

Though developed relatively recently, this cognitive explanation of goal setting effects has received support in the sport psychology literature (Burton, 1989, 1992). Swimmers who were higher in their abilities to set performance-oriented goals were less anxious and showed greater improvements in their performances over the course of a season (Burton, 1989). This research and theory suggests that performance goals have a greater effect on enhancing performance than outcome goals, and that it is the effect on psychological states that makes goals effective.

The motivational and cognitive explanations for the effectiveness of goal setting give insight into how goals can affect performance. But, do goals work? The next section reviews the research support for the effectiveness of goal setting in sport.

Effectiveness of Goal Setting

The research on the effectiveness of goal settings in industrial/organizational settings is voluminous and supportive. Hundreds of studies conducted with thousands of subjects have shown goal setting to be a viable and effective method for increasing performance (Locke & Latham, 1990). A comprehensive review of this literature showed that specific, challenging goals were superior to "do-your-best" goals in 183 of 201 studies and that challenging goals had a greater positive effect on performance than easy goals in 175 of 192 studies (Locke & Latham, 1990). With this overwhelming support for the effectiveness of goal setting in industrial/organizational settings, one would expect similar results in the sport psychology literature. In fact, it has been argued that goal setting in sport settings may be more effective than in industrial/organizational settings because the measurement of performance is often more objective and accurate (e.g., tenths of a second, the huge number of specific scores and statistics related to performance) (Locke & Latham, 1985). However, studies examining different characteristics of goal setting in sport settings have been inconsistent in their support. A review of these studies specifically examined the characteristics of goal specificity, goal difficulty, and goal proximity as they relate to sport performance (Weinberg, 1994). This review showed mixed support for these different characteristics of goals, with many studies showing no relationship between these characteristics of goals and subsequent performance. A more statistically based review of the literature used meta-analysis to investigate the effectiveness of goal setting in sport (Kyllo & Landers, 1995). **Meta-analysis** is a procedure that combines the results of many studies to determine what can be concluded from the all the research that is conducted. The meta-analysis conducted for goal setting in sport indicated that there is a positive performance effect for setting goals, but the specific characteristics of what makes an effective goal were not clear from this review (Kyllo & Landers, 1995).

Several researchers have identified methodological problems with the investigations of goal setting that may explain why the results are not more supportive (Locke, 1991, 1994; Weinberg, 1994; Weinberg & Weigand, 1993). The primary difficulty in much of the sport-related research is spontaneous goal setting by control groups. Research designs usually compare performances of a goal setting group with a control group told to "do your best." A positive effect for goal setting would be greater performance improvement for the goal group when compared to the do-your-best group. Unfortunately, many subjects performing sport-related tasks in do-your-best groups tend to set their own goals and therefore improve their performance as much as the subjects in goal setting groups. As many as 83 percent of the subjects in do-your-best control groups set their own goals (Weinberg, 1994). Thus, the control groups against which goal groups are compared are often just as goal-oriented, and significant differences between the groups are not found. Other methodological problems such as subjects adopting personal goals different from those that were assigned, lack of commitment to the assigned goals, and spontaneous competition between subjects all have contributed to the lack of consistently significant findings in the sport-related goal setting research (Weinberg, 1994). Current and future researchers must overcome these methodological flaws to clearly demonstrate the nuances involved in effective goal setting in sport.

Implication for Intervention

Though the research support for the specifics of goal setting in sport is still evolving, this does not mean that goal setting cannot be effectively used to enhance performance. Goal setting is a flexible intervention that can be applied to any aspect of sport performance. Goals can be set for specific sport skills, conditioning, nutrition, and psychological skills. There are ten characteristics of a well-designed goal setting program that are supported by research and practice (Weinberg, 1995):

1. Goals should be specific and described in clear, measurable, behavioral terms. "I will improve my free-throw percentage by 5–7 percent by practicing an extra 20 minutes per practice and focusing on my release and follow-through." You will notice in this example that the target goal (5–7 percent) is not an exact number but a range. This range, or goal window, maintains the specificity of the goal yet recognizes that sport performance is often subject to minor, natural fluctuations (O'Block & Evans, 1984).
2. Goals should be challenging but realistic. Consultation with coaches, athletes, and other professionals can help determine what level of a goal would be challenging yet attainable.
3. Set both long- and short-term goals. Long-term goals provide the direction and ultimate destination of a training program. Short-term goals provide the daily and weekly motivation and positive feedback.
4. Set goals for practice and competition. Practice goals can focus on specific skills that will build to the achievement of competitive goals.
5. Write goals down and review them periodically. Writing down goals and placing them where they will be seen regularly (e.g., in the locker room, on the refrigerator) will serve as a reminder of the goals and help to maintain focus on them.
6. Develop strategies to accomplish goals. It is not enough to write down specific, challenging goals; plans must be made to attain them. As progress is made toward each goal, the plan can be altered or modified as needed.
7. Set performance goals as opposed to outcome goals. Achieving performance goals is more within an athlete's control and can help to reduce anxiety and build self-confidence. Performance goals also more directly focus attention on what needs to be done rather than on the outcome of performance.

8. Set individual and team goals. Depending on the sport and the particular goal, both team goals and individual goals should be set. These must be compatible because the role a player has on a team may not be conducive to particular individual goals. For example, a football running back whose main role is to block should not set a goal to have a 1,000-yard rushing season.
9. Provide social support for goals. Support from coaches, other players, family members, and friends can be an important asset in accomplishing goals (Hardy, Richman, & Rosenfeld, 1991). These sources of social support can provide additional motivation and understanding for the attainment of goals.
10. Evaluate goals periodically. As progress is made, goals may need to be modified to maintain their optimal effectiveness. By periodically evaluating progress toward goals, they can be altered (e.g., made more or less difficult) to maximize their motivational effect.

Adhering to these guidelines can help design an effective and comprehensive goal setting plan to cover all relevant aspects of athletic performance. Goal setting can be a tremendous asset to achieving excellence in sport, but, as with the other interventions covered in this chapter, it is a more complex process than it may appear and requires practice and training. With careful application of sound goal setting principles, a well-designed goal program can help athletes effectively improve their performances and realize their dreams.

Info Box

Goal setting is most effective if the goals are specific, challenging within reason, and performance based. These types of goals can increase motivation, reduce anxiety, and increase self-confidence in athletes, which will ultimately result in successful performances.

Arousal and Sport Performance

The fire and brimstone locker room speech has been used for decades as a means to get athletes to the "appropriate" physiological and emotional energy level for peak performance. The assumption underlying these motivational talks is that more excitement and extremely high energy levels are related to better performances. Sport psychologists have questioned the validity of this assumption and have conducted extensive investigations into the relationship between performance and levels of activation (Gould & Udry, 1994). Because the theories and research pertaining to the arousal–performance relationship are covered elsewhere, this section will focus on research concerning the effectiveness of arousal control techniques and specific implications for interventions.

Effectiveness of Arousal Control Techniques

Arousal control is often advocated as an intervention, but rigorous investigations of specific arousal control interventions are rare. Studies that have been conducted can be categorized into those focused on the effects of increasing arousal and those focused on the effects of decreasing arousal.

Increasing Arousal.   Few studies have been conducted to investigate the effects of increasing arousal, probably because athletes experience problems with overarousal and anxiety more frequently than underarousal. A recent review of research in this area found that psyching-up strategies, such as getting mad and charged up, enhanced performance on strength tasks but were not effective on tasks requiring more skill and timing (Gould & Udry, 1994). This illustrates that different tasks may require specific levels of arousal for effective performance. More theoretically driven and ecologically valid research is needed, however, before firm conclusions can be drawn about the effective use of arousal increasing interventions.

Reducing Arousal.   A substantial amount of research has been conducted on the effects of arousal reduction strategies on performance, and a recent review has grouped these studies into four categories: (1) biofeedback techniques, (2) relaxation strategies, (3) cognitive–behavioral interventions, and (4) mental preparation routines (Gould & Udry, 1994). The first three of these techniques are all well-recognized for reducing arousal; however, it is the subsequent effect on performance that has been of interest to sport psychologists.

Biofeedback is a technique that provides individuals with information about their physiology that is not normally available to them. Through this feedback, they learn to control these processes. Typical physiological measures used in biofeedback are heart rate, blood pressure, electromyogram (EMG), electrodermal (EDR), and electroencephalogram (EEG). In a review of biofeedback research in sports, 83 percent of the studies examined showed improvement of some kind (Zaichkowski & Fuchs, 1988), although other researchers have pointed to serious methodological flaws with many of these studies (Gould & Udry, 1994). One problem is that biofeedback often is only one component of a more comprehensive intervention program, and determining if the effects are due to the biofeedback or some other aspect of the intervention is difficult. Another difficulty is that the level of the physiological processes needed for optimal performance is often not known, so while the individual may learn to control these processes through biofeedback, he or she may not know what level is required to excel at a particular task (Petruzzello, Landers, & Salazar, 1991). Biofeedback shows promise as a technique for controlling arousal, but details about how this can be used to optimize performance are still unknown.

Relaxation strategies are often a component of psychological interventions, but research support for their effects on performance is not substantial. Similar to the biofeedback research, relaxation is often one component of a multifaceted intervention package, and evaluating the effects of relaxation alone are difficult. A meta-analysis of intervention strategies found support for relaxation-based interventions, but causality could be inferred from only two of the studies (Greenspan & Feltz, 1989), and causality in these studies could not be specifically attributed to relaxation techniques. A further complication in evaluating relaxation and its relationship to performance is that learning to relax may bring about other psychological changes, such as increases in sense of mastery and self-efficacy, and it may be these changes that affect performance (Gould & Udry, 1994). More focused research is needed on the specific effects of relaxation and on different relaxation techniques to determine their effects on performance.

Reviews of research investigating cognitive–behavioral techniques have consistently found positive effects for arousal regulation and anxiety reduction (Meichenbaum, 1985; Smith, 1980; Suinn, 1994). These techniques are the mainstay for many anxiety reduction programs within and outside of sport. Recent reviews of performance enhancement interventions have also shown effectiveness for cognitive–behavioral techniques (Greenspan & Feltz, 1989; Vealey, 1994), but many of these studies were focused on performance enhancement and not specifically designed to evaluate the effects of arousal reduction. As with the research on biofeedback and relaxation, the independent effects of reduced arousal through cognitive–behavioral interventions on performance are difficult to ascertain.

A relatively new area of investigation concerning arousal management is the effects of preperformance routines (Gould & Udry, 1994). These routines are systematic patterns of thoughts and actions that are utilized by athletes to prepare themselves for an upcoming performance. Part of the justification for these routines is their supposed ability to regulate the arousal level of the athlete to the appropriate level. There is preliminary support that these techniques can help athletes improve their performance, but specific evidence for the arousal controlling aspect of the routines is lacking (Crews, 1993; Crews & Boutcher, 1987). Preperformance routines and their potential impact on performance will be discussed in greater detail later in this chapter.

In summary, there is some evidence that performance may be enhanced by many of the techniques used to regulate arousal. Cognitive techniques in particular have support for their efficacy in enhancing performance. However, attributing increases in performance specifically to changes in arousal is not possible in many of these studies. More theoretically driven studies designed to specifically examine the effects of arousal management are needed to provide support for the arousal–performance relationship.

Implications for Intervention

From the preceding discussion of the research support for the efficacy of arousal control techniques to enhance performance, it may appear that little is known for certain. Guidelines and practical suggestions for intervention with athletes, however, can be derived not only from the research evidence but also from theoretical implications, the experience of athletes, and practicing sport psychologists.

One recommendation is to recognize that different tasks require different levels of arousal and that individuals vary in the level of arousal they find to be optimal. This suggests that each athlete must determine what level of arousal is best in different situations and that there is no "right" level of arousal for everybody. Research on the effectiveness of cognitive interventions suggests that arousal is not purely a physiological characteristic but includes a cognitive component. It may be necessary to increase some components of arousal (e.g., physiological arousal) and decrease other components (e.g., cognitive anxiety) to achieve an optimal arousal state (Gould & Krane, 1992). This suggests athletes must be equipped with a variety of arousal management techniques to increase or decrease the multiple components of arousal. Cognitive arousal can be regulated through the use of psyching up self-talk if arousal is too low or through cognitive restructuring if arousal is too high (Caudill, Weinberg, & Jackson, 1983). Physiological arousal can be raised through energizing activity or high-energy body language (Taylor, 1995). Physiological arousal that is too high can be lowered by one of many relaxation techniques. An example of Jacobsonian relaxation (Jacobson, 1938), a common relaxation technique, is presented in Figure 10.1.

Arousal regulation is more complex than "Just relax; you'll do better," or "Are you ready to go out there and fight?" With attention to which levels of arousal are optimal for each athlete and each specific settings, sport psychologists can design strategies to help athletes reach the state of arousal that will be most effective for them. The regulation of arousal is an important component of any sport psychology intervention package.

Info Box

You must be able to control your simply physical processes before you can control complex motor patterns involved in athletic performance. For example, athletes must be able to regulate their breathing before they can focus on executing a skill. The use of biofeedback techniques, relaxation strategies, and cognitive restructuring can help athletes learn to control their arousal level before and during competition.

Imagery

Imagery is often viewed as the cornerstone of sport psychology interventions. Famous athletes such as Jack Nicklaus (professional golfer), Greg Louganis (Olympic diver), and Jerry

FIGURE 10.1   *Progressive Muscle Relaxation (Jacobson, 1938).*

Progressive muscle relaxation (PMR) is based on the finding that muscles become more relaxed after they have been tensed. PMR involves systematically tensing and relaxing the major muscle groups until all the muscle groups have been tensed and relaxed. Either read and follow the instructions below or have someone read the instructions to you slowly and clearly.

Sit as comfortably as you can, and focus your attention on the muscles in the back of your neck. Tighten and contract those muscles and hold this contraction for about 3 seconds (pause). Focus on the feeling of tension in this group of muscles. Now relax, and pay attention to feeling of relaxation as the muscles let go of the tension. Repeat this contraction for 3 seconds (pause)... and relax, paying attention to this relaxed state. Now move your attention to your facial muscles, and tense these muscle into a grimace, and hold this for 3 seconds (pause). Focus on this feeling of tension...and relax, paying close attention to this feeling of relaxation. Repeat this process of tension for 3 seconds (pause)...and relax.

This basic procedure of tensing, holding the tension, and relaxing is repeated for both arms, both hands, back, stomach, buttocks, both legs, and both feet. The process is then repeated for the whole body, tensing and then relaxing all the muscles of the body. If particular muscles are involved in specific tasks to be executed, such as the hands or the legs, these muscle groups can be focused on more fully during the relaxation procedure. Depending on how completely the procedure is followed, PMR may take as long as 30–40 minutes. However, with continued practice, a state of deep relaxation may be attained very quickly when needed.

Rice (NFL wide receiver) report using imagery to help them perform their best. Imagery has been advocated as a tool for enhancing the learning of athletic skills, improving the performance of well-learned skills, coping with competitive stress, psyching up prior to a competition, accelerating recovery from injury, and for other issues related to sports performance (Sheikh & Korn, 1994). But what exactly is imagery, how does it work, and how is it applied to sports performance?

Imagery has many synonyms, such as visualization, covert practice, mental rehearsal, mental practice, and "playing the game in your head." Though these terms may not be completely interchangeable, they all refer to a mental process with several specific characteristics (Murphy & Jowdy, 1992). First, imagery is experienced as very similar to actual sensory or perceptual events. When vividly imagining a particular scene, event, or movement, it is like "seeing" your surroundings or "feeling" the movement. This imagining of a scene can be like watching yourself in a movie (called external perspective) or like seeing the scene from your own eyes (called internal perspective). Second, imagery is different from daydreaming or dreaming because you are consciously aware of the process and have some control over the content of the imagery. Third, imagery does not involve actual stimulus. There does not need to be a scene, situation, or any movement—it all takes place in your imagination.

A misconception about imagery is that it only involves "seeing" the image in your mind. Some sport psychologists advocate the use of all the senses, not just the sense of sight, to increase the vividness of the experience (Harris & Harris, 1984; Murphy, 1996; Orlick, 1986, 1990). Images can include the smell of the grass, the sweat in the locker room, or the chlorine in the water; the sound of the crack of the bat, the swish of the golf swing, or the roar of the crowd; the feel of the pedals under your feet, the grip on the handle, or the ball in your hand; the kinesthetic sense of the pivot to the basket, the sprint toward the finish, or the swing of the racquet; and even the taste of salt on your lips, the freshness of the air, or the mouth guard in your mouth. Imagery in this context refers to all of your imagination, including the senses of sight, hearing, taste, smell, touch, and kinesthesis. The term *imagery* will be used throughout this chapter to refer to this rich interpretation of imagination.

Theoretical Bases for Imagery Processes

A number of theories attempt to explain how imagery functions to improve performance, and imagery has been studied by researchers in various fields for most of this century (for a review, see Murphy & Jowdy, 1992). Most imagery theory development focuses on the use of imagery as a mental practice technique—the imager mentally rehearses a particular skill or imagines reacting to a specific situation. Though these theories have their shortcomings, they do provide frameworks for understanding how imagery may work as a performance enhancement strategy.

Psychoneuromuscular Theory. This theory proposes that when imagining a particular movement pattern, the brain sends out signals to the muscles that are duplicates of the signals used to actually produce the movement, although the neuromuscular activation is substantially smaller in magnitude. For example, when a swimmer visualizes performing the backstroke, these images produce a low-level activation of the nerves and muscles involved in actually swimming the backstroke. The theory postulates that these low levels of activation are sufficient to affect the motor pattern or schema in the motor cortex responsible for the execution of the movement. Therefore, rehearsing a skill in your imagination, like the backstroke, could affect your ability to perform the movement.

There is substantial evidence that muscles are activated to a slight degree when imagining a particular movement. Imagining activities such as downhill skiing, riding, rowing, and baseball has been shown to mimic the pattern of neuromuscular activity when actually performing the same skills (Bird, 1984; Suinn, 1980). However, it is not clear that this low level of neuromuscular activation is the actual cause of any subsequent improvement in performance. There is evidence that the effect that imagery has on performance is better explained by changes in the central nervous system rather than at a neuromuscular level (Murphy & Jowdy, 1992). For example, imagining the backstroke may cause low-level neuromuscular activation, but the imagery also affects how one thinks about the backstroke, integrates the components of the stroke, and even plans a race. This suggests the neuromuscular activation detected during imagery may be an effect of the imagery but is not necessarily the cause of any beneficial effects of the imagery practice.

Symbolic Learning Theory.   This theory postulates that imagery functions primarily at a cognitive level, allowing the performer to mentally rehearse the symbolic elements of a task. The sequencing of movements, spatial considerations, decision making, and movement planning can all be refined by mental practice. A skier can imagine a slalom course and by doing so can rehearse entries into turns and make decisions about speed without ever putting on the boots; this experience could clearly help performance. It is this symbolic encoding of information that produces the beneficial effects of imagery, according to this theory.

Two bodies of research offer support for this interpretation of mental practice effects. There is a large body of literature demonstrating that skills that are higher in cognitive content are affected more by mental practice than skills that are more purely motoric or strength-related (Feltz & Landers, 1983). There is also support from studies investigating the relationship of mental practice at different stages of learning. Early stages of learning require greater attention to cognitive and symbolic content and require more information processing than later stages of learning (Fitts, 1962). Therefore, you would expect mental practice, if it enhances the mental processing component of movement, to have a greater effect at early stages of learning. Indeed, this is what several researchers have found (Wrisberg & Ragsdale, 1979; Minas, 1980).

The major shortcoming of the symbolic learning theory explanation of imagery is that although it proposes that imagery affects performance at a cognitive level, it offers little information regarding how imagery affects this cognitive processing. The exact content and nature of the imagery used in many studies is not clearly described, so conclusions about what components of the imagery are related to cognitive changes cannot be determined. It is also unclear if imagery aids in the encoding of the motor program, the retrieval of the motor program, or the performance of the skill (Murphy & Jowdy, 1992).

Information Processing Theory.   It has been suggested that theories from cognitive and clinical psychology may be useful for examining the effectiveness of imagery as a performance enhancement tool (Murphy & Jowdy, 1992). One such theory is psychophysiological information processing theory (Lang, 1977, 1979). This theory states that an image is an organized set of propositions contained in the brain. This set of propositions contains two types of statements: stimulus propositions that describe the content of the imagined scenario and response propositions that describe the imager's response to the scenario. For example, a basketball player may imagine the crowd noise, sweaty palms, and nervousness prior to stepping to the foul line with 0.5 seconds left and the score tied (stimulus propositions). The player may also imagine the feel of the ball, appropriate arm and leg movements, and seeing and hearing the ball hit nothing but net (response propositions). Information processing theory emphasizes that both types of propositions are important for imagery to have an effect on performance. This theory has received support from research on phobia and anxiety interventions (Lang, 1977, 1979) and sport-specific studies (Hecker & Kaczor, 1988, Murphy & Jowdy, 1992; Suinn, 1983). This theory has clear implications for imagery interventions because it asserts that the content of the imagery must include both stimulus and response components to be effective.

Triple-Code Theory. This theory specifies three major components to imagery: the image itself, the somatic response of the imager, and the meaning of the image to the imager (Ahsen, 1984). The first two components are similar to those proposed by informational processing theory: the stimulus of the image and the somatic response to the image. The addition of the meaning of the image for the individual is crucial because people will interpret images according to their own experiences and personalities. For example, a veteran tennis player who has experienced many tournaments may easily imagine serving the first serve of a tournament with confidence and ease, but a novice's image of the first serve of the tournament may be accompanied by anxiety and trepidation. This variation in meaning acknowledges that no two people, even given the same imagery instructions, will have the same imagery experience.

Though an adequate, comprehensive theory of imagery and its relationship to performance has yet to be developed and tested, there are several tentative conclusions that can be drawn from our current understanding (Gould & Damarjian, 1995). First, it is doubtful that imagery produces its effect entirely through a neuromuscular mechanism. A more likely explanation is that higher levels of cognitive processing are involved. Second, for imagery to be successful, it might be necessary for this higher level of processing to include both stimulus and response types of propositions. Third, the meaning of the imagery to the individual is also an important factor and must be carefully evaluated to understand the effect of the imagery on subsequent performance.

Effectiveness of Imagery as an Intervention

Sport psychologists have conducted many studies to investigate the effectiveness of imagery interventions. These studies fall into four major categories: (1) comparisons of successful and less successful athletes on their use of imagery, (2) examinations of factors that mediate the effectiveness of imagery interventions, (3) investigations of imagery to prepare for a performance, and (4) studies of mental practice (Gould & Damarjian, 1995; Murphy & Jowdy, 1992).

Comparing Successful and Less Successful Athletes. One way to evaluate the effectiveness of imagery is to compare a group of successful athletes with a group of less successful athletes on their use of imagery. For example, athletes selected for the Olympic team at tryouts were compared to the athletes who were not chosen (Mahoney & Avener, 1977). These types of studies have shown that successful athletes tend to dream of success in their events, use internal imagery, and use imagery to problem solve more than their less successful counterparts (Murphy, 1994). This type of study, however, provides only weak support for the benefits of imagery due to the correlational nature of the design. These studies provide no evidence that the use of imagery reported by more successful athletes caused their success, and they give little indication of how imagery might be related to their success. Further experimental research is needed on what role, if any, imagery plays in developing successful athletes.

Mediating Factors in Imagery Effectiveness. Many of factors may contribute to the effectiveness of an imagery intervention. Specific considerations that have been studied by sport psychologists are (1) imagery ability, (2) imagery perspective, (3) image outcome, and (4) the use of relaxation (Murphy & Jowdy, 1992).

Imagery ability is composed of two components: the clarity and realism of the image, referred to as vividness, and the ability of the imager to control the content and action of the imagery, referred to as controllability. Several studies have found that more successful athletes were better at imagery (i.e., had higher levels of vividness and controllability; Highlen & Bennett, 1983; Meyers et al., 1979). These results suggest that imagery ability may be an important factor in imagery interventions; however, these studies are correlational in nature, and causation cannot be inferred. Further research is needed on the effect of imagery ability on intervention effectiveness and on how imagery skills can be enhanced.

Imagery perspective refers to the point of view of the imagery. Imagery from an external perspective is like watching a movie. You see the events and yourself performing as if you were an external observer. Imagery from an internal perspective is perceiving the image from inside your own body. You are the eye behind the camera, and you see and feel everything from the perspective of the actual performer. Research examining the effects of different imagery perspectives has not shown a conclusive advantage of one perspective over the other (Gould & Damarjian, 1995; Murphy & Jowdy, 1992; Hardy, 1997; Hardy & Callow, 1999). It is possible that the different perspectives operate through different mechanisms, and these mechanisms may have different effects. Internal imagery may be more beneficial for movement and technique, and external imagery may be better for problem solving and building confidence (Gould & Damarjian, 1995; Murphy & Jowdy, 1992), though currently this is speculative and there is no evidence to support this differential effect.

The **outcome of the image** is an interesting variable that has received little investigation. Because imagery interventions are usually focused on enhancing performance, the images used are typically of success-related activities. This makes intuitive sense and has support from research because studies using imagery of a negative outcome have consistently shown a detrimental effect on performance (Powell, 1973; Woolfolk, Parrish, & Murphy, 1985). This is a particularly important finding when combined with the controllability research described earlier. An athlete with poor imagery control may not be able to maintain a success-oriented image, and if the image transforms into failure, it could have a strong negative effect on performance. This reemphasizes the need for skill in controlling images and for research on teaching controllability.

The majority of imagery-based interventions advocate relaxation as an integral component of the use of imagery. A review of the research findings, however, shows little support for relaxation adding to the effectiveness of imagery (Murphy, 1994; Murphy & Jowdy, 1992). This suggests that relaxation may have benefits to athletic performance (see the previous section on Arousal and Sport Performance), but it may not be a critical mediating variable for the effect of imagery on performance. Relaxation is often advocated by practitioners as a means of reducing distractions and creating a conducive atmosphere for quality imagery, but this belief has received little research support.

Effectiveness of Imagery to Prepare for Competition. Imagery is often used by athletes prior to a competition to psych themselves up or to become appropriately focused for a competition. This often involves imagining successful completion of the task (e.g., a flawless downhill skiing run, a successful first serve in tennis) immediately before the performance. Unfortunately, the research concerning this strategy has been equivocal (Murphy, 1994; Murphy & Jowdy, 1992). This should not be interpreted to mean that imagery as a preperformance strategy does not work. The studies investigating preperformance imagery, however, have serious shortcomings, and most have not taken into account the mediating variables discussed previously. The consistent use of this technique by athletes, particularly successful athletes, suggests that it is effective. More sophisticated research that recognizes the mediating effects of imagery ability, differing task demands, and individual differences is needed to further our understanding of how and why imagery is useful as a preperformance strategy.

Effectiveness of Mental Practice. Imagery is often used as an aid to learning and subsequently performing a skill. This is distinguished from the precompetition use of imagery, because mental practice is used to learn and perfect the skill. This type of mental rehearsal has been extensively researched, and overall there is a positive effect for participating in mental practice (Feltz & Landers, 1983; Weinberg, 1981). The research suggests that mental practice is better than no practice at all, but mental practice is not as good as actual practice. A combination of actual practice and mental practice will probably have the most beneficial effects (Murphy, 1994).

These reviews of the research literature provide some support for the efficacy of imagery as an intervention technique, highlight the important variables that need to be considered, and give guidance for designing effective imagery programs.

Implications for Intervention

Theory development about imagery and performance enhancement is still in a relatively formative stage. What is known from theory and research combined with the rich clinical lore in the use of imagery suggests several factors that can enhance the use of imagery (Gould & Damarjian, 1995; Murphy & Jowdy, 1992; Orlick, 1986, 1990; Sheikh & Korn, 1994; Weinberg & Gould, 1995).

One consistent recommendation is that imagery is a skill, and like any other skill needs to be practiced and refined. Exercises for controlling images and increasing their vividness have been developed by several practitioners (Korn, 1994; Martens, 1987; Sheikh, Sheikh, & Moleski, 1994; Weinberg & Gould, 1995). As mentioned at the beginning of this section, images should include as many relevant senses as possible because this likely improves the vividness of the images. Images should also be constructed from both internal and external perspectives, because they may each have unique beneficial effects on performance. Other recommendations that have less theoretical or research support yet are often advocated by practitioners are to imagine in real time, to use imagery logs to chart performance, to use audio and/or videotapes as reinforcers or imagery stimuli, to use cues or triggers to create and remember specific images, and to use relaxation to facilitate imagery (Gould & Damarjian, 1994).

Another recommendation is to use images not only to learn specific sport skills but also to learn coping skills (Murphy, 1996; Orlick, 1980). Using imagery to learn or enhance the performance of sport skills is often termed **mastery imagery,** because it is used to master a particular skill or movement. **Coping imagery** is used to develop coping skills or to problem solve for particular situations or events. Imagining executing the proper technique and movement of a free throw is an example of mastery imagery. Imagining a free throw at the end of a tied game while successfully dealing with the crowd noise, pressure from the coach, tired legs, heavy breathing, and maintaining concentration and technique is an example of coping imagery. Coping imagery can be especially useful for dealing with conditions that you cannot duplicate in practice, such as bad weather, unfamiliar environments, or unexpected setbacks. You can practice coming from behind in your imagination many times before actually being behind in reality.

Imagery is perhaps one of the most flexible psychological skills an athlete can possess. It has been used for skill acquisition, skill maintenance, examining performance problems, arousal regulation, confidence building, injury rehabilitation, and pain management (Gould & Damarjian, 1994; Sheikh & Korn, 1994). It has been recommended for use during practice, prior to competition, during competition, and after competition (Janssen & Sheikh, 1994). In fact, it is hard to think of a psychological or sport skill for which it has not been used, and it can be regarded as an essential psychological skill for successful athletes.

Info Box

Imagery ability is a psychological skill that must be rehearsed to be most effective. An athlete may favor an imagery perspective; however, it may be most effective to develop both an internal and an external view. Similarly, coping imagery and mastery imagery both have unique applications that must be practiced. In general, imagery can be effective in reducing arousal, focusing attention, and even perfecting a technique.

Cognitive Interventions

Although interventions such as goal setting, imagery, and arousal control probably can be classified as cognitive in nature, there are specific interventions used by sport psychologists that directly relate to how athletes think. Research has shown that elite athletes use different cognitive strategies and may think differently than their nonelite counterparts (Gould, Eklund, & Jackson, 1992a, 1992b; Gould, Finch, & Jackson, 1993; Gould, Weiss, & Weinberg, 1981; Highlen & Bennett, 1979; Williams & Krane, 1993). Successful athletes tend to have fewer negative thoughts, fewer self-doubts, more task-related thoughts, more positive expectancies, and a more positive focus. These findings suggest that helping athletes to think in a more positive, task-oriented manner would be beneficial to their performance. Sport psychologists have adapted the techniques of cognitive interventions from the fields of counseling and clinical psychology to help athletes enhance their performance. This section reviews the theory underlying these applications and discusses designing effective performance enhancement programs based on cognitive interventions.

Theoretical Bases of Cognitive Interventions

Many of the cognitive techniques used by sport psychologists have been adapted from the field of cognitive therapy (Silva, 1982). Cognitive therapy has several different schools of thought and specific interventions (e.g., Beck, 1976; Ellis & Harper, 1975; Meichenbaum,

Thoughts predispose behaviors. Think quick!

1977), but the underlying principles are closely related (Dobson & Block, 1988). Cognitive interventions are based on three basic assumptions. The first assumption is that individuals have belief systems, sometimes called cognitive schemas, and also have particular styles of information processing. These cognitive structures and processes determine how individuals interpret their environment and circumstances. It is this interpretation, not the actual events, that determines how people feel and behave in particular situations. The second assumption of cognitive techniques is that these schemas and information processing styles can be examined and altered if necessary. The third assumption is that changes in cognitive schemas and styles of information processing will result in emotional and/or behavioral changes. Interventions based on cognitive techniques typically involve a process of discovery and exploration of current patterns of thinking, followed by a restructuring of thoughts to facilitate the desired emotional or behavioral change. Although cognitive techniques were initially formulated to help individuals overcome psychological difficulties (Freeman et al., 1990), they are readily adaptable to athletes' performance-related concerns.

For example, a gifted tennis player exerts full effort against only equal or superior players. When facing lesser opponents, this player relies on greater skill and talent. This player competes well against superior opponents but often plays poorly when facing opponents that should be easily defeated. This player frequently loses these "easy" matches and does not understand why. This player's belief system ("I should be able to rely on my talent to defeat lesser opponents and shouldn't have to try very hard") directly affects performance in these matches and ultimately affects the outcome. A cognitive-based intervention would help this player examine the underlying belief system and its relationship to subsequent behavior and performance. Then it would help the player develop new beliefs to maintain consistent effort and performance.

Cognitive therapy theorists and practitioners have identified common distortions of thinking that contribute to psychological distress (Beck, 1976; Burns, 1980). These distortions become more prevalent when an individual is under stress and can cause self-defeating assumptions, incorrect interpretations of situations, harsh self-judgments, and inadequate coping strategies (Weishaar & Beck, 1983). Many sporting situations are stressful, and these cognitive distortions are often prevalent in the minds of athletes and can lead to decreases in performance (Gauron, 1984). Ten common categories of distortions have been identified by Burns and are listed below. Note that a particular distortion may have characteristics of several categories and that the examples may fall into more than one category.

1. All-or-nothing-thinking—tending to look at things in black-or-white, win-or-lose categories. If performances are not perfect, they are viewed as a total failures. "If I don't win the championship, I am a failure as an athlete and a failure as a human being."
2. Overgeneralization—a single negative event is viewed as a certain, never-ending pattern of defeat. This often creates a self-fulfilling prophecy. "I missed another backhand. I haven't hit a backhand all day. My backhand is worthless."
3. Mental filter—a tendency to notice and focus on the negatives and lose sight of the positives. It is very difficult to accept positive feedback with this type of thinking. Coach: "You looked good out there today; keep up the good work!" Athlete: "I am still messing up my crossover dribble, so I wasn't very good in practice today."
4. Discounting the positive—insisting that your positive qualities do not count and that your negative qualities are more important. Continually focusing on the negative can

undermine confidence and self-esteem. "I may have a good first serve, but that doesn't matter when my ground strokes are so poor."

5. Jumping to conclusions—making a negative interpretation even though there are no facts to support this judgment. It is difficult to maintain optimism and motivation with this type of thinking. There are two types of this distortion: (a) Mind reading—assuming people are reacting negatively when there is no evidence of this. "My teammates probably think I'm no good because I missed that last shot." (b) Fortune telling—arbitrarily predicting that things will turn out badly in the future. "I missed that opening, and I probably won't get another chance and will lose the game!"

6. Magnification or minimization—blowing things out of proportion, usually your mistakes or your opponents strengths, and shrinking the importance of other things, usually your strengths or your opponents weaknesses. It is difficult to realistically evaluate your strengths and weaknesses and determine appropriate strategies when thinking this way. "Wow! What amazing form that guy has. I'll never be able to compete against him." or "It's not that important that my jump shot is good; the rest of my game is so terrible."

7. Emotional reasoning—reasoning from your feelings about something. Sports performances can generate many strong feelings, but these feelings may not be an accurate reflection of your abilities. "I feel lousy for losing that match, so I must really be lousy."

8. Should statements—criticizing or motivating yourself by telling yourself you "should," "ought," or "must" do something or be a certain way. Failing to obey these statements results in guilt, shame, or anger at yourself. "I must win this match, or I am no good."

9. Labeling—identifying yourself with shortcomings. Rather than examining your behavior, you label yourself with a characteristic. "I screwed up, so I'm a screw-up." "I lost that close match, so I must be a choker."

10. Personalization and blame—taking all the responsibility for an outcome or event that clearly was not entirely your responsibility. This can create high levels of anxiety and decreased motivation over time. "If I had made that last putt, out team would have won. It's all my fault we lost."

The result of these distortions is a pattern of dysfunctional thinking and an unrealistic, negative appraisal of capabilities and situation, which can lead to ineffective behavior and poor performances. The goal of cognitive interventions is to more realistically and effectively appraise the individual and the situation, which will lead to more effective behavioral responses.

Many techniques can be classified as cognitive interventions, including imagery, thought stopping, positive affirmations, cognitive restructuring, hypnosis, and self-talk. These techniques assume underlying inappropriate or ineffective thought processes and attempt to give these processes a more positive and realistic orientation. Imagery has already been discussed, and hypnosis is a widely known intervention, but the others may require brief descriptions. **Thought stopping** is a technique used to interrupt the process of dysfunctional thinking that results from one or several of the cognitive distortions. The first step in thought stopping is to identify a person's common cognitive distortions. With these cognitive distortions identified, whenever the individual recognizes that his or her thinking has become distorted, he or she stops the train of thought. Common methods of stopping the pattern of dysfunctional thinking are wearing a rubber band on the wrist and snapping it, or imagining a bright red stop sign. These methods allow the individual to stop and re-assess the situation in a more realistic manner. Simply stopping the train of thought may be enough to bring about a positive change, but often thought stopping is used in conjunction with some other type of cognitive intervention. Thought stopping can be followed by pos-itive affirmations, which are self-statements that contradict the typical negative thinking of cognitive distortions. Such phrases as "I am confident," "I am talented," or "I will succeed" may serve to diffuse the effect of negative thinking. Another technique for addressing cog-nitive distortions is **cognitive restructuring,** which is a more sophisticated approach that first uncovers the beliefs an individual holds about himself or herself and then attempts to change these beliefs through the gathering of evidence or logical reasoning. These tech-niques are common in the field of counseling and psychology but have received little re-search attention in the sport psychology literature.

One approach that has been receiving attention in sport psychology research and prac-tice is the use of **self-talk.** Self-talk is the voice or internal dialogue that takes place in the mind of an individual. The examples cited in the listing of cognitive distortions are descriptions of self-talk that can be disrupting to performance. In line with the assumptions of cognitive inter-ventions, examining the self-talk of individuals is a way to assess their belief systems, and changing patterns of self-talk is a way to alter dysfunctional belief systems. For this reason, self-talk has been examined by sport psychologists as a way to understand what makes elite athletes successful and as a technique to bring about improvements in performance.

Sport psychologists have compared successful with less successful athletes on their use of self-talk and generally have found that successful athletes use more self-talk of vary-ing types (content-based, positive, and negative) than less successful athletes (Gould, Ek-lund, & Jackson, 1992a, 1992b; Highlen & Bennett, 1983; Orlick & Partington, 1988), though some researchers have found no difference in self-talk between successful and less successful athletes (Rotella et al., 1980) or between best and worst performances (Dagrou, Gauvin, & Halliwell, 1991). A review of experimental research examining the effects of self-talk has shown that positive self-talk is related to better performances or sometimes to no improvement in performance, but negative self-talk is related to worse performances (Van Raalte et al., 1994). The results of these experimental studies suggest that if athletes alter their patterns of self-talk from negative to positive, they may experience an increase in performance. From the theory of cognitive interventions just described, this change in performance is probably due to a change in the athletes' belief systems from a self-defeat-ing orientation to a more self-affirming and task-focused orientation.

Analyzing self-talk can not only be diagnostic of underlying irrational thoughts and cognitive distortions but can also serve as a guide to effective interventions. Cognitive techniques are popular ways to address these performance-related psychological character-istics, but the question remains, "Do they work?" The next section discusses research on the effectiveness of cognitive interventions.

Effectiveness of Cognitive Techniques

Cognitive techniques have received a great deal of positive support in the psychological lit-erature as a therapeutic technique (Beck, 1991), and evidence is beginning to mount in the sport psychology literature as well. One review of performance enhancement studies examined twenty-three different interventions, including cognitive techniques. In general, it showed support of improvements in performance for the cognitive-based interventions (Greenspan & Feltz, 1989). A more recent extension of this review showed that the majority of studies examining cognitive and cognitive–behavioral interventions demonstrated performance improvements for these techniques (Vealey, 1994). Although there are criticisms of the studies evaluating these intervention programs, such as lack of appropriate control groups, poor manipulation checks, and few measures of the long-term effectiveness of these interventions, the overwhelming support from the counseling and therapy literature and the growing support from the performance enhancement literature suggest that these techniques provide useful and practical guidelines for helping athletes improve their performances.

Implications for Intervention

Theory and research suggest that changing distorted, negative, and self-defeating cognitions to more realistic, positive, and self-affirming ones will probably bring about an improvement in performance. This change can be facilitated by careful examination of the belief systems and styles of information processing in athletes. A few simple questions can help determine the rationality or effectiveness of particular beliefs (Steinmetz et al., 1980): (1) Are the beliefs based on objective reality? (2) Are they helpful to you? (3) Are they useful in reducing interpersonal conflict? (4) Do they help you reach your goals? (5) Do they reduce emotional conflict? If the answer to any of these questions is "no," the belief is probably not effective or rational, and emotions and behavior can probably be improved by examining and modifying this belief.

Distortions in thinking can be examined by identifying the type of distortion outlined in the previous section. When discovered, these distortions can be replaced with more facilitative, realistic appraisals of the situation. It should be emphasized that cognitive schemas and styles of information processing are probably firmly entrenched in the minds of athletes, and changing them requires great effort, energy, and focused attention. Like physical skills learned by exceptional athletes, learning to think in a positive and productive manner requires practice, patience, and a commitment to excellence. Cognitive techniques can help athletes learn these skills, and research shows that they can contribute to greater performance.

Info Box

Our behaviors are physical manifestations of our thoughts. Our thoughts are psychological manifestations of our beliefs. Consequently, to change athletes' behaviors, cognitive restructuring must occur. However, this may be difficult if the athlete does not believe in the thoughts he or she has restructured. A challenge to every sport psychologist is to help the athlete to believe in the intervention.

Preparation for Competition

The interventions discussed in this chapter are the tools that sport psychologists typically use to help enhance an athlete's performance. However, they should not be viewed as independent and separate options for performance enhancement and are often used in combination to bring about performance change. In fact, there are intervention packages that combine several components into an integrated system (e.g., visuo-motor behavior rehearsal [VMBR; Suinn, 1972, 1977], imageletics [Cautela & Samdperil, 1989]). One creative combination of interventions is the **preperformance routine.** Preperformance routines are sets of carefully planned, well thought out, and practiced activities that are used prior to a performance to help an athlete prepare effectively. These routines have a number of distinct positive effects (Taylor, 1995). Routines can enhance an athlete's comfort level with the performance situation. Through previous practice with the routine, the athlete has become familiar with and accustomed to the preparation for the activity. Routines also allow the athlete to have greater control over activities prior to performance, which can decrease the likelihood of distractions. By rigorously using routines as part of practice, athletes can develop consistency of thought, feeling, and behavior prior to performing.

Some sport psychologists advocate planning the entire day of a competition as part of the competitive plan (Orlick, 1986; Taylor, 1995), with flexibility for free time and changes if necessary. The extent of these plans varies with the specific needs of the activity and the personality of the athlete. As the time for competition approaches, these plans progress from inspecting and readying equipment, to physical warm-ups, to becoming mentally prepared for performance. The mental preparation phase of the routine is when the interventions discussed in this chapter play the most prominent role. The specific content of these mental preparation routines varies greatly according to the individual demands of the sport and the personal preferences and needs of the athlete. They may contain psyching-up strategies and energetic imagery if the player and the sport require high levels of activation, or they may contain relaxation and calm, focusing imagery if that is more appropriate to the situation. In general, the routines are designed to focus an athlete on the essentials of the performance, not the outcome, which parallels the performance–outcome dimension of effective goal setting. Routines are typically a combination of arousal adjusting techniques (relaxation or psyching-up strategies), success- and mastery-oriented imagery, and self-talk designed to maintain proper focus, increase confidence, and reach or maintain an optimum psychological set (see Fig. 10.2 for an example).

Research has shown preperformance routines to be effective for improving performance in golf (Cohn, Rotella, & Lloyd, 1990) and in football (Ravizza & Osborne, 1991), and they are applicable to most sporting situations (Orlick, 1986). As research into the combined effects of various intervention strategies during the preperformance period continues, sport psychologists will be able to more effectively tailor these interventions to the needs of the individual athlete and to the demands of particular sporting situations.

Conclusion

This chapter examined the pillars of most sport psychology interventions—goal setting, arousal regulation, imagery, and cognitive–behavioral techniques. Research support for each of these interventions is growing, and as the research becomes more sophisticated, our understanding of the many mediating factors affecting the efficacy of these interventions will improve. The theoretical understanding and knowledge from professional practice provide guidelines for the effective use of each of these interventions. Athletes

FIGURE 10.2 *Outline of a Preperformance Routine for a Tennis Player with a Match the Next Afternoon.*

This routine is designed to help alter the athlete's focus from general preparation for the next afternoon's tennis match to specific readiness immediately before the first serve. The details of the goals, self-talk, and imagery to be used will have been carefully prepared in advance. If written out in detail, a comprehensive plan that includes the specifics of physical warm-up, arousal control, goal review, imagery, and self-talk would cover several pages.

Night Before
- Eat a nutritious meal.
- Make any necessary checks of equipment and scheduling for the next day.
- Socialize with teammates.
- Go to bed early.

Morning
- Eat a light breakfast.
- Light stretching and jogging to loosen up.
- Practice with teammates. Focus on general warm-up and acclimating to the playing conditions and environment.
- Mentally review goals for the match.
- Spend time using previously prepared positive imagery.
- Listen to relaxing music through headphones.

Prior to Match
- Specific physical warm-up for match.
- Last-minute tactical review.
- Use positive thoughts and self-talk to maintain confidence and focus.
- Review specific goals—focus on process goals.
- Mentally assess arousal level and adjust if necessary (relax or psych up).
- Use previously designed imagery to prepare for the first serve.

probably set goals, regulate their arousal, imagine themselves in competition, and think about themselves in various ways prior to any consultation with a sport psychologist. Sport psychologists use their knowledge about sport and athletes to help participants set effective goals, regulate arousal appropriately, use imagery wisely, and think productively. Excelling at sports, or any activity, requires paying attention to all aspects of the task, and sport psychologists have developed the effective tools covered in this chapter to help athletes enhance the psychological skills needed for successful sport performance.

Key Terms (in order of appearance)

goal setting	cognitive explanation	meta-analysis
goal	of goal setting	imagery
motivational explanation	outcome goal	psychoneuromuscular theory
of goal setting	performance goal	symbolic learning theory

information processing theory
triple-code theory
imagery ability
imagery perspective

outcome of the image
mastery imagery
coping imagery
thought stopping

cognitive restructuring
self-talk
preperformance routine

References

Ahsen, A. (1984). ISM: The triple code model for imagery and psychophysiology. *Journal of Mental Imagery, 8,* 15–42.

Beck, A. T. (1976). *Cognitive therapy and the emotional disorders.* New York: International Universities Press.

Beck, A. T. (1991). Cognitive therapy: A 30-year retrospective. *American Psychologist, 46,* 368–375.

Bird, E. I. (1984). EMG quantification of mental practice. *Perceptual and Motor Skills, 59,* 899–906.

Burns, D. D. (1980). *Feeling good: The new mood therapy.* New York: Morrow.

Burton, D. (1989). Winning isn't everything: Examining the impact of performance goals on collegiate swimmers' cognitions and performance. *The Sport Psychologist, 3,* 105–132.

Burton, D. (1992). The Jekyll/Hyde nature of goals: Reconceptualizing goal setting in sport. In T. Horn (Ed.), *Advances in sport psychology* (pp. 267–297). Champaign, IL: Human Kinetics.

Caudill, D., Weinberg, R., & Jackson, A. (1983) Psyching-up and track athletes. A preliminary investigation. *Journal of Sport Psychology, 5,* 231–235.

Cautela, J. R., & Samdperil, L. (1989). Imageletics: The application of covert conditioning to athletic performance. *Journal of Applied Sport Psychology, 1,* 82–97.

Cohn, P. J., Rotella, R. J., & Lloyd, J. W. (1990). Effects of a cognitive behavioral intervention on the pre-shot routine and performance in golf. *The Sport Psychologist, 4,* 33–47.

Crews, D. (1993). Self-regulation strategies in sport and exercise. In R. Singer, M. Murphy, & L. Tennant (Eds.), *Handbook on research in sport psychology* (pp. 557–567). New York: MacMillan.

Crews, D., & Boutcher, S. (1987). The effects of structured preshot behaviors on beginning golf performance. *Perceptual and Motor Skills, 9,* 51–58.

Dagrou, E., Gauvin, L., & Halliwell, W. (1991). La préparation mentale des athlètes invoiriens: Pratiques courantes et perspectives de recherche [Mental preparation of Ivory Coast athletes: Current practice and research perspectives]. *International Journal of Sport Psychology, 22,* 15–34.

Dobson, K. S., & Block, L. (1988). Historical and philosophical bases of the cognitive–behavioral therapies. In K. S. Dobson (Ed.), *Handbook of cognitive behavioral therapies* (pp. 3–34). New York: Guilford.

Ellis, A. E., & Harper, R. A. (1975). *A new guide to rational living.* Englewood Cliffs, NJ: Prentice Hall.

Feltz, D. L., & Landers, D. M. (1983). The effects of mental practice on motor skill learning and performance: A meta-analysis. *Journal of Sport Psychology, 5,* 25–57.

Fitts, D. M. (1962). Skill training. In R. Glaser (Ed.), *Training research and education* (pp. 177–199). Pittsburgh: Univ. of Pittsburgh Press.

Freeman, A. M., Pretzer, J. L., Fleming, B., & Simon, K. M. (1990). *Clinical applications of cognitive therapy.* New York: Plenum.

Gauron, E. F. (1984). *Mental training for peak performance.* Lansing, NY: Sport Science Associates.

Gould, D., & Damarjian, N. (1995), Imagery training for peak performance. In J. Van Raalte & B. Brewer (Eds.), *Exploring sport and exercise psychology* (pp. 25–50). Washington, DC: American Psychological Association.

Gould, D., Eklund, R. C., & Jackson, S. A. (1992a). 1988 U.S. Olympic wrestling excellence: I. Mental preparation, precompetitive cognition, and affect. *The Sport Psychologist, 6,* 358–382.

Gould, D., Eklund, R. C., & Jackson, S. A. (1992b). 1988 U.S. Olympic wrestling excellence: II. Thoughts and affect occurring during competition. *The Sport Psychologist, 6,* 383–402.

Gould, D., Finch, L. M., & Jackson, S. A. (1993). Coping strategies used by national champion figure skaters. *Research Quarterly for Exercise and Sport, 64,* 453–468.

Gould, D., & Krane, V. (1992). The arousal–athletic performance relationship: Current status and future directions. In T. Horn (Ed.), *Advances in sport psychology* (pp. 119–142). Champaign, IL: Human Kinetics.

Gould, D., & Udry, E. (1994). Psychological skills for enhancing performance: Arousal regulation strategies. *Medicine and Science in Sports and Exercise, 26,* 478–485.

Gould, D., Weiss, M., & Weinberg, R. (1981). Psychological characteristics of successful and nonsuccessful Big Ten Wrestlers. *Journal of Sport Psychology, 3,* 69–81.

Greenspan, M. J., & Feltz, D. L. (1989). Psychological interventions with athletes in competitive situations: A review. *The Sport Psychologist, 3,* 219–236.

Hardy, C. H., Richman, J. M., & Rosenfeld, L. B. (1991). The role of social support in the life stress/injury relationship. *The Sport Psychologist, 5,* 128–139.

Hardy, L. (1997). The Coleman Roberts Griffith address: Three myths about applied consultancy work. *Journal of Applied Sport Psychology, 9,* 277–294.

Hardy, L., & Callow, N. (1999). Efficacy of external and internal visual imagery perspectives for the enhancement of performance on tasks in which form is important. *Journal of Sport and Exercise Psychology, 21,* 95–112.

Harris, D. V., & Harris, B. L. (1984). *The athlete's guide to sports psychology: Mental skills for physical people.* Champaign, IL: Human Kinetics.

Hecker, J. E., & Kaczor, L. M. (1988). Application of imagery theory to sport psychology: Some preliminary findings. *Journal of Sport Psychology, 8,* 105–111.

Highlen, P. S., & Bennett, B. B. (1979). Psychological characteristics of successful and nonsuccessful elite wrestlers: An exploratory study. *Journal of Sport Psychology, 1,* 123–137.

Highlen, P. S., & Bennett, B. B. (1983). Elite divers and wrestlers: A comparison between open- and closed-skill athletes. *Journal of Sport Psychology, 5,* 390–409.

Jacobson, E. (1938). *Progressive relaxation,* 2nd ed. Chicago: University of Chicago Press.

Janssen, J. J., & Sheikh, A. A. (1994). Enhancing athletic performance through imagery: An overview. In A. Sheikh & E. Korn (Eds.), *Imagery in sports and physical performance* (pp. 1–22). Amityville, NY: Baywood.

Korn, E. R. (1994). Mental imagery in enhancing performance: Theory and practical exercises. In A. Sheikh & E. Korn (Eds.), *Imagery in sports and physical performance* (pp. 201–230). Amityville, NY: Baywood.

Kyllo, L. B., & Landers, D. M. (1995). Goal setting in sport and exercise: A research synthesis to resolve the controversy. *Journal of Sport & Exercise Psychology, 17,* 117–137.

Lang, P. J. (1977). Imagery in therapy: An information-processing analysis of fear. *Behavior Therapy, 8,* 862–886.

Lang, P. J. (1979). A bio-informational theory of emotional imagery. *Psychophysiology, 17,* 495–512.

Locke, E. A. (1991). Problems with goal-setting research in sports—and their solutions. *Journal of Sport & Exercise Psychology, 13,* 311–316.

Locke, E. A. (1994). Comments on Weinberg and Weigand. *Journal of Sport & Exercise Psychology, 16,* 212–215.

Locke, E. A., & Latham, G. P. (1985). The application of goal setting to sports. *Journal of Sport Psychology, 7,* 205–222.

Locke, E. A., & Latham, G. P. (1990). *A theory of goal setting and task performance.* Englewood Cliffs, NJ: Prentice Hall.

Locke, E. A., Shaw, K. N., Saari, L. M., & Latham, G. P. (1981). Goals setting and task performance. *Psychological Bulletin, 90,* 125–152.

Mahoney, M. J., & Avener, M. (1977). Psychology of the elite athlete: An exploratory study. *Cognitive Therapy and Research, 1,* 135–141.

Martens, R. (1987). *Coaches guide to sport psychology.* Champaign, IL: Human Kinetics.

Meichenbaum, D. (1977). *Cognitive–behavior modification.* New York: Plenum.

Meichenbaum, D. (1985). *Stress inoculation training.* New York: Pergamon.

Meyers, A. W., Cooke, C. J., Cullen, J., & Liles, L. (1979). Psychological aspects of athletic competitors: A replication across sports. *Cognitive Therapy and Research, 3,* 361–366.

Minas, S. C. (1980). Mental practice of a complex perceptual-motor skill. *Journal of Human Studies, 4,* 102–107.

Murphy, S. (1996). *The achievement zone.* New York: Putnam.

Murphy, S. M. (1994). Imagery interventions in sport. *Medicine and Science in Sports and Exercise, 26,* 486–494.

Murphy, S. M., & Jowdy, D. P. (1992). Imagery and mental practice. In T. Horn (Ed.), *Advances in sport psychology* (pp. 221–250). Champaign, IL: Human Kinetics.

O'Block, F. R., & Evans, F. H. (1984). Goal-setting as a motivational technique. In J. M. Silva III & R. S. Weinberg (Eds.), *Psychological foundations of sport* (pp. 188–196). Champaign, IL: Human Kinetics.

Orlick, T. (1980). *In pursuit of excellence.* Champaign, IL: Human Kinetics.

Orlick, T. (1986). *Psyching for sport: Mental training for athletes.* Champaign IL: Leisure.

Orlick, T. (1990). *In pursuit of excellence: How to win in sport and life through mental training.* Champaign IL: Leisure.

Orlick, T., & Partington, J. (1988). Mental links to excellence. *The Sport Psychologist, 2,* 105–130.

Petruzzello, S. J., Landers, D. M., & Salazar, W. (1991). Biofeedback and sport/exercise performance: Applications and limitations. *Behavior Therapy, 22,* 379–392.

Powell, G. E. (1973). Negative and positive mental practice in motor skill acquisition. *Perceptual and Motor Skills, 37,* 312.

Ravizza, K., & Osborne, T. (1991). Nebraska's 3 R's: One-play-at-a-time preperformance routine for collegiate football. *The Sport Psychologist, 5,* 256–265.

Rotella, R. J., Gansneder, B., Ojala, D., & Billing, J. (1980). Cognitions and coping strategies of elite skiers: An exploratory study of young developing athletes. *Journal of Sport Psychology, 2,* 350–354.

Sheikh, A. A., & Korn, E. R. (Eds.). (1994). *Imagery in sports and physical performance.* Amityville, NY: Baywood.

Sheikh, A. A., Sheikh, K. S., & Moleski, L. M. (1994). Improving imaging abilities. In A. Sheikh & E. Korn (Eds.), *Imagery in sports and physical performance* (pp. 231–248). Amityville, NY: Baywood.

Silva, J. M., III. (1982). Competitive sport environments: Performance enhancement through cognitive intervention. *Behavior Modification, 6,* 443–463.

Smith, R. (1980). A cognitive–affective approach to stress management training for athletes. In C. Nadeau, W. Halliwell, R. Newell, & G. Roberts (Eds.), *Psychology of motor behavior and sport.* Champaign, IL: Human Kinetics.

Steinmetz, J., Blankenship, J., Brown, L., Hall, D., & Miller, G. (1980). *Managing stress before it manages you.* Palo Alto, CA: Bull.

Suinn, R. M. (1972). Behavioral rehearsal training for ski racers. *Behavior Therapy, 3,* 519–520.

Suinn, R. M. (1977). Behavioral methods at the Winter Olympic Games. *Behavior Therapy, 8,* 283–284.

Suinn, R. M. (1980). Psychology and sports performance: Principles and applications. In R. Suinn (Ed.), *Psychology in sports: Methods and applications* (pp. 26–36). Minneapolis: Burgess.

Suinn, R. M. (1983). Imagery and sports. In A. A. Sheikh (Ed.), *Imagery: Current theory, research, and application* (pp. 507–534). New York: Wiley.

Suinn, R. M. (1994). Visualization in sports. In A. Sheikh & E. Korn (Eds.), *Imagery in sports and physical performance* (pp. 23–42). Amityville, NY: Baywood.

Taylor, J. (1995). Intensity regulation and athletic performance. In J. L. Van Raalte & B. W. Brewer (Eds.), *Exploring sport and exercise psychology* (pp. 75–106). Washington, DC: American Psychological Association.

Van Raalte, J. L., Brewer, B. W., Rivera, P. M., & Petitpas, A. J. (1994). The relationship between observable self-talk and competitive junior tennis players' match performance. *Journal of Sport and Exercise Psychology, 16,* 400–415.

Vealey, R. S. (1994). Current status and prominent issues in sport psychology interventions. *Medicine and Science in Sports and Exercise, 26,* 495–502.

Weinberg, R. S. (1981). The relationship between mental preparation strategies and motor performance: A review and critique. *Quest, 33,* 195–213.

Weinberg, R. S. (1994). Goal setting and performance in sport and exercise settings: A synthesis and critique. *Medicine and Science in Sport and Exercise, 26,* 469–477.

Weinberg, R. S. (1995). Goal setting in sport and exercise: Research to practice. In J. L. Van Raalte & B. W. Brewer (Eds.), *Exploring sport and exercise psychology* (pp. 3–24). Washington, DC: American Psychological Association.

Weinberg, R. S., & Gould, D. (1995). *Foundations of sport and exercise psychology.* Champaign, IL: Human Kinetics.

Weinberg, R., & Weigand, D. (1993). Goal setting in sport and exercise: A reaction to Locke. *Journal of Sport and Exercise Psychology, 15,* 88–96.

Weishaar, M. E., & Beck, A. T. (1983). Cognitive therapy. In W. Dryden & W. L. Golden (Eds.), *Cognitive–behavioral approaches to psychotherapy* (pp. 61–91). Cambridge, England: Hemisphere.

Williams, J. M., & Krane, V. (1993). Psychological characteristics of peak performance. In J. M. Williams (Ed.), *Applied sport psychology: Personal growth to peak performance* (pp. 137–147). Mountain View, CA: Mayfield.

Woolfolk, R., Parrish, W., & Murphy, S. M. (1985). The effects of positive and negative imagery on motor skill performance. *Cognitive Therapy and Research, 9,* 335–341.

Wrisberg, C. A., & Ragsdale, M. R. (1979). Cognitive demand and practice level: Factors in the mental practice of motor skills. *Journal of Human Movement Studies, 5,* 201–208.

Zaichkowski, L., & Fuchs, C. (1988). Biofeedback applications in exercise and athletic performance. *Exercise and Sport Sciences Review, 16,* 381–421.

11

Psychological Interventions for the Injured Athlete

Allen Cornelius

Springfield College

- Psychological and environmental precursors of sport injury exist. Certain personality factors, level of life stress, and the stress response of an athlete can help to predict injury.
- Psychological reactions to injury are explained from three theoretical models: Kubler-Ross's Grief Model, the Affective Cycle model, and the cognitive appraisal models.
- Several considerations must be made when planning the intervention for an injured athlete, including the strength of the athletic identity, the nature of the injury, coping skills of athletes, the existence of secondary gain, social support, and situational factors.
- Versatile psychological interventions such as goal setting, imagery training, cognitive restructuring, and relaxation are employed when consulting injured athletes; however, knowing the injury and rehabilitation process, managing pain, and establishing social support are also important.

Sport Injury Interventions

> *Life is Absurd. Just when I begin to put it all together, I pull this muscle. I'm so depressed. Why me? Why now? I'll never be able to get to this place again. I'm so afraid I'll never fully recover. Is there any doctor who can help me get going? The stress is unbearable, to say nothing of the physical pain itself. It's just not fair. I feel like dying. A terrible loss (Lynch, 1988, p. 161).*

An elite marathon runner spoke these disheartening words following a severe groin injury two weeks before the 1984 Olympic Trials. The words graphically describe the psy-

Being able to perform at a high level after injury is an emotional and psychological challenge.

chological trauma that often accompanies a physical injury. Severe psychological reactions as identified in the quotation above, such as depression, fear, hopelessness, and anxiety, may have a more serious impact on an athlete's life than the physical limitations of the injury. Physical rehabilitation of injuries has evolved into a complex field of study, but treatments for psychological recovery of injured athletes have just begun to be explored and developed. This chapter's main focus is the psychological interventions used in the treatment of athletic injuries. However, sport psychologists also are interested in several other aspects of athletic injuries, such as possible precursors of injury and psychological reactions to injury. This chapter, therefore, is divided into three sections. The first section describes the current knowledge on psychological precursors to injury, specifically personality variables and the life stress–injury relationship. The second section examines current models of psychological reaction to injury, focusing on grief models and cognitive appraisal models. The third section presents interventions for assisting athletes with their recovery from physical injury.

Precursors of Sport Injury

A survey in the United Kingdom revealed that sport and exercise cause approximately one-third of all injuries experienced (Uitenbroek, 1996). It has been reported that 3 to 5 million nonfatal athletic injuries occur each year in the United States (Kraus & Conroy, 1984). Another study suggested that over 4 million sports-related injuries in children and adolescents occur each year, with 36 percent of all injuries for this age group related to sport and recreation (Bijur et al., 1995). Recent data from the Consumer Product Safety Commission indicate approximately 2 million hospital emergency room cases are the result of sport-related injuries (NEISS Data Highlights, 1998). With this volume of athletic injuries each year, attempts to identify risk factors that are related to injuries are highly warranted. Sport psychologists have expended substantial effort to identify psychological factors that may predispose certain athletes to injury. If such factors exist and can be identified, preventive measures could be taken for these at-risk athletes to reduce the probability that they will be injured. Two potential precursors that have received significant attention in the research literature are personality factors and life stress events.

Personality Factors.   Sport psychologists have postulated that certain personality traits relate to an athlete being prone to injury. A common way to examine these relationships has been to give athletes a personality test prior to the season and then document who becomes injured during the season. The personality characteristics of the injured athletes are then compared to the characteristics of those who were not injured.

A common personality test used for this type of analysis is the 16 PF (1967), a standardized psychological test that measures 16 distinct dimensions of personality. For example, one dimension varies from Reserved to Outgoing, describing people who are detached, critical, and cool as **Reserved** and people who are warmhearted, easygoing, and participating as **Outgoing.** Another dimension categorizes people who are self-reliant, realistic, and no-nonsense as **Tough-minded,** and those who are dependent, overprotected, and sensitive as **Tender-minded.** The 16 PF can provide a fairly comprehensive psychological profile that then can be used to examine which personality characteristics are related to injury proneness.

In a typical study of this type (Jackson et al., 1978), the 16 PF was administered to 110 high school football players at the beginning of the season. At the end of the season, the 16 PF profiles of the injured players were compared to those of the noninjured players. The personality characteristics of the more seriously injured athletes also were examined. The results indicated that athletes who were more Tender-minded were more likely to experience injury than athletes who were Tough-minded. The results also indicated that athletes who were more Reserved experienced more severe injuries than athletes who were more Outgoing.

Other studies have used different psychological measures to examine a wide variety of athletic populations. Pooling the findings from these studies reveals a few common traits that consistently emerge as indicating a proneness to injury (Silva & Hardy, 1991). The traits of tender-mindedness, introversion, and various indicators of poor psychological adjustment (e.g., guilt, depression, low self-concept) have been consistently related to an increased likelihood of injury. According to Silva and Hardy (1991), research points to a few personality traits that may be related to risk for injury, but it is premature to conclude that our knowledge in this area is broad enough to formulate sound predictions and interventions. Many studies in this area have serious methodological flaws, such as lack of a theoretical basis, poor statistical analysis, poor definition of injury, and an overreliance on male populations. Research is continuing in this area, and perhaps in the future sport psychologists will be able to accurately predict injury risk from personality profile information. Researchers have been examining other avenues for predicting an athlete's risk of injury such as the life stress–injury relationship.

Life Stress. **Life stress** can be thought of as the amount of stress people experience in reaction to the events in their lives. This stress can result from different kinds of events, such as the death of a loved one, moving to a new city, changing jobs, going away to college, or any other change that requires some adaptation or coping response. The relationship between life stress and illness or injury is based on the belief that greater levels of stress eventually wear down an individual's ability to adapt or cope, and injury or illness will result. This trend for extreme or prolonged high levels of stress to be related to greater susceptibility to injury and illness has been supported in the research literature (Rahe & Arthur, 1978).

In addition to the depletion of coping resources proposed in the life stress–illness research, athletes have another factor that influences their risk for injury. Attempting to cope with life stress may disrupt the attentional focus needed for sport performance, thus placing athletes with high levels of life stress at a greater risk for injury (Bramwell et al., 1975). The narrowing of perceptual focus for individuals with high life stress when placed in a stressful condition has received preliminary research support (Andersen, 1988; Williams & Andersen, 1997; Williams, Tonyman, & Anderson, 1990, 1991), which suggests that perceptual narrowing may be a contributing factor to injury risk for athletes with high life stress.

Investigations with athletes have mirrored the findings in the life stress–illness relationship, showing that athletes who experience higher levels of overall life stress may be more prone to injury (Bramwell, Masuda, & Wagner, 1975; Cryan & Alles, 1983). More sophisticated analysis has partitioned the life stress experienced by athletes into total life stress, positive life stress, and negative life stress (Coddington & Troxel, 1980; Hardy & Reihl, 1988; May et al., 1985; Passer & Seese, 1983). The majority of these studies have indicated that it is primarily the negative component of life stress that is predictive of increased incidence of injury, although several recent studies have indicated that positive life stress may also be related to injury occurrence (Blackwell & McCullagh, 1990; Hanson, McCullagh, & Tonyman, 1992; Petrie, 1993). In a comprehensive review of the life stress–injury relationship in athletes, Williams and Andersen (1998) concluded that 27 of the 30 studies conducted by that time supported a relationship between life stress and injury.

Despite the consistency of support for a significant life stress–injury relationship, some studies have found only limited support for such a relationship (Passer & Seese, 1983; Williams, Tonyman, & Wadsworth, 1986). For example, Passer and Seese found that for NCAA Division II athletes, negative life stress was higher for injured athletes than for noninjured athletes. For Division I athletes, however, there was no significant difference between the injured and noninjured athletes in any life stress measures. This discrepancy in the research findings was addressed by Anderson and Williams (1988), who proposed that a direct link between life stress and injury occurrence was an insufficient explanation. These researchers emphasized that it is the **stress response** of athletes that may or may not place them at risk for injury. This stress response is determined not only by life stress demands, as examined in earlier research, but also by how athletes perceive these demands and their ability to cope with them. Athletes' perceptions are influenced by a variety of factors, such as personality factors and coping resources, that, in combination with their life stress levels, will be related to the risk of injury. For example, in a study of high school male and female athletes, athletes with low levels of coping skills and low levels of social support showed the strongest relationship between life stress and injury (Smith, Smoll, & Ptacek, 1990). Many diverse variables such as trait anxiety and playing status have been proposed as potential moderators of the life stress–injury relationship (Petrie, 1993). Williams and Andersen (1998; Anderson & Williams, 1988) have proposed a model that incorporates the variety of potential influences on the life stress–injury relationship, including personality variables (e.g., locus of control, trait anxiety), coping resources, history of stressors, the stress response of the individual, and the potential effect of any interventions (see Fig. 11.1). Research on the interrelationships depicted in this model is growing (Williams & Andersen, 1998), and as our understanding of the complexities of the life stress–injury relationship increases, targeted interventions for those athletes at risk may become possible.

Both personality factors and life stress–injury relationships have potential merit for predicting risk of injury. Neither of these approaches, however, has reached a level of sophistication that would warrant using them as screening measures for injury risk. Even if sport psychologists were able to predict which athletes might become injured, how these athletes react to their injuries remains a topic of key importance. This issue is discussed in the next section.

Psychological Reactions to Injury

Athletes' emotional reactions to injury can vary from devastation to mild annoyance depending on many factors. Though a majority of athletes cope well with injury, a substantial

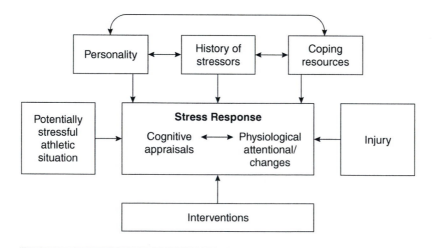

FIGURE 11.1   *The Revised Model of Life Stress and Injury (Williams & Andersen, 1998).*

minority, approximately 10–20 percent (Wiese-Bjornstal et al., 1998), exhibit extreme psychological disturbance that may require clinical intervention. Sport psychologists have been studying the psychological experiences of athletes who become injured. Two models have emerged from these investigations—a grief model that asserts injury is experienced as some type of loss and a cognitive appraisal model that views injury as a psychological stressor.

Grief Model. Athletes' reactions to injuries and the accompanying changes in lifestyle can be experienced as loss. There may be loss of physical functioning due to the injury, loss of identity as an athlete, loss of socialization with teammates, loss of income, and so on. Sport psychologists have noted the parallels between the loss reactions experienced by injured athletes and the grief reactions typical of other serious psychological losses (Pedersen, 1986; Rotella & Heyman, 1986). In perhaps the most widely quoted description of psychological reaction to loss, **Kubler-Ross** (1969) proposed that **five stages of grief**—denial, anger, bargaining, depression, and acceptance—are commonly experienced by individuals following a major loss.

These stages characterize some of the emotional experiences of injured athletes (Silva & Hardy, 1991). Denial consists of downplaying or ignoring the significance of the injury and involves an unrealistic belief in rapid recovery. As the reality of the severity of the injury becomes more apparent, athletes may become angry at teammates, opponents, coaches, trainers, the world, and themselves. This sense of anger is followed by a bargaining stage in which athletes rationalize or make promises contingent on a quick recovery. As the futility of this coping strategy becomes apparent, injured athletes may enter a period of depression in which they reflect on the losses resulting from their injury. This stage may be characterized by crying, feelings of despair and hopelessness, withdrawal, and social isolation. Eventually, as the injury is treated and recovery is seen as a possibility, this period of depression is replaced by an acceptance of the injury and its implications and focus switches to more positive steps for recovery.

Kubler-Ross's (1969) five-stage model is only one of several models of the grief reaction. Alternative stage models exist, with different numbers of stages and different descriptions of the stages (Averill, 1968; Brown & Stoudemine, 1983). There is debate, however, about the applicability of these stage models (Evans & Hardy, 1995). Many of the stage models of grief are based on the reactions of terminally or seriously ill patients, and the experience of injury for athletes may not be the same (Smith, Scott, & Wiese, 1990). Support for emotional reactions other than those proposed in stage models has been offered by a study monitoring the emotional reactions of seventy-two injured recreational athletes from the onset of the injury to return to activity (Smith et al., 1990). Using the Emotional Response of Athletes to Injury Questionnaire (ERAIQ; Smith et al., 1990) and the Profile of Mood States (POMS; 1971), injured athletes initially showed elevated levels of frustration, depression, tension, and anger. These responses did not fluctuate in a stage-like manner, but the overall global mood disturbance remained for approximately 1 month following the injury, and then the athletes' moods appeared to return to normal levels. A similar study used the POMS and an open-ended questionnaire to monitor five athletes for 4 weeks following their injury (McDonald & Hardy, 1990). These athletes showed an initial total mood disturbance similar to the previous study, but over the 4-week period a two-stage process emerged. The initial global mood disturbance moderated significantly after about 1 week and was followed by a period of adaptation and acceptance. These two stages were described (1) as shock, panic, disorganization, and helplessness, followed by (2) a task-focused approach to rehabilitation, adaptation to their limitations, and eager expectation to return to competition.

A variation of the stage models of reaction to injury has been proposed that recognizes that emotional responses to injury may not progress in a stage-like manner. The **affective cycle** (Heil, 1993) was derived from the original work of Kubler-Ross (1969) yet proposes a repeating cycle of the affective states of distress, denial, and determined coping. The **distress** portion of the cycle describes the disrupting and disorganizing impact of the injury on the athlete's emotional state. It includes shock, anger, bargaining, anxiety, depression, isolation, guilt, humiliation, preoccupation, and helplessness. Rather than depicting these reactions as occurring in stages, this model includes the totality of the emotional response as one component. The second component is **denial,** which includes disbelief and distorting the reality of the severity of the injury. Depending on the severity of the injury and the degree of the denial, this use of denial may be an effective coping mechanism for the athlete, or it may interfere with the rehabilitation process. The third stage is **determined coping,** which includes acceptance of the severity of the injury and the injury's impact on the athlete's short- and long-term goals. Determined coping involves the use of effective coping responses and efficiently working through the recovery process. The affective cycle model does not view the psychological reaction to injury as proceeding through linear stages, but shifts can occur from denial to distress to determined coping and back again many times and in any order. One component probably dominates at any given time, but there is constant fluctuation depending on situational influences and the cognitive activity of the athlete.

For example, the viewing of game films can often trigger the distress portion of the cycle, yet during actual physical rehabilitation, the athlete may exhibit realistic determined coping. As healing progresses, there is a shift toward the determined coping component and a lessening of distress and denial. The affective cycle was derived from theory, research, and practice and has much intuitive appeal, but it has not been tested directly and remains in need of research support.

Reviews of grief models applied to the experience of athletic injury have identified a number of limitations (Brewer, 1994; Evans & Hardy, 1995). In addition to citing several methodological issues in the research (lack of consistent definitions of injury, use of invalidated measures, lack of prospective longitudinal designs, and lack of theory testing), these authors conclude there is little empirical support for a consistent, stage-like progression of reactions to injury. However, this is not to say these models are completely without merit. With more sophisticated, theory driven research, there may be some components of a grief model that will help to explain the psychological reactions of athletes who have been injured.

Cognitive Appraisal Models.   A major shortcoming of the stage models of grief reactions to injury is their failure to account for individual differences in injury perception. To account for these differences in perceptions, models of reaction to injury have been proposed that view the injury as a stimulus or a stressor (Brewer, 1994; Wiese-Bjornstal & Smith, 1993). The first step in these models portrays the injury as an objective demand that must be evaluated by the athlete. The next step in the sequence is the athlete's cognitive appraisals of the situation and his or her ability to cope with the injury. Brewer identified two sets of variables that influence the cognitive appraisal of an injury. Personal factors are individual characteristics of the athlete such as trait anxiety, self-esteem, coping skills, and injury history. Situational factors are circumstances surrounding the injury and the athlete's environment, such as the severity and duration of the injury, social support, life stress levels, and time of season. These two sets of variables will interact to influence how the injury will be perceived. For example, an athlete with high trait anxiety and low self-esteem (personal factors) might perceive an injury as very threatening, yet if he or she has a good social support network and low life stress (situational factors), the perception of the injury may not be as scary. The final step in these models shows how the cognitive appraisal directly influences the athlete's emotional and behavioral responses to the injury. For example, if the cognitive response is plagued with doubt and thoughts of severe negative outcomes, the emotional response probably will be a more serious emotional disturbance. If, on the other hand, the cognitions are of a more positive nature, the emotional reaction to the injury is likely to be less severe.

Using the concepts of cognitive appraisal models, Wiese-Bjornstal and colleagues (1998) designed a model specific to athletes' reactions to injuries. These researchers synthesized the findings from research on the previously discussed components of personal factors, situational factors, cognitive appraisal, and behavioral and emotional responses, and they offer preliminary support for many of the components of this model. Although research into the specifics of cognitive appraisal models is in its infancy, these models can provide a useful framework for understanding the psychological reaction of athletes to injury. They also have the benefit of providing theoretical guidance for interventions, because many of the personal and situational factors can be modified (e.g., improving social support systems).

What is clear from the research in this area is that athletes often have a strong emotional reaction to becoming injured. This component is often overlooked in their rehabilitation and treatment. Often the physical injury itself is the focus of the treatment, and the athlete must cope with the emotional healing on his or her own. The next sections present the current thinking on providing a psychological component to rehabilitation from an injury.

Info Box

In order to establish an intervention strategy, the sport psychologist must consider the emotional stage the athlete is in. An athlete may need to work through distress or denial before he or she can engage in determined coping. The sport psychologist must also consider the cognitive appraisal of the injured athlete, which may give insight into the emotional state being experienced.

Considerations Prior to Planning the Intervention

The various descriptions of athletes' psychological reactions to injury presented in the previous section present a complex mix of factors affecting how a particular athlete may respond to being injured. A thorough understanding of these factors and how they may interact with the intervention process is necessary before an effective intervention program can be designed. A number of these factors are discussed on the following page.

Identification with the Athlete Role

The degree to which an athlete identifies with the role of athlete will have a significant impact on his or her psychological reaction to an injury (Petitpas & Danish, 1994). For example, a recreational athlete who sprains an ankle and has to miss practice and competition for a few weeks may view the injury as only a mild annoyance. A varsity athlete who gains pride and a sense of identity from participation in sport may view a sprained ankle and the missed practices and competitions as a serious stressor and may have strong emotional reactions. Serious injuries and extensive reductions in participation may have a profound impact when an individual's identification with the role of athlete is high. Empirical support for this relationship was presented in a series of studies with football players (Brewer, 1993). These studies showed that athletes with strong and exclusive identification with their role as athletes suffered more serious depressed mood following an injury than did athletes with less investment in their athlete role. This relationship between athletic identity and severity of emotional reaction to injury suggests that athletes who identify strongly with their role as an athlete may require more intensive treatment. Therefore, a clear assessment of the investment in the role of athlete is needed before an intervention can be effectively designed and carried out.

Nature of the Injury

Another important variable to consider is the actual nature of the injury. Injuries can be examined according to five factors: severity, onset, course, history, and type (Petitpas & Danish, 1994). The severity of an injury can range from temporary, with full recovery expected in a short time, to career-ending or even life-threatening. The severity of an injury often affects athletes' perceptions of control and predictability, which in turn affect their emotional responses. The onset of an injury can be either sudden and unexpected or gradual. Sudden onset can be very traumatic and may require a crisis management approach initially; a gradual onset may be subtler and the emotional responses not as apparent, but they still may be severe. The course of the injury is another important factor. The course of an injury can be progressive, constant, or episodic (Petitpas & Danish, 1994). An injury with a progressive course moves toward either recovery or more serious disability, with a clear course and prognosis. The responses of athletes to this type of injury may fluctuate dramatically through the course of treatment but should eventually moderate if moving toward recovery. Athletes with a constant course injury must cope with an injury that is stable; it is not going to improve but will likely not deteriorate. Depending on the severity of the injury, a minor adjustment of playing style may be all that is required. For a more severe injury, the athlete may have to accept that participation in sport may no longer be possible. Injuries can also be episodic, with symptom-free periods alternating with flare-ups of the symptoms. With these types of injuries, the athlete must cope not only with the injury when it is symptomatic but also with the fear of it returning periodically.

The athlete's injury history can be an important variable for predicting reactions to the injury and planning interventions. An athlete who experiences a first injury—with the pain, uncertainty, and rehabilitation process all being new experiences—may require more education, support, and intervention than will an "injury veteran," who may have learned how to cope and probably will have developed the skills needed to negotiate the healing process. The type of injury and the treatment required may also have an important impact on the athlete. For example, an athlete with a clearly visible injury, requiring a cast or crutches, may get sympathy and understanding from friends and teammates. An athlete with an injury that is less visible may not receive the same type of support, although the injury could be more serious (Petitpas & Danish, 1994).

Coping Skills of Athletes

The coping skills athletes bring to bear on their injury experience will have a direct effect on their reaction to the injury as well as on their ability to deal with the rehabilitation process. Coping skills can be divided into three categories: appraisal-focused coping, problem-focused coping, and emotion-focused coping (Tunks & Bellissimo, 1988). Appraisal-focused coping is skill in finding meaning in a crisis and evaluating what is at stake. An injured athlete with good appraisal-focused coping may view time away from practice and competition because of an injury as an opportunity to spend more time with family, study strategy and tactics, or pursue other endeavors. Problem-focused coping is dealing with the reality of the problem and designing and implementing plans to address the issue. Injured athletes with good problem-focused coping skills will seek out information from trainers, comply with their rehabilitation program, and stay focused on what needs to be done to return to competition. Emotion-focused coping addresses the emotional reaction to the incident and strives to return the individual to emotional equilibrium. An athlete with solid emotion-focused coping skills has effective means of dealing with the anger, disappointment, and other emotions associated with the injury.

Ideally, an athlete coping with an injury has adequate levels of all three types of coping skills. Overreliance on one type of skill can be problematic (Petitpas & Danish, 1994). For example, an athlete with good problem-focused skills may believe he is progressing well because he is diligent in his rehabilitation, but he may not be facing the emotional consequences of his injury. Similarly, an athlete may become overinvolved and focused on dealing with the emotional aftermath of the injury and fail to adequately address the physical recovery process. A thorough understanding of an athlete's total coping resources provides a guide for understanding the most effective targets of interventions.

Secondary Gain

An athlete may view an injury as beneficial, and this **secondary gain** can severely compromise the recovery process. Avoidance of painful practices, saving face in response to challenging competition, or passive aggressiveness against parental or coach pressure are examples of possible motivations for sabotaging attempts to recover from an injury. The attention and sympathy from coaches, teammates, friends, and family members may also backfire and become an incentive to delay recovery. Recognizing the benefits of the injury and developing strategies to compensate for these may be a necessary part of an intervention plan (Petitpas & Danish, 1994).

Social Support

The social support network of an injured athlete is an important component of his or her physical and emotional recovery. This support system can facilitate recovery by offering understanding and encouragement or can inhibit recovery by being overprotective, frightened, or applying pressure to return too soon. Assisting an athlete's recovery from injury often requires not only assessment of his or her social support resources but also often direct intervention with these resources. Coaches, trainers, friends, family, and teammates may need guidance about how best to respond to an injured athlete, and particularly about how to respond to the various emotions the athlete may be experiencing.

Situational Factors

A variety of situational factors interact when an injury occurs that influence how an athlete responds and what types of treatment planning are required. The type of sport, the length of the season, the amount of playing time, the athlete's performance level, the role on the team (both the position played and any leadership role), and the player's age are all important factors to consider. A key consideration in examining these factors is that it is not simply the objective nature of these factors, but the athlete's perception of these factors that is important. For example, suppose an athlete who is viewed by the coach as a key player on the team is injured in the final push to the playoffs and is out for the rest of the season. The athlete responds to the injury with little emotion and begins planning for the rehabilitation process. The coach fails to understand how this key player can take the injury and missing the playoff race so lightly. The athlete did not believe he or she was a key player on the team, however, and did not believe the team would suffer. The perception of this athlete was very different from the coach's perception and may have been different from the reality of the situation, but it is the athlete's perception of the circumstances that is vital to understanding reaction to the injury and to developing a treatment plan for recovery.

Info Box

The sport psychology intervention may be very challenging if the injured athlete views his or her primary identity as an athlete, has a severe injury, lacks coping skills, or lacks social support. In addition, an athlete may feel pressure from the coaches or teammates to return to competition or may feel that the injury relieves the pressure of having to consistently perform well. Psychological assessment of the injured athlete will provide direction for forming an intervention strategy.

Psychological Interventions Following Injury

As described in the previous section, the reactions of athletes to injury can have a wide variety of characteristics. If an athlete who has been injured seeks out assistance from a sport psychologist to help cope with the injury or assist in the recovery process, what can this athlete expect?

Assessment Considerations

Before planning any psychological interventions following an injury, it is important to carefully assess how the athlete is responding emotionally, the factors that may be contributing to the athlete's reaction, and possible sources of strength the athlete brings to the recovery process. The most effective method of conducting this assessment is through an in-depth interview with the athlete (Wiese-Bjornstal & Smith, 1993; Heil, 1993). This interview should assess factors preceding the injury, details of the injury, and the circumstances following the injury. The factors assessed in the interview will closely parallel the personal and situational factors considered in the cognitive appraisal models discussed previously.

A comprehensive guideline for conducting an assessment interview is the Emotional Response of Athletes to Injury Questionnaire (ERAIQ; Smith et al., 1990). The ERAIQ is an interview guide that assesses preinjury factors (sports played, hours per week spent in practice, reasons for being involved in sport, recent life stress prior to the injury, etc.), factors concerning the injury itself (how, when, and where the injury occurred, the severity of the injury, etc.), and factors related to recovery from the injury (emotional reactions, details on the rehabilitation program, sources of social support, estimated time of recovery, etc.). The ERAIQ or interviews assessing similar information will provide a detailed description of the factors related to recovery. The information gained should guide subsequent interventions, and will identify warning signs of a poor adjustment to injury (see Fig. 11.2).

Another important component of the initial assessment is establishing rapport between the sport psychologist and the injured athlete (Petitpas, 1996). The athlete should be given an opportunity to voice his or her concerns, opinions, attitudes, and feelings about the injury. The athlete should feel listened to and believe that the sport psychologist understands his or her particular circumstances. Basically, the athlete must feel that he or she can trust the sport psychologist, and that the sport psychologist has the expertise to provide assistance in the recovery process.

Intervention Techniques

Two words of caution are needed before presenting the interventions for injured athletes. Helping an athlete cope with injury can be a very complex process. The myriad factors re-

---

FIGURE 11.2 *Signs of a Poor Psychological Adjustment to Injury (Petitpas & Danish, 1995).*

- Evidence of anger, depression, confusion, or apathy.
- Obsession with the question, "When will I be able to play again?"
- Denial, reflected in remarks such as, "Things are going great," "The injury is no big deal," or other remarks that lead you to believe that the athlete is making an extraordinary effort to convince you that the injury does not matter.
- A history of coming back too fast from injuries.
- Exaggerated storytelling or bragging about accomplishments in or out of sport.
- Dwelling on minor somatic complaints.
- Remarks about letting the team down or feeling guilty about not being able to contribute.
- Dependence on the therapist or the therapy process or "just hanging around the training room" too much.
- Withdrawal from teammates, coaches, friends, family, or therapist.
- Rapid mood swings or striking changes in affect or behavior.
- Statements that indicate a feeling of helplessness to impact recovery.

---

lated to an athlete's response to being injured and the intense emotional reactions that are possible make this challenging work. Facilitating an athlete's recovery from injury is more than using a collection of techniques, although these techniques are often an integral part of the recovery process. Examining the various techniques separately and in isolation from the process of working with an injured athlete presents the interventions as somewhat simplistic. This is far from the truth. The effective use of these techniques within a trusting relationship can approach more of an art than a science. Please consider the remainder of this chapter with this caveat in mind.

The second caution regards the paucity of research support for many of the interventions presented. Providing psychological services to injured athletes is a relatively new field, and testing the efficacy of interventions is just beginning. The majority of the interventions have a rich history in other fields such as counseling and performance enhancement interventions (see Chapter 10), so there is justification for their use. A review of the available research is presented at the end of this section.

After the initial assessment and a working relationship have been established, the sport psychologist and the athlete must plan how to best facilitate the recovery process. The remainder of this chapter focuses on interventions for injured athletes who are able to recover and return to competition. Many of the interventions to be discussed are adaptable to career-ending injuries, but the examples cited are geared toward recovery and reentry into competition.

Sport psychologists and athletic trainers have advocated various intervention programs for assisting athletes with their psychological recovery from injury (Eldridge, 1983; Heil, 1993; Lynch, 1988; Pedersen, 1986; Rotella, 1988; Rotella & Heyman, 1986; Smith, Scott, & Wiese, 1990; Weiss & Troxel, 1986; Wiese, Weiss, & Yukelson, 1991; Yukelson, 1986). Many commonalities exist in the approaches outlined, and a number of important themes are consistently emphasized by these practitioners. The four components common to all the approaches are education, goal setting, psychological skills training, and social support. Fortunately, these themes are centered on skills that are familiar to many athletes, and with practice these sport-related psychological skills can be transferred to the injury recovery process.

Education.   The educational component consists of accurate information gathering and effective communication skills. Athletic trainers are vital participants in this stage, because they are the primary information source for the athlete. Good athletic trainers are skilled in translating the medical terminology concerning the injury and the rehabilitation process into terms that athletes can understand. The athlete needs to understand specifics about the cause, physical consequences, and psychological reactions that may be related to the injury in clear, non-ambiguous terms (Heil, 1993). The athlete should also be given a sense of the healing process and how physical therapy will aid recovery. It is unreasonable to expect athletes to cope well with injuries they do not understand, and information about the injury and the process of rehabilitation will help them regain the sense of control that the injury may have compromised.

Information about the injury and the rehabilitation process is in the hands of athletic trainers and medical personnel, and athletes may have to be assertive in their pursuit of this information. If they are passive and only accept the information that is given, they may not receive it in a clear and understandable way. Alternative sources, such as books, journals, and second opinions, should be pursued as supplements to the original information. The more knowledgeable athletes are about their injuries, the better they will understand and be able to cope with the rehabilitation process.

Another useful educational component to emphasize is that many of the same skills and qualities that have made athletes successful in their sport can be used during the rehabilitation process (Weiss & Troxel, 1986; Wiese & Weiss, 1987). Maintaining motivation, coping with pain, long hours of practice, and putting out maximal effort are all skills that athletes use in their competitive lives. Drawing parallels between their sport skills and the rehabilitation process will help to instill confidence in their ability to recover from the injury.

Goal Setting.   A skill seen as crucial to many of the psychological treatment plans is goal setting (Heil, 1993; Weiss & Troxel, 1986; Wiese & Weiss, 1987; Yukelson, 1986). Heil outlined nine characteristics of goals that are facilitative to the injury recovery process. **Rehabilitation goals** should be specific and measurable; be stated in positive language; be challenging but realistic; have short-, intermediate-, and long-term components; be monitored and evaluated; have outcome goals linked to process goals; be personalized and internalized; have sport goals linked to life goals; and have a timetable for completion. Many of these characteristics of goal setting were described in Chapter 10. Athletes who are familiar with the goal-setting process in their sport will be able to transfer these skills to their rehabilitation program. Factors specific to injury recovery may hinder the effectiveness of goal setting related to rehabilitation, even if the athlete is a skilled goal setter (Heil, 1993). The recovery process is often a new experience for the athlete, and they may lack knowledge about the specifics required of rehabilitation. This reemphasizes the need for proper education about the process of rehabilitation so the athlete can understand the rationale for particular goals leading to recovery. Another possible barrier to goal attainment is a lack of skill at particular rehabilitation exercises. Athletes may need to be taught specific rehabilitation regimens, and goals may need to be modified depending on their familiarity with the procedures. Other influences may complicate the goal attainment process, such as fear of reinjury or pain tolerance, and need to be addressed for goal setting to be effective.

Specific rehabilitation goals should be formulated by the athlete in conjunction with the athletic trainer and periodically monitored and revised if needed. This continued feedback provides the athlete with a measure of his or her progress and provides structure to the recovery process. A physical rehabilitation goal that could be posted on an athlete's locker would be, "I will be able to lift three repetitions at 20 pounds of resistance with my injured leg by next Friday" (Wiese & Weiss, 1987, p. 325). The specific daily exercises needed to reach this goal would accompany it. This process provides a sense of control over the recovery process as well as continued accomplishments of which the athlete can be proud.

Additional goals not related to recovery may be useful during the rehabilitation process. The time-out from athletic activities that often accompanies injury can leave athletes aimless and unmotivated. Setting goals for other areas of their lives can be beneficial. For college athletes, this may be an ideal time to focus on schoolwork and academic pursuits. For professional athletes, this may be a time to spend more energy on family, hobbies, or other activities that often must be given less attention than their sport. This could also be an ideal time to become more knowledgeable about their sport by scouting opponents, developing strategies, analyzing game films, and so on. All these pursuits are easily incorporated into a goal setting program.

Imagery Training.   Imagery can be a useful adjunct to the recovery process in a number of ways. Four types of imagery that may help athletes cope with their injuries are mastery, coping, emotive, and body rehearsal (Rotella & Heyman, 1986). **Mastery imagery** is the visualization of successfully carrying out the physical therapy and returning to competition. This can be directly tied to the goals that the athlete has set by visualizing the accomplishment of each goal. **Coping imagery** involves mentally rehearsing anticipated problematic situations and effectively dealing with them. For example, mentally rehearsing and visualizing adaptive responses to the pain of rehabilitation prepares the athlete for the times when this occurs. **Emotive imagery** enables athletes to rehearse positive emotional responses to anticipated events. The athlete could imagine returning to competition and feeling excited and energized. The previous three types of imagery are similar to the imagery used by athletes to enhance their performance (see Chapter 10), but body rehearsal imagery is a little different. **Body rehearsal** involves mentally imaging the injury and what is happening during the rehabilitation process. Information about the anatomy of the injury and the healing process is important for this type of imagery. Using this knowledge, the athlete can accurately visualize the healing process of fractured bones getting stronger, joints working smoothly, and so on. Several sport psychologists advocate body rehearsal imagery (Green, 1993; Ievleva & Orlick, 1991; Lynch, 1988; Rotella & Heyman, 1986; Smith, Scott, & Wiese, 1990), although the efficacy of this type of imagery is not established and the mechanisms through which it may work are not clearly understood.

   Imagery can also be detrimental to the recovery process, depending on the particular images the athlete visualizes. For example, replaying the original injury over and over and picturing the pain and agony of rehabilitation may make the rehabilitation more difficult (Green, 1993; Ievleva & Orlick, 1991). This suggests that the athlete should be taught techniques for directing images toward more positive and self-reinforcing themes. One program to help athletes control their imagery recommends starting with outcome-oriented imagery and then shifting toward process-oriented tasks (Green, 1993). The outcome imagery helps the athlete see a clear, positive goal, which helps the athlete stay focused and motivated. This outcome imagery is followed by process imagery, which emphasizes the tasks needed to accomplish this goal. Such a program would begin with the athlete visualizing a complete recovery and return to competition. Once the athlete has mastered this and can readily see himself or herself healthy, the imagery practice shifts toward the tasks that are required to reach this complete rehabilitation. For example, images of successfully executing rehabilitation tasks, getting rid of crutches, casts, and braces, and the first return to practice could be visualized in this process-oriented imagery practice. (See Fig. 11.3 for an example of an imagery program.)

   As with goal setting, imagery practice can be broadened to encompass more than just the rehabilitation of the injury. Physical skills, specific plays, and competition-related activities can be mentally rehearsed so the athlete is prepared to return to competition when the injury is healed.

Cognitive Techniques.   Many of the performance enhancement models for athletes based on cognitive interventions (see Chapter 10) can be readily adapted to the treatment of injury. The belief systems of injured athletes can hinder the healing process ("I will never recover.") or facilitate recovery ("This is a setback, but nothing I can't overcome."). Many sport psy-

FIGURE 11.3 *Example of an Imagery Program for a Basketball Player Recovering from Knee Injury (Green, 1994).*

Script #1:   "Knee at 90 degrees, I want to be a success story" (following surgery, getting out of bed and out of the hospital; establishing images of desired outcome).

Script #2:   "Strut your stuff" (getting off crutches, watching other people walk, establishing own gait).

Script #3:   "Hurt to get better" (progression of physical therapy that includes, in part, weight training, electric stimulation, stationary bike, stair master).

Script #4:   "Spring forward" (running at 75 percent, jumping exercises, increasing workload).

Script #5:   "Let's play" (pickup games).

Script #6:   "Dribble, drive, and dive!" (playing with no fear of failure).

Script #7:   "No brace" (the final stage due to school policy of mandatory use of brace following an injury).

chologists advocate the examination of injured athletes' self-talk for information regarding their beliefs about the injury (Ievleva & Orlick, 1991; Rotella & Heyman, 1986; Smith, Scott, & Wiese, 1990; Weiss & Troxel, 1986; Wiese & Weiss, 1987). By recognizing self-defeating inner dialogues and replacing these with more positive responses, athletes can modify their beliefs about the injury, become more action focused, and progress more rapidly in their healing process (Ievleva & Orlick, 1991). An inner dialogue that is plagued with **self-defeating talk** would contain phrases like, "This hurts too much to be beneficial," "These exercises will probably cause me more harm than good," and "I can't see any progress," which reflect negative beliefs about the rehabilitation process (Rotella, 1988). An effective use of **positive self-talk** would recognize the detrimental nature of these beliefs and respond to them with statements like, "These exercises hurt, but it's OK—they'll pay off," "I'll be competing soon because I'm doing these exercises," and "I know there will be plateaus in the process, and I will have to work through them." This self-talk refocuses athletes on the positive aspect of their training and gives them a greater sense of control over their recovery. Figure 11.4 on page 240 contains examples of positive self-talk and negative self-talk taken from a study investigating the differences between fast healing and slow healing athletes (Ievleva & Orlick, 1991). The self-talk of the athletes who healed more rapidly was characterized by a more affirming and positive outlook, but those athletes who healed more slowly tended to whine and complain about themselves and their misfortune in their self-talk.

Another use of cognitive interventions in the treatment of injury is coping with pain. A lot of pain is often associated with rehabilitation from injury. Without effective methods for coping with this pain, adherence to rehabilitation can be compromised. There are two general categories of cognitive pain management techniques—associative and dissociative (Heil, 1993). **Associative techniques** actually focus on the pain and try to reinterpret or reevaluate it. For example, an athlete may be trained to see the pain as a positive sign of the effort expended in the rehabilitative process. **Dissociative techniques** are more common and usually involve distraction from the pain. Athletes can distract themselves from the pain by listening to music, counting backwards from one hundred, imagining a peaceful and serene setting, or some other stimulus that takes the focus of attention away from the pain.

FIGURE 11.4   *Example of Positive Self-Talk and Negative Self-Talk Related to Injury Rehabilitation (Ievleva & Orlick, 1993).*

Positive Self-Talk
    How can I make the most out of what I can do now?
    I can beat this thing.
    I can do anything.
    I can do it. I can beat the odds and recover sooner than normal.
    I want to go spring skiing. I'll be totally healed by then.
    I have to work to get my leg as strong as the other one.
    It's feeling pretty good.
    It's getting better all the time.

Negative Self-Talk
    It's probably going to take forever to get better.
    I'll never make up for lost time.
    What a stupid thing to do—dumb mistake.
    What a useless body.
    It will never be as strong again.
    Stupid fool! Stupid injury! Stupid leg!
    There is nothing good about this, and there is nothing I can do about it.
    Why me?

Relaxation.   The ability to relax is an important skill for many athletic performances, and it can be readily applied to many aspects of injury recovery. Relaxation can physiologically calm the body when it is experiencing a great amount of stress, as is often the case after an injury or when undergoing physical rehabilitation. Relaxation also increases the circulation of blood, which leads to more effective healing of tissues (Benson, 1975). Relaxation can also be used as a distracting technique to cope with pain because relaxation diverts attention away from worry and tension associated with injury (Weiss & Troxel, 1986). Several different types of relaxation protocols such as Jacobson's (1938) progressive muscle relaxation, Benson's (1975) relaxation response, and various meditative techniques have been suggested as useful for injury recovery.

Social Support.   Social support for injured athletes has been consistently advocated as a means for assisting them in the recovery process (Heil, 1993; Lynch, 1988; Weiss & Troxel, 1986; Wiese & Weiss, 1987). Social support has been categorized into six types: listening, technical appreciation, technical challenge, emotional support, emotional challenge, and shared social reality (Rosenfeld, Richman, & Hardy, 1989) (See Fig. 11.5 for descriptions.) These sources of support come from a variety of individuals because no one person can provide all these types of support. For example, technical support and technical challenge can be provided only by individuals with expertise in the specific activity. Coaches and other teammates typically provide this type of support for sport-related tasks; trainers and other medical personnel must supply these types of support for the tasks of rehabilita-

FIGURE 11.5 *Types of Social Support for Injured Athletes (Heil, 1993).*

Listening

Listening in a nonjudgmental way to the concerns and feelings of another, as well as empathic sharing of joys and sorrows.

Technical Appreciation

Acknowledgment of good performance, based on technical understanding of the tasks in question.

Technical Challenge

Encouragement to meet performance goals by those who have a technical understanding of the tasks in question.

Emotional Support

Active support of an athlete through emotionally demanding circumstances (without necessarily taking his or her side).

Emotional Challenge

Encouragement to meet and overcome obstacles that are emotionally demanding.

Shared Social Reality

Sharing of similar experiences, values, and views that provide a basis for self-evaluation through social comparison.

---

tion. The emotional support and emotional challenge sources of social support can come from friends, parents, and significant others. The shared social reality category of support needs to come from others who have the same experience and background, such as other injured athletes or athletes who have recovered from injury. A clear deficit in one of these areas of social support can inhibit the recovery process, and it may be necessary for a sport psychologist to provide guidance to the various members of an athlete's support network (coaches, family, teammates, friends, etc.) about how to provide the social support the athlete requires.

Sources of support present in the athlete's life preinjury should be maintained during the postinjury rehabilitation period. Strategies to accomplish this include keeping the athlete as involved with the team as possible, attending practices when feasible, and generally helping to maintain his or her identity with the team (Heil, 1993). An additional strategy is to provide social support by the use of a peer model, which "partners" an injured athletes with an athlete who has successfully recovered from the same type of injury (Wiese & Weiss, 1987). This peer athlete can be a model for the injured athlete, providing information about surgery and recovery, motivational strategies, pain coping strategies, and potential roadblocks in the recovery process (Flint, 1993). This peer athlete should be chosen carefully so that the two athletes can relate to one another and each benefit from the relationship.

A further source of social support is the use of support groups (Wiese & Weiss, 1987). These groups bring injured athletes together to discuss their frustrations, concerns, and emotions with other athletes who may be experiencing similar problems. These groups can be a source of most of the categories of social support and can help the injured athlete feel less alone, aid in maintaining motivation, and provide a group of similar others with which to share experiences. These groups can also carry out many psychological interventions to aid injured athletes in their recovery process. Education, goal setting, imagery, relaxation, and cognitive interventions can all be carried out in a group format. Injury support groups, therefore, can fulfill a variety of functions in addition to the supportive nature of group treatment.

Info Box

While injury provides a unique and challenging situation for sport psychologists, the intervention techniques are similar to other situations that arise out of competition. Goal setting, imagery, cognitive restructuring, positive self-talk, and relaxation can all be instrumental in the rehabilitation process. Sport psychologists can also encourage athletes to learn about their injuries, can teach pain management strategies, and can direct athletes to social support groups.

Research Support for Injury Interventions

Although solid research support for many interventions used with injured athletes is sparse, there have been studies supporting their efficacy. A recent review (Cupal, 1998) divided this research into two types—studies examining prevention interventions and studies examining rehabilitation interventions. Prevention interventions are derived from the life stress–injury research and use stress-reduction techniques to reduce injury prevalence. For example, Kerr and Goss (1996) used a stress management program with elite gymnasts and found that the group of gymnasts who participated in the program had lower stress levels and fewer injuries than a control group. Although only three other studies have examined the efficacy of this type of preventive intervention (Davis, 1991; May & Brown, 1989; Schomer, 1990), they all showed a positive effect for reducing the incidence of injury.

Cupal (1998) reviewed thirteen studies that investigated the efficacy of various interventions with athletes who have been injured. Several of these studies examined the effectiveness of biofeedback training (see Chapter 10), but other interventions included stress management training, relaxation, guided imagery, goal setting, and attention control strategies. All of the studies in this review demonstrated some type of positive outcome, including earlier strength gains, increased physical functioning, reduced pain, less state anxiety, and less reinjury anxiety.

These studies provide preliminary evidence for the effectiveness of interventions to prevent or rehabilitate athletic injuries, but there are several shortcomings to the research in this area. The majority of rehabilitative studies have focused on athletes with knee injuries, and little is known about the success of interventions with other types of injuries (Brewer, 1998). Few of the studies incorporated control groups in their designs, so attributing the cause of any positive outcome to the intervention is problematic. Further difficulties in investigating these interventions are the vast number of personal, situational, and injury-related variables that could influence the rehabilitation process. Many more carefully designed studies are needed to fully understand which interventions and which specific components of these interventions are effective for each type of injury, person, and situation that is encountered.

Conclusion

The psychological impact of an injury can be devastating to an athlete. Both personality and levels of life stress may contribute to the likelihood that an athlete will be injured, but research has not yet been able to demonstrate a detailed understanding of the psychological components related to injury risk. After an injury, athletes experience a wide range of emotions, which appear to be determined by a variety of personal and situational factors. Some athletes are able to cope well with the injury and the process of recovery, while others suffer serious disturbances in mood including depression, anger, frustration, and tension. Sport psychologists have adapted many of the skills from their performance enhancement expertise to assist injured athletes in the recovery process. Education about the injury and the rehabilitation process, goal setting, relaxation, imagery, cognitive techniques as well as providing social support have been recommended to help athletes cope with injury and the rehabilitation process. Research support for the effectiveness of these interventions is mounting, but more study is needed to document the success of these interventions to assist athletes in their physical and psychological recovery from injury.

Key Terms *(in order of appearance)*

reserved	five stages of grief	coping imagery
outgoing	affective cycle	emotive imagery
tough-minded	distress	body rehearsal
tender-minded	denial	self-defeating talk
life stress	determined coping	positive self-talk
stress response	secondary gain	associative technique
grief model	rehabilitation goal	dissociative technique
Kubler-Ross	mastery imagery	

References

16 PF. (1967). Champaign, IL: Institute for Personality and Ability Testing.

Andersen, M. B. (1988). "Psychosocial factors and changes in peripheral vision, muscle tension, and fine motor skulls during stress." Ph. D. diss., University of Arizona.

Andersen, M. B., & Williams, J. M. (1988). A model of stress and athletic injury: Prediction and prevention. *Journal of Sport & Exercise Psychology, 10,* 294–306.

Averill, J. A. (1968). Grief: Its nature and significance. *Psychological Bulletin, 70,* 721–748.

Benson, H. (1975). *The relaxation response.* New York: Morrow.

Bijur, P. E., Trumble, A., Harel, Y., Overpeck, M. D., Jones, D., & Scheidt, P. C. (1995). Sports and recreation injuries in US children and adolescents. *Archives of Pediatric and Adolescent Medicine, 149,* 1009–1016.

Blackwell, B., & McCullagh, P. (1990). The relationship of athletic injury to life stress, competitive anxiety, and coping resources. *Athletic Training, 25,* 23–27.

Bramwell, S. T., Masuda, M., Wagner, N. N., & Holmes, T. H. (1975). Psychosocial factors in athletic injuries. *Journal of Human Stress, 2,* 6–20.

Brewer, B. W. (1993). Self-identity and specific vulnerability to depressed mood. *Journal of Personality, 61,* 343–364.

Brewer, B. W. (1994). Review and critique of models of psychological adjustment to athletic injury. *Journal of Applied Sport Psychology, 6,* 87–100.

Brewer, B. W. (1998). Psychological application in clinical sports medicine: Current status and future directions. *Journal of Clinical Psychology in Medical Settings, 5,* 91–102.

Brown, T. J., & Stoudemine, A. G. (1983). Normal and pathological grief. *Journal of the American Medical Association, 250*(3), 378–382.

Coddington, R. D., & Troxel, J. R. (1980). The effects of emotional factors on football injury rates—A pilot study. *Journal of Sports Medicine and Physical Fitness, 21,* 55–61.

Cryan, P. D., & Alles, W. F. (1983). The relationship between stress and college football injuries. *Journal of Sports Medicine, 23,* 52–58.

Cupal, D. D. (1998). Psychological interventions in sport injury prevention and rehabilitation. *Journal of Applied Sport Psychology, 10,* 103–123.

Davis, J. (1991). Sports injuries and stress management: An opportunity for research. *The Sport Psychologist, 5,* 175–182.

Eldridge, W. D. (1983). The importance of psychotherapy for athletically related orthopedic injuries among adults. *International Journal of Sport Psychology, 14,* 203–211.

Evans, L., & Hardy, L. (1995). Sport injury and grief responses: A review. *Journal of Sport & Exercise Psychology, 17,* 227–245.

Flint, F. A. (1993). Seeing helps believing: Modeling in injury rehabilitation. In D. Pargman (Ed.), *Psychological bases of sport injuries* (pp. 183–198). Morgantown, WV: Fitness Information Technologies.

Green, L. B. (1993). The use of imagery in the rehabilitation of injured athletes. In D. Pargman (Ed.), *Psychological bases of sport injuries* (pp. 199–218). Morgantown, WV: Fitness Information Technologies.

Hanson. S. J., McCullagh, P., & Tonyman, P. (1992). The relationship of personality characteristics, life stress, and coping resources to athletic injury. *Journal of Sport & Exercise Psychology, 14,* 262–272.

Hardy, C. J., & Reihl, R. E. (1988). An examination of the life stress–injury relationship among non-contact sport participants. *Behavioral Medicine, 14,* 113–118.

Heil, J. (1993). *Psychology of sport injury.* Champaign, IL: Human Kinetics.

Ievleva, L., & Orlick, T. (1991). Mental links to enhanced healing: An exploratory study. *The Sport Psychologist, 5,* 25–40.

Ievleva, L., & Orlick, T. (1993). Mental paths to enhance recovery from a sports injury. In D. Pargman (Ed.), *Psychological bases of sport injuries* (pp. 219–245). Morgantown, WV: Fitness Information Technologies.

Jackson, D. W., Jarrett, H., Bailey, D., Kausek, J., Swanson, J., & Powell, J. W. (1978). Injury prediction in the young athlete: A preliminary study. *American Journal of Sports Medicine, 6,* 6–14.

Jacobson, E. (1938). *Progressive relaxation.* Chicago: Univ. of Chicago Press.

Kerr, G., & Goss, J. (1996). The effects of a stress management program on injuries and stress levels. *Journal of Applied Sport Psychology, 8,* 109–117.

Kraus, J. F., & Conroy, C. (1984). Mortality and morbidity from injuries in sports and recreation. *Annual Review of Public Health, 5,* 163–192.

Kubler-Ross, E. (1969). *On death and dying.* London: MacMillan.

Lynch, G. P. (1988). Athletic injuries and the practicing sport psychologist: Practical guidelines for assisting athletes. *The Sport Psychologist, 2,* 161–167.

McDonald, S. A., & Hardy, C. J. (1990). Affective response patterns of the injured athlete: An exploratory analysis. *The Sport Psychologist, 4,* 261–274.

May, J. R., & Brown, L. (1989). Delivery of psychological services to the U.S. alpine ski team prior to and during the Olympics in Calgary. *The Sport Psychologist, 2,* 161–167.

May, J. R., Veach, T. L, Southand, S. W, & Herring, M. W. (1985). The effects of life change on injuries, illness, and performance in elite athletes. In N. K. Butts, T. T. Gushiken & B. Zarin (Eds.), *The elite athlete* (pp. 171–179). Jamaica, NY: Spectrum.

NEISS data highlights. (1998, Fall). *Consumer Product Safety Review, 3*(1), 4–6.

Passer, M. W., & Seese, M. D. (1983). Life stress and athletic injury: Examination of positive versus negative events and three moderator variables. *Journal of Human Stress, 10,* 11–16.

Pedersen, P. (1986). The grief response and injury: A special challenge for athletes and athletic trainers. *Athletic Training, 21,* 312–314.

Petitpas, A. J. (1996). Counseling interventions in applied sport psychology. In J. L. Van Raalte & B. W. Brewer (Eds.), *Exploring exercise and sport psychology* (pp. 189–204). Washington, DC: American Psychological Association.

Petitpas, A., & Danish, S. J. (1994). Caring for injured athletes. In S. Murphy (Ed.), *Sport psychology interventions* (pp. 255–281). Champaign, IL: Human Kinetics.

Petrie, T. A. (1993). Coping skills, competitive trait anxiety, and playing status: Moderating effects on the life stress–injury relationship. *Journal of Sport & Exercise Psychology, 15,* 261–274.

POMS. (1971). San Diego: Educational and Industrial Testing Service.

Rahe, R. H., & Arthur, R. J. (1978). Life change and illness studies: Past history and future directions. *Journal of Human Stress, 5,* 3–15.

Rosenfeld, L. B., Richman, J. M., & Hardy, C. J. (1989). Examining social support networks among athletes: Description and relationship to stress. *The Sport Psychologist, 3,* 23–33.

Rotella, R. J. (1988). Psychological care of the injured athlete. In D. N. Kuland (Ed.), *The injured athlete* (pp. 151–164). Philadelphia: Lippincott.

Rotella, R. J., & Heyman, S. R. (1986). Stress, injury, and the psychological rehabilitation of athletes. In J. M. Williams (Ed.), *Applied sport psychology* (pp. 343–364). Mountain View, CA: Mayfield.

Schomer, H. H. (1990). A cognitive strategy training programme for marathon runners: Ten case studies. *South African Journal for Research in Sport, Physical Education, and Recreation, 13,* 47–78.

Silva, J. M., & Hardy, C. J. (1991). The sport psychologist: Psychological aspects of injury in sport. In F. O. Mueller & A. Ryan (Eds.), *The sports medicine team and athletic injury prevention* (pp. 114–132). Philadelphia: Davis.

Smith, A. M., Scott, S. G., O'Fallon, W., & Young, M. L. (1990). The emotional responses of athletes to injury. *Mayo Clinic Proceedings, 65,* 38–50.

Smith, A. M., Scott, S. G., & Wiese, D. M. (1990). The psychological effects of sports injuries. *Sports Medicine, 9,* 352–369.

Smith, R. E., Smoll, F. L., & Ptacek, J. T. (1990). Conjunctive moderator variables in vulnerability and resiliency research: Life stress, social support, and coping skills and adolescent sport injuries. *Journal of Personality and Social Psychology, 5,* 360–369.

Tunks, T., & Bellissimo, A. (1988). Coping with the coping concept: A brief comment. *Pain, 34,* 171–174.

Uitenbroek, D. (1996). Sports, exercise, and other causes of injuries: Results of a population survey. *Research Quarterly for Exercise and Sport, 67,* 380–385.

Weiss, M. R., & Troxel, R. K. (1986). Psychology of the injured athlete. *Athletic Training, 21*(2), 104–109.

Wiese-Bjornstal, D. M., & Smith, A. M. (1993) Counseling strategies for enhanced recovery of injured athletes within a team approach. In D. Pargman (Ed.), *Psychological bases of sport injuries* (pp. 149–182). Morgantown, WV: Fitness Information Technologies.

Wiese-Bjornstal, D. M., Smith, A. M., Shaffer, S. M., & Morrey, M. A. (1998). An integrated model of response to sport injury: Psychological and sociological dynamics. *Journal of Applied Sport Psychology, 10,* 46–69.

Wiese, D. M., & Weiss, M. R. (1987). Psychological rehabilitation and physical injury: Implications for the sports medicine team. *The Sport Psychologist, 1,* 318–330.

Wiese, D. M., Weiss, M. R., & Yukelson, D. P. (1991). Sport psychology in the training room: A survey of athletic trainers. *The Sport Psychologist, 5,* 15–24.

Williams, J. M., & Andersen, M. B. (1997). Psychosocial influences on central and peripheral vision and reaction time during demanding tasks. *Behavioral Medicine, 22,* 160–167.

Williams, J. M., & Andersen, M. B. (1998). Psychosocial antecedents of sport injury: Review and critique of the stress and injury model. *Journal of Applied Sport Psychology, 10,* 5–25.

Williams, J. M., Tonyman, P., & Andersen, M. B., (1990). Effects of life-event stress on anxiety and peripheral narrowing. *Behavioral Medicine, 16,* 174–181

Williams, J. M., Tonyman, P., & Andersen, M. B., (1991). Effects of stressors and coping resources on anxiety and peripheral narrowing in recreational athletes. *Journal of Applied Sport Psychology, 3,* 126–141.

Williams, J. M., Tonyman, P., & Wadsworth, W. A. (1986). Relationship of life stress to injury in intercollegiate volleyball. *Journal of Human Stress, 12,* 38–43.

Yukelson, D. (1986). Psychology of sports and the injured athlete. In D. B. Bernhardt (Ed.), *Sports physical therapy* (pp. 173–195). New York: Churchill Livingstone.

12

Enhancing Sport Performance: The Role of Confidence and Concentration

Luis Manzo

The University of Notre Dame

- Definitions of several key components, including sport confidence, self-efficacy, and dispositional optimism, can clarify the psychological construct of confidence in sport.
- A lack of confidence can be identified as learned helplessness, which is related to the explanatory style of an athlete.
- Several guidelines exist for developing an athlete's self-confidence; however, the development and maintenance of a high level of self-confidence is challenging.
- Concentration and attention are important in athletic performance, as explained by the attentional style theory.
- The relationship among anxiety, arousal, and attention may explain possible attention-related performance problems.
- Several intervention techniques can facilitate the improvement of concentration in sport.

> *This game is all confidence, and, you know, sometimes it's scary. When I'm at my best, I can do just about anything I want, and no one can stop me. I feel I'm in total control of everything.*
>
> —Larry Bird (Callahan, 1985, 52)

For decades, athletes of all ages and competitive levels have sought the feeling of confidence described by Larry Bird. Even in sport psychology's infancy, Griffith (1928) suggested that it is confidence that instills the hope and drive in an athlete to persevere

Kicking a game-winning goal with millions of spectators watching requires both confidence and concentration.

even when faced with overwhelming adversity. These early insights have been substantiated by modern sport psychologists who have demonstrated that athletes with a high degree of confidence perform better in a variety of athletic situations than those who lack confidence (Barling & Abel, 1983; Holloway, Beuter, & Duda, 1988; Lee, 1982; Martin & Gill, 1991; Matheson & Mathes, 1991; Vealey, 1986; Sinclair & Vealey, 1989). Despite these insights, however, the field lacks a comprehensive understanding of confidence and of what it is about this variable that has such a powerful effect on performance.

What Is Confidence?

Since Griffith's early writings, many sport psychologists have contributed descriptive understandings of confidence (Cook, 1992; Orlick, 1990). Confidence has been described as "the inner knowledge that assures you that you can achieve your goal(s)" (Bennett & Pravitz, 1987, p. 133). Athletes often equate confidence with a "gut" feeling that you either have or do not have (Kauss, 1980). In its purest form, confidence can be described as "the acceptance of your abilities" (Orlick, 1990, p. 88). Although few athletes would argue with these descriptions of confidence, sport psychologists still lack a true understanding of confidence.

So what is wrong with our understanding of confidence? Bandura (1997) argues that "confidence is a nondescript term that refers to the strength of belief but does not necessarily specify what the certainty is about" (p. 382). Additionally, Bandura is critical of the word *confidence* because it is merely a catchword in sports rather than a theoretical construct embedded in a theoretical system" (p. 382). Thus, Bandura takes issue with the fact that confidence, as we know it in sport psychology, is a construct that is devoid of any theory or structure to outline a comprehensive understanding.

For the purposes of this chapter, **confidence** is defined as possessing an optimistic attitude and the belief that one's actions will have an impact on the outcome of a situation. The interaction of optimism and belief in competence enhances one's belief that he or she can successfully fulfill the demands of a sport situation.

What Is Sport Confidence?

The study of self-confidence within the domain of athletics, or what is commonly referred to as "sport confidence," has traditionally drawn heavily from Bandura's (1977) self-efficacy theory. Self-efficacy is an individual's judgment of his or her capabilities to organize and execute a specific course of action required to attain a desired performance (Bandura, 1997). Vealey (1986) describes a sport-specific form of self-efficacy labeled "sport confidence." **Sport confidence** is defined as "the belief or degree of certainty individuals possess about their ability to be successful in sport" (Vealey, 1986, p. 222). However, Vealey's definition of sport confidence does not appear to adequately differentiate itself from self-efficacy. It should be noted that Vealey's definition of sport confidence is conceptualized as a global construct rather than the task-specific construct Bandura (1986) uses for self-efficacy. Additionally, Vealey's definition of sport confidence is vague in terms of how "success" is defined.

The astute reader may have noticed that self-efficacy and sport confidence tend to be used interchangeably. However, although self-efficacy and sport confidence share some similarities (e.g., a belief that one has the capabilities to be successful), sport confidence embodies a frame of mind (i.e., a positive attitude and sense of personal control) that subsequently impacts the individual in a variety of athletic situations and tasks.

There are two widely used measures of sport confidence: The Trait Sport Confidence Inventory (TSCI; Vealey, 1986) and the self-confidence subcomponent of the Cognitive State Anxiety Inventory-2 (CSAI-2; Martens, Vealey, & Burton, 1990). The TSCI was developed by Vealey (1986) to measure an athlete's trait level of sport confidence. Similar to the TSCI, the State Sport Confidence Inventory (SSCI; Vealey, 1986) was developed to assess an athlete's state level of sport confidence. These measures of sport confidence are essentially global measures of self-efficacy that have been tailored to the domain of sport.

The self-confidence subcomponent of the CSAI-2 (Martens, Vealey, & Burton, 1990) is a nine-item subscale that appears to measure the absence of cognitive anxiety. Because some literature suggests that the absence of cognitive anxiety is associated with high levels of self-confidence, the authors of the CSAI-2 named this subcomponent "self-confidence."

It is currently clear that the study of sport confidence is based on Bandura's self-efficacy theory. To have a full understanding of sport confidence, therefore, it is necessary to understand self-efficacy theory and why research has demonstrated it to be such a compelling construct.

Info Box

Confidence is often portrayed in the media as a highly transitional psychological construct that increases or decreases with each minor successful or unsuccessful performance. However, although performances have the potential to affect confidence, in actuality confidence has a greater effect on performance. Larry Bird performed consistently at a high level because he brought a high level of confidence to his performances. He did not allow his performance to dictate his confidence.

Self-Efficacy

Central to the understanding of *self-efficacy* is the clarification that it is not concerned with the skills one has, but rather the judgment one makes regarding what he or she can do with whatever skills he or she possesses (Bandura, 1986). Additionally, self-efficacy is not a global personality trait; it is a task-specific belief that fluctuates from situation to situation, context to context (Bandura, 1986). Efficacy expectations are derived from four sources of information: performance accomplishments, (e.g., doing well during an athletic event), vicarious experiences, (e.g., seeing peers and role models doing well in athletics), verbal persuasion, (e.g., receiving encouragement and support from significant others), and emotional arousal, (e.g., arousal associated with participating in athletic events; Bandura, 1977). It should be noted, however, that efficacy information obtained from these sources does not automatically influence one's self-efficacy (Schunk & Carbonari, 1984). For such information to have any relevance in terms of one's efficacy beliefs, it must be cognitively processed (Bandura, 1992). The impact this information will have on an individual's judgments of self-efficacy depends on how it is "cognitively appraised" by the individual.

Self-efficacy theory is compelling, because it has tremendous explanatory power and yet is simple to understand. If you believe in your abilities, the probability of achieving what you set out to do is higher than if you do not believe in your abilities. With skills and abilities held constant, self-efficacy is a significant determinant of performance (Schunk & Carbonari, 1984). Judgments of self-efficacy have been shown to increase performance of phobic activities (Bandura, Reese, & Adams, 1982), alleviate anxiety, and facilitate therapeutic change (Williams, Dooseman, & Kliefield, 1984). Additionally, sport psychologists have demonstrated that a high degree of self-efficacy is an essential component of successful athletic performance. Weinberg, Gould, and Jackson (1979) found that individuals with a high level of self-efficacy performed better on a leg extension task than individuals with a lower level of self-efficacy. In the face of failure, highly self-efficacious individuals are more persistent, whereas the performance of the low self-efficacious individuals decreased. Weinberg and colleagues (1981) also found that individuals who had a high level of preexisting self-efficacy expected to and actually did perform significantly better on a leg extension task than those who had lower preexisting levels of self-efficacy. These findings have also been documented in actual sporting situations. Lee (1982) indicated that gymnasts perform to their level of expectation. Gymnasts with high levels of self-efficacy predict that they will do well in competition and perform up to their expectations, whereas gymnasts with low levels of self-efficacy perform poorly.

It is this subjective and very personal cognitive appraisal process that produces differential levels of self-efficacy from the same efficacy building experiences. For example, a baseball player who comes to the plate and hits a home run, only to attribute this success to a mistake made by the pitcher, experiences little if any increase in his or her self-efficacy. A player who hits a home run and attributes this success to hard work, practice, and skill, however, will likely experience an increase in perceived self-efficacy.

The cognitive appraisal process, which is central to one's self-efficacy, involves the ascription of causes to the various efficacy-building experiences one may encounter. This entails not only evaluating the outcome of the event but also weighing such factors as task difficulty, effort expended, the number of external aids received, the situational circumstances surrounding the event, and the temporal pattern of one's success and failures (Bandura et al., 1980). This cognitive appraisal process is a vital component in the development of efficacy beliefs. Thus, a full understanding of self-efficacy and sport confidence requires an understanding of this appraisal process. The next section explores an approach to sport confidence that integrates a broader understanding of this cognitive appraisal process.

A Theoretical Approach to Sport Confidence

Despite recent advances in the study of sport confidence, sport psychologists still lack a comprehensive understanding of sport confidence. Surely, self-efficacy theory has outlined the activities that will enhance an athlete's sport confidence. Yet, the field lacks a clear understanding of how this information is transformed into the confidence Larry Bird described at the start of this chapter.

Based on the personal accounts of athletes at all competitive levels as well as a review of the existing literature and theories, Manzo and Silva (1993) developed a theoretical model for sport confidence. This model is based on three underlying constructs: dispositional optimism (having a positive attitude), perceived control (the belief that an expectancy is under one's control), and perceived competence (the degree to which one believes that he or she can successfully fulfill the demands of a sport situation).

Dispositional optimism is a system of cognitive schemas whose common dominator is positive expectations about the future (Scheier & Carver, 1985; Beck et al., 1974). Optimists are individuals who generally believe that good things will happen to them whether or not they cause these good things to occur (Scheier & Carver, 1985).

Perception of control also is a decisive component of sport confidence and likely the most affected by one's perception of the world. Perceived control is: how we understand why certain outcomes occur, how much we believe that our own attributes cause these outcomes, and how much we believe other individuals cause these outcomes (Connell, 1985). The construct of **perceived competence** is in its purest form is one's self-efficacy beliefs for a variety of sport tasks.

Based on this conceptualization of sport confidence, researchers developed a theory-driven measure of sport confidence called the Carolina Sport Confidence Inventory (CSCI). The CSCI is a paper-and-pencil measure of sport confidence, and research has demonstrated very favorable psychometric properties for this measure (Manzo, Silva, & Mink, 2001).

A closer examination of the constructs proposed in this model suggest two broad categories: self-efficacy itself and the cognitive appraisal mechanism used to evaluate efficacy-building information. Perceived competence in this context appears to represent self-efficacy, whereas dispositional optimism and perceived control represent the cognitive appraisal mechanism used to evaluate self-efficacy–building experiences. Thus, to have a complete understanding of sport confidence we must know two pieces of information: (1) the athlete's self-efficacy for a specific task and (2) the perceptual filter through which the athlete evaluates the efficacy-building experiences that have resulted in his or her existing level of self-efficacy.

Bandura (1997) views self-efficacy as a contextual construct and argues that people do not approach tasks devoid of any notion about themselves and the world around them. Only through transactional experiences do individuals evolve a structured self-system that contains a rich semantic network (Bandura, 1992). This self-schemata affects how individuals interpret, organize, and transform information, thus impacting one's efficacy beliefs that develop. Two people who differ in the way they view the world, in terms of their dispositional optimism and perceived control, will make different efficacy judgments from the same efficacy building experience. Thus, two athletes who differ in terms of their dispositional optimism and perceived control will derive different efficacy beliefs from the same experience. For example, consider the case of two baseball players who are both struggling with their hitting and who have identical experiences hitting lines drives that are caught by outfielders. The player with a high degree of dispositional optimism and perceived control will likely see such an at bat as a success, because she or he made good contact with the ball, thus experiencing an increase in his or her self-efficacy. The individual who has lower levels of dispositional optimism and perceived control, however, will likely see this at bat as just another failure and inability to break out of a hitting slump. This interpretation will result in lower levels of self-efficacy. The individual with a high level of dispositional optimism and perceived control will likely attend to the positive aspects of the experience and may remain more persistent in the belief that he or she can get a hit. Unfortunately, the individual with low levels of dispositional optimism and perceived control will likely focus on the negative aspects of the performance and may begin to develop a stronger belief that he or she can't get a hit.

To understand sport confidence, it is essential to know the causal attributions athletes make during success and failure experiences. The impact these attributions have on how individuals view their athletic abilities and accomplishments play an influential role in the formulation of an athlete's sport confidence. These attributions also inform individuals about whether their actions have an impact on future outcomes. To understand this attributional process, an examination of the construct of explanatory style is necessary.

Learned Helplessness and Explanatory Style

Explanatory style is the way a person habitually explains good and bad events. It is through understanding these explanations that psychologists can account for the vast amount of individual differences in human behavior. Explanatory style grew out of the learned helplessness research conducted during the mid 1960s (Peterson, Maier, & Seligman, 1993).

Learned helplessness occurs when an individual perceives a noncontingency between his or her actions and subsequent outcomes. This leads to the expectation that future outcomes will not be contingent on his or her actions and ultimately leads to passive behavior (Peterson, Maier, & Seligman, 1993). The classic demonstration of learned helplessness involved exposing a group of dogs to a series of unavoidable electric shocks and another group of dogs to avoidable shocks. After 24 hours, these dogs were placed in a shuttle box. The shuttle box was divided in two by a small barrier that the dogs could easily jump. On one side of the box, the dogs received electric shock. To escape the shock, all the dogs needed to do was jump the barrier to the other side of the box. Those dogs exposed to the escapable shock easily navigated their way across the barrier to safety. The dogs that were exposed to the unavoidable shocks made no attempt to escape the shocks and simply sat passively enduring them. Maier and Seligman (1976) proposed that the dogs exposed to unavoidable shock learned to be helpless. They learned that the electric shocks were independent of their responses. The theory of learned helplessness was developed from numerous studies demonstrating similar effects. Such helplessness could also apply to a sport context, for example, the gymnast who believes that regardless of the fact that she sticks her landings and has a flawless performance, the judges will score her lower than former Olympic gymnasts or well-established gymnasts may eventually stop working hard in practice because she believes "the favorites always win; gymnastics is so political. It's who knows you, not what you do or how you really perform."

Unfortunately, learned helplessness theory seemed inadequate to explain human behavior in the presence of uncontrollable events. It failed to account for the range of reactions that people display in response to them (Peterson, Buchanan, & Seligman, 1995). In addition, only two-thirds of the people exposed to uncontrollable events became helpless. For some reason, a third of the people did not. Of those who did become helpless, some bounced back right away; others never recovered. Some were helpless only in the very situation in which they learned to be helpless; others generalized their helplessness to new situations (Seligman, 1990). Learned helplessness theorists had difficulty making sense of these findings. The attempt to incorporate them into learned helplessness theory provided the impetus for the attributional reformulation of learned helplessness, which was called explanatory style (Abramson, Seligman, & Teasdale, 1978).

Info Box

Learned helplessness is sometimes exhibited in sport competition. Athletes often perceive that they are performing to the best of their capabilities, yet they do not observe the desired result. Athletes who have this perception are likely to attribute failure to reasons outside of their control, such as officiating, injury, or even luck or fate. They concede that the outcome is out of their control, which is a form of decreased confidence.

Explanatory Style: A Reformulation of Learned Helplessness

Lyn Abramson, Martin Seligman, and John Teasdale reformulated learned helplessness theory in 1978. They proposed that when people encounter an uncontrollable event, they ask themselves why it happened. The causal attributions embedded in an individual's response to such events set the parameters for the feelings of helplessness or competence that follow (Peterson, Buchanan, & Seligman, 1995). This reformulation left the original model of helplessness intact by maintaining that uncontrollable events produce motivational and behavioral deficits when events produce an expectation that one's future responses are independent of future outcomes. However, the reformulation suggests that these motivational and behavioral deficits are also influenced by the causal attributions the individual makes the uncontrollable event (Peterson, Buchanan, & Seligman, 1995). Abramson, Seligman, and Teasdale (1978) considered there to be three types of causal attributions that are crucial to the reformulation. These dimensions determine **explanatory style:** internal versus external, stable versus unstable, and global versus specific.

Internal Versus External.   The internal versus external dimension contrasts the attributions of "it's me," an internal attribution, to "it is someone else," an external attribution. In the face of uncontrollability, an internal attribution fosters a loss of self-esteem, whereas an external attribution leaves one's self-esteem intact.

Stable Versus Unstable.   The distinction between a stable attribution ("It's going to last forever") versus an unstable attribution ("It's short-lived") influences one's expectations for future successes or failures. In the face of uncontrollability, a stable attribution produces enduring helplessness and passivity, whereas an unstable attribution produces primarily temporary deficits.

Global Versus Specific.   A global attribution ("It's going to affect everything that happens to me") versus a specific attribution ("It's only going to influence this situation") speaks to the generalizability of the helpless deficits. A global attribution for a bad event elicits passive behaviors in many areas of the individual's life, whereas a specific attribution contains the helpless behaviors to one particular domain.

In the face of a negative event, the combination of internal, stable, and global attributions for the cause of that event will form a pessimistic explanatory style. Such a person is also likely to make external, unstable, and specific attributions for the causes of positive events. The flip side of these attributions forms an optimistic explanatory style. Therefore, a person with an optimistic explanatory style will make external, unstable, and specific attributions for negative events and internal, stable, and global attributions for positive events. For example, a basketball player with an optimistic explanatory style who misses the game-winning shot may explain his miss in the following manner: the opposing team's defense was excellent (external), it was a long shot with a 50/50 chance of going in (unstable), and the defense forced him to shoot off balance on that particular shot (specific).

An optimistic explanatory style can provide a striking advantage in the workplace, on the athletic field, and in the classroom. The reformulation predicts that those individuals who habitually attribute negative events to internal, stable, and global causes and positive events to external, unstable, and specific causes (a pessimistic explanatory style) are at greater risk for helplessness deficits than those individuals with a positive or optimistic explanatory style (Schulman, 1995). Explanatory style affects achievement in the following way. The explanation one makes for successes and failures eventually leads to expectations that affect their reactions to future success and failures. These expectations lead to self-fulfilling prophecies that either enhance or undermine one's performance. For example, the swimmer with an optimistic explanatory style who loses a close race is likely to become motivated to practice harder and enhance his swimming technique and fitness, whereas the swimmer with a pessimistic explanatory style is likely to not look forward to practice the next week and become reluctant to pursue ways that could improve his swimming.

Researchers have demonstrated the influential role an optimistic explanatory style can have in the world of sports. Whether it is on the basketball court, on the baseball diamond, or in the swimming pool, having an optimistic explanatory style not only is an asset but also gives an athlete a competitive edge (Rettew & Reivich, 1995; Seligman et al., 1990).

Rettew and Reivich (1995) describe a pair of studies that convincingly illustrate the importance of an athlete's explanatory style. These studies examined the impact of an optimistic or pessimistic explanatory style in professional basketball and baseball. To study the effect an optimistic explanatory style in the NBA, the researchers derived a team's explanatory style score for each of five teams in the Atlantic Division. The independent variable in this study was explanatory style as measured by a technique that analyzes the content of written and spoken material. The performance of each team following a defeat during the target season served as the dependent variable. The season following the assessment of a team's explanatory style served as the target season. In addition to control for the disparity in ability that existed among these teams, the Las Vegas point spread was used as a measure of a team's talent. As hypothesized, those "teams with a more optimistic explanatory style for bad events performed significantly better in games following a loss than teams with a pessimistic explanatory style" (p. 176). This supports the notion that how an athlete views failure or the loss of a game predicts his or her performance after a negative event (Rettew & Reivich, 1995).

Using the same technique employed in the basketball study, Rettew and Reivich (1995) assessed the explanatory style of twelve National League baseball clubs. The teams' winning percentage in the season following the measurement of explanatory style served as the dependent variable. As in the basketball study, they found that teams with an optimistic explanatory style won more games than teams with a more pessimistic explanatory style.

The importance of an optimistic explanatory style is perhaps best illustrated in a study by Seligman and colleagues (1990). They studied thirty-three collegiate swimmers (fourteen male, nineteen female). Each swimmer's explanatory style was assessed using a self-report measure, the Attributional Style Questionnaire (Peterson et al., 1982). Additionally, at the beginning of the season the coaches rated each swimmer on how well he or she would perform after a defeat. The swimmers were then asked to swim their best event. After the swimmers completed their best events, coaches provided false feedback indicating that the athlete had performed slower than his of her actual time. The athletes were given 30 minutes to rest and then were asked to swim their event again. The results indicated that the swimmers with an optimistic explanatory style did as well or better after the bogus defeat then they did in their first swim. Those swimmers with pessimistic explanatory styles performed considerably slower. In addition, this study suggested that swimmers with a pessimistic explanatory style are more likely to perform below their coaches' expectations during the season than those swimmers with optimistic explanatory styles.

Self-Efficacy and Explanatory Style

Despite the family resemblance between self-efficacy and explanatory style (e.g., both are cognitive, both are related to successful performance and to how individuals meet the demands of the world), striking theoretical distinctions can be made between these two constructs (Peterson & Stunkard, 1992). Self-efficacy theory is deeply rooted in the ways individuals use cues from their environment, their thoughts, and their feelings to develop beliefs in their abilities. Explanatory style, on the other hand, is a global trait that is described as "the tendency to offer similar sorts of explanations for different events" (Peterson, Buchanan, & Seligman, 1995, p. 2). Simply stated, explanatory style is viewed as the lens through which an individual makes sense of his or her world.

It is proposed that an athlete's explanatory style may influence how he or she processes their experiences and, therefore, the degree to which efficacy beliefs benefit from these experiences. Thus, an individual with an optimistic explanatory style will display greater judgments of perceived self-efficacy than an individual with a pessimistic explanatory style. The individual with a pessimistic explanatory style will fail to benefit from efficacy-building experiences. The individual with an optimistic explanatory style will likely attend to the positive aspects of the experience, attributing successful experiences to superior personal skills and abilities. The individual with a pessimistic explanatory style probably will focus on the negative aspects of his or her performance, attributing success to external forces. Thus, to truly understand "sport confidence," or sport-specific self-efficacy, it is essential to understand how athletes process information to result in the positive feelings of control and effortlessness described in Larry Bird's quote at the beginning of this chapter.

Guidelines for Developing Self-Confidence in Sport

The perspective of sport confidence offered by Manzo and Silva (1993, 1994) is an understanding of sport confidence based in theory. This position contends that self-efficacy and explanatory style interact to form an athlete's sport confidence; thus, interventions designed to enhance self-efficacy and alter explanatory style should cultivate feelings of sport confidence within the athlete.

Developing Self-Efficacy

Bandura (1997) suggests that judgments of self-efficacy are generated via four sources of efficacy information (past performance accomplishments, vicarious experiences, verbal persuasion, and physiological arousal); thus, athletes should be aware of how to utilize these sources of self-efficacy.

"Nothing Breeds Success Like Success"

As this statement suggests, if an athlete wants to develop sport confidence, it is imperative that the athlete be in the position to have successful efficacy-building experiences (Miller, 1991). For example, a football coach can reward effort and good performance even if it does not always result in the desired outcome. The coach must be realistic, however, and should be careful not to reinforce mediocrity.

Visualize Success

By practicing positive imagery, athletes can develop images of themselves performing successfully and create a template in their "mind's eye" of positive past performances and expectations of good performances (success in the future).

Choose Positive Models

Modeling can serve as a rich source of self-efficacy information and should be used when appropriate. When selecting a model, it is important to choose one with which the athlete can easily identify (e.g., a college freshman using a highly skilled junior or senior as a model, college players using former teammates who are now playing in the pros).

Implement Positive Self-Talk

Some of the most powerful and influential messages are those that come from within, our "inner voice." Thus, covert conditioning can be a valuable source of verbal persuasion. However, such self-talk should maintain a positive perspective. This entails structuring statements to emphasize the execution of a desired performance as opposed to an undesired one (e.g., for a baseball player to "Connect with the ball," as opposed to "Don't strike out."). Additionally, it is useful to have athletes keep self-talk logs so that they become more aware of the content and tone of their self-talk.

Understand Arousal

Depending on how an athlete interprets the "butterflies" in his or her stomach can have a dramatic impact on performance. Those that perceive these "butterflies" as a sign of weakness and indicators of self-doubt are setting themselves up for failure. However, the athlete who interprets such physiological arousal as a sign that his body is getting ready for the physical demand required by their sport is priming himself for success. Thus, athletes need to be encouraged to become more aware of how their body feels when they are relaxed and when they are anxious. Practicing a differential progressive muscle relaxation exercise could assist some athletes to achieve this discrimination.

Becoming an Optimist

Optimists believe they can have an impact on the outcome of events. Additionally, optimists possess an attributional framework that is internal, stable, and global for positive events and external, unstable, and specific for negative events.

Own Your Success

Individuals who lack confidence often "explain away" their successes. If an athlete is to develop an optimistic explanatory style, he or she need to begin to internalize their successes. This can be accomplished with the help of a "Sport Confidence" log in which the athlete keeps a diary of his or her personal achievements made during training and competition (Miller, 1991). The log can identify specific training and competition behaviors the athlete exhibited that contributed to a successful performance. Taking responsibility for your success and understanding what you need to correct when you fail are both important aspects of the process of internal attributions.

View Failures as Changeable

Overall, athletes should take responsibility for their actions (internal attributions) to the extent that they are able to recognize the mistakes that lead to poor performances or failure. It is important that the athlete views these mistakes as changeable. However, if the athlete is unaware of the aspects of his or her performance that caused the unsuccessful outcome, the athlete would benefit best from an external attribution. For example, the figure skater who skates a "career best" program, yet receives low scores for no apparent reason, would benefit from attributing his or her scores to inconsistent judging (external attribution) rather than to lack of ability. An external attribution in this example will avoid reducing motivation and/or decreasing effort in future practices and competitions. The key is being able to recognize the actions that are under one's control, which if changed would result in improved performance and an increased probability of success. Thus, if an athlete is unaware of what he or she did incorrectly that led to failure and is oblivious as to how to correct his or her behaviors, the athlete's sport confidence would best be served by an external attribution that would insulate their sport confidence. However, once the athlete becomes aware of the steps he or she needs to take to improve performance, an external attribution would no longer serve this function. Such an attribution would then be merely one way the athlete is avoiding his or her responsibility, and the probability of modifying practice with competitive behavior to increase success is reduced.

Take Control of Your Situation

Instrumental to developing an optimistic explanatory style is believing that one's actions will have an impact on subsequent results. Thus, athletes need to develop ways to take control over their situations. Developing performance goal windows and having precompetitive plans are examples of how athletes can monitor and make subsequent adjustments to their behavior and performance in competition.

Info Box

Athletes can develop self-confidence in many ways; however, it is not an easy process. Self-confidence is not given by other people. It must be developed by the athletes themselves through strong mental training and self-discipline.

Challenges to the Athlete in Developing and Maintaining Self-Confidence

The challenge facing athletes who wish to develop or maintain a desired level of sport confidence is ownership. By ownership, it is meant that "confidence is a choice" (Cook, 1992).

Confidence is a choice that each athlete has to make each and every day. Each day athletes make decisions that earn them the right to be confident. For example, athletes who spend extra time conditioning their bodies and honing their skills earn the right to approach competitions with the belief that they have done everything they could to prepare, whereas the athletes who loaf on their workouts probably will entertain self-doubts in their abilities as competition nears because they know they could have trained more effectively. Athletes earn the right to be confident by being in top physical condition and approaching each practice and training session as an opportunity to improve their skills and abilities. Confidence is not a commodity that is easily bestowed on another or taken away at a coach's whim. The notion that athletes "lose" their confidence or that "coaches do not give their athletes any confidence," needs to be dismissed, and athletes need to recognize the ways in which they are *choosing* to give their confidence away.

Implication for the Athlete: Performing with or without Confidence

The positive relationship between sport confidence and successful performance has been demonstrated in numerous settings, research investigations, cases studies, and anecdotal evidence. Clearly, an athlete who approaches competition with a confident attitude has a distinct advantage over an athlete who is not confident. Athletes who are confident display a greater sense of resiliency, which enables them to endure hardships and respond positively to setbacks, whereas the athlete who lacks confidence is likely to allow even minor setbacks to result in a subsequent deterioration in performance. In many ways, competing with true confidence gives an athlete an advantage over the athlete who does not compete with confidence, even if the confident athlete possesses less "physical talent"—like a Larry Bird.

Imagine an athlete who does possess exceptional physical talent as well as self-confidence. Will that athlete consistently perform well enough to achieve success? If the athlete is motivated, confident, and physically talented, he or she must still be able to perform skills without distraction. High levels of self-confidence are beneficial to performance; however, an athlete should never overestimate his or her ability in competition and become mentally lazy. The challenge to the athlete is to have realistic self-confidence as well as the ability to maintain concentration on the task at hand. No better example may exist of this combination of physical ability, high self-confidence, and concentration ability than Michael Jordan.

> *As fast as the game moves, his mind moves faster. He is able to analyze the game frame by frame, as if the play unfolds in slow motion. He can sustain concentration in each frame of the game. If an opposing player loses his concentration for a split second— blam! Michael grabs the advantage.*
>
> —Isaiah Thomas (1998, p. 58)

Concentration

As the statement by Isaiah Thomas illustrates, one of the reasons Michael Jordan is considered the greatest basketball player to ever have played the game is his uncanny ability to sustain his concentration. Generally, concentration is referred to as "the skill of focusing one's attention on the function or task at hand" (Dorfman & Kuehl, 1989, p. 152). More specifically, concentration can be viewed as focusing on task-relevant cues, while at the same time not attending to task-irrelevant cues (Burke, 1992; Weinberg & Gould, 1995).

Nideffer (1976) proposed that to fully understand concentration, we need to view it as the product of two interacting dimensions representing width and directionality. Attentional width varies from broad to narrow and corresponds to the amount of information that is attended to within one's environment. More concretely, attentional width refers to the number of elements a person can focus on at any given moment (Moran, 1996). A broad attentional focus suggests the athlete is aware of a wide variety of cues within his or her environment. This type of focus contrasts with a narrow attentional focus, which indicates the athlete is attending to one or two cues within the environmental array. Directionality, on the other hand, is concerned with the target of one's attention. Thus, directionality differentiates whether the athlete is focusing on cues that are internally based (cues from within the athlete, such as muscle tension and self-talk) or externally based (cues in the environment, such as noise or poor weather conditions). The interaction of the dimensions of width and directionally form four types of concentration: Broad External (BE), Narrow External (NE), Broad Internal (BI), and Narrow Internal (NI).

Broad External (BE)

Broad external concentration is the attentional focus an athlete engages in while "assessing" the situation (Burke, 1992). The focus is centered externally and on many cues within the environment. For example, a broad external focus is often used when a point guard who is leading a fast break scans the court to determine which of his or her teammates is open for an easy score. Such a focus requires the ability to integrate a variety of different environmental cues at the same time.

Narrow External (NE)

Narrow external concentration is best characterized as "object focus" attention (Burke, 1992). Here the athlete is focused on one or two primary cues. This is the type of concentration the athlete should be in while executing a particular skill. Although the direction of this concentration remains external to the individual, this form of concentration contrasts with broad external because the athlete is focusing only on one or two essential cues required to complete a particular task. Thus, the baseball player who comes to the plate would benefit by focusing on the speed and placement of the ball.

Broad Internal (BI)

This form of concentration characterizes the attentional focus present when an athlete is "analyzing" the sport situation (Burke, 1992). Thus, the athlete it considering a variety of cues that entails using his or her ability to integrate a multitude of different thoughts and feelings. Here the athlete is likely to be developing different scenarios in his or her mind in an attempt to figure out a "game plan" or the best course of action to take to meet the task demands at hand, for example, the point guard whose team is down by three points with less than a minute to go in the game who weighs the necessity of setting up a teammate for a quick three-point shot.

Narrow Internal (NI)

Narrow internal concentration is a "thought-focused" attention (Burke, 1992). The athlete focusing on only one or two cues, which are primarily internal, demonstrates this type of concentration. This is the type of attentional focus the athlete engages in when mentally preparing for competition, such as a diver mentally rehearses the sequence of twists and turns for the next dive.

Nideffer (1976) expanded this understanding of concentration into attentional style theory. Attentional style theory is the foundation of Attention Control Training (ACT). Attention control training embodies a multifaceted approach that enables the sport psychologist, coach, or athlete to identify attentional strengths and weaknesses to facilitate the construction of interventions (Nideffer & Simon-Sagal, 1988). The eight principles of ACT are outlined in Table 12.1.

Attentional style theory suggests that of the four attentional styles described, each individual has a "preferred attentional style" that is tabled across sport settings. Additionally, Nideffer and Simon-Sagal (1998) assert that different sports and different sport skills require different attentional styles. For example, while bringing the ball down the court, a basketball

TABLE 12.1 *Eight Principles of Attentional Control Training (ACT).*

1. Athletes need to be able to engage in four types of attention (BE, NI, NE, NI).
2. Different sport situations will make different attentional demands on an athlete. Therefore, the athlete must be able to shift to the appropriate type of concentration to match changing attentional demands.
3. Under optimal conditions, the average person can meet the concentration demands of a wide variety of performance situations.
4. Attentional characteristics are at times trait-like, having predictive validity in any number of situations. At other times, they are state-like, situationally determined and modified through training.
5. The individual's ability to perform effectively as the dominant concentration style becomes more trait-like depends on two factors (1) the appropriateness of the dominant attentional style and (2) the level of confidence within the particular performance situation.
6. The phenomenon of choking—of having performance progressively deteriorate—occurs as physiological arousal increases, causing attention to involuntarily narrow and become more internally focused.
7. Alterations in physiological arousal affect concentration. Thus, systematic manipulation of physiological arousal is one way of gaining some control over concentration.
8. Alterations in the focus of attention affect physiological arousal. Thus the systematic manipulation of concentration is one way to gain some control over arousal (e.g., muscular tension levels, heart rate, respiration rate).

Nideffer & Simon-Sagal, 1988, p. 297.

player may need to have a broad external focus, whereas when he or she is shooting a free throw, a narrow external focus would be necessary. Furthermore, optimal performance is dependent on the compatibility between an athlete's attentional style and the attentional demand of their sport. Thus, when there is a discrepancy between the athlete's attentional style and the task demand of the sport, poor performance is likely to result (Moran, 1996). However, the most striking aspect of this attentional style theory is that as an athlete's arousal increases he or she is likely to experience an involuntarily narrowing of attentional focus, increased distractibility, and reduced attentional flexibility.

Info Box

According to theory, each athlete exhibits an attentional style. Performance is enhanced when the attentional style of the athlete is compatible with the task being performed. Because the majority of sports present a variety of tasks within competition, it is important for athletes to develop the ability to shift through the attentional dimensions to align the task with the attentional style that is best suited.

Attention

To understand how arousal can affect an athlete's attention and subsequently his or her concentration, it is necessary to take a closer look at what is meant by *attention*. Often attention is described as a "zoom lens" (Orlick, 1990) or, more fittingly, a beam of light that is responsible for bringing a portion of our sensory world to the forefront and allows our information processing systems to make sense of it. However, like the beam of light that emanates from a flashlight, one's attentional focus is limited by the width of the beam. Thus, our attentional system is charged with the task of selecting sensory input from the environment (Zimbardo, 1992).

Moran (1996) contends that attention is a multifaceted construct that embodies the ability to selectively attend to information, engage in mental "time-sharing," and regulate one's level of alertness. The notion of attention being selective is thought to serve a protective function, preventing individuals from being overwhelmed by the myriad of environmental information. Similarly, the concept of "time-sharing" illustrates the ability to spread one's attentional resources efficiently across a variety of tasks to complete complex motor behaviors, such as driving a car. Finally, attention has become synonymous with a "brief and usually involuntary, state of alertness or preparedness for action" (Moran, 1996, p. 42). Thus, being attentive to one's environment means being "aroused," and a lack of arousal is associated with a reduced sensitivity to one's surroundings (Moran, 1996).

Arousal, Anxiety, and Attentional Narrowing

As Moran (1996) and Nideffer (1976) have suggested, one's level of arousal influences one's attentional focus. Simply stated, arousal can be conceptualized as a state of alertness.

In the truest sense, arousal is a physiological process involving organs under the control of the autonomic nervous system (Cox, 1985). This activation of the organism can be viewed as varying on a continuum from deep sleep to extreme excitation (Malmo, 1959). Weinberg and Gould (1995) characterized the lack of arousal on this continuum as a state that is devoid of activation and closely resembles coma, whereas the state of complete arousal is representative of a state of frenzy or the fight-or-flight response. In light of this information, a more comprehensive definition of arousal is "a nonemotional physiological state of readiness to perform physically, intellectually, or perceptually" (Wann, 1997, p. 133).

Physiologically, a high level of arousal is reflected by increases in an athlete's heart rate, respiration, blood pressure, sweating, and muscle tension (Cox, 1985). However, arousal in itself is neither positive nor negative. It is the way in which an athlete makes sense of or interprets arousal that gives it a positive of negative valence. The best way to understand how the athlete's thoughts can affect his or her level of activation is to revisit the classic analogy proposed by Martens (1974). He compared the energy created by one's increases in arousal to the accelerator of an automobile. When the car is in neutral, the revolutions per minute of the engine can be varied along a continuum from low to high depending on how much pressure is exerted on the accelerator. However, the direction of the car is unaffected unless the car is placed in gear. Thus, the athlete who interprets "butterflies" in his stomach as a sign that he is unprepared for the challenges his opponent presents is likely to suffer performance decrements. This contrasts with the athlete who views these same "butterflies" as a sign that her body is ready and prepared for competition.

Based on this understanding of arousal, it appears that at the upper end of the continuum, arousal can take either a positive or a negative connotation. When a high level of arousal has a negative flavor, the athlete experiences stress or anxiety. Specifically, anxiety is the emotional impact or cognitive dimension of being overaroused (Gould & Krane, 1992), which is associated with an unpleasant emotional experience.

Spielberger (1975) differentiates between state and trait anxiety. State anxiety is defined as an immediate emotional state characterized by feelings of apprehension, nervousness, fear, and tension. Trait anxiety, on the other hand, is a predisposition to interpret relatively nonthreatening stimuli as threatening and thus to respond with a high level of state anxiety.

Additionally, anxiety can be viewed as having two distinct components. Davidson and Schwartz (1976) distinguish between cognitive and somatic anxiety. Cognitive anxiety is the component of anxiety that is primarily associated with one's thought processes. Somatic anxiety is essentially the body's physiological reaction to anxiety, such as shakiness, sweating, and increased heart rate.

Anxiety affects athletic performance negatively by causing muscle tension and coordination deficits. Anxiety alters an athlete's attentional/concentrational focus by restricting the scope of the attention span and the direction of the concentrational beam (Moran, 1996). Lacey (1967) suggests that there is a physiological distinction between an attentional focus that is focused inward and one that is fixed on environmental cues. Lacey found that if focus is tuned to cues in the environment, the individual will experience a reduction in his or her heart rate. As the attentional focus turns to internal cues, his or her heart rate increases (Lacey, 1967). Athletes who are anxious are likely to attend to internal stimuli rather than external environmental cues while performing complex tasks under pressure (Moran, 1996).

As athletes focus inwardly, they begin to worry about potential failures, which reduces the attentional resources available to concentrate on task relevant cues.

This turning inward is often regarded as attentional narrowing. Easterbrook's (1959) cue utilization theory suggests that as arousal increases, an athlete's attentional focus narrows, resulting in a reduction of incidental environmental cues that are processed. Such narrowing can become extremely hazardous during complex tasks that require the integration of multiple cues that are essential to successfully execute a task. As attentional narrowing occurs, the athlete is likely to ignore vital information as well as task irrelevant cues. Under normal levels of arousal, one's attentional field is optimal. However, under stressful conditions when the athlete is likely to become overaroused, his or her attentional focus tends to narrow, thus causing the athlete to disregard important stimuli in his environment. On the other hand, when the athlete is underaroused, her attentional focus broadens. Now, the athlete is attending to cues within her environment that are irrelevant to the task at hand (Nideffer, 1976).

Choking

The most notable concentrational problem probably is the phenomenon known to coaches and athletes as choking. Choking occurs when an athlete is unable to regain control over his or her performance as it progressively deteriorates (Weinberg & Gould, 1995). Unfortunately, choking is likely to occur when the athlete is in a situation that is extremely important to him or her. Choking is characterized by a series of physiological reactions such as increases in heart rate, respiration, sweating, as well as disturbances in fine-motor coordination and timing due to tensing of one's muscles. However, it is the attentional deficits that the athlete experiences that is so destructive to the athletic performance. As the choke cycle progresses, the athlete's attention shifts from cues within the environment that are essential to completing the task at hand to an internal attentional focus, which is often characterized by self-doubts and negative self-talk. Additionally, the athlete's ability to shift one attentional focus to another is compromised.

Info Box

Arousal has the capacity to negatively affect performance through attentional processes. Low arousal levels allow the athlete to divert attention away from the self, causing a very broad focus that may often include task-irrelevant stimuli. On the contrary, high arousal forces the athlete to shift his or her attention to a narrow and often internal focus, which may lead to the disregard of important task-relevant stimuli.

Improving Concentration

Several techniques can improve athletes' concentration. Athletes can enhance their concentration by developing strategies to help them focus on task-relevant cues while ignoring task-irrelevant cues. Such strategies as competing in the "here and now," goal setting, establishing precompetitive routines, and using cue words are very helpful. Attention control training also suggests it is possible to improve one's concentration by regulating one's arousal through the use of deep breathing and progressive muscle relaxation exercises. The following strategies and exercises are designed to target either focusing one's concentration or reducing one's arousal.

Just Be: Performing in the "Here and Now"

Sport psychologists, athletes, and coaches have long advocated that to unlock true potential and be in "the zone," it is necessary to perform in the "here and now." For example, for baseball, Hanson and Ravizza (1995, p. 45) epitomize this approach when they suggest "play the game one pitch at a time."

Goldberg (1998) asserts that performing in the "here and now" entails making sure you are in the right "time zone." Consider, the difficulties a traveler experiences when he or she flies from New York City to Paris. Such a trip involves crossing several time zone and is likely to cause jet lag. This occurs because although the traveler may physically be in Paris, his or her mind is still 8 hours behind in New York City. Just as the traveler experiences jet lag, the athlete who dwells on past events or future outcomes experiences concentration deficits because his or her body is not in sync with his or her mind. The athlete who comes to the plate thinking about the pitch that got away or how his teammates will carry him off the field when he hits the winning home run is setting himself up for failure. Each time an athlete goes out to practice or compete, she can choose to be in one of three time zones: past, present, or future. Focusing on past at bats places the athlete's focus in the past, whereas thinking about the next game shifts her focus into the future. It is only when the athlete is focused in the present and on the task at hand that the mind and body are in sync and prepared to exert full potential.

Goal Setting

An effective means of staying in the "here and now" and thus improving concentration is goal setting. Athletes who set process goals or goals that focus on improvements relative to their own standards of performance (e.g., improving a free throw percentage from 75 percent to 80 percent) as opposed to goals that focus on desired outcome (e.g., going undefeated and winning the championship) are more focused and better prepared to reach their potentials. Goal setting enhances concentration because it not only motivates and directs energy but also specifies which task-relevant thoughts and actions are most important (Moran, 1996). Essentially, goals improve concentration by providing a sense of purpose and centering the attentional "spotlight."

Precompetitive Routines

In addition to effective goal setting, preperformance plans or precompetitive routines are also effective ways to focus attention. Precompetitive routines help to ensure that athletes perform in a flow state. This routine is a detailed series of events that an athlete goes through as he or she prepares for practice or competition. Such routines could include proper stretching, warm-up exercises, and mental preparation exercises. They are effective if they are focused on task-relevant thoughts and actions. When routines are excessively long or have no "technical function" in the execution of the skill (Moran, 1996, p. 188), they are often considered rituals or superstitions. Superstitions imply that performance is contingent on external sources (e.g., wearing black socks); however, precompetitive routines are actions the athlete controls that prepare him or her to perform.

Precompetitive routines are believed to enhance an athlete's concentration in several ways. They require athletes to engage in thoughts and actions that focus their attentional "spot light" on the task at hand. Precompetitive routines help reduce distractions and worry that may hinder them from entering the "zone." Additionally, precompetitive routines help prevent "warm-up" decrements, a phenomenon that occurs when an athlete's performance drops following a period of rest. Precompetitive routines prevent such decrements by helping athletes maintain physical and psychic intensity during the lulls that precede competition (Moran, 1996).

Self-Talk and Cue Words

Saying the right things to yourself can often facilitate getting in "the zone" and staying there. But what are the right things? For all practical purposes, when we are thinking, we are engaging ourselves in conversation. This is what is commonly called self-talk. Self-talk can either enhance or hinder an athlete's performance. Negative self-talk is any thought that detracts from the task at hand or any disparaging or critical statement about yourself or your performance. On the other hand, positive self-talk is any comment that keeps one focused and improves performance. Thus, although a positive affirmation, such as "I am a good person," can improve one's self-esteem, in the heat of competition such thoughts may actually hinder an athlete's performance to the extent that it detracts from his or her focus on the task at hand.

Murphy (1996) suggests that self-talk should take the form of performance or cue words. These cue words should be "simple, positive, and focus on one's strengths" (p. 165). Additionally, cue words are most effective if they enhance "mechanical efficacy" and encourage proper technique (e.g., strong, steady and follow through). Furthermore, cue words such as "full power" or "blastoff" can be used to instill a particular mood, such as confidence or intensity, which many athletes believe is necessary for optimal performance.

Diaphragmatic Breathing

Although a relatively simple technique, diaphragmatic or "belly breathing" is believed to enhance concentration because it is an effective means of preventing anxiety. When executed properly, diaphragmatic breathing counteracts anxiety because it requires the athlete to pay conscious attention to breathing. Focus on breathing in itself reduces anxiety, because it is impossible to focus on breathing and worries at the same time.

Diaphragmatic breathing encourages athletes to take breaths that require them to make the most efficient use of their lungs. This is accomplished by asking them to imagine that their lungs are divided into three chambers. Athletes then begin concentrating on filling the bottom section of the lungs, followed by the middle and then the top. This is successfully completed if at the end of each breath the stomach appears distended, which occurs because the diaphragm, the muscle that separates the lungs from the abdominal cavity, is forced down into the abdominal cavity as the lungs begin to fill up with air. Hence the name *diaphragmatic breathing*. Each breath should be inhaled in a smooth and gradual fashion and held for approximately 5–6 seconds (Williams & Harris, 1998).

In addition to regulating breathing, athletes can improve their concentration by developing a better sense of how their body feels during relaxed and tense states. Jacobson's (1938) progressive muscular relaxation is one effective technique that helps individuals develop such an awareness. Through the systematic tensing and relaxing of all the major muscle groups in the body, progressive muscular relaxation is designed to teach athletes to focus their attention on the somatic sensations of relaxation and tension (Weinberg, 1998).

Simulation Training

Simulation training can provide athletes with the opportunity to practice their concentrational skills. By simulating real-life competitive situations, athletes can examine how their concentration is likely to change for better or for worse during competition. Furthermore, athletes can then practice refocusing techniques (e.g., deep breathing, cue words) when they feel their attention shifting involuntarily.

Focusing Exercises

Exercises that provide the athlete with the opportunity to practice maintaining and shifting attentional focus can be extremely beneficial. Such an exercise could entail focusing upon an object that is relevant to the sport (e.g., a ball) while repeating "ball" or "focus" (Burke, 1992). Additionally, the athlete could be encouraged to practice shifting attention from competing visual and auditory cues. This is done by identifying several different visual and auditory cues in the environment and progressively focusing on each one separately and then, eventually, all the cues simultaneously.

Imagery

Imagery has the potential to both strengthen the attentional resources and create a relaxed state within the athlete. To strengthen concentration, engage athletes in imagery that allows them to practice voluntarily shifting their attentional focus. Imagery can also be used to instill a state of relaxation by having athletes visualize calm and relaxing settings.

Conclusion

Two of the characteristics that help elite athletes, such as Michael Jordan, perform at peak potential are a high level of self-confidence and the ability to harness attentional focus. This chapter examined self-confidence and sport confidence, as well as the related concepts of self-efficacy and dispositional optimism. In the absence of confidence, learned helplessness can occur because of explanatory style. High levels of self-confidence have many beneficial effects on performance. Consequently, several guidelines to develop self-confidence were presented. The chapter continued with a focus on concentration and how

Concentration is a skill that athletes can develop and improve.

this skill can be cultivated and mastered. Our discussion of concentration began with a basic description of this concept, focusing on Nideffer's (1976) conceptualization that concentration is a construct that is best characterized by four attentional styles (BE, NE, BI, NI). This focus on attentional style naturally led to a discussion exploring the relationship between concentration and attention. We examined the effect arousal can have on concentration, and finally we offered a variety of techniques to enhance concentration.

Key Terms *(in order of appearance)*

confidence	dispositional optimism	learned helplessness
sport confidence	perception of control	explanatory style
self-efficacy	perceived competence	

References

Abramson, L. Y., Seligman, M. E. P., & Teasdale, J. D. (1978). Learned helplessness in humans: Critique and reformulation. *Journal of Abnormal Psychology, 87,* 49–74.

Bandura, A. (1977). Self-efficacy: Toward a unifying theory of behavioral change. *Psychological Bulletin, 84,* 191–215.

Bandura, A. (1986). *Social foundations of thought and action: A social cognitive theory.* Englewood Cliffs, NJ: Prentice Hall.

Bandura, A. (1992). On rectifying the comparative anatomy of perceived control: Comments on "cognates of personal control." *Applied and Preventive Psychology, 1,* 121–126.

Bandura, A. (1997). *Self-efficacy: The exercise of personal control.* New York: Freeman.

Bandura, A., Adams, N. E., Hardy, A. B., & Howells, G. N. (1980). Tests of the generality of self-efficacy theory. *Cognitive Therapy and Research, 4,* 39–66.

Bandura, A., Reese, L., & Adams, N. E. (1982). Microanalysis of action and fear arousal as a function of differential levels of perceived self-efficacy. *Journal of Personality and Social Psychology, 43,* 5–21.

Barling, J., & Abel, M. (1983). Self-efficacy beliefs and tennis performance. *Cognitive Therapy and Research, 7,* 265–272.

Beck, A. T., Weissmann, A., Lester, D., & Trexler, L. (1974). The measurement of pessimism: The hopelessness scale. *Journal of Consulting and Clinical Psychology, 42,* 861–865.

Bennett, J. G., & Pravitz, J. E. (1987). *The profile of a winner: Advanced mental training for athletes.* Ithaca, NY: Sport Science International.

Burke, K. L. (1992). Concentration. *Sport psychology training bulletin: For coaches, athletes, & parents, 4*(1) 1–8.

Callahan, T. (1985). Masters of their game. *Time,* March 18, 52–60.

Connell, J. P. (1985). A new multidimensional measure of children's perceptions of control. *Child Development, 56,* 1018–1041.

Cook, D. L. "Understanding and enhancing confidence in athletes: From research to practice." Paper presented at the annual meeting of the Association for the Advancement of Applied Sport Psychology. Colorado Springs, CO, October, 1992.

Cox, R. H. (1985). *Sport psychology: Concepts and applications.* Dubuque, IA: Wm. C. Brown.

Davidson, R. J., & Schwartz, G. E. (1976). The psychobiology of relaxation and related stress: A multi-process theory. In D. I. Mostofsky (Ed.), *Behavior control and modification of physiological activity* (pp. 339–442). Englewood Cliffs, NJ: Prentice Hall.

Dorfman, H. A., & Kuehl, K. (1989). *The mental game of baseball: A guide to peak performance.* South Bend, IN: Diamond Communications.

Easterbrook, J. A. (1959). The effect of emotion on cue utilization and the organization of behavior. *Psychological Bulletin, 66,* 183–201.

Goldberg, A. S. (1998). *Sports slump busting: 10 steps to mental toughness and peak performance.* Champaign, IL: Human Kinetics.

Gould, D., & Krane, V. (1992). The arousal-athletic performance relationship: Current status and future directions. In T. Horn (Ed.), *Advances in sport psychology* (pp. 119–141). Champaign, IL: Human Kinetics.

Griffith, C. R. (1928). *Psychology and athletics: A general survey for athletes and coaches.* New York: Scribner's.

Holloway, J. B., Beuter, A., & Duda, J. L. (1988). Self-efficacy and training strength in adolescent girls. *Journal of Applied Sport Psychology, 18,* 699–719.

Jacobson, E. (1938). *Progressive relaxation.* Chicago: Univ. of Chicago Press.

Kauss, D. R. (1980). *Peak performance: Mental game plans for maximizing your athletic potential.* Englewood Cliffs, NJ: Prentice Hall.

Lacey, J. I. (1967). Somatic response patterning and stress: Some revisions of activation theory. In M. H. Appley & R. Trumbull (Eds.), *Psychological stress: Issues and research* (pp. 170–179). New York: Appleton-Century-Crofts.

Lan, L. Y., & Gill, D. L. (1984). The relationship among self-efficacy, stress responses, and a cognitive feedback manipulation. *Journal of Sport Psychology, 6,* 227–238.

Lee, C. (1982). Self-efficacy as a predictor of performance in competitive gymnastics. *Journal of Sport Psychology, 4,* 404–409.

McAuley, E. (1985). State anxiety: Antecedents or result of sport performance. *Journal of Sport Behavior, 8,* 71–77.

Maier, S. F., & Seligman, M. E. P. (1976). Learned helplessness: Theory and evidence. *Journal of Experimental Psychology: General, 105,* 3–46.

Malmo, R. B. (1959). Activation: A neuropsychological dimension. *Psychological Review, 66,* 367–386.

Manzo, L. G., & Silva, J. M. "Applying self-confidence research to competitive sport." Paper presented at the North Carolina Alliance of Health, Physical Education, Recreation, and Dance Conference, Greensboro, North Carolina, November 1993.

Manzo, L. G., & Silva, J. M. "Construction and initial validation of the Carolina Sport Confidence Inventory." Paper presented at the annual conference of the Association for the Advancement of Applied Sport Psychology, Lake Tahoe, Nevada, October 1994.

Manzo, L. G., Silva, J. M., & Mink, R. (2001, in press). "Sport confidence: A theory generated measure." *Journal of Applied Sport Psychology.*

Martens, R. (1974). Arousal and motor performance. In J. H. Wilmore (Ed.), *Exercise and sport science reviews.* New York: Academic.

Martens, R., Vealey, R. S., & Burton, B. (1990). *Competitive anxiety in sport.* Champaign, IL: Human Kinetics.

Martin, J. J., & Gill, D. L. (1991). The relationship among competitive orientation, sport confidence, self-efficacy, anxiety, and performance. *Journal of Sport and Exercise Psychology, 13,* 149–159.

Matheson, H., & Mathes, S. (1991). Influence of performance setting, experience and difficulty of routine on the precompetition anxiety and self-confidence of high school female gymnasts. *Perceptual and Motor Skills, 72,* 1099–1105.

Miller, M. (1991). Building sport confidence. *Sport psychology Training Bulletin: An educational resource for athletes, coaches, & parents, 2,* (5), 1–6.

Moran, A. P. (1996). *The psychology of concentration in sport performers: A cognitive analysis.* East Sussex, UK: Psychology.

Murphy, S. (1996). *The achievement zone: An 8-step guide to peak performance in all areas of life.* New York: Berkley.

Nideffer, R. M. (1976). *The inner athlete.* New York: Cromwell.

Nideffer, R. M., & Simon-Sagal, M. (1998). Concentration and attention control training. In J. Williams (Ed.). *Applied sport psychology: Personal growth to peak performance,* 3rd ed., (pp. 296–315). Mountain View CA: London.

Orlick, T. (1990). *In pursuit of excellence: How to win in sport and life through mental training,* 2nd ed. Champaign, IL: Leisure.

Peterson, C., Buchanan, G. M., & Seligman, M. E. P. (1995). Explanatory style: History and evolution of the field. In G. M. Buchanan & M. E. P. Seligman (Eds.), *Explanatory Style.* Hillsdale, NJ: Erlbaum.

Peterson, C., Maier, S. F., & Seligman, M. E. P. (1993). *Learned helplessness: A theory for the age of personal control.* New York: Oxford Univ. press.

Peterson, C., Semmel, A., Von Beyer, C., Abramson, L. Y., Metalsky, G. I., & Seligman, M. E. P. (1982). The attributional style questionaire. *Cognitive Therapy and Research, 6,* 287–300.

Peterson, C., & Stunkard, A. J. (1992). Cognates of personal control: Locus of control, self-efficacy, and explanatory style. *Applied and Preventative Psychology, 1,* 111–117.

Ravizza, K., & Hanson, T. (1995). *Heads-up baseball: Playing the game one pitch at a time.* Chicago, IL: Contemporary Books.

Rettew, D., & Reivich, K. (1995). Sports and explanatory style. In G. M. Buchanan & M. E. P. Seligman (Eds.), *Explanatory Style.* Hillsdale, NJ: Erlbaum.

Schulman, P. (1995). Explanatory style and achievement in school and work. In G. M. Buchanan & M. E. P. Seligman (Eds.), *Explanatory Style.* Hillsdale, NJ: Erlbaum.

Scheier, M. F., & Carver, C. S. (1985). Optimism, coping, and health: Assessment and implications of generalized outcome expectancies. *Health Psychology, 4,* 219–247.

Schunk, D. H., & Carbonari, J. P. (1984). Self-efficacy models. In J. D. Matarazzo, S. M. Weiss, J. A. Herd, N. E. Miller & S. M. Weiss (Eds.), *Behavioral health: A handbook of health enhancement and disease prevention.* New York: Wiley.

Seligman, M. E. P. (1990). *Learned optimism.* New York: Pocket Books.

Seligman, M. E. P., Nolen-Hoeksema, S., Thornton, N., & Thornton, K. M. (1990). Explanatory style as a mechanism of disappointing athletic performance. *Psychological Science, 1,* 143–146.

Sinclair, D. A., & Vealey, R. S. (1989). Effects of coaches' expectations and feedback on the self-perceptions of athletes. *Journal of Sport Behavior, 12,* 77–91.

Spielberger, C. D. (1975). Anxiety: State-trait process. In C. D. Spielberger & I. G. Sarason (Eds.), *Stress and anxiety,* Vol. 1 (pp. 115–143). New York: Hemisphere.

Spence, K. W. (1956). *Behavior theory and conditioning.* New Haven, CT: Yale Univ. Press.

Taylor, J. (1987). Predicting athletic performance with self-confidence and somatic and cognitive anxiety as a function of motor and physiological requirements in six sports. *Journal of Personality, 55,* 139–153.

Thomas, I. (1998). One of a kind: Focus. *ESPN The Magazine,* June 29, 58.

Vealey, R. S. (1986). Conceptualization of sport-confidence and competitive orientation: Preliminary investigation and instrument development. *Journal of Sport Psychology, 8,* 221–246.

Wann, D. (1997). *Sport psychology.* Upper Saddle River, NJ: Prentice Hall.

Weinberg, R., Gould, D., & Jackson, A. (1979). Expectations and performance: An empirical test of Bandura's self-efficacy theory. *Journal of Sport Psychology, 1,* 320–331.

Weinberg, R. S. (1998). *The mental advantage: Developing your psychological skills in tennis.* Champaign, IL: Human Kinetics.

Weinberg, R. S., & Gould, D. (1995). *Foundations of sport and exercise psychology.* Champaign, IL: Human Kinetics.

Weinberg, R. S., Gould, D., Yukelson, D., & Jackson, A. (1981).The effects of preexisting and manipulated self-efficacy on a competitive muscular endurance task. *Journal of Sport Psychology, 4,* 345–354.

Williams, J., & Harris, D. V. (1998). Relaxation and energizing techniques for regulation. In J. Williams (Ed.), *Applied sport psychology: Personal growth to peak performance,* 3rd ed., (pp. 219–236). Mountain View, CA: London.

Williams, S. L., Dooseman, G., & Kliefield (1984). Comparative effectiveness of guided mastery and exposure treatments for intractable phobias. *Journal of Consulting and Clinical Psychology, 42,* 505–518.

Zimbardo, P. (1992). *Psychology and life,* 13th ed. New York: Harper Collins.

13

Group Dynamics: The Influence of the Team in Sport

Julie Partridge and Diane E. Stevens

The University of North Carolina at Chapel Hill

- Differences exist between a collection of individuals and a group.
- The characteristics of group members and the size of the group influence performance and motivation.
- All groups conform to a general group structure.
- Group processes and how they are influenced by group composition and group structure are explained.

Think for a moment about the way you behave in different situations. Do you behave differently in the classroom than when you are alone in your room or with friends? Are you more reserved with family members than with others? Are you more assertive when you participate in sport than when playing with your brothers or sisters? These questions demonstrate the thrust of this chapter: group pressures, influences, and dynamics can result in behavior that may be different than that exhibited in dyads or situations in which an individual acts alone. Given the highly interdependent nature of sport teams, the topic of group dynamics is of vital importance to sport psychology. **Group dynamics** is the scientific study of behavior in groups, and is designed to advance our knowledge about the nature of groups, group development, and the interrelationships between groups and the individual (Johnson & Johnson, 1997). This chapter is designed to introduce the reader to some of the factors of group dynamics that are fundamental to the sport team.

Info Box

By understanding group dynamics, we develop an understanding of people's behavior in a group.

Every successful team is more than a collection of individuals.

Introduction to Group Dynamics

The concept of people behaving differently in groups than they do individually is certainly not unique to sport. The study of groups and group dynamics is an important topic to explore, especially when considering the number and diversity of groups that individuals will join over the course of their lives (e.g., family, college classes, sport teams). Given the pervasiveness of the group's influence on an individual's beliefs, feelings, and thoughts, it is not surprising that the study of group dynamics has received a large amount of attention from researchers, particularly in the area of the social psychology of sport (Widmeyer, Brawley, & Carron, 1992).

Pioneer work in social psychology conducted by Norman Triplett (1897) studied **audience effects,** a term that refers to the consequences of behavior performed in the presence of others. A bicycling enthusiast, Triplett noticed that cyclists achieved different speeds during races when competing against the clock than when being "paced" by another cyclist. Intrigued by this observation, he conducted an experiment examining cycling times under three conditions: unpaced (against a clock); paced (against a clock but also with a pacer); and paced competition (against another competitor). Triplett found that the cyclists in the paced condition rode faster than in either of the other two conditions. Triplett's research provided evidence for social facilitation: the improvement in performance when others are present.

Over the years, numerous studies have examined how the presence of others influences performance both in coacting tasks (e.g., jogging with a friend, eating with a friend in the cafeteria) and audience tasks (e.g., shooting a free throw in front of spectators). Results of this line of research showed that the presence of others did not always lend itself to improved performance. These equivocal results led Robert Zajonc (1965) to explore the issue of audience effects more closely. Studies were classified according to two dimensions. The first contrasted tasks that were *simple* for the subject to perform (dribbling a ball) with those that were *complex* (dribbling a ball while running down the court and making a shot). It was concluded that that presence of others facilitates performance of simple tasks and inhibits performance of complex tasks. The second dimension divided tasks into those that required *dominant responses* (habitual to the performer) and *nondominant responses* (less likely to be enacted). Zajonc concluded that the presence of others increases an individual's tendency to perform the dominant response and decreases the tendency to perform the nondominant response. This conclusion was labeled **social facilitation theory.**

This theory holds many practical implications for groups of people in everyday life (e.g., students taking a test). If you know your material well, the increased pressure associated with taking a test will result in your writing down the correct answers. Conversely, if you do not know your material well, that same pressure may result in a lesser performance because your dominant response is not the correct response. The implications for sport teams are numerous as well. Think of the experience of a wide receiver in football who must catch a ball over his shoulder while running at full speed and eluding a defensive back while 60,000 people are watching from the stands and millions more on TV. It is crucial for an athlete's dominant response to be the correct one, because it is most likely to be exhibited in situations in which an audience is present.

Info Box

People will perform habitual behaviors when in the presence of others, regardless of whether this response is the correct (or desired) one.

Although social facilitation theory has been important in bridging the gap between research from social psychology to sport psychology, the study of group dynamics as it relates to a sport environment is certainly not limited to audience effects. The knowledge of how a group functions is of prime importance to athletes, coaches, and sport psychologists. Despite this, a modest amount of scholarly research on group dynamics in sport has been conducted, the majority of which has focused on cohesion or leadership (Landers, Boutcher, & Way, 1986).

Group dynamics is an important area of study because of the extensive amount of experience individuals in our society have with groups of people. Furthermore, sport teams provide researchers with fertile research opportunities, and the pervasiveness of sport in our culture invites further examination of the factors that might affect the overall behavior of the group and the individual members' satisfaction and performance levels. Before examining the underlying processes that affect the group structure in sport, we must first define the term *group*.

Group Defined

Although the concept of a group is familiar to most people, creating a true definition of what constitutes a group can be more difficult. For example, it may seem apparent that volleyball teams, fraternities, or service clubs should be considered "groups," but what about people who are watching a movie at a theater or people playing a pickup game of basketball? Would the latter two examples constitute a group? A collection of individuals does not necessarily guarantee that a group has been formed. Several criteria must be met before a collection of individuals may be called a group. The characteristics that differentiate a sport team from a collection of individuals have been summarized by Carron and Hausenblas (1998; see Table 13.1).

Foundations of Group Behavior

Much of this text is devoted to developing an understanding of what guides individual behavior, such as an athlete's personality, anxiety, motivation, emotion, and confidence.

TABLE 13.1 *Characteristics of a Group (Tuckman, 1965; Tuckman & Jensen, 1972).*

Collective identity	Members see themselves as distinct from other teams.
Common fate	Regardless of individual performance, members win or lose as a team.
Sense of shared purpose	Collectively, a team wants to win.
Structured patterns of interaction	Patterns of interaction develop between certain players or coaches.
Structured modes of communication	Terms used in sport (*blitz, neutral zone trap*) are understandable to team members.
Personal and task interdependence	Dependence on others to play a team sport.
Member self-categorization	Members consider themselves to be part of the team.
Interpersonal attraction	Members socialize with each other.

However, an individual's behavior in a group setting may differ from how he or she acts when alone. Those interested in sport psychology need to understand the foundations of group behavior (just as they need to understand the foundations of individual behavior). These foundations include attention to group composition (e.g., the characteristics of group members), the group environment (e.g., group size), and the structure of the group (e.g., group development roles, norms, status). By understanding these concepts, team effectiveness and cohesiveness may be enhanced.

Group Composition

The characteristics of the members of a group have an important effect on how the group performs. It has been suggested that the composition of the group influences other variables (e.g., communication, cohesion) which in turn influence group productivity (Widmeyer, 1990). The variability in the **group's composition**—the degree of homogeneity versus heterogeneity—has been examined across two specific domains. First, the personal attributes (physical characteristics, race, personality, values) and psychological characteristics of group members have been examined. Second, the skills and abilities of group members have been examined. Results of this line of inquiry are discussed next.

Personal Attributes. Is a team comprising members with similar personal attributes more successful than a team with more diverse individual qualities? In an early study, Eitzen (1973) examined whether differences in personal attributes influenced clique formation and goal attainment in high school basketball players. The personal attributes measured included: father's occupation, prestige in the community, place of residence, and religion. Eitzen found that the more homogeneous the team members were around these attributes, the fewer cliques formed and the greater the chance of goal attainment. Despite this finding, other research examining the personal attributes of members and performance has been mixed (Clement & Schiereck, 1973; Klein & Christiansen, 1969). Thus, no clear effect has been found of team member homogeneity versus heterogeneity around personal attributes.

Skills and Abilities. A second line of research has examined group member's homogeneity versus heterogeneity around the skills and abilities of group members. Research has shown that groups composed of members with diverse skills and abilities outperform those where there is greater uniformity of skills (Jackson, 1992; Jones, 1974). Carron (1988) has suggested that heterogeneity of ability is particularly important in sports where athletes have distinct tasks. Softball involves hitting, pitching, running, throwing, and catching. A softball team may struggle because they do not have athletes with the skills needed to get the job done. Thus, a group's performance depends, in part, on its members' abilities.

Group Environment—Group Size

Groups vary considerably in size. A volleyball team consists of about twelve people, a baseball team about 25, and a football team may have over 80 members. The number on a sport team can indirectly influence individual behavior and the group's overall behavior. Increasing the size of a team can result in many positive consequences. For example, the chance of finding quality athletes is enhanced, as is the likelihood of the athletes expanding their social network. Conversely, the size of a team can lead to negative consequences and unfavorable attitudes of group members, such as increased perceptions of crowding, anxiety, and decreased member satisfaction and cohesion (Carron, 1990).

Steiner's Model of Productivity.   Steiner (1972) proposed a model to account for how changes in size influence team efficiency and performance (see Fig. 13.1). According to Steiner, the potential productivity of a group increases as the number of group members increases. The presence of more individuals provides the group or team with a larger number of potential resources. In a sport environment, the chance of finding skilled players for *all* positions increases. Eventually, with further increases in group size, group productivity plateaus (all positions have been adequately filled), and further increases in group size do not impact group performance.

As a group's size increases, the efficiency of group processes suffers. Interactions among team members become more difficult, as does the coordination of many team functions. It becomes more difficult to schedule team meetings, and designing effective practices becomes more complicated. Thus, even when a group possesses all the resources they need, faulty group processes may prevent them from being as successful as they could be.

Steiner's (1972) model also proposes that as the number of members on a team increases, so too does the actual productivity of the team. However, once the team's size extends beyond the optimal level, decreases in performance are likely to occur. Eventually, the size of the group becomes so large that it is ineffective. Individual members of the team decrease their productivity as the size of the team increases.

Ringelmann Effect.   Max Ringelmann, a French agricultural engineer, conducted one of the earliest studies of the impact of group size on performance. Through a series of experiments, Ringelmann (1913) discovered that additive tasks (tasks that require the summing together of individual inputs to produce a group outcome) resulted in decreased individual productivity. Tug-of-war, applauding at a concert, or working with others on a group project are all examples of additive tasks. In addition, Ringelmann found that by increasing the number of individuals in a group, the productivity decreased proportionally. For example, if one person could push 100 pounds across a floor, simple math should tell

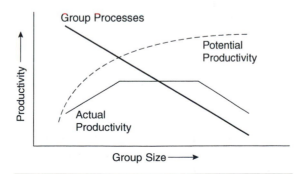

FIGURE 13.1   *Steiner's Model of Group Productivity.*

us that two people (of similar ability) should be able to push 200 pounds, and four people should push 400 pounds. However, increasing the group's size *decreased* the group's overall efficiency, so the two-person group did not push 200 pounds, but 175. The four-person group pushed only 340. The tendency for groups to become less effective as the size of the group increases has been termed the **Ringelmann effect.**

Why might people fail to be as productive as they could be when in a group? Steiner (1972) identified two possible causes. First, coordination losses that result from inefficient interactions or coordination between team members affect performance. On a task like tug-of-war, people might start pulling at different times, which would affect overall performance. Second, Steiner proposed that individuals may be less motivated to work hard when working in a group. The reduction of effort by individuals working in a group is called **social loafing** (Williams, Harkins, & Latané, 1981).

Latané, Williams, and Harkins (1979) attempted to determine the relative importance of coordination losses and decreased motivation on noise production (e.g., how loudly can you shout). Subjects were asked to shout as loudly as possible with one or five other people shouting with them. However, the subjects were deceived, and in fact, there were no other individuals shouting with them. Any reduction in productivity could not be the result of coordination losses because they were the only ones shouting. Decreases in productivity were then attributed to reduced individual effort. Latané, Williams, and Harkins found that productivity reached 82 percent and 74 percent of its capacity when subjects thought they were shouting alongside one or five other individuals, respectively. These findings demonstrated the importance of individual motivation as a cause of social loafing.

There are several implications for social loafing in an athletic setting. In many sport situations, the team's success is dependent on each individual giving his or her maximal effort. If the right offensive tackle gives 100 percent during a series of downs, but the right guard does not, social loafing is occurring. Consequently, the performance of the offensive line overall may suffer. Social loafing is rarely an isolated phenomenon on a team. The reduction of effort is often contagious, and it may cause dissension among team members. Potential reasons for social loafing are identified in Table 13.2.

Info Box

The number of players on a team has profound implications for individual athlete motivation and performance. When in a group, individuals may not exert as much effort. As a consequence, performance of that group suffers.

TABLE 13.2   *Why Do Audience Effects Occur?*

- Increased arousal—The presence of others results in increased arousal levels.
- Evaluation apprehension—When others are watching, we fear failure and embarrassment.
- Distraction—Less focused on task-relevant stimuli.
- Interferes with learning—May inhibit the dominant response.

Strategies for Reducing Social Loafing.   Several strategies have been identified that may reduce the occurrence of social loafing (Hardy, 1990). First, acknowledge all team members' contributions to the overall performance of the team. This strategy may help to establish a definite contingency between individual effort and recognition. Second, develop respect among players, not only for the starters but for members of the practice squad as well. It is important that those who do not receive the "glory" associated with competition also be recognized for their part in developing the team. Third, when possible, have team members work on interesting and/or challenging tasks. Finally, teams may also wish to assist individual goal-setting and monitoring programs. By holding individuals accountable for their performances and improvements, the tendency to "loaf" may be reduced.

Group Structure

To accurately examine groups, one must look beyond individual member characteristics and examine the group's basic structure. **Group structure** refers to the stable pattern of interaction among team members (Johnson & Johnson, 1997) that emerges in all groups. For example, patterns of communication are identified, leaders emerge, roles are filled, and rules governing the team are set. The group structure holds important implications for development of team cohesion (Carron, 1988). Cohesion may be enhanced on teams where attention to the components of group structure have been addressed. Four key structural patterns will be discussed and examined in this chapter—group development, group roles, norms, and status.

Group Development.   **Group development** can be described as a process in which a collection of individuals, with minimal ties to one another, develop over time into a cohesive unit, complete with identity, structure, norms, and roles (Brower, 1996). Group development, then, is a dynamic process that is continual until the team is disbanded. Most people can remember how they felt about a team that they participated on when first meeting the members, when competing together, and when the season was over. These stages are each associated with various emotions (e.g., nervousness, excitement), interpersonal relationships, and member behavior. Models of group development can generally be classified as linear (team development advances to each successive stage with no regression to a previous stage) or pendular (team development swings back and forth between stages). Regardless of which model of group development is employed, researchers generally believe that groups pass through five phases (Robbins, 1992; Wheelan & Hochburger, 1996).

Tuckman (1965) and Tuckman and Jensen (1965, 1977) proposed the most common model of group development. According to these researchers, the evolution of a group can be conceptualized as occurring in five developmental stages: *forming, storming, norming, performing,* and *adjourning* (see Table 13.3 on page 280). The time spent in each stage differs for each group, and some groups may never develop through each stage.

Forming.   Forming is the initial stage of team development. It occurs when team members begin to familiarize themselves with other members of the group. During this stage, relationships among group members are often awkward because individuals are often reserved in their interactions with people that they know little or nothing about. Members must also deal with their own uncertainty regarding their roles in the group. The forming

TABLE 13.3   *Stages of Group Development.*

Stage	Interpersonal Relations	Member Behavior
Forming	Explore relationships Familiarity develops	Task exploration Methods to achieve task
Storming	Rebellion between members and leader	Resistance arises
Norming	Feelings of unity Roles develop	Agreement on how to achieve goals
Performing	Relationships stabilized Mutual cooperation	Emphasis on performance
Adjourning	Contact decreases Reduced dependency Regret	Completion of the task

stage is an opportunity for team members to begin to identify and explore interpersonal relationships with each other and with coaches. Problems in the forming stage may occur when team members do not identify with other team members or feel as though they are competing with teammates.

Storming.   The second stage of team development, storming is characterized (as you might guess from the name) by rebellion against team leaders and coaches, conflicts among team members, and resistance to group control. Storming arises as individuals begin to assert themselves into roles on the team and struggle to define group goals. Much of the conflict is interpersonal, and coaches play a big role in helping the team resolve conflicts. Athletes' strengths and weaknesses must be evaluated honestly and their roles on the team clarified. By communicating these evaluations to each team member in an objective manner, coaches may reduce the amount of stress experienced by the team members, resulting in decreased hostility among group members. Conflict that is resolved successfully can help to bind a team together, and the team can move successfully to the next stage. Conflict that is not resolved can result in a team that does not achieve its full potential.

Norming.   After resolving the turmoil of the previous stage, teams enter the third stage of team development, norming, which is characterized by team unity and stability. Members communicate more openly and norms emerge more clearly. Finally, members of the team begin to solidify their roles, and recognition of other members' roles is heightened. Increased role clarity can promote mutual respect between members and can increase group cohesion and collective striving toward the performance of group goals.

Performing.   In the fourth stage of team development, performing, the group structure is fully accepted and functional. Teams in this stage are focused on very specific team goals and usually perform at high levels. The energies of the team members are channeled into performing their individual roles in a way that will benefit the team, and players assist each other in ways that will facilitate team performance.

Adjourning.   The final stage of team development is adjourning. The disbanding of a team can occur in one of two ways. The most common is when a team disbands because of a planned dissolution. No athletic season goes on forever, and a planned dissolution occurs when a team has played the final game of its schedule. When team members go through a planned dissolution, athletes are believed to have fewer difficulties adjusting to life away from the team (Forsyth, 1990). Team members psychologically prepare for dissolution by discussing the accomplishments of the group as well as the individual members. However, the dissolution may be spontaneous, in which the introduction of an unforeseen conflict requires the team to disband. Spontaneous dissolution can be highly stressful, particularly in situations in which the team members have had little or no advance warning. Forsyth notes that the impending demise of the group can create anxiety among its members, who may anticipate that they will miss the structure and social support of the group.

In the initial stages of group development, team leaders should focus on group goals and how each team member contributes to the overall good of the team. During the adjourning stage, team leaders can help to alleviate some of the stress and negative feelings associated with the termination of a team by facilitating appreciation among the group members for the accomplishments of individuals. Thus, the focus of attention has shifted from the group to the individual. Coaches and leaders may also oversee group sessions in which team members discuss their experiences with the group, express any concerns about the team's termination, and share any plans for the future (Flapan & Fenchel, 1987).

Group Roles.   A **role** is a shared expectation for behavior that serves to differentiate group members. Each role defines the behaviors expected of an athlete who occupies a given position on the team. The understanding of role behavior would be simplified if each of us occupied only one role. This is not the case. Most people have many different roles to play in their lives. One man could be a father, an accountant, a runner, and a youth league coach all at the same time. Similarly, an athlete may have several different roles on his or her team. All athletes have a position that they play—this is one role. However, an athlete may also be a team leader, a source of social support, and serve as an example to other team members. Further, the behaviors required to fulfill each role differ. If a team is to be successful, individuals must recognize, accept, and perform the roles within the team structure. The importance of roles was highlighted by the 1999 Los Angeles Lakers of the National Basketball Association. On the Lakers roster were league superstars such as Shaquille O'Neal, Kobe Bryant, and (for a time) Dennis Rodman. The team was in contention for the championship but fell far short of expectations. Once of the most common reasons cited was that team members refused to accept their assigned roles. Disagreement surfaced as to who should be the "go-to" man—the one to take the ball to the basket.

For a team to successfully achieve its goals, it is important for each individual to perform the requirements of his or her role. An individual's view of how he or she is supposed to act in a given situation is called *role perception*. People engage in certain types of behaviors based on how they believe they are supposed to act in a given situation. Significant others (e.g., coaches, teammates, other occupants of the role) provide individuals with important information about how to behave in each role occupied. If the way an athlete views his or her role is comparable to the way others view the role, then *role clarity* should emerge. Role clarity results from each athlete knowing how his or her role contributes to the overall goals of the team and how the role affects the behavior of their teammates. Take the example of a freshman football player whose coach expects him to specialize on kick returns. Although this individual would like to be the starting tailback, he understands that he has not yet earned that position. Therefore, if he has achieved role clarity, he can now focus his attention on performing his assigned role to the best of his ability.

Role acceptance is also necessary for effective role performance to occur. Even if a role is clear to an athlete, he or she may not accept that role. A person occupying the position of an "enforcer" in hockey may wish to fulfill the role of goal-scorer. Dissatisfaction with the responsibilities of a role can lead to poor individual performance and, consequently, poor overall team performance and loss of the role.

Role Conflict.   In some instances, group members may find themselves occupying contradictory roles. In other instances, an individual does not believe that he or she has the time, ability, or motivation to fulfill the requirements of a role. When any of these circumstances arise, role conflict may occur. A variety of role conflicts may exist, and Carron (1988) has identified three of the most common (see Table 13.4).

What are the consequences of role conflict? First, if an individual fails to fulfill the duties of his or her role, the performance of the team probably will suffer. This conflict is present when a person does not have the proper abilities (e.g., does not have the speed required to be a base stealer) motivation, time, or understanding to execute the responsibilities of their role (Carron, 1988). In addition, it is likely that individual athlete satisfaction will decrease. It is not surprising that an athlete who is experiencing role conflict will not enjoy participating on the team.

Info Box

Role acceptance is facilitated when athletes have a good understanding of what their roles on a team are and the behaviors needed to fulfill the roles are clear.

TABLE 13.4 *Role Conflict in Sport.*

Conflict type	Cause	Example
Intrarole	Single role produces contradictory demands on person in that role.	A football player who is first instructed to be aggressive, then is reprimanded when he receives penalties for his aggressive style of play.
Interrole	Conflicting expectancies between two roles that are occupied by the same individual.	Player-manager in baseball whose responsibilities (i.e., to the players and the front office) may be conflicting at times.
Person-role	Person is either unable unwilling to carry out the duties of the role to which he or she has been assigned.	Athlete who is moved to a new position on a team in college.

Group Norms. Roles serve to differentiate team members, but norms integrate team members. **Norms** are structured rules that govern the manner in which the group is organized and maintained. Mott (1965) identified four different types of norms (see Table 13.5). The time that practice starts, communications style with coaches, and acceptable versus unacceptable behavior are examples of formalized norms that typically are set by the organization and/or coaches. However, the majority of norms are informal and develop over time. Norms (whether formal or informal) structure individuals' behavior and judgment in group settings and establish standards of behavior for the group or team. Group norms are often implemented to serve as a substitute for more formal interventions. For example, if a team has a norm that prohibits drinking, and an individual breaks that norm, the team may punish the individual without direct interaction from the coaches/administration. Norms are put into place to specify how members should behave. Should individuals violate certain norms, pressure is typically applied to bring their behavior into conformity with group standards. Thus, group norms help to maintain behavioral consistency among group members.

Why Are Norms Important? Groups do not establish norms for every conceivable situation. For example, most teams do not tell athletes what music they can listen to, what they are to eat, or how they are to dress outside of team functions. The norms that are enforced tend to be those that are important to the successful functioning of the team (Robbins, 1992). A norm is considered important if it:

1. *Facilitates the team's success.* Teams look for norms that facilitate the chances of their being successful. Practice and weight training schedules and absence policies from practice are examples of norms that may enhance the chances of a team's success.
2. *Increases the predictability of team members' behavior.* Norms designed to increase predictability enable team members to anticipate each other's actions and prepare appropriate responses if deviant behavior occurs. Norms that state exactly when practice is to start, when team members are to arrive at the bus for away games, and

TABLE 13.5 *Types of Norms.*

Norm	*Definition*	*Example*
Prescribed	Identifies behaviors that are inappropriate for group members.	How much time a goalie should spend after practice taking shots on goal.
Proscribed	Establishes behaviors that are *not* acceptable to group members.	Swimmers who determine that no one should stay out late the night before a meet.
Permissive	Determines behaviors that are permitted, but not expected, of group members.	Umpires who change the strike zone to be smaller than the rule book states.
Preference	Reflects behaviors that are preferred, but not required, of group members.	Sandlot football players who will not call all the possible penalties in a game because it disrupts the flow of the game.

dress code rules will all enhance the chances that team members will show up on time for practice and travel and will be dressed appropriately.

3. *Reduces the potential for embarrassing interpersonal problems.* Norms are important to ensure the satisfaction of the members and prevent as much interpersonal discomfort as possible. Team norms about what time to show up for travel prevent athletes from missing the bus.

4. *Promotes the central values of the group.* Norms that encourage the group's values and distinctive identity help to solidify and maintain the group. For example, team uniforms and dress codes help to distinguish a team from those not part of the team.

How Are Norms Developed and Maintained?   Norms gradually develop as group members learn what behaviors are necessary for the team to function effectively. According to Robbins (1992), most norms develop in one of the following four ways:

1. *Explicit statements*—often by a coach or a team leader. The coach may specifically say to team members that there will be no swearing during practice, that team members are required to wear a tie when they travel, or that any athlete who is late to practice will be required to run hills at the end of practice.

2. *Critical events in the team's history*—Previous events set an important precedent. For example, in warmup before an ice hockey game a few years ago, a player who was not wearing his helmet got hit in the head with a puck and ended his career. Based on this accident, wearing a helmet at any time when on the ice became a requirement.

3. *Primacy*—The first behavior pattern that emerges frequently sets group expectations. If one athlete claims a locker, it is unacceptable for another athlete to claim that same locker space.

4. *Carryout behaviors*—Group members often bring expectations from other groups to which they have belonged. These behaviors may be incompatible with the current group situation, and norms will need to be explicitly stated to ensure that incongruent behaviors do not continue within the group setting.

Norms that evolve in groups must be functional to the success of that group. Once established, norms become part of the group's structure. The individuals responsible for the adoption of the norm (or the circumstance that resulted in its development) may be in the past, but the norm remains resistant to change. New members of the group are encouraged to adopt the prevailing norms. Forsyth (1990) identified three factors that aid in the maintenance of team norms within the structure of the group (see Table 13.6).

Info Box

Norms are essential to team functioning. Norms should be established to include team practices and meetings, effort, attitude, and member relationships.

Status of Individual Members.   If you were asked to describe some of the characteristics that contribute to status on an athletic team, you would probably list qualities such as

TABLE 13.6 *How Norms Are Maintained.*

Influence	Result
Normative influences	Cause consistency of thoughts, feelings, and actions. Members will perceive a sense of obligation to honor the norms.
Informational influences	Opinions are changed after learning the opinions of others.
Interpersonal influences	Bargaining and persuasion (perhaps even threats) are used to convince people to conform and maintain norms.

physical ability, experience, persistence, leadership, and mental toughness. **Status** refers to the degree to which an individual's contribution is crucial to the success and prestige of the group, how much power that individual has, and the extent to which the person embodies some idealized or admired characteristic (Johnson & Johnson, 1997). Status can be acquired formally through titles such as "captain," the position played, or the amount of money earned or informally from playing experience, age, race, or sex. Jacob and Carron (1997) found the most important factors contributing to status on sport teams were competitive experience, performance ability, and team role (e.g., captain/cocaptain).

Individual status has definite implications for the team as a whole and can influence several aspects of the group's performance. Higher status individuals on a team are more likely to be tolerated within the hierarchy of the group and are less likely to be affected by such things as peer pressure to conform to the standards and beliefs of the group, because high status individuals are less likely to expect to receive punishment for their actions (Johnson & Allen, 1972). High status individuals also have a greater impact on group decisions and judgment patterns than do their low status teammates. Their input is considered the most important and relevant to ensuring the effectiveness of the group as a whole. Conversely, individuals who hold positions of low status in the group are largely ignored with respect to any suggestions they give to the group. This disregard for the contributions of low status individuals occurs regardless of whether their input is helpful to the group.

Implications for Group Membership

Thus far, the core foundational components of group dynamics have been identified (group composition, group environment, and group structure). These components, in turn, influence other group variables such as cohesion and a variety of group processes. Understanding and developing cohesion in a group will be addressed separately in Chapter 14. **Group processes** influence the effectiveness of a group and represent the dynamic interactions that are characteristic of group membership (Carron & Hausenblas, 1998). Group processes are not directly influenced by the composition, structure, or cohesiveness of a team, but they are more effective when these variables have been considered. The group processes introduced in this section include: collective efficacy, social support, and groupthink. Although this list is not exhaustive, it highlights some important considerations for athletes and coaches when examining the overall effectiveness of their team.

Collective Efficacy

Behaviors such as persistence, effort, and mastery are believed to be motivated by efficacy beliefs (Bandura, 1997). Self-efficacy is the belief in one's capability to produce a given level of performance. It has been found to be a consistent predictor of sport and exercise behavior (Moritz et al., in press). Bandura (1986) extended the concept of individual self-efficacy to include the group. **Collective efficacy** is a team's collective expectation for success. It is based on team members' judgments of their team's capabilities. A baseball player who rates his belief in his ability to hit .300 for the season is assessing self-efficacy. When asked to rate his belief in the team's ability to hit .300 for the season, collective efficacy is being assessed.

Bandura (1977) asserts that collective efficacy should be a better predictor of team performance in sports where a high degree of interdependence exists (e.g., soccer, football, lacrosse) compared to sports where team performance is more a function of individual member performance (e.g., equestrian, wrestling). Research has supported the role of collective efficacy in enhanced performance in laboratory (Hodges & Carron, 1992; Lichacz & Partington, 1996) and field experiments (Feltz & Lirgg, in press; Spink, 1990). Thus, developing collective efficacy on a team may be of particular importance to effective team functioning.

Social Support

A supportive environment is one in which an individual feels respected and encouraged by others. A teammate who listens without judgment, provides advice, or stays after practice to help you work on a difficult skill provides different examples of social support. In fact, support can take many forms (see Table 13.7; Pines, Aronson, & Kafry, 1981; Rosenfeld & Richman, 1997). Social support has been found to be positively related to physical and mental well-being (Ganster & Victor, 1988), cohesion (Weiss & Fredrichs, 1986; Westre & Weiss, 1991), and satisfaction (Schliesman, 1987).

Both coaches and athletes have highlighted the importance of a supportive training environment. Côté and Salmela (1996) reported that 58 percent of the coaches surveyed preferred a supportive training style. When the types of support offered by intercollegiate coaches was investigated, Rosenfeld, Richmond and Hardy (1989) found that primarily technical appreciation and technical support were given. Teammates offered technical challenge support almost exclusively. From this study, it appears that those in the athletic environment offer only a few of the types of support identified. Sources outside the athletic environment provided frequent and diverse types of support, with friends being identified most often. Given the benefits of a supportive environment, groups need to be aware of the quality and the quantity of support given.

Groupthink

Not all group processes are positive to overall team effectiveness. Group membership often results in pressures for conformity to goals, ideals, and perceptions. Janis (1972) suggested that conformity leads to faulty judgments by team members, a phenomenon he labeled groupthink. As such, **groupthink** is characterized by a style of thinking that overrides

TABLE 13.7 *Types of Social Support Provided by Groups*

Type of Support	Characteristics
Emotional challenge	The perception that another is challenging an individual to persist and achieve goals.
Emotional support	The perception that another is providing comfort and care.
Listening support	The perception that another individual is listening without judgment.
Personal assistance support	The perception that another is providing various services (e.g., laundry, errands) designed to help the individual.
Tangible assistance support	The perception that an individual is providing assistance that is neither emotional nor task oriented (e.g., financial aid, gifts).
Task appreciation support	The perception that others acknowledge and appreciate the work being performed.
Task challenge support	The perception that others are challenging an individual to achieve more or perform better.
Social reality support	The perception that a similar other is helping confirm an individual's perception of the social world.

group members' motivation to realistically assess alternative behaviors. Groupthink interferes with effective group decision making and is most likely to occur when certain characteristics are present. These include: high levels of cohesion, teams which are relatively isolated from outside influences, autocratic leadership, and homogeneity around personal attributes (Janis & Mann, 1977). Janis suggests that if only one cause of groupthink is present, it is unlikely that the group will suffer from poor decision making. If two or more of the causes are present within a team, the likelihood of groupthink is greater.

Pressures for conformity result in groupthink, which interferes with effective decision making. As an example, consider what could happen as members of an extremely successful softball team (Team A) prepare for a game against a less talented opponent (Team B). Team A's team members believe that they will easily beat Team B and do not adequately prepare during practice. The illusion of invulnerability is prevalent throughout the entire team, and the lack of preparation results in an upset victory for Team B.

Groupthink can have a negative impact on team performance. The repression of individual skills in an effort to conform to the group ideal seriously restricts the diversity of team talent. Groupthink also limits the flexibility of the team's performance by lowering individual creativity. If a basketball team is experiencing groupthink, an individual player will be much less likely to implement creative decision-making strategies because the team dictates the "accepted" way to approach athletic situations. Groupthink may also facilitate illusions of invulnerability among team members. Individuals think that the beliefs and morals endorsed by the group are correct because all team members appear to support these beliefs. Personal pressure to conform has been identified as another symptom of groupthink (Forsyth, 1990). Peer pressure appears in all groups, but it may be especially powerful when groupthink occurs. Examples of the dangerous (and potentially fatal) outcomes of groupthink can be found in weight-dependent sports, such as wrestling and gymnastics, in which substantial pressure exists to maintain a certain weight. The potential consequences of this pressure on the athlete are virtually ignored. Finally, groupthink can decrease the openness of the group members and may hinder their growth potential. When individual creativity is stifled and one belief is pervasive in a group/team setting, the possibility of independent thought is greatly reduced.

Info Box

> With group membership comes a pressure to conform to the values, behaviors, and attitudes of the team. In certain instances, conformity can lead to poor decision-making ability by team members.

Conclusion

The majority of research in sport psychology has examined the relationship between psychological variables and individual behavior. However, much of sport competition occurs in a group setting. Of considerable importance is the finding that behavior differs when an individual is alone, in a dyad, or in a group. Consequently, the examination and study of group dynamics cannot be ignored. The purpose of this chapter was to synthesize theory and research on group dynamics to identify basic concepts that influence team functioning. The following two chapters build on this foundation by highlighting the importance of cohesion in sport. Chapter 15 will tie the previous two chapters together and examine team building as a strategy to develop team effectiveness. Several strategies designed to improve team functioning will also be introduced.

Key Terms (in order of appearance) _____

group dynamics	social loafing	status
audience effect	group structure	group process
social facilitation theory	group development	collective efficacy
group composition	role	social support
Ringelmann effect	norm	groupthink

References _____

Bandura, A. (1977). Self-efficacy: Toward a unifying theory of behavioral change. *Psychological Review, 84*, 191–215.

Bandura, A. (1982). Self-efficacy mechanism in human agency. *American Psychologist, 37*, 122–147.

Bandura, A. (1986). *Social foundations of thought and action. A social cognitive theory.* Englewood Cliffs: Prentice Hall.

Bandura, A. (1997). *Self-efficacy: The exercise of control.* New York: Freeman.

Brower, A. M. (1996). Group development as constructed social reality revisited: The construction of small groups. *The Journal of Contemporary Human Services,* 336–344.

Carron, A. V. (1988). *Group dynamics in sport.* London, Ontario: Spodym.

Carron, A. V. (1990). Group size in sport and physical activity: Social psychological and performance consequences. *International Journal of Sport Psychology, 21,* 286–304.

Carron, A. V., & Hausenblas, H. A. (1998). *Group dynamics in sport,* 2nd ed. Morgantown, WV: Fitness Information Technology.

Clement, D., & Schiereck, J. (1973). Sex composition and group performance in a visual signal detection task. *Memory and Cognition, 1,* 251–255.

Côté, J., & Salmela, J. H. (1996). The organizational tasks of high-performance gymnastics coaches. *The Sport Psychologist, 10*(3), 247–260.

Eitzen, S. (1973). The effect of group structure on the success of athletic teams. *International Review of Sport Sociology, 8,* 7–17.

Feltz, D. L., & Lirgg, C. D. (in press). Perceived team and player efficacy in hockey. *Journal of Applied Psychology.*

Flapan, D., & Fenchel, G. H. (1987). Terminations. *Group, 11,* 131–143.

Forsyth, D. R. (1990). *Group dynamics,* 2nd ed. Belmont, CA: Brooks/Cole.

Ganster, D. C., & Victor, B. (1988). The impact of social support on mental and physical health. *British Journal of Medical Psychology, 69,* 615–622.

Hardy, C. J. (1990). Social loafing: Motivational losses in collective performance. *International Journal of Sport Psychology, 21,* 305–327.

Hodges, L., & Carron, A. V. (1992). Collective efficacy and group performance. *International Journal of Sport Psychology, 23,* 48–59.

Jackson, S. (1992). Team composition in organizational settings: Issues in managing an increasingly diverse work force. In S. Worchel, W. Wood, & J. Simpson (Eds.), *Group processes and productivity* (pp. 138–173). Newbury Park, CA: Sage.

Janis, I. J. (1972). *Victims of groupthink.* Boston: Houghton-Miffin.

Janis, I. J., & Mann, L. (1977). *Decision making: A psychological analysis of conflict, choice, and commitment.* New York: Free Press.

Jacob, C. S., & Carron, A. V. (1997). The sources of status on sport teams. *International Journal of Sport Psychology, 27,* 369–382.

Johnson, D. W., & Allen, S. (1972). Deviation from organizational norms concerning the relations between status and power. *Sociological Quarterly, 13,* 174–182.

Johnson, D. W., & Johnson, F. P. (1997). *Joining together: Group theory and group skills,* 6th ed. Needham Heights, MA: Allyn & Bacon.

Jones, M. (1974). Regressing group on individual effectiveness. *Organizational Behavior and Human Performance, 11,* 426–451.

Klein, M., & Christiansen, G. (1969). Group composition, group structure and group effectiveness of basketball teams. In J. W. Joy & G. S. Keynon (Eds.), *Sport, culture, and society* (pp. 397–408). New York: MacMillan.

Landers, D. M., Boutcher, S. H., & Way, M. Q. (1986). The history and status of the Journal of Sport Psychology: 1979–1985. *Journal of Sport Psychology, 8,* 149–163.

Latané, B., Williams, K., & Harkins, S. (1979). Many hands make light work: The causes and consequences of social loafing. *Journal of Personality and Social Psychology, 37,* 822–832.

Lichacz, F. M., & Partington, J. T. (1996). Collective efficacy and true performance. *International Journal of Sport Psychology, 27,* 146–158.

Mills, T. M. (1984). *The sociology of small groups,* 2nd ed. Englewood Cliffs, NJ: Prentice Hall.

Moritz, S. E., Feltz, D. L., Mack, D., & Faurbach, K. L. (in press). The relation of self-efficacy measures to sport and exercise performance: A meta-analytic review. *Research Quarterly for Exercise and Sport.*

Mott, P. E. (1965). *The organization of society.* Englewood Cliffs, NJ: Prentice Hall.

Pines, A. M., Aronson, E., & Kafry, D. (1981). *Burnout.* New York: Free Press.

Ringelmann, M. (1913). Research on animate sources of power: The work of man. *Annals de l'Institut National Agronomique, 2e serie-tome XII,* 1–40.

Robbins, S. P. (1992). *Essentials of Organizational Behavior,* 3rd ed. Englewood Cliffs, NJ: Prentice Hall.

Rosenfeld, L. B., & Richman, J. M. (1997). Developing effective social support: Team building and the social support process. *Journal of Applied Sport Psychology, 9*(1), 133–153.

Rosenfeld, L. B., Richman, J. M., & Hardy, C. J. (1989). An examination of social support networks among athletes: Description and relationship to stress. *Sport Psychologist, 3,* 23–33.

Schliesman, E. S. (1987). Relationship between the congruence of preferred and actual leadership behavior and subordinate satisfaction with leadership. *Journal of Sport Behavior, 10(3),* 157–166.

Spink, K. S. (1990). Group cohesion and collective efficacy of volleyball teams. *Journal of Sport and Exercise Psychology, 12,* 301–311.

Steiner, I. D. (1972). *Group processes and productivity.* New York: Academic.

Triplett, N. (1897). The dynamogenic factor in pacemaking and competition. *American Journal of Psychology, 9,* 507–533.

Tuckman, B. W. (1965). Developmental sequences in small groups. *Psychological Bulletin, 63,* 384–399.

Tuckman, B. W., & Jensen, M. A. (1977). Stages of small group development revisited. *Group and Organizational Studies, 2,* 419–427.

Weiss, M. R., & Fredrichs, W. D. (1986). The influence of leader behaviors, coach attributes, institutional variables on performance and satisfaction of collegiate basketball teams. *Journal of Sport Psychology, 8,* 332–346.

Westre, K. R., & Weiss, M. R. (1991). The relationship between perceived coaching behaviors and group cohesion in high school football teams. *Sport Psychologist, 5,* 41–54.

Wheelan, S. A., & Hochburger, J. M. (1996). Validation studies of the group development questionnaire. *Small Group Research, 27*(1), 143–170.

Widmeyer, W. N. (1990). Group composition in sport. *International Journal of Sport Psychology, 21,* 264–285.

Widmeyer, W. N., Brawley, L. R., & Carron, A. V. (1990). The impact of group size in sport. *Journal of Sport and Exercise Psychology, 12,* 177–190.

Widmeyer, W. N., Brawley, L. R., & Carron, A. V. (1992). Group dynamics in sport. In T. S. Horn (Ed.), *Advances in Sport Psychology.* Champaign, IL: Human Kinetics.

Williams, K. D., Harkins, S., & Latané, B. (1981). Identifiability as a deterrent to social loafing: Two cheering experiments. *Journal of Personality and Social Psychology, 40,* 303–311.

Zajonc, R. B. (1965). Social facilitation. *Science, 149,* 269–274.

14

The Science of Developing Cohesion

Diane E. Stevens

The University of North Carolina at Chapel Hill

- Distinguish between the two dimensions of cohesion (group–individual and task–social).
- Understand the factors associated with cohesion.
- Understand the performance–cohesion relationship.

We have all studied the field of chemistry. Chemistry is the science of the elements. This science deals with the properties and chemical reactions of elements and their compounds. Chemistry also includes the study of how these elements and compounds can be combined to form a more complex substance. A simple reaction known as combustion is also considered a chemical reaction.

Chemistry is important for any sport team to develop. We often think of chemistry as cohesion. In developing cohesion, coaches often look at the individual characteristics (e.g., personality) of the athletes on the team and determine how well they will fit together. In the end, coaches hope that the individual team members will form a well-functioning group that may be thought of as a more complex substance. At times, however, individuals do not bind together well and a team breaks up (combustion). So essential is cohesion to team functioning that it is considered by some social scientists to be the most important group variable (Golembiewski, 1962; Lott & Lott, 1965).

What Is Cohesion?

It is likely that we can each recall a team we have been on that was cohesive and one that was not. Cohesive groups are unified around a common goal, and team members enjoy socializing with each other. Noncohesive groups are characterized by tension and dislike among team members. But what about team members who enjoy interacting with one another but have no common goal? Or they have a common goal, but team members do not

Individual performances often occur within the context of a group.

interact with each other? Are these teams cohesive? It depends on how you define and measure the construct.

Cohesion as a Force That Binds People Together

Group cohesion initially was defined as "the total field of forces which act on members to remain in the group" (Festinger, Schachter, & Back, 1950, p. 164). Two factors that contribute to group cohesiveness are the attractiveness of the group and the ability of the group to help its members achieve their goals. According to this definition, cohesion was seen as the strength of the bond that holds members in a group. Groups that are cohesive are bound together, and those that are not drift apart.

Cohesion as Interpersonal Attraction

Lott and Lott (1965) conceptualized cohesion as a "group property that is inferred from the number and strength of mutual positive attitudes among the members of a group" (p. 259). Similarly, Olson, Sprenkle, and Russell (1979) defined cohesion as the "emotional bonding members have with one another" (p. 5). In essence, members remain with a group because they like one another. Attraction may also extend to the level of the group and not necessarily to specific team members (Bollen & Hoyle, 1990; Dion, 1990). An individual may be attracted to the idea that they belong to a group. The status and social identity that results from group membership is appealing for many individuals.

Cohesion as a Common Purpose

Others believe that cohesion is more a function of members' willingness to work together to achieve their goals than interpersonal attraction between team members. For example, Goodman, Ravlin, and Schminke (1987) defined cohesion as "the commitment of members to the group task" (p. 149). Teams that remain together do so because of the underlying objective or goal.

Cohesion as a Multidimensional Construct

Cota and colleagues (1995) argued that cohesion is a multidimensional construct that encompasses both interpersonal attraction and working toward a unified purpose. Consistent with this belief, Carron, Brawley, and Widmeyer (1998) defined **cohesion** as "a dynamic process which is reflected in the tendency for a group to stick together and remain united in the pursuit of its instrumental objectives and/or for the satisfaction of member affective needs" (p. 213). A group may be cohesive because team members like each other or because of a powerful sense of belonging to the group. Another group may be cohesive because of a common purpose. Reasons for remaining part of the team are never static. Initially, an athlete may join a team because he or she wants to play soccer (and you can only play if you are on a team). However, once on the team relationships are established with other members and common goals are identified. Whatever the reason for remaining part of the team, the group has become a cohesive unit.

Info Box

Cohesion is a multidimensional construct. Task cohesion reflects the degree to which individual team members work toward a common goal. Social cohesion reflects the degree of interpersonal attraction between team members.

The Assessment of Cohesion

The different definitions of cohesion have led researchers to measure the construct in a variety of ways. The Group Environment Questionnaire (GEQ; Carron, Widmeyer, & Brawley, 1985) is the most common assessment tool in sport research. The GEQ is based on the Conceptual Model of Cohesion, which identified two dimensions of cohesion—individual–group and task–social (see Fig. 14.1 on page 294). The individual–group dimension reflects that a member can be committed to other members and/or the group itself. **Group Integration** represents the members' perceptions of the group as a totality. How close is the group as a whole? Is the group unified about its objectives? **Individual Attraction** to

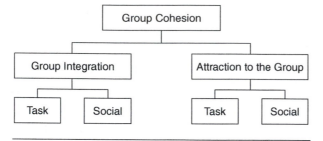

FIGURE 14.1   *Conceptual Model of Cohesion (Carron & Hausenblas, 1998).*

the group represents a member's personal involvement and attraction to the group. Am I accepted in the group? Does the team provide me with opportunities for athletic development?

The task–social dimension reflects that a member can be interested in the goals of a group and/or the social relationships in a group. On sport teams, members are concerned with group performance, productivity, and achievement. Shared concerns about the task help to bind the team together into a cohesive unit. The social aspects of the group revolve around mutual friendships and shared feelings of togetherness. The four related dimensions result in the following cohesion factors: Group Integration-Task and Social (GI-T and GI-S) and Individual Attraction to the Group Task and Social (ATG-T and ATG-S). Carron, Widmeyer, and Brawley (1985) suggested that each dimension could be sufficient to encourage athletes to remain with their team.

Info Box

In addition to the task–social dimension, cohesion can be measured at the level of the individual and the group.

Correlates of Cohesion

Which factors contribute to the development of cohesion among a group of athletes? According to Carron and Hausenblas (1998), these factors are a product of the environment surrounding the team, individual member attributes, leadership characteristics, and team variables (see Fig. 14.2). They note that while these factors contribute to the development of cohesion, their relationship is likely reciprocal. That is, cohesion influences team confidence, and team confidence influences cohesion. Similarly, individual member satisfaction is related to cohesion, and perceptions of cohesion to member satisfaction.

Environmental Factors

Environmental factors exist in the social setting, the physical environment, and various structural aspects of the group. In a classic study, Festinger, Schachter, and Back (1950)

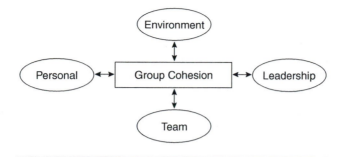

FIGURE 14.2 *Framework for Examining the Correlates of Group Cohesion (Carron & Hausenblas, 1998).*

demonstrated the power of **proximity** to the development of cohesion through examining the social relationships between married students living in dorms. Results of this study found that physical proximity (i.e., living close to one another) is of prime importance to the development of friendships. People are more likely to form friendships with those living close to them than with those who live further away. In sport, Rainey and Schweickert (1988) found that members of a baseball team who travel together report higher levels of social cohesion than members who are unable to travel. The proximity associated with traveling together and subsequent increased interaction among team members may have facilitated the development of cohesion.

Why do people form groups with those that are more proximal to them? Researchers note that groups tend to form as people interact with the same people with frequency (Moreland, 1987) and that liking is increased toward those we see on a regular basis (Bornstein, Leone, & Galley, 1987). When team members are physically close to one another, perceptions of cohesion may develop because of increased opportunities to interact and communicate.

Distinctiveness is a second environmental variable related to the development of cohesion. As a group of individuals becomes more separate (or distinct) from other groups, feelings of pride and belonging develop. Distinctiveness on a sport team can be achieved in many ways. Ask team members what song characterizes the group. A variety of suggestions may arise, but one song might make such an impact that it can trigger a sense of identity. (Remember the song "We Are Family"?). These and many other strategies (team uniforms, team parties, slogans) are used in sport help to create a sense of belonging to one group and a sense of distinctiveness from another.

The **size** of the group also influences the development of cohesion. As the size of a group increases, it becomes more difficult to communicate effectively with group members and coordinate team activities (Steiner, 1972). As such, social and task cohesion may be influenced by the number of players on a team. Also remember, not all players get to see significant playing time. As a coach, you want to make sure there are enough players to survive illness and/or injury but not so many that the chemistry of the team is affected. It may be more difficult for reserve players to remain motivated and committed. These feelings may spill over to other team members and become disruptive to team functioning.

To investigate this issue, Widmeyer, Brawley, and Carron (1990, study 1) manipulated the size of a team in a 10-week 3-on-3 basketball league. Teams were formed with 3,

6, or 9 members. Perceptions of task and social cohesion were measured at the end of the third and tenth weeks. Results indicated that task cohesion decreased as the roster size increased and that social cohesion was the highest in the 6-member team.

Carron and Hausenblas (1998) identify that **contractual responsibilities,** such as eligibility, athletic scholarships, or transfer rules, may impact cohesion. Contractual responsibilities bind an athlete to a team and hold the group together. In recent years, numerous examples of athletes being dissatisfied with their contractual obligations to their team have surfaced (e.g., Joey Galloway, Alexi Yashin). As a result, players have missed training camp (or part of the season) or have demanded a trade to another team. Unfortunately, these disputes are not private because the media chronicles the tensions between athletes and management.

Contractual obligations also impact cohesion at lower levels of sport. Consider the high school athlete who is unhappy with his or her coach, playing time, or position. Essentially, the athlete has two options—either quit the team or persist despite being dissatisfied. It is a rare instance when an athlete transfers to a different school to play for a different coach or in the hope of increased playing time.

Info Box

Numerous environmental factors contribute to the development of cohesion on a team. This highlights the importance of attention to normative factors that keep a team together.

Personal Factors

Diversity is to be expected when a group of individuals form a sport team. Players have different personalities and may come from different cultural and socioecomonic backgrounds. The role of personal characteristics to the development of cohesion has intrigued researchers. One personal factor often cited is **similarity** of team members around personal attributes. Eitzen (1973) revealed that the more similar a team is around these variables, the greater the perception of cohesion. More recent research (Widmeyer, Silva, & Hardy, 1992; Widmeyer & Williams, 1991) noted that similarity around personal attributes was not related to increased cohesion.

Individual athlete **satisfaction** has been identified as one of the most important personal factors related to cohesion (Carron & Chelladurai, 1981; Hackner & Williams, 1981; Martens & Petersen, 1971). In a study of 132 female intercollegiate field hockey players, Williams and Hackner (1982) identified a circular relationship between cohesion and satisfaction. Higher levels of cohesion increased future satisfaction, and higher levels of satisfaction increased future cohesion. Widmeyer and Williams (1991) proposed that satisfaction may be a particularly important correlate of cohesion in coacting sports because satisfaction was found to be the best predictor of task and social cohesion in female intercollegiate golf teams.

Athletes make many personal **sacrifices** to participate in sport. Sacrifices may occur within sport (e.g., playing a different position, being a bench player) or outside sport (e.g., less time for family and work). The extent to which an individual sacrifices for his or her team demonstrates commitment by showing others that the team is important. Prapavessis and Carron (1997) examined whether sacrifice resulted in increased cohesion in 127 male cricket players. Participants were asked to rate the extent to which they and their teammates made sacrifices for the team. Sacrifice, both within and outside sport, were related to perceptions of cohesion. Similarly, higher levels of task and social cohesion led to greater sacrifice behavior by team members.

Social loafing is the reduction in individual effort when people work in groups versus when they work alone (Latané, Williams, & Harkins, 1979) Various strategies have been proposed to offset the effects of social loafing (cf. Hardy, 1990). Cohesion has been identified as potentially offsetting the negative effects of individual reduction of effort. Ideally, if members are united in the pursuit of a common goal, then individual members should be less likely to reduce effort. When cohesion is high, the desire for group success is increased and group motives may surpass individual motives. This belief has been supported by research showing that cohesive groups loaf less than noncohesive ones (Everett, Smith, & Williams, 1992; Karau & Williams, 1993), and individual member work output is greater when perceptions of cohesiveness are higher (Prapavessis & Carron, 1997).

Before taking a test, have you said, "I didn't study much last night because I had to work"? Or before a game, have you thought, "I haven't had much time to prepare for this competition because of school commitments"? These are examples of self-handicaps. **Self-handicapping** involves adopting or claiming impediments that reduce the probability of success and provide a plausible excuse for failure (Leary, 1995). Self-handicaps also serve to protect self-esteem because performance is attributed to other causes and not to ability. The relationship between cohesion and self-handicapping has recently received attention (Carron, Prapavessis, & Grove, 1994; Hausenblas & Carron, 1996). These researchers found that high trait self-handicappers (i.e., those who frequently self-handicap) who participate on highly cohesive teams reported making fewer excuses for their performance. Therefore, cohesion serves to moderate the relationship between the trait of self-handicapping and the use of self-handicapping strategies.

Info Box

To help a team remain cohesive, personal factors must be considered, and especially athlete satisfaction.

Leadership Factors

The third influence on cohesion is leadership. Carron and Hausenblas (1998) identified the complex interrelationships among the coach, the athlete, and cohesion. When the coach–team relationship is good, the coach is considered to be a powerful member of the team. If the team is in direct conflict with the coach, the coach is excluded from membership in the group and team members may actively employ their own agenda. Where a significant amount of conflict exists between the team and the coach, members may actively unite against the coach in an attempt to have them removed from the position.

Being an effective coach is about more than knowing the "X's and O's." Many people are able to teach the physical skills and tactics necessary to be successful. A coach who does not clarify group goals or who does not offer suggestions aimed at accomplishing the group task, however, will not lead a cohesive group. A coach who does not clarify individual member roles or is not an effective communicator will find uniting a team to be extremely challenging. Therefore, one of the most important qualities of an effective coach is the ability to develop a strong sense of cohesion.

Decision making style is an important aspect of developing cohesion. Johnson and Johnson (1997) identify many different types of decision-making styles, ranging from autocratic (leader makes all decisions without consulting the group members in any way) to democratic (a collective opinion arrived at by the entire group). Although the latter type of decision making is the most time-consuming, these researchers note that it is the most effective for producing an innovative and high-quality decision. In sport, democratic decision-making styles are associated with increased levels of cohesion (Carron & Chelladurai, 1981; Westre & Weiss, 1991). Coaches will want to carefully consider the pros and cons of various decision-making styles. Certainly, there is not always time to get all the team members' opinions before making a decision (e.g., in a game); however, surveying athlete's opinions on matters such as goal setting, athlete leadership, and team norms may foster individual member commitment and cohesion.

The **compatibility** between coach and athlete is also related to the level of cohesiveness. Carron and Chelladurai (1981) examined the three motivational orientations proposed by Bass (1962; i.e., task, social, self). Task and social motivation are similar to task and social cohesion, respectively. Self-motivation is reflected in the personal satisfaction derived from performing up to one's ability. The most important predictors of an athlete's perceptions of cohesiveness were compatibility between the athlete and his coach on task motivation.

Info Box

The coach plays an integral role in establishing an environment that is conducive to the development of cohesion. Although a coach may contribute to perceptions of cohesion, specific behaviors may negatively affect its development.

Team Factors

Team factors are found in the structure of a group. They are a stable pattern of interaction between team members (Johnson & Johnson, 1997). Team factors include stage of development, team stability, norms, and status.

Stage of Development

In Chapter 13, the ways in which a team tends to develop were outlined. Remember forming, storming, norming, performing, and adjourning (Tuckman, 1965; Tuckman & Jensen, 1977)? A coach or sport psychologist can use these stages of team development to guide and anticipate a team's progression. It also makes intuitive sense that perceptions of cohesion change as the team progresses through each stage of development. To test this notion, Stevenson and Durand-Bush (1999) assessed cohesion on a university football team at two times during the course of a season. Prior to each administration, the coach was asked to identify the stage of group development (time 1 was identified as norming, and time 2 was performing). Recall that norming is the stage in which cohesiveness and group roles are established. The relationships between players are stabilized, and the focus of the group is on the task during the performing stage. It was found that players reported higher levels of social integration and were more focused on the group's task during the performing stage. No changes were found across the measures of individual attraction to the group (either task or social) in these stages. Differences between types of cohesion were also found at each stage. While in the norming stage, the players reported higher levels of social cohesion than task cohesion. The opposite was true for the performing stage, where players reported higher levels of task cohesion. These results can be useful to help the coach and sport psychologist understand players' feelings and how to aid in progression from one stage to the next.

Stability

Team cohesion is fostered by minimal turnover. Turnover often cannot be helped and can occur because of injury, graduation, and age restrictions. **Team stability** refers to the duration of time team members have remained together. The longer a group has been together and the greater the opportunity to interact with each other, the greater are the perceptions of cohesiveness. Similarly, the more cohesive a group becomes, the less likely it is that members will choose to leave. A growing body of research has found that intention to continue sport participation is positively related to cohesion in youth sport (Carron, Widmeyer, & Brawley, 1985), recreational teams (Robinson & Carron, 1982; Spink, 1995, Study 1), exercise settings (Spink & Carron, 1992, 1993, 1994), and elite female competitors (Spink, 1995, Study 2). Of particular interest is the finding that it is the social aspect of cohesion that is the best predictor of the intention to continue. Thus, a coach who is interested in keeping a team together should focus not only on the accomplishment of the task but on the social aspects of the group as well.

Turnover also has much to do with athlete satisfaction. As a coach, the key to reducing turnover may be to make athletes feel like valued members of the team and that there is room for individual improvement. Team members can contribute to minimal turnover by recognizing the contributions of all players (regardless of the role they play) and their needs.

The short-term stability–cohesion relationship was also assessed by Brawley, Widmeyer, and Carron (1988). These researchers assessed the relationship between cohesion and the *group's resistance to disruption*. An open-ended format was used in which athletes were asked to suggest potential disruptive events and rate the degree of disruption. Results demonstrated that more cohesive groups reported a disruptive event to have less impact on the team. This relationship held for elite and recreational teams and members of exercise classes.

Norms

Norms are also associated with increased cohesiveness through increased individual attraction to the group and the development of a team identity (Smith & Smoll, 1997; Zander,

Appreciating team members' accomplishments facilitates team stability by minimizing dissention and interpersonal conflict.

1982). **Norms** are explicit or implicit rules that are established to regulate the behavior of team members. Examples of explicit group norms are dress codes, practice times, and communication patterns between athletes and coaches. Implicit team norms include giving maximal effort in practice and games and being on time.

Norms are formed in areas that have some significance for the group. As such, norms for performance are often established and can be thought of as acceptable levels of performance established by the group (Misumi, 1985). For example, a softball team might establish a performance norm for batting between .300 and .310. According to Stodgill (1972), the group's performance norms are key moderators in the relationship between performance and cohesion (see Fig. 14.3). If group cohesiveness is high and the norm for productivity is high, performance will be enhanced. Conversely, if cohesion is high and the group norm for productivity is low, performance will be negatively affected. Within sport teams, performance norms have been found to be positively related to cohesion (Kim, 1995; Kim & Sugiyama, 1992).

Status

Every member of a team would like to see a substantial amount of playing time. Unfortunately, this is rarely the case. On many teams, some people perform unappreciated jobs to

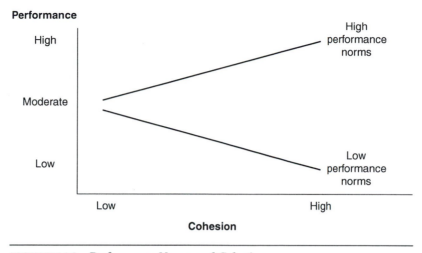

FIGURE 14.3 *Performance Norms and Cohesion.*

help the team achieve its goal. When we think of our favorite sport team, who do we remember? The great home run hitter or perhaps the athlete who was able to make the kill? These are the "glory" positions. But, what about the person who laid the sacrifice bunt to advance the runner? Or the backcourt player who provided the perfect pass to the setter? Players who receive even less recognition are not rewarded with substantial (if any) playing time. These are benchwarmers or nonstarters who are essential to the team because they train and develop the starters each and every day.

Can the benchwarmers, in fact, influence team chemistry? It is logical to assume that if a player is unhappy with his role or perceives that another player is undeservedly receiving playing time, their attitude could influence cohesion. As such, the relationship between starting status and cohesion has been addressed. Gruber and Gray (1982) and Granito and Rainey (1988) found that starters reported stronger perceptions of cohesion than did nonstarters.

Spink (1992) found the relationship between starting status and cohesion to be more complex because team success moderated this relationship. Starters and nonstarters of less successful teams were found to differ on perceptions of task cohesion. On successful teams, this difference disappeared. Starters and nonstarters reported similar levels of cohesion. It is always important to make every player feel like a valued member of the team, but it may be more important for the development of cohesion to attend to this on less successful teams.

Info Box

Group characteristics influence cohesion. Consequently, factors such as stage of development, norms, stability, and status must be effectively addressed.

Performance

Do more cohesive teams outperform those that are less cohesive? In an attempt to resolve this question, Mullen and Cooper (1994) conducted a meta-analytic review (a synthesis of previous research) that encompassed cohesion literature across a variety of settings—laboratory groups, work groups, military units, and of course sport teams. Results supported the existence of a significant relationship between cohesion and performance. This was especially true for sport teams, because the relationship between variables was stronger than that found in other types of groups.

Mullen and Cooper also explored which aspect of cohesion makes groups perform more effectively. Is it the cohesiveness surrounding interpersonal attraction, group pride, or commitment to the task? They found that when cohesion was assessed by commitment to the task (i.e., task cohesion), the cohesion–performance relationship was strongest. Interpersonal attraction and group pride were not negatively related to performance, but these types of cohesion did not influence cohesion to the same extent.

We know that cohesion influences performance. However, can performance also influence cohesion? Mullen and Cooper addressed this issue and also examined the relative strength of each relationship. These researchers tried to determine whether early season cohesion is more strongly related to midseason performance than early season performance is to midseason cohesion. It was found that the relationship between early season performance and future cohesion is somewhat stronger than the relationship between early season cohesion and future performance. In essence, performance success is likely to relate to increased team chemistry. Teams that are not successful should therefore develop chemistry to increase their chances of being more successful.

The final issue addressed by Mullen and Cooper relates to the task of the group. Cohesion obviously is important in team sports. These sports are classified as **interactive sports** because successful performance is dependent on interaction between team members. Performance in many sports, such as wrestling, track, and gymnastics, does not rely on that of a teammate (although they train together and interact with each other). These sports are generally classified as individual or **coactive sports.** Is cohesion more important to develop on interacting teams than coacting? According to Mullen and Cooper, the answer is no. Cohesion was associated with higher levels of performance across all task types.

Info Box

The cohesion–performance relationship is complex; task cohesion both predicts performance and is predicted by performance. The cohesion–performance relationship is observed for interacting and coacting sports.

Conclusion

Cohesion is an elusive quality that all members of sport organizations would like to foster in their teams. However, team members do not always get along. Athletes report resentment toward team members, conflicts with their coach, and personal struggles with commitment. You should not always expect tranquility and cohesion on a team, but how a team resolves these issues is of prime importance. Strategies designed to address the development of cohesion are discussed in Chapter 15, which focuses specifically on team building.

Key Terms (in order of appearance)

cohesion	contractual responsibilities	coach-athlete compatibility
group integration	personal factors	team factors
individual attraction	similarity	stage of development
task cohesion	satisfaction	team stability
social cohesion	sacrifice	norm
environmental factors	social loafing	status
proximity	self-handicapping	performance
distinctiveness	leadership factors	interactive sport
size	decision making	coactive sport

References

Bass, B. M. (1962). *The orientation inventory.* Palo Alto, CA: Consulting Psychologists.

Bollen, K. A., & Hoyle, R. H. (1990). Perceived cohesion: A conceptual and empirical examination. *Social Forces, 69,* 479–504.

Bornstein, R. F., Leone, D. R., & Galley, D. J. (1987). The generalizability of subliminal mere exposure effects: Influence of stimuli perceived without awareness on social behavior. *Journal of Personality and Social Behavior, 53,* 1070–1079.

Brawley, L. R., Widmeyer, W. N., & Carron, A. V. (1988). Exploring the relationship between cohesion and group resistance to disruption. *Journal of Sport & Exercise Psychology, 10,* 199–213.

Carron, A. V., Brawley, L. R., & Widmeyer, W. N. (1998). The measurement of cohesiveness in sport groups. In J. L. Duda (Ed.), *Advancements in sport and exercise measurement* (pp. 213–226). Morgantown, WV: Fitness Information Technology.

Carron, A. V., & Chelladurai, P. (1981). The dynamics of group cohesion in sport. *Journal of Sport Psychology, 3,* 123–139.

Carron, A. V., & Hausenblas, H. A. (1998). *Group dynamics in sport.* Morgantown, WV: Fitness Information Technology.

Carron, A. V., Prapavessis, H., & Grove, J. R. (1994). Group effects and self-handicapping. *Journal of Sport and Exercise Psychology, 16,* 246–258.

Carron, A. V., Widmeyer, W. N., & Brawley, L. R. (1985). The development of an instrument to assess cohesion in sport teams: The group environment questionnaire. *Journal of Sport Psychology, 7,* 244–266.

Cota, A. A., Evans, C. R., Dion, K. L., Kilik, L., & Langman, R. S. (1995). The structure of group cohesion. *Personality and Social Psychology Bulletin, 21,* 572–580.

Dion, K. L. (1990). Group morale. In R. Brown (Ed.), *The Marshal Cavendish encyclopedia of personal relationships: Human behavior, How groups work,* Vol. 15 (pp. 1854–1864). Oxford: Cavendish.

Eitzen, D. S. (1973). The effect of group structure on the success of athletic teams. *International Review of Sport Sociology, 8,* 7–17.

Everett, J. J., Smith, R. E., & Williams, K. D. (1992). Effects of team cohesion and identifiability on social loafing in relay swimming performance. *International Journal of Sport Psychology, 23,* 311–324.

Festinger, L., Schachter, S., & Back, K. (1950). *Social pressures in informal groups: A study of human factors in housing.* New York: Harper.

Forsyth, D. R. (1999). *Group Dynamics,* 3rd ed. Belmont, CA: Brooks/Cole Wadsworth.

Golembiewski, R. (1962). *The small group.* Chicago: Univ. of Illinois Press.

Goodman, P. S., Ravlin, E., & Schminke, M. (1987). Understanding groups in organizations. In L. L. Cummings & B. M. Staw (Eds.), *Research in organizational behavior,* Vol. 9 (pp. 121–173). Greenwich, CT: JAI.

Granito, V. J., & Rainey, D. W. (1988). Differences in cohesion between high school and college football teams and starters and non-starters. *Perceptual and Motor Skills, 66,* 471–477.

Gruber, J. J., & Gray, R. R. (1982). Responses to forces influencing cohesion as a function of players status and level of male varsity basketball competition. *Research Quarterly for Exercise and Sport, 53*(1), 27–36.

Hardy, C. J. (1990). Social loafing: Motivational losses in collective performance. *International Journal of Sport Psychology, 21,* 305–327.

Hausenblas, H. A., & Carron, A. V. (1997). Group cohesion and self-handicapping in female and male athletes. *Journal of Sport and Exercise Psychology, 18,* 132–143.

Johnson, D. W., & Johnson, F. P. (1997). *Joining together: Group theory and group skills,* 6th ed. Needham, MA: Allyn & Bacon.

Karau, S. J., & Williams, K. D. (1993). Social loafing: A meta-analytic review and theoretical integration. *Journal of Personality and Social Psychology, 65,* 681–706.

Kim, M. S. (1995). Performance norms and performance by teams in basketball competition. *Perceptual and Motor Skills, 80*(3), 770.

Kim, M. S., & Sugiyama, Y. (1992). The relation of performance norms and cohesiveness for Japanese school athletic teams. *Perceptual and Motor Skills, 74,* 1096–1098.

Latané, B., Williams, K., & Harkins, S. (1979). Many hands make light work: The causes and consequences of social loafing. *Journal of Personality and Social Psychology, 37,* 822–832.

Leary, M. R. (1995). *Self-presentation: Impression management and interpersonal behavior.* Boulder, CO: Westview.

Lott, A. J., & Lott, B. E. (1965). Group cohesiveness as interpersonal attraction: A review of the relationships with antecedent and consequent variables. *Psychological Bulletin, 64,* 259–309.

Martens, R., & Peterson, J. (1971). Group cohesiveness as a determinant of success and member satisfaction in team performance. *International Review of Sport Sociology, 6,* 49–71.

Misumi, J. (1985). *The behavior science of leadership.* Ann Arbor: Univ. of Michigan Press.

Moreland, R. L. (1987). The formation of small groups. *Review of Personality and Social Psychology, 8,* 80–110.

Mullen, B., & Cooper, C. (1994). The relation between group cohesiveness and performance: An integration. *Psychological Bulletin, 115*(2), 210–227.

Olsen, D. H., Russell, C. S., & Spenkle, D. H. (1979). Circumplex model of marital and family systems: 1. Cohesion and adaptability dimensions, family types, and clinical applications. *Family Process, 18,* 3–28.

Prapavessis, H., & Carron, A. V. (1997). Sacrifice, cohesion, and conformity to norms in sport teams. *Group Dynamics: Theory, Research, and Practice, 1*(3), 231–240.

Prapavessis, H., & Carron, A. V. (1997). Cohesion and work output. *Small Group Research, 28*(2), 294–301.

Rainey, D. W., & Schweickert, G. J. (1988). An exploratory study of team cohesion before and after a spring trip. *The Sport Psychologist, 2,* 314–317.

Robinson, T. T., & Carron, A. V. (1982). Personal and situational factors associated with dropping out versus maintaining participation in competitive sport. *Journal of Sport Psychology, 4,* 364–379.

Smith, R. E., & Smoll, F. L. (1997). Coach mediated team building in youth sports. *Journal of Applied Sport Psychology, 9*(1), 114–132.

Spink, K. S. (1992). Group cohesion and starting status in successful and less successful elite volleyball teams. *Journal of Sport Sciences, 10,* 379–388.

Spink K. S. (1995). Cohesion and intention to participate of female sport team athletes. *Journal of Sport & Exercise Psychology, 17,* 416–427.

Spink, K. S., & Carron, A. V. (1992). Group cohesion and adherence in exercise classes. *Journal of Sport & Exercise Psychology, 14,* 78–86.

Spink, K. S., & Carron, A. V. (1993). The effects of team building on the adherence patterns of female exercise participants. *Journal of Sport & Exercise Psychology, 15,* 39–49.

Spink, K. S., & Carron, A. V. (1994). Group cohesion effects in exercise groups. *Small Group Research, 25,* 26–42.

Stodgill, R. M. (1972). Group productivity, drive, and cohesiveness. *Organizational Behavior and Human Performance, 8,* 26–43.

Steiner, I. D. (1972). *Group processes and productivity.* New York: Academic.

Stevenson, M., & Durand-Bush, N. (1999). The relationship between the development of a university football team and cohesion over a season. *AVANTE, 5*(2), 90–100.

Tuckman, B. W. (1965). Developmental sequences in small groups. *Psychological Bulletin, 63,* 384–399.

Tuckman, B. W., & Jensen, M. A. (1977). Stages of small group development revisited. *Group and Organizational Studies, 2,* 419–427.

Westre, K. R., & Weiss, M. R. (1991). The relationship between perceived coaching behaviors and group cohesion in high school football teams. *The Sport Psychologist, 8,* 332–346.

Widmeyer, W. N., Brawley, L. R., & Carron, A. V. (1990). The impact of group size in sport. *Journal of Sport and Exercise Psychology, 12,* 177–190.

Widmeyer, W. N., Silva, J. M., & Hardy, C. J. *The nature of group goals in sport teams: A phenomenological approach.* Paper presented at the Association for the Advancement of Applied Sport Psychology, Colorado Springs, CO, 1992.

Widmeyer, W. N., & Williams, J. M. (1991). Predicting cohesion in a coacting sport. *Small Group Research, 22,* 548–570.

Williams, J. M., & Hackner, C. M. (1982). Causal relationships among cohesion, satisfaction and performance in women's intercollegiate field hockey teams. *Journal of Sport Psychology, 4,* 324–337.

Zander, A. (1982). *Making groups effective.* San Fransico: Jossey-Bass.

15

Building the Effective Team

Diane E. Stevens

The University of North Carolina at Chapel Hill

- The concept of team building is discussed as an effective group intervention strategy to improve teamwork.
- Two team-building approaches that may be adopted for sport are discussed.
- Characteristics of effective teams are identified.
- Specific team building strategies for each characteristic are developed.

Chemistry is superior to talent for the team's success.

—Anson Carter, as a Boston Bruin

Talent alone is not enough. They used to tell me you have to use your five best players, but I've found that you win with the five who fit together best

—Red Auerbach (as quoted in Williams, 1997, p. 30)

How do you build an effective team? One way was highlighted by the 1992 U.S. Men's Olympic Basketball Team. For the first time, professional basketball players were allowed to compete for Olympic glory. By selecting the best professional players in the country, the team dominated all opponents and easily won the Gold. Olympic 4 × 100 and 4 × 400 relay teams also historically comprised the fastest athletes in the country. This method of team formation has recently been extended to ice hockey. In the 1998 Winter Olympics, professional hockey players were allowed to compete for the Gold for the first time. Are these teams successful? Sometimes. This raises the following question: When successful, are these teams victorious because of their ability to work well together, or because each individual member has spectacular athletic talent? This question may never be adequately answered.

When building a team, not every coach is able to select the best athletes in the country. Most teams comprise the best athletes available. In this case, availability may be restricted because of factors such as geographic limitations, financial constraints, the number of scholarships available, and willingness to participate. Teams put together through this method typically must be *developed* to be successful. The effective team in this case is able to take advantage of the various abilities, backgrounds, and interests of its members and form a unified team with a shared sense of purpose. Zander (1985) identified team unity (or cohesiveness) as one of the fundamental components of effective teamwork. A team that succeeds as the result of development may do so because of *extraordinary teamwork* and not extraordinary individual talent.

However, simply assembling a group of athletes to form a team does not ensure that the athletes will work well together. Teamwork is not something that magically appears. Many teams fail to develop to their full potential, whereas others exceed all expectations, in part because athletes have learned to play well together. Consider the 1995 New Jersey Devils of the National Hockey League, who, to the surprise of most, won the Stanley Cup without one superstar player on its roster. The team was said to be successful because all members bought into their coaches' unique style of play (the neutral zone trap) and played as a team. The following year, the Devils did not live up to expectations because they failed to make the playoffs. This example illustrates that teamwork, or its lack, is a dynamic attribute.

To help facilitate consistency in teamwork, organizational settings often use team-building strategies. The concept of team building has only recently been introduced into the sporting environment. Typical sport psychology interventions have focused on the development of the individual athlete (e.g., anxiety reduction, arousal regulation, imagery), yet relatively little attention has focused on enhancing overall team functioning. It is somewhat surprising that sport teams have not been introduced earlier to team-building concepts. Sport teams share many similarities with other groups in which individual members are required to work together (e.g., common goals, sense of shared purpose, group motivation), and team building may facilitate performance.

What Is Team Building?

Team building is the deliberate process of facilitating the development of an effective and close group. Beer (1980) conceptualized team building as a process intervention (i.e., a series of ongoing interventions designed to target and improve team functioning). Team building aims to help individuals and groups examine and act on their behavior and relationships. Thus, team building interventions attempt to influence team effectiveness toward task and social purposes to develop a cohesive team. Once potentially harmful behaviors are identified, team-building strategies aid team members to overcome these deficiencies. Team building typically focuses on one or more of the areas mentioned in Table 15.1 on page 308.

The primary focus of team-building efforts should be task related and not focus exclusively on improving the relationships between team members (Beckhard, 1972). Interpersonal problems often result from other issues of team functioning. For example, if two team members perceive their roles on a team to be similar, the relationship between these two individuals may suffer. A "Band-Aid" solution focuses only on the improvement among relationships between these team members. The cause of the problem is not being adequately addressed and is likely to resurface. Thus, initial team-building sessions are often more effective if they focus on task rather than relationship issues.

TABLE 15.1 *Purposes of Team Building.*

1. To set team goals and to ensure their accomplishment is clear.
2. To ensure that team members' roles are clearly understood.
3. To examine the way in which the team functions (norms, communication, etc.).
4. To examine the relationships among team members.
5. To ensure that team meetings and practices are efficient.
6. To diagnose potential weaknesses and minimize their influences.
7. To ensure that leadership is coherent, visionary, and acceptable.

Adapted from Beckhard, 1972; Woodcock & Wilson, 1994.

Info Box

Team-building interventions are designed to help a team become more effective. Team-building strategies are typically designed to resolve task-related areas of functioning, but interpersonal relationships can also be their target.

Process of Team Building

Team building in sport psychology has typically been conducted according to either an *indirect* or a *direct* approach. In the indirect approach, the sport psychologist serves a more educational role. The sport psychologist trains the coach in concepts related to group dynamics and specific strategies to enhance team effectiveness. The coach then becomes the team builder as he or she imparts the material to the team. In the direct approach, the sport psychologist assumes a more active role in the team-building process and works directly with the athletes and the coaching staff to implement team-building strategies. Each of these approaches to team building is discussed in more detail next.

Indirect Approach to Team Building

The indirect approach to team building may be ideal for educating coaches about how to facilitate the development of a cohesive team. It may also be beneficial when time, geographical restrictions, or financial constraints limit the involvement of the sport psychologist in the team-building process. Carron and Dennis (1998) outlined a four-stage process for conducting indirect team building in sport:

1. *The introductory stage* introduces group leaders/coaches to the importance of group cohesion and its benefits. For example, the relationship between team cohesiveness and improved coach/athlete relations may be discussed.
2. *The conceptual stage* is used to facilitate communication about issues related to group dynamics, to highlight the importance and interrelatedness of various components of the team-building process, and to identify possible areas of intervention.

3. During the *practical stage* the coaches brainstorm to develop *specific* strategies that address problems in team functioning that are specific to their team. Ultimately, these strategies are used to help develop cohesiveness.
4. In the *intervention stage,* the strategies developed during the practical stage are implemented and maintained by the coaches.

Is the Indirect Approach Effective?

The indirect approach to team building has been found to increase cohesiveness in exercise settings (Carron & Spink, 1993; Spink & Carron, 1992). Fitness leaders used team-building strategies to help promote adherence to an exercise program and cohesiveness among exercise participants. The types of intervention strategies employed include making the group distinct from other exercise classes, developing group norms and increased partner exercises to improve interaction among participants, and asking some participants to make sacrifices for the group.

In one sport example, Prapavessis, Carron, and Spink (1996) involved soccer coaches in a team-building workshop. The strategies learned in the workshop were to be used by the coaches throughout the preseason and the 6-week regular season. At the end of this period, cohesion was not found to differ between teams whose coaches engaged in the workshop and those whose coaches did not.

Info Box

The indirect approach to team building involves the coach and sport psychologist in developing strategies for use with the team. This approach has been found to be effective for developing cohesion and increased adherence rates in exercise classes.

Direct Approach to Team Building

The majority of team-building interventions conducted in organizational psychology are based on an *action research* model (see Fig. 15.1 on page 310; Beckhard, 1972; Beer, 1976). This model focuses on enhancing team performance by improving team processes (e.g., communication, roles). The first step involves the assessment of current team procedures and overall functioning through the use of interviews, personal observations, and/or questionnaires with the coaching staff and athletes. The sport psychologist then plans and implements changes to improve productivity and effectiveness. Finally, team functioning is reassessed to determine whether further changes are needed. Two unique features of a direct approach to team building distinguish it from the indirect approach. First, the sport psychologist is actively involved in all stages of the team-building process. Second, team members are also actively involved at each stage. Team members are typically involved in the diagnoses of team functioning, planning change, and the evaluation of the effectiveness of the interventions. Through the involvement of team members, change is not forced, and favorable consequences are more likely to result.

FIGURE 15.1   *The Action Research Model of Team Building Applied to Sport (adapted from Woodcock & Francis, 1994).*

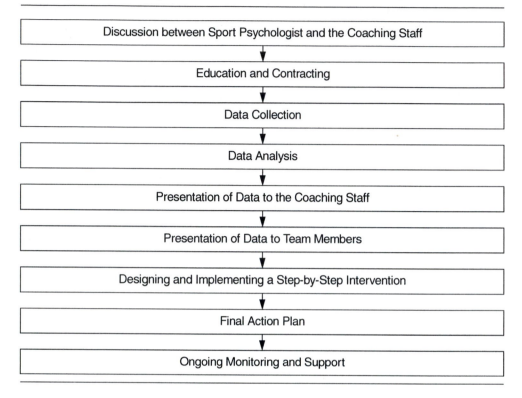

| Discussion between Sport Psychologist and the Coaching Staff |
| Education and Contracting |
| Data Collection |
| Data Analysis |
| Presentation of Data to the Coaching Staff |
| Presentation of Data to Team Members |
| Designing and Implementing a Step-by-Step Intervention |
| Final Action Plan |
| Ongoing Monitoring and Support |

Discussion with the Coaching Staff.   Coaches play an important role in any direct-approach team-building intervention. It is recommended that the coaching staff be active participants in the team-building process. Thus, the sport psychologist must ensure that the team-building approach is understood, accepted, and supported by the coaching staff. This is accomplished through the clarification of responsibilities of the coaches in the team-building process. The coaches must also be willing to evaluate their role in team functioning, because they are capable of contributing to problems in overall team functioning (e.g., coaching behaviors, communication patterns). Therefore, coaches, as well as athletes, must be willing to examine how their behaviors contribute to overall team effectiveness. If the coach is not committed to the team-building process, the feasibility of the intervention should be reassessed to determine whether change in team functioning can be facilitated without coach involvement.

An exploratory meeting with coaches can also provide additional information and/or resources to help the sport psychologist in the team-building process. Important areas of information that can be gathered have been suggested by Recardo and colleagues (1996) and include:

• Identify the characteristics of team members (age, experience, education, etc.).
• Identify the nature of the sport (interdependent or interacting sport).

- Identify problem areas and concerns.
- Identify which athletes are most influential to the task and social aspects of team functioning.
- Identify the atmosphere of the team (communication patterns, trust among members, conflicts, clique formation, etc.).
- Identify the best approach for data collection.

Education and Contracting. In this phase, the team-building process is outlined to team members. Most team-building sessions require that the sport psychologist present ideas, concepts, and frameworks inherent in group dynamics. A solid knowledge of the theory and practice of the concepts that lead to successful functioning may lead team members to a deeper understanding of their current team's situation. Informative questions that could be asked include "What makes a successful team?" "How do you think this team could improve its functioning?" and "What problems does the team feel it has?"

It is important for team members to have an explicit understanding of their roles and responsibilities and those of the sport psychologist as well (see Table 15.2). Team members must be willing to open themselves up to the team-building process and commit the time necessary to improve team functioning. Although some reservations and uncertainties are to be expected, support by all team members increases the probability of a successful outcome.

The issue of confidentiality between athletes and the sport psychologist should also be discussed at this stage. Confidentiality is often dependent on the extent to which the coach is involved in the team-building process. If the coach is not involved, then confidentiality is ensured. However, it is recommended that the coach maintain a role in the team-building process. In this case, athletes should be made aware that the coach may be informed of themes identified (by the athletes or sport psychologist) for improvement and the result of any intervention. At no time, however, will the coach be informed of individual athlete responses. The ultimate goal of this stage is to gain commitment from team members to the team-building process.

TABLE 15.2 *The Functions of a Sport Psychologist in the Team-Building Process.*

DO	*DON'T*
• Collect data about team effectiveness	• Usurp leadership
• Observe functioning of the team	• *Tell* team members what is wrong (help identify problems)
• Provide a clear and objective view of team functioning	• Make decisions for the team
• Select activities to help facilitate team functioning	• Make the team dependent on the continued presence of the sport psychologist
• Give feedback	
• Provide guidance to coaches and athletes	
• Encourage the team to review the impact of their behavior	
• Convey optimism	

Data Collection. To fully serve the team, the sport psychologist must collect objective and comprehensive data regarding the team's functioning. Brawley and Paskevich (1997) recommend that data be collected along two dimensions: overall group functioning (e.g., cohesion, norms) and the social environment of the team (e.g., social setting, cliques). Specific characteristics of the team may also influence the data collection process (Beer, 1980; Brawley & Paskevich, 1997). These factors include the size of the team, the level of cohesion, the degree of social interaction among team members, and potential barriers to intervention. The stage of development is one of the primary characteristics of the team to consider. In newly formed teams, confusion may exist regarding norms, roles, and coaching styles. In this case, the team-building interventions should serve a clarifying functioning. Within teams that have been together for a longer period of time, the style of functioning should be in place (whether it be effective or not). Those that are working effectively for the team need not be addressed. Those that are ineffective may need to be addressed in depth during the intervention (stage 7). Possible assessment areas for any team include cohesion, leadership, social support, goal setting, communication, conflict, norms, and roles.

Sport psychologists can gather information on team functioning through semistructured interviews, personal observation, and/or questionnaires. With small teams, a confidential interview with each athlete may be of particular benefit. One-on-one interviews may not be feasible with larger teams, but several small group interviews could be conducted to gather the needed information. Important goals of the interview process are to:

- Identify athletes' attitudes regarding team functioning (e.g., performance, satisfaction).
- Identify how well individual needs are being met by team involvement.
- Identify potential problem areas.

Collecting data through personal interviews has several benefits and limitations (Carron & Widmeyer, 1996). First, trust and rapport are more likely to be facilitated between the sport psychologist and athlete through face-to-face communication. Secondly, athlete understanding is ensured through the use of clarifying questions. One salient limitation of the interview method is the amount of time required to conduct detailed personal interviews.

Data about team functioning can also be collected through the use of valid, sport-specific questionnaires. Many such scales have been developed, including the Group Environment Questionnaire (Carron, Widmeyer, & Brawley, 1985), the Leadership Scale for Sport (Chelladurai & Carron, 1981; Chelladurai & Saleh, 1978), and the Social Support Scale (Richman, Rosenfeld, & Hardy, 1993). Where valid instruments do not exist (e.g., role assessment), tests can be constructed that target the team processes you wish to assess. As with the interview method, researchers have identified various benefits and limitations of using questionnaires for team building (Carron & Widmeyer, 1996). One benefit is the ability to gather a large amount of data quickly. Second, questionnaires provide respondents with anonymity, which may be more conducive to athletes' responding to the items honestly. Limitations of this method include the impersonal nature of questionnaires, response bias, and the difficulty of verifying athlete understanding.

Data Analysis. When interview techniques are employed, it is particularly important to group various ideas identified by individual team members into themes and subthemes.

When questionnaires are employed, statistical analyses are performed and accurate interpretation of the data helps to provide important information about the team's level of functioning. Whichever method is employed, the sport psychologist must be well trained in qualitative and quantitative analyses to ensure accurate interpretation.

During this stage, key issues must be identified (e.g., lack of communication, poor interpersonal relationships) to fully assess the most *prominent* problem interfering with team functioning. Thus, the *root causes* of the problems, rather than simply addressing the symptoms, must be critically examined. For example, one athlete may feel as though role confusion is a salient problem on the team. Perhaps the coach has failed to clearly discuss role behavior with the athletes, and the confusion experienced by the athletes is a function of ineffective communication patterns that need to be addressed prior to examining roles on the team.

Presentation of Data to the Coaching Staff. To verify the results obtained in data analysis, the sport psychologist may choose to inform the coaching staff of his or her findings. In cases where the sport psychologist is working closely with the coaching staff, a general summary of the findings should be provided. From this, additional information and/or verification of findings can be generated.

Presentation of Data to All Team Members. In this stage, team builders present concrete data to the group. Caution must be taken to ensure that the team is not overwhelmed with data and that team members can easily grasp the concepts presented. The issues identified to be the most important to overall team effectiveness should be dealt with first in the intervention stage.

Step-by-Step Intervention. The most important stage in the team-building process, and often the longest, is intervention. At this stage, the sport psychologist is responsible for educating, facilitating discussion (both at the level of the individual athlete and in small groups), and helping the team facilitate changes that can be monitored over the course of the season. The sport psychologist must have an action plan (i.e., interventions designed specifically to enhance team effectiveness) and assist team members to overcome the identified problems. Interventions must be relevant and directly applicable to the specific team. Examples of team-building interventions are developing role clarity, establishing norms, and conflict resolution. Interventions must center on the best way of focusing the team's development energy on blockages and development opportunities. Creating a positive environment by developing not only the relationships among team members but also knowledge is of particular importance. The role of the facilitator is to bring up stressful situations, maintain a supportive environment, and challenge prevailing thoughts. Ultimately, however, individuals will change *only when they want to.* Completion of this stage may take many months.

Final Action Planning. In this stage of the team-building process, a comprehensive summary of the interventions conducted in previous sessions is provided. Final interviews and/or questionnaire assessment should occur to determine whether the desired changes took place compared to baseline levels, which were assessed in stage 3. Team members are told of future involvement with the sport psychologist and that the progress of the team will be continually monitored.

Ongoing Monitoring and Support.   Follow-up meetings should be conducted with coaches and athletes at 3–6 months to assess progress. Continued support should be offered to assist the team to overcome difficulties and continue to work together openly and effectively. The sport psychologist also needs to be responsible and review their performance. Areas of improvement should be identified, and intervention techniques that were particularly effective should be highlighted.

Is the Direct Approach Effective?

The effectiveness of direct team-building interventions in business and industry has received both anecdotal and empirical support (Woodcock & Francis, 1994). In a review of thirteen team-building studies in industry, Sundstrom, DeMeuse, and Futrell (1990) reported that 80 percent of the interventions resulted in improved effectiveness across numerous group variables (e.g., communication, cooperation, cohesion, satisfaction). However, the benefits of team-building strategies on performance are less conclusive. Performance was found to improve in four of nine studies in which it was measured. Thus, while the direct approach to team-building has been found to be effective in enhancing group processes, its effectiveness on performance is unclear.

One study that utilized a direct approach to team-building examined the effectiveness of a series of interventions on an equestrian team (Bloom & Mack, 1999). Before the intervention, cohesion was assessed by the GEQ (Carron, Widmeyer, & Brawley, 1985) and semistructured interviews with the head coach and athletes. Based on the results of this information, six team-building sessions were carried out and included developing athlete leadership, readdressing norms for interpersonal relationships, establishing better communication patterns, being chosen for competition, and preparation for competition. Although no changes were evident across the measure of cohesion, athletes' perceptions of team functioning improved from their preintervention evaluations.

Info Box

The coach, sport psychologist, and the team develop an ongoing relationship when using the direct approach to team building. The effectiveness of this approach to sport teams has not yet been determined.

Other Team-Building Research in Sport

Not all team-building research in sport has been conducted according to the indirect or the direct approach. McClure and Foster (1991) examined the effectiveness of a 15-week team-building intervention on perceptions of cohesiveness and role clarity and on acceptance in a small sample of intercollegiate gymnasts. Team members were randomly assigned to either a team-building group or a control group. The team-building sessions were unstructured. They were designed so that team members could discuss their feelings concerning themselves and their teammates and were not designed to target specific aspects of group functioning. Cohesion was found to increase compared to the control group following the intervention.

Cogan and Petrie (1995) examined the efficacy of a season-long team building (again with intercollegiate gymnasts). The program was designed to increase perceptions of cohesion and to decrease anxiety. Questionnaires were administered to the athletes six times over the course of the season (three in preseason and three during the competitive season). Results revealed some changes in cohesion and anxiety between specific time periods, but cohesion and anxiety did not differ between the first and final administration of the questionnaires.

Characteristics of Effective Groups

Chemistry, while harder to spot than talent, is even more important. What we call chemistry is really a combination of a lot of factors: ability and skill levels, drive, ambition, emotional makeup, values, communication, and people skills. Chemistry is not easy to assess until you actually put the team together under real world conditions. Often you have to experiment a few times, adding this, subtracting that in order to get just the right chemistry going

—Williams, 1997, p. 30

Reflect on a team you were on that was successful. Now reflect on a team that you were on that was not successful. What were some of the differences between these teams? The question of what makes a team successful has challenged researchers interested in group dynamics and team-building for years (Fisher & Thomas, 1996; Johnson & Johnson, 1997; Reddy & Jamison, 1988; Salmela, 1996). These researchers have identified several common themes characteristic of successful teams.

The following section builds on the concepts discussed in the previous chapters in this section. With the theoretical and empirical foundation established, now the focus needs to be placed on applied group dynamics. Many factors contribute to team cohesiveness (which in turn impacts many group and individual variables): How can cohesion be enhanced? How can roles be clarified? How are norms established or changed? Specific team-building intervention strategies are discussed that are designed to facilitate team success. For each intervention, a direct approach to team-building is assumed. Some of the suggested interventions have not been empirically tested by sport scientists to determine their effectiveness. Despite this, all proposed interventions are grounded in theoretical and empirical evidence from organizational and sport psychology as well as practical evidence from the team-building literature.

Info Box

Many factors must be considered when trying to establish an effective team. Attention to only one factor may not be sufficient, so the strengths and weaknesses of each team must be evaluated to determine where improvements can be made.

TABLE 15.3   *Team Vision—the Orlando Magic of the National Basketball Association.*

The vision of the Orlando Magic is to be recognized as the professional sports model of the twenty-first century by exemplifying the principles and practices of a championship organization in both the sport and business of basketball. We intend to achieve world-class status as a franchise through unwavering commitment to integrity, service, quality, and consumer value, while emphasizing the partnership among our community, our fans, our coaches, our players, our staff, and our owners.

Adapted from Williams, 1997.

Creating a Vision

The most successful teams begin with somebody's dream. Successful coaches are able to create a **team vision** of what they perceive to be possible if all team members work together toward a common purpose (Desjardins, 1996; Fisher & Thomas, 1996; Sundstrom, DeMeuser, & Futrell, 1990). The vision often includes perceptions of athletic ability, personal character, values, and motivation of the individuals who make up the team. Table 15.3 is an example of the vision of an organization. A vision not only unites team members around the task of the group but also may enhance emotional commitment. The vision provides the coaching staff with direction and influences everything from short- and long-term planning to team selection and goal setting.

TABLE 15.4   *Team-Building Strategy for Developing a Team Vision.*

1. Coaches Meeting—Begin with the End
- Ensure that the view of the future is clear, reasonable, and accepted by all members of the coaching staff. Accept input from all coaches to ensure their commitment to the future of the team.
- Develop clear strategies for attaining the vision (who to draft, which offensive style of play, etc.).

2. Team Meeting—Develop Ownership
- Bring vision to all team members. Accept input.
- Discuss how each member contributes to the team's future.
- Discuss what will change under this direction for the future (what will be done differently, new competencies developed, etc.).

3. Connect Daily Activities to the Accomplishment of the Vision

4. Provide for Evaluation of the Vision
- How is the team progressing toward the vision?

Adapted from Fisher & Thomas, 1996.

This shared vision of the future must be clearly communicated to team members. Athletes become the "keepers of the vision." Only through their effort can the vision be attained. Team commitment to the vision is essential because it may help to bind diverse athletes together of form a united group. Without commitment, athletes may deliberately pull against the vision because team goals may be incompatible with individual goals. Table 15.4 outlines a strategy to help facilitate the development and acceptance of team vision. Goal setting and role commitment are essential to achieve the vision.

Acceptance and Commitment to Group Goals

Once a clear direction for the team has been established and accepted by all team members, it is possible to set group goals designed to achieve the vision. **Group goals** are shared perceptions that refer to a desirable state of the group as a unit (Mills, 1984). Examples of group goals are a baseball team wanting to score an average of five runs per game or a hockey team wanting to score on 25 percent of their powerplays. The team vision and the goals should not be confused. The vision is larger and grander than goals. Goals are generally more focused on performance (see Fig. 15.2 for an example). Although goal setting is

---

SOFTBALL TEAM GOALS

1. Team Batting Average (BA)	285–305	5. Number of Runs Scored (RS)	4–6
2. On-Base Percentage (OB%)	340–360	6. Number of Runners Left on Base (ROB)	3–5
3. Fielding Percentage (Field%)	.96–.97	7. ERA	.09–1.2
4. Number of Runs Allowed (RA)	≤ 3		

SEGMENT 1

	Minnesota		Triangle Classic							S. Carolina		
	Game 1	Game 2	Game 1	Game 2	Game 3	Game 4	Game 5	Game 6	Game 7	Game 1	Game 2	Segment 1 Average
BA 285–305												
OB% 340–360												
Field% .96–.97												
RA ≤ 3												
RS 4–6												
ROB 3–5												
ERA .09–1.2												

FIGURE 15.2 *Team Goal Setting Example (adapted from Mack & Bloom, 1999).*

essential for providing direction and motivating the team, a strategy in which the goals are monitored to determine progress is equally important.

Two ways of developing group goals have been identified in the sport psychology literature. The first outlines a process whereby the athletes, along with the sport psychologist, identify areas of performance in which the team needs to improve to be successful (Carron & Widmeyer, 1996; Widmeyer & DuCharme, 1997). This strategy is developed through an educational, workshop, and monitoring phase (see Table 15.5 on page 319).

Team performance profiling has also been identified as an effective tool to facilitate team goal setting (Dale & Wrisberg, 1996; Yukelson, 1997). Performance profiling was developed as a means of enhancing the athlete's self-awareness about performance preparation (Butler, 1991; Butler & Hardy, 1992). Dale and Wrisberg used performance profiling techniques with team sport athletes to develop group goals. Athletes were asked to identify the characteristics (physical, mental, tactical, attitude) of an effective team in their sport. Examples of characteristics identified were winning attitude, communicating well on court, sound fundamentals, and mental toughness. Team members were then asked to rate their team (compared to the ideal) on these qualities along a ten-point scale. The head coach was also asked to rate his or her perceptions of the team across these dimensions. Group goals were made based on those characteristics in which a large discrepancy existed between current and ideal performance. Significant improvements across these characteristics were made over the course of the season. Using team performance profiling may be an effective way to identify and achieve group goals.

Defined and Accepted Roles

> *I knew that the only way to win consistently was to give everybody—from the stars to the number 12 player on the bench—a vital role on the team.*
>
> —Phil Jackson, Coach, Los Angeles Lakers

To make a successful team, each athlete must believe that he or she makes a difference. The **role** that each team member plays in goal attainment and how his or her role fits into the overall vision must be clarified. Effective communication on the part of the coach is paramount to aid in role clarity. For an athlete to give his or her best effort, the specific role must be clear and the expectations that others have for that role must be clearly understood.

What happens when a person does not like an assigned role? This is not an uncommon phenomenon. It is not surprising that some athletes do not enjoy the role of the "bench player," "goon," or "sixth man." However, in highly interdependent sports, many diversified roles are essential to team functioning. Athletes are competent in specialized areas that are highlighted by the roles they play on the team.

The challenge is getting the athletes to accept the need for diversity to enhance team functioning (and ultimately achieve the team's vision). Coaches who are able to build respect for diversity in all team members and also develop unity of purpose may have a particularly effective team. Table 15.6 on page 321 outlines a team-building strategy that may be used to develop role clarity and role acceptance. The strategy is designed around each athlete identifying his or her role(s) on the team. Questions are asked regarding role clarity, importance, commitment, and acceptance of each role. Small group discussions take place

TABLE 15.5   *Team-Building Strategy to Develop a Team Goal-Setting Program.*

1. Examine the Vision of the Team

The vision often becomes the *long-term outcome goal* of the team.

2. Educational Phase

Educate players concerning goal setting:

- The relationship between goal setting and performance.
- Qualities of effective goals.

Identify types of goals that can be set:

Performance outcome—divide the season into segments. If the season is 30 games long, divide into six 5-game segments. Determine the winning percentage for each segment that will allow the team to achieve the long-term outcome goal (e.g., win three of every five games).

Performance—identifies ways of achieving short-term performance outcome goals. What needs to be done in order to win three of five games? Effective power plays, low error rate, and number of sacks per game are examples of performance goals.

Process—targets established for the component actions that make up the short-term performance goals. What percentage of powerplay opportunities should be scored on?

3. Workshop Phase

Establish a Method of Achieving the Long-Term Outcome Goal.
Involve all team members in establishing goals—enhances acceptance of group goals.

a. Performance goals—ask each athlete to write down what he or she thinks are the most important performance goals to focus on.

b. Divide athletes into odd-numbered heterogeneous groups (e.g., starters/nonstarters; offensive/defensive specialists) where they are asked to come to a consensus about what the performance goals should be.

c. Record each group's desired goals on a blackboard. Discrepancies are discussed among team members. The team adopts the most frequently cited goals.

d. Process goals—set target levels for each performance goal. Provide athletes with a list of previous years' statistics to serve as a guide. Target levels are set both individually and collectively.

e. Record the target level for each group. When discrepancies exist between groups, stimulate discussion until consensus is reached.

4. Monitoring Goal Progress

Post performance goals in the dressing room for each game and average across each segment.

Adapted from Widmeyer & Carron, 1996; Widmeyer & DuCharme, 1997.

Helping every player understand his or her role contributes to building an effective team.

to determine whether teammates see that athlete's role any differently. Discussions regarding the importance of each athlete's role are also facilitated in an attempt to highlight the importance of each person to team functioning.

Supportive Environment

A **supportive environment** in which team members can excel develops when athletes feel respected and encouraged by their coaches and teammates. In fact, a supportive environment often surrounds teams that achieve greatness (Bloom, 1996; Fisher & Thomas, 1996). However, it appears as though a supportive environment may not be the norm in many sport teams. Research has found that coaches and teammates provide less social support than do friends (Richman, Rosenfeld, & Hardy, 1989). In addition, the type of support offered by coaches and teammates tends to be related solely to sport performance. This finding may be a reflection of the nature of competitive sport. Within any team, there are always rivals (i.e., other team members may want to occupy your position). For example, if you are a starter, the bench players will not play as long as you are healthy and playing well. Where

TABLE 15.6   *Team-Building Strategy for Developing Clearly Defined and Accepted Roles.*

1. **Coach Responsibilities**—to clearly define what is expected of each athlete. Once every team member understands the pattern of behavior that is expected, each person knows how he or she contributes to the team.

2. **Educational Phase**—to describe the importance of roles to overall team functioning. Develop an understanding of the concepts of role clarity, role acceptance, and role commitment.

3. **Workshop Phase**

    Individual team members—ask individual team members to respond to the questions:*

    What is your primary role on this team?
    Which teammates are most dependent on your successfully completing this role?
    What are the specific functions of your primary role?
    How does this role contribute to the team's vision?
    How clear are you about your role?
    How much do you like this role?
    How important is this role to the success of the team?
    How committed are you to this role?

    Have athletes answer all questions for all secondary and tertiary roles as well.

4. **Group Discussion**—helps individual athlete clarify his or her roles and how others value their roles.

    a. Divide athletes into odd-numbered heterogeneous groups to facilitate a discussion on team roles.

    b. Ask team members to state what they think each other's roles on the team are.

    c. Discuss the importance of each role to overall team functioning.

    d. Encourage the athlete to write down any additional information to serve as a reminder of the roles he or she occupies.

    * Questions 5 through 8 are rated according to the following scale (*1 = not at all* to *9 = extremely*)

Adapted from Widmeyer & Carron, 1996; Mumma, 1994.

there is too much intrateam competition, it is unlikely that a supportive environment will exist. Supportive rivalries need to be developed so that athletes are challenged to make each other better (and consequently make the team better).

Team members may need to be taught to provide each other with social support that is not just sport related. When this occurs, they probably will enhance their communication and share a deeper commitment to team goals and to the team "vision." Social support may be critical to building a successful team. This strategy in Table 15.7 on page 322 is designed to assess the types of social support provided by team members and how often. Based on team responses, different types of social support are discussed and ways of enhancing and diversifying types of social support are identified.

TABLE 15.7   *Team-Building Strategy to Enhance Social Support among Team Members.*

1. **Assessment**—The Social Support Survey (SSS; Richman et al., 1993) should be completed to examine the nature of, and satisfaction with, social support received by team members. Based on the results of the survey, strengths and weaknesses of members social support network can be identified.

2. **Education**—Identify the multidimensional nature of social support. Provide team members with the results.

3. **Intervention**—Based on team weaknesses, have team members identify specific strategies designed to enhance specific types of social support. With the help of the sport psychologist, have the team determine the feasibility of the proposed interventions.

4. **Implementation**—Coaches and athletes implement the strategies discussed in the intervention phase.

5. **Evaluation**—Readminister the SSS to determine the effectiveness of the intervention and the current level of members' social support.

Adapted from Rosenfeld & Richman, 1997.

Communication

Effective communication may be the most important ingredient in developing and maintaining effective teamwork (Williams, 1997). After all, how can teamwork develop without communication? Effective teams devote time and energy to building communication networks. Effective communication often entails team members' willingness to receive feedback from others. Miscommunication often results in wasted time and energy, poor performance, and/or poor interpersonal relationships. A team that experiences difficulties in communication style may benefit from team-building sessions designed to foster improved communication patterns.

When conducting team-building communication sessions, it is important to highlight two distinct areas: effective listening skills and effective group discussion (Sullivan, 1993). Developing *effective listening skills* is particularly important because listening conveys *value,* not only to what is being said but also to the person who is sending the information. Most of us engage in "selective hearing"—we hear only what we want to hear. When a person is heard, their importance to others is often reaffirmed. If a person believes they matter, they feel they make a difference.

The ability to *effectively communicate as a group* is another valuable tool. When communicating with one person, it is relatively easy to ensure understanding and evaluate attitude and motivation. However, as the number of members in a group increases, effective communication becomes more problematic. Within a large group there are numerous values, opinions, listening styles, and ideas that need to be addressed to come to a consensus. Properties of effective listening and group discussion skills are summarized in Table 15.8.

Communication patterns in game situations are often very different from those experienced in practice, team meetings, or other areas of life. In a structured environment, it is

TABLE 15.8 *Team Building Strategy to Effective Communication Patterns.*

Building Effective Listening Skills
- Maintain eye contact
- Ask clarifying questions
- Understand; don't argue
- Check to make sure everyone has had a chance to speak
- Paraphrase to ensure understanding
- Try to respect speaker's point of view
- Maintain an open and relaxed body posture
- Before giving/offering advice, ask if it is wanted
- Use congruent verbal and nonverbal messages

Effective Group Discussion
- Respect the thoughts, feelings, and experiences of others
- Use first-person singular pronouns ("I" or "my")
- Do not judge others
- Do not feel pressure to speak if you do not want to
- Do not discount others' thoughts
- Do not monopolize the conversation
- Do not try to change somebody's mind
- Respect silence—some need time to think before responding

Adapted from Sullivan, 1993.

relatively easy to take the time necessary to communicate openly and accurately once you have the skills to do so. In competition, however, time is of the essence and communication patterns are more likely to be nonverbal. The communicator cannot always take the time to ensure understanding or acceptance of the message. The team needs to nail down a standard procedure for communication (e.g., signs, signals, set plays) because during competitions accurate information and communication are essential

Team strategy meetings should be set up to discuss ways in which to facilitate communication in competitive situations. First, the coach must identify the "show time" moments of the game to all team members (Fisher & Thomas, 1996). Examples of these important moments include third down and long, stealing a base, changing offensive alignment, and the pitch to be thrown. Second, the information that needs to be shared and to whom the information should be given needs to be identified. Should only those directly affected (e.g., the base runner stealing) be informed? Or should those indirectly affected (e.g., the batter) also be notified of what his or her teammate is doing? The coaching staff typically makes these decisions. Third, a routinized method for sharing the information must be developed. It is not practical (or smart) for a baseball manager to yell across the field, "Steal!" Signals must be developed and learned so that the manager can communicate his or her intentions to the base runner. Another method of communication in "show time" moments involves an athlete bringing plays in from the sideline. The final step to effective communication in game situations is confirmation of the received information. Accurately performing the desired play sometimes is confirmation enough; at other times, a more formalized procedure may be developed (i.e., a nod of the head).

Once these communication patterns have been established and learned by all team members, it is extremely important to practice this style of communication in simulated competitive situations. Miscommunication during games often will result in undesired consequences, such as poor performance, frustration by athletes, and conflict.

Norms

Effective teams have norms and rules of behavior agreed on by all members (Bassin, 1988). Unfortunately, most teams do not establish written rules for team behavior, attitude, and member interactions. Remember, norms serve many purposes (e.g., provide consistency, reduce ambiguity) and reflect the core values of the team. They must be formalized so that each team member has a clear understanding of what is expected of him or her and the consequences of norm violation.

Table 15.9 outlines a strategy for the development of team norms. The first stage of the intervention is designed to examine the norms that currently exist. Following a discussion on the importance and benefits of norms, the team is asked to come up with a revised list of team norms. New norms may also be identified at this stage. Following a group discussion, during which the feasibility and acceptance of the norms are evaluated, the new or revised norms should be put into place. The team norms should be reviewed periodically to determine their effectiveness.

An important aspect of establishing team norms is norm violations. Team members should help develop policies for discipline in these instances. Discussion should center on who should play the role of disciplinarian, what is acceptable punishment, and the role of the coaching staff. Bassin (1988) commented that norms are more likely to be accepted when team members are instrumental in their development and have a say in the punishment for violations.

Conclusion

> *Team chemistry is the most fragile of all mixtures. You never know how you get it, and you never know why you lost it. But when you've got it, you know you've got it—and when you don't you know that too.*
>
> —Joe Axelson, NBA General Manager (quoted in Williams, 1997, p. 30)

Teamwork is critical to performance and athlete satisfaction, but effective teamwork does not develop naturally. Further, effective teamwork is not easy to assess until you place team members together. That doesn't mean there is nothing you can do to help teamwork develop. The purpose of this chapter was to introduce indirect and direct methods to conduct team building and to identify specific strategies to deal with problems that can affect any team. Although many of these strategies require additional testing, they offer a solid starting point for developing overall team effectiveness. Inherent in all these strategies is the involvement of team members in diagnosing and planning change. The role of the sport

TABLE 15.9 *Team-Building Strategy to Develop Team Norms.*

1. **Norm Assessment**

   Identify and examine the team's current norms (if any) through discussion with coaches and team members.

2. **Educational Phase**

   Educate team members about the benefits of norms, what they accomplish, and the types of norms that can be set (effort, communication, conflict, etc.).

3. **Workshop Phase**

   Setting Team Norms

   - Have individual team members make a list of behaviors they would like to see team members adopt. Remind team members that norms should be something valued by the team and something that can be observed.
   - Divide team members into heterogeneous groups to discuss the norms written by each individual member. Ask each group to come to a consensus regarding proposed team norms.
   - Ask each group to state their norms. Write down each norm for the entire team to review.
   - Facilitate group discussion on team norms. Which are desirable? Which are achievable? Do any of the proposed norms need to be modified? Have all areas where norms could be set been addressed?
   - Reach group consensus on which norms to adopt.

   Disciplinary Action against Norm Violation

   - Have team members decide among themselves what the penalty should be if any of the team norms are violated. Examples of disciplinary actions could be financial, extra work, missed game, etc. Penalties should be implemented that promote self-discipline and not embarrass the athlete in front of teammates.

   Have team norms (and their disciplinary actions) typed and a copy given to all team members.

4. **Review Team Norms**

   After a few months, review the current team norms to determine their feasibility. If necessary, establish new norms or modify old ones.

psychologist is to educate, to determine the feasibility of proposed changes, and to facilitate change. The goal of the proposed team-building strategies is to improve the effectiveness of a team in the long run by improving the process by which members work together. Ultimately, these strategies should lead to enhanced cohesion within the team.

Key Terms (in order of appearance) _____

team building	characteristics of an	role
indirect approach to	effective group	supportive environment
team building	team vision	communication
direct approach to team building	group goal	norm

References _____

Bassin, M. (1988). Teamwork at General Foods: New and improved. *Personnel Journal, 67*(5), 62–70.

Beckhard, R. (1972). *Organizational development.* Reading MA: Addison-Wesley.

Beer, M. (1976). The technology of organization development. In M. Dunnette (Ed.), *Handbook of industrial and organizational psychology* (pp. 937–994). Chicago: Rand McNally.

Beer, M. (1980). *Organizational change and development: A systems review.* Glenview, IL: Scott, Foresman.

Bloom, G. A. (1996). Life at the Top: Philosophies of Success. In J. H. Salmela (Ed.) *Great job coach: Getting the edge from proven winners* (pp. 37–65). Ottawa, ON: Potentium.

Bloom, G. A., & Mack, D. E. (1999). *Improving team effectiveness: A direct approach to team-building.* Ms. submitted for publication.

Brawley, L. R., & Paskevich, D. M. (1997). Conducting team-building research in the context of sport and exercise. *Journal of Applied Sport Psychology, 9*(1), 11–40.

Butler, R. J. (1991). Amateur boxing and sport science II: Psychology. *Coaching Focus, 18,* 14–15.

Butler, R. J., & Hardy, L. (1992). The performance profile: Theory and application. *The Sport Psychologist, 6,* 253–264.

Carron, A. V., & Dennis, P. W. (1998). The sport team as an effective group. In J. M. Williams (Ed.), *Applied Sport Psychology: Personal growth to peak performance* (pp. 127–141). Mountain View, CA: Mayfield.

Carron, A. V., & Spink, K. S. (1993). Team building in an exercise setting. *The Sport Psychologist, 7,* 8–18.

Carron, A. V., & Widmeyer, W. N. (1996). Team building in sport and exercise. Workshop presented at the Association for the Advancement of Applied Sport Psychology, Williamsburg, VA.

Carron, A. V., Widmeyer, W. N., & Brawley, L. R. (1985). The development of an instrument to assess cohesion in sport teams: The Group Environment Questionnaire. *Journal of Sport Psychology, 7,* 244–266.

Chelladurai, P., & Carron, A. V. (1981). Applicability to youth sports of the Leadership Scale for Sport. *Perceptual and Motor Skills, 53,* 361–362.

Chelladurai, P., & Saleh, S. D. (1978). Preferred leadership in sports. *Canadian Journal of Applied Sport Sciences, 3,* 85–92.

Cogan, K. D., & Petrie, T. A. (1995). Sport consultation: An evaluation of a season-long intervention with female collegiate gymnasts. *The Sport Psychologist, 9,* 282–296.

Dale, G. A., & Wrisberg, C. A. (1996). The use of a performance profiling technique in a team setting: Getting the athletes and coach on the same page. *The Sport Psychologist, 10,* 261–277.

Desjardins, G. (1996). The Mission. In J. H. Salmela (Ed.), *Great job coach: Getting the edge from proven winners* (pp. 67–100). Ottawa, ON: Potentium.

Fisher, B., & Thomas, B. (1996). *Ream dream teams: Seven practices used by world-class leaders to achieve extraordinary results.* Delray Beach, FL: St Lucie.

Johnson, D. W., & Johnson, F. P. (1997). *Joining together: Group theory and group skills, 6th ed.* Boston, MA: Allyn & Bacon.

Mack, D. E., & Bloom, G. A. (1999). *Team building in sport.* Ms. submitted for publication.

McClure, B. A., & Foster, C. D. (1991). Group work as a method of promoting cohesiveness within a women's gymnastics team. *Perceptual and Motor Skills, 73,* 307–313.

Mills, T. M. (1984). *The sociology of small groups,* 2nd ed. Englewood Cliffs, NJ: Prentice Hall.

Mumma, F. S. (1994). *What makes your team tick? Team-work and team-roles.* King of Prussia, PA: HDRQ.

Prapavessis, H., Carron, A. V., & Spink, K. S. (1996). Team building in sport. *International Journal of Sport Psychology, 27,* 269–285.

Recardo, R. J., Wade, D., Mention, C. A., & Jolly, J. A. (1996). *Teams: Who needs them and why?* Houston, TX: Gulf.

Reddy, W. B., & Jamison, K. (1988). *Team building: Blueprints for productivity and satisfaction.* San Diego, CA: University Associates.

Richman, J. M., Rosenfeld, L. R., & Hardy, C. J. (1989). The social support survey: An initial evaluation of a clinical measure and practice model of the social support process. *Research on Social Work Practice, 3,* 288–311.

Rosenfeld, L. R., & Richman, J. M. (1997). Developing effective social support: Team building and the social support process. *Journal of Applied Sport Psychology, 9,* 133–153.

Salmela, J. H. (1996). *Great job coach: Getting the edge from proven winners.* Ottawa, ON: Potentium.

Spink, K. S., & Carron, A. V. (1992). Group cohesion and adherence in exercise classes. *Journal of Sport and Exercise Psychology, 14,* 78–96.

Sullivan, P. A. (1993). Communication skills training for interactive sports. *The Sport Psychologist, 7,* 79–91.

Sundstrom, E., DeMeuse, K. P., & Futrell, D. (1990). Work team: Applications and effectiveness. *American Psychologist, 45*(2), 120–133.

Widmeyer, W. N., & DuCharme, K. (1997). Team building through team goal setting. *Journal of Applied Sport Psychology, 9,* 97–113.

Williams, P. (1997). *The magic of teamwork: Proven principles for building a winning team.* Nashville TN: Thomas Nelson.

Woodcock, M., & Francis, D. (1994). *Team building.* Hampshire, England: Aldershot.

Yukelson, D. (1997). Principles of effective team-building interventions in sport: A direct services approach at Penn State University. *Journal of Applied Sport Psychology, 9,* 73–96.

16

The Nature, Prevalence, and Consequences of Aggression in Sport

W. Neil Widmeyer, Kim D. Dorsch, Steven R. Bray, and E. J. McGuire

University of Waterloo

- Aggression is defined and distinguished from legitimate acts of assertion in sport.
- The challenge of measuring aggression is discussed and conclusions and recommendations are offered.
- The pervasiveness and prevalence of aggression in sport is discussed and is compared to the pervasiveness and prevalence of aggression in the general society.
- Many consequences of aggression exist in sport, including consequences to the recipient, the aggressor, the observers of the sport, and the sport itself.

Aggression: The Meaning of the Term

> When a word becomes so diffusely applied that it is used both of the competitive striving of the footballer and the bloody violence of a murderer, it ought to be dropped or more closely defined.
>
> —Storr, 1968, p. x

Indeed, the noun *aggression* and its adjectival form *aggressive* are used in a wide variety of ways. In the world of business, an aggressive salesperson is revered. Likewise, in baseball an aggressive base runner is admired. In these contexts, the term *aggressive* refers to the individual's drive (i.e., his or her proactiveness). However, the social scientist would contend that in these examples the term *aggressive* is being applied incorrectly.

Aggression or assertion: Do you know the difference?

Labeling an Act as "Aggressive"

Despite Bandura's (1973) caution that attempting to define a concept such as aggression "represents an invitation for a stroll through a semantic jungle" (p. 2), we will make an effort to respond to Storr's appeal to "more closely define" this construct. In an attempt to accomplish this task, social scientists have chosen to define the term **aggression** as overt verbal or physical acts that are intended to either psychologically or physically injure another living organism (Silva, 1980). **Violence** refers to acts of extreme physical aggression. Based on Silva's definition, references to "an aggressive salesperson" or "an aggressive baserunner" are inappropriate. Although these phrases are meant to convey the notion of the pursuit of goals through vigorous and determined action, they are not meant to suggest that harm is intended. Thus, they are more aptly described as "assertive" behavior.

Assertive behaviors are exhibited with no intent to harm another person. Indeed, many forceful behaviors in sport are permitted by the rules and, for the most part, are not intended to injure an opponent (e.g., a body check in ice hockey, a tackle in football). These behaviors often involve the use of heightened verbal or physical force and are often confused with truly aggressive behaviors. Silva (1979) labeled this forceful yet acceptable behavior as "proactive assertion." In sport, proactive assertive behaviors are task oriented (i.e., offensive or defensive), in accord with the rules of the game and involve force but no intent to injure.

Aggressive behaviors, on the other hand, are nonaccidental and can often be classified according to the primary reinforcement sought through the act. For example, if the behavior is performed solely for the purpose of harming an individual, such as when an annoyed hockey player slashes an opponent with his stick, that action is labeled **hostile (or reactive) aggression** (Husman & Silva, 1984). The primary reinforcement in this situation is seeing pain or injury inflicted on the target. Thus, this type of aggressive behavior is an end, rather than a means. When the intentionally harmful behavior is used as a means to an end, however, such as putting a viscious hit on a star quarterback to eliminate him from the game, it is labeled **instrumental aggression.** The primary reinforcement in this case is a tangible reward, such as praise or victory (Husman & Silva, 1984). It is important to keep in mind that even though the ultimate goal of instrumental aggression is not injury, the intent to harm remains an integral facet of the aggressor's motivation in performing the action.

Info Box

Sportscasters frequently will suggest that an athlete play more "aggressively" during a game. Given that the term *aggressive behavior* is defined primarily as a behavior intended to harm, sportscasters' casual use of the term is inappropriate. Forceful and determined behavior that is not intended to harm is often praised in sport but is often mislabeled as "aggressive" behavior. The more appropriate descriptor is "assertive" behavior.

The "intent to do harm" is the primary criterion in distinguishing aggressive from assertive behavior, but it is not the only basis for a behavior to be labeled aggressive. The act must also be perceived to be antinormative; in other words, it must violate a prevailing cultural norm (Brown & Tedeschi, 1976; Mummendey, Bornewasser, Löschper, & Linneweber, 1982; Mummendey, Linneweber, & Löschper, 1984a). DeRidder (1985) tested this assertion by presenting scenarios in which the aggressive behavior was either a violation or nonviolation of a situation-specific norm. He found subjects were more likely to label an act as aggressive and see it as motivated by malevolent intent when it was not in accord with the accepted values and behavior of the individual's culture or subculture. Thus, the second criterion for an act to be labeled aggressive is the perception that it is antinormative.

The third criterion for an act to be labeled aggressive is the perception of injury occurring to the victim. Löschper, Mummendey, Linneweber, and Bornewasser (1984) set out to determine how the three criteria (i.e., the actor's intent to harm, the perceived negative norm violation, and the perceived injury to the victim) influenced judgments of and reactions to various behaviors. They constructed eight scenarios (combinations of low and high levels of each of the three criteria) designed to be familiar to school-age subjects in a school setting. Results indicated that perceptions of norm violation and intent to injure influenced the ratings of aggressiveness and the punishment deserved. The severity of injury was found to affect only the perceiver's willingness to sanction the behavior. A combination of high intent and high deviation from the norm resulted in a judgment of the act as aggressive and non-sanctionable. However, this interaction was not independent of the level of injury. If an intended action only slightly violated a norm or if the norm violation was unclear, then the degree of injury provided the extra information for the labeling process. In addition, the combination of injury and norm violation was not sufficient to influence the interpretation of the action. Löschper and colleagues (1984) concluded, "in order to come to a definite definition of an action and a selection of appropriate reactions, evaluation of the actor's intent must be possible" (p. 398). Thus, even though this study showed that perceived intent had the most impact on the labeling of an act as aggressive, the criteria of perceived norm violation and the perceived injury to the victim were also involved in this process. It must be stressed that the judge's perception of the actor's intent and his or her perception of the norm violation are necessary and sufficient criteria for labeling an act as aggressive. The perception of injury to the victim aids in interpretation only when norm violation is slight or unclear.

Evaluation of these three criteria is also influenced by the perceiver's position relative to the act (Mummendey et al., 1982). In any social interaction involving aggression, there is always an actor (perpetrator) and a receiver (victim). Judgment regarding the aggressiveness of the act will depend on one's point of view. The actor will view his or her action as appropriate, whereas the victim will perceive the same action as inappropriate (Mummendey et al., 1982; Mummendey, Linneweber, and Löschper, 1984b). However, individuals other than the actor and the victim often see the behaviors. An observer's interpretation of an act depends on whether the observer is psychologically closer to the actor or the victim. An individual with a positive attitude toward the actor will view the aggressive act more favorably than another individual who is more emotionally aligned with the victim.

A classic study by Hastorf and Cantril (1954) demonstrated that the group to which an observer belongs affects their perception of not just a single behavior, but a series of behaviors, in this case an entire football game played between Dartmouth and Princeton universities. In an exceptionally physical game, the number of infractions witnessed and the amount of aggression perceived by two groups of fans were entirely different based on the affiliation of the observer. Thus, it can be concluded that direct involvement, as well as psychological affiliation with either the actor or victim, influences the perception of the aggressiveness of an act or series of actions.

Every social behavior occurs within a social context. Hence, evaluations of an act as aggressive are also modified by the perceived context in which the act occurs. Specific to research in aggression is the potential influence of context on the determination of intent. Intent is not a property of the behavior itself but must be inferred by the observer (Brown & Tedeschi, 1976). For this inference to be made by a judge, the circumstances before, during, and after the act (i.e., context) need to be examined (daGloria & DeRidder, 1977). In other words, if the harmful intention of the actor is unclear, as is often the case, other factors in the situation (e.g., the actors' and the victims' previous behaviors) and factors within the observer (e.g., his or her own experience with the activity [e.g., football]) will influence the observer's judgment of the aggressiveness of the behavior.

The previous discussion leads to the suggestion that some aggressive acts may even be considered "legitimate" in certain situations. A **legitimate act** is one in which the behavior has been deemed acceptable in the given circumstances (context). To be able to make a judgment regarding the legitimacy of an act, the observer must make a comparison of the act in question with appropriate normative standards. The extent to which the act is deemed acceptable or unacceptable within those circumstances determines the rating of the act on the previously specified definitional dimensions of aggressive behavior (Forgas, Brown, & Menyhart, 1980). When the acceptability of the act is clear, there is no need to justify the reasons that the behavior was committed; thus, the action is legitimate. The justification is "built-in" to the event—it develops as part of the event in process (Ball-Rokeach, 1972). For example, in North American society there exists a norm concerning the right of an individual to defend himself or herself. In sport, this norm applies to the protection of teammates and especially to the protection of one's goaltender. Therefore, the use of aggressive behavior is justified when such protection is necessary. However, when the acceptability of the act is more clouded, the need to justify (i.e., give reasons for) the behavior becomes more important. A **justification** can be viewed as an explanation for or a rationalization of a behavior (Ball-Rokeach, 1972) and is usually provided as a method for achieving some greater "morally worthy" end (Mees, 1990), such as discipline. For example, in a study of child abuse, the majority of the abusers justified their actions by saying that the child had been defiant and they (the abusers) had been under considerable stress (Dietrich, Berkowitz, Kadushin, & McGloin, 1990). Thus, we can see that justifications are used as a means to avoid the dissonance felt when one perceives an aggressive act to be antinormative yet acceptable.

Generally, information regarding justifications for an act is obtained by the observer through the context within which the act occurs. This information then influences perceptions of the extent to which the actor intended to harm the victim. A justification serves to shift responsibility, at least partially, away from the actor to the victim, to a third party, to chance, or to some societal goal achieved by the act (Darley, Klossen, & Zanna, 1978). Indeed, justification of aggressive behavior lies at the heart of the criminal justice system. Often, contextual information provides a justification for an unacceptable aggressive act by shifting the perception of responsibility for the act away from the actor and onto the victim. In other words, the intention of the actor, and thus the perception of the amount of aggression, portrayed in the act can be influenced through the justification of the behavior.

In summary, it is clear that the perception of aggressive behavior is a function of the perceptions of (a) intent to injure either physically or psychologically, (b) norm deviation, and (c) severity of injury. Both the perspective of the judge (i.e., actor, victim, or observer) and the context surrounding the behavior modify these perceptions. Once perceptions of the aggressiveness of an act have been determined, the observer is able to assess the perceived legitimacy of such behaviors. Perceptions of legitimacy appear to be based on the acceptability of the act compared to situation-specific norms and on evaluations of the justifications provided for why the behavior was committed. Because of the complexity in identifying an aggressive behavior, much controversy surrounds how to actually measure this phenomenon. The following section describes some of the methods that have been utilized to accomplish this goal.

Measuring Aggression

> *When you cannot measure it,*
> *When you cannot express it in numbers,*
> *Your knowledge is of a meager and unsatisfactory kind.*
>
> —Lord Kelvin

The measurement of any construct involves operationalizing its conceptual definition. Thus, the measurement of aggression requires the operationalizing of "behavior designed to physically or psychologically harm another." A true assessment of any behavior, for example, exercise involvement, entails measuring both the frequency and intensity of the behavior, but most research conducted in naturalistic settings has measured only the frequency of behaviors such as smoking, alcohol consumption, and lovemaking. This same observation can be made for the assessment of aggression. Specifically, the aggression/ violence present in a city or nation has been expressed with crime statistics listing the *number* of homicides, beatings, rapes, and incidents of child abuse per capita occurring during a specific period of time. One can appreciate that numbers obtained from municipal or national records certainly underestimate the true incidence of these heinous actions because many victims are reluctant to report such attacks. In addition, it should be noted that statistics are usually kept only for extreme acts of aggression, whereas behaviors such as barroom brawls and verbal insults are never recorded even though they often do represent attempts to harm another.

When social scientists have examined aggression in laboratory experiments, they have employed indicators such as the number of times a child has struck a BoBo doll (e.g., Bandura, 1965) and the number and/or intensity of shocks or intense noise a subject has administered to an experimenter's accomplice (e.g., Geen & Donnerstein, 1983). From subjects' behavior in these contrived situations, reviewers sometimes infer how aggressively an individual will behave in real-life settings.

When researchers have examined aggression in naturalistic settings such as the school classroom, they have not typically measured behavior but rather have assessed the personality trait of aggressiveness. Evaluations have sometimes been made subjectively by teachers and researchers, and at other times, standardized paper-and-pencil inventories or projective tests have been administered to assess individuals. Unfortunately, teachers are often biased, inventories are inappropriate for the population (e.g., Minnesota Multiphasic Personality Inventory, or MMPI), and projective tests (e.g., TAT) are difficult to interpret. Thus, it appears, at this time, that investigators of aggression in society are unable to provide sport scientists with definitive instruments for measuring aggression.

Two Measurement Perspectives: External and Internal

Aggressive behavior in sport is examined largely from two perspectives: external and internal. In the external perspective, aggressive behavior is observed and measured with no consideration of the actor's feelings or cognitions. However, because an individual's intent to do harm is a central facet of the conceptual definition of aggression, an internal perspective has also been shown to be of value. From this standpoint, past research has examined an individual's desire to behave aggressively as well as an individual's perceptions of aggressive acts. These methodologies are described in the following paragraphs.

External Perspective.   One of the methodologies utilizing the **external perspective** closely resembles the measurement of aggressive behavior in society at large. Just as crime statistics have been cited as an indicator of the extent of aggression in the larger society, penalty statistics have been used as such an indicator in sport. For example, investigations of sport aggression have recorded the fouls in basketball (e.g., Harrel, 1980), yellow and

TABLE 16.1 *Player-Identified Aggressive Penalties in Ice Hockey.*

Charging	Elbowing	High sticking	Butt ending	Checking from behind
Boarding	Roughing	Slashing	Spearing	Head butting
Kneeing	Fighting	Cross checking	Instigating	

Source: Widmeyer & Birch (1984) and Widmeyer & McGuire (1997).

red cards in soccer (e.g., LeFebvre & Passer, 1974), and penalties in ice hockey (e.g., Widmeyer & Birch, 1984). The basic premise behind the use of this type of indicator is that penalties represent the observations of trained observers (i.e., game officials). Undoubtedly, several problems are associated with such measures. First, not all penalties represent acts of aggression. For example, "delay of game" and "too many players on the field/ice" penalties do not reflect behavior designed to harm another. Recognizing this problem, researchers of sport aggression have designated certain infractions as "aggressive penalties" and others as "nonaggressive penalties." For the most part, solely the researcher has made these delineations. For example, early researcher-devised lists of aggressive penalties in ice hockey (e.g., Wankel, 1973) included such questionably aggressive hockey actions as interference and tripping. Later attempts to more accurately determine which acts reflected an intent to harm by ice hockey players (e.g., Widmeyer & Birch, 1984) heeded Sherif and Sherif's (1969) plea to include subjects as active agents in the research process. Specifically, Widmeyer and Birch (1984) provided a list of all hockey infractions to forty professional players asking them to indicate the percentage of time they used each of these behaviors in an attempt to harm an opponent either physically or psychologically. Using 80 percent of the time as their criterion, Widmeyer and Birch (1984) identified eleven penalties as aggressive (see Table 16.1). A more recent polling of twenty-five professional hockey players (Widmeyer & McGuire, 1997) has added the infractions of instigating, head-butting, and checking from behind to this list of aggressive penalties in the sport of ice hockey. Using a similar protocol in football (participants as active agents and an 80 percent criterion), Widmeyer (1997) surveyed thirty varsity football players to produce the list of aggressive football penalties seen in Table 16.2.

A second problem associated with the use of penalties is that the game officials do not see all infractions. This is especially true of those infractions that occur "behind the play." To gain an appreciation of the extent of this problem, Katorji and Cahoon (1992) had three trained observers, sitting at different areas in an arena, independently record all infractions they witnessed in ten Junior "B" ice hockey games. In addition to strong interob-

TABLE 16.2 *Player-Identified Aggressive Penalties in Football.*

Unnecessary roughness	Roughing passer/kicker
Late hit	Unsportsmanlike conduct

Source: Widmeyer (1997).

server reliability ($r = .87$), the researchers witnessed only 5.2 percent more incidents of aggression than did the game officials. It was concluded that at this level of hockey, unobserved infractions did not constitute a major problem when penalties were used as indicators of aggression. It is unlikely that such a problem of omission occurs more frequently at levels of hockey above that of Junior "B" (i.e., professional leagues), where officials have more training and experience. However, this is not to say that the problem does not exist when assessing aggression with penalties in minor hockey and/or in other sports. Various sports (e.g., hockey, basketball) have taken this possibility into consideration, though, and are attempting to minimize the number of unobserved infractions by implementing systems in which multiple individuals are used to officiate at sporting contests.

Info Box

Using penalties as a measurement of aggression can be problematic for many reasons. Distinguishing an aggressive penalty from a nonaggressive penalty can be difficult. In addition, some infractions go unobserved and thus unpenalized.

A second approach utilized when assessing aggressive behavior from an external perspective was devised by Houston and Widmeyer (1987) in their examination of the aggression occurring in ringette. In this sport, females wearing ice skates attempt to move a Velcro ring by means of a nonbladed stick into an opponent's net. Houston and Widmeyer (1987) had 17- to 22-year-old players and their coaches independently rate the five most and five least aggressive players on their team. In addition, they had players rate their own aggressiveness. Although they found that coaches' and players' ratings of teammates were highly correlated, they did not find a strong relationship between players' ratings of themselves and those of their teammates. This finding was pronounced among the smaller players on the team who saw themselves as more aggressive than did the other members of the team. It could be that smaller players were overestimating their own aggressiveness or that other players were underestimating the aggressiveness of their small teammates.

Taking this methodology into minor league hockey, Dorsch and Widmeyer (1993) asked players aged 12–13 and their coaches to identify individuals on their team who were the most likely to attempt to physically harm and those who were the most likely to attempt to psychologically harm opposing players. Strong relationships were found between actual aggressive behavior (aggressive penalties) and those perceived as most likely to injure ($r = .57, p < .001$) and most likely to intimidate ($r = .48, p < .001$). These findings suggest some degree of convergent validity for the external methods of measuring aggression.

Internal Perspective.   Another tactic used in the measurement of aggressive behavior is to focus on an **internal perspective,** examining those factors that are internal to the individual, such as the individual's desire to aggress and individual's perceptions of aggressive acts. With respect to the first technique, Brice (1990) asked university ice hockey players how frequently they wanted to physically harm or psychologically intimidate an opponent during a competitive season. It was determined that slightly over 30 percent of all university players wanted to physically injure an opponent and 69.5 percent desired to psychologically intimidate opposing players at least once per game or more. Dorsch and Widmeyer (1993) employed this same measure in their study of PeeWee ice hockey players. Approximately 39 percent of all these 12- to 13-year-old boys stated that they desired to physically injure an opponent at least once per game and approximately 78 percent of these young athletes stated that they wished to psychologically intimidate an opponent at least once per game. In the discussion of these results, the researchers proposed that some of these youngsters might have overestimated their aggressive desires in an attempt to present a macho image of themselves. Data from six investigations utilizing this technique to assess the aggressive feelings of male and female athletes in a wide variety of sports at various levels of competition are presented in the next section. Although an argument could be made against the validity of this measurement technique by stating that not all aggressive feelings lead to aggressive behavior, nor does all aggressive behavior have to be preceded by aggressive feelings, Dorsch and Widmeyer (1993) did find that as an athlete's stated desire to behave in an aggressive manner (either physically or psychologically) increased, so did his or her actual aggressive behaviors. Thus, despite the shortcomings of this measurement technique, it does have utility, especially when the opportunity to view or produce an actual aggressive response is not possible.

Another measurement approach that utilizes the internal perspective involves determining the athlete's perceptions of the legitimacy of various sport behaviors. Past research examining perceptions of legitimacy of sport behaviors have utilized written scenarios (e.g., Duda, Olson, & Templin, 1990) or 35-mm slides (e.g., Bredemeier, 1985; Silva, 1983). Silva (1983) found perceptions of legitimacy to vary as a function of subject gender, the amount of physical contact involved in the sport that the subject played, the highest competitive level of organized sport the subject played, and the number of years the subject had participated in organized sport. Specifically, males who played in more physical sports for longer periods of time at higher competitive levels were the most likely to perceive the rule-violating (i.e., aggressive) behaviors depicted in the slides as legitimate. These two methodologies (written scenarios and static depictions of aggressive acts) equate legitimacy of aggressive behaviors with the individuals' perceptions of acceptability. However, as stated previously, three criteria are needed to label an act as aggressive: perceived intent, perceived degree of norm violation, and perceived degree of injury to the victim. Perceptions of acceptability are based on a comparison with the prevailing norms within the situation. Perceived legitimacy of aggressive acts may also be influenced by a justification of the intent of the actor. Therefore, it is believed that both measures (acceptability and justifiability) are necessary when perceptions of legitimacy are being assessed.

Further, as discussed previously in this chapter, contextual information is also an important factor when labeling an act as aggressive. Taking all these issues into consideration, Dorsch and colleagues (1996) developed a videotape depicting aggressive actions to assess ice hockey athletes' perceptions of an actor's intent, the justifiability of the actor's intent, and the acceptability of the actor's behavior. They found that contextual material significantly lowers perceptions of the intent to physically and psychologically harm when nonaggressive stimuli (e.g., a clean body check) are presented and heightens these perceptions when aggressive stimuli (e.g., a high-stick infraction) are presented. In addition,

Dorsch and Widmeyer (1993) discovered that when the force and the speed of the aggressive act can be seen along with antecedent and consequent contextual information, the intent of the actor is less justifiable than if this information is not present. Subsequently, Dorsch and colleagues (1996) concluded that because contextual information is an important modifier of observers' perceptions of actors' intentions, this information should be taken into consideration when examining the legitimacy of aggressive behaviors.

Conclusions and Recommendations Regarding the Measurement of Aggression

Based on the information presented in this chapter, the following conclusions and recommendations are made for the measurement of aggression in sport:

1. The most obvious conclusion is that the measurement of aggressive behavior is an extremely complex task. The many methodologies that exist are categorized as being from either an external or an internal perspective.
2. Many aggressive feelings do not result in aggressive behaviors, and many aggressive behaviors are not preceded by aggressive feelings. Therefore, it is recommended that the researchers distinguish between and measure both these aspects of aggression.
3. Intent to harm can mean the intent to physically injure and/or the intent to psychologically injure (i.e., intimidate). Therefore, both these manifestations of aggression need to be assessed.
4. Because a key component in the labeling of an action as aggressive is the degree of norm violation, only those individuals who are privy to these sport-specific norms are able to identify those behaviors that are truly intended to harm. Therefore, it is recommended that the study participants be utilized as active agents in defining what is aggression in their sport.
5. Colburn's (1985) research into the legitimacy of various acts in ice hockey has revealed that fist fights are viewed by players of this sport as legitimate and are generally not considered by them to be aggressive acts. However, if players from a different sport (e.g., basketball) were asked to rate the acceptability of a hockey fist fight, their perceptions may be extremely negative. Thus, it is important to consider the sport-specific normative rules when examining perceptions of aggression and legitimacy of aggressive behaviors.
6. Finally, the findings of Dorsch and colleagues (1996) suggest that contextual information is an important modifier of observers' perceptions of actors' intentions. As such, contextual information should be taken into consideration when studying aggressive behaviors. Further, because context has an influence on observers' perceptions of intent, stimulus presentations should be manipulated on the basis of intent, rather than on the severity of injury occurring to the victim.

Despite the complexities and problems associated with the assessment of aggression, it is apparent that conceptual clarification and methodological refinements have taken place. Thus, we do have tools to determine the extent of this behavior in sport.

Pervasiveness and Prevalence of Aggression

When introducing any topic to a class, professors usually give some indication of the topic's pervasiveness and/or prevalence (i.e., try to show that the topic is important and, therefore, worthy of study). Authors often take this approach in an effort to justify a topic's inclusion in their book. This section begins with a brief picture of the pervasiveness/prevalence of aggression/violence in society at large. Then, we present indicators of the pervasiveness/ prevalence of aggression/violence in sport.

Although many people use the words *aggression* and *violence* interchangeably, social scientists distinguish between them. Simply stated, violence is extreme physical aggression. As far as pervasiveness and prevalence are concerned, although they seem similar, each has a distinct meaning. **Pervasiveness** refers to how widespread a phenomenon is, and **prevalence** refers to its frequency or extent. Although many authors speak about the pervasiveness of aggression and/or violence, typically they provide data concerning only the prevalence of this behavior.

Pervasiveness and Prevalence of Aggression in Society

To gain some perspective on the pervasiveness and prevalence of physical aggression or violence in sport, it is essential to demonstrate the extent of violent behavior in society at large. Specifically, if violent behaviors such as assault, robbery, rape, and murder are relatively commonplace in society, the prevalence of aggressive acts such as fighting in ice hockey, brutal tackles in football, and the fracturing of limbs in the Ultimate Fighting Challenge may be seen as more normative by sports participants and society at large. With this in mind, it is important to outline the pervasiveness and prevalence of violence in society before presenting the extent of such behavior in sport.

We contend that aggression pervades daily life in North America. It is said that most behavior is learned in the home. If Strauss, Gelles, and Sternmetz (1980) are correct in their estimation that "Overall, every other home in America is the scene of family violence at least once a year," then we can understand why aggression is so prominent today. We hear of elementary school students carrying weapons and secondary schools employing police to protect students and teachers. Teen gangs, which were once a local phenomenon, are now nationwide. Violence pervades the media. On television, children see Wile E. Coyote trying to end the life of the Roadrunner. Popular movies such as *Boyz in the Hood, Terminator,* and *Hoodlum* not only depict violence but also glorify it. This is not surprising, given that a prominent director, Oliver Stone, recently stated with some pride, "I shoot good violence...I know I do." A recent phenomenon on our highways is road rage, the desire to physically or psychologically harm someone in another automobile. The pervasiveness of violence is no more apparent than when our "keepers of the peace," our police, engage in brutal acts such as the Rodney King beating. No longer can violence be thought of as something that occurs only in limited areas of a few large cities. Rather, it must be recognized that this behavior takes place in the homes, schools, streets, and roads of every city, town, and village in North America.

The most recent crime statistics for both the United States (United States Department of Justice Bureau of Statistics, 1998) and Canada (Juristat: Canadian Centre for Justice Statistics, 1996) exhibit decreasing trends in overall violent crime (i.e., total number of rapes, homicides, aggravated and simple assaults, and robberies) over the past 3 years. Specifically, the rate of overall violent crime in the United States was down almost 20 percent (41.5 attacks per 1000 population) in 1996 from 51.1 attacks per 1000 in 1994. In Canada, these attacks decreased from 10.7 per 1000 in 1993 to 9.7 per 1000 in 1996. In the United States, the total incidence of violent crime in 1996 was approximately 3.2 million, compared to over 4 million in 1993 and 3.6 million in 1973. The volume of violent crime in Canada, a country with a population approximately one-tenth that of the United States, dropped from 310,000 incidents in 1993 to 291,000 in 1996. Whereas violent crime in Canada and the United States reached a peak in 1993–1994, present rates have not only declined rapidly but also represent a 25-year low.

The good news is that violent crime is decreasing, but the bad news is that violent crime is still very prevalent within our society. Specifically, there were more than 21,000 murders, almost 100,000 rapes, and over one million aggravated assaults in the United States in 1995 alone. Add to these data the fact that many such crimes go unreported and that other acts of aggression, ranging from verbal assaults to muggings to child/wife abuse, go unrecorded. Thus, despite evidence that violent crime has decreased in society over recent years, the amount of violent crime that is still taking place today is staggering.

Some important questions that arise from recent statistics are (a) why is such a rapid decrease in violent crime occurring now? (b) will the decreasing trends continue? and (c) what implications do these trends have for aggressive behavior in sport? Obviously, addressing the first two questions is beyond the scope of this chapter. We are definitely interested, however, in knowing whether or not this trend of decreasing violent crime in society is being or will be replicated in the world of sport.

Info Box

Violent crime has steadily decreased in recent years, but violence is still prevalent in society.

Pervasiveness and Prevalence of Aggression in Sport

It was once commonly believed that sport aggression occurred only in collision (e.g., football, soccer, rugby, hockey) or combative sports (e.g., boxing, wrestling). However, we hear male tennis players proclaim that the only way to play mixed doubles is to hit the first few balls "as hard and as accurately as possible at the female opponent." Baseball announcers speak of "playing a little chin music" when alluding to the fact that pitchers are throwing balls at batters' heads in an attempt to intimidate them. There have been international water polo matches in which the water was red with blood. Even the refined game of cricket has experienced violence. At a recent international match, a player went into the crowd to physically attack a spectator. Sport violence does not occur only at the elite level where competitors are entertaining paying spectators. It has been reported that "Little League sport coaches settle altercations with their fists, and one father murdered a coach in a dispute over playing time" (Weinberg & Gould, 1995, p. 467). Also, Smith (1983) describes aggressive behavior that occurs among 9- and 10-year-old hockey players at the house league level. This behavior is by no means a folly of youth, because it seems to be a regular occurrence in "oldtimers" hockey games. Thus, it appears that almost no sport, at any level, is immune to violence. But are the anecdotes we hear isolated incidents or are they normative behavior? In other words, how prevalent is violence in sport?

The sport parallel to societal crime statistics is assessed penalties. Earlier it was noted that since not all penalties reflect an "intent to harm," a more valid reflection of aggression would be "aggressive penalties." Thus, attempts have been made to make athletes active agents in identifying the infractions that usually reflect their intentions to harm an opponent in ice hockey (Widmeyer & Birch, 1984) and in football (Widmeyer, 1997). As expected, McGuire (1990) found that there were more aggressive penalty minutes per game ($M = 11.1$) in professional ice hockey (NHL) than did Dorsch & Widmeyer (1993) at the PeeWee level ($M = 5.0$), where players are typically 12 and 13 years old. What is surprising to some is that at the Junior "B" level, where players range in age from 16 to 19 years, the most aggressive penalties took place ($M = 19.7$). In explaining this finding, those in the hockey world point out that (a) professionals, being more mature, are concerned about not injuring themselves and therefore shortening their lucrative careers and (b) many of the juniors believe that their aggression will help them gain access to the professional ranks. Although we have no comparative data on female ice hockey players, a study conducted in the similar sport of ringette indicated that the average number of comparable aggressive penalties per game assessed to these 15- to 17-year-old females was 3.25 (Houston & Widmeyer, 1987). Direct gender comparisons cannot be made because of age and sport differences, but it appears that the females were less aggressive. A close examination of their penalties indicates they were more instrumental than hostile.

In the previous section, it was noted that although societal violence is high, certain crime statistics suggest that it is on the decline. Does the same trend exist in sport? From Table 16.3, we can see that in both professional hockey and Canadian University football there have been minor yearly changes but no overall trends over the past 3 years.

Researchers sometimes make inaccurate judgments regarding whether there is an intent to injure involved in a particular action. Therefore, some researchers have directly asked athletes how frequently they wanted to physically injure and psychologically harm their opponents. A summary of results from several investigations is presented in Tables 16.4 on page 341 and 16.5 on page 341. It is not surprising that for all sports at all levels, the frequency of wanting to physically injure opponents is less than that of wanting to intimidate them. This suggests that athletes perceive intimidation to be more acceptable than

TABLE 16.3 *Aggressive Penalties Per Game 1994–1997*

Professional Ice Hockey		*University Football*	
1994–95	7.74	1994	3.6
1995–96	6.63	1995	3.0
1996–97	7.09	1996	3.1
		1997	4.0

Source: Widmeyer, W. N. (1998). Frequency of aggressive penalties in professional ice hockey and university football 1994–1997 (unpublished manuscript).

TABLE 16.4 *Frequency of Wanting to Physically Injure Opponents.*

	At Least Once Per Game (%)	Never (%)
University hockey (Brice, 1990)	31.0	6.4
PeeWee hockey (Dorsch & Widmeyer, 1993)	38.8	0.0
University female field hockey (Widmeyer, 1995)	11.9	39.2
University male soccer (Widmeyer, 1995)	50.1	0.0
University female soccer (Widmeyer, 1995)	13.4	26.7
University male basketball (Widmeyer, 1995)	22.9	11.1
University female basketball (Widmeyer, 1995)	11.1	55.6
University hockey (Widmeyer, Dorsch, & Sanzole, 1995)	24.1	9.5
High school male hockey (Sanszole, 1995)	77.7	7.5
High school male soccer (Sanszole, 1995)	31.8	22.7
High school male basketball (Sanszole, 1995)	32.2	21.6
High school male volleyball (Sanszole, 1995)	40.1	30.4
High school male football (Sanszole, 1995)	77.1	8.4
High school female field hockey (Sanszole, 1995)	47.1	21.0
High school female soccer (Sanszole, 1995)	40.2	24.3
High school female basketball (Sanszole, 1995)	60.6	15.2
High school female volleyball (Sanszole, 1995)	18.7	35.4

TABLE 16.5 *Frequency of Wanting to Psychologically Harm Opponents.*

	At Least Once Per Game (%)	Never (%)
University hockey (Brice, 1990)	69.0	0.0
PeeWee hockey (Dorsch & Widmeyer, 1993)	76.6	0.0
University female field hockey (Widmeyer, 1995)	60.6	6.8
University male soccer (Widmeyer, 1995)	83.3	8.3
University female soccer (Widmeyer, 1995)	66.6	20.0
University male basketball (Widmeyer, 1995)	88.8	0.0
University female basketball (Sanszole, 1995)	44.4	0.0
University hockey (Widmeyer, Dorsch, & Sanzole, 1995)	80.1	7.5
High school male hockey (Sanszole, 1995)	84.2	7.6
High school male soccer (Sanszole, 1995)	54.6	9.1
High school male basketball (Sanszole, 1995)	75.6	5.4
High school male volleyball (Sanszole, 1995)	70.0	10.0
High school male football (Sanszole, 1995)	89.5	0.0
High school female field hockey (Sanszole, 1995)	54.4	10.5
High school female soccer (Sanszole, 1995)	64.5	18.7
High school female basketball (Sanszole, 1995)	60.7	18.2
High school female volleyball (Sanszole, 1995)	47.9	19.8

attempts to injure. The high values for PeeWee hockey players and male high school athletes are no doubt inflated by the normative attitude that pressures these adolescents to appear macho. Thus, we believe their values are overestimates of their true feelings. We do not perceive that this same norm is operating among male university athletes, and thus we are somewhat shocked by how frequently these athletes want not only to intimidate but also to actually physically harm their opponents. Because of the relative recent development of this measure of aggression, we have no temporal data to determine whether these feelings are increasing, declining, or remaining rather constant over time.

Info Box

Athletes engage in aggressive behavior more often to intimidate their opponents than to physically injure their opponents.

Consequences of Sport Aggression

Undoubtedly, the reason that aggression has been researched so frequently by social scientists is because of their awareness and concern over the dire consequences that aggression can have for society. This awareness/concern has prompted researchers to investigate the causes of aggression so that these precipitous conditions can be minimized and, in turn, ensuing aggression reduced. In Chapter 17, we outline numerous explanations for the occurrence of aggression in sport. Then, in Chapter 18, we present prescriptions for the control of this undesirable behavior. But why is this behavior "undesirable" for sport? At this point, our purpose is to describe the consequences that result from sport aggression. Sport aggression has consequences for (a) the recipient of the aggression, (b) the aggressor, (c) the viewer of the aggression, and (d) the sport in which the aggression takes place. Each of these consequence areas is now examined.

Consequences of Sport Aggression for the Recipient

Those who are on the receiving end of sport aggression can encounter one or more of the following consequences: injury, intimidation, and altered arousal level. **Injury** is a frequent consequence for the target of aggression in any setting. Injury statistics presented for sport often are simply linked to participation in that activity and not identified as being the consequence of aggression that occurred in the sport. For example, Messner (1990) found that when he asked a former professional football star how tall he was, he got this rather surprising reply:

> Oh I used to be about 6'2"—I'm about six even right now. All the vertebrae in my neck, probably from the pounding and stuff, used to be further apart—just the constant pounding and jarring. It hurts all the time. I hurt all the time. (p. 211)

From this account, we do not know if MacArther Lane's injuries and chronic pain, which he attributed to "constant pounding and jarring," were due to the aggressive behavior of an opponent, his own aggressive behavior toward others (e.g., spear blocking), or legal contact by himself or opponents. It is our suspicion that all three of these sources contributed to his injuries, but it is impossible to determine exactly how much of the harm done to him was due to the aggression of others.

Numerous researchers have investigated the impact of aggression on injury in sport. Studies have shown that boxers who have been knocked out suffer head injuries ranging from mild to serious concussions (e.g., Casson, Sham, Campbell, Tralau & Domenic, 1982). Pashby (1989) reports that during the 1974–75 season there were 257 eye injuries and 43 blinded eyes in Canadian ice hockey. Although a likely assumption is that such boxing and hockey injuries were caused by an opponent, rather than by the athlete himself, it cannot be determined whether they were the result of intentional attempts to injure, accidental contact, or sanctioned assertive behaviors by the opposition. Hayes (1975) found that 15 percent of all injuries that occurred in Canadian and American university ice hockey were "penalty related." His findings imply that these injuries were related to intentional harm doing, they may have been caused by acts such as tripping and interference, which are illegal but do not represent attempts to harm. Park and Castaldi (1980) found that of the injuries received by Junior "B" hockey teams, 8 percent were due to slashing and 3 percent to fighting. It is safe to conclude that these injuries were the result of opponent aggression. However, we can't tell how much of the additional 48 percent "body contact" and 4 percent "stick-related" injuries resulted from aggression or from assertive or accidental behavior. Tator and Edmonds (1986) report that of the 117 spinal injuries that occurred in minor hockey between 1966 and 1986, 26.5 percent were due to an illegal check from behind, an act usually considered to reflect aggression by an opponent. More recently, Katorji and Cahoon (1992) learned from their interviews of trainers and players that 59 percent of injuries afflicting Junior "B" hockey players over twenty games were the result of their opponents' aggressive acts. Although these investigations do not allow us to determine the exact amount and the full extent of the injuries that result from sport aggression, it seems clear that injury is a major consequence of this behavior. In addition, it should be noted that we do have evidence that individuals desire to physically harm an opponent (see Table 16.4).

Intimidation is another consequence for the recipient of aggression. However, quantifying psychological harm is far more difficult than quantifying physical harm. Intimidation cannot be seen directly, as can an unconscious body, a lacerated face, or a broken jaw. To complicate matters, there is a cultural norm operating within most sports that dictates that one never allows one's opponents, teammates, coaches, fans or anyone else (including researchers) to know that one has been frightened by an opponent. Yet, when we see a football receiver alter his route to avoid contact with a safety or a hockey player hesitate to go into the corner to pursue the puck, we infer that these players have been intimidated. In the sport world, it is said that these players "hear the footsteps." Intimidation has even become commonplace in "noncontact sports." In baseball, pitchers are throwing more balls at batters to intimidate them than ever before. In a 1997 game between the Montreal Expos and the Atlanta Braves, there were no fewer than twelve incidents of "chin music" played by three different pitchers. Although it is unlikely that players would tell us they have been intimidated for fear of being seen as less macho, we can determine whether athletes want to intimidate their opponents. This desire has been documented in sports ranging from hockey to volleyball at levels ranging from PeeWee to university (Table 16.5). Thus, even though we don't know exactly how much intimidation results from sport aggression, we know that athletes consciously set out to achieve this consequence.

Elevated arousal level occurs with individuals when others attack them. The question is: "How detrimental/beneficial is this heightened arousal?" Although heightened arousal can have intrapersonal (e.g., ulcers) or interpersonal (e.g., irritability with others) consequences, it is most often examined in sport in regard to its impact on performance. The impact of heightened arousal on performance cannot be determined until it is known how aroused the individual was before being attacked. For example, if an individual were at optimal arousal level, the increased arousal brought about by the opponent's aggression would push the recipient beyond his or her optimal level and thus cause a poorer performance. However, if the recipient had been at a less than optimal level of arousal, the increased arousal due to aggression may have brought him or her to his or her optimal level and therefore improved his or her performance. In warming up, football linemen often physically hit teammates in an effort to raise their arousal level.

Consequences for the Aggressor

While attempting to harm others, aggressors can themselves experience consequences. These include injury, penalization, and altered success. Injury is a reality that all aggressors must face. There is ample evidence that individuals can hurt themselves while aggressing. For example, in football and hockey it is not uncommon for a player to break a hand while attempting to strike an opponent with a fist. The aggressor can also be injured when the opponent retaliates. Katorji and Cahoon (1992) found that 27 percent of the injuries to Junior "B" hockey players occurred while they were trying to harm an opponent. Although we cannot tell what percentage of these injuries were due to the aggressors' actions and what percentage resulted from retaliation, we do know that injury to self was a consequence of the players' aggression.

Penalization is the most frequent consequence for individuals who act aggressively. Penalization in sport can range from receiving a yellow or red card to being banished from the playing surface to having criminal charges levied against the aggressor. Penalization for aggressive behavior in individual sports, such as boxing, wrestling, and tennis, is a consequence for only the individual who aggressed. However, in team sports, such as hockey, football, and lacrosse, the entire team is penalized for the individual's aggressive behavior. For example, when a football player grabs the facemask of an opponent, his or her team is penalized 15 yards. Likewise, when a hockey player slashes an opponent, his or her team must play "shorthanded" for the next 2 or 5 minutes. In every sport, with the exception of boxing and hockey, the act of fighting results in an automatic ejection from the game. Some professional hockey owners have stated that if hockey players were ejected for fighting, then more illegal stick work would take place. Although no solid evidence supports this contention, university hockey, which is one of the few levels where fighting does result in game expulsion plus one further game suspension, is purported to have a great deal of illegal stick work.

Penalization is designed to deter aggressive behavior by reducing the aggressing team's chances for success. Although penalties can achieve this goal directly by forcing the aggressing team to go further to score a touchdown or to score with only five players instead of six, they also achieve this end indirectly. The morale of a team is severely damaged when one of their players causes a 90-yard runback of a kick to be called back because of an illegal block from behind or when a hockey player's attack on an opponent causes the team's regular forward line combinations to be altered during and after "killing a penalty." The effect this weakening of morale caused by penalization can have on team performance is discussed next.

Info Box

Aggressive athletes may be faced with many adverse consequences, including injury or penalization. Injury and penalization have the capacity to negatively influence performance directly by reducing the opportunity for participation as well as indirectly by reducing team morale.

Is success a consequence of aggression in sport? In other words, does behaving aggressively help teams to win and individual players to be more successful? In the first edition of this text (Silva & Weinberg, 1984), an entire chapter was devoted to aggression–performance outcome relationships. That chapter began by demonstrating that fans, coaches, and players all believe that aggression helps one to be successful in sport. Next, theories were advanced to explain why aggression–performance relationships probably exist. Finally, research was presented to demonstrate the strength and consistency of the aggression–performance outcome relationship in sport. Although all of this material is not repeated here, an explanation of why and how aggression and performance are related is presented along with some key research findings.

Steiner's (1972) **theory of group productivity** can help the reader understand why aggression can influence performance. Specifically, the theory states that a group's actual productivity is equal to its potential productivity minus its process losses of motivation and coordination. A team's aggression can weaken its opponent's potential productivity through intimidation or injury and, therefore, enhance its own performance outcome. On the other hand, if a team is penalized for its aggression, its own potential productivity is reduced and thus its own performance lessened. Never was this more apparent in professional sport than in the 1997 NBA playoff series between the New York Knicks and the Miami Heat. After being up three games to one, five key members of the New York team and only one member of the Miami team were ejected from game five and suspended for the next two games for their part in an end-of-game brawl. As a result of this penalization, the weakened Knicks went on to lose the next three games and the series. Aggression can also influence process losses. If team aggression becomes the team's rallying point, as it did with the 1975 Philadelphia Flyers ice hockey team, it can unite and motivate the team. If, however, so much penalization results from a team's aggression that some players rarely get an opportunity to play, their cohesion and motivation decline and in turn so does their performance. Aggression can also influence the group processes of the recipient. It may inspire the opponent to rally against the attack, or it may be so defeating that it weakens unity and motivation. Thus, Steiner's (1972) theory of group productivity does explain how aggression could influence team success, but it does not indicate whether it actually does improve or impede this success. To answer this question, we need to know if the penalization was severe enough to weaken the aggressor more than the opponent was weakened by injury and intimidation. Also, we need to know how the aggression influenced the unity and motivation of both the aggressor and the recipient.

Research has examined aggression–performance outcome relationships at both the individual and the team levels. Penalties assessed to individuals have been correlated with indicators of individual performance, such as goals scored and assists made. Russell (1974), along with McCarthy and Kelly (1978a, 1978b), found that this analysis yielded a positive relationship between aggression and performance of hockey players. Widmeyer and Birch (1979) demonstrated that the relationship was curvilinear in that highly successful (all-star) university ice hockey players were either extremely aggressive or extremely nonaggressive, whereas less successful (not all-stars) were moderately aggressive. The fact that the majority of the highly aggressive all-stars were defensemen and most of the nonaggressive all-stars were forwards implies that successful defensemen are more aggressive than nonsuccessful defensemen but that successful forwards are less aggressive than nonsuccessful forwards. In a more controlled experiment, Silva (1979) demonstrated that subjects who were aggressive performed more poorly on a pegboard task and in a three-on-three game of basketball than did subjects who were not aggressive. Silva concluded that arousal, which generally accompanies aggression, can interfere with an individual's concentration, which in turn can interfere with performance.

The results of examinations of aggression–performance outcome relationships at the team level appear as equivocal as those found at the individual level. Andrews (1974) demonstrated a significant positive relationship ($r = .64$) between the number of penalties teams accumulated and their order of finishing in the National Hockey League. Cullen and Cullen (1975) found that the mean number of penalties assessed to college hockey teams that were winning was greater than for those that were losing. European handball teams that were winning likewise committed more fouls than did losing teams (Albrecht, 1979). In contrast, Volkamer (1971) demonstrated that German soccer teams that lost committed more fouls than did teams that won. However, nonsignificant results were found in the Belgian soccer league (LeFebvre & Passer, 1974), in English First Division Soccer (Underwood & Whitwood, 1986), in women's softball (Sachs, 1978), and in men's university ice hockey (Wankel, 1973; Widmeyer & Birch, 1979). Widmeyer and Birch (1981) analyzed four seasons of data from the National Hockey League and found no relationship between level of aggression and level of performance of the teams. However, subsequent analyses revealed that there was a positive relationship ($r = .48$) between aggression in the first period and performance outcome, and a negative relationship ($r = -.28$) between aggression in the third period and performance outcome. The first finding was interpreted as evidence that aggression committed early in a contest can be instrumental in bringing about success, possibly through injury and/or intimidation of the opponent. The second finding implied that aggression is also a behavioral response, which can be a reaction to the frustration of losing and/or as a retaliatory mechanism to received aggression.

The correlational nature of most investigations of the aggression–performance outcome relationship makes it difficult to ascertain whether aggression influences performance outcome or whether performance outcome influences aggression. The temporal nature of the Widmeyer and Birch (1981) investigation suggests that both influences are operating.

In Chapter 17, the influence of performance outcome on aggression is examined more fully when discussing the impact of frustration.

Consequences of Aggression for the Viewer of Aggression

What happens to individuals who see others aggress? This question is the basis for examining the effect of participant aggression on spectator aggression. The classic laboratory research of Bandura and Walters (1963), involving a BoBo doll, demonstrated that individuals who witness violence learn how to be violent regardless of reinforcement to the model. However, the viewer was more likely to behave aggressively if he or she saw the model rewarded or if the viewer was rewarded for approximating the behavior.

The impact of participant aggression on spectator aggression has also been examined with field studies conducted at sporting contests. Typically, the aggressive feelings of the spectators are assessed with a questionnaire or interview prior to and following an athletic event. Often the pre–post response differences obtained from spectators attending aggressive sports events are compared with those taken at nonaggressive sporting events. For example, Turner (1970) found that after watching basketball and football, the aggressive feelings of fans increased; however, there was no pre–post difference for those viewing a wrestling match. Likewise, after watching football, the aggression of fans rose, but after watching gymnastics, there was no difference (Goldstein & Arms, 1971). Arms, Russell, and Sandilands (1979) found that the aggressiveness of fans watching wrestling did increase as it did for hockey fans, but for those attending a swim meet, there were no changes. When comparing reactions of spectators to an "especially violent" hockey game with those who attended a "relatively nonviolent" contest, Russell (1981) found that the former group had stronger feelings of hostility. The point is made in Chapter 17 that although these studies demonstrate the consequences that participant aggression has for the viewer, they could also be considered as examples of how aggression is learned (i.e., as antecedents of aggression).

Consequences of Aggression for the Sport

Does the existence of aggression in a sport make the sport better or worse, more popular or less popular? Those who would say that aggression benefits the sport in which it occurs would likely assert that aggression has a positive impact on attendance. Cliff Fletcher, former president of the Calgary Flames, stated, "The bottom line is that there are a lot of fans who like fighting" (Rosner, 1989, p. 18). Likewise, Conn Smythe, the legendary owner of the Toronto Maple Leafs, is purported to have said in response to complaints about hockey violence in the 1940s, "Yes we are going to have to stamp this out—or else people are going to keep on buying tickets" (Rosner, 1989, p. 19). Lou Nanne, president of the Minnesota North Stars observed, "There's definitely a segment of fans who want to see it, and then there's a segment of fans who don't come to games because they don't like it.... The big question we have to determine is: Which is the greatest segment?" (Rosner, 1989, p. 19). In one of the few empirical investigations of this impact of player aggression on fan attendance, Russell (1986) found no relationship between attendance at Western Junior Hockey League games and the amount of aggression expressed by the teams in their previous game.

Notwithstanding Rodney Dangerfield's classic comment "I went to the fights the other night and a hockey game broke out," hockey is not the only sport to have its image tarnished by aggression. Recently, *Sports Illustrated* devoted considerable space in its December 15, 1997, issue to the impact of violence in the sport of basketball. They drew the readers' attention to such acts as Latrell Sprewell's attack on his coach, P. J. Carlesimo, and Charles Barkley throwing a fan through a plate glass window. The authors made their point with the following story.

> You're 13 years old, and you're a true believer in the NBA. But this season it has been hard to keep the faith. Real hard.
> You don't quite know what to make of this Latrell Sprewell–P. J. Carlesimo thing, but you know players aren't supposed to choke their coaches, not even in football. You still like Scottie Pippen, but you can't figure out why he's trashing the Chicago Bulls.—Nor are you sure why the Raptors' coach, Darrell Walker, gave the finger to a fan in Utah the other night.
> And Michael says he's quitting.
> You've seen all of Shaq's movies—you loved it when he called himself a "genie with an attitude"—but you're wondering why he had to slap a harmless schmuck like Utah's Greg Ostertag after a shootaround. You love seeing Charles Barkley fuss and fume on the court because he's another old guy who can really play. But you wonder why he threw a guy through a barroom window.
> And Michael says he's quitting. (McCallum, 1997, p. 68)

Thus, hockey is not the only sport that has been stained by violence.

Sport ends, where violence begins. (Néron Report, 1977, p. *v*)

Key Terms (in order of appearance)

aggression	justification	intimidation
violence	external perspective	elevated arousal level
assertive behavior	internal perspective	penalization
hostile (or reactive) aggression	pervasiveness	Steiner's theory of
instrumental aggression	prevalence	group productivity
legitimate act	injury	

References

Albrecht, D. (1979). Zursportartspezifischen aggression in Wettkampfspeil. *Sportwissenshaft, 9,* 78–91.

Andrews, R. (1974). A Spearman Rank Order Correlation for 18 NHL teams. *National Hockey League Guide: 1974.* New York: National Hockey League.

Arms, R. L., Russell, G. W., & Sandilands (1979). Effects on the hostility of spectators of viewing aggressive sports. *Social Psychology Quarterly, 42,* 275–279.

Ball-Rokeach, S. J. (1972). The legitimation of violence. In J. F. Short Jr. & M. E. Wolfgang (Eds.), *Collective violence.* Chicago: Aldine-Atherton.

Bandura, A. (1973). *Aggression: A social learning analysis.* Englewood Cliffs, NJ: Prentice Hall.

Bandura, A., & Walters, R. H. (1959). *Adolescent aggression.* New York: Ronald.

Bredemeier, B. J. (1985). Moral reasoning and the perceived legitimacy of intentionally injurious sport acts. *Journal of Sport Psychology, 7,* 110–124.

Brice, J. G. (1990). "Frustration in ice hockey: Extent, antecedents and consequences." Unpublished master's thesis, University of Waterloo, Waterloo, ON.

Brown, R. C., & Tedeschi, J. T. (1976). Determinants of perceived aggression. *Journal of Social Psychology, 100,* 77–87.

Colburn, K. (1985). Honor, ritual, and violence in ice hockey. *Canadian Journal of Sociology, 10,* 153–170.

Cullen, J. B., & Cullen, F. T. (1975). The structural and contextual conditions of group norm violation: Some implications from the game of ice hockey. *International Review of Sport Sociology, 10,* 69–78.

Da Gloria, J., & de Ridder, R. (1977). Aggression in dyadic interaction. *European Journal of Social Psychology, 1,* 189–219.

Darley, J. M., Klosson, E. C., & Zanna, M. P. (1978). Intentions and their context in the moral judgments of children and adults. *Child Development, 49,* 66–74.

De Ridder, R. (1985). Normative considerations in the labeling of harmful behavior as aggressive. *Journal of Social Psychology, 125*(5), 659–666.

Dietrich, D., Berkowitz, L., Kadushin, A., & McCloion, J. (1990). Some factors influencing abusers' justification of their child abuse. *Child Abuse and Neglect, 14,* 337–345.

Dorsch, K. D., & Widmeyer, W. N. "The extent and antecedents of aggression in Pee Wee ice hockey." Paper presented at the annual meeting of the North American Society for the Psychology of Sport and Physical Activity, Brainard, MN, June 1993.

Dorsch, K. D., & Widmeyer, W. N. (1996). The influence of contextual information of observer's perceptions of actors' intentions to harm others. *Aggressive Behavior, 22,* 183–193.

Dorsch, K. D., Widmeyer, W. N., Paskevich, D. M., & Brawley, L. R. (1996). Exploring relationships among collective efficacy, norms for aggression, cohesion, and aggressive behavior in junior hockey. *Journal of Applied Sport Psychology, 8,* 555.

Duda, J., Olsen, L., & Templin, T. (1990). The relationship of task and ego orientation to sportsmanship attitudes and the perceived legitimacy of injurious acts. *Research Quarterly for Exercise and Sport, 62,* 79–87.

Duda, J. L., Olsen, L. K., & Templin, T. (1991). The relationship of task and ego orientation to sportsmanship attitudes and the perceived legitimacy of aggressive acts. *Research Quarterly for Exercise and Sport, 62,* 79–87.

Forgas, J. P., Brown, L. B., & Menyhart, J. (1980). Dimensions of aggression; The perception of aggressive episodes. *British Journal of Social and Clinical Psychology, 19,* 215–227.

Goldstein, J. H., & Arms, R. L. (1971). Effects of observing athletic contests on hostility. *Sociometry, 34,* 83–90.

Green, R., & Donnerstein, E. (1983). *Human aggression: Theoretical and empirical reviews, vol. 1.* New York: Academic Press.

Harrel, W. A. (1980). Aggression by high school basketball players: An observational study of the effects of opponents' aggression and frustration inducing factors. *International Journal of Sport Psychology, 11,* 290–298.

Hastorf, A. H., & Cantril, H. (1954). They saw a game: A case study. *Journal of Abnormal Psychology, 49,* 129–134.

Hayes, D. (1975). Hockey injuries: How, why, where and when? *The Physician and Sportsmedicine, 3,* 61–65.

Houston, B., & Widmeyer, W. N. "Factors influencing the learning of aggression in sport by females." Paper presented at the meeting of the North American Society for Psychology of Sport and Physical Activity, Vancouver, BC, June 1987.

Husman, B. F., & Silva, J. M. (1984). Aggression in sport: Definitional and theoretical considerations. In J. M. Silva & R. S. Weinberg (Eds.), *Psychological Foundations of Sport* (pp. 246–260). Champaign, IL: Human Kinetics.

Katorji, J. K., & Cahoon, M. A. "The relationship between aggression and injury in Junior 'B' Hockey." Unpublished MS., Univ. of Waterloo, Waterloo, ON, 1992.

LeFebvre, L. M., & Passer, M. W. (1974). The effects of game location and importance on aggression in team sport. *International Journal of Sport Psychology, 5,* 102–110.

Loschper, G., Mummendeym, A., Linneweber, V., & Bornewasser, M. (1984). The judgement of behavior as aggressive and sanctionable. *European Journal of Social Psychology, 14,* 391–404.

McCarthy, J. F., & Kelly, B. R. (1978a). Aggression, performance variables, and anger self-report in ice hockey players. *Journal of Psychology, 99,* 97–101.

McCarthy, J. F., & Kelly, B. (1978b). Aggressive behavior and its effect on performance over time in ice hockey athletes: An archival study. *Journal of Sport Psychology, 9,* 90–96.

McCallum, J. "Foul trouble." *Sports Illustrated, 87*(24), December 15, 1997, 68–69.

McGuire, E. J. (1990). "Antecedents of aggressive behavior in professional ice hockey." Unpublished doctoral dissertation, University of Waterloo, Waterloo, ON.

Mees, U. (1990). Constitutive elements in the concept of human aggression. *Aggressive Behavior, 16,* 285–295.

Messner, M. A. (1990). When bodies are weapons: Masculinity and violence in sport. *International Review for Sociology of Sport, 25,* 203–217.

Mummedey, A., Bornewasser, M., Loschper, G., & Linneweber, V. (1982). Defining interactions as aggressive in specific contexts. *Aggressive Behavior, 8,* 224–228.

Mummedey, A., Linneweber, V., & Loschper, G. (1984a). Aggression: From act to interaction. In A. Mummedy (Ed.), *Social psychology of aggression: From individual behavior to social interaction.* Berlin: Springer-Verlag.

Mummedey, A., Linneweber, V., & Loschper, G. (1984b). Actor or victim of aggression: Divergent perspectives—diverent evaluations. *European Journal of Social Psychology, 14,* 297–311.

Néron, G. E. (1977). *Violence in hockey: The final report of the Study Committee on violence in minor hockey in Quebec.* Quebec: Government of Quebec.

Park, R. D., & Castaldi, C. R. (1980). Injuries in junior ice hockey. *Physician and Sports Medicine, 3,* 81–86.

Pashby, T. (1989). Epidemiology of eye injuries in hockey. In C. R. Castaldi & E. F. Hoerner (Eds.), *Safety in ice hockey.* Philadelphia: ASTM.

Rosner, D. (1989, February 1989) "The fight for riches." *Sports Inc., 11,* 18–21.

Russell, G. W. (1974). Machiavellianism, locus of control, aggression, performance, and precautionary behavior in ice hockey. *Human Relations, 27,* 825–837.

Russell, G. W. (1981). Spectator moods at an aggressive sports event. *Journal of Sport Psychology, 3,* 217–227.

Russell, G. W. (1986). Does sports violence increase box office receipts? *International Journal of Sport Psychology, 17,* 173–183.

Sachs, M. L. (1978). An analyses of aggression in female softball players. *Review of Sport and Leisure, 3,* 85–97.

Sanszole, M. "The extent, antecedents and response to sport frustration by high school students." Unpublished honors thesis, University of Waterloo, Waterloo, ON, 1995.

Shaw, M. E., & Costanzo, P. R. (1982). *Theories of social psychology,* 2nd ed. Toronto: McGraw Hill.

Sherif, M., & Sherif, C. W. (1969). *Social psychology.* New York: Harper and Row.

Singer, R. N., Murphy, M., & Tennant, L. K. (1993). *Handbook of research on sport psychology.* New York: MacMillan.

Silva, J. M. (1979). Behavioral and situational factors affecting concentration and skill performance. *Journal of Sport Psychology, 1,* 221–227.

Silva. J. M. (1980). Understanding aggressive behavior and its effects on athletic performance. In W. F. Straub (Ed.), *Sport psychology: An analysis of athletic behavior.* Ithaca, NY: Movement Publications.

Silva, J. M. (1983). The perceived legitimacy of rule violating behavior in sport. *Journal of Sport Psychology, 5,* 438–448.

Silva, J. M., & Weinberg, R. S. (1984). *Psychological Foundations of Sport.* Champaign, IL: Human Kinetics.

Smith, M. D. (1983). *Violence and sport.* Toronto: Butterworth.

Statistics Canada. (1997). *Canadian crime statistics, 1996.* Ottawa: Juristat, Canadian Centre for Justice Statistics.

Steiner, I. D. (1972). *Group process and productivity.* New York: Academic Press.

Storr, A. (1968). *Human Aggression.* London: Penguin.

Tator, C. H., Edmonds, V. E., & Lapczak. (1989). Spinal injuries in ice hockey: A review of 182 North American cases and analysis of etiologic factors. In C. R. Castaldi, P. J. Bishop, & E. F. Horner (Eds.), *Safety in ice hockey 2* (pp. 11–20). Philadelphia: ASTM.

Turner, E. T. (1970). Effects of viewing college football, basketball, and wrestling on the elicited aggressive responses of male spectators. *Medicine and Science in Sports, 2,* 100–105.

Underwood, G. L., & Whitwood, J. R. (1980). Aggression in sport: A study of an English first division soccer team. *FIEP Bulletin, 50,* 31–39.

U.S. Department of Justice. (1998). *Bureau of Justice statistics 1997* [online]. www.ojp.usdoj-gov/bjs.

Volkamer, M. (1970). Investigation into aggressiveness in the competitive social system. *Sportwissenshaft, 1,* 33–64.

Wankel, L. M. (1973, October). An examination of illegal aggression in intercollegiate hockey. *Proceedings: Fourth Canadian Psycho-Motor Learning and Sports Psychology Symposium* (pp. 531–544). Waterloo, ON: Univ. of Waterloo.

Weinberg, R. S., & Gould, D. (1995). *Foundations of Sport and Exercise Psychology.* Champaign, IL: Human Kinetics.

Widmeyer, W. N. "'Aggressive Penalties' in university football." Unpublished MS., Univ. of Waterloo, Waterloo, ON, 1997.

Widmeyer, W. N., & Birch, J. S. (1979). The relationship between aggression and performance outcome in ice hockey. *Canadian Journal of Applied Sport Sciences, 4,* 91–94.

Widmeyer, W. N., & Birch, J. S. (1984). Aggression in professional ice hockey: A strategy for success or reaction to failure? *Journal of Psychology, 117,* 77–84.

Widmeyer, W. N., & McGuire, E. J. "'Aggressive penalties' as perceived by professional hockey players." Unpublished MS., Univ. of Waterloo, Waterloo, ON, 1997.

Widmeyer, W. N., Dorsch, K. D., Sanzsole, M. "Gender differences in the extent, antecedents of, and responses to frustration in sport." Paper presented at the annual meeting of the North American Society for Psychology of Sport and Physical Activity, Monterey, CA, June 1995.

17

Explanations for the Occurrence of Aggression

Theories and Research

W. Neil Widmeyer, Steven R. Bray, Kim D. Dorsch, and E. J. McGuire

University of Waterloo

- Aggression relates to such broad perspectives as instinct theory, biological theories, personal difference theories, and social learning theory. These explain the occurrence of aggression in general terms, as though aggression is a trait.
- Aggression is also explained by self-presentation and role theories, which examine aggression as dependent on the social context present.
- Aggression is also explained by theories related to the specific sport situation, including the frustration level present, the need for retaliation, and annoyance.
- Personal and situational factors also moderate aggression.

Why Does Aggression Occur in Sport?

While outlining the consequences of aggressive behavior in Chapter 16, examples of aggression that have recently occurred in the professional sports of basketball (New York Knicks versus Miami Heat), baseball (Montreal Expos versus Atlanta Braves), and ice hockey (Colorado Avalanche versus Detroit Red Wings) were described. Why do these and other acts of violence occur in sport? A number of athletes, most fans, and every media person have views (some would even say "the answer") as to why these behaviors took place. Although post hoc opinions have been expressed in many specific ways, most could be encompassed by the following ten explanations.

1. "They were just born that way."
2. "Athletes have too much testosterone."

3. "It was a frustrating situation."
4. "They were just getting even."
5. "The other team was a thorn in their side all night."
6. "They believed it was going to help them."
7. "It's the type of people who play those sports."
8. "They did it to show others their toughness."
9. "They had to do it. It's part of their job."
10. "They were doing it for their teammates."

Some of these explanations (1, 2, 6, and 7) reflect "grand theories" of psychology (i.e., instinct theory, biological theories, personal difference theories, and social learning theory, respectively). Others (8, 9) represent the "middle-range theories" of self-presentation and role theory. The remaining explanations (3, 4, 5, and 10) are very specific to the prediction of aggressive behavior. Although some social scientists would not grant the status of theory to these explanations, Shaw and Costanzo (1982) would likely refer to the frustration, annoyance, attack, and group explanations as "specialized theories." In the remainder of this chapter, these ten theoretical explanations of why aggression occurs in sport are outlined, and the empirical evidence supporting or refuting each of these theories is presented.

"They were just born that way":
The Instinct Theory of Aggression

The earliest explanation of why humans engage in aggressive behavior involved **instincts,** inborn behavioral tendencies that cause people to act in certain ways. According to this viewpoint, certain people are "born to be bad." This notion was espoused in the early part of this century by personality theorists, most notably Sigmund Freud (1925), and later by ethologists such as Konrad Lorenz (1966). Today, support for the instinct perspective is almost nonexistent, for three reasons. First, so many (10,000 plus) different instincts were identified that experimental psychologists found the concept too impractical to examine. Second, explanations of behavior based on instinct were circular in nature. Because so many men were seen hunting, for example, it was concluded that there was a hunting instinct in males. At the same time, however, it was said that because men possessed a hunting instinct, men hunted. Finally, considerable opposition was mounted by learning theorists to the ethologists who generalized from animal to human behavior. It is safe to conclude that, because of widespread recognition of the existence and power of human reason and volition, instinct theories have little support today and certainly can be of little use in understanding aggression in sport.

Sport has been connected to one aspect of instinct theory, however: the notion of catharsis. Instinct theorists believed that when individuals behave aggressively or observe aggressive behavior, they release their built-up aggressive feelings. The relief felt through the supposed lowering of aggressive feelings was referred to as a **catharsis,** a word derived from the Greek term *katharsis,* which means to purge/cleanse the body. It was believed by some people that sport was a healthy, controlled environment for such purging to take place (Menninger, 1948). This view is reflected in Stokes's (1958) comments: "It is obvious that considerable aggression is used in hitting, kicking, and flinging the ball; indeed here lies the principal opportunity for the catharsis of aggression" (p. 241). However, Husman and Silva (1984) reported that Berkowitz (1970) "stated rather emphatically that no valid experimental findings support the contention that the need to aggress is lowered by observing others behave in an aggressive manner or by behaving aggressively oneself. Rather, the tendency to aggress may actually be enhanced by this type of activity" (p. 253).

Findings from research examining catharsis in sport could be described as equivocal. Johnson and Hutton (1955), Martin (1976), and Smolev (1976) demonstrated less aggression in athletes following competition. On the other hand, the investigations of Stone (1950), Ryan (1970), and Zillman, Katcher, and Milavsky (1972) showed that aggression increased following physical activity. One could question whether any of these studies actually tested catharsis. Most of them simply looked at how competing or participating in vigorous exercise influenced aggressive levels, but they did not clearly determine whether behaving aggressively leads to lower aggressive feelings. In his examination of catharsis theory in football, Bennett (1991) went so far as to say that "educators realize the sport actually increases aggression but hide behind the outdated hypothesis about catharsis to perpetuate the sport" (p. 415). Berkowitz (1965) concluded, "Sport has considerable value for our society, but we shouldn't justify it as a safe outlet for pent up violent urges" (p. 328). Venting anger may (a) cause the aggressor to worry about retaliation, (b) cause the aggressor to feel guilty, and (c) work the aggressor up to feel more hostile. Thus, it appears that behaving aggressively tends to exercise (and develop) rather than exorcise hostility.

The notion of **vicarious catharsis** (i.e., feeling less aggressive after watching someone else aggress) seems even more difficult to accept. Accepting such an idea is tantamount to believing that when a hungry person sees someone else eating, the observer feels less hungry. It seems that the observer would in fact become hungrier. Chapter 16 demonstrated that a consequence of player aggression is increased aggression by the observer. This finding held when the observer was actually present at the sporting event (e.g., Arms, Russell, & Sandilands, 1979) or was viewing the contest on television (e.g., Celozzi, Kazelskis, & Gutsch, 1982). Russell (1981) points out that "this pattern of findings is entirely consistent with reviews of laboratory research which conclude that displays of aggression generally increase aggression in onlookers" (p. 217).

"Athletes have too much testosterone":
Biological Theories of Aggression

Those who propose that aggression is primarily physiologically based identify two supportive mechanisms: brain pathology and blood chemistry. Concerning the former, it has been shown that aggressive behavior is often characteristic of people with brain tumors and that aggressive behavior can be elicited by stimulating various parts of the brain. The association of blood chemistry with aggression is linked primarily to aromatized testosterone and aggressive behavior. In their review, Bahrke, Vesalis, and Wright (1990) state, "While a relationship between endogenous testosterone levels and aggressive behavior has been observed in various animal species it is less consistent in humans. It can be concluded that, although the use of exogenous anabolic-androgenic steroids may have psychological effects in some patients and athletes, the effects are variable, transient upon continuation of the drugs and appear to be related to type, but not dose, of anabolic-androgenic steroids administered" (p. 303). Testosterone may, indeed, cause individuals to be aggressive, but it is difficult to explain why people who possess high levels of this steroid are aggressive in some situations and not in others. It is also hard to explain why people who possess little or low amounts of testosterone, for example, females, can be aggressive.

Rarely have biological/physiological theories been drawn on to explain aggression in sport. One exception concerns steroid use, most notably by weightlifters, football players, and track athletes. The links between steroid use and feelings of aggressiveness and between steroid use and aggressive behavior have been frequently documented among athletes (e.g., Yates, Perry, & Murray, 1992). For the most part, research with athletes who take steroids has shown that use of this form of testosterone is associated with frequent episodes of anger that is of greater intensity and duration and a hostile attitude toward others (Lefavi, Reeve, & Newland, 1990). It has also been found that the use of anabolic steroids among athletes is related to the number of fights, the amount of verbal aggression, and violence toward significant others (Choi & Pope, 1994). For the most part, athletes' aggression that has been recorded has taken place in the laboratory, the home, or some other nonsport setting. Conspicuously absent is solid evidence that steroid users are more aggressive than nonsteroid users while competing in their sport. This is not to say that they are not aggressive. We certainly think they would be, but to date there is little evidence to support this intuitively appealing notion.

Info Box

Limited support for biological theories of aggression has been provided through examination of steroid users. However, no conclusive evidence suggests that aggressive acts in competition are related to elevated testosterone levels.

"It was a frustrating situation":
Frustration Theories of Aggression

The third major theoretical viewpoint is often referred to as the **frustration–aggression hypothesis.** Frustration is a feeling of helplessness that develops within individuals when one or more of their goals are blocked. The original version, which proposed that all aggression is the result of frustration and that frustration always leads to aggression (Dollard et al., 1939), was long ago abandoned. Reformulations by Berkowitz (1962, 1989), however, have found some support. The newer versions recognize that certain aggression could have causes other than frustration and that frustration could lead to behaviors other than aggression (e.g., withdrawal). In fact, Berkowitz said that when frustration occurs, it usually produces the emotional reaction of anger that does not automatically lead to aggression but rather to a readiness to aggress. Berkowitz even went so far as to accept the idea that a cognitive evaluation of the situation influences the extent to which frustration produces these negative feelings. In this vein, Alcock, Carment, and Sadava (1998) pointed out that "people are also more likely to be upset and attack their frustrators if they think they have been deliberately and wrongfully kept from attaining their goal than if they perceive the interference to be accidental" (p. 342). Although Berkowitz's modifications made the theory more palatable, some scholars have been reluctant to accept the frustration–aggression hypothesis because it implies that an inborn mechanism accounts for the frustration–anger link. On the other hand, some scholars, while acknowledging that this theory does not explain instrumental aggression, are quite satisfied that it does shed light on the occurrence of hostile (or "reactive") aggression.

Does a Frustration–Aggression Relationship Exist in Sport?   Berkowitz's (1983) notion that not all aggression is the result of frustration and that frustration does not always lead to aggression was demonstrated in Brice's (1990) findings from intercollegiate ice hockey. Specifically, he found that only 22 percent of the time when feeling the desire to physically injure and only 14 percent of the time when wanting to intimidate had the players been experiencing frustration. Conversely, when frustrated, the most frequent response, by 52 percent of the players, was to try harder, whereas only 7.6 percent said they would aggress and only 5.9 percent admitted that they actually had engaged in such behavior. Although these results demonstrate a limited impact of frustration on aggression, they do not rule out the existence of a relationship between these variables. In fact, Brice (1990) found significant correlations between feeling frustrated and wanting to physically injure an opponent ($r = .20, p = .04$) and between feeling frustrated and wanting to intimidate an opponent ($r = .22, p = .03$).

That much sport aggression is attributable to frustration is not difficult to accept, given that sport is a highly organized form of competitive interaction. In such interaction, one competitor's gain represents the other competitor's loss. A basic objective in sport, consequently, is to keep one's opponent from achieving his or her goal; in other words, to thwart him or her. Thus, competition can be perceived as a frustrating situation and, therefore, an antecedent of aggression.

Many researchers have examined the effects of competition on aggression. In their classic field study, Sherif and Sherif (1953) demonstrated that when competition was introduced into a camp setting, friendships were destroyed, hostilities were created, and aggressive behavior escalated. Nelson, Gelfand, and Hartmann (1969) found that children were more aggressive after playing competitive games than after engaging in noncompetitive games, even if they won most of the competitive contests. In his laboratory experiment, Leith (1977) showed that competitive physical activity elicits more aggression than does cooperative physical activity or a control situation. In their two experiments using video games, Anderson and Morrow (1994) found that by simply thinking about competition, "we spontaneously think about aggressive behaviors, negative emotions, and conflict, whereas when we think about cooperation, we think about friendly behaviors, pleasant emotions, and working together" (p. 1029).

If competition produces aggression, then more frequent competition against the same opponent should produce more aggression than less frequent competition. Widmeyer and McGuire (1996) demonstrated this hypothesis. Their examination of 9,318 aggressive incidents across 840 NHL games showed that more aggression occurred in intradivisional games, in which teams played each other seven or eight times, than in interdivisional games, in which teams competed against each other only three times over a 6-month season. The aggression that accompanied more frequent competition between two teams may not have been reflecting more frustration but rather more hatred caused by more intense rivalries. In fact, the researchers explained their results with **social conflict theory** (Sherif et al., 1961), which proposes that when there is a long-term struggle for limited resources, ri-

Players often exhibit aggressive behavior when they are obstructed from achieving their goals.

valry between the competing units develops, which leads to conflict. Applying this theory to hockey, Widmeyer and McGuire (1996) reasoned that players do not feel the same animosity toward an opponent whom they encounter every 2 months as they do toward one they face every 3 weeks. Given this rationale, perhaps we should be advancing another explanation for aggression.

Info Box

Frequency of competition between teams is directly related to the amount of aggression observed by these teams. Accordingly, conference games would most likely contain more aggressive behavior than nonconference games.

"They hate each other":
Rivalry as an Explanation for Aggression

Most investigations of the frustration–aggression link in sport have compared the amount of aggression occurring in situations that the researcher presumed were frustrating with that taking place in situations believed not to be frustrating. **Situations presumed to be frustrating** include losing, losing at home, losing late in a contest, losing by a large margin, losing to an opponent you should be beating, losing to an opponent you are outplaying, and being prohibited from performing your skills.

Losing and frustration have been linked because of the premise that the basic objective in sport is to win. It is reasoned, therefore, that when one's goal of winning is being blocked (i.e., thwarted), one feels frustrated and hence behaves aggressively. The majority of investigators of this notion have compared the aggression of the game winners with that of the losers, rather than contrasting the team's aggression exhibited when they were losing with that exhibited when they were winning or tied.

One of the earliest examinations of the notion that losing is frustrating and leads to more aggression was carried out by Volkamer (1971) who analyzed 1,986 soccer matches. He found that losers received more penalties and personal warnings than did winners. In a laboratory study, Leith (1989) found that subjects who lost a competitive game administered more shocks than those who won. In contrast, Cullen and Cullen (1975) found that winning junior hockey teams committed more norm violations (all penalties) than did losers. Studies conducted by Wankel (1973) and Widmeyer and Birch (1979, 1984) in which only "aggressive penalties" were examined found no differences in the aggressive behavior of winners and losers. In all of the aforementioned studies, comparisons of aggression were made between the teams that were the ultimate losers of the game and the teams that were the ultimate winners. Lefebvre and Passer (1974) argued that because infractions occur continuously throughout a contest, a more sensitive analysis and a better test of the frustration-aggression hypothesis would be one that determined whether more infractions were committed by teams (even the ultimate winner) when they were in a "losing state" during a contest than when they were in a "winning state." These researchers found that although more soccer infractions were committed by teams in a losing state ($n = 27$) than in a winning ($n = 19$) or tied ($n = 19$) state, the differences were not significant. McGuire (1990) tested LeFebvre and Passer's notion in a more elaborate study that examined 9,318 aggressive incidents occurring in the National Hockey League during the 1988–1989 season. He did not find that more aggressive acts were committed by teams that were losing than by those who were winning. These results suggest that losing is not sufficiently frustrating to cause individuals, at least at this professional level, to become aggressive.

An early study by Martin (1976) that examined the effects of winning and losing on various types of aggression seems to have been overlooked by many reviewers of the sport aggression literature. Martin interpreted his finding of lowered aggression by basketball players following a victory as support for catharsis theory. This contention must be questioned, because aggression during the contest was never assessed. However, his finding that wrestlers' aggressiveness increased following a loss, whereas that of basketball players did not, is intriguing. His suggestion that losing may produce more frustration for the individual sport athlete who is solely responsible for this performance than for the team sport athlete who can "rationalize his loss on extraneous factors" needs to be examined further. It is interesting to note that all the studies reviewed above, which did not show that losing was frustrating, were conducted in team sports, whereas the laboratory studies that showed that losing was frustrating examined individual participants.

Losing at home could be perceived as more frustrating than losing away from home because of the generally accepted notion that teams win a greater percentage of their games at home; therefore, a loss at home would be perceived as more devastating. Although several investigations have compared the aggression of home teams with that of visiting teams (e.g., Glamser, 1990), rarely has the aggression of teams that were losing at home been compared with that of teams that were losing away from home. One exception is the study by McGuire (1990), who found that among professional ice hockey teams, those losing at home were no more aggressive than those that were losing away from home were. The results from this one study suggest that losing at home, at least at the professional level, is no more frustrating than is losing away from home.

Losing late in a game would appear to be more frustrating than losing early in a game. This supposition is based on the notion that when one is losing early in a contest, one does not feel as helpless as when one is losing and realizing at the same time that "time is running out." Several studies (e.g., Wankel, 1973; Kelly & McCarthy, 1979; Russell & Drewry, 1976) have shown that more aggressive penalties occur in the latter stages of a game than during the early and middle stages. This finding is surprising because a commonly accepted norm in ice hockey is that during the later stages of a game the referee puts away his whistle and "lets the teams' play decide the outcome." It could be that such a norm operates only when games are close or that there is so much aggression late in a game that even with the norm operating, there is still more aggression in the later stages of games. Russell and Drewry (1976) explained the increasing aggression later in games with the notion that aggression begets aggression. McGuire (1990) compared the aggression of teams that were losing in the first 10 minutes, middle 10 minutes, and last 10 minutes of professional hockey games and found no significant differences. Thus, it appears that losing late is no more frustrating than losing early, or at least it is not sufficiently more frustrating to cause more aggression.

Losing by a large margin would certainly seem to evoke the cognition of one's goals being blocked and ensuing feelings of helplessness (frustration) thus leading to aggressive behavior. Earlier studies (Wankel, 1973; Harrel, 1980; Goginsky, 1989) looked at the combined number of aggressive incidents during different score differential situations. Although these results generally supported the hypothesis that more aggressive behavior occurs when there is a greater score differential, they do not provide an adequate test of the frustration–aggression hypothesis. To rectify this shortcoming, McGuire (1990) examined how score differential impacted on the aggression of losing teams only. He found that significantly more aggressive infractions were committed by the losing team when the score differential was three or more goals than when it was only one or two goals. In a much smaller-scale study, Cullen and Cullen (1975) found the intriguing result that winning teams commit more norm violations (total penalties) when only one or two or when greater than five goals separate the two teams, whereas losing teams commit more violations when three or four goals separate the teams. These two studies support the notion that losing by a large margin is frustrating and can lead to aggression.

Info Box

Obviously, losing can be very frustrating, and losing by a large margin can be embarrassing and frustrating. Whether this frustration is translated into aggression may depend on whether the losing team feels that aggression will have an effect. There may be a point at which athletes who are frustrated by a huge point deficit do not engage in aggressive behavior as a result of learned helplessness. Why waste energy aggressing if the point spread is too great to overcome?

Losing to an opponent you should be beating and losing to an opponent you are outplaying would seem to frustrate athletes. Indeed, Brice (1990) found that the frustration experienced in both these situations was significantly greater ($M = 7.7$ and 7.2, respectively, on 9-point Likert scales) than that found for losing in general ($M = 5.6$). Brice explained his results in light of Berkowitz's (1987) findings that unjustified frustrations produce elevated levels of aggressive behavior. Undoubtedly, losing to a team you should be beating and losing to a team that you are outplaying do not seem to be justifiable situations, whereas losing can be justified when these conditions do not exist.

Not being able to perform one's skills appears to be frustrating for both teams and individuals. When a team can keep the opposing team from executing their offense, they tend to frustrate their opponent. This is evident in ice hockey when the team that is ahead "rags" the puck (passes it around without shooting) and in football when the winning team "runs out the clock" with a methodical "ground game." In the sport of basketball, such a potentially frustrating situation was substantially reduced by the implementation of a shot clock, whereby the offensive team must shoot the ball before 30 (or 24) seconds expire. At the individual level, two manifestations of not being able to play one's game seem very frustrating. In the one case, talented offensive players like Wayne Gretzky in hockey and Jerry Rice in football are kept from demonstrating their talent by the clutching, grabbing, and holding techniques of inferior defensive players. When these illegal impediments persist and go unpunished, they are likely to be extremely frustrating. Indeed, Widmeyer, Dorsch, and Sanszole (1995), using 9-point Likert scales, found that being restrained (e.g., held by one's jersey) was the second leading cause of feeling frustrated by both high school ($M = 6.9$) and university athletes ($M = 6.7$) in the sports of soccer, basketball, hockey, lacrosse, rugby, and football. Likewise, a player seeing another player on his or her team whom he or she perceives to have less talent than themselves receiving more playing time can be extremely frustrated. It is more likely in this case that any ensuing anger and/or aggressive feelings would be directed toward the coach or the teammate, rather than the opposition. Although all these manifestations of not being able to play appear to be very frustrating, their effect on aggression has not been empirically examined.

What, then, is frustrating to athletes? In analyzing responses to the open-ended question "What are some of the things that happen during the course of a game that make you feel frustrated?" Brice (1990) found that the most frequent response had to do with the athlete's own poor play. Specifically, 48 percent of the players said that making unforced errors and missing easy goals were the most common causes of their feelings of frustration. Reasons such as bad calls by the referee (15 percent), poor play by teammates (12 percent), and "not getting the breaks" (12 percent) were cited much less frequently. Some might argue that the feelings experienced when one's own play does not meet expectations is not really frustration because they do not stem from someone thwarting the player's goal. Granted, these examples of poor performance were not caused by interference by others. It could be argued, however, that they represent examples of one's goal attainment being blocked by oneself. In an examination of more than 600 high school and 100 university athletes, Sanszole (1995) demonstrated, with sport-specific 9-point Likert items, that one's own mistakes (e.g., missing the open net/goal/receiver) produced more frustration ($M = 7.3$) than did a similar mistake made by a teammate ($M = 5.6$) or being "robbed" by the outstanding play of an opponent (e.g., spectacular save or perfect pass; $M = 5.4$).

Frustration and Aggression in Sport: A Summary.   Based on research conducted to date, it can be concluded that losing, losing at home, and losing late in the contest were not perceived to be highly frustrating by high school and university athletes and did not cause professional hockey players to behave aggressively. On the other hand, losing by a large margin, losing to an opponent you are outplaying and/or an opponent who is inferior, along with not being allowed to perform one's skills, and playing poorly were frustrating situations for athletes. Because only the first of the frustrating situations has been shown empirically to lead to more aggression in sport, the other conditions definitely warrant research attention. However, simply determining if there is more aggression when these situations occur than when they do not might not adequately test the frustration–aggression relationship.

As noted earlier, in most investigations of the relationship between frustration and aggression, the researchers establish a condition that they believe is frustrating and then compare the amount of aggression that occurs when this condition has been created with the amount that takes place when the condition does not exist. This approach possesses at least two problems. First, there is no verification that the researcher-determined situation is, in fact, frustrating. Second, because no attempt is made to test Berkowitz's (1983) notion that feelings of frustration lead to feelings of anger, the relationship between anger and feelings of aggressiveness cannot be determined. In his attempt to rectify these shortcomings, Brice (1990) not only asked athletes what they found frustrating but also tested a model that proposed various links among feelings of frustration, anger, desire to physically injure, and desire to intimidate. He found significant relationships between (a) feeling frustrated and wanting to intimidate an opponent ($r = .22$; $p = .03$), (b) feeling frustrated and wanting to physically injure an opponent ($r = .20$, $p = .04$), (c) feeling frustrated and feeling angry ($r = .36$; $p = .001$), (d) feeling angry and wanting to intimidate an opponent ($r = .46$; $p = .001$), and (e) feeling angry and wanting to physically injure an opponent ($r = .46$, $p = .001$). Although not formally tested with the Baron and Kenny (1986) technique, it would appear, given the relationships outlined earlier, that anger mediates the relationship between frustration and aggressive feelings.

"They were just getting even":
Retaliation as an Explanation for Aggression

It is surprising that **retaliation** is not typically listed as a theory or at least as a major explanation for aggression. In fact, Jaffe and Yinon (1979) indicated that "Aggressive instigation has been amply demonstrated to be a most potent antecedent of aggressive behavior, if not the most important one (Bandura, 1973; Dollard et al., 1939)" (p. 178). Similarly, A. H. Buss (1961) argued that attack was a far more powerful cause of aggression than was frustration. This contention was demonstrated by Gentry (1970), who found that attack produced both more anger and more aggression than did a goal blockage condition. Given these results, we were surprised that not one of fifteen texts dealing with social psychology in general or specifically devoted to aggression proposed retaliation as a theory of aggression.

The words *retaliation* and *revenge* are used often in the world of sport. The late Michael Smith (1983) in his book *Violence and Sport* outlined a "violence precipitates violence hypothesis." Although he provided evidence from the sports of basketball, football, soccer, and ice hockey to support this hypothesis, each of these investigations was conducted on crowd rather than on player/team violence. Harrel (1980), in his investigation of high school basketball players, found that opponents' aggression was the strongest predictor of player aggression ($R^2 = .62$). The assumed frustrating conditions of low free throw and field goal shooting percentages and high turnovers were not significant predictors of aggression. Brice (1990) found that the most often cited reason for wanting to physically harm an opponent, which was given by 83 percent of the university hockey players he studied, was that the opponent had attempted to injure them personally and/or another member of their team. It is interesting to note, however, that this factor was almost never cited as a reason for wanting to intimidate an opponent. In the more recent and more extensive study conducted by Sanszole (1995), retaliation was the number one reason given ($M = 49$ percent) for wanting to injure an opponent by both male and female high school athletes. In addition, this study supported Brice's (1990) notion that retaliation was not a major reason for wanting to intimidate an opponent. The results of these studies indicate that both the desire to retaliate (Brice, 1990; Sanszole, 1995) and actual retaliation (Harrel, 1980) exist in sport and that the goal of retaliatory actions is physical injury and not intimidation.

Retaliation seems most likely to occur in contact sports. In fact, Zillman, Johnson, and Day (1974) demonstrated that contact sport athletes behaved more aggressively than noncontact sport athletes did. To accommodate this result, they proposed, "It may be argued that contact-sport athletes actually exhibited superior coping, but that in spite of feeling less emotional anger, they experienced little reluctance to aggress against their tormentor" (p. 151). Corner and Widmeyer (1983) reasoned that retaliation was most likely to occur in contact sports when athletes had not been in the sport long enough to perceive that the contact was "simply part of the game." These researchers, therefore, compared the aggressive penalty minutes per game across ten games accumulated by PeeWee hockey players (12-year-olds), whose league prohibited body contact, with those levied to Minor Bantams (13-year-olds), who played in a contact league. Although it could be argued that age was a confound, it is unlikely that it accounted for the large difference in the accumulated aggressive penalty minutes per game between the groups (PeeWee $M = 2.71$; Minor Bantams $M = 4.75$). These results might suggest that retaliation is occurring in response to the contact, legal or otherwise, by the opposition, but they also reflect proactive efforts by the Minor Bantams to physically harm and/or intimidate their opponents. The retaliation explanation is supported by Sanszole (1995), who found that wanting to injure an opponent because they attacked you or one of your teammates was cited more frequently in the contact sports of rugby, football, soccer, field hockey, and ice hockey ($M = 58\%$) than in the noncontact sport of volleyball ($M = 26\%$) or the semicontact sport of basketball ($M = 44\%$) where opportunities to aggress are much less.

Whenever the notion is raised in class that aggression in sport often occurs in response to previous aggression by one's opponent, at least one student always asks, "But why did the opponent aggress in the first place?" This is a good question. Answering it leads us into proactive, rather than reactive, reasons for aggressing.

"The other team was a thorn in their side all night":
Annoyance as an Explanation for Aggression

Sometimes in everyday life, individuals become angry with others and want to inflict harm on them, not because the other attacked or frustrated them, but simply because they were annoying. Someone honking his or her horn at you when you are sitting in your stalled car at a busy intersection can be very annoying and consequently anger-provoking. **Annoyances** in sport can take many forms. These include mannerisms of an opponent, inconsistent calls by an official, and taunting by opposing players, coaches, or spectators. Brice (1990) found that officiating was a source of anger among university hockey players; however, none of the other irritants have, to the best of our knowledge, been examined empirically in sport. Nevertheless, there are many anecdotal accounts of athletes being angered and aggressing because of the annoyances they encountered from others. For example, it is well known that many opposing players and fans were upset with the brashness and antics of tennis player John McEnroe and football player Deion Sanders. Also, although players come to expect "trash talk" from opponents and criticism from fans, these annoyances often lead to aggression. Each season there are accounts of football, hockey, and sometimes basketball players who climb into the stands to attack fans whose insults have exceeded the players' tolerance levels. In 2000, such behavior took place at the international level in the "gentlemanly" game of cricket. We typically think of these annoyances as stemming from the opposition, but recently the taunts of a player's own coach caused him to behave violently. Some argue that verbal insults, whether from opposing players, fans, or coaches, or even from one's own, represent another form of attack and therefore do not warrant separate treatment in this chapter. However, we believe that brashness, cockiness, stalling behavior, and other annoying mannerisms of an opponent cannot be construed as an attack and therefore do deserve separate treatment.

"They believed it was going to help them":
The Social Learning Theory of Aggression

According to **social learning theory,** aggression, like any other social behavior, is learned. It is proposed that such learning occurs as a result of either direct or indirect (vicarious) reinforcement. Simply stated, this theory says that people will learn and/or perform a behavior that they believe will bring them a reward, either because they have been rewarded in the past for performing a similar behavior or because they have seen others rewarded for performing that behavior. This viewpoint proposes that people learn not only how to aggress, but also when and against whom to aggress.

Much research has been conducted outside sport that demonstrates that when aggression is reinforced, it is repeated. Davitz (1952) found that children who had been praised for aggressive behavior in the past were more likely to behave aggressively when frustrated than were children who were praised for behaving cooperatively. Loew (1967) showed that subjects who were given approval for making hostile verbal statements were more likely to physically attack another person than were those not given such approval. It should be noted that these investigations and the classic BoBo doll studies by Bandura and Walters (1959) were conducted before the universal establishment of ethics committees for conducting research. It is fortunate that these studies could not be carried out today, but the "good news" is that they did show that by rewarding individuals for behaving aggressively, one can get them to behave aggressively.

Is sport aggression the result of learning? In answering this question, we will determine whether sport aggression is learned and/or exhibited through direct reinforcement and whether it is the result of indirect (or vicarious) reinforcement that accompanies modeled aggression.

Is sport aggression learned through direct reinforcement? In other words, does athlete X aggress in situation Y because he had been reinforced for aggressing in that or a similar situation in the past? As one might imagine, recent research on this question, whether in the laboratory or the field, is somewhat sparse because of ethical concerns associated with providing inducements to subjects to behave in a violent fashion. Consequently, most investigations of this question are retrospective rather than prospective in nature.

The behavior of athletes, like that of anyone else, is reinforced when that behavior receives approval from others, particularly if those others are seen as being significant by the athlete. In 1974, Smith surveyed minor hockey players and discovered that those who engaged in fighting believed that significant others approved of this behavior. Clark and colleagues (1978) found that minor hockey players believed that their parents approved of their aggressive behavior. Teenage hockey players studied by Vaz (1972) indicated that their coaches encouraged physically aggressive play and even taught them how to fight. In their study of female ringette players, Houston and Widmeyer (1987) demonstrated that the amount of praise players reported receiving for having aggressed in the past was a significant predictor of the athletes' present aggression. In none of these four studies was actual reinforcement for aggression assessed. The variable examined instead was the athlete's perceptions of past reinforcement for aggression.

Approval and praise are not the only possible reinforcers of aggression. Many athletes aggress because they believe that their past success was due to their aggression. Smith (1978) found that 76 percent of minor hockey players believed that success came to them because of their aggression. Players' beliefs that aggression can bring success were demonstrated by Luxbacher (1986), who found that athletes who believed that winning was very important to their coaches exhibited high levels of reactive aggression. Houston (1986) demonstrated that players' perceptions that their past success was due to aggression was the second best predictor ($R^2 = 16\%$) of their present aggression. Again, it must be pointed out that it is not actual past success for aggressing that reinforces the athletes, but rather the athletes' perceptions of past success due to their aggression.

Is sport aggression learned through **vicarious reinforcement**? In other words, do athletes behave aggressively because they have seen others rewarded for aggressing? Because of ethical concerns, there have been no prospective examinations of this question. Youth hockey players reported that they learned illegal tactics from professional players (Nash & Lerner, 1981). Mungo and Feltz (1985) noted that 93.4 percent of youth football players indicated that they had learned at least one aggressive act from college or professional players. In these two studies, the young athletes who observed their significant others aggress did not report seeing them rewarded. The fact that these role models were playing at the professional level, however, could have been interpreted by the youngsters as a significant reinforcement. Houston and Widmeyer (1987) did not find that seeing a significant other aggress was a significant predictor of aggression among female ringette players. It should be noted, however, that only one of the 82 players indicated that they ever saw their significant other behave aggressively. One of the consequences of aggression that was identified in Chapter 17 was the learning of aggression by viewers of aggression (i.e., spectators). Although the findings presented were treated as consequences of participant aggression, the results could also be viewed as antecedents of spectator aggression. As such, these investigations represent examples of the effects of modeled aggression.

One does not have to witness violence firsthand to learn and subsequently demonstrate such behavior. In fact, it appears that more research has been conducted on the impact of secondary consumption of violence (i.e., seeing violence through the eyes of the media). Although his imitation of the violent behavior John Hinkley, Jr. saw in the movie "Taxi Driver" has prompted some research into the effect of "silver screen" violence on its viewers, the majority of media violence investigations have examined the impact of television violence. A limited number of recent studies have looked at video games and Internet surfing influence the aggression of viewers (e.g., Ballard & Wiest, 1996).

Although not as extensive as the research that examined the effects of viewing nonsport violence, studies have been conducted on the impact of sport violence portrayed through different media. Perhaps the earliest investigations were the laboratory studies that examined the responses of subjects who viewed the aggression that Kirk Douglas demonstrated as a boxer in the movie "Champion" (Geen & Berkowitz, 1967). More recently, archival studies have shown that watching championship prizefights on television correlates with homicide increases (Miller, Heath, & Phillips, 1983). Homicides were also shown to be related to the viewing of televised National Football League games (White, 1989). As was the case with boxing, more homicides took place in the geographic area surrounding the losing team than in that of the winning team. While these findings are extremely interesting, it should be kept in mind that the relationships are simply correlational, and therefore causation cannot be assumed. In one laboratory study, subjects who viewed televised violence in ice hockey were more aggressive than those who had not viewed the aggressive segment but simply discussed hockey (Celozzi, Kazelskis, & Gutsch, 1982). Numerous studies demonstrate that individuals are more aggressive after participating in video games (e.g., Schutte, Malouff, & Post-Gordon, 1988). Although it has been shown that playing video games and watching violent television aroused children equally, it is noted that viewing is a passive behavior, whereas video game players "actively mete out and receive destruction and death" (Cooper & Mackie, 1986). Recent warnings have been issued regarding the impact that pornography displayed on the internet can have on children. Perhaps similar warnings should be issued regarding the dangers of violent video games.

Social Learning and Aggression in Sport: A Final Note. Sometimes the phrase "social learning of aggression" is misleading because it conveys the notion that this instrumental approach applies only to the acquisition (i.e., learning) of aggressive responses and not to their elicitation. Certainly, one learns how to behave aggressively through shaping or by watching others behave aggressively. Reinforcement, however, direct or vicarious, teaches the principle that "aggression pays." This value is responsible for aggressive behavior occurring long after the initial means of aggressing are learned.

Although there may not be solid evidence obtained through prospective studies to demonstrate that athletes aggress because they have been rewarded for aggression in the past, some evidence suggests that athletes' aggression is related to their perceptions of having received reinforcement (approval, success) for their past aggressive behavior. In addition, some research indicates that athletes aggress because they have seen role models aggress. Finally, investigations demonstrate that aggression is learned from sport violence that occurs at games, in the movies, on television, and perhaps even in video games and on the Internet.

Info Box

Aggressive behavior is learned behavior and has the capacity to be reinforced directly or indirectly (vicariously). Given this fact, sport related mass media should be sensitive to which acts they present and how they present those acts. Commentators of televised competitions should make a point of distinguishing between legitimate acts of assertion and aggression instead of continually using the term *aggression* flippantly.

"It's the type of people who play those sports": Individual Difference Theories of Aggression

Although the majority of research on aggression in sport has focused on situational factors, thought to be frustrating or instrumental to success, other research has examined personal factors, such as achievement motivation and moral development, as possible antecedents of aggression. Specifically, sport researchers have applied Achievement Motivation Theory (Nicholls, 1984) and stage theories of moral development (e.g., Haan, 1985; Kohlberg, 1976) to the study of aggression in sport.

Achievement Motivation Theory. **Achievement Motivation Theory,** according to Nicholls (1989), proposes that in achievement situations, subjective success is determined by two factors: task and ego involvement. Individuals whose perceptions of ability are based on task involvement focus on being actively engaged in the task, improving skills, and mastering tasks. Ego-involved individuals, however, base perceptions of their ability on comparison of abilities to others. Nicholls (1989) suggests that in sport situations, where the emphasis is on winning, individuals who are high in ego orientation may often display maladaptive achievement behaviors. Specifically, ego-oriented individuals are more likely to display behaviors such as breaking or bending rules to their advantage and aggressing against opponents in attempts to "win at all costs" and demonstrate superior ability. Duda (1993) went so far as to argue that individuals who are high in ego orientation might utilize aggressive behavior to display competence at a sport. Individuals who perceive themselves as inferior in terms of ability may achieve success through physical dominance of their opponents, where it might otherwise be unattainable if they relied on skill alone. Recent research by Duda and colleagues (Duda, Olsen, & Templin, 1991; Huston & Duda, 1991; cited in Duda, 1993) examined the relationship between sport achievement orientation and aggression. Duda, Olsen, and Templin (1991) found that ego orientation was positively associated with perceived legitimacy of both aggressive behavior and cheating in a sample of high school basketball players. In a similar study, Huston and Duda (1991; cited in Duda, 1993) found that collegiate football players' ego orientation was positively related to their acceptance of aggressive and potentially injurious behaviors, even when years of competitive experience and level of competition were not. This line of research supports the notion that ego-involved athletes are more aggressive than those who are task-involved.

Moral Development and Aggression.   Another personal factor that has been linked to aggressive behavior is the **moral development** of the aggressor. The basic premise of this association is that individuals aggress because they have not matured enough to recognize the needs and wants of others, so they do not realize that they are doing wrong to others. Although the notion that individuals progress through a series of stages of moral development was first advanced by Kohlberg (1969; 1976) and also by Hahn (1977), it was Bredemeier and Shields, along with their colleagues, who examined stages of moral development in sport. These researchers have compared the moral development of athletes and nonathletes, and they have also looked at how moral development relates to the aggressiveness of athletes.

In 1984, Bredemeier and Shields reported that the aggressiveness of college basketball players, as rated by their coaches, was inversely related to their moral development. These researchers found that stage of moral reasoning was lowest among college basketball players when compared to college nonathletes and college athletes participating in noncontact sports (i.e., swimmers). Bredemeier and colleagues (1986) found that the moral development of children in grades 4–7 was negatively related to children's tendencies to aggress and their participation and interest in contact sports. In a second study (Bredemeier et al., 1987), children aged 9–13 were shown a series of slides depicting potentially injurious acts in sport contexts. Although children perceived the people in all of the slides to be at risk of injury, results revealed a negative relationship between children's moral reasoning and the number of slides judged to be legitimate behaviors. Bredemeier (1994) examined the relationship between children's moral reasoning and submissive, assertive, and aggressive action tendencies. Children's reported tendencies to act submissively or assertively were significantly related to their moral maturity. However, moral maturity was negatively related to physical and nonphysical aggressive tendencies in both sport and everyday life situations. Regression analyses indicated, furthermore, that children's level of moral reasoning for sport and everyday life predicted between 13 and 18 percent of the variance in their physical and nonphysical action tendencies in conflict situations.

Stephens and Bredemeier (1996) recently found that the two personal factors of achievement motive and level of moral development jointly influence aggression. They assessed the achievement orientations of youth soccer players and their coaches as well as players' moral reasoning and perceptions of their team's norms for collective aggressiveness. Analyses revealed that although players' perceptions of their team's proaggression norm was the strongest predictor of their likelihood to aggress ($R^2 = 29\%$), players' achievement orientation and their stage of moral development explained significant additional variance in their likelihood to aggress.

Findings from these studies suggest an inverse relationship between athletes' stage of moral development and their aggressive behavior. Although it could be that individuals of lower moral development elect to participate in aggressive sports, it could also be that participation in aggressive sports causes moral development to regress. How much each of these possibilities is contributing to the moral development–sport aggression relationship has yet to be determined.

Info Box

Although the details of the relationship are not known, athletes who exhibit a low level of moral development are more likely to engage in aggressive behavior than athletes who have developed further morally.

"They did it to show their toughness":
Self-Presentation Explanation of Aggression

Self-presentation involves disclosing aspects of oneself to others. An early theory in this area by Jones and Wortman (1973) proposed that self-presentation was a tactic of **ingratiation.** In other words, individuals disclosed aspects of themselves to others to make themselves appear more attractive. Many sport scientists believe that some athletes in contact sports behave aggressively to convey an image of toughness to opponents, coaches, teammates, fans, and the media. The objective of this presentation may be (a) to intimidate their opponent, (b) to secure a position on their team, (c) to be noticed by professional scouts, or (d) to give themselves a self-identity that pleases them. Research of self-presentation in sport is somewhat sparse and often indirect.

In his qualitative analysis of professional hockey players, Gallmeier (1987) discovered that these athletes put on a "game face" and "staged" emotions before, during, and after games. Wann (1997) found that intercollegiate ice hockey and football teams whose players had their names printed on their uniforms were more aggressive than teams that did not have names printed their jerseys. He interpreted his results as supporting self-presentation theory as opposed to deindividuation. Earlier support for self-presentation theory came from McGuire's (1990) research. He found that professional ice hockey players who did not wear face masks and thus made their identity clear to others were more aggressive than those who did wear masks. At the group level, certain teams have promoted the image that they were aggressive. In professional football, for example, the Oakland Raiders wore black uniforms and prided themselves on being vicious tacklers. One of their players, Jack Tatum, even wrote a book entitled *They Call Me Assassin* (Tatum & Kushner, 1979). The Detroit Pistons presented themselves as "bad boys" in professional basketball. In professional ice hockey, several teams have consciously portrayed an image of toughness. Undoubtedly, no team was more successful at this presentation than the Philadelphia Flyers of the 1970s. This team took pride in being known as the "Broad Street Bullies." The portrayal of being an aggressive team at the group level is done for any or all of the reasons advanced earlier for why individuals present this image. Another reason advanced for group presentation of aggressiveness, however, is that the team uses the image as a rallying factor to bring their members closer.

"They had to do it...it's part of their job": Role Theories of Aggression

Roles are generally thought of as a set of prescriptions that define the desired behavior of a person who occupies a specific position (Biddle & Thomas, 1966). **Role theory** (Biddle, 1979) proposes that individuals engage in certain behaviors because they are fulfilling some of their role prescriptions. The questions of interest in this section are how and how much does a role influence aggression.

Roles in sport teams are designed and integrated to create effective team systems for offense and defense. Individual players not only are trained to carry out their role functions but also are often recruited onto a team to fill a needed role on the basis of their abilities. Both formal and informal roles can exist on teams. Formal roles, such as team captain, refer to those behaviors established by the group directly, but informal roles, such as "team clown," evolve from interactions among members in the team environment.

The "policeman" or "enforcer" in ice hockey is perhaps the most commonly identified aggressive role in sport. To the unsocialized observer, the occupant of this role is often labeled a "goon," but the violence associated with professional hockey dictates that a player functioning in this role is a necessity. The role of the enforcer may not be formally defined and may vary greatly from team to team. In professional hockey, however, Carron (1988) suggests that it is often assumed that a team cannot be successful without someone in a "policeman" role. Commentaries on the importance of the hockey enforcer to team effectiveness are certainly not rare. For example, Goyens and Turowetz (1986) stated, "The player who fights for his teammates, or is at least willing to drop his gloves so that less pugilistic players are free to do what they do best, is as essential to a team as any other player" (pp. 200–201). Indeed, the "policeman" role has been acclaimed to be as important to effective team functioning in ice hockey as that of a leading goal scorer. One legendary policeman, John Ferguson of the Montreal Canadiens, recounted, "One year the Canadiens veterans voted me the most valuable player and that was the year Cournoyer led the team in scoring. What impressed me was that in the Canadiens scheme of things you could be a leader not only as a goal scorer but also as an aggressor" (Goyens & Turowetz, 1986, p. 201). Within some teams, aggressiveness is clearly an important component of some players' role responsibilities.

It seems logical that those in defensive positions on teams would be more aggressive than those performing offensive roles. Indeed, Widmeyer and Birch (1979) found that ice hockey defensemen were more aggressive than forwards.

That one's role in any organization influences one's behavior is not surprising. Consequently, aggression occurring in sport can be attributed, at least in part, to athletes fulfilling their roles (i.e., simply doing their jobs). To date, research has shown that the roles of defenseman and enforcer influence aggression in the sport of ice hockey.

Info Box

Many sports have developed roles that require aggressive behavior. The athletes who carry out these roles are often asked to push the limits of the constitutive rules of the game to intimidate the opponent. In some cases, these athletes are used to "test the officials"; in extreme cases, they are called on by coaches to physically damage a key opponent (i.e., take out the quarterback).

"They were doing it for their teammates":
Group Influences on Aggressive Behavior

Although a great deal of competitive sport, and hence sport aggression, occurs at the individual level, the majority of athletes participate in some form of group or team competition (Widmeyer, Brawley, & Carron, 1992). Most social psychological researchers readily admit that an individual's behavior is highly influenced by his or her membership in groups. Yet, most research examining the causes of aggression in sport has been conducted at the individual level, virtually ignoring the contribution of the group or team to which the individual belongs.

As an extension of their research examining the links between an individual's moral development and aggressive behavior, Shields and Bredemeier (1995) proposed that the "moral atmosphere" within a team setting is a significant contextual mediator of team behavior. Central to this notion of moral atmosphere is the presence of a set of collective norms regarding team members' behavior. These **group norms** are specific behavioral expectations (Carron, 1988; Power, Higgins, & Kohlberg, 1989) that govern the behavior of group members and represent the group's consensus about what is considered acceptable. In sport, norms pertaining to deviant (i.e., aggressive) behaviors have "become so important that participants in many sports must learn not only the written rules, but the unwritten or normative rules of their sport in order to be successful" (p. 438). Indeed, in the sport of ice hockey, many researchers (e.g., Cullen & Cullen, 1975; Faulkner, 1974; Vaz, 1972, 1977) have suggested that aggressive behavior is accepted to achieve success at both the individual and team levels. Once accepted, the performance of these behaviors then becomes expected (i.e., normative).

In a study of girls' youth soccer, Stephens (1995) found that the best predictor of players' self-described likelihood to engage in aggressive behaviors was their belief that teammates would play unfairly (i.e., their group norms). Similarly, Shields and colleagues, (1995) discovered that norms regarding cheating and aggression in baseball and softball teams were higher (a) at the college level than at the high school level, (b) for males, (c) for athletes with more experience in the sport, (d) for players on a winning team, and (e) for nonstarters. These findings lend support to the notion that perceived collective norms may indeed influence actual or intended aggressive behaviors.

As the performance of aggressive behaviors becomes increasingly accepted, team members begin to develop perceptions about their team's ability to successfully execute these behaviors in a strategic manner. In other words, as is the case with any offensive or defensive skill, a team may develop a sense of its collective competence concerning its ability to perform aggressive skills (i.e., **collective efficacy for aggression**). In a study of male ice hockey teams, Dorsch (1997) found that perceptions of collective efficacy for strategic aggression did, in fact, predict future team aggressive behavior. The most interesting aspect of this research was that it showed that perceptions of collective efficacy for aggressive skills were more similar among team members than between teams, thus reflecting a group phenomenon.

It has further been speculated that the amount of **team cohesion** may influence both norms and actual aggressive behavior (Dorsch, 1997; Shields & Bredemeier, 1995). It is postulated that as teams become more cohesive, the beliefs regarding the appropriateness of aggressive behavior become increasingly shared among group members. Subsequently, as groups become more cohesive, sanctions for not complying with the behavioral standards set by the group (i.e., the group norms) may become stronger. It may be that a high level of cohesion must exist for collective norms about aggressive behavior to influence the actual performance of such behaviors. In a test of this hypothesis, Shields and colleagues (1995) found task cohesion to be positively related to expectations that peers would cheat and aggress. Similarly, Dorsch and colleagues (1996) discovered that perceptions of task cohesion in elite junior ice hockey teams significantly discriminated between teams that were either high or low in actual aggressive behaviors. Taken together, these findings serve as preliminary support to indicate a relationship between group cohesion and aggressive behavior.

The limited research on group factors suggests that group norms, group efficacy, and group cohesion are associated with group aggression. Other factors, such as group composition and group leadership, no doubt also have an impact on aggression in sport.

Factors That Moderate These Explanations of Aggression

Attack, frustration, reinforcement, self-presentation motives, and other factors discussed in this chapter may lead to aggression in sport. Other variables, however, may not bring about aggression themselves but may modify the effect of the more direct influences. Although it cannot be said that being from a lower socioeconomic class makes one more aggressive than being from an upper class, for example, it is possible that the frustration–aggression link is stronger for lower-class individuals than for those from the upper class. Modifiers of relationships, which Baron and Kenny (1986) refer to as *moderators,* can be categorized as either personal or situational factors.

Personal Moderators of Aggressive Behaviors

The most frequently examined personal moderators in aggression research are gender, age, and socioeconomic class.

Gender as a Moderator of Aggression.   Biological theories, social learning theory, and role theory all predict that males exhibit more aggression than do females. However, various meta-analytic reviews (e.g., Hyde, 1984; Eagly & Steffen, 1986) indicate that gender differences are inconsistent across studies. "The tendency for men to aggress more than women was more pronounced for aggression that produces pain or physical injury than for aggression that produces psychological or social harm" (Eagly & Steffen, 1986, p. 309).

Most sport aggression studies have examined male athletes. Although a few researchers have studied aggression in female athletes, rarely has the aggression in male and female athletes been compared in the same study. One exception (Silva, 1983) compared male and female athletes' and nonathletes' perceptions of the legitimacy of various potentially injurious rule-violating behaviors. He found that males rated the behaviors as more acceptable than did females. This acceptability by males increased with their participation in sport, but the acceptance of sport aggression was actually greater among female nonathletes than female athletes. Silva concluded that socialization in sport appears to legitimize rule-violating aggressive behavior for males, but the same socialization impact was not found for females. Widmeyer and colleagues (1995) recently found that male intercollegiate athletes felt more frustrated during competition than did female athletes. Although both genders were frustrated by their own poor play, males were more frustrated by losing than were females. The moderating effect of gender was demonstrated by the fact that when both genders were frustrated, males became more angered and more frequently wanted to injure an opponent than did females. When frustrated, the most frequent response by females was to try harder.

Age as a Moderator of Aggression.   Different studies have examined the aggression of children, adolescents, and adults, but rarely has the aggression of these different age groups been compared in the same study. It could be hypothesized that given the same amount of frustration, attack, or annoyance, older individuals would aggress less than younger ones. This assumption is based on the belief that as people mature, they develop more effective coping mechanisms. In support of this prediction, Sanszole (1995) found that, when frustrated in their sport, high school athletes were more angered ($M = 5.6$ vs. 5.1 on a 9-point Likert scale) and wanted to hurt opponents more often ($M = 19.6\%$ vs. 11.6%) than did university athletes of the same gender in the same sport. However, a more complete answer may have been uncovered by recent cross-sectional national survey of 18- to 90-year-olds. This investigation showed a significant curvilinear relationship between age and scores on the Cook-Medley Hostility Scale, with values being lowest for individuals between the ages of 30 and 60 (Barefoot et al., 1991).

Social Class as a Moderator of Aggression.   Lower-class individuals are frequently portrayed as aggressing more than members of higher social classes. Verbal aggression and utilitarian motives were more characteristic of middle- and upper-class characters" (Gecas, 1970; p. 680). Is this an accurate depiction? A review by Brounfield (1986) concludes that the relationship between social class and aggression depends on the measure of social class used. When social class is assessed by occupation and education level, it has only a moderate relationship to aggressive behavior; unemployment and welfare status, however, are highly correlated with violent behavior. To date, little or no research has examined how social class relates to aggression in sport. If a hockey team were frustrated because they were losing by a large margin late in a contest, would the players who came from an extremely poor background be more likely to aggress than would those from a higher social class? This is an interesting question and one that should be answered to identify individuals who are at high risk of aggressing.

Situational Moderators of Aggression

When discussing the likelihood that individuals who feel aggressive will behave aggressively, four conditions usually are identified. These moderating situations are (1) characteristics of the target, (2) the presence of weapons, (3) belonging to a group, and (4) the presence of others. The environmental variables of noise, crowding, and temperature, however, have also been examined as moderators of antecedent aggression relationships.

Characteristics of the Target as a Moderator of Aggression.   It has been said that, given the same amount of provocation, an individual is more likely to aggress against an enemy than against a friend or someone who is unknown. Much of the research on this factor involves the manipulation of the race of a hypothetical target. It generally has been shown that whites, when not provoked, tend to aggress more frequently against whites, but if they have been provoked, they tend to aggress more against blacks (Rogers & Prentice-Dunn, 1981). In explaining the violence that an almost all-black University of Minnesota basketball team directed toward an almost all-white Ohio State team, the race of their opponents has often been cited as much as the frustration of losing to a team they should have been beating. Research has generally shown that males direct more retaliative aggression toward male than female targets (Taylor & Smith, 1974). It would be interesting to see whether this finding replicates in coed basketball, soccer, and ice hockey. Another characteristic of the target that has influenced the extent to which provocation leads to aggression is the degree to which an individual is perceived as human. If the target is seen as less human or less real, he or she is less likely to be aggressed against. For example, it has been shown that soldiers will not hesitate to shoot at an enemy who is 150 yards away, but if the target is so close that his or her facial features are clear, soldiers are reluctant to fire their weapons. This suggests that although a full face shield offers protection to a football or hockey player, such deindividuation may make him a more likely target of aggressive behavior.

The Presence of Weapons as a Moderator of Aggression.   It has been shown that the mere presence of a gun increased the punishment that an angry subject administered to a tormentor (Berkowitz & LePage, 1967). This suggests that "guns not only permit violence, but they also stimulate it." The fact that the badminton racquet did not elicit much retaliatory aggression in the Berkowitz and LePage experiments may give some solace to those who are concerned about violence in sport. One must ask, however, could a hockey stick be perceived as a weapon? Would less aggression occur if the stick were removed and the game became more like soccer on ice? Perhaps then the skate would be perceived to be a weapon.

Belonging to a Group as a Moderator of Aggression.   If an individual who is attacked, frustrated, or annoyed by another belongs to a group, he or she is more likely to aggress than if no affiliation existed. The impact of group norms, collective efficacy, and group cohesion has already been outlined. Group membership might increase the likelihood of aggressive behavior because the aggressor believes he or she will be protected by his or her group from retaliation or that he or she must "save face" in front of the group members. The moderating effect of group membership explains gang wars, why the fights that occur in hockey rarely involve only two combatants, and why so many bench-clearing brawls take place in baseball.

The Presence of Others as a Moderator of Aggression.   Intuitively, it seems that having others around would deter individuals from being aggressive out of fear of reprisal. We know, however, that serial killers enjoy publicity and that street gangs behave violently in open view of others. Although many have wondered why none of the thirty-eight onlookers came to the aid of Kitty Genovese when she was being brutally attacked for 35 minutes, rarely does anyone ask why the attacker carried on with so many people around. Would there be less violence in hockey games or football matches if no spectators were present?

Environmental Factors as Moderators of Aggression.   Environmental factors believed to influence the relationship between a predictor variable (e.g., frustration) and a criterion variable (e.g., aggressive behavior) include noise, crowding, and temperature. In the case of noise, considerable laboratory evidence suggests that people who have been angered are more prone to act aggressively when exposed to a noisy environment than angry people in a no-noise circumstance (e.g., Geen & O'Neal, 1969). Thus, we would expect that when a visiting professional football team is losing by a large margin in Denver's Mile High Stadium, which is noted for its noise, the visitor would be more likely to aggress than if he were playing in a less noisy environment. Crowding, or density, has also been proposed as exerting influence on aggressiveness. Russell (1983) reported that crowd size was negatively related to the aggression of visiting teams. Russell explains this finding as follows: "as crowds grow ever larger and more ominous, competing responses of avoidance supersede aggression at the top of the visitors' behavioral hierarchy" (p. 13). A considerable body of archival and field research has examined the relationship between temperature and violence in society (cf. Anderson, 1989). Research on violent crimes has shown, for example, that murder rates are higher in countries situated in southern latitudes and that, within any country, violent crime occurs most frequently during the hottest times of the year (Anderson, 1989).

One study has examined the aggression–temperature relationship in baseball (Riefman, Larrick, & Fein, 1991). Findings revealed a significant positive correlation (r's ranged from .09 to .11) between game temperature and the number of hit batters. When games were played at lower temperatures (e.g., 70 to 79°F), relatively few batters were hit, but when game temperature started to climb, so did the incidence of hit batters.

The existing research linking environmental factors to aggression is far from conclusive. Current perspectives suggest that the influence of environmental factors on aggression is not direct; rather, conditions such as noise, heat, and crowding enhance anger and aggression in an already frustrated or annoyed individual. However, future research is necessary to more fully determine the extent of these relationships.

Conclusion

In this chapter, we reiterated the instinct, biological, frustration, and social learning theoretical explanations for the occurrence of aggression. We presented findings of sport research that have tested these explanations during the last 14 years. In addition, we proposed six other explanations about why aggression occurs in sport. Simply stated, these are:

1. Athletes aggress because they have been aggressed against.
2. Athletes aggress because their opponents have annoyed them.
3. Athletes aggress because they are highly ego oriented and/or they have a low level of moral development.

4. Athletes aggress to show others how tough they are.

5. Athletes aggress because they see it as part of their role.

6. Athletes aggress because of group pressures.

Some of these explanations have been tested and supported empirically in sport more frequently than others. The relative importance of each reason varies according to the situation. More than one of these explanations probably applies in each specific incident of athletic aggression. Some factors may influence aggression indirectly by moderating the effects of the more direct influences (e.g., frustration, annoyance, attack) identified by the ten major explanations. Moderating variables are either personal or situational. The sex, age, and socioeconomic status of the potential aggressor are personal moderators. Situational variables described are the characteristics of the target, the presence of weapons, the presence of onlookers, group membership, and the environmental factors of crowding, noise, and temperature. Logical arguments can be presented about why each of these variables might modify (moderate) the relationship between the antecedent conditions and aggression, but rarely have their moderating effects been systematically examined, especially in sport.

Key Terms (in order of appearance)

instinct theory of aggression	situations presumed	self-presentation
instinct	to be frustrating	ingratiation
catharsis	retaliation	role
vicarious catharsis	annoyance	role theory
biological theories of aggression	social learning theory	group norm
frustration–aggression	vicarious reinforcement	collective efficacy for aggression
hypothesis	achievement motivation theory	team cohesion
social conflict theory	moral development	

References

Alcock, J. E., Carment, D. W., & Sadava, S. W. (1998). *A textbook of social psychology* (4th ed.). Scarborough, ON: Prentice Hall Allyn & Bacon Canada.

Anderson, C. A. (1989). Temperature and aggression: Ubiquitous effects of heat on occurrence of human violence. *Psychological Bulletin, 106,* 74–96.

Anderson, C. A., & Morrow, M. (1994). Competitive aggression without interaction: Effects of competitive versus cooperative instructions on aggressive behavior in video games. *Personality and Social Psychology Bulletin,* 1020–1030.

Arms, R. L., Russell, G. W., & Sandilands (1979). Effects on the hostility of spectators of viewing aggressive sports. *Social Psychology Quarterly, 42,* 275–279.

Bahrke, M. S., Vesalis, C. E., & Wright, J. E. (1990). Psychological and behavioral effects of endogenous testosterone levels and anabolic-androgenic steroids among males: A review. *Sports Medicine, 10,* 303–337.

Ballard, M. E., & Wiest, J. R. (1996). Mortal Kombat ™: The effects of violent video game play on males' hostility and cardiovascular responding. *Journal of Applied Social Psychology, 26,* 717–730.

Bandura, A. (1973). *Aggression: A social learning analysis.* Englewood Cliffs, NJ: Prentice Hall.

Bandura, A., & Walters, R. H. (1959). *Adolescent Aggression.* New York: Ronald.

Barefoot, J. C., Peterson, B. L., Dahlstrom, W. G., Siegler, I. C., Anderson, N. B., & Williams, R. B. (1991). Hostility patterns and health implications: Correlates of Cook-Medley Hostility scale scores in a national survey. *Health Psychology, 10,* 18–24.

Baron, R. M., & Kenny, D. A. (1986). The moderator-mediator variable distinction in social psychology research: Conceptual, strategic and statistical considerations. *Journal of Personality and Social Psychology, 51,* 1173–1182.

Bennett, J. C. (1991). The irrationality of the catharsis theory of aggression as justification for educators" support of interscholastic football. *Perceptual and Motor Skills, 72,* 415–418.

Berkowitz, L. (1962). *Aggression: A social psychological analysis.* New York: McGraw Hill.

Berkowitz, L. (1965). Some aspects of observed aggression. *Journal of Personality and Social Psychology, 2,* 359–369.

Berkowitz, L. (1970). Experimental investigation of hostility catharsis. *Journal of Consulting and Clinical Psychology, 35,* 1–7.

Berkowitz, L. (1983). Aversively stimulated aggression: Some parallels and difference in research with animals and humans. *American Psychologist, 38,* 1135–1144.

Berkowitz, L. (1987). Frustration, appraisals, and aversively stimulated aggression. *Aggressive Behavior, 7,* 3–11.

Berkowitz, L. (1989). Frustration-aggression hypothesis: Examination and reformulation. *Psychological Bulletin, 106,* 59–73.

Berkowitz, L., & LePage, A. (1967). Weapons as aggression-eliciting stimuli. *Journal of Personality and Social Psychology, 7,* 202–207.

Biddle, B. J., & Thomas, E. J. (1966). *Role theory: Concepts and research.* New York: Wiley.

Biddle, B. J. (1979). *Role theory: Expectations, identities, and behaviors.* New York: Academic.

Bredemeier, B. (1994). Children's moral reasoning and their assertive, aggressive, and submissive tendencies in sport and daily life. *Journal of Sport and Exercise Psychology, 16,* 1–14.

Bredemeier, B., & Shields, D. (1984). The utility of moral stage analysis in the understanding of athletic aggression. *Sociology of Sport Journal, 1,* 138–149.

Bredemeier, B., Weiss, M., Shields, D., & Cooper, B. (1986). The relationship of sport involvement with children's moral reasoning and aggressive tendencies. *Journal of Sport Psychology, 8,* 304–318.

Bredemeier, B., Weiss, M., Shields, D., & Cooper, B. (1987). The relationship between children's legitimacy judgements and their moral reasoning, aggressive tendencies, and sport involvement. *Sociology of Sport Journal, 4,* 48–60.

Brownfield, D. (1986). Social class and violent behavior. *Criminology, 24,* 421–438.

Buss, A. H. (1961). *The Psychology of Aggression.* New York: Wiley.

Carron, A. V. (1988). *Group dynamics in sport.* London, ON: Spodym.

Celozzi, M. J., Kazelskis, R., & Gutsch, K. U. (1982). The relationship between viewing televised violence in ice hockey and subsequent levels of personal aggression. *Journal of Sport Behavior, 4,* 157–162.

Choi, P. Y., & Pope, H. G. (1994). Violence toward women and illicit androgenic-anabolic steroid use. *Annals of Clinical Psychiatry, 6,* 21–25.

Clark, W. J., Vaz, E., Vetere, V., & Ward, T. A. (1978). Illegal aggression in minor league hockey: A causal model. In F. Landry & W. Orban (Eds.), *Ice hockey research, development and new concepts* (pp. 81–88). Miami, FL: Symposium Specialists.

Cooper, J., & Mackie, D. (1986). Video games and aggression in children. *Journal of Applied Social Psychology, 16,* 726–744.

Corner, P. A., & Widmeyer, W. N. "Minor hockey: A social situation where the check always bounces (back)." Paper presented at the meeting of the North American Society for the Sociology of Sport, St. Louis, MO, October 1983.

Cullen, J. B., & Cullen, F. T. (1975). The structural and contextual conditions of group norm violation: Some implications from the game of ice hockey. *International Review of Sport Sociology, 10,* 69–78.

Davitz, J. R. (1952). The effects of previous training on post-frustration behavior. *Journal of Abnormal and Social Psychology, 47,* 309–315.

Dollard, J. C., Doob, L., Miller, N., Mowrer, O. H., & Sears, R. R. (1939). *Frustration and aggression.* New Haven, CT: Yale Univ. Press.

Dorsch, K. D. "Examining aggressive behavior from a group perspective." Ph.D. diss., University of Waterloo, Waterloo, Ontario, 1997.

Dorsch, K. D., Widmeyer, W. N., Paskevich, D. M., & Brawley, L. R. (1996). Exploring relationships among collective efficacy, norms for aggression, cohesion, and aggressive behavior in junior hockey. *Journal of Applied Sport Psychology, 8,* 555.

Duda, J. L. (1993). Goals: A social-cognitive approach to the study of achievement motivation in sport. In R. N. Singer, M. Murphy, & L. K. Tennant (Eds.), *Handbook of research on sport psychology* (pp. 421–436). New York: MacMillan.

Duda, J. L., Olsen, L. K., & Templin, T (1991). The relationship of task and ego orientation to sportsmanship attitudes and the perceived legitimacy of aggressive acts. *Research Quarterly for Exercise and Sport, 62,* 79–87.

Eagly, A. H., & Steffen, V. I. (1986). Gender and aggressive behavior: A meta-analytic review of the social psychological literature. *Psychological Bulletin, 100,* 309–330.

Faulkner, R. R. (1974). Making violence by doing work: Selves, situations, and the world of professional hockey. *Sociology of Work and Occupations, 1,* 288–312.

Freud, S. (1925). *Collected papers.* London, UK: Hogarth Press.

Gallmeier, C. P. (1987). Putting on the game face: The staging of emotions in professional hockey. *Sociology of Sport Journal, 4,* 347–362.

Geen, R. G., & Berkowitz, L. (1967). Some conditions facilitating the occurrence of aggression after the observation of violence. *Journal of Personality, 35,* 666–676.

Geen, R. G., & O'Neal, E. C. (1969). Activation of cue-elicited aggression by general arousal. *Journal of Personality and Social Psychology, 11,* 289–292.

Gentry, W. D. (1970). Effects of frustration, attack and prior aggressive training on overt aggression and vascular processes. *Journal of Personality and Social Psychology, 16,* 718–725.

Glamser, F. D. (1990). Contest location, player misconduct, and race: A case from English soccer. *Journal of Sport Behavior, 13*(1), 41–49.

Goginsky, A. M. (1989). "Microcosmic characteristics of aggression in professional ice hockey." Master's thesis. Pennsylvania State University, State College, PA, 1989.

Goyens, C., & Turowetz, A. (1986). *Lions in winter.* Scarborough, ON: Prentice Hall.

Haan, N. (1985). Process of moral development: Cognition or social disequilibrium. *Developmental Psychology, 21,* 996–1006.

Harrel, W. A. (1980). Aggression by high school basketball players: An observational study of the effects of opponents' aggression and frustration inducing factors. *International Journal of Sport Psychology, 11,* 290–298.

Houston, B. Y. (1986). Factors influencing the learning of aggression in sport by females. Unpublished master's thesis. University of Waterloo, Waterloo, Ontario.

Houston, B., & Widmeyer, W. N. "Factors influencing the learning of aggression in sport by females." Paper presented at the meeting of the North American Society for Psychology of Sport and Physical Activity, Vancouver, BC, June 1987.

Husman, B. F., & Silva, J. M. (1984). Aggression in sport: Definitional and theoretical considerations. In J. M. Silva & R. S. Weinberg (Eds.), *Psychological Foundations of Sport* (pp. 246–260). Champaign, IL: Human Kinetics.

Huston, L., & Duda, J. L. "The relationship of goal orientation and competitive level to the endorsement of aggressive acts in football." Paper submitted for publication, 1991.

Hyde, J. S. (1984). How large are gender differences in aggression? A developmental meta-analyses. *Developmental Psychology, 20,* 722–736.

Jaffe, Y., & Yinon, Y. (1979). Retaliatory aggression in individuals and groups. *European Journal of Social Psychology, 9,* 177–186.

Johnson, W. R., & Hutton, D. H. (1955). Effects of combative sport upon personality dynamics as measured by a projective test. *Research Quarterly, 26,* 49–53.

Jones, E. E., & Wortman, C. (1973). *Ingratiation: An attributional perspective.* Morrestown, NJ: General Learning.

Kelly, B. R., & McCarthy, J. F. (1979). Personality dimensions of aggression: Its relationship to time and place of action in ice hockey. *Human Relations, 32,* 219–225.

Kohlberg, L. (1976). Moral stages and moralization: The cognitive-developmental approach. In T. Lickona (Ed.), *Moral development and behavior: Theory, research, and social issues* (pp. 31–53). New York: Holt, Rinehart, and Winston.

Lefavi, R. G., Reeve, T. G., Newland, C. M. (1990). Relationship between anabolic steroid use and selected psychological parameters in male body builders. *Journal of Sport Behavior, 13,* 157–166.

LeFebvre, L. M., & Passer, M. W. (1974). The effects of game location and importance on aggression in team sport. *International Journal of Sport Psychology, 5,* 102–110.

Leith, L. M. "An experimental analysis of the effect of direct and vicarious participation in physical activity on subject aggressiveness." Unpublished doctoral dissertation. University of Alberta, 1977.

Leith, L. M. (1989). The effect of various physical activities, outcome, and emotional arousal on subject aggression scores. *International Journal of Sport Psychology, 20,* 57–66.

Loew, C. A. (1967). Acquisition of a hostile attitude and its relationship to aggressive behavior. *Journal of Personality and Social Psychology, 5,* 335–341.

Lorenz, K. (1966). *On aggression.* New York: Harcourt, Brace & World.

Luxbacher, J. (1972). Violence in sport. *Coaching Review, 15,* 14–17.

Luxbacher, J. A. (1986). Violence in sports: An examination of the theories of aggression, and how the coach can influence the degree of violence displayed in sport. *Coaching Review, 9,* 14–17.

Martin, L. A. (1976). Effects of competition upon the aggressive responses of college basketball players and wrestlers. *Research Quarterly, 47,* 388–393.

McGuire, E. J. "Antecedents of aggressive behavior in professional ice hockey." Ph.D. diss. University of Waterloo, Waterloo, ON, 1990.

Menninger, W. C. (1948). Recreation and mental health. *Recreation, 42,* 340–346.

Mungo, D. A., & Feltz, D. L. (1985). The social learning of aggression in youth football in the United States. *Canadian Journal of Applied Sport Science, 10,* 26–35.

Nash, J. E., & Lerner, E. (1981). Learning violence from the pros: Violence in youth hockey. *Youth and Society A Quarterly Journal, 13,* 229–244.

Nelson, J., Gelfand, D., & Hartmann, D. (1969). Children's aggression following competition and exposure to an aggressive model. *Child Development, 40,* 1085–1097.

Nicholls, J. G. (1984). Achievement motivation: Conceptions of ability, subjective experience, task choice, and performance. *Psychological Review, 91,* 328–346.

Power, F. C., Higgins, A., & Kohlberg, L. (1989). *Lawrence Kohlberg's approach to moral education.* New York: Columbia Univ. Press.

Riefman, A. S., Larrick, R. P., & Fein, S. (1991). Temper and temperature on the diamond: The heat-aggression relationship in major league baseball. *Personality and Social Psychology Bulletin, 17,* 580–585.

Rogers, R. W., & Prentice-Dunn, S. (1981). Deindividuation and angle mediated inter-racial aggression: Unmasking regressive racism. *Journal of Personality and Social Psychology, 41,* 63–73.

Russell, G. W. (1981). Spectator moods at an aggressive sports event. *Journal of Sport Psychology, 3,* 217–227.

Russell, G. W., & Drewry, B. R. (1976). Crowd size and competitive aspects of aggression in ice hockey: An archival study. *Human Relations, 29,* 723–735.

Ryan, E. (1970). The cathartic effect of vigorous motor activity on aggressive behavior. *Research Quarterly, 41,* 542–551.

Sanszole, M. (1995). "The extent, antecedents and response to sport frustration by high school students." Unpublished honors thesis, University of Waterloo, Waterloo, ON, 1995.

Schutte, N. S., Malouff, J. M., & Post-Gordon, J. C. (1988). Effects of playing video games on children's aggression and other behaviors. *Journal of Applied Social Psychology, 18,* 454–460.

Sherif, M., Harvey, O. J., White, B. J., Hood, W. R., & Sherif, C. W. (1961). *Intergroup cooperation and conflict: The robbers cave experiment.* Norman, OK: Institute of Group Relations.

Sherif, M., & Sherif, C. W. (1953). *Groups in Harmony and Tension: An integration of studies in intergroup behavior.* New York: Harper & Row.

Shields, D. L. L., & Bredemeier, B. J. L. (1995). *Character development and physical activity.* Champaign, IL: Human Kinetics.

Shields, D. L. L., Bredemeier, B. J. L., Gardner, D. E., & Bostrom, A. (1995). Leadership, cohesion, and team norms regarding cheating and aggression. *Sociology of Sport Journal, 12,* 324–336.

Silva, J. M. (1983). The perceived legitimacy of rule violating behavior in sport. *Journal of Sport Psychology, 5,* 438–448.

Smith, M. D. (1974). Significant others' influence on the assaultive behavior of young hockey players. *International Review of Sport Sociology,* 45–56.

Smith, M. D. (1983). *Violence and sport.* Toronto: Butterworth.

Smith, M. D. (1978). From professional to youth hockey violence: The role of mass media. In M. Garnmon & A. Beyer (Eds.), *Violence in Canada.* Toronto, ON: Methuen.

Smolev, B. (1976). The relationship between sport and aggression. *The humanistic and mental aspects of sport, exercise, and recreation.* Chicago, IL: American Medical Association.

Stephens, D. E. (1995). Judgements about lying, hurting, and cheating in youth sport: Variations in patterns of predictors for female and male soccer players. *Journal of Applied Sport Psychology, 7,* S111.

Stephens, D. E., & Bredemeier, B. (1996). Moral atmosphere and judgements about aggression in girl's soccer: Relationships among moral and motivational variables. *Journal of Sport and Exercise Psychology, 18,* 158–173.

Stokes, J. P. (1958). Psycho-analytical reflections on development of ball games. In I. A. Nathan (Ed.), *Sport and sociology.* London, UK: Bowes and Bowes.

Stone, A. "The effect of sanctioned overt aggression on total instigation to aggressive responses." Honors thesis, Harvard University. Cambridge, MA 1950.

Tatum, J., & Kushner, B. (1979). *They call me assassin.* New York: Everest House.

Taylor, S. P., & Smith, I. (1974). Aggression as a function of sex of the victim and male subject's attitude toward women. *Psychological Reports, 35,* 1095–1098.

Vaz, E. W. (1972). The culture of young hockey players: Some initial observations In A. W. Taylor (Ed.), *Training, scientific basis and application.* Springfield, IL: Charles C. Thomas.

Vaz, E. W. (1977). Institutionalized rule violation in professional hockey: Perspective and control systems. *J. Can. Assoc. Health Phys. Ed. & Rec., 43*(3), 6–16.

Volkamer, M. (1971). Investigation into aggressiveness in the competitive social system. *Sportwissenshaft, 1,* 33–64.

Wankel, L. M. "An examination of illegal aggression in intercollegiate hockey." *Proceedings: Fourth Canadian Psycho-Motor Learning and Sports Psychology Symposium* (pp. 531–544). University of Waterloo, Waterloo, ON, October 1973.

Wann, D. L. "The relationship between players' names on uniforms and athletic aggression." Paper presented at the meeting of the Association for the Advancement of Applied Sport Psychology, San Diego, CA, September 1997.

White, G. F. (1989). Media and violence: The case of professional football championship games. *Aggressive Behavior, 15,* 423–433.

Widmeyer, W. N., & Birch, J. S. (1979). The relationship between aggression and performance outcome in ice hockey. *Canadian Journal of Applied Sport Sciences, 4,* 91–94.

Widmeyer, W. N., & Birch, J. S. (1984). Aggression in professional ice hockey: A strategy for success or reaction to failure? *Journal of Psychology, 117,* 77–84.

Widmeyer, W. N., Brawley, L. R., & Carron, A. V. (1992). Group dynamics in sport. In T. Horn (Ed.), *Advances in Sport Psychology.* Champaign, IL: Human Kinetics.

Widmeyer, W. N., Dorsch, K. D., Sanszole, M. "Gender differences in the extent, antecedents of, and responses to frustration in sport." Paper presented at the annual meeting of the North American Society for Psychology of Sport at Physical Activity, Monterey, CA, June 1995.

Widmeyer, W. N., & McGuire, E. J. (1997). Frequency of competition and aggression in professional ice hockey. *International Journal of Sport Psychology, 26,* 57–60.

Yates, W. R., Perry, P., & Murray, S. (1992). Aggression and hostility in anabolic steroid users. *Biological Psychiatry, 31,* 1232–1234.

Zillman, D., Johnson, R. C., & Day, K. D. (1974). Provoked and unprovoked aggressiveness in athletes. *Journal of Research in Personality, 8,* 139–152.

Zillman, D., Katcher, A. H., & Milavsky, B. (1972). Excitation transfer from physical exercise to subsequent aggressive behavior. *Journal of Experimental Social Psychology, 8,* 247–259.

18

Reducing Aggression in Sport

W. Neil Widmeyer

University of Waterloo

- Reducing frustration through altering the situation or the athlete can reduce aggression.
- Reducing annoyance and attacks through such intervention techniques as cognitive restructuring or desensitization can reduce aggression.
- A reduction in rivalry can have a reducing effect on athlete aggression.
- Several techniques are presented for reducing aggression in accordance with social learning theory, including punishment, time-out techniques, reducing rewards for aggression, reinforcing assertion, and reducing the modeling of aggression.
- Personal factors such as goal orientation and moral development can be examined and altered to reduce aggression.
- Altering member's roles, athlete self-presentation, or using other group techniques can reduce aggression within groups.
- This chapter provides recommendations directly to responsible sport-specific parties, including league administration and officials, media, coaches, and parents.

> *Hey Hey, Ho Ho*
> *Da Violence Gotta Go*

> —Madeline MacIntyre (1997)

Concern over societal violence comes from many sources. Never was the prevalence of this concern more apparent to me than when I overheard my two-and-a-half-year-old granddaughter, Madi, chanting the adage above. Although many would like to see violence "go" (i.e., go away), such a goal is very unrealistic. A more feasible objective would be the reduction of this undesirable behavior. A logical approach to reducing aggression would be one that involves reducing (i.e., minimizing) conditions that have been found or theorized to lead to aggression. Thus, the explanations and findings presented in Chapter 17 are the basis for advancing prescriptions designed to reduce aggression in sport.

By staying focused on legitimate actions, athletes can reduce the incidence of aggressive behavior in sport.

Reducing Aggression by Reducing Instinctual and Biological Factors

Reducing aggressive instincts seems both unlikely and unprofitable. Because instincts are innate and do not explain why aggression occurs at some times and not at others, it seems strange to suggest that we can draw on instinct theory to help reduce aggression. The very fact that instincts cannot explain aggression, however, can be used in reducing sport aggression. Athletes often will tell media personnel, coaches, and even parents, "I can't help it that I lose it out there. That's the way I am." Regardless of whether athletes truly believe this "explanation" or simply use it as an excuse for their actions, these players must be educated by their parents and coaches that they cannot rationalize their behavior as instinctual. Athletes must be taught to accept responsibility for their actions and to deal with their feelings from logical and moral perspectives.

Reducing biological factors also appears to have limited potential as an approach to reducing aggression in sport. The hormone testosterone is the biological factor most frequently discussed in relation to aggression. It would appear that reducing testosterone would reduce aggressive urges. Indeed, it has been shown (Rubin, 1987) that castration of those convicted of sexual assault caused a reduction in these individuals' sexual thoughts and their likelihood of sexually assaulting again. No evidence exists, however, that this measure reduced nonsexual aggression. Even if such a technique were effective in reducing other forms of violence, it is certainly not a practical approach to reducing aggression in sport. Efforts can be made, however, to reduce the testosterone that athletes receive via anabolic steroids. Although there are certainly enough other reasons for reducing and hopefully eliminating these illegal substances from sport, the testosterone-aggression link provides sport administrators and coaches with more justification for banning these drugs.

Reducing Aggression by Reducing Frustration

Reducing frustration can be accomplished through two general approaches. One approach involves altering the situation, and the other focuses on changing the individual.

Alter the Situation

Altering the situation to reduce frustration can take several forms. Although the clutching and grabbing that occur in contact sports may be perceived as annoyances, they could also be viewed as frustrating situations. Regardless of how they are seen, reducing these behaviors should reduce aggression in sport. One situation that is clearly frustrating and that has been reduced in some sports is preventing the opponent from performing. In basketball, the introduction of rules designed to ensure that the ball is (1) shot before 24 or 30 seconds expire, (2) brought across the mid-court line before 10 seconds expire, and (3) advanced toward the basket while in the front court have all been instituted to avoid stalling tactics that are very frustrating to opponents. Likewise, in Canadian University football the clock stops on every play during the last 2 minutes of a game to reduce the likelihood of the winning team being able to "run out the clock"—a situation that frustrates the losing team. Losing by a large margin is the situational variable that consistently produces a significant amount of frustration and aggression in sport. Although winning by a large margin has also been strongly related to aggression, winning by a large margin is not likely to be construed as being frustrating. Reducing the number of "blowout" games can be accomplished by reducing the talent disparity among competing teams. In the professional ranks, parity is pursued yearly by such procedures as having weaker teams draft the new players first, having supplemental drafts for only the weaker teams, and allowing stronger teams to "protect" only a core member of players. More conscientious efforts must be made by those who are responsible for establishing minor leagues to ensure that teams are more equal in ability. When it is evident that teams are not equal, then different leagues (e.g., "A," "B," & "C" divisions), each containing fewer and more equal-ability teams, should be established. Even with equal-ability teams, sometimes games have large score discrepancies. To avoid this situation, which leads both the losing and the winning teams to aggress, the contest should be stopped. In some leagues of some sports, this is referred to as a "mercy rule." In a scheme proposed by Widmeyer, McGuire, and Dorsch (1994) for minor hockey, the game would be awarded to the opposition if a team were losing by five goals in the first period, four goals in the second period, or three goals in the third period. All three interventions require implementation by league administrators and monitoring by game officials. Coaches', parents', and players' contributions to reducing aggression by reducing frustration are more likely to be made at the personal (i.e., player) level.

Alter the Player

Altering the player to reduce frustration should be based on determinations of what frustrates different athletes at different levels in different sports. We have found some interindividual differences, but one universal source of frustration is displeasure with one's own play. To avoid this feeling, a player must play better and/or alter perceptions of his or her play. To help athletes play better, the fundamental skills of the game must be taught better and more frequently. Better teaching can result when coaches are better trained and certified by some mechanism, such as the Levels 1–4 Coaching Certification Program that operates in Canada. To ensure more frequent teaching, the number of games must be reduced (an intervention that also reduces aggression by reducing rivalry) and the number of practices increased. Practice should involve not only scrimmages and team drills, but rather should focus, especially at younger age levels, on the teaching, practicing, and goal setting of individual skills. Players can and should be taught realistic perceptions and expectations regarding their performance. Players' performances should be monitored closely (e.g., shots taken, shots made, turnovers), and success should be perceived in **relative terms** (i.e., improvement) rather than in **absolute outcomes** (e.g., points). Next, realistic goals for upcoming contests should be established. Both players and coaches should be involved in this process. Finally, efforts must be made to increase players' tolerance of frustration so that they will not respond aggressively. Players must learn not only to expect frustration but also how to handle it when it occurs. Thus, coaches should simulate frustrating situations during practice, such as having some players clutch and grab others or establishing unequal teams for scrimmages. Through such techniques, players can learn how to handle frustration in an environment in which the coach has the opportunity to stop play and teach alternative coping strategies. In essence, these techniques represent a form of frustration inoculation.

Reducing Aggression by Reducing Annoyance and Attacks

There seems to be an attitude held by officials in several sports that "We can't penalize everything, so we'll let the 'small stuff' go and just penalize the severe infractions." What these officials fail to consider is that if the "small stuff" were stopped, many of the "severe infractions" would not occur. The "small stuff" in basketball, football, soccer, and ice hockey ranges from holding on to an opponent's jersey to physical jabs. When these acts are "let go," they usually escalate (e.g., the holding becomes more frequent, the jabs become more severe). When the recipients can no longer tolerate these annoying behaviors and attacks, he or she usually retaliates with a definitive act of violence. Because these responses are typically penalized, rather than the series of acts that caused them, coaches constantly tell their players, "Instigate. Don't Retaliate." This advice may reduce penalization, but it is not an effective guideline for reducing aggression.

Despite considerable evidence to show that verbal aggression leads to physical aggression, verbal attacks in the form of "trash talking" are escalating in sport. This verbal aggression is difficult to detect, but when it is witnessed, it must be immediately and severely punished. In addition, coaches must make athletes understand that engaging in trash talking can interfere with one's own focus on performance and may cause retaliatory injurious actions.

Aggression often occurs in contact sports because athletes interpret legal assertive actions toward them as intentions to harm and, therefore, retaliate with acts of aggression. Three approaches can and should be taken in such sports to reduce this retaliatory aggression. At the minor levels, all body contact must be minimized. In the sport of ice hockey, body checking is not allowed until the players reach the age of 12. On January 30, 1998, the Canadian Hockey Association passed a proposal that allows this intentional contact to occur at the novice (8-year-old) level. Arguments for such a change include "body checking is a part of the game of hockey" and "if there is body checking, there will be less illegal stick work." The argument to the first contention is that minor hockey does not have to be a mirror of professional hockey to be an enjoyable experience. The response to the second argument is that there is no solid evidence that increased body contact results in fewer stick infractions. It may well be that players use their sticks to retaliate against a heavy body check. Thus, body checking should not be allowed until the players are 15 years of age. Not only is this procedure likely to reduce aggression (Corner & Widmeyer, 1983), but also it should increase the players' chances of perfecting skills sanctioned by the sport (e.g., passing, skating, shooting). *Cognitive restructuring* can also be used to reduce retaliatory aggression. Athletes should be taught to perceive that not all contact by opponents is meant to harm them. When it is apparent that the opponent did intend harm, however, the victim must learn that often this behavior is nothing personal and that the individual is simply behaving as he was instructed. If cognitive restructuring fails, then players should be exposed to some form of violence *desensitization.* During team practices, athletes can be exposed to an ever-increasing amount of aggressive attacks and taught nonretaliatory behaviors (e.g., withdrawal, effort toward other behaviors).

Reducing Aggression by Reducing Rivalry

Anthropologist Margaret Mead is credited with distinguishing between competition and rivalry. *Competition* involves a striving for scarce rewards and/or a social comparison process, and *rivalry* is behavior designed to beat another. Chapter 17 pointed out that the more frequent the competition between the same opponents, the more likely conflict, rivalry, and aggression are to occur (Widmeyer & McGuire, 1996). This contact-conflict-rivalry-hatred-aggression chain operates in sport, especially when unbalanced schedules exist. Although unbalanced schedules produce the rivalries that benefit gate receipts in professional sport, playing the same opponent on several occasions also leads to aggression-producing animosities. These animosities are especially likely to develop when teams compete frequently against each other over a brief period of time. This situation occurs in professional football when there are back-to-back games involving two teams from the same division. An even more extreme example is the "120-minute" game that occurs in ice hockey when a team, such as Toronto, plays another, such as Detroit, in Toronto on Saturday night and again in Detroit on Sunday night. It has been found that these two-game series are especially violent (Widmeyer & Birch, 1984). League officials at all levels should avoid highly unbalanced schedules and back-to-back games. In minor leagues, teams should play all opponents less frequently and practice more often to develop skills and discipline.

The desire to beat an opponent whom (a) you have played recently, (b) you are situated close to, and/or (c) you view as a traditional rival is a feeling that is difficult to alter. Nevertheless, steps can be taken to reduce the hatred associated with the desire to beat another. The media certainly must be convinced that they should not foster hatred between teams and among competitors. Neither the media nor coaches should attempt to motivate players by creating the image of the opposition as the evil enemy. Instead, coaches should adopt a more positive approach by emphasizing execution of their own team's offense, defense, and work habits. No data are available on his players' lack of hatred; however, such an approach proved to be an effective strategy for performance success with John Wooden's UCLA basketball teams during the 1960s and 1970s.

Reducing Aggression through Social Learning

It was noted earlier that social learning occurs through either direct or indirect (i.e., vicarious) reinforcement. Direct reinforcement involves presenting rewards or administering punishments to individuals learning or performing a behavior (e.g., aggression). Indirect or vicarious reinforcement involves seeing another individual (i.e., a model) reinforced or punished for a behavior (e.g., aggression). The logic behind vicarious reinforcement is "If I do what the model did, the same consequences will occur to me." The impact that punishing and rewarding athletes directly as well as those they watch has on the athletes' aggressive behavior in their sport is examined next.

Punishment

Punishment as a method of reducing aggression has gone through cycles of support. Even though, for centuries, societies have had severe punishment for violent crime, psychologists in the first half of the twentieth century thought that punishment was rather ineffective and produced only a temporary reduction in violent behavior. However, a number of researchers (e.g., Bower & Hilgard, 1981) propose that punishment can have both a powerful and a permanent effect on behavior provided that (a) the punishment follows the objectionable conduct almost immediately, (b) the punishment is of sufficient magnitude to be aversive to the aggressor, and (c) the contingency between the behavior and the punishment is clear to the recipient. Unfortunately, in our society a great deal of time elapses before a criminal offense is brought to trial and eventually a sentence is handed down. Punishment also is substantially reduced through plea-bargaining and the parole system. Finally, notwithstanding the precedent system of law, inconsistencies in laws across states/ provinces, counties, and judges often make the crime-punishment contingency very unclear. Given these conditions, it is not surprising that many social scientists remain pessimistic about the effective means of punishment in reducing violence in society.

Is punishment effective in reducing violence in sport? Although on some occasions films are sent to league commissioners for purposes of punishing an act of sport violence "after the fact," for the most part punishment in the form of penalization is immediate in sport. The severity of punishment for sport aggression, however, can definitely be questioned. The awarding of (a) two foul shots in basketball for taking the legs out from under a player to prevent a basket, (b) five or even fifteen yards for grabbing the face mask of an opponent in football, (c) a yellow or red card to a soccer player for charging an opponent, and (d) a two thousand-dollar fine to an athlete earning over $1 million when he or she pushes an official hardly seem severe enough forms of punishment to deter these behaviors in the future. More severe punishment must be meted out for these and other acts of aggression in sport. Giving the basketball player's team an automatic three points and possession of the ball, the football player's team a 25- to 35-yard penalty, the soccer player's team a penalty kick, and the professional athlete a fifteen-thousand-dollar fine seems more likely to deter athletes from performing these aggressive behaviors in the future. Fighting in any sport at any level most definitely should result in immediate expulsion from that contest and an automatic suspension from the next game, as it does at the university level in ice hockey.

Are players in sport completely aware of the contingency that exists between their behavior and any ensuing penalization? A norm appears to be operating in certain sports whereby the experience of the players moderates the enforcement of the rules by game officials. For example, it is commonly accepted in baseball that veteran hitters have a smaller strike zone than do "rookie" players. In professional soccer, football, and ice hockey, certain "stars," such as Maradero, Rice, and Gretzky, appear to "get away with" more illegal acts than do less prominent players. Another norm that appears to operate in sport, especially in ice hockey, is that during the later stages of a game, the referee "puts away the whistle." In other words, the referee does not penalize infractions in the late stages of the third period that would be penalized in the first or second periods. Inconsistency in meting out punishment occurs not only across players and time of the game but also across officials. Some referees at every level of ice hockey are renowned for "letting the players decide the game." Such officials rarely call any penalties on any players at any time in a game. With these types of inconsistencies, it is difficult, if not impossible, for players to learn the contingency between their behavior and how it will be penalized. It is no wonder that the present penalization scheme is an ineffective form of punishment.

The world of sport recognizes and is concerned about the imperfections in its methods of punishing violence. In his report on violence in minor hockey, McMurtry (1974) made the following plea:

> It is imperative that the standard of referees be upgraded to ensure that:
> (a) they apply the rules of the game;
> (b) they are consistent;
> (c) they have the respect of the players, coaches, and fans; and
> (d) there is a uniform philosophy towards the game of ice hockey (p. 39).

To help ensure that these conditions existed, McMurtry proposed more programs for certifying referees and urged that referees be given support by various associations, coaches, and players. No doubt this support must start from the top (i.e., with league officials).

"Time Out" Technique

Instead of punishing children who misbehave, often teachers and/or parents utilize a *"time out" technique* that removes the child from the disturbing situation. Some might view the penalization system in hockey as a form of "time out," but the offender usually perceives it as a punishment. In fact, it is primarily a punishment to the offender's team, which must play shorthanded for a period of time. It has been reported that when former Swedish tennis great Bjorn Borg was a young boy and threw temper tantrums on the court, his parents would take his tennis racquet from him. This form of "time out" must have worked, because Borg went on to become known as "the iceman"—the epitome of self-control. It is quite conceivable that other forms of "time outs" could be effective in curbing aggressive behavior of young athletes in other sports.

Reduce Rewards for Aggressive Behaviors

Not only is aggression not punished frequently and severely enough in sport, but also sometimes it is even rewarded. Thus, reducing rewards for aggression represents another strategy for reducing aggression. Rewards for aggression ranging from praise to money come from teammates, coaches, fans, the media, and even parents. It is doubtful that all these reinforcements can be eliminated or even substantially reduced. Nevertheless, steps must be taken to achieve this objective. League officials should begin by demanding that all coaches be certified and by making it known that any coach who encourages or rewards aggression by his players will be punished. The first occurrence of such behavior should result in a one- or two-game suspension; a second offense should carry a one-year expulsion from coaching. Coaches must also see to it that others, namely parents and teammates, do not encourage or reward aggression. Parents should be spoken to immediately following the game and told that such behavior is not tolerated; a second occurrence should result in the parent's banishment from all home games during the rest of the season. In the case of teammates, first offenders should be severely chastised and receive reduced playing time, and second offenders should be banished from that game and the following one. Although reinforcements of aggression are not always seen, when they are witnessed, they must be punished immediately and consistently.

Reward Nonaggressive, Proactive Assertive Behaviors

Rewarding nonaggressive behavior can sometimes be as effective in reducing aggression as punishing or not rewarding aggressive behavior. Positive reinforcement for nonaggressive behavior can range from simple recognition to tangible rewards. Nonaggressive behavior can take several forms, including (1) "great moves," such as those performed by Michael Jordan or Barry Sanders; (2) tremendous and/or constant effort, such as that displayed by the forward who never quits trying to dig the puck out of the corner or the linebacker who never stops pursuing the ball carrier; (3) acts of courage, such as those of Silken Laumann, the rower who pursued her dream of a gold medal despite having a badly injured leg; (4) unselfish play that occurs when a player who has a clear shot at the basket passes the ball to a teammate who has a slightly better shot; and (5) acts of sportsmanship, such as efforts to avoid collisions with opposing goaltenders and attempts to help an opponent who is injured.

How can the reinforcement of such acts occur? It can take place before the fact through encouragement to emulate such behavior, or it can occur after the fact through rewards. Prebehavior encouragement can come about by having still pictures posted in the dressing room depicting role models performing these types of behavior, by drawing attention to such behavior by professional athletes when the team is watching television, or with a simple, "Did you see the move that Vince Carter put on Glen Rice last night?" Encouragement does not have to be tied to vicarious reinforcement of role models; it can be very direct. For example, a coach can say, "Why don't you stay for 10 minutes after practice, and I'll help you perfect that 'spin' move that Michael Jordan uses." After-the-fact reinforcement is most effective when it is immediate. Thus, even though the coaching staff is constantly thinking about offensive and defensive strategies, they should make efforts to acknowledge great moves, persistent effort, acts of courage, unselfish play, and/or sportsmanship as soon as the player comes to the bench. Exceptional examples of these behaviors should be acknowledged in the dressing room after the game.

Formal recognition of outstanding game play exists in many sports. The presentation of the game ball in football and the selection of three stars in ice hockey are excellent examples of this reinforcement. Interestingly enough, many leagues of hockey have added a "grinder" award to recognize hard work during the game. Acknowledging the recipient of this award after the three stars have been identified increases its value. Finally, teams and leagues should establish trophies for seasonlong demonstrations of effort and sportsmanship to go along with awards for performance.

Nonaggressive play can and should also be recognized at the team level. Dr. Edmund Vaz (1982), a sociologist with a strong interest in "cleaning up" minor ice hockey, has proposed an elaborate scoring system that would reward nonaggressive play. A much simpler system has been adopted in Quebec minor hockey leagues. In addition to the usual two points for a win and one point for a tie, each team can earn an additional point if they have less than five penalties assessed. Administrators and coaches in these leagues have found that teams have been very eager to earn their sportsmanship point, and penalty minutes have consequently significantly decreased.

Reduce the Modeling of Aggression

Decreasing the modeling of aggression can help in reducing future aggressive behaviors. As already indicated, when one sees a behavior performed by another (i.e., model) being rewarded, one is likely to replicate that behavior. When the model is a role model (e.g., a professional athlete), one is all the more likely to learn and in turn perform that behavior. To reduce the learning and performance of aggression by young viewers, portrayals of rewarded aggression must be reduced. This objective can best be achieved by cooperation from the media. Television networks have done a great deal to reduce the showing of the champagne parties that occur in dressing rooms following a championship game victory. They must also be responsible for not replaying acts of violence in sport. In fact, they should institute a policy of going away from fights. Networks and sportscasters should be encouraged to show more positive footage. In other words, the "plays of the day" should be more glorified. Specifically, the "Greatest Goals" should replace the "Greatest Fights." In addition, "Rock 'em,

Sock'em" videos should carry a rating that requires parental guidance. Other efforts should be made by the media to deglorify sport violence. Publishing books such as *They Call Me Assassin* (Tatum & Kushner, 1979) and assigning nicknames to players such as "The Grim Reaper" (Stu Grimson) or "Charley" (Dave Manson) must be treated as irresponsible journalism. Responsibility for not modeling aggression also lies with professional athletes. These heroes of youth must be constantly reminded by their league office, their own team's management, the players' association, and the media that their words and actions influence the beliefs and behavior of thousand of youngsters. When a professional athlete makes claims, such as one rather violent professional basketball player did, such as "I ain't no role model," he must be severely chastised by his league, team, fellow athletes, and the media.

Modeled behavior is more frequently copied when the behavior is rewarded. Therefore, radio and television announcers must be educated not to praise the aggressive play they report. When parents attend games or watch them on television with their children and violence takes place, these significant others must not reinforce the behavior through praise or laughter or even by ignoring it. Instead, they must seize this "teachable moment" to educate their children about the unacceptability of the viewed behavior.

Several steps can be taken to minimize the aggression that occurs among spectators who view aggressive behavior. These steps include (1) limiting the sale of alcohol to the first two-thirds of a game (e.g., six innings in baseball, two periods in hockey), (2) using air-conditioning to keep the temperature of indoor stadiums below 75°F, and/or (3) having the public address announcer diffuse any aggressive feelings among fans with humor and/or music. Instead of playing The Nylon's "Na Na Na Na Hey Hey Hey Goodbye" to the frustrated losing players and their fans, substitute "We'll be missing you," or use this time to play birthday wishes or ask trivia questions.

Reducing Aggression by Altering Personal Factors

To this point, the recommendations for reducing aggression in sport have, for the most part, involved altering situational factors. The question now is whether personal factors can be altered to reduce aggression. In Chapter 17, two personal factors associated with aggression, goal orientation and level of moral development, were identified. Suggestions will now be provided about how each of these factors can be altered to reduce aggression.

Alter Goal Orientations

Altering goal orientations has been achieved in at least one study. Lloyd and Fox (1990) conducted a 6-week intervention study in which the behavior of an exercise class leader was manipulated to promote either task- or ego-orientation among female class participants. In one class, the instructor's feedback involved comparisons among participants (**ego-orientation**), and in the other, feedback was directed at individual self-improvement (**task-orientation**). Participants in the social-comparison condition, who were initially low in ego-involvement, demonstrated an increase in their ego-involvement. However, girls who were initially high in ego-orientation and were exposed to the task-oriented condition showed a decrease in their ego-orientation. In addition, participants in the task-orientation condition exhibited higher motivation. These results provide some preliminary evidence that ego-orientations can be changed. If athletes receive and are encouraged to focus on feedback in relation to self-referenced standards of performance, it may help change the perceptions and behavior of ego-oriented athletes who think achieving goals by illegitimate means is acceptable.

Altering Moral Development

Moral development has also been altered in at least three studies. In the first study (Bredemeier et al., 1986), youth summer campers (ages 5–7 years) were randomly assigned to one of three conditions: a control group, social learning, or structural developmental. In the control condition, children followed a standard physical education curriculum that encouraged conformity to rules and teachers' instructions. Instructors in the social learning group modeled and provided reinforcement for prosocial behavior among the campers. Children in the structural developmental condition participated in peer-oriented moral dialogue that was facilitated by their instructors when moral dilemmas arose in class. Results showed that over a 6-week intervention period, children in the social learning and structural developmental conditions demonstrated significant gains in moral reasoning maturity. Children in the control condition did not show significant changes in moral reasoning over the duration of the study.

A study by Romance, Weiss, and Bockoven (1986) examined the efficacy of an 8-week intervention on the moral development of older (10 years) elementary school children. Children in the control condition participated in daily physical education classes according to their school's normal curriculum. In the experimental condition, students followed a regular physical education program but also took part in activities in which they identified and discussed rules and behaviors that affected them and others. After discussing rules and behaviors, students had input into establishing guidelines for moral behavior in the gymnasium. A comparison of pretest and posttest scores of moral reasoning, level showed that children in the experimental condition exhibited significant gains in moral reasoning for sport and life dilemmas and overall moral reasoning, while the control group showed no differences. Significant differences were also found between the experimental and control groups for life, sport, and overall moral reasoning at the end of the intervention program, when initial moral reasoning levels were controlled for.

In a more recent study, Gibbons, Ebbeck, and Weiss (1995) investigated the effectiveness of a 7-month moral development intervention in an elementary school population (grades 4–6). The study involved a comparison of three conditions: (1) a control condition for which pupils received the standard school curriculum, (2) physical education intervention that focused on moral development in physical education classes only, and (3) all classes intervention that implemented a moral development curriculum in every subject. The moral development intervention was the Fair Play for Kids (1990) intervention program, which consisted of several teaching strategies designed to promote fair play and moral growth (cf. Gibbons, Ebbeck, & Weiss, 1995). When the data were examined at the class level ($N = 18$), no pretest differences were evident between groups; however, posttest scores revealed significantly higher levels of moral judgment, reasoning, and intention in the moral development classes (i.e., physical education and all classes) compared with the control condition. At the individual level of analysis ($N = 452$), students in the control condition scored significantly higher than other students on the pretest of moral reasoning, but no other differences emerged. On examination of the posttest data, participants in the moral development condition were significantly higher than controls for moral judgment, reasoning, intention, and prosocial behavior. No differences between the physical education only and all classes intervention conditions emerged for any of the dependent variables.

The combined findings of these three studies suggest that moral development can be altered using both social learning (i.e., modeling) and structural developmental interventions designed to encourage fair resolution of moral dilemmas, problem solving, and communication. The success of the intervention programs is tempered by their solid theoretical grounding. Unfortunately, none of these studies reported follow-up results for their participants, so neither the long-term nor the lasting effects of the interventions are known. What can be said, however, is that when children participated in an environment that encouraged their moral development, their level of moral development was enriched. Although children's aggression was not a focus in these studies, they do provide examples of how physical educators and coaches can have a positive influence on one of the personal factors that has been associated with aggression in sport.

Reducing Aggression by Altering Members' Roles

It has been demonstrated that defensive hockey players are more aggressive than offensive players (e.g., Widmeyer & Birch, 1979). Although protecting the goal might require more assertive play than scoring on the opposition, the defensive role does not necessitate the levels of aggression currently employed by athletes in these positions. Efforts should be made to reward nonaggressive defensive play (e.g., the "poke check" in hockey, interceptions in football). In addition, coaches should encourage their defensive players to improve their offensive skills. Bobby Orr was an outstanding defenseman in professional hockey, not because of his ability to inflict harm on opponents, but rather because of his ability to make significant contributions to his team's offense while still performing his defensive role in a nonaggressive fashion. The media, coaches, and parents should promote such a player as a role model for young defensive players.

There should be no place on any team or in any sport for a "goon"—someone who has a position not because of technical skill, but rather because of his or her ability to inflict harm on opponents. Coaches say that they have to carry such a "role player" on their team to protect their nonaggressive skilled players. Obviously, harsher rules must be established by league administrators and strictly enforced by game officials to ensure that the goon is not needed and that his or her presence is viewed as a detriment to the team as a result of costly penalization and having one less skilled player on the roster. If "goonish" behavior were severely punished at minor levels and at the same time all players were encouraged to develop the technical skills of their sport, it is unlikely that we would see the role of goon existing at higher levels of sport.

Reducing Aggression by Altering Self-Presentation

Chapter 17 reported that college football and hockey players whose names were on their jerseys were more aggressive than those whose names were not displayed. Wann (1997) interpreted these findings as supporting a self-presentational perspective as opposed to a deindividuation theory. He pointed out that the results apply only to aggressive sports and would predict the opposite results in nonaggressive sports. The implications of these findings appear to be that if we want to reduce aggression in sport, we should not allow names on jerseys of athletes playing aggressive sports and require this identification in nonaggressive sports. Likewise, based on Frank and Gilovich's (1988) discovery that football players who wore black were more aggressive, one would oppose the wearing of all black uniforms in aggressive sports. McGuire's (1990) finding that professional hockey players who wore face shields were the least aggressive seems more difficult to apply. The mandatory use of face shields is an excellent safety precaution; however, it seems unlikely that making their use mandatory would make aggressive players behave less aggressively. In fact, some could argue that they might use the face shields as a weapon or at least as a form of protection while aggressing.

Reducing Aggression by Group Techniques

Chapter 17 stated that membership in a group can influence an individual member's behavior. In any group, norms exist concerning the ways that members are expected to think, feel, and behave. Such norms definitely exist on sport teams in regard to aggression. Just as members of the group construct norms, so also the group as a whole and/or some of its influential members can alter the norms of the group. For example, highly skilled members of a team might decide to create a norm that their team is a "scoring machine," and thereby emphasize improving offensive skills. Likewise, a coach might decide that aggression is not a suitable tactic for success and that he is going to give playing time to skilled players rather than "goons." Both of these revised group norms are likely to lead to a reduction in team aggression.

It was previously mentioned that people do what they believe they can do well. We know that a group perception exists regarding the group's ability to successfully use aggression as a tactic. Because this perception exists and is socially learned through membership in the group, it should be able to be reduced through these means as well. As Bandura (1997) points out, a group's belief in their collective competence to perform certain behaviors undoubtedly influences their choice, effort, and persistence with these behaviors. Thus, if we are able to reduce a team's collective efficacy regarding their ability to use strategic aggression, we should be able to reduce the performance of this behavior.

Reducing Aggression in Sport: Specific Responsibilities

Scholars should be pleased that the prescriptions for reducing sport aggression were based on theoretical and empirical knowledge of the factors that bring about aggression. However, practitioners might argue that the prescriptions were lost among the theories and the research. Thus, we now propose specific recommendations for (1) administrators/officials, (2) the media, (3) coaches, and (4) parents. Some recommendations apply at all levels of sport; others are meant only for youth sport.

Recommendations for League Administrators and Game Officials to Reduce Aggression in Sport

1. *Penalize all aggressive behavior.* (Remember, the "small stuff" leads to the "big stuff.") Increase the number of officials so that more aggression can be seen (e.g., two referees in hockey).
2. *Penalize aggression more severely* at all levels (e.g., more "time outs" in youth sport, larger fines in professional sport).
3. *Penalize consistently,* regardless of the status of the athlete or the time in the game.
4. *Reduce disparity* among competing teams (e.g., have reverse drafting, supplemental drafts). In minor sport, institute a "mercy rule" to stop games in which the score becomes too disparate.
5. Institute rules that prevent winning teams from *"running out the clock"* late in a game.
6. Award points for nonaggressive play in minor sport (e.g., Vaz system).
7. Impress on *professional athletes* in the sport that they ***are*** *role models* for youth.
8. Institute rules to *decrease body contact* in youth sport.
9. Institute rules to *minimize "trash talking."*
10. Minimize *unbalanced schedules* and *avoid back-to-back games.*
11. Implement better and more frequent *screening for anabolic steroid use.* Institute *stricter punishment* for athletes who use these substances.

Recommendations for the Media to Reduce Sport Aggression

1. *Do not replay* sport aggression. Pan away from brawls.
2. *Do not glorify* aggression in sport.
3. *Glorify nonaggressive play* (great moves) and nonaggressive players (Wayne Gretzky).
4. *Do not promote rivalries* by building up opponents as enemies.
5. *Educate* athletes at all levels regarding the *consequences of anabolic steroids.*

Recommendations for Coaches to Reduce Sport Aggression

1. *Do not encourage or reward aggression* by players.
2. Give your players a *"time out"* for being aggressive.
3. *Punish* youth players who encourage their teammates to aggress.
4. *Encourage and reward nonaggressive play* (e.g., great moves, effort, unselfish play, courage, sportsmanship).
5. Have and give players *realistic expectations* for performance.
6. *Teach skills* more and scrimmage less. Institute new and challenging drills.
7. *Develop task-* rather than *ego-orientation* in your minor athletes.
8. *Encourage moral development* in minor athletes.
9. *Foster a group norm of improving oneself,* rather than beating the opposition.
10. *Never build up an opponent as the enemy.*
11. *Teach athletes to be responsible* for their actions.
12. Use an inoculation approach to *develop tolerance to frustration, annoyance, and attacks* during practice.

13. *Do not allow "trash talking."* Explain how it detracts from one's focus.
14. Teach athletes to *expect frustration, annoyance, and attack* and not to perceive these conditions as personal attacks but simply the opponents doing their jobs.
15. *Educate* players regarding the *consequences of anabolic steroid use.*

Recommendations for Parents to Reduce Sport Aggression

1. *Never encourage or reward aggression* by your child.
2. Give your child a *"time out"* for aggressive behavior, including trash talking.
3. *Reinforce nonaggressive behavior* by your child.
4. Hold up *nonaggressive models* to your child.
5. Foster *moral development* in your child.
6. Develop *task- rather than ego-orientation* in children.
7. *Never build up an opponent as the enemy.*
8. *Teach* your child *responsibility* for his or her actions.
9. Have *realistic goals* for your child's performance.
10. *Educate* your child regarding the *consequences of anabolic steroid use.*

Conclusion

Following is a brief summary of the information presented in Chapters 16 to 18 regarding aggression in sport.

1. Aggression is antinormative behavior designed to harm another living organism, physically and/or psychologically.
2. Aggression has been measured by quantifying behaviors (external approach) and by asking individuals their desire and/or intention to physically injure and/or intimidate another (internal approach). Because of measurement flaws with each approach, multiple measures are recommended for validity.
3. Aggression takes place in almost every sport, at all age levels, among both males and females, and at various levels of competition. It is especially prevalent in highly competitive sports that allow body contact.
4. Sport aggression has consequences for the recipient (injury, intimidation, and altered arousal level), the aggressor (penalization, injury, and performance outcome changes), the viewer (learning of aggression), and the sport (hurts image).
5. Ten theories were advanced to explain why aggression occurs in sport. These explanations ranged from grand theories (e.g., instinct, social learning) to middle-range theories (e.g., role theory, self-presentation) to specialized theories (e.g., retaliation). Antecedents of aggression were identified based on findings of research when each of these explanations was tested in sport settings.
6. Finally, based on the theoretically and empirically derived antecedents of aggression, various recommendations were offered for the reduction of aggression in sport and directed to sport administrators/officials, the media, coaches, and parents. It is hoped that a better understanding of sport aggression will lead to a significant reduction in this undesirable behavior.

Key Terms (in order of appearance)

relative term
absolute outcome
cognitive restructuring
desensitization

competition
rivalry
punishment
"time out" technique

ego-orientation
task-orientation

References

Bandura, A. (1997). *Self-efficacy: The exercise of control.* New York: Freeman.

Bower, G. H., & Hilgard, E. R. (1981). *Theories of Learning,* 5th ed. Englewood Cliffs, NJ: Prentice Hall.

Bredemeier, B. J., Weiss, M. R., Shields, D. L., & Shewchuk, R. M. (1986). Promoting moral growth in a summer sport camp: The implementation of theoretically grounded instructional strategies. *Journal of Moral Education, 15,* 212–220.

Corner, P. A., & Widmeyer, W. N. "Minor hockey: A social situation where the check always bounces (back)." Paper presented at the meeting of the North American Society for the Sociology of Sport, St. Louis, MO, October 1983.

Frank, M. C., & Gilovich, T. (1988). The dark side of self- and social perception: Black uniforms and aggression in professional sports. *Journal of Personality and Social Psychology, 54,* 74–85.

Gibbons, S. L., Ebbeck, V., & Weiss, M. R. (1995). Fair Play for Kids: Effects on the moral development of children in physical education. *Research Quarterly for Exercise and Sport, 66*(3), 247–255.

Lloyd, L., & Fox, K. R. "The effect of contrasting interventions on the exercise achievement orientation and motivation of adolescent girls." Paper presented at the meetings of the British Associate for the Sport Sciences, Cardiff, Wales, September 1990.

McGuire, E. J. "Antecedents of aggressive behavior in professional ice hockey." Ph.D. diss., University of Waterloo, Waterloo, ON, 1990.

McMurtry, W. R. (1974). *Investigation and inquiry into violence in amateur hockey.* Toronto-Ontario Ministry of Community and Social Services.

Romance, T. J., Weiss, M. R., & Bockoven, J. (1986). A program to promote moral development through elementary school physical education. *Journal of Teaching in Physical Education, 5,* 126–136.

Rubin, R. T. (1987). The neuroendocrinology and neurochemistry of antisocial behavior. In S. Mednick, T. Moffitt, & S. Stack (Eds.), *The causes of crime* (pp. 239–262). Cambridge, UK: Cambridge Univ. Press.

Tatum, J., & Kushner, B. (1979). *They call me assassin.* New York: Everest House.

Vaz, E. W. (1982). *The professionalization of young hockey players.* Lincoln, NE: Univ. of Nebraska Press.

Wann, D. L. "The relationship between players' names on uniforms and athletic aggression." Paper presented at the meeting of the Association for the Advancement of Applied Sport Psychology, San Diego, CA, September 1997.

Widmeyer, W. N., & Birch, J. S. (1979). The relationship between aggression and performance outcome in ice hockey. *Canadian Journal of Applied Sport Sciences, 4,* 91–94.

Widmeyer, W. N., & Birch, J. S. (1984). Aggression in profession ice hockey: A strategy for success or reaction to failure? *Journal of Psychology, 117,* 77–84.

Widmeyer, W. N., & McGuire, E. J. (1996). Frequency of competition and aggression in professional ice hockey. *International Journal of Sport Psychology, 26.*

Widmeyer, W. N., McGuire, E. J., & Dorsch, K. (1994). Aggression. *Sport Psychology Training Bulletin, 4*(5) 1–8.

19

The Revolution of Women in Sport

Barbara Osborne
The University of North Carolina at Chapel Hill

- This chapter develops enhanced understanding of the history of women's participation in sport.
- The chronological history is developed to modern times, facilitating increased awareness of women's current opportunities for participation in sport.
- The physiological similarities and differences between male and female athletes are discussed.

We are in the midst of a revolution—a revolution of girls and women who are exercising their right to be physically active and compete in the world of sport. Recent successes of American women in the Women's World Cup and Olympic Games has focused the public's attention on creating opportunity for women to excel in sport. To understand fully the current phenomenon, it is important to look at the history of women's participation in athletics. Although women have always sought competitive opportunities, the dominant culture generally sought to keep women out of sport. The most cited reasons to prevent women from participating have been threats associated with exercise and women's ability to reproduce. Physiological differences between men and women do exist, but no physical differences prevent women from participating. Tremendous strides have been taken, particularly in the last two decades, to overcome the historical barriers and appreciate the physical benefits of athletic participation for women. This chapter focuses on the history of women's participation in sport and the physiological benefits of sport participation.

A History of Women in Sport

The name of this chapter was originally Evolution of Women in Sport. It is not women in sport who have evolved, however, but the dominant culture that is coming full circle to once again accept women as equal. More than 3,500 years ago, women in ancient civiliza-

Women have made great strides over the last twenty-five years in the race for equality in sport.

tions were competing in sport. Partnership societies, where both men and women were valued for their contributions, were the norm. Women had equal status with men and participated in all activities. On the island of Crete, one of the last existing partnership societies, women drove chariots, hunted, and engaged in bull grappling, an event that involved vaulting over a large, live bull. Even before the ancient Olympic Games, women competed in an athletic festival called the Herean Games, honoring the goddess Hera. For over 1000 years, footraces were the most popular events for women and girls in Greece (Costa & Guthrie, 1994).

Between 4300 and 600 B.C., patriarchal societies, structured with male leadership and control, began to dominate. The ancient Greeks worshipped goddesses, but mortal sportswomen were heralded as well. In Sparta, both girls and boys were physically educated and trained. The Spartan philosophy was that strong, healthy women would produce strong, healthy babies for the society. In Athens, however, the culture dictated that women avoid strenuous activity and spend their time making themselves and their surroundings beautiful (Costa & Guthrie, 1994).

In medieval times, the civilized world had evolved into a racial and cultural unity that was primarily influenced by the Roman Catholic Church and the feudal system. Women's participation in sport varied according to social class, but women of all groups generally competed in some form of physical activity. Women of the nobility participated with men in archery, and they ice skated, jousted, and played a sort of hand tennis. In contrast, the women of the lower social groups used most of their physical strength to complete the chores of daily survival. These women found ways to satisfy their natural desire for competition, however, in contests at fairs and religious festivals.

Info Box

Until the sixteenth century, sport participation and competition was a valued and accepted form of expression for women.

With the emergence of Protestant sects in the 1500s, physical competition began to be viewed as sinful. Psychologists suggest that Puritans disapproved of sport because it provided means for spontaneous expression of undisciplined impulses (Oglesby, 1978). By the end of the sixteenth century, only women of nobility had the means and approval to participate in sporting activities.

Seventeenth- and eighteenth-century society considered women as ornaments to be pampered. By this time, society had excluded women from the workforce. Women had no property rights, no ownership rights, and legally did not exist as persons separate from their husbands or fathers. Sport had evolved to include highly structured games with rules (Costa & Guthrie, 1994). The activities that men and women engaged in were still determined more by social class and rural or urban location than by gender. Cricket, boxing, bull baiting, horse racing, and rowing were the preferred sports of the upper class, and the lower classes enjoyed cockfighting, bowling, billiards, shuffleboard, and football (soccer). The most widespread athletic competition for women was still foot racing, and races for women were much more frequently held than were races for men. Women also competed in early football (soccer) matches, with teams composed of married women competing against unmarried women, or women of one town competing against the women of another town (Costa & Guthrie, 1994).

The first known female professional athletes emerged during the late 1700s. Footraces and rowing competitions often featured significant cash prizes. Margaret Evans of North Wales earned a living as a wrestler. She began her career wrestling women but soon took on men. Her career ended when her promoters could no longer find a man to wrestle her, and no person would bet against her. Boxing matches between women were also popular during this time and often drew much larger crowds than matches between men (Costa & Guthrie, 1994).

In the newly established American colonies, women were scarce, and physical stamina and prowess were valued. Women worked alongside men, and only the fittest survived. Struggles for survival left little time for recreation or socialization. As communities became more established, life assumed a pattern similar to that in England. Cities formed and grew, and having a social life became a possibility because people were less isolated. Dancing was the primary recreation of the upper class, and horse and foot racing maintained popularity. In the Puritan colonies, however, little if any recreation was ever permitted.

In the early 1800s, life in rural American was physically demanding for both men and women. Women were actively engaged in the survival of their farms and families, but they still engaged in recreational activities such as horseback riding and skating. Urban women of means, on the other hand, were frail and sickly as a result of the cultural restrictions placed on their activities. The dominant cultural standard, known as the Cult of Domesticity, defined and promoted women's roles as mothers and moral guardians of society. Women were thought to be physically and mentally inferior to men but to have superior moral standards. They were placed on pedestals for their high morals, but this elevated status actually signaled a historical step backward for women. In London and Paris, Mary Wollstonecraft, an early feminist, advocated for the education of women and promoted independence and equality. Wollstonecraft criticized the highly restricted and idealized place that women held in society. Wollstonecraft's ideas were embraced by educators in the United States (Oglesby, 1978).

During the mid 1800s, the women's suffrage movement grew. Political debate about freedom and the rights of slaves also spawned the first feminists, who sought freedom for women from the Cult of Domesticity. Women became politically active and joined abolitionist groups. Amelia Bloomer led the attempt at dress reform for women—cutting off her long skirts to knee length and exposing pantalets that covered the lower leg. Feminists also sought birth control and fought for better conditions for working women in the mills. They began to demand entry into higher education and male professions, such as teaching and medicine. Women's schools were founded, including the Troy Female Seminary in New York and Mt. Holyoke seminary in Massachusetts. To combat the generally poor health of women, the founders of these institutions encouraged their students to participate in gymnastics, dancing, horseback riding, and walking.

Historically, whenever women have made forward strides, the dominant culture has fought vigorously to make them step back. Opponents of women's education argued that college was too strenuous for women, that overstudy would give girls brain fever. They also claimed that such mind stress would make women too weak to have children (Oglesby, 1978). Ironically, two men undertook the task of disproving these arguments. Matthew Vassar founded Vassar College in Poughkeepsie, New York, in 1865, and Henry Fowle Durant founded Wellesley College in Wellesley, Massachusetts, in 1875. Both men used sport as part of their plans to show that young women could engage in college work equal to that of young men. The curricula at Vassar and Wellesley included gymnastics, bowling, riding, boating, swimming, tennis, and ice skating.

Physical activity did improve and maintain the health of the students; however, the general routine of exercises did not hold their interest. In 1876, Vassar College allowed students to play a sport in place of physical education. By the 1890s, team sports were an established part of the physical education curriculum. Basketball, volleyball, and field hockey became the dominant component of college physical education programs. In 1896, the first women's intercollegiate basketball game took place between the University of California–Berkeley and Stanford University. Men were not allowed to spectate. Women's participation in physical activity and competition had gained acceptance, but it was still not socially acceptable for men to see women engaging in these activities (Costa & Guthrie, 1994).

In the late 1800s, sports for women not only were accepted at women's colleges but also were gaining acceptance in philanthropic agencies, private clubs, and community programs. After centuries of restrictions, there appeared to be a frenzy of sport activities among women. The seeds of change had been planted, and the more women did, the more they wished to do (Oglesby, 1978). The invention of the bicycle seemed to symbolize this revolution of activity. Both men and women rode and enjoyed the bicycle from its inception. For women, the bicycle also brought mobility; women could travel much further and faster by bicycle than on foot, thereby expanding their potential experiences. Although naysayers proclaimed that bicycle riding was physically harmful for women, women rode in exhibitions and even formed professional cycling teams.

The end of the 1800s brought a higher level of organization and sophistication to women's sport. Women's sport clubs were established, such as the Staten Island Ladies Athletic Club. Women regularly competed in darts, archery, golf, and tennis. In 1885, a national golf championship for women was held, and in 1887, women competed in their first national tennis championship. At the same time, Baron Pierre de Coubertin was reestablishing the most visible display of athletic competition in the modern world. In 1896, the first modern **Olympic Games** were held in Athens, Greece. De Coubertin sought to model his modern Olympic games after the ancient Greek festivals. All Olympic events were for men only, and de Coubertin justified keeping women out of the competition based on the history of the ancient Olympics as gender-segregated events. Nevertheless, a woman named Melpomene requested permission to enter the marathon. Olympic officials denied her entry, but Melpomene ran the distance from Marathon to Athens anyway, in 4½ hours, accompanied by cyclists to witness the event (Cohen, 1993).

Info Box

Through the 1800s, female participation in physical activity gained increasing acceptance in social organizations.

Pierre de Coubertin actively lobbied to keep women out of the Olympic games. He proclaimed that women who engaged in sport destroyed their feminine charm and that allowing females to compete would feminize sport, diminishing its value to the men who competed. Ironically, it was de Coubertin's poor control over the management of the games that allowed the first female participants. Although de Coubertin represented the

Olympic philosophy, it was the organizing committee of the host city that set the Olympic schedule. Local organizers of the Paris games allowed twelve women to compete in golf and tennis at the II Olympiad in 1900. Archery was offered for women in St. Louis in 1904. Women's opportunities were greatly expanded in London in 1908, as they competed in skating, tennis, archery, gymnastics, and aquatics. The 1912 games in Helsinki limited women to tennis, gymnastics, and swimming. All Olympic competition for women was limited to exhibition status, and female competitors were not recognized as Olympians. Both male and female participants of the early games were wealthy individuals who had the time and the means to travel (Cohen, 1993).

In response to de Coubertin's campaign to keep women out of the Olympics, a French woman, Alice Miliat, founded the federation Sportive Feminine Internationale and organized the Women's World Games. International Olympic organizers had consistently refused to add official women's track and field events to the schedule, so Miliat provided a platform for women to display their competitive abilities in the most traditional women's competitive events. The first Women's World Games in Paris were a resounding success, with more than 20,000 spectators on the first day. The success of the Games also attracted the attention of the International Olympic Committee (IOC). The IOC desired sole control over Olympic-format competition on the international level. They responded by offering the first official women's events in the Olympic program in 1924, although limiting women's participation in the traditional exhibition sports.

Track and field events for women were officially added to the Olympic program in 1928, and women were allowed to compete in an 800-meter race. The all-male IOC continued to lobby against expanding the women's program and recruited the media to spread its propaganda. The media reported that five women dropped out of the race, and five more collapsed at the finish line. In fact, nine women started the race, all finished, none collapsed from exhaustion at the finish line, and the winner set a world record. Nonetheless, the IOC used the gross misrepresentation by the media to declare that the 800-meter event was too demanding for women and dropped the event from the Olympic program. The longest track event contested by women in the Olympic Games for the next 32 years would be the 200 meters (Cohen, 1993).

In the United States, the Roaring 20s offered prosperity and increased leisure time, making sport possible for many women. In 1919, women had legally obtained the right to vote. Clothing became less restrictive, with short bloomers for active sports and one-piece brief bathing suits. The accomplishments of individual athletes drew worldwide attention. Suzanne Lenglen changed the game of tennis, bringing functional clothing, a short hairdo, and a complete game to the court. Lenglen was as well known as Babe Ruth or Jack Dempsey and drew larger crowds at Wimbledon than any of the male competitors. Helen Willis of California raised the competitive standard in tennis in the United States. Her strong serves and powerful ground strokes kept her undefeated in singles matches for 5 years. The Lenglen-Willis match at Cannes in 1925 was world news, with Lenglen winning the match, 6–3, 8–6 (Smith, 1998). In 1926, Gertrude Ederle also captured the world's attention by swimming the English Channel, bettering the men's record by 2 hours.

Acceptance of the twentieth-century sportswoman also brought exploitation. Newspapers, real estate firms, and advertising agencies discovered that photographs of athletic women in their wet, one-piece swimsuits increased sales significantly. Women physical educators criticized the inappropriate use of women in sport for "cheesecake" advertising. In 1920, the Association of Directors of Physical Education for College Women denounced intercollegiate athletics as leading to commercialization and professionalization. Women's competitive sport took a step backward as the female leaders promoted a new athletic philosophy encouraging broad-based participation and denouncing elite competition. In 1923, a Women's Division of the National Amateur Athletic Federation was formed. It stressed sport opportunities for all girls, protection from exploitation, enjoyment of sports, female leadership, health, and the necessity for international competition to be approved by the federation. Women's intercollegiate athletics competition was virtually eliminated in favor of "playdays," a format in which teams were formed at random with members of every school represented on each team. The Committee on Women's Athletics and the Women's Division of the National Amateur Athletic Federation supported these events and opposed programs such as the Olympic Games.

The 1930s brought renewed interest in sport for the average woman. City leagues, industrial leagues, and public recreation programs provided more opportunities for participation. Industry embraced sport as a means of improving the health of the workforce, lowering absence rates, and increasing loyalty to employers. Team sports developed cooperation and team spirit that would carry over to the production line. Sponsoring women's athletic teams also demonstrated a company's progressive attitude and was used as a public relations tool. Basketball was the most visible of the industrial league sports. Many girls had played high school basketball and wished to continue playing as adults. Textile mills in the south began to hire women with athletic skills to enhance the performance of their teams. The best female athletes in the industrial leagues were semiprofessionals, who were paid regular wages while they were training and on competitive road trips. The salaries of female athlete-employees were often higher than those of the average worker.

The industrial leagues also recognized the sex appeal of their women's teams. Women's bodies were used for their publicity value. The company provided tight-fitting uniforms with the company name prominently displayed across the chest. When the Dallas Cyclones basketball team shortened their uniform shorts, attendance increased from an average of 150 spectators per game to over 5,000 viewers. Savvy industrialists recognized the commercial value associated with flashy displays of the female body and used sex appeal for product promotion. Although women had increased opportunities to participate and financially benefit from their participation in sport, recognition and acceptance were related to their physical appearance and ability to conform to the sexual stereotype of femininity rather than to their athletic achievements (Costa & Guthrie, 1994).

Throughout the 1940s, women continued to break barriers. Kathryn Dewey led her four-man bobsled team past the all-male competition to the U.S. National Championship title. Instead of promoting increased participation for women, the male leadership of the bobsled federation immediately passed a rule to prevent women from further competition, thus ensuring no further humiliation of the male competitors. Women were also breaking barriers in education as they began to be admitted at public colleges and universities. Golf continued at the forefront of women's sport in the United States, and the first national collegiate golf tournament, organized by women's physical educators at Ohio State University, took place in 1941. At the same time, black colleges embraced women's athletics and were the first to offer female athletes work-study grants to pursue their education.

World War II had a dramatic impact on American society. Women poured into the workforce to replace the male workers who went to war and to increase the production of goods necessary to support the war effort. In 1943, Philip K. Wrigley, owner of the Chicago Cubs, formed the All-American Girls Professional Baseball League. The league was conceived as a substitute for men's baseball while the professional male athletes were in military service. It was a success, with more than 500 women participating over 12 years and drawing more than a million fans. But the success of the league was not without its setbacks for women in sport. The owners of the teams were not interested in developing women's competitive skills and creating a quality baseball product, but rather in providing a product that would conform to the customs, values, and mores of mainstream Americans. Players were measured more by their appearance than by their ability. Only healthy, attractive, all-American girls were signed to contracts. These athletes were required to attend mandatory charm school lessons at night, where they learned how to apply makeup and to drink tea properly. They were not allowed to wear shorts or slacks in public, although the uniforms they were required to wear had extremely short skirts and were not at all functional for playing ball. Ironically, while the league owners wanted their players to be feminine, they also demanded much more from them physically than they expected from male players. The women played games every day, with a squad of up to sixteen players. Everyone played all positions, and they often played hurt. They were also expected to be spectacular, not just make the out or win the game.

The 1950s brought affluence back to the American public. Colleges and universities experienced a huge increase in the number of women submitting applications, and women were able to obtain a college degree with only slightly more difficulty than men of this time. However, college women of this decade seemed to lack interest in sport. Society had embraced a pseudo-return of the Cult of Domesticity—women were expected to get married and be good wives, mothers, and homemakers. Even though more women than ever were obtaining college degrees, women's career options were still extremely limited. If a college woman was interested in sport, her only career option was to become a physical education teacher. Social standards also dictated which sports were acceptable (ladylike) and unacceptable (unladylike) for women to participate in. The ladylike sports were swimming, gymnastics, riding, skiing, and tennis. Softball, basketball, and track were considered unladylike. The feminity of athletes participating in these sports was questioned, which discouraged many from participating. The International Amateur Athletic Federation also chose to support the popular social conception that female athletes were not feminine by instituting a sex test. Beginning in 1968, female Olympians were required to prove that they were biologically women to be allowed to compete. No test designed to demonstrate "masculinity" was ever required of male athletes.

The 1960s represented significant social change in American society. Students protested the war in Vietnam and challenged traditional societal values. The sixties also brought change to the women's Olympic program. In 1960, the women's 800-meter event was reinstated, and in 1964, volleyball was introduced as the first women's team sport in the Olympic Games. In the United States, the Committee on Women's Athletics had absorbed the Women's Division of the National Amateur Athletic Federation and was reorganized as the Division of Girls and Women's Sports (DGWS). At the same time, the United States Olympic Development Committee organized a Women's Board to increase opportunities for women and girls in athletics. Together, DGWS and the Women's Board of the Development Committee of the USOC sponsored a series of National Institutes on Sport. Sessions promoted the latest coaching strategies and fostered interest in developing higher level skills. These workshops signified a turning point for women's sport. As physical educators who had attended the workshops conducted statewide programs of their own, a network of skilled female coaches was developed; they used their knowledge and skills to develop highly trained, competitive athletes. As female athletes became more skilled, they sought more opportunities to compete.

Until the late 1960s, the theme of DGWS had been a sport for every girl and every girl in a sport. This philosophy promoted broad-based participation and sacrificed high-level competition. In 1967, DGWS formed a Commission on Intercollegiate Athletics for Women to provide a framework for appropriate intercollegiate athletic opportunities for women, including national championships. As a result, the Association for Intercollegiate Athletics for Women (AIAW) was formed in 1971 to provide guidelines for women's competitive athletics and conduct national championships. The AIAW sought to be a student-centered, education-oriented model for intercollegiate athletics competition. In the first year, 276 institutions joined, and membership grew to 971 schools. More than 750 state, regional, and national competitions were held for women each year in nineteen different sports at three competitive levels. The organization recognized the abuses they perceived in men's intercollegiate athletics and struggled to create safeguards against those abuses within women's sport. The AIAW fought the NCAA lobby against Title IX and helped to define the Title IX regulations.

Throughout the 1970s, the AIAW sought to increase competitive opportunities for college women. Previously, the physical education department, not the athletics program, sponsored the typical women's college team. The coach was often a physical education teacher who volunteered her own time, and athletes often provided their own equipment and uniforms and paid their own travel expenses. The teams played a limited five- or six-game schedule. Players set up the playing field and cleaned up afterward. The AIAW struggled with the ideal of having the right to develop programs in the best interest of female athletes and the pressure to develop programs identical to those that the athletics department offered for men.

In 1972, Congress passed **Title IX** of the Educational Amendments Act. Heralded as the single most significant piece of legislation to affect the direction of women in sport, Title IX prohibits gender discrimination in education in one simple sentence: "No person in the United States shall, on the basis of sex, be excluded from participation in, be denied the benefits of, or be subjected to discrimination under any education program or activity receiving Federal financial assistance" (U.S. Department of Health, Education and Welfare, 1975.) The NCAA lobbied Congress to exclude intercollegiate athletics from Title IX jurisdiction. Senator John Tower of Texas authored an amendment to prevent intercollegiate athletics programs from having to comply with the act. When this failed, a second draft of the amendment tried to exclude revenue sports from Title IX jurisdiction. The Senate-House conference committee defeated the amendment, arguing that the department of Health, Education and Welfare was best qualified to consider the nature of intercollegiate sports while developing Title IX regulations. The first legal challenge to Title IX was brought by the NCAA on behalf of its members. In *NCAA v. Califano,* the NCAA sought relief for invalidation of Title IX regulations with respect to sex discrimination in athletics. Ironically, after using every legal means available to prevent application of Title IX to intercollegiate athletics, the NCAA used the threat of Title IX enforcement to gain control of women's intercollegiate sport.

By 1981, the accomplishments of the AIAW were a serious threat to the power structure and status quo of intercollegiate athletics as governed by the NCAA. The NCAA had been content to let women's teams exist within the physical education framework. They lobbied in Congress against Title IX out of concern that funds needed to support women's programs would drain resources from the men's programs. The leaders of the AIAW advocated radical ideals contrary to the standard operations of the NCAA, such as legislation to provide only need-based financial aid to student-athletes, instead of athletics scholarships. During the 1981 convention, the NCAA leadership convinced athletics directors that compliance with Title IX required that men's and women's athletics programs be combined. To gain control of the women's intercollegiate athletics programs, the NCAA voted to offer women's championships of their own. The NCAA offered to host women's championships without an increase in institutional membership dues, whereas the AIAW was supported almost entirely by a separate membership fee structure. The NCAA also reimbursed schools for their expenses incurred in championships competition, but schools were required to pay their own way to compete in AIAW championships. Within 6 months, the AIAW experienced a 20 percent loss of membership and a 32 percent drop in championship participation and lost almost half of their Division I members. In 1982, the AIAW voted to disband.

Globally, women's opportunities in the Olympic movement continued to grow. The 1984 Games in Los Angeles were known as the "Olympiad of the American Woman" because the Eastern bloc boycott allowed American women to establish many "firsts." Although Melpomene had completed the Olympic marathon almost 100 years earlier, Joan Benoit won the "first" women's Olympic marathon in 2:24:52. Women's events were added at 3000 meters on the track and 49 miles in cycling and in synchronized swimming. Valerie Brisco-Hooks became the first woman to win both the 200-meter and 400-meter events. The women's basketball team won its first gold medal for USA, and a woman served as an official for an Olympic basketball game.

Financial prosperity, increased leisure time and money for sport, growing concern for development of Olympic athletes, and the approval of national collegiate championships contributed to the impression that our culture was beginning to accept women's sports (Costa & Guthrie, 1994). At the same time that American women were capturing the attention of the world in the 1984 Olympic Games, however, the Supreme Court made a decision that would set back the progress of girls sports in the schools. The Court ruled that the word "program" used in Title IX regulations should be defined as any subunit of an institution. Under this interpretation, if a particular department within an institution did not receive federal funding, that department would not be required to comply with the requirements of Title IX, even though the institution received federal funds. Several colleges immediately cut scholarships for their female athletes, and coaches and athletes who had filed suits under Title IX had their complaint files closed. This was only a temporary setback for most women's programs because the legislature stepped up to protect the intent of Title IX and include application on an institution-wide basis by passing the Civil Rights Restoration Act in 1987. This act also restored strength to the administrative enforcement of Title

IX by allowing the Office of Civil Rights to effectively investigate and impose penalties on institutions that are not in compliance. During the 1990s, Title IX became even more effective, as female students started filing lawsuits and the courts determined that they could be awarded monetary damages.

Throughout the 1990s, unprecedented numbers of women engaged in sport. The effects of Title IX are far-reaching because girls have had the opportunity to grow in sport from youth leagues, through scholastic programs, intercollegiate programs, and professional leagues. In 1992, the 10,000-meter racewalk was added to the women's Olympic program, not equaling the men's competition at 20k and 50k, yet providing an additional sporting opportunity. Global attention was focused on the 1996 Olympic Games in Atlanta with the success of American women in team competition. Team USA brought home the gold in basketball, soccer, and the first softball competition. The number of girls participating in high school sports in 1996 increased to 2.37 million, up from only 300,000 in 1972, the year Title IX was enacted. Women's intercollegiate athletics programs continue to grow, with 2,239 new women's sports programs added between 1978 and 1996. However, 581 women's programs also were eliminated during that time, resulting in a net gain of 1,658 programs (Sabo, 1998). The 1999 Women's World Cup established new records for spectators of a women-only sporting event. The largest crowd ever for a women's only event, 9,185 spectators watched the USA defeat China in the championship match. The 1990s also saw the birth of a successful women's professional basketball league with the Women's National Basketball Association and the introduction of women's professional football. These gains in professional women's sport are counterbalanced, however, by the short life span of the American Basketball League and the Women's Professional Softball League.

Info Box

The diverse sporting opportunities available to women have resulted in widespread growth in participation.

Examination of the history of women's participation in sport reveals several themes that were used to keep women from competing. Primarily, women were told that it was unhealthy to participate in rigorous physical activity. Research has contributed significantly to dispelling the myths that participation in sport is physically dangerous for women.

Physiology

Historically, women have been portrayed as victims of their own **physiology.** Women have been told that they are weak and inferior and that exercise will damage their reproductive organs (Cohen, 1993). Consequently, many women relinquished power over their own bodies to the social order—they believed that they were weak and powerless. Over the years, women have learned that they are not inherently frail but that subordinate cultural roles have made them weak. Through that knowledge, they have grown stronger physically as well as socially.

Physiologically there is more difference within each sex than there are between the sexes (Harris, 1973). Height, weight, shoulder and hip width measurements, muscular development, and levels of testosterone and estrogen all overlap substantially when comparing men and women. Men's sexual organs are external and vulnerable to injury, whereas women's sex organs are internal and well protected. Interestingly, the health risks of sport participation related to reproductive health have never been advanced as a reason for men to forgo activity.

Before age 12, virtually no sex-related differences exist in the physiology of boys and girls. Up to age 10, girls grow and develop muscular strength and speed faster than boys and are 12 to 18 months ahead of boys in the maturation of bone tissue (Holloway & Baechle, 1990). Although the skeletal and muscular structures of boys and girls are similar, girls grow and slightly develop earlier than boys. Differences have been found in strength. In a study of prekindergarten children, girls showed significantly less upper body strength than boys of the same age and size (Holloway & Baechle, 1990). Although there is no physiological reason for girls to be weaker than boys at this age, there is a cultural impact. The daily activities in which girls engage from an early age generally limit their upper body development. Another explanation is that society has low expectations for girls' physical performance, so girls do not give priority to developing physical skill (Rozdilsky, Wilkinson, & Williamson, 1992).

During puberty, girls mature faster than boys. As a result, boys' transition is longer, which accounts for larger body size overall. The changes in the testosterone/estrogen balance in puberty also result in greater muscle mass for most men and a higher percentage body fat for most women (Wells, 1991). During puberty, girls' sport involvement drops dramatically. There is no known physiological reason for this phenomenon, which is known as the puberty barrier. Psychologists speculate that this rejection of sport is due to role conflicts, and others suggest that fewer sports opportunities exist for adolescent girls, making participation more difficult (Anshel, 1994).

At maturity, women's performance is generally lower than men's performance in most physiological measurements. Body composition has an impact on physical performance because higher ratios of muscle mass to body fat generally result in increased strength and power. Body fat is essential for survival, but sex-specific fat, which is necessary for female reproduction, is four times that required for men. Percentage body fat for the average woman ranges from 20 to 30 percent, while men's percentage of body fat ranges from 15 to 18 percent (Wilmore, 1983). The percentage of fat in the female is an important factor in coaching, teaching, and implementing conditioning programs. Work capacity, endurance, and athletic performance are all affected by the high fat-to-muscle ratio. Understanding the physiological need for women to have a higher body fat percentage is critical for coaches of female athletes. Many coaches have unrealistic notions about the relationship between body fat and performance and set unhealthy weight goals for their athletes. Female athletes should not be encouraged to reduce body fat to levels similar to those of male athletes—dangerously low levels of body fat have serious health implications for women.

Aerobic capacity measures the ability to use oxygen to provide energy for physical tasks. Because women generally have smaller hearts, smaller lungs, lower hemoglobin counts, and less muscle mass than men, their aerobic capacity test results are also lower. It is interesting to note that the average woman has an aerobic capacity approximately 15–20 percent lower than that of the average man, but the difference in aerobic capacity of male and female world record holders drops to just 8–10 percent difference (Cohen, 1993). These statistics indicate that lifestyle probably has more to do with the differences in performance than biology.

Anaerobic threshold is the percentage of aerobic capacity that can be sustained for a period of time without substantially increasing lactic acid. Men and women with similar training generally reach anaerobic threshold at the same percentage of maximum aerobic capacity. However, because women generally have a lower aerobic capacity, their absolute work rate is also lower. Similarly, because women generally have lower anaerobic capacity, their ability to achieve maximum high-intensity effort for a short period of time is lower, due to lower muscle mass, although there is no difference between the muscle concentrations of enzymes per unit of muscle of men and women (Cohen, 1993).

Strength differences between men and women are considerably greater than the differences in aerobic and anaerobic power. Women have only half the upper body strength of men and up to 80 percent of their lower body strength. Most of this difference is related to the size of the muscle. The quality of muscle tissues is identical in men and women, as is the distribution of muscle fiber type. When strength is expressed relative to body mass and lean body mass, the difference in strength between men and women is greatly reduced (Holloway and Baechle, 1990). Lesser muscle strength should not prohibit females' participation in sport, but accommodating the difference can make sport a more rewarding experience for female participants. For example, in basketball creating a smaller, lighter ball for the women's game has allowed for more control, faster play, less fatigue, and a more exciting game.

Men and women's physiological **response to exercise** is identical. During exercise, both men and women experience increased heart rate, cardiac output, ventilation, and metabolism. Through training, men and women can increase their aerobic and anaerobic capacity, strength, speed, and muscle mass and decrease body fat. Lower testosterone levels limit women's ability to develop excessive muscle mass, but regular training decreases the differences between men's and women's performance (Wells, 1991). Although in general women achieve lower levels of performance than men, it is inappropriate to compare men's and women's sport performances. Lightweight boxers and wrestlers are not viewed as less skilled than their heavyweight counterparts, and women should not be looked on as inferior for having smaller bodies or less strength. Females need to be encouraged to participate and compete and not be compared to male standards of achievement.

The idea that exercise will damage female reproductive organs or somehow prohibit fertility has existed from the beginning of time. Only the ancient Spartans seem to have recognized the need for women to be healthy to bear healthy children. Modern societies have tried to shelter women from physical exercise so that they will have enough strength to bear children. This faulty logic was not really questioned until the nineteenth century. It is known that girls who begin training at a young age experience delays in the onset of puberty and menstruation. There is no evidence that this delay, typically of 6 months to 2½ years, has any effect on reproductive functions. Once they experience menarche, most athletes report that menstruation has no effect on performance. Some athletes may experience retention of "water weight" and its physical implications—bloating and slight weight increase—which can have an impact on performance. Some studies have shown that regular exercise decreases the incidence of painful menstrual periods. Other studies have shown that athletes who are younger, are highly motivated, train intensively, or have particularly low body fat experience disruptions in their regular cycle, resulting in oligomenorrhea or in loss of menstruation, known as amenorrhea (Wells, 1991; Sanborn, 1986). Amenorrhea is not a convenient by-product of training but a serious medical condition. Most women regain normal menstrual function when they decrease their training intensity; however, prolonged lack of menstruation may result in loss of bone mineral density, or osteoporosis. Osteoporosis is a gradual loss of bone calcium that occurs with age. Ironically, physical activity actually decreases the rate of bone density loss in postmenopausal women. Menopause, the natural cessation of menses, has no impact on the ability to exercise (Wells, 1991).

Women of the early 1900s were often confined to bed rest while pregnant, but studies show that women who exercise during pregnancy increase their fitness level with little or no risk to themselves or the fetus. Pregnant women experience physiological changes in most of their body systems: increased blood volume, cardiac output, ventilation, heart rate, and metabolic rate. It is generally agreed that exercise should be of low to moderate intensity and that pregnant women should avoid contact or high-risk sports. There is no consensus on how moderate the exercise should be or how long it should be engaged in (Sady, 1989).

Contrary to the historical belief that sport was unhealthy for women, the health benefits of physical activity are now well documented. For example, a 1997 study conducted by the President's Council on Physical Fitness concluded that sports participation improves the physical health of girls in terms of increased resistance to cold and flu, decreased blood pressure and cholesterol, and lowered risk for obesity and osteoporosis. Recent studies indicate that aerobic workouts of only 20 minutes, three times per week decrease the risk of cardiovascular disease. Over a women's reproductive lifetime, 1 to 3 hours of exercise a week can bring a 20 to 30 percent reduction in the risk of breast cancer, and 4 or more hours of exercise a week can reduce the risk almost 60 percent (Women's Sports Facts, 1995).

Pierre de Coubertin, the founder of the Olympic Games, believed that if women could not play on equal terms with men, they should not be allowed to compete at all. Although some women are able to compete with men in the same arena (e.g. racecar drivers, jockeys, equestrians, ultradistance performers), because of physiological differences it is unlikely that women can compete equally with men in activities that are related to speed and strength. With increased opportunities, however, the gap between men's and women's physical performance will continue to narrow. Although physiology is partially responsible for the variation in men's and women's performance, psychological and sociological influences also have significant impact on physical performance (Hudson, 1994). These influences are discussed in detail in Chapter 20.

Conclusion

The revolution of women in sport is ongoing; it is a revolution of participation, and the number of women participating in organized sport, fitness, and recreation is continually increasing. Society has also accepted, and indeed now promotes, the health benefits of women's physical activity. But women have not achieved equity or equality in sport yet. Although Title IX was enacted almost 30 years ago, only one-third of college athletes are women, and less than 25 percent of the money spent on college athletics is for women's programs. The percentage of female coaches and athletics administrators continues to decline, and the salaries of women's team coaches are still significantly lower than those for coaches of men's teams. The NCAA, football coaches associations, and other political action groups, such as Common Cause, continue to lobby for changes in the regulation of Title IX. Women's sport growth through traditional organizations such as the Olympics is agonizingly slow, and with few opportunities for women in leadership positions within these organizations, more rapid growth is unlikely. Female athletes continue to be compared to their male counterparts. Once the comparisons have stopped, when women are comfortable with the bodies and are judged by their achievement, the evolution of women in sport will be complete and equality will be achieved.

Key Terms (in order of appearance)

Olympic Games	aerobic capacity	response to exercise
Title IX	anaerobic threshold	
physiology	strength differences	

References

Anshel, M. H. (1994). *Sport psychology: From theory to practice.* Scottsdale, AR: Gersuch Scarsbrick.

Costa, D. M., & Guthrie, S. R. (1994). *Women and sport: Interdisciplinary perspectives.* Champaign, IL: Human Kinetics.

Cohen, G. L. (1993). *Women in sport: Issues and controversies.* Newbury Park, CA: Sage.

Harris, D. V. (1973, March–April). Women in sports: Some misconceptions. *Journal of Sports Medicine,* 15–17.

Harris, D. V. (1987). The female athlete. In J. R. May & M. J. Asken (Eds.), *Sport psychology* (pp. 99–115). Costa Mesa, CA: PMA.

Holloway, J. B., & Baechle, T. R. (1990). Strength training for female athletes: A review of selected aspects. *Sports Medicine, 9,* 216–228.

Hudson, J. L. (1994). It's mostly a matter of metric. In D. M. Costa & S. R. Guthrie (Eds.), *Women and sport: Interdisciplinary perspectives* (p. 1435). Champaign, IL: Human Kinetics Publishers.

Ogelsby, C. (1978). *Women and sport: From myth to reality.* Philadelphia: Lea & Febiger.

Rozdilsky, R., Wilkinson, S., and Williamson, K. "The perpetuation of sexism through physical fitness testing." Paper presented at AAHPERD annual meeting, Indianapolis, IN, 1992.

Sabo, D. (1998). *Gender equity report card.* New York: Women's Sports Foundation.

Sady, S. P., & Carpenter, M. W. (1989). Aerobic exercise during pregnancy: Special considerations. *Sports Medicine, 7,* 357–375.

Sanborn, C. H. (1986). Athletic amenorrhea. In *Female endurance athletes* (pp. 125-148). Champaign, IL: Human Kinetics Publishers.

Smith, L. (1998). *Nike is a goddess.* New York: Atlantic Monthly.

U.S. Department of Health, Education and Welfare, Office for Civil Rights. (1975). Final Title IX Regulations.

Wells, C. L. (1991). *Women, sport and performance: A physiological perspective,* 2nd ed. Champaign, IL: Human Kinetics.

Wilmore, J. B. (1983). Body composition in sport and exercise: Directions for future research. *Medicine and Science in Sports and Exercise, 15*(1), 21–31.

Women's Sports Facts. (1995, September 25). Compiled by the Women's Sports Foundation. Available: www.womenssportsfoundation.org

20

Psychosocial Issues and the Female Athlete

Diane E. Stevens
Brock University

Barbara Osborne and Jamie Robbins
The University of North Carolina at Chapel Hill

- This chapter details the sociocultural influences on female sport participation.
- The chapter provides a discussion about the influence of masculinization of the female athlete and the concern that homosexuality has on perceptions and participation.
- We examine the perceptual influences of females on sport participation.
- We discuss many differences in gender on achievement orientation and expectations.

A recent Nike commercial pitted Mia Hamm against Michael Jordan in soccer, basketball, tennis, sprints, and Tae Kwon Do while the song "Anything you can do, I can do better" was heard in the background. This advertisement demonstrates the strides that women's athletics have made in the past few years.

Not only is the female athlete more recognized and accepted in today's athletic world, but also women have broken down barriers in sports traditionally considered to be "men's only." Janet Guthrie became the first woman to race in the Indianapolis 500 in 1977. Goalie Manon Rheaume became the first female to play in the National Hockey League. Close to 800 high school female athletes are now competing in football (Sports Illustrated, 1996). In 1997, the National Basketball Association hired two female referees to officiate in the league. Finally, in 1998 women's ice hockey became an Olympic sport, which further challenged the dichotomy between masculine and feminine sports. Sports are not just for the boys anymore.

Chapter 19 outlined the historical and physiological differences attributed to sport and gender. The physiological approach to examining differences between men and women was identified as too narrow because it assumes that a unidimensional factor (i.e., biology) is responsible for differences in behavior. This chapter moves beyond the recognition of biological differences and examines more significant issues, such as the influence of sociological and psychological factors on female sport participation.

Social Barriers to Women in Sport

Cultural influences and societal expectations have a tremendous influence on girls' decisions to become athletes. Society often views sport as "masculine." Historically, participation in sports has been an essential part of a boy's identity and transition into "manhood." This labeling has been a deterrent for many girls and women who fear participation in sports diminishes their femininity. Cultural definitions of masculinity and femininity, as well as the relationship between gender roles and socially acceptable behavior, play an important part in the choices that girls and women make in deciding whether to participate in sports and in which sports to participate. Perception of gender roles may be the greatest barrier to the aspiring female athlete (Harris, 1987).

Gender Role Orientation

Gender role orientation researchers began studying individual behavior as a reflection of culturally defined standards of masculinity and femininity. They assumed that females

Women have demonstrated the ability to compete at a high level in all sports.

possess certain personality characteristics and males possess others. This line of research was advanced separately by the development of the Bem Sex Role Inventory (BSRI; Bem, 1974) and the Personality Attributes Questionnaire (PAQ; Spence & Helmreich, 1978). The development of these questionnaires challenged two long-standing beliefs. First, the idea that the personality characteristics of masculinity and femininity are linked to biological sex was challenged. Bem argued that although socially acceptable, there is no reason for men to possess only masculine characteristics and women to possess only feminine characteristics. Second, the belief that personality constructs are unidimensional was examined. Bem dismissed original models of gender roles and introduced an approach that looked at both personality characteristics and an individual's behavior.

The BSRI is a sixty-item instrument that asks respondents to indicate how well each attribute listed describes them. Twenty of the attributes reflect the culturally defined characteristics of masculinity (e.g., independence, assertiveness), twenty attributes reflect characteristics of femininity (e.g., nurturance, understanding), and twenty of the items are defined as neither masculine nor feminine. Those who scored high on both masculine and feminine attributes are called **androgynous,** and those who scored high on only a single dimension are sex typed as either masculine or feminine. Individuals who scored low on both types of attributes are labeled as undifferentiated. According to Bem, those classified as androgynous (high on both masculine and feminine characteristics) were more well adjusted, more adaptable, and more flexible than their sex-typed counterparts (Bem, 1974).

Research on female athletes classified them as either masculine or androgynous based on the BSRI and the PAQ (Colker & Widom, 1980; Del Rey & Sheppard, 1981; Harris & Jennings, 1977). Subsequent investigations differentiated athletes by sport. Findings demonstrated that both male and female team sport competitors were more likely to score high on masculinity or androgyny than on femininity (Wrisberg, Draper, & Everett, 1988). However, female athletes who participated in individual sports scored high on femininity, while their male counterparts were distributed evenly across three groups.

Info Box

Both male and female athletes possess traits typically characterized as masculine and feminine.

Family has been identified the most important influence regarding gender roles. (Achincloss, 1984; Bloom, 1985; Watkins & Montgomery, 1989). Parents choose the toys that their children play with. They reward their children for appropriate behavior and punish them for inappropriate behavior. Parents often treat their sons and daughters differently, engaging in physical play with their sons and cuddling in a more sedentary way with their daughters. Very young children are able to distinguish subtle differences in their parents' attitudes about what types of activities are acceptable for boys and for girls, thus subconsciously encouraging them to choose "appropriate" activities (Power & Parke, 1986).

The family must provide powerful and positive social influences in early childhood for girls to overcome traditional sexism in sport (Gordon, 1988). Female athletes have disproportionately more parents who were former athletes when compared to female nonathletes (Anshel, 1994). Girls are likely to select sports identical to those in which their mothers are currently active or formerly participated. However, fathers have been identified as the most important influence on daughters' participation (Cohen, 1993). Parents who value sports and leadership activity provide support and reinforcement for their daughters, allowing them to resolve their gender identify conflicts (Goldberg & Chandler, 1991).

Gender role orientation research was extended to include the notion of **role conflict** in the female athlete. Traditionally, sport has been considered a masculine activity because it requires physical qualities such as strength and fitness and reinforces attributes such as competitiveness and assertive behavior. These qualities have traditionally been valued and encouraged in males but not in females. Researchers suggested that female athletes might find the role of athlete incompatible with being female, the result of which is role conflict. Sage and Loudermilk (1979) examined this question in a sample of intercollegiate athletes. Twenty percent of their sample reported that they experienced a large degree of role conflict. A greater percentage (41 percent) of the female athletes competing in traditional masculine sports reported more of a role conflict than those in traditionally feminine sports (34 percent). Some suggested that women resolved this conflict by overemphasizing their femininity outside the sports arena (Del Rey, 1978). Others went as far as claiming that this conflict contributed to women's use of alcohol (Wetzig, 1990). Follow-up studies, however, failed to find that role conflict was of any real concern for female athletes (Allison & Butler, 1984; Anthrop & Allison, 1983).

Although gender role research helped shift the focus away from biological and genetic determinants of behavior, it has suffered from several methodological and theoretical limitations of its own. Bem (1993) acknowledged gender role research as an individualistic approach that ignores the larger historical and societal forces that have created inequality between the sexes. In addition, even though androgyny was meant to eliminate gender polarization, the BSRI may actually perpetuate the masculine–feminine dichotomy by again providing for distinct classifications (Gill, 1994). In other words, the inventory itself classifies people as masculine, feminine, or androgynous based on which traits they possess and does little to show similarities.

Gender role research has also been criticized for not recognizing the importance of situational factors in the sport setting (Gill, 1994). For example, many gender role studies were organized around comparisons of athletes and nonathletes. Those who participated in athletics generally scored higher on instrumental (masculine) attributes, and nonparticipants scored higher on the expressive (feminine) dimension. The use of the BSRI and PAQ may have perpetuated this finding because both categorize competitiveness (i.e., instrumental, assertive behavior) as a masculine attribute. It would be expected, therefore, that the female athlete would score higher on masculinity because this dimension includes various attributes considered significant to an athlete's ultimate success.

Homosexuality

Martina Hingis won the 1999 Australian Open by beating an unseeded Amelie Mouresmo in straight sets. Controversy surrounded Mouresmo's participation because Hingis and Lindsay Davenport suggested she played tennis with a man's strength. Hingis even commented to reporters that Mouresmo was "half a man." Mouresmo was hounded by the media, who hoped for a response to these comments or those concerning her relationship with another woman. This example demonstrates the stereotype that sport masculinizes the female athlete, which is really a twofold issue concerning both the appearance and sexuality of the female athlete. Because sport has traditionally been defined as a male preserve, female participants who acquire the skills necessary to become physically proficient have also taken on more "masculine" traits in the process. Because many of these traits have become associated with lesbianism, many female athletes have also been suspected of **homosexuality** (Cahn, 1994). Whereas a woman's sexuality, or more specifically heterosexuality, is often perceived to be jeopardized by participation in sports, a man's is perceived to be validated or strengthened by such behavior.

The myth attached to female athletes and sexuality suggests either that sport participation changes the sexual orientation of females or that lesbians are attracted to sport. The attitude has been demonstrated by coaches, athletes, and the media. Penn State basketball coach Rene Portland publicly stated that she did not allow lesbians on her team. Olympic gold medalist Dot Richardson wrote that "dealing with the stereotype [that of being a lesbian] was going to be the hardest part of being a top level female athlete" (Richardson, 1997, p. 40). These stigmatizations often lead to conformist attitudes and ultimately may persuade some individuals to act in traditional ways in an attempt to avoid being labeled or stereotyped. Men may be dissuaded from participating in dance or gymnastics, for example, and women may avoid sports that emphasize physical contact, force, and strength.

Many cultures teach fear or condemnation of homosexuality. In an attempt to compensate for an association with masculinity, women in sport often try to promote a feminine image and focus public attention on individual athletes who meet cultural standards of beauty (Creedon, 1994). Professional women's sports, college athletics teams, and individual athletes have taken a step beyond femininity to pose and promote their athletes in glamour shots. Even the Women's Sports Foundation provides an opportunity for athletes to receive free hairstyling and makeup application before the annual awards dinner.

The issue of lesbians in sport is often ignored or labeled an "image" problem. Women's golf has combated an "image problem" since its inception in the 1940s. The pioneers of women's professional golf were independent women. Every time they stood to the tee, they were making a statement to the world that they were competitive athletes. They were all single and chose their golf careers instead of families. Prize money was limited and sponsorship virtually nonexistent, so they traveled in small groups, sharing transportation and lodging. All of these behaviors—independence, competitiveness, fraternization— were contrary to societal expectations of women, so it was assumed that these women must be lesbians. In the 1970s, the LPGA hired a marketing professional to improve the "image" of women's golf. The tour had difficulty attracting sponsors and raising tour purses because of constant complaints that the women on the tour were too mannish. Broadcasters constantly criticized the golfers' physical appearance, and one broadcaster actually announced that lesbians in the sport hurt women's golf. Sex appeal was introduced to the tour with cheesecake posters of Laura Baugh and Jan Stephenson, and players in swimsuits and evening gowns posed for glamour shots in the LPGA *Fairway* magazine (Smith, 1998).

Association of athleticism with lesbians and the use of the lesbian label has been a powerful tool to prevent women from engaging in sport. Homosexuality has no relationship to sport and does not influence athletic performance. So why is homophobia so significant to women's participation in sport? In general, society tries to avoid association with

TABLE 20.1   *Suggestions for Combating Homophobia in Sport.*

- Respect the sexual preference of every athlete.
- Hold workshops to address the issue of homophobia.
- Generate guidelines and rules about sexual relationships for all athletes, heterosexual or homosexual.
- Realize that homosexuals may be more accepting of heterosexuals than heterosexuals are of homosexuals.
- Remember that sexual preference is not a predictor of athletic performance.
- Respect the right to privacy for all team members, and realize that homosexuals may not want to publicly admit their sexual preferences.
- Avoid jokes or making fun of homosexuals.
- View athletes as individuals and then as athletes.
- Recognize the ways in which fear of being called a lesbian or associating with lesbians controls all women in sport.
- Become aware of and change the ways that homophobia limits your choice of activities, friends, and speaking out against antigay actions.
- Insist that sport governing organizations and coaches associations take a stand against homophobia and discrimination against lesbian coaches and athletes.
- Monitor your own stereotyped beliefs about homosexuals and commit yourself to unlearning them.

Source: Adapted from Griffin, 1992; Rotella & Murray, 1991.

homosexuality (Griffin, 1993). Parents who believe that participating in sport will influence their child's sexual preferences will not allow their child the opportunity to compete (Rotella & Murray, 1991). Athletes who are psychologically and morally unable to deal with other athletes who are perceived to be homosexual will not join that team or are more likely to quit the team to avoid the stigma of association.

An understanding of sexuality is inherent in the study of gender and sport. Sport participation compels us to understand the physical body. Further, no scientific evidence shows that participating in sport causes lesbianism. It is important to understand that homosexuality is not a problem in sport—discrimination against homosexuals and fear of homosexuality are problems. Recommendations have been proposed to help individuals actively deal with the issue of homosexuality (see Table 20.1; Griffin, 1993; Rotella & Murray, 1991).

Info Box

Compulsory heterosexuality is the norm in sport. People must resist this bias to overcome homophobia.

Self-Perceptions as Barriers for Women in Sport

Social barriers are not the only obstacles that women have had to overcome to engage in sport. Certain personal barriers operate independently (or in combination with social barriers) to shape the experience of sport for women. Many of these barriers center on the physique and athletes' concerns over presenting themselves favorably to others. How athletes perceive themselves and how others view them may have a great impact on continued participation. An athlete who is able to effectively deal with these concerns or minimize their influence will likely derive greater enjoyment from the sport experience. Specific barriers discussed are body image, self-presentation, social physique anxiety, and eating-disordered behaviors.

Body Image

The conception of physical attractiveness in others and ourselves is learned. Family, society, culture, and the media influence this learning process, which results in tremendous pressure on individuals to present their appearance in a positive manner. A lean and fit physique is considered ideal for women, but a lean and muscular physique is ideal for men. Society offers significant rewards to those considered attractive. They are thought to be more intelligent and successful than individuals rated as unattractive (Steiner-Adair, 1987). Further, attractive individuals have been found to receive preferential treatment from teachers (Martinek, 1981) and in the workplace (Cash & Kilcullen, 1985). Is it any wonder that many men and women seek to alter their appearance in hopes of being more physically attractive? They gain and lose weight, change hairstyles, wear the latest stylish clothing, and use cosmetics.

One's physique is not easy to alter because it is determined in part by genetics. The inability to obtain the perfect body has led to the prevalence of body image disturbances in many members of our society. Cash and Pruzinsky (1990) have defined **body image** as "the internal, subjective representations of physical appearance and bodily experience" (p. xi). In a national survey, Cash and Henry (1995) found that 48 percent of women negatively evaluated their appearance. Many factors impact how an individual views his or her body, including perceptions (assessing how accurately we perceive our bodies), affect (our feelings about our bodies), cognition (thoughts and attitudes about our bodies), behavior–lifestyle (eating and exercise habits), and protective strategies (wearing loose clothing) related to body image (Bane & McAuley, 1998).

One of the behavioral strategies often used to improve perception of body image is physical activity. Physical activity can result in numerous physical and psychological changes. Reductions in body fat percentage, improved muscle tone, enhanced self-esteem, and physical competence can all result from regular exercise participation. As such, is exercise an effective strategy to reduce body image disturbances? Or does the struggle to attain physical perfection contribute to body image disturbances? In a summary of existing research, Bane and McAuley (1998) report that exercise is not always an effective strategy for improving body image for people in the general population.

Although many people choose to exercise for a variety of reasons, exercise is obviously integral to any athletes' training. Sport offers the opportunity to develop feelings of physical competence while striving toward the challenge of competition. Perceived body image has been examined to determine whether sport participation results in improved body image. Athletes have been found to have improved body image perceptions compared to similar aged populations (Warren et al., 1989; Wilkins, Boland, & Albinson, 1993). Therefore, sport appears to offer female athletes psychological protection surrounding body image.

Info Box

The relationship between enhanced body image and exercise participation is equivocal in the general population. Athletes, however, report improved body image compared to that of the general population.

Self-Presentation

Self-presentation refers to the processes people use to monitor and control how they are perceived and evaluated by others (Schlenker, 1980). The impressions left on others has implications for friendships, job success, and romantic involvement. Self-presentation involves the selective presentation and omission of aspects of the self to create desired impressions and avoid undesired impressions (Leary, 1992). Baumeister (1982) suggested two reasons for engaging in self-presentational behaviors. The first centers on the attainment of rewards. Others (e.g., employers, coaches) often control whether we are given rewards. By presenting ourselves favorably to others, we may be more likely to achieve that reward. The second reason is related to the goal of achieving our ideal self. People generally have an idea of how they ultimately would like to be (e.g., the ideal self) or be perceived. The ideal self may center on being attractive, intelligent, humorous, or athletic. Self-presentational behaviors can be used to make the public image comparable to the ideal self.

Leary (1992) outlines numerous avenues in sport and exercise whereby individuals may feel pressure to present themselves in a desirable manner. The potential exists for athletes to convey negative images to important others, including coaches, teammates, and audience members. Being perceived as incompetent, unprepared, or unable to handle the pressure of sport competition is just one of the risks athletes take. Sport competition trait anxiety (i.e., the tendency to perceive threat and to experience anxiety in sport competition) has been examined as a self-presentational process, with interesting implications for the female athlete (Martin & Mack, 1996). These researchers assessed 146 undergraduate students across two measures of self-presentation (i.e., social physique anxiety and physical self-presentation) and determined their relations to sport competition trait anxiety. The self-presentational variables were significantly correlated with the trait anxiety for females only. Regression analyses revealed that approximately 21 percent of the variance in trait anxiety was accounted for by these self-presentational variables. It was concluded that self-presentational concerns have implications on sport competition trait anxiety for females only.

Info Box

Concern over others' impressions is a significant contributor to competition anxiety in female athletes.

Social Physique Anxiety

One self-presentational construct that has received considerable attention in the sport and exercise literature is **social physique anxiety** (SPA). SPA refers to the "anxiety that people experience in response to others' evaluations of their physiques" (Hart, Leary, & Rejeski, 1989, p. 94). Although related to body image, SPA specifically deals with the anxiety that occurs as a result of actual or perceived body evaluation from others. Some people who are disinterested in others' opinions or those who perceive that their bodies will be evaluated favorably may rarely experience SPA.

As previously mentioned, sport provides considerable opportunity to be evaluated by others. One's physique is not exempt from such scrutiny. In subjectively evaluated sports, transmitting a positive impression of one's physique (e.g., bodylines, grace) even plays a role in the evaluation of performance. As such, social physique anxiety in female athletes has intrigued researchers. Results have shown that female athletes report moderate levels of social physique anxiety (Hausenblas & Mack, in press; McAuley & Burman, 1993; Reel & Gill, 1996). Consequently, anxiety from others' evaluation of their physique does not appear to be a concern for most female athletes. Hausenblas and Mack (in press) also reported that athletes in a subjectively evaluated sport (e.g., diving) reported lower levels of SPA than an athletic control or a nonathletic control. One plausible explanation for this finding may be that athletes in subjectively evaluated sports become desensitized to physique anxiety because of repeated exposure to evaluation during practice and competition. In addition, perhaps athletes whose physique does not conform to that thought to be necessary for performance in subjectively evaluated sports withdraw from participation. Finally, perhaps athletes in subjectively evaluated sports enjoy their physiques.

Eating Disorders

Leanness has become equated with sport performance. Athletes participating in certain sports are considered advantaged if they maintain a lean physique. When athletes become obsessed about their weight, they may engage in unsafe weight loss practices, including pathogenic weight control methods and/or eating-disordered behavior. A study by Burkes-Miller and Black (1988) outlined the common weight loss techniques used by male and female athletes. Of the 695 athletes surveyed, 59 percent used excessive exercise as a means of controlling their weight. Other prevalent practices included: restricted dietary intake (24 percent); fasting for at least 24 hours (12 percent); laxative or diuretic use (7 percent); and self-induced vomiting (6 percent). The extent to which athletes will adopt unhealthy means to control their weight therefore needs to be a concern for coaches and family members.

Anorexia nervosa and bulimia are the two most common **eating disorders.** According to the Diagnostic and Statistical Manual of Mental Disorders (American Psychiatric Association, 1994) some of the characteristics of **anorexia** are:

- weight loss leading to maintaining a body weight 15 percent below what is expected for age and height norms
- intense fear of gaining weight
- disturbance in perception of body weight, size, or shape
- the absence of three consecutive menstrual cycles in females

Characteristics of **bulimia** include:

- recurrent episodes of binge eating
- perceptions that eating behavior cannot be controlled during binge episodes

- regularly engaging in various methods to prevent weight gain (e.g., self-induced vomiting, the use of laxatives or diuretics, fasting, vigorous exercise)
- a minimum of two binge episodes a week over a 3-month period
- persistent overconcern with body shape and weight (American Psychiatric Association, 1994)

Are eating disorders a problem in sport? Many studies have been conducted to determine whether athletes are more at risk for eating disorders than are nonathletes (Ashley et al., 1996; Burkes-Miller & Black, 1988; Stoutjesdyk & Jevne, 1993; Sundgot-Borgen, 1994). Whether athletes are more likely to experience eating-disordered behavior is equivocal, however. Stoutjesdyk and Jevne studied collegiate athletes competing in a variety of sports. Over 10 percent of the athletes studied were classified as at risk for anorexia, which is comparable to that reported for collegiate nonathletes. Conversely, Sundgot-Borgen surveyed 522 elite female athletes ranging in age from 12 to 35. Of those responding, 22.4 percent were classified as "at risk" for eating disorders. Finally, Wilkins, Boland, and Albinson (1993) found that athletes were less likely to report symptoms associated with eating-disordered behavior compared with a nonathletic control group. These researchers suggest that sport participation may provide protection for the athlete from the onset of eating disorders.

Prevalence rates for anorexia and bulimia seem to be sport specific. Athletes in sports that emphasize leanness have been shown to be at greater risk for eating disorders than other athletic group (Borgen & Corbin, 1987; Petrie, 1993; Terry & Waite, 1996). These sports can be separated into the following three categories:

1. subjectively evaluated sports, in which aesthetic appearance is evaluated (e.g., figure skating, gymnastics, diving)
2. endurance sports, in which lowering body weight can maximize performance (e.g., cross-country running, cross-country skiing)
3. weight-dependent sports, which incorporate weight classifications (e.g., judo, rowing)

Petrie (1993) reported that over 60 percent of intercollegiate gymnasts engaged in some form of eating-disordered behaviors. Terry and Waite (1996) revealed that lightweight rowers scored significantly higher on the measure of eating disorders than did heavyweight rowers. Coaches, athletes, and parents in these sports need to be aware of the added pressure for maintaining a lean physique. Perhaps through understanding, incidence rates of eating disorders in sports such as gymnastics and distance running can be reduced.

Risk Factors for Eating-Disordered Behavior.   Sundgot-Borgen (1994) conducted detailed interviews of 103 female athletes classified as "at risk" for eating disorders and of 30 control athletes. The purpose of the interviews was to determine potential risk factors associated with the development of eating-disordered behavior. Prolonged periods of dieting or a history of weight fluctuations was reported by 38 percent of the sample. Other factors that triggered changes in eating patterns included a new coach (30 percent); injury/illness (23 percent); casual comments by others concerning weight (19 percent); leaving home to train (10 percent); and problems in an interpersonal relationship (10 percent). It is obvious that the factors associated with eating disordered behavior are both personal and environmental.

TABLE 20.2   *Behavioral Recommendations for Coaches in the Prevention of Eating Disorders.*

- Emphasize fitness goals rather than body weight goals.
- Avoid careless remarks about weight.
- Avoid always associating weight loss with performance.
- Do not have group weigh-ins.
- Do not punish athletes for not making weight.

Source: Gender and Sport, p. 30.

Sundgot-Borgen (1994) also asked athletes why they started dieting. Not surprisingly, 100 percent of the athletes cited improved performance. It is of particular interest that the majority (67 percent) of coaches recommended that the athlete lose weight. As such, the role of the coach is critical in shaping the attitudes and behaviors of athletes concerning eating and sport performance. Coaches must understand their powerful influences on the athlete. Some athletes may go to pathogenic measures to please their coach and enhance performance. Swoap and Murphy (1995) outline some recommendations for coaches to reduce the risk of their athletes developing eating disorders (see Table 20.2).

Leary, Tchividjian, and Kraxberger (1994) suggested that self-presentational concerns may be another antecedent to eating disorders. This suggestion appears conceivable because people's concerns with how they are regarded by others may increase their risk of pathological eating behaviors in an attempt to convey a positive impression. Further, Bulik and colleagues (1991) noted that eating-disordered individuals report a fear of negative evaluation. Taken together, an individual's anxiety of physique evaluation (i.e., social physique anxiety) and eating-disordered behavior may be linked. Research has supported this relationship in that measures of eating disorders were found to predict social physique anxiety (Hausenblas & Mack, in press; Reel & Gill, 1996). Therefore, persistent concerns over others' evaluation of their physique may lead some individuals to engage in eating-disordered behavior.

Info Box

Sport participation does not cause eating-disordered behavior. However, specific characteristics about the individual and the environment may predispose athletes to engage in eating-disordered behaviors. These characteristics need to be recognized and, where possible, controlled.

Gender and Sport Achievement

The introduction of achievement research to the sport setting mirrored a more general trend that was taking place in psychology. In this line of research, expectation perceptions, self-confidence, and socialization influences were emphasized over biological or personality differences as factors that might affect performance levels. Initially, gender differences in achievement were ignored because research was conducted with only male samples. It was not until Horner (1972) completed her widely publicized dissertation on women's "fear of success" that gender and its relation to achievement became a prominent theme in research literature. Specifically, Horner argued that success had negative consequences for women. She claimed that, to achieve success, a woman must behave in ways that are in direct conflict with the ideal feminine image. She further argued that this conflict triggers the **fear of success** motive, which leads to increased anxiety levels and avoidance behavior. When examined in an athletic setting, McElroy and Willis (1979) found no evidence to support fear of success in female athletes. In fact, attitudes surrounding achievement were similar to those found in male athletes. "Fear of success" has been discredited because it relies on stereotypical attitudes toward women's success.

Further studies of achievement motivation looked at multidimensional measures of **achievement orientation.** This allowed researchers to detect more specific ways in which thought processes differ between men and women. For example, Gill and Deeter (1988) developed the Sport Orientation Questionnaire, which was designed to assess achievement behavior across three dimensions; competitiveness, win orientation, and goal orientation. Those who score high in competitiveness are motivated to participate in competitive sports and strive for success. Individuals high in win orientation are outcome oriented and focus on interpersonal comparison. Goal orientation is an emphasis on achieving personal performance goals in competitive situations. When administered to male and female athletes, consistent gender differences were found: males scored higher than females on competitiveness and win orientation, and females scored higher on goal orientation (Duda, 1986; McNally & Orlick, 1975; Weinberg & Jackson, 1979).

Info Box

Male athletes are generally more motivated to win, whereas females are more motivated to achieve personal goals for performance.

Most recently, those attempting to explain gender differences in achievement orientation have looked at cognitive processes (e.g., self-perception, expectations, perceived competence). Researchers are beginning to understand that how well one expects to perform is often a fairly accurate indication of how well one actually does perform (Bandura, 1977; Crandall, 1969; Feltz, 1988; Roberts, 1984). Studies investigating gender differences in expectations have found that women typically report lower expectations of success and make fewer achievement-oriented attributions. These gender differences, however, were not found to apply equally across all situations and tasks. Various studies show that women actually lower their expectations of success the most when the task is perceived as masculine, when ambiguous feedback is provided, and when social comparison is emphasized (Corbin, 1981; Corbin, Steward, & Blair, 1981; Corbin et al., 1983; Lenney, 1977).

By integrating results of previous studies, Eccles and Harold (1991) proposed a developmental model that identified how socialization influences, social context, and interpersonal cognitive variables interact in producing gender differences in sport participation and achievement. Expectations and values are identified as the primary determinants of achievement behavior and are influenced by a variety of sociocultural and individual factors (e.g., aptitude, temperament, talent). The model proposes that participation in an activity, such as sport, is based on an individual's beliefs about his or her ability, interpretation of that ability, incentive depending on possible gains and losses, and expectations of success. These factors are all influenced by both personal traits and socialization. Participation in achievement settings and expectations of success, therefore, are influenced by a combination of socialization, situational, and personal factors.

Info Box

Gender differences in sport are the result of numerous factors, including expectations, socialization, cultural norms, and individual differences.

Researchers using this model have identified a variety of interesting gender differences in athletic achievement. Eccles and Harold (1991) examined the role of child belief systems toward sport involvement. Adolescent boys were found to place more value on sport participation, and they believed that they were more capable in sports than did adolescent girls. These differences were found to develop at a very young age, which may influence the amount of free time boys and girls spend playing sports. Girls will play sports as long as they perceive themselves to be above average in skill level and ability, while much lesser skilled boys will continue to play sports. The study also found that girls and boys rated sports as a more sex-typed activity than math or reading. These ratings correlated highly with ratings of their own ability in sports, which suggests that gender stereotypes influence sport confidence.

The influence of parental socialization on children's sport involvement cannot be ignored. Jacobs and Eccles (1992) examined the relationship between a mother's stereotypic beliefs, perceptions of her children's abilities, and her children's self-perceptions. Findings revealed that mothers overestimated or underestimated their child's ability based on gender stereotypes. Mothers perceived their sons to have more athletic ability than their daughters, which may reflect a sex difference in sport competition and participation. In addition, a mother's perception of her child's ability influenced the child's perception of his or her own ability. Brustad (1996) studied the contribution of parental socialization processes and gender to a child's interest in physical activity among a lower socioeconomic population. He also found a significant relationship between parental socialization and a child's perceived physical competence and attraction to physical activity. Parental encouragement was the most influential factor for boys, and parental enjoyment was the most significant variable for the girls. Gender differences also emerged in terms of attitude toward physical exertion, whereby vigorous physical activity was regarded as more gender appropriate for boys than girls. The studies, using the Expectancy Value Model of Motivation (Eccles & Harold, 1991), suggest that gender influences achievement through the values and expectations that boys and girls are taught and acquire through various socialization influences.

Conclusion

Arguments against women's sport participation persist. One hundred years ago, girls and women were denied the right to play sports because it was believed that they would do irreparable harm to their reproductive organs. This argument has been dispelled, but new myths designed to keep girls from playing sports have been advanced. Rarely are these myths purported for the male athlete. For example, unhealthy weight reduction practices are rarely cited to dissuade boys from participation in wrestling, and male interest in sport is always assumed. When confronted with these myths, people need to remember why it is so important for women to have the same opportunities as men.

The power of the socialization process on behavior was highlighted in this chapter. Boys and girls are socialized to think that gendered role expectations are appropriate. The expectations of significant others influence how we view ourselves, how others view us, and our perceptions of others. This has implications for self-concept, body image, and eating-disordered behavior. Finally, differences in expectations may influence differences in achievement patterns and confidence for males and females.

Key Terms (in order of appearance)

gender role orientation	body image	anorexia
androgyny	self-presentation	bulimia
role conflict	social physique anxiety	fear of success
homosexuality	eating disorders	achievement orientation

References

Achincloss, E. (1984). *The new agenda: A blueprint for the future of women's sports.* San Francisco: The Women's Sports Foundation.

Allison, M., & Butler, B. (1984). Role conflict and the elite female athlete: Empirical findings and conceptual dilemmas. *International Review for Sociology of Sport, 19,* 157–167.

American Psychiatric Association. (1994). *Diagnostic and statistical manual of mental disorders,* 4th ed. Washington, DC: American Psychiatric Association.

Anshel, M. H. (1994). *Sport psychology: From theory to practice.* Scottsdale, AZ: Gorsch Scarisbrick, Publishers.

Anthrop, J., & Allison, M. (1983). Role conflict and the high school female athlete. *Research Quarterly, 54,* 104–111.

Ashley, C. D., Smith, J. F., Robinson, J. B., & Richardson, M. T. (1996). Disordered eating in female collegiate athletes and collegiate females in an advanced program of study: A preliminary investigation. *International Journal of Sport Nutrition, 6,* 391–401.

Bandura, A. (1977). Self-efficacy: Toward a unifying theory of behavior change. *Psychological Review, 84,* 191–215.

Bane, S., & McAuley, E. (1998). Body image and exercise. In J. L. Duda (Ed.), *Advances in sport and exercise psychology measurement* (pp. 331–322). Morgantown, WV: Fitness Information Technology.

Baumeister, R. F. (1982). A self-presentational view of social phenomena. *Psychological Bulletin, 91,* 3–26.

Bem, S. L. (1974). The measurement of psychological androgyny. *Journal of Consulting and Clinical Psychology, 42,* 155–162.

Bem, S. L. (1993). *The lenses of gender.* New Haven, CT: Yale Univ. Press.

Bloom, B. S. (1985). *Developing talent in young people.* New York: Ballentine.

Borgen, J. S., & Corbin, C. B. (1987). Eating disorders among female athletes. *Physician and Sportsmedicine, 15,* 89–95.

Brustad, R. J. (1996). Attraction to physical activity in urban schoolchildren: Parental socialization and gender influences. *Research Quarterly for Exercise and Sport, 67,* 316–323.

Bulik, C. M., Beidel, D. C., Duchmann, E., Weltzin, T. E., & Kaye, W. E. (1991). An analysis of social anxiety in anorexic, bulimic, social phobic, and control women. *Journal of Psychopathology and Behavioral Assessment, 13,* 199–211.

Burkes-Miller, M. E., & Black, D. R. (1988). Male and female college athletes: Prevalence of anorexia nervosa and bulimia nervosa. *Athletic Training, 2,* 137–140.

Cahn, S. K. (1994). *Coming on strong: Gender and sexuality in twentieth-century women's sport.* Cambridge, MA: Harvard Univ. Press.

Cahn, S. K. (1994). Crushes, competition, and closets: The emergence of homophobia in women's physical education. In S. Birrell & C. Cole (Eds.), *Women, sport, and culture* (pp. 327–340). Champaign, IL: Human Kinetics.

Cash, T. C., & Henry, P. E. (1995). Women's body images: The results of a national survey in the U.S.A. *Sex Roles, 33,* 19–28.

Cash, T. C., & Kilcullen, R. (1985). The eye of the beholder: Susceptibility to sexism and beautyism in evaluation of managerial applications. *Journal of Applied Social Psychology, 15,* 591–605.

Cash, T. C., & Pruzinsky, T. (1990). *Body images: Development, deviance, and change.* New York: Guilford.

Cohen, G. (1993). *Women in sport: Issues and controversies.* Newbury Park, CA: Sage.

Colker, R., & Widom, C. S. (1980). Correlates of female athletic participation. *Sex Roles, 6,* 47–53.

Corbin, C. B. (1981). Sex of subject, sex of opponent, and opponent ability as factors affecting self-confidence in a competitive situation. *Journal of Sport Psychology, 3,* 265–270.

Corbin, C. B., Landers, D. M., Feltz, D. L., & Senior, K. (1983). Sex differences in performance estimates: Female lack of confidence vs. male boastfulness. *Research Quarterly for Exercise and Sport, 54,* 407–410.

Corbin, C. B., Steward, M. J., & Blair, W. O. (1981). Self-confidence and motor performance of preadolescent boys and girls in different feedback situations. *Journal of Sport Psychology, 3,* 30–34.

Crandall, V. C. (1969). Sex differences in expectancy of intellectual and academic reinforcement. In C. P. Smith (Ed.), *Achievement motives in children* (pp. 11–45). New York: Russell Sage.

Creedon, P. J. (1994). *Women, media and sport: Challenging gender values.* Newbury Park, CA: Sage.

Davis, L. R. (1997). *The swimsuit issue and sport: Hegemonic masculinity in Sports Illustrated.* Albany, NY: State Univ. of New York Press.

Del Rey, P. (1978). The apologetic and women in sport. In C. Ogelsby (Ed.), *Women and sport: From myth to reality* (pp. 107–111). Philadelphia: Lea & Febiger.

Del Rey, P., & Sheppard, S. (1981). Relationship of psychological androgyny in female athletes to self-esteem. *International Journal of Sport Psychology, 12,* 165–175.

Department of Education. (1997). Title IX: 25 years of progress [On-line]. Available: http://www.ed.gov/pubs/TitleIX/.

Duda, J. L. (1986). A cross-cultural analysis of achievement motivation in sport and the classroom. In L. VanderVeldon & J. Humphrey (Eds.), *Current selected research in the psychology and sociology of sport* (pp. 115–132). New York: AMS.

Duncan, M. C. (1990). Sport photographs and sexual difference: Images of women and men in the 1984 and 1988 Olympic games. *Sociology of Sport Journal, 7,* 22–43.

Duncan, M. C., & Hasbrook, C. A. (1988). Denial of power in televised women's sports. *Sociology of Sport Journal, 5*(1), 1–21.

Duncan, M. C., Messner, M. A., Williams, L., Jensen, K., & Wilson, W. (1990). *Gender stereotyping in televised sports.* Los Angeles, CA: Amateur Athletic Foundation.

Eccles, J. S., & Harold, R. D. (1991). Gender differences in sport involvement: Applying the Eccles expectancy-value model. *Journal of Applied Sport Psychology, 3,* 7–35.

Eitzen, S., & Sage, G. (1993). *Sociology of North American sport.* Dubuque, IA: Wm. C. Brown.

Feltz, D. L. (1988). Self-confidence and sports performance. In K. Pandolf (Ed.), *Exercise and sport sciences reviews,* Vol. 16 (pp. 423–457). New York: Macmillan.

Gill, D. L. (1994). Psychological perspectives on women in sport and exercise. In D. M. Costa & S. R. Guthrie (Eds.), *Women and sport: Interdisciplinary perspectives* (pp. 253–284). Champaign, IL: Human Kinetics.

Gill, D. L., & Deeter, T. E. (1988). Development of the Sport Orientation Questionnaire. *Research Quarterly for Exercise and Sport, 59,* 191–202.

Goldberg, A. D., & Chandler, J. L. (1991). Sport participation among adolescent girls: Role conflict of multiple roles. *Sex Roles, 25,* 213–224.

Gordon, S. (1998). Talent development of the elite sportswomen: A retrospective picture of the process. In K. Dyer (Ed.), *Sportswomen toward 2000: A celebration* (pp. 113–124). Adelaide, Australia: Hyde Park Press.

Griffin, P. (1993). Homophobia in women's sports: The fear that divides us. In G. L. Cohen (Ed.), *Women in sport: Issues and controversies* (pp. 193–203). Newbury Park, CA: Sage.

Hall, M. A. (1990). How should we theorize gender in the context of sport? In M. A. Messner & D. F. Sabo (Eds.), *Sport, men, and the gender order: Critical feminist perspectives* (pp. 223–239). Champaign, IL: Human Kinetics.

Harris, D. V. (1987). The female athlete. In J. R. May and M. J. Asken (Eds.), *Sport psychology* (pp. 99–115). Costa Mesa, CA: PMA Publishing.

Harris, D. V., & Jennings, S. E. (1977). Self-perceptions of female distance runners. *Annals of the New York Academy of Sciences, 301,* 808–815.

Hart, E. A., Leary, M. R., & Rejeski, W. J. (1989). The measurement of social physique anxiety. *Journal of Sport & Exercise Psychology, 11,* 94–104.

Hausenblas, H. A., & Mack, D. E. (in press). Social physique anxiety and eating disorder correlates among female athletic and nonathletic populations. *Journal of Sport Behavior.*

Horner, M. S. (1972). Toward an understanding of achievement-related conflicts in women. *Journal of Social Issues, 28,* 157–176.

Hudson, J. L. (1994). It's mostly a matter of metric. In D. M. Costa & S. R. Guthrie (Eds.), *Women and sport: Interdisciplinary perspectives* (pp. 145–162). Champaign, IL: Human Kinetics.

Intercollegiate. (1997). Gender equity report card. Women's Sport Foundation [On-line]. Available: http://www.lifetimetv.com/WoSport/stage/GENE,Q97.

Jacobs, J. E., & Eccles, J. S. (1992). The impact of mothers' gender-role stereotypic beliefs on mothers' and children's ability perceptions. *Journal of Personality and Social Psychology, 6,* 932–944.

Johnson, M. D. (1994). Disordered eating in active and athletic women. *Clinics in Sports Medicine, 13,* 355–369.

Leary, M. R. (1992). Self-presentational processes in exercise and sport. *Journal of Sport and Exercise Psychology, 14,* 399–351.

Leary, M. R., Tchividjian, L. R., & Kraxberger, B. E. (1994). Self-presentation can be hazardous to your health: Impression management and health risk. *Health Psychology, 13,* 461–470.

Lenney, E. (1977). Women's self-confidence in achievement settings. *Psychological Bulletin, 84,* 1–13.

Martin, K. A., & Mack, D. (1996). Relationships between physical self-presentation and sport competition trait anxiety: A preliminary study. *Journal of Sport and Exercise Psychology, 25,* 1049–1053.

Martinek, T. (1981). Physical attractiveness: Effects on teacher expectations and dyadic interactions in elementary age children. *Journal of Sport Psychology, 3,* 196–205.

McAuley, E., & Burman, G. (1993). The social physique anxiety scale: Construct validity in adolescent females. *Medicine and Science in Sports and Exercise, 25*(9), 1049–1053.

McElroy, M. A., & Willis, J. D. (1979). Women and the achievement conflict in sport: A preliminary study. *Journal of Sport Psychology, 1,* 241–247.

McNally, J., & Orlick, T. (1975). Cooperative sport structures: A preliminary analysis. *Mouvement, 7,* 267–271.

Messner, M. A. (1992). *Power at play: Sports and the problem of masculinity.* Boston: Beacon.

Nelson, M. B. (1994). *The stronger women get, the more men love football.* New York: The Hearst Corporation.

Petrie, T. A. (1993). Disordered eating in female collegiate gymnasts: Prevalence and personality/attitudinal correlates. *Journal of Sport and Exercise Psychology, 15,* 424–436.

Power, T. G., & Parke, R. D. (1986). Patterns of early socialization. Mother- and father-infant interactions in the home. *International Journal of Behavioral Development, 9,* 331–341.

The President's Council on Physical Fitness and Sports. (1997). Physical activity and sport in the lives of girls.

Reel, J. J., & Gill, D. L. (1996). Psychosocial factors related to eating disorders among high school and college female cheerleaders. *The Sport Psychologist, 10,* 195–206.

Richardson, D. (1997, Spring). Sex, lies and softball. *Sports Illustrated for Women,* 40.

Roberts, G. C. (1984). Toward a new theory of motivation in sport: The role of perceived ability. In J. M. Silva & R. S. Weinberg (Eds.), *Psychological foundations of sport* (pp. 214–228). Champaign, IL: Human Kinetics.

Rotella, R. J., & Murray, M. (1991). Homophobia, the world of sport, and sport psychology consulting. *The Sport Psychologist, 5,* 355–364.

Sabo, D. (1988). Psychosocial impact of athletic participation on American women: Facts and fables. *Journal of Sport and Social Issues, 12,* 83–96.

Sage, G. H., & Loudermilk, S. (1979). The female athlete and role conflict. *Research Quarterly, 50,* 88–96.

Schlenker, B. R. (1980). *Impression management: The self-concept, social identity, and interpersonal relations.* Monterey, CA: Brooks/Cole.

Selby, R., Weinsten, H. M., & Bird, T. S. (1990). The health of university athletes: Attitudes, behavior and stressors. *Journal of American College Health, 39,* 11–18.

Smith, L. (1998). *Nike is a goddess.* New York: Atlantic Monthly.

Spence, J. T., & Helmreich, R. L. (1978). *Masculinity and femininity.* Austin, TX: Univ. of Texas Press.

Sports Illustrated, December 9, 1996.

Steiner-Adair, C. (1987). Weightism: A new form of prejudice. *Newsletter of National Anorexic Aid Society Inc., 10,* 1–2.

Stoutjesdyk, D., & Jevne, R. (1993). Eating disorders among high performance athletes. *Journal of Youth and Adolescence, 22*(3), 271–282.

Sundgot-Borgen, J. (1994). Risk and trigger factors for the development of eating disorders in female athletes. *Official Journal of the American College of Sports Medicine,* 414–419.

Swoap, R. A., & Murphy, S. M. (1995). Eating disorders and weight management in athletes. In S. M. Murphy (Ed.), *Sport Psychology Interventions.* Champaign, IL: Human Kinetics.

Terry, P. C., & Waite, J. (1996). Eating attitudes and body shape perceptions among elite rowers: Effects of age, gender and weight category. *The Australian Journal of Science and Medicine in Sport, 28(1),* 3–6.

Warren, B., Blessing, D., & Staton, A. (1990). Disordered eating patterns in competitve female athletes. *International Journal of Eating Disorders, 9,* 565–569.

Watkins, B., & Montgomery, A. B. (1989). Conceptions of athletic excellence among children and adolescents. *Child Development, 60,* 1362–1372.

Weight, L. M., & Noakes, T. D. (1987). Is running an analog of anorexia? A survey of the incidence of eating disorders in female distance runners. *Medicine and Science in Sports and Exercise, 19,* 213–217.

Weinberg, R. S., & Jackson, A. (1979). Effects of competitions, success/failure, and sex on intrinsic motivation. *Research Quarterly, 50,* 494–502.

Wetzig, D. L. (1990). Sex-role conflict in female athletes: A possible marker for alcoholism. *Journal of Alcohol and Drug Addiction, 35*(5), 45–53.

Wilkins, J. A., Boland, F. J., & Albinson, J. (1993). A comparison of male and female university athletes and nonathletes on eating disorder indices: Are athletes protected? *Journal of Sport Behavior, 14*(2), 129–143.

Women's Sports Foundation. *Sport and teen pregnancy: Executive summary,* July 1998.

Wrisberg, C. A., Draper, M. V., & Everett, J. J. (1988). Sex role orientations of male and female collegiate athletes from selected individual and sport teams. *Sex Roles, 19,* 81–90.

21

Coaching the Female Athlete

Barbara Osborne
The University of North Carolina at Chapel Hill

- This chapter describes the factors that contribute to the effective coaching of the female athlete.
- Several sources of motivation for the female athlete are presented.
- Coaches should consider the unique communication needs of female athletes.
- Team-building helps female athletes achieve peak performance.
- A description of unethical abuses of the coach–athlete relationship is included.

After the United States National Soccer Team won the 1999 World Cup, coach Tony DiCiccio was asked the secret of his success. He credited his star forward, Mia Hamm, with his approach for coaching women: Train us like men, but treat us like women.

Many coaches believe that there is no difference in coaching male and female athletes. As with physiological differences, there is probably more variation in the unique characteristics of the athletes within each sex than there are differences between the sexes. Both male and female athletes are willing to sacrifice time and energy, risk injury, endure pain, and feel the pressures and tensions of competitive sport (Anshel, 1994). Both men and women require coaches to provide direction in physical conditioning, skill development, and metal preparation. Both male and female athletes need respect, communication, physical activity, competition, and close relationships with teammates. Both male and female athletes enjoy winning, and both can become upset when they lose.

However, the female experience in sport is different from the experience of a male. Women have historically been discouraged from participating in physical activity and competitive sport. Parents, teachers, and coaches generally have lower expectations for female athletes than for male athletes. Although there is no physiological basis, societal expectations are illustrated by the President's Physical Fitness Test standards, which are lower for prepubescent girls than boys. Girls' middle school and high school cross-country races are often shorter than the boys' races, and in some youth soccer leagues, girls play 25-minute halves, while the same-aged boys are playing 35 minutes.

Are female and male athletes motivated by the same rewards and punishments.

Motivating the Female Athlete

Societal values and sex role stereotyping have a significant impact on whether a female participates in sports. These constructs affect the athlete's perceptions of her abilities, the importance she places on participating in sport, her perceptions about the proper roles for men and women in society, and her incentive to demonstrate competence and achieve goals (Eccles & Harold, 1991). Female athletes have been found to be more assertive, dominant, self-sufficient, independent, aggressive, intelligent, reserved, and achievement-oriented than nonathletes. All these traits are needed to overcome the societal stigma of being a woman in the man's world of sport (Williams, 1978).

It is a myth that women are not motivated to achieve as athletes. To overcome the obstacles found in society, female athletes are likely to be as mature and motivated as male competitors. Although there are differences in the sources that motivate male and female athletes, again, there are probably more differences between female nonathletes and female athletes than between male and female athletes (Cratty, 1983). For women, the sport experience is personal. Female athletes are more likely to participate for personal satisfaction and self-gratification than male athletes are. They tend to engage in tasks they perceive as desirable and achievable and measure success or failure based on their perceived ability and expectations. Female athletes who believe that their success was obtained because of their high ability or work effort will be more likely to continue in sports (Gill, 1984). The coach working with female athletes needs to recognize the female athlete's need for self-satisfaction and provide the athlete with tasks, such as new skills or timed goals, that fall within her capability (Eccles & Harold, 1991). Confidence, self-esteem, and the **motivation** to continue participation come from experiencing some degree of success on a regular basis.

Creating Community within the Team

Anson Dorrance, the head women's soccer coach at the University of North Carolina at Chapel Hill, is statistically the most successful coach in women's sport. In 20 years of coaching women's soccer at UNC, his teams have won twelve Atlantic Coast Conference Championships, one NAIA Championship in 1981, and sixteen NCAA Championships. Dorrance is recognized for his success and unique philosophy in leading, motivating, and coaching female athletes. Also the former head coach of the men's soccer team at UNC, Dorrance absolutely believes that men and women need to be coached differently.

Dorrance has identified the need to create **team community** within a women's team as essential to achieving success, as well as one of the greatest challenges of coaching female athletes. Athletic teams are generally perceived as a hierarchy, with the coach at the top and assistant coaches, captains or team leaders, star athletes and starters, significant reserves, and practice players filling out the ladder. Dorrance strives to create an environment in which everyone is valued equally, although they are not equal in skill, speed, or contributions on the field.

Dorrance explains his philosophy of building a team community by retelling a story by one of his favorite authors, Scott Peck. Peck describes his experiences at an elite private school in New England, where everyone was judged by how much money their fathers made, what kind of car they drove, what label of clothing they wore, and any other status or materialistic measurement. Peck hated the way that the "haves" always scorned those who were not as wealthy and successful. Peck later attended a Quaker school. A huge range of intellectual and socioeconomic ability was represented, yet everyone was treated equally and valued for their unique contributions. Peck loved the environment that the Quaker school provided. Dorrance has tried to create a genuine community, like that of the Quaker school, in his teams at Carolina.

Colleen Hacker, sports psychologist for the U.S. Women's National Soccer Team, also stresses the importance of good **team chemistry** for women's teams to be successful (Gregg, 1999). Hacker strives to make all the players on the national team feel as though they are equal by exposing their vulnerabilities. By showing the members of the team that everyone is vulnerable, the team is able to learn that one person's strength makes up for another teammate's weakness (Gregg, 1999). It is critical that individual leaders within the team not be allowed to use athletes' vulnerabilities to separate the team into cliques. When teammates appreciate the role that each member plays on the team and value each member's contributions, the female athlete has a greater investment in the success of the team. The athlete is no longer competing for herself but is also performing for her teammates.

In his book *Training Soccer Champions,* Dorrance (1996) discusses the need for internal team leadership in building team community and the need for the coach to lead the team as well. Dorrance advocates use of a positive tone and supportive body language when dealing with female athletes. Although male athletes will listen to what the coach says and interpret the words, female athletes will watch the coach, look at the coach's body language, listen to the coach's tone of voice, and decipher the message regardless of the words the coach is saying (Dorrance, 1996). Coaches of female athletes may need to adjust their **communication style** to facilitate better reception of the intended message by the female athlete.

Male athletes and female athletes react differently to criticism. When a coach is criticizing the team for a poor performance, male athletes externalize the criticism. The male athlete assumes that his performance was great and that everyone else on the team was horrible. On the other hand, female athletes take the exact same words from the coach and internalize them. Each female athlete assumes that every criticism and negative word is directed personally at her. She is less inclined to take credit for favorable performance outcomes and tends to take more than her share of the blame for negative outcomes (Dorrance, 1996).

Anshel (1994) supports Dorrance's beliefs that women need to be treated differently from male athletes. The in-your-face coaching techniques of Vince Lombardi or Bobby Knight would not yield successful results for women's teams. Female athletes do not respond productively to coaches' negative comments. No female athlete surveyed in Anshel's (1994) study indicated a favorable attitude or improved performance after receiving negative comments or verbal abuse from the coach. Women are more intrinsically motivated than men (Eccles & Harold, 1991), so negative comments are contrary to having a positive experience. Anger and hostility are barriers to creating an atmosphere that fosters female competitors' need for affiliation.

Dorrance (1996) claims that you have to drive men, but you can lead women. Male **leadership style** is done through status, reputation, and intimidation. Traditionally, many successful men's coaches dominated their athletes, intimidated them, and used the superior strength of their personality over the athletes. They demanded performance from men, and they got it. On the other hand, contemporary coaches find that women perform if they have respect for the coach. This respect comes from the relationship between the coach and the athlete. The female athlete wants to know that the coach cares for her as a person. She is beyond the superficiality of athletics and recognizes that human qualities are more important than athletics ability (Dorrance, 1996).

Info Box

Female athletes may need to be coached differently. Attention to achievement motivation, effective and supportive verbal and nonverbal communication, and developing a team community based on respect are essential ingredients to getting the most out of female athletes.

Coach–Athlete Relationships

Female athletes can benefit from a personal connection with the coach. Rakel Karvelson, a 1999 graduate of the UNC women's soccer team, provided insight to Dorrance when she told him that "women will never care how much you know until they know how much you care" (Dorrance, 1996, p. 43). Female athletes internalize their sport experience. They need to feel secure and trust the coach to allow the coach to lead them to peak performance.

Does the gender of the coach matter? A survey of female high school basketball players indicated a preference for a male coach, except when given the choice between an unsuccessful male coach and a successful female coach. Even in that scenario, almost half of the female athletes still preferred the male coach (Williams and Parkhouse, 1988). In sports that are considered individual sports, as compared to team sports, athletes have been found to prefer coaches of the same gender (Medwechuk & Crossman, 1994; Frankl & Babbitt, 1998). It is likely that female athletes' preferences for a male coach reflect cultural expectations of men in authority positions. Male dominance in women's sports reinforces the notion that men have the ultimate authority to teach sports (Nelson, 1994). Female athletes are also more familiar with male coaches because of a lack of female coaches as role models.

Both male and female coaches can be equally effective in communicating with and leading female athletes. The coach must have the ability to show empathy, warmth, a sense of humor, and mutual respect (Anshel, 1994). However, the personal management style of most women may actually be more desirable for successful coaching than the management traits exhibited by men. Qualities such as sympathy, sensitivity, and lack of killer instinct, which have been criticized as female weaknesses, may actually enable women to get the best performance out of their athletes.

Coaches, Athletes, and Sexual Abuse

The close, trusting relationship between coach and female athlete may be necessary for the athlete to achieve peak performance, but this closeness may also lead to abuse. The athlete may spend more time with her coach than any other significant person in her life, including parents, teachers, or peers. During this time, the coach and the athlete share goals and dreams, as well as success and disappointment. Through this experience, they develop an emotional bond. This bond is generally necessary for female athletes to trust the coach to lead them to maximum performance. However, the athlete's intense feelings and desires sometimes become fixated on the coach as an extension of the intimate trust and the intense focus on the functioning of the athlete's body to maximize performance.

Does the gender of the coach affect the dynamics of the coach-athlete relationship?

Female athletes seem to be particularly vulnerable to their male coaches because they are culturally conditioned to please male authority figures (Bloom, 1985). Male coaches are often an extended father figure for some female competitors (Greendorfer, 1992). The athlete is looking for attention and approval, and pleasing the coach ensures patriarchal approval. In other cases, the athlete equates her intense emotional attachment to her coach with the only other female–male relationship she understands—that of lovers. In this situation, it is the coach's responsibility to ignore the crush. The coach has a duty to nurture the athlete's physical, social, and emotional development in sport and ignore the desires that go beyond that.

No figures exist on how many coaches have relationships with their athletes. Within the athletics community are many anecdotal stories. In every sport, someone knows of at least one coach–athlete couple. Statistics indicate that other similar professional–subordinate relationships are common. Studies show that between 20 and 30 percent of college students have been approached sexually by professors (Nelson, 1994). Another relationship that has similar trust and respect characteristics is that of the psychologist and patient. Studies indicate that almost 10 percent of psychologists have had sex with a patient (Nelson, 1994). Given the sexual energy in an athletics environment, it is possible that coach–athlete relationships are significantly more prevalent.

Info Box

Parents, athletes, and coaches need to be aware of the potential for sexual abuse.

One possible explanation for the prevalence of coach–athlete relationships is that the opportunity exists. High school and middle school athletic coaches are not closely monitored. No national certification process for coaches exists, and no training in psychology or ethics is required. Most coaches at all levels of sport are men, and many them are either insensitive to the emotional needs of adolescent girls or are simply ignorant of them (Bloom, 1999).

Another explanation is that the relationship satisfies the coach's needs. Many middle-aged men are fighting insecurities about aging or their masculinity. They spend endless hours working in a close physically and emotionally charged environment. The attention and adoration of young, physically fit women can be intoxicating. In this situation, it is easy for the coach to believe that he is satisfying the athlete's needs instead of succumbing to his own.

Having a sexual relationship with an athlete is an abuse of the coach's power (Seefeldt, 1998). Intimate relationships should be a balance of equal partners sharing needs and desires. In a coach–athlete relationship, the coach has all the control. The coach decides what the athlete does in training; dictates diet, weight, and sleep requirements; and determines who plays and who sits. The imbalance of power makes it impossible for each partner to have equal status. The athlete is always a subordinate who needs someone to guide and direct her progress, and the coach is always the director.

It is often argued that as long as the coach and the athlete are consenting adults, their relationship is a personal issue, not a public agenda for the world to scrutinize. Coach–athlete relationships are never just personal. First, the coach's relationship with an athlete is not personal, it is professional. Second, this relationship is not between just the coach and the consenting athlete; it affects the entire team. When a coach goes beyond the necessary emotional connection with the athlete and creates a sexual connection, the trust of other athletes on the team is destroyed. The coach and athlete often try to hide their relationship, which creates secrets and sets up barriers within the team. Teammates may be forced to deal with jealousy, feelings of betrayal, or agendas other than performance.

Coach–athlete relationships are also defended as "true love" by pointing to the many marriages that result. It is unprofessional to allow the sexuality of human movement and the excitement of performance to be perceived as "love." The success rate of coach–athlete relationships is not high (Hornak & Hornak, 1993). Most of these relationships fail because the athlete grows up, is no longer dependent on the coach, and recognizes that marriage is a two-way street (Nelson, 1994).

Lesbian Relationships. Although the threat of the lesbian coach as sexual predator is often used as a recruiting smear or scare tactic, the truth is that lesbian coach–athlete relationships are rare. Of sexual exploitation by professionals 96 percent occurs between a man in power and a woman under his guidance. The other 4 percent involves male–male, female–male, and female–female relationships. Although the threat of lesbian coach–athlete relationships is rare, the punishment imposed on lesbian coaches is overwhelmingly disproportionate. Most male coaches who are involved in inappropriate relationships with their athletes are reprimanded, but most female coaches who are involved in inappropriate relationships with their athletes are fired. The harmful effects of **sexual abuse** in a coach–athlete relationship are no more or less damaging when the coach is a woman.

Dealing with Sexual Abuse

Most female athletes do not question a coach's actions or motives, even when they know that the behavior is inappropriate. Some female athletes may have a fragile self-image and blame themselves for the coach's behavior. Supervisors need to more closely monitor the contact and relationships of coaches with their athletes. Punishments for male coaches who behave inappropriately need to be more severe. Parents also need to monitor the coach–athlete relationship, communicate with their daughters, and encourage them to speak up to the coach if the coach's behavior makes them uncomfortable. Athletes also have legal recourse to address inappropriate sexual behavior. If the athlete is not of the legal age of consent, statutory rape charges should be filed. Sexual harassment complaints may be filed under Title IX of the Education Act, which allows for monetary damages.

Recommendations for athletics organizations, administrators, coaches, and athletes in dealing with sexual harassment and abuse include the following:

- Establish a clear policy statement on sexual harassment, including grievance procedures and investigative and disciplinary guidelines.
- Expressly prohibit intimate coach–athlete relationships, and enforce punishment of those whose conduct violates this rule.
- Educate athletics administrators, coaches, and staff about the definition of sexual harassment, and provide examples of specific behaviors. Emphasize the damaging impact that intimate relationships between coaches and athletes have on the athlete and the team, as well as on the coach's professional reputation and career.
- Educate the athlete about the dangers of "consensual" relationships with coaches. Emphasize the department policies, the negative impact on the athlete and the team, and the specific ways to report abusive situations.
- Designate an individual for athletes and staff to go to if concerns about intimate relationships or sexual harassment arise, and guarantee complete confidentiality.

- Carefully conduct a complete background search on all new hires.
- Properly supervise all personnel so that the opportunity for abusive situations does not exist.

Sexual harassment is one of the barriers to full female participation in sport that still exists. Lenskyj (1990) indicates that sexual harassment is an obstacle to women's potential to develop and define sport in woman-centered terms. Men use harassment to oppress and marginalize those who threaten their power base in sport, which may include limitations on access to facilities, training, or coaching (Lenskyj, 1990). Sexual harassment also interferes with women's sport performance. Female athletes may feel humiliated, powerless, frustrated, and guilty, causing them both physical and psychological stress. Athletes may choose to drop out of sport to remove themselves from the harassment.

Conclusion

Very little scientific research has been conducted on coaching the female athlete. As discussed in Chapter 20, female athletes differ from male athletes in achievement orientation, motivation, and gender role perceptions. Little has been done to acknowledge how coaches can address these differences to advance women's performance. Building a team community was discussed as one way to maximize female athletes' commitment to peak performance. Differences in communicating with female athletes and the need for a close, professional coach–athlete relationship were also discussed. Future research might focus on whether female athletes truly have different needs from male athletes or whether coaches are merely perpetuating the societal stereotypes surrounding the emotional differences between men and women. Studies need to be conducted on the impact of various coaching and communication styles on the performance of female athletes. Research should also look at the needs of female athletes in individual sports versus those who compete on a team. It should not be assumed that women can achieve athletic success through the same methods that have been successful for men. However, as more and more women participate, breaking through the physical, social, and psychological barriers historically imposed on them, the old theories may prove to be invalid for the female athlete of the new millennium.

Key Terms *(in order of appearance)* _____

motivation	communication style	sexual harassment
team community	leadership style	
team chemistry	sexual abuse	

References _____

Anshel, M. H. (1994). *Sport Psychology: From theory to practice,* 2nd ed. Scottdale, AZ: Gorsuch Scarisbrick.

Bloom, B. S. (1985). *Developing talent in young people.* New York: Ballantine.

Bloom, M. "When athletes are one sex, and coaches are the other." *New York Times,* June 13, 1999, 20.

Cratty, B. J. (1983). *Psychology in contemporary sport: Guidelines for coaches and athletes.* Englewood Cliffs, NJ: Prentice Hall.

Dorrance, A., with Nash, T. (1996). *Training soccer champions.* Apex, NC: JTC Sports, Inc.

Eccles, J. S., & Harold, R. D. (1991). Gender differences in sport involvement: Applying the Eccles' expectancy-value model. *Journal of Applied Sport Psychology, 3,* 7–35.

Frankl, D., & Babbitt, D. G., III (1998). Gender bias: A study of high school track and field athletes' perceptions of hypothetical male and female head coaches. *Journal of Sport Behavior, 21,* 396.

Gill, D. C. (1984). Individual and group performance in sport. In Silva, J. M., & Weinberg, R. S. (Eds.), *Psychological Foundations of Sport.* Champaign, IL: Human Kinetics Publishers.

Greendorfer, S. L. (1992). Gender bias in theoretical perspectives: The case of female socialization into sport. *Psychology of Women Quarterly, 11,* 327–340.

Gregg, L. (1999). *The Champion Within.* Apex, NC: JTC Sports, Inc.

Hornak, J. N., & Hornak, J. E. (1993, May/June). Coach and player: Ethics and dangers of dual relationships. *Journal of Physical Education, Recreation, and Dance,* 84–86.

Lenskyj, H. (1990). Power and play: Gender and sexuality issues in sport and physical activity. *International Review for the Sociology of Sport, 25*(3), 235–243.

Medwechuk, N., & Crossman, J. (1994). Effects of gender bias on the evaluation of male and female swim coaches. *Perceptual and Motor Skills, 78,* 163–169.

Nelson, M. B. (1991). *Are we winning yet? How women are changing sports and sports are changing women.* New York: Random House.

Nelson, M. B. (1994). *The stronger women get, the more men love football.* Orlando, FL: Harcourt Brace.

Seefeldt, V. (1998). Understanding sexual harassment and the abuse of power in athletic settings [On-line]. Available: *http://edweb3.educ.nsu.edu/ysi/spotlightfall98/understandsex.ht*

Williams, J. M. (1978). Personality characteristics of the successful female athlete. In W. F. Straub (Ed.), *Sport psychology: An analysis of athlete behavior,* 2nd ed., pp. 353–359

Williams, J. M., & Parkhouse, B. L. (1988). Social learning theory as a foundation for examining sex bias in evaluation of coaches. *Journal of Sport and Exercise Psychology, 10,* 322–333.

22

Coaching Demands and Responsibilities of Expert Coaches

Gordon Bloom

McGill University

- Practical experience, such as mentoring, being an athlete, observing coaches, or attending clinics, tends to be more critical than formal education in the development of expert coaches.
- Both Trait Theory and Behavioral Theory explain leadership, which is an important characteristic of expert coaches.
- The Multidimensional Model of Leadership suggests that the success of coaches results from the interaction between the coach and the athlete or athletes and is not based solely on what leadership the coach brings to the team.
- Although each athlete or team is unique, the Coaching Model provides a general structure that increases the likelihood of a coach being successful, including abilities to organize, train, and guide the athlete or team through all phases of competition.

Because people can see what coaches are doing during games, they agree that the best coaches are often effective strategists. Rarely, however, is the public privy to what coaches do before and after games or how much of their lives they give to the sport they love. For example, what personal sacrifices have they made? How much time do they spend preparing for games and practices? What are their views on building team cohesion? How do they analyze their games? These questions all lead to a larger one: "What are the most important demands and responsibilities of expert coaches?" This chapter will answer these questions. First, a number of recommendations will be listed for becoming a top coach, such as the importance of mentoring, hard work, strong leadership, and communication skills. This will be followed by a historical look at early forms of empirical research

The relationship between the coach and the athlete should not be underestimated.

in the coaching domain, such as the work of Chelladurai and colleagues (e.g., Chelladurai, 1978, 1980; Chelladurai & Saleh, 1978, 1980), as well as Smith and Smoll and their associates (e.g., Smith, Smoll, & Barnett, 1995; Smith, Smoll, & Curtis, 1978, 1979; Smith, Smoll, & Hunt, 1977). After this, two recent bodies of coaching research will be explored; one focuses on individual sport coaches, and another examines team sport coaches. All the information in this chapter is intended to explain what it takes to become an expert coach, including the different demands and responsibilities of this noble profession.

Personal Preparation

A large number of children and adults probably wonder how they can increase the likelihood of becoming the next Vince Lombardi, Sparky Anderson, Pat Summitt, or Pat Riley. Unlike a doctor, lawyer, or university professor, there is no definite path to follow in the United States for becoming a top coach. In fact, Martens (1986) stated the estimated 3 million coaches in the United States actually receive very little formal education and training. Let's examine some recent literature on expert coaches to provide guidelines and suggestions for becoming a successful coach.

Coaches' Needs

Gould and colleagues (Gould et al., 1987, 1989, 1990) examined a number of elite coaches' needs in a series of studies that looked at areas such as coach education, coach development, and the use of psychological strategies. The data were gathered from two samples of top coaches: one of these consisted of 130 U.S. national, Olympic, and Pan American coaches from a variety of sports, and the other included more than 100 collegiate wrestling coaches. The methodology for the studies varied from an open-ended questionnaire that assessed the coaches' general information, educational background, participation in coaching science courses, and opinions about coaching and coach education to a questionnaire that assessed coaches' perceptions of athletes' psychological skills, such as self-efficacy, individual motivation, positive attitude, and mental toughness. All three studies using this data contributed important information that offered suggestions for improving the coaching profession as well as for future research in this domain.

One of the findings, which was particularly disturbing to most academics, was that coaching textbooks and seminars were the least important sources of coaching information (Gould et al., 1990). The elite coaches thought the two most important knowledge sources that helped them develop their coaching styles were coaching experience and observing other successful coaches (Gould et al., 1990). The coaches also believed there were no definite sets of concepts or principles to follow in their profession. On the other hand, the coaches "overwhelmingly supported" the need for a more structured coaching education program that would extend beyond coaching manuals and incorporate practical mentoring programs and the value of experiential knowledge. Finally, little or no differences emerged between male and female coaches and coaches of different sports. This led Gould and colleagues (1990) to conclude that elite coaches are a fairly homogenous group in terms of their background and needs.

Bloom, Salmela, and Schinke (1995) conducted a similar study to that of Gould and associates (1989), except they used a different methodology and their sample consisted of expert Canadian coaches. Bloom and colleagues interviewed expert team sport coaches to elicit their recommendations regarding the best methods for acquiring coaching knowledge. The results revealed that expert coaches believed that more emphasis was needed in the following four areas: (1) attending clinics, seminars, and symposia where coaches could interact and exchange ideas with other coaches, (2) learning through hands-on experience with more elite coaches, (3) passive observation of other coaches from the bleachers, standing on the sidelines, or sitting within hearing distance of the coach, and (4) the creation of a structured mentoring program.

Many of the conclusions from their sample of expert Canadian coaches concurred with those reached by Gould and associates (1990) in their study of elite American coaches. One exception worth noting was Bloom and colleagues' emphasis on a structured and formalized mentoring program. The interviewed coaches said the most valuable and enriching coaching knowledge was acquired while they were being mentored by someone who was recognized as an expert in his or her sport. Many of the current and former national team sport coaches still referred to their mentor for advice, having developed a lifelong relationship with him or her. In sum, the research cited in this section reveals that coaching development programs still have a lot of work ahead of them in both Canada and the United States to formalize their approaches toward mentoring. However, this outlook can only improve if those who are at the top of their profession are continuously asked to offer their advice and also are willing to contribute their time to the worthy development of coach education.

Mentoring

The research discussed previously alluded to the importance of **mentoring** in the development of elite coaches, but it did not explicitly examine this phenomenon. Bloom and associates (1998) recently looked at the mentoring experiences of expert team sport coaches. More specifically, the intent of their study was to determine whether any of the current and past top university and Olympic coaches of Canada were mentored through their development as athletes and subsequently as coaches, and if in turn they mentored other athletes and coaches during their careers. It was believed that mentoring occurs when a coach willingly invests time in the personal development of the athlete, when a trusting relationship evolves, when needs and interests are fulfilled, and when imitation of behavior takes place.

The results of their research showed that mentoring is an ongoing process in sport. Almost all these present expert coaches were mentored when they were young athletes and again later as beginning and intermediate coaches. The knowledge and experience they acquired from their expert coaches helped them shape their eventual coaching style and philosophy. Because of their positive experiences, these coaches were willing to mentor young athletes and coaches as well. Unfortunately, there was no set path for acquiring a mentor coach. According to these coaches, it was simply a case of being in the right place at the right time, which might explain why many expert coaches are supporting the need for more formalized mentoring programs.

Athletic Experiences

Two recent bodies of research (Miller, Bloom, & Salmela, 1996; Schinke, Bloom, & Salmela, 1995) examined the characteristics of expert Canadian coaches while they were still athletes. A look at these two studies reveals some variables that suggest that certain characteristics of future elite coaches are evident and developing while they are still performing as athletes.

Schinke and colleagues (1995) interviewed six elite Canadian basketball coaches of men and women to examine their evolution from their first athletic experiences to their present coaching positions. The results of their study revealed seven chronological career stages of these coaches, which were labeled as: (1) early sport participation, (2) national elite sport, (3) international elite sport, (4) novice coaching, (5) developmental coaching, (6) national elite coaching, and (7) international coaching. The first three stages related to the athletic careers of these coaches, and the latter four stages demonstrated the evolution process in the coaching ranks.

Early sport participation referred to the experiences of these coaches when they were beginner and early competitive athletes. They were influenced by their own initial love of sport, as well as parents, sport instructors, and their accessibility to physical resources. Because of their commitment and progression in sport, all these individuals progressed to the next level of development, defined as national elite sport. At this level, the athletes either represented their university or state in national level competitions or competed in the lower levels of professional basketball. Sport now became an obsession as opposed to a recreational activity. Most of the athletes' spare time was spent playing basketball or another team sport. The final stage of their athletic development was defined as international elite sport. To qualify for this stage, the performer had to be a member of their country's Olympic or national team. Two of the six coaches sampled in this study reached this level. According to the researchers, "While it could not be inferred that performing at this level was a prerequisite for future coaching success, the high level of commitment required at the international level apparently contributed to the progression of these coaches" (Schinke, Bloom, & Salmela, 1995, p. 55). An important conclusion that can be gathered from this study is that the acquisition of coaching knowledge follows a fairly consistent developmental process that is rooted in the early athletic experiences of the participants. Although these coaches were not superstar athletes, they did attain high levels of athletic success that undoubtedly influenced their coaching style and philosophy.

While the previous study outlined the stages of athletic development of expert coaches, Miller, Bloom, and Salmela (1996) identified three distinct categories of athletic leadership that were found among a group of twenty-one expert Canadian team sport coaches who were interviewed for their study. First, the expert coaches exhibited strong personalities as athletes that were accentuated by a tenacious work ethic in training. Many of these future coaches were wholeheartedly committed to the pursuit of excellence in all areas of their sport. Second, many of the coaches had been assistants or team captains with their youth and competitive teams. In fact, their own coaches, who often gave them considerable responsibility, recognized many of their leadership skills. Finally, many of these individuals began to coach younger teams as they advanced to higher levels of competition. This usually began in high school, when many would return to assist their local or community coaches. While in college, some returned to help their high school coaches. The skills that these individuals were acquiring would help promote their initiation to high-level coaching positions. The results of this study show that it is never too early for aspiring coaches to acquire the skills and experiences needed to reach a higher level of standing within the coaching domain.

Although there may not be a clear and definitive path for aspiring coaches to follow, this section has identified a number of ways by which one can enhance the likelihood of becoming a coach. They include the importance of being mentored, acquiring hands-on coaching experience, engaging in high levels of competition as an athlete, exhibiting a strong work ethic, and volunteering time as an assistant coach for youth sport teams. Having identified the personal preparation of a coach, it now becomes important to examine some of the models relating to all areas of coaching.

Info Box

Although academic training may be of some benefit in coaching, it does not seem to measure up to practical experiences. Experiencing coaches as an athlete, being mentored, discussing ideas with current coaches, passively observing coaches on the job, or actually engaging in coaching all increase the likelihood of becoming a successful coach.

Historical Research in Coaching

Coakley (1990) reported the word *coach* first came into existence following the American Civil War. Before that time, *coach* was an English word that described a person who taught manners and academic subjects (Coakley, 1990). Since the 1870s, coaching sports has emerged as a profession in which winning and making money for wealthy owners and universities have become a top priority for many organizations (Michener, 1980). On the other hand, some profiles of successful coaches have shown that there can be much more to coaching than winning games and making money for team owners (Walton, 1992; Wooden, 1988). Martens (1990) stated that although coaches historically focused on tactics and techniques, they have recently expanded their knowledge bases to include areas such as sport psychology, sport pedagogy, sport physiology, and sport management. Some of the first forms of empirical research on coaching in the sport psychology domain will now be summarized, beginning with trait versus behavioral models of coaching.

Trait Versus Behavioral Models

One of the most repeated questions by young and aspiring coaches is: "Are certain individuals born with characteristics that predispose them toward a career in coaching?" Although the answer to that question is negative, the topic has led to some interesting debates among academics and nonacademics. The most important characteristic for coaches is leadership. Like a university dean, company president, or ranking army officer, a successful coach is expected to be a good leader. Walton (1992) noted that football coach Woody Hayes felt this component was so important that he always carried with him a list of what he considered to be the ten virtues and characteristics of a good leader (see Fig. 22.1 on page 444).

Many of the early researchers who studied leadership felt that individuals were born with a set of universal personality and leadership qualities and characteristics that are essential for (coaching) success. These theorists supported **trait theories of leadership.** Other theorists believe that leadership characteristics can be learned and developed and that they depend to a large extent on the current situation. These individuals support the

FIGURE 22.1   *Woody Hayes' Ten Virtues and Characteristics of a Good Leader.*

Positive image, character and integrity
Mental toughness, to endure and rebound
Communication skills
To not underestimate the role of the leader
To know your limits and be yourself
Preparation, including anticipation
Accessibility and visibility
Confidence
Ability to inititate interaction
To not underestimate the spiritual power of people

---

behavior theories of leadership. This section of the chapter examines the opposing views of coaching leadership.

Trait Theory.   Traits have been defined as "stable internal structures that served as predispositions to behavior and could therefore be used as adequate predictors of behavior" (Sherman & Fazio, 1983, p. 310). Although the trait theory cannot guarantee that a person will respond in a certain way every time, it does suggest an increased likelihood of predicting certain recurring behaviors or responses across situations and over time. From a sporting context, proponents of this theory believe that certain individuals are born to coach because they display specific personality profiles that distinguish them from other individuals.

Trait theories of leadership originated in the 1920s, when scientists and civilians were interested in the makeup of great leaders in business and industry. The prevalence of war probably had a great deal to do with this curiosity. At the time, many people both in and outside academia wanted to believe that all you had to do was administer a personality inventory to find out who would be a successful leader. The ramifications of this way of thinking about sports could be highly detrimental. Imagine if team owners chose their head coaches based solely on the results of personality tests. Fortunately, after World War II many academics began to disassociate themselves from this thought process.

At that time, the most thorough and in-depth review of the research on the trait theory of leadership came from Stodgill (1948). In reviewing more than 100 research studies, Stodgill concluded that there was little support for personality variables, such as intelligence, independence, and self-confidence, as they relate to trait theory of leadership. Many have suggested that Stodgill's comprehensive review convinced the scientific community to abandon their support of the trait theory of leadership. Furthermore, from a trait theory perspective, few consistent findings in the sporting domain have emerged for ideal coach or athlete leadership skills. In other words, John Elway and Brett Favre, two of the NFL's premier quarterbacks in the 1990s, displayed opposite styles of athletic leadership and still led their teams to Super Bowl victories. Elway prefers a more even-tempered and calm approach to the game, and Favre is seen as someone who exhibits a "looser" style of leadership and shows more emotion and excitement.

Behavioral Theory. Trait theories pose that great leaders are born. Behavior theories propose the opposite, that great leaders can be made or developed simply by learning the necessary skills of other great leaders. The latter approach would obviously be the one favored by most coaches, because it suggests that anyone can learn to be a great leader. The surge of research on behavioral leadership came from Ohio State University in the early 1950s, resulting in two significant contributions. The first was the identification of two important underlying factors that characterize the behaviors of leaders: consideration and initiating structure. Through **consideration** a leader displays behaviors such as trust, friendship, respect, two-way communication, and concern for subordinates. **Initiating structure** refers to more task-oriented behaviors. Leaders are concerned with setting up rules, methods of production, means of communication, and organization to achieve team goals. Although these two behaviors are considered to be independent of one another, aspiring coaches might want to consider incorporating elements of both behaviors into their coaching repertoires.

The second major contribution from Ohio State researchers was the development of a scale, named the Leader Behavior Description Questionnaire (LBDQ), for measuring behavior research. The LBDQ is completed by athletes or subordinates to describe how they feel about their leaders' or coaches' behavior in certain situations, such as their levels of communication and consideration. The LBDQ has exhibited high rates of validity and reliability (Schriesheim & Stodgill, 1975) and has been used in a number of sport-related studies (e.g., Danielson, Zelhart, & Drake, 1975; Snyder, 1990).

Coaching Leadership

Chelladurai's (1978, 1980) pioneering work on leadership in sport led to the creation of the **Multidimensional Model of Leadership** (see Fig. 22.2 on page 446). Created specifically for athletic situations, Chelladurai's model conceptualizes leadership as an interactional process. In his model, three forms of coaches' behaviors affect team performance and satisfaction: required behavior, behavior preferred by athletes, and actual behavior. The three variables are influenced by "antecedent" variables, which include characteristics of the situation, the coach, and the athletes (members). Ideal performance and athlete satisfaction are positively related to the degree of congruence among the three forms of coach behaviors.

Required behaviors are those that are expected of coaches and that adhere to certain standards or norms. For example, coaches are expected to behave in a certain respectful manner toward the media or opposition players and coaches. However, a head coach at Brigham Young University, because of its religious affiliation, is required to adhere to the same moral standards as all other employees within the university. **Preferred leader behaviors** occur when coaches learn to act in a certain way based on either the athletes' preferences or on the past history of the organization for which they work. Thus, head coaches who work for team owners such as Al Davis, George Steinbrenner, or Jerry Jones understand ahead of time that the owner likes to have a say in all team matters, including coaching decisions. Athletes on George Steinbrenner's baseball team know that Steinbrenner is

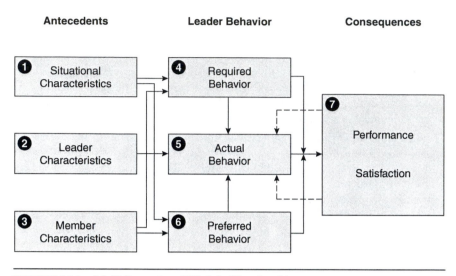

FIGURE 22.2 *Multidimensional Model of Leadership.*

likely to publicly criticize them if they do not perform to his expectations. Athletes and coaches on these teams must understand and respond to this style of leadership if they are to succeed. Finally, **actual leader behaviors** are the behaviors that the coach exhibits, regardless of team standards. This form of behavior also provides the opportunity to explain how antecedent variables influence actual coach behaviors. For example, the same coach might act differently if he or she is coaching professional athletes rather than recreational or high school athletes. Professional athletes are expected to devote themselves wholeheartedly to their sport; if they don't, the coach can release or punish them. Along the same line, the athletes behave differently at these levels, which in turn influences the manner in which the coach behaves. In sum, the characteristics of the situation, the coach, and the athletes all have an impact on the three types of required leader behaviors.

Over the years, researchers have tested a number of hypotheses stemming from the Multidimensional Model in some very interesting and unique ways. One of them focused on the **Leadership Scale for Sport (LSS)** (Chelladurai & Saleh, 1978, 1980), a reliable sport-specific instrument used to test the applicability of the Multidimensional Model of Leadership. The LSS provides information in three areas: the athletes' preferences for specific coaching behaviors, the athletes' perceptions of their coaches leadership behaviors, and the coaches' perceptions of their own behaviors. The large number of studies using the Multidimensional Model is one indication of its relevance in the sport setting. Another is that it has been translated into Finnish, French, Japanese, Korean, Portuguese, and Swedish. The LSS consists of the following five dimensions of coaches' leadership behaviors:

1. *Training:* Coaching behaviors geared toward improving the performance of the athlete through a rigorous and structured training program.
2. *Democratic behavior:* Coaching behavior that gives the athlete a greater say in decisions pertaining to leading the team (during games and practices).

3. *Autocratic behavior:* Coaching behavior that gives the coach sole responsibility for running the team.
4. *Social support:* Coaching behavior that includes a general concern for the well-being of the athletes.
5. *Positive feedback:* Coaching behavior used to reward and praise athletes for their work.

A number of studies have used the LSS to examine different outcomes of the coach/athlete relationship, such as the athlete's satisfaction with the coach's performance (e.g., Chelladurai, 1984; Chelladurai et al., 1988; Dwyer & Fischer, 1990). Dwyer and Fischer (1990), for example, looked at leadership styles of wrestling coaches as a predictor of athlete satisfaction. An important finding was that wrestlers were most satisfied with their coaches' leadership behaviors if the coaches were perceived to exhibit greater amounts of positive feedback and training/instruction and lower levels of autocratic behavior. It should be noted, however, that athletes' satisfaction with their coaches' leadership skills varies by sport and by the skill level of the athlete. One general conclusion can be drawn: compared to their lower-skilled counterparts, highly skilled athletes prefer their coaches to act as teachers/trainers and providers of positive feedback, and they prefer coaches who have a democratic style. The LSS has also been used to examine cross-cultural differences in coaching behaviors. Chelladurai and colleagues (1988) examined differences in coaching behaviors and satisfaction between Canadian and Japanese athletes. The results of their study indicated that male Japanese athletes preferred autocratic behavior and social support from their coaches, but Canadian athletes preferred training and instruction-type behavior. These preferences may indicate that culture plays a crucial role in understanding effective leadership.

Another interesting dimension of the LSS concerns the outcome of team performance. Weiss and Friedrichs (1986) are among the few researchers who have examined this issue. They solicited 251 American collegiate basketball players and 23 coaches to study a number of variables related to team performance, as measured by win-loss record. The results, which surprised the authors, showed that only the dimension of social support was significant, but in a negative fashion. Thus, higher levels of social support were associated with lower winning percentages. It could not be concluded, however, that higher levels of social support caused the team to lose. Perhaps teams that perform poorly require more social support from their leaders. The authors cautioned that more work is needed in this area.

These studies present the results of only a small fraction of the many examinations of the LSS relating to important components of the coach–athlete relationship. It can be concluded that team performance and athlete satisfaction is highest if the three types of leader behavior agree or are congruent. In other words, a coach will excel if he or she exhibits leadership qualities that are in line with his or her particular situation. A modern sport example would be Phil Jackson, the former head coach of the Chicago Bulls basketball team. It wasn't until Jackson brought his own style of leadership, one that stressed team success, that the Bulls began to win their string of world championships. Although this was certainly not the only reason for the Bulls' success, it can reasonably be concluded that it did have an impact. In fact, it appears that once the athletes accepted, and even embraced, Jackson's leadership style, the team's satisfaction and performance increased. Nevertheless, Chelladurai (1993) has referred to the research in this area as "piecemeal," primarily because all segments of the multidimensional model have yet to be explored. It was suggested that future studies more closely examine causal linkages of the results, the experiences and insights of both coaches and athletes, and the operational definitions of some leader behaviors, specifically when the team is the unit of analysis.

Info Box

An important characteristic of effective coaching is leadership. In general, effective coaches integrate the ability to provide a rigorous training structure with democracy, support, and positive feedback. However, coaches must find a balance that provides for cultural and situational considerations.

Coach–Athlete Interactions

A related area of research to Chelladurai's is the work of Smith, Smoll, and colleagues, who conducted several studies dealing with the relationships and interactions between youth sport coaches and athletes (Smith, Smoll, & Barnett, 1995; Smith, Smoll, & Curtis, 1978, 1979; Smith, Smoll, & Hunt, 1977). Smith and Smoll were initially interested in a number of coach–athlete interactions, such as what coaches do and how often they exhibit the behaviors of encouragement, punishment, instruction, and organization. A major difference between this line of research and the preceding one was the measurement. While Chelladurai and colleagues used questionnaires, Smith, Smoll, and associates observed and recorded coaches' behaviors through the development of a standardized scoring system. Although this research deals with youth sport coaches, it provides important information about ideal behaviors that can be useful for coaches at all levels.

Smith and Smoll's research led to the creation of the **Coaching Behavior Assessment System** (CBAS), probably the most well-known behavior observation instrument for coding coaches' behaviors during games and practices. In the first of many studies, Smith, Smoll, and Hunt (1977) developed the CBAS from direct observation of youth sport coaches and unveiled twelve behavioral dimensions that can be classified into two categories. The first, the coach's **reactive behaviors,** included immediate coach reactions to player or team mistakes, desirable performances, or misbehaviors. The second category, the coach's **spontaneous behaviors,** dealt with either relevant or irrelevant behaviors exhibited during a game that were not in response to an observable preceding event.

The purpose of their research was to create a training program for youth sport coaches based on the results of the CBAS. In the first of their studies, Smith, Smoll, and Curtis (1978, 1979) observed fifty-one little league coaches over 201 games and approximately 1,000 behaviors of each coach. A total of 542 players, aged 8–15, were also interviewed. The strength of this research was that it emphasized actual coach behaviors by allowing athletes the opportunity to assess and recall the coaches' behaviors and their overall sporting experiences. Smith, Smoll, and Curtis then trained seventeen observers over a 4-week period to use the CBAS to measure and observe coaches.

One particularly interesting finding from their research was that the coach was an important factor in the development of young athletes. For example, two observed behavioral dimensions from the CBAS, supportiveness and instructiveness, were positively related to the players' attitudes toward their coach, sport, and teammates (Smith, Smoll, Curtis, 1979). Their research also revealed that trained and untrained coaches differed in their behaviors. Trained coaches communicated more effectively than untrained coaches, were evaluated more positively by players, and saw their players acquire significant increases in self-esteem from the previous year.

Smith, Smoll, and their colleagues have continued to use adapted versions of the CBAS to study a variety of youth sport coaches in different areas, such as coaches' effect on athlete enjoyment (Smith et al., 1983) and coaches' effect on athletes' self-esteem (Smith & Smoll, 1990). In the first of these two studies, it was found that, in general, coaching behaviors had a significant impact on players' enjoyment of their sport, team solidarity, evaluation of coaches, and self-esteem (Smith et al., 1983). Furthermore, coaches who provided more mistake-contingent technical instruction, less punishment, less general feedback, and who engaged in fewer controlling behaviors were rated more positively by athletes. In the second study cited, Smith and Smoll (1990) found that children who were low in self-esteem responded more favorably to coaches who were reinforcing and encouraging and negatively to coaches who were not supportive.

In conclusion, the work of Smith, Smoll, and their colleagues has added a great deal of practical knowledge to the training methods of youth sport coaches. While this section only summarized a small segment of their work, it can be seen that certain ideal behaviors exist for youth sport coaches (remain positive, encouraging, and stress fundamentals) and that youth sport coaches can be trained to exhibit these ideal behaviors.

Recent Research in Coaching

The 1990s have witnessed a growth of empirical research in the coaching domain, much of which was influenced by the preceding bodies of research. Sport psychologist John Salmela, his colleagues, and graduate students at the University of Ottawa have led a great deal of the current research on coaching. This research has followed a qualitative format, one that involved in-depth interviews with a coach and the researcher. This method allowed the coaches to express their thoughts, feelings, emotions, and knowledge in a nonthreatening and unstructured manner. For example, Côté, Salmela, and colleagues (Côté, 1993; Côté & Salmela, 1996; Côté, Salmela, & Russell, 1995; Côté et al., 1995) studied the knowledge of expert individual (i.e., gymnastic) coaches; Bloom, Salmela, and collaborators (Bloom, Durand-Bush, & Salmela, 1997; Bloom et al., 1998; Bloom, Schinke, & Salmela, 1997; Miller, Bloom, & Salmela, 1996; Schinke, Bloom, & Salmela, 1995) investigated similar information of expert team sport (i.e., basketball, volleyball, field hockey, ice hockey) coaches. Recently, John Salmela supervised research of Luiz Carlos Moraes (1998) that examined expert coaches of combat (judo) sports. Although the two research projects had different goals and looked at different sports, there were a number of similarities. This included categorizing coaches' demands, responsibilities, and knowledge into three primary and three peripheral topics. Each of these six categories will be addressed in this part of the chapter, including differences between individual and team sport coaches. This section will also include a discussion of the Coaching Model (Côté, 1993; Côté et al., 1995) and an explanation of the Coaching Process (Bloom, 1997). Before proceeding, it is necessary to provide a brief overview of the structure of these two bodies of research.

Research on Expert Individual Sport Coaches

Jean Côté, John Salmela, and their colleagues (Côté & Salmela, 1996; Côté, Salmela, & Russell, 1995; Côté et al., 1995) interviewed 17 Canadian high-performance gymnastic coaches with a framework that allowed them to explore and conceptualize the structure of the coaches' knowledge without imposing any boundaries on what or how the coaches responded. All coaches had accumulated a minimum of 10 years of coaching experience, produced at least one international and two national level athletes, and were identified by their national coaching association as the top in their country. An analysis of this data resulted in the creation of the **Coaching Model (CM)** consisting of three primary components of coaching, labeled as organization, training, and competition, as well as three peripheral components, labeled as coach's characteristics, gymnast's personal characteristics, and contextual factors. Two other factors, the coach's goal and belief in the athlete's potential, completed the model (Fig. 22.3).

The Coaching Model.   Côté and colleagues' (1995) creation of the CM was significant because it was the first theoretical framework for explaining which factors were most important for coaches as well as the relationships among these factors. While earlier research from Chelladurai (1978, 1980, 1984) and Smith, Smoll, and their associates (1977, 1978, 1990) identified models to investigate forms of coaching, such as leadership and the coaches' interactions during training and competition, they did not provide a conceptual framework that included broader variables involved in coaching. This point was alluded to in the results of an earlier study that listed the educational needs of American coaches (Gould et al., 1990, p. 342). In particular, Gould and associates found that "one disconcert-

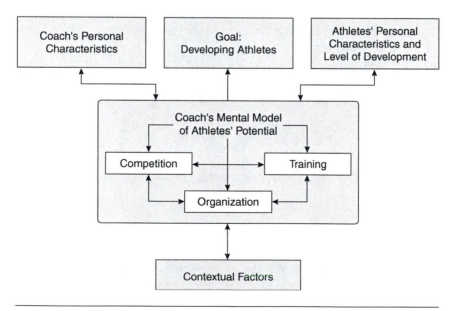

FIGURE 22.3   *The Coaching Model*

ing finding was that less than half of the coaches sampled felt that there exists a well-defined set of concepts and principles for coaches." Côté and colleagues (1995, p. 2) noted further that "without a general model of coaching, the knowledge accumulated through research remains disconnected information related to how and why coaches work as they do." It seems safe to surmise, therefore, that the CM will have a significant impact on all future forms of research carried out in the coaching domain.

Research on Expert Team Sport Coaches

John Salmela (1996) and Gordon Bloom (1997) led research at the University of Ottawa on expert team sport coaches. Salmela (1996) interviewed 22 of Canada's leading team sport coaches using an interview technique similar to the one employed by Côté and colleagues. The intent of Salmela's research was to uncover each coach's knowledge, including whether commonalties emerged across coaches and sports. He was interested in their evolution from athlete to novice coach to expert coach. Moreover, what experiences and opportunities did these coaches share and what were their common philosophies in the areas of organization, training, and competition? The coaches were chosen by international sport governing bodies based on a number of criteria, including coaching for at least 10 years, producing top athletes and teams, and achieving recognition from peers. The coaches were involved in the sports of ice hockey, field hockey, volleyball, and basketball, and represented men and women who had coached at the professional, Olympic, and collegiate levels. Bloom (1997) also examined team sport coaches; however, this research did not include any athletic or early coaching experiences. It focused on identifying the characteristics, knowledge, and strategies of expert coaches, and then conceptualizing the relationships between these categories.

Primary Categories of Coaches Knowledge

Research from both individual and team sport coaches identified three primary categories of a coach's knowledge: organization, training, and competition. The following discussion will explain and define each of the primary categories, including their internal makeup and any differences between individual and team sport coaches.

Organization

Organization is a prerequisite step to help coaches prepare for training and competition. It is the coaches' organizational skills that allow a season to be seen from the broadest perspective and then to sequence events through a planned process. Côté and Salmela (1996, p. 250) defined organization as "the knowledge used by coaches to establish optimal training and competition conditions by structuring and coordinating various coaching tasks."

Organization always has been represented as an important component in the success of teams or athletes, even if the exact term has not been used in most coaching textbooks, empirical studies, or autobiographies. For example, Douge and Hastie (1993) reviewed five approaches for examining coaching effectiveness, and all of them included what could be labeled as organizational tasks. Lacy and colleagues (Lacy & Darst, 1985; Lacy & Goldston,

1990) examined the behaviors of successful coaches during practice sessions. Through the use of a systematic observation procedure, they revealed two important categories of knowledge for top high school coaches: instruction and organization. Martens' (1990) textbook on coaching provides one of the best accounts of organization because it devotes two chapters to the planning skills of coaches. Coaches were encouraged to invest time in planning their activities, and three steps were listed for effectively developing a seasonal plan. First, coaches should establish their instructional goals. Second, they should select the subject matter needed to achieve each goal. Finally, they should organize the subject matter for instruction. After the coaches mapped out their plan for the season, two final steps were recommended. Coaches first should evaluate their athletes' initial level of skill and knowledge, and then they should orient their drills toward areas that need improvement.

The studies from Côté, Salmela, Bloom, and their colleagues all explicitly listed organization as a crucial variable for the success of any individual or team sport. The internal makeup of this category differed somewhat with these studies, which probably had more to do with the different demands inherent with team and individual sports than with a different understanding of the term. In their study of individual sport coaches, Côté and Salmela (1996) listed five subcomponents of organization: (1) working with parents, (2) working with assistants, (3) helping gymnasts with personal concerns, (4) planning training, (5) monitoring weight and esthetics. Salmela (1996) and Bloom (1997), on the other hand, listed eight organizational components of team sport coaches in their research: (1) the vision, (2) planning, (3) team selection, (4) goal setting, (5) team rules, (6) building team cohesion, (7) administrative concerns, (8) working with support staff.

The research on individual sport coaches listed categories that dealt with one-on-one relationships between coaches and their athletes. For example, working with parents, helping gymnasts with personal concerns (e.g., relationships with family members, personal and social lives, education, and retirement from sport), and monitoring weight/esthetics (only discussed by coaches of female gymnasts) all require a large amount of a coach's time and energy, something that probably isn't possible if dealing with a team of anywhere from 10 to 60 athletes. This difference also might be explained by the age of elite gymnasts, usually much younger than top performers from other sports. Gymnastic coaches, therefore, must have a great deal more interaction and communication with the athletes' parents compared to most other elite sports.

The main similarity between individual and team sport coaches was the importance placed on planning. All coaches felt it was important to plan ahead; this included quadrennial plans for Olympic coaches as well as seasonal, monthly, weekly, and daily plans for all coaches. The seven other organizational categories mentioned by team sport coaches directly relate to the dynamics involved with team sports, beginning with "the vision."

The Vision.   The most important subcomponent of organization for team sports was labeled as "**the vision.**" All team sport coaches felt very strongly about beginning any season or championship quest by clearly outlining the mission for their team and the steps necessary to achieve success. Without an explicit plan or vision from the coach, the team is unlikely to excel. Although basketball coach Phil Jackson is most known for implementing the Triangle Offense in helping lead the Chicago Bulls to a number of NBA championships in the 1990s, what many individuals fail to realize is the vision that he first had for his team in relation to Michael Jordan, their star player.

> I flashed back to 1989 when I took over as head coach and had talked to Michael about how I wanted him to share the spotlight with his teammates so the team could grow and flourish. In those days he was a gifted young athlete with enormous confidence in his own abilities that had to be cajoled into making sacrifices for the team. Now he was an older, wiser player who understood that it wasn't brilliant individual performances that made great teams, but the energy that's unleashed when players put their egos aside and work toward a common goal. (Jackson & Delehanty, 1995, p. 21)

Former Northwestern University head football coach Gary Barnett provides another example of the importance of setting a vision for your athletes. Barnett took over a floundering football program in the early 1990s, one that set a record of 49 consecutive losses. Within 4 years, Barnett had led his Northwestern Wildcats football team to the Rose Bowl.

> Early on, we also created two Mission Statements that we now print in our media guide, which also is for recruiting.
>
> Our mission is to take the student-athlete where he cannot take himself. We will foster an environment that teaches young men to:
>
> 1. Relentlessly pursue and win The Big Ten Championship!
> 2. Appreciate and embrace cultural diversity.
> 3. Achieve an exemplary foundation of leadership and academic success.
>
> Our mission is based on the values of family, successful attitudes, and team chemistry. We believe in honesty, integrity, strength of character, care, and confidence. We embrace a commitment to excellence, loyalty, selflessness, trust, and humility. We teach overcoming adversity, establishing priorities, goal setting, and the value of diversity. (Barnett & Gregorian, 1996, p. 19)

Although setting a clear vision is very important for team sport coaches, motivating the athletes to buy into this vision is equally as important (Bloom, 1997; Salmela, 1996). When the athletes buy into their coaches' plan or vision, and the talent is present, the results are likely to end up as they did with Phil Jackson and the Chicago Bulls (i.e., winning many championships). Consider the following quote from one of the ice hockey coaches in Salmela's (1996, p. 70) research:

> One of the things I now feel is important is to try and make sure you can create the same vision in the minds of all your players. I have heard some people talk about it, saying "There is the North Star, we all want to follow the North Star." With the National Junior Team we wanted to win the gold medal. Once we had established the goal, I tried to make sure my athletes knew there were lots of different paths to that gold medal, that there was no set way of doing it. The key to getting there is the decision as a group that we are going to follow one way, and the guy who has been designated to set that direction is the coach.

The other six categories mentioned by the team sport coaches—team selection, team rules, team cohesion, goal setting, administrative concerns, dealing with support staff—all relate to factors that will help the team function as a more complete and synchronized machine. The only category that might not be easily understood is administrative concerns. This dealt with money issues, finding housing for athletes, recruiting, athletic scholarships, and interactions with the university and/or sport governing bodies. In conclusion, coaches who are organized will have solid foundations from which to begin their seasons, including more effective training sessions.

Training

Quality training or practicing is an important time for most coaches. This is an opportunity to display their knowledge and skills to help their athletes prepare for competition. An old saying supports the significance of effective training time: "Practice doesn't make perfect; perfect practice makes perfect."

A great deal of research has been carried out in the sport sciences to look at different components or aspects of training. A popular method of gathering data in this area is known as **systematic observation.** Tharp and Gallimore (1976) carried out the first sport study using this method when they examined the practice sessions of legendary basketball coach John Wooden. Tharp and Gallimore (1976, p. 75) noted that although some successful college coaches "see their roles mostly as group facilitators or emotional managers, or even administrators, Wooden's system of basketball requires teaching and learning, everything from complex set-offense options to how to pull up your socks on right." They also found that most of Wooden's comments were instructional, meaning they were verbal cues relating to the basic fundamentals of playing basketball. Furthermore, Wooden seldom used positive statements in coaching although his negative statements were consistently followed by instructions, and he rarely used physical or negative punishment.

Lacy and associates (Lacy & Darst, 1985; Lacy & Goldston, 1990) used a similar methodology for acquiring data on the practice sessions of high school head coaches. They concluded that half of the coaches' behaviors were instructional in nature. More recently, Bloom, Crumpton, and Anderson (1999) coded the coaching behaviors of Fresno State basketball coach Jerry Tarkanian throughout the course of a season. Using a modified version of Tharp and Gallimore's (1976) instrument that further divided the instruction category into technical, tactical, and other measures, Bloom, Crumpton, and Anderson found that tactical instructions represented almost one-third of Tarkanian's coaching behaviors during practices. The next closest category, called hustles, where the coach was encouraging his players to work harder, had a frequency that was almost half that of tactical instructions.

It is important to consider that all of the coaches observed in these studies used their practice sessions to improve various elements of their athletes' technical and tactical skills. The old school of thinking, one that involves an extensive physical training component and excessive verbal abuse, appears to have been replaced by more effective, learner-friendly training sessions.

Although the studies on individual and team sport coaches defined training in a similar manner, the subcomponents contained within this category differed. In Côté, Salmela, and Russell's (1995) work on expert gymnastic coaches, training was broken down into the following five categories: (1) technical skills, (2) mental skills, (3) intervention style, (4) simulation, (5) coach involvement. Salmela (1996) and Bloom (1997) divided training into four equally important categories that are the most commonly recognized: (1) physical training, (2) technical training, (3) tactical training, (4) mental training.

Physical Training. **Physical training** is the area in which athletes' respiratory, energy, and muscular systems are prepared from aerobic, anaerobic, flexibility, and strength perspectives. The sole purpose of this component is to train the athletes' physical strength, endurance, and conditioning so they will perform well in competition. Coaches are adamant in their feelings about the importance of hard, strenuous training, using practices that are up-tempo and fast-moving (Bloom, 1997; Salmela, 1996).

Tactical Training. The area that deals with teaching the cognitive strategies used by coaches to outsmart their opponents is known as **tactical training.** It was apparent that the coaches carefully crafted their practice environment with plays and strategies. An important part of tactical training was simulating the game situations of their opponents (Bloom, 1997; Salmela, 1996).

Technical Training. A third element of training, technical aspects or the skill-based dimension, appears to be the most obvious pedagogical part of coaching. **Technical training** occurs when coaches provide instruction to their athletes that will enhance the learning of individual motor skills or interactive team maneuvers. It was important to these coaches that all their players received some form of individual attention to help them reach their athletic potential (Bloom, 1997; Côté, Salmela, & Russell, 1995; Salmela, 1996).

Mental Training. A final segment of training included **mental training.** The brain is trained to think and react optimally in pressure situations. The expert coaches all incorporated some form of mental training into their athletes' regimens, although some gave it more priority than others. Many of the coaches felt it was important as well to hire a sport psychologist to work with their team on the finer aspects of mental training, such as motivation, controlling anxiety, and visualization techniques (Bloom, 1997; Côté, Salmela, & Russell, 1995; Salmela, 1996).

Competition

It should come as no surprise to see competition listed as one of the three primary categories of coaching, along with training and organization. This category relates to those tasks that take place throughout the day of competition. While early research on competition focused on youth sport coaches (e.g., Smith, Smoll, & Curtis, 1978, 1979; Smith, Smoll, & Hunt, 1977), recently some empirical sources on expert coaches have contributed to the body of knowledge in this area (e.g., Bloom, Durand-Bush, & Salmela, 1997; Côté, Salmela, & Russell, 1995; Salmela, 1996).

Côté, Salmela, and Russell (1995) broke down the competition category for expert gymnastic coaches into the competition site, the competition floor, and trial competitions. Competition site included all the time spent by coaches during a competition day, weekend, or week that was not spent immediately before, during, or after an event. The competition floor encompassed all of the time spent by the gymnasts immediately before, during,

Attention to the finer points of the game is often the responsibility of the expert coach.

or after an event. Trial competitions were defined as "real competitions" in which the gymnasts participated that would help them become more confident and technically strong.

Research on team sport coaches' interactions before, during, and after competitions has been even more extensive than research on individual sport coaches (e.g., Bloom, 1997; Bloom, Durand-Bush, & Salmela, 1997; Salmela, 1996). This probably can be attributed to the complexity and importance of team sport coaches' activities before, during, and after competition. In team sports, for example, coaches play an active role during competition, whereas in individual sports (skiing, equestrian, figure skating, or gymnastics) coaches act more as passive observers, because there are no athlete substitutions, time-outs, and few interactions with officials. It seems safe to surmise that although studies on individual and team sport coaches defined competition in a similar manner (pre-, during, and postcompetition), only data from team sport coaches necessitated a more in-depth analysis of this area of coaching.

Precompetition. Precompetition routines of team sport coaches involve their tasks from the moment they wake up on the morning of game day until they arrive on-site. These duties are further divided into those related to the team and those related to the coaches themselves. In the former, coaches focus on the early morning routines of their athletes, helping them mentally prepare for the game and organizing team meetings. Early morning routines refer to such activities as pregame meals, transportation, and team routines, all thought by coaches to increase the closeness of the team.

Another area within precompetition was the personal preparation coaches provided for themselves. The quality of their coaching performance often was affected by the amount of preparation accomplished earlier in the day. It was found that expert team sport coaches had their own routines on game day, including preparing their minds and bodies early in the day, mentally rehearsing for the upcoming game, arriving early at the competition site, and adhering to specific procedures during the pregame warm-up of their players. The following two quotes from Salmela (1996, pp. 147–149) highlight these points:

> I do a lot of things, like a daily run. On game day, that run is very important to me because it is my quiet time to think. No phones and nothing but me and my dog. He doesn't talk; he just runs. That's great....

> I have a specific plan for myself during the game. During my preparation, I try to go through the things I think I am going to do. It is like practicing my game plan. I try to run through some scenarios, saying, "If this doesn't work, then I will do this." I don't get too locked in because too many things can happen.

Two final areas contained within the precompetition routines of expert team sport coaches were the pregame warm-up and the pregame pep talk. With respect to the warm-up, the coaches stressed the importance of having one that was well-run, professional, and cohesive. They wanted their athletes to use this time to mentally prepare themselves for the upcoming contest. During the time of their team's warm-up, the coaches either scouted their opponents or rested in the coaches' room. The second category contained within precompetition was the pregame pep talk. While many individuals still believe in the old rah-rah inspirational type of pep talk, one that was made famous by Knute Rockne's "Win one for the Gipper" speech, these coaches felt otherwise. Like Martens (1987) and Cox (1994) earlier, the results of these studies (Bloom, Durand-Bush, & Salmela, 1997; Salmela, 1996) revealed that coaches preferred a calm, even-tempered pregame pep talk. They believe their athletes have individual needs and arousal levels that would be differentially affected by a high-spirited pep talk. The coaches' final words were process-centered and reviewed three or four of the most important points stressed in the previous week's preparation.

During Competition.   Salmela's (1996) textbook revealed a number of important areas once the competition began. In fact, it was found that team sport coaches still had significant responsibilities because the slightest edge might make the difference between victory and defeat. The information related to the strategic use of time-outs and substitutions, judicious interactions with game officials, providing athletes with appropriate playing time, and the effective use of intermission breaks. The coaches' understanding of sport went beyond the basic textbook strategies. They reported what might be considered an uncanny ability, while reading the game, to notice what few others did. Most of the factors just listed do not apply to coaches of individual sports because they generally take a passive approach during competition.

Postcompetition.   Postcompetition activities of expert team sport coaches dealt with four areas: how the coaches handled the outcome, how they coped with their own emotions, what they did and said in the locker room, and their postgame evaluation (Bloom, Durand-Bush, & Salmela, 1997; Salmela, 1996). The content and focus of the postcompetition meeting depended both on the outcome and on the coaches' perceptions of whether the team played well or poorly. For example, when the team won and played well, coaches emphasized effort and performance, not just outcome. Second, when they won but played poorly, coaches stressed areas needing improvement and acknowledged those individuals who gave a solid effort. Coaches felt that winning was the priority, and whenever the team won, the athletes should savor it, no matter how poorly the coaches thought they had played.

Losses depended on whether the coaches felt the players performed up to their capabilities. For example, when the team lost but played well, the expert team sport coaches said it was important to remain encouraging, focusing on the positive aspects of their performance. However, when the team lost and played poorly, most of these coaches felt it was best to say little to their players because the players usually weren't in a receptive mode and they themselves worried about saying something they would later regret. The coaches had to hold back their natural tendency to correct any flaws or errors that they noticed during the game. They felt the best time for this was at the next training session, not immediately after a game.

After the contest, the expert team sport coaches also had to deal with their own emotions before entering the locker room. Many chose to take some time for themselves in order to "wind down." This is another significant difference between individual and team sport coaches. While the former are generally unobtrusive observers, the latter play an active role in the contest and often experience the same emotions as many of their athletes. After gathering their thoughts, the coaches were ready to enter the locker room. Most coaches said very little because they realized that both they and their athletes still were very emotional. They especially were aware that they shouldn't single out any individual player. One reason for not analyzing the game in the locker room was that the coaches wanted to complete a thorough postgame evaluation, something that took place within 24 hours of the match. The expert team sport coaches were cognizant of the importance of consulting a number of resources, such as videos of the contest, statistics, and assistant coaches, before finalizing the postgame evaluation.

Info Box

Knowledge about training athletes physically, technically, tactically, and mentally is the responsibility of the coach, as is approaching competition and leading the athlete or team through it. However, organizational abilities are even more crucial in coaching. Developing a season-long strategy, slamming individual practice days, and preparating for competition require the coaches to establish a "vision" of what their team has the potential to accomplish.

Peripheral Categories of Coaches Knowledge

Côté and colleagues' (1995) CM detailed the importance of the three primary categories of organization, training, and competition. It also explained how the primary categories are directly affected by their interactions with three peripheral components called the coach's characteristics, athlete's characteristics, and contextual factors. These three categories will now be defined and explained.

Coaches' Characteristics

Côté and associates (1995) defined the **coaches' characteristics** as any variables that are part of the coach's philosophy, perceptions, beliefs, or personal life that could influence any or all of the three primary categories. Bloom (1997) and Salmela's (1996) coaches' characteristics dealt with the coach's continuing passion for acquiring knowledge, the maturation process of coaching, the necessity of hard work, and the ability to find the right coaching style.

A common trait to emerge from team sport coaches was their continued quest for acquiring more coaching knowledge (Bloom, 1997; Salmela, 1996). No matter how long they had been coaching, there was consensus that one never should stop learning. Attending coaching clinics, gaining coaching experience, and interacting with peers were some of the most important methods of learning. Along the same line, the coaches in both Bloom and Salmela's research explicitly stated the value of a strong work ethic. Many of these coaches noted how they work in a very competitive field, and the only way to succeed is by working harder than their colleagues work. This may mean sacrificing a long weekend with one's family to recruit or not going to the movies because the only film these coaches have time to watch are game films. Finally, the coaches discussed the importance of developing a personalized coaching style. Coaches felt that to succeed, they had to develop a coaching style that best suited their personality. Emulating other successful coaches was not always the best way to proceed.

Athletes' Characteristics

Côté and colleagues (1995) defined the **athletes' characteristics** as any variables relating to the athlete's stage of learning, personal abilities, and other personal characteristics that could affect the three primary categories. Bloom's (1997) and Salmela's (1996) understanding of this category was similar in many respects. In particular, athletes characteristics dealt with the importance of helping athletes' grow both inside and outside of sport, respecting athletes, the type of (professional) relationship coaches have with their athletes, and ways to establish the ideal learning environment for athletes.

An important finding from both of these studies of expert coaches was that they sought to improve their athletes' lives both inside and outside of sport, in other words to develop the whole person. The coaches were concerned about the personal success of their athletes once their sporting careers were over. The following quote illustrates this point:

> The idea is you want to develop independent thinking, creative, responsible individuals who can make decisions when they leave. Clearly, it's incumbent upon the athlete to develop self-discipline and properly manage their time and priorities. There will be ups and downs, pitfalls along the way, but in the end, if they've survived a rigorous, demanding, and intense athletic involvement, and if they've also done well academically, achieving their degree, what more rewarding experience could you ask for? (Salmela, 1996, p. 50)

In contrast to the similarities, there were some differences between the individual and team sport coaches in this category. Not surprisingly, the difference is directly attributable to the different demands of individual and team sports. Whereas individual sport coaches can divert all of their attention to one athlete all of the time and thus create more personal decisions around a single athlete, team sport coaches must be aware of how their interactions relate to the overall organization and effectiveness of the team.

Contextual Factors

Côté and associates (1995, p. 12) defined **contextual factors** as "unstable factors, aside from the athletes and the coach, such as working conditions, that need to be considered when intervening in the organization, training, and competition components." These also could be defined as situationally specific variables. Bloom (1997) and Salmela (1996) have listed a number of contextual factors that include the university, the professional, and the family context. Depending on the advantages or disadvantages inherent within each of these components, a coach or team's win–loss record could be greatly influenced. For example, a team in the university setting can gain a significant advantage over other schools if it receives more to fund scholarships and to purchase new equipment.

The team sport coaches alluded to a number of different variables or constraints that were present in different environments, such as the collegiate, international, professional, or Olympic contexts (Bloom, 1997; Salmela, 1996). For example, when traveling internationally overseas, the coaches must prepare their teams with more than just tactics and techniques. They also must study the culture, food, and political climate. Other interesting scenarios greeted coaches of professional sport teams. Many of these coaches found themselves dealing with athletes who were making more money than they were, and, in some cases, who had more control or power over team decisions than they did. They also had to deal with management who sometimes wanted certain players to receive more playing time due to their contractual status. These were variables that often received little or no attention in the minor league or collegiate contexts.

One final area was the influence of the family on the lives of the coaches. In fact, Salmela (1996) provides one of the most candid portrayals of the problems facing coaches—trying to establish a solid family life. Many of these coaches were divorced or chose not to get married because many of them traveled for 200 days of the year. This was a sacrifice they chose to make, and one that they believed helped them progress up the coaching ranks. On the other hand, there was a glimmer of hope provided by the coaches who remained married. Most of them stated that marrying a former athlete or fellow coach was the ideal solution or marrying a spouse who clearly understood the sacrifices that they would have to make.

The Coaching Process

An important contribution from the research on expert coaches (Bloom, 1997; Côté, Salmela, & Russell, 1995) was the way it explained the relationship between the primary and peripheral categories. The term "**coaching process**" refers to the manner in which the six categories affect one another. Although Côté and associates' (1995) results were analogous to those carried out on expert team sport coaches, there were some differences other than those dealing with the dynamics between the two types of sports. The most important related to the primary objective of the two studies. Côté and colleagues' research examined factors affecting the knowledge of coaches for developing elite gymnasts, which ultimately led to the creation of the CM. The CM did not provide a detailed analysis of how the coaches' interpersonal characteristics, such as their quest for knowledge and personal growth, affected their interactions in the other five categories. Thus, a primary goal of the research on expert team sport coaches was to uncover the characteristics that made these coaches special, including how the characteristics explained the coaches' interactions within the organizational, training, and competition elements, as well as athlete interactions and adaptations to different coaching contexts (Bloom, 1997).

Bloom (1997) found that the coaches' interpersonal characteristics infused energy and directed the other five categories. These coaches were totally possessed with all aspects of their profession, including becoming the best coach possible. Although this was labeled as a peripheral category, it is very important because it affects such crucial areas as how coaches acquire coaching knowledge and how it has shaped their interactions with athletes and other individuals involved within their sport. For example, if coaches are rigid and unwilling to learn, they are likely to encounter problems in the central areas of organization, training, and competition. On the other hand, coaches who choose to attend clinics, seminars, and symposia to update their knowledge and who regularly exchange information with their peers will probably have more interesting practices, more detailed seasonal plans, and more success at competitions. In addition, coaches with more intricate personal approaches to coaching, such as working harder and communicating more effectively, should have happier players who will produce better results during competition (Bloom, 1997).

Conclusion and Recommendations

This chapter has explained the demands and responsibilities of expert coaches, including how coaches can begin to acquire coaching knowledge when they are athletes and beginner coaches. Côté and colleagues' (1995) CM helped to identify the primary and peripheral aspects of a coach's profession, especially coaches of individual sports. Bloom's (1997) and Salmela's (1996) research on team sport coaches found that although the larger picture remained unchanged with the same six categories emerging, some differences did exist. Most prominently, Bloom's (1997) research outlined how the coaches' personal characteristics are a starting point for understanding how the coaching process works. Expert team sport coaches were driven by a persistent quest for personal growth, learning, and development. This drive and determination often led to achievement in their profession.

Although research in coaching has progressed significantly in the last decade, there is still much more to be accomplished. With the increase in salaries of such professional coaches as Rick Pitino and Pat Riley in basketball, Tony LaRussa and Jim Leyland in baseball, Scotty Bowman in hockey, and Bill Parcells in football combined with the recent empirical surge of studies in sport psychology, one can expect research in this unique domain to continually move forward. Until that time, the following recommendations and key points are offered:

1. Developing coaches should acquire hands-on coaching experience, observe other successful coaches, attend clinics, seminars, and symposia, and, most importantly, acquire a mentor coach.
2. The acquisition of coaching knowledge begins with one's athletic experiences.
3. A balance among the three types of coaching leadership (required, preferred, actual) produces ideal team performance and athlete satisfaction.
4. Youth sport coaches can be trained to exhibit the ideal characteristics for athlete performance and satisfaction.
5. Recent research has indicated that top coaches are not born with certain leadership qualities; these characteristics can be learned.
6. The CM represents an important development in the research on coaching psychology because it is the first theoretical framework for explaining which factors are most important in this domain.
7. Strong organizational skills are important assets for coaches of all levels.
8. It is important to have a plan or vision for the team that is verbally expressed to the athletes at the beginning of each season.
9. It is necessary to master knowledge of the physical, tactical, technical, and mental components of training.
10. Coaches meticulously prepare both themselves and their athletes for upcoming competitions.
11. Coaches prefer an even-tempered pregame pep talk.
12. Coaches assess their team's performance based on the outcome and their perception of the team's effort.
13. Coaches say very little to their team at the completion of the contest, preferring to first thoroughly analyze the match.

14. Coaches stress the importance of continuous learning.
15. Successful coaches attribute a great deal of their success to hard work and dedication.
16. Coaches are concerned with the personal development of their athletes.
17. Successful coaches are able to adapt to different contexts.
18. Marriage and family for successful coaches requires great sacrifices that need to be clearly outlined to a potential spouse.
19. Coaches' interpersonal characteristics plays a large part in their interactions and adaptations to the different areas of their profession.

Acknowledgments.   Appreciation is extended to John H. Salmela and Richard W. Francis for their insightful feedback on earlier drafts of this chapter.

Key Terms (in order of appearance)

mentoring
trait theories of leadership
behavior theories of leadership
consideration
initiating structure
Multidimensional Model
    of Leadership
required behavior
preferred leader behavior

actual leader behavior
Leadership Scale for Sport (LSS)
Coaching Behavior Assessment
    System (CBAS)
reactive behavior
spontaneous behavior
Coaching Model (CM)
organization
"the vision"

systematic observation
physical training
tactical training
technical training
mental training
coaches' characteristic
athletes' characteristic
contextual factor
"coaching process"

References

Barnett, G., & Gregorian, V. (1996). *High hopes: Taking the purple to Pasadena.* New York: Warner.

Bloom, G. A. "Characteristics, strategies, and knowledge of expert team sport coaches." Ph.D. diss., University of Ottawa, Ottawa, Ontario, Canada, 1997.

Bloom, G. A., Crumpton, R., & Anderson, J. E. (1999). A systematic observation study of the teaching behaviors of an expert basketball coach. *The Sport Psychologist, 13,* 157–170.

Bloom, G. A., Durand-Bush, N., & Salmela, J. H. (1997). Pre- and postcompetition routines of expert coaches of team sports. *The Sport Psychologist, 11,* 127–141.

Bloom, G. A., Durand-Bush, N., Schinke, R. J., & Salmela, J. H. (1998). The importance of mentoring in the development of coaches and athletes. *International Journal of Sport Psychology, 29*(3), 267–281.

Bloom, G. A., Salmela, J. H., & Schinke, R. J. (1995). Expert coaches' views on the training of developing coaches. In R. Vanfraechem-Raway & Y. Vanden Auweele (Eds.), *Proceedings of the Ninth European Congress on Sport Psychology* (pp. 401–408). Brussels, Belgium: Free University of Brussels.

Bloom, G. A., Schinke, R. J., & Salmela, J. H. (1997). The development of communication skills by elite basketball coaches. *Coaching and Sport Science Journal, 2*(3), 3–10.

Chelladurai, P. "A contingency model of leadership in athletics." Ph.D. diss., University of Waterloo, Waterloo, Ontario, Canada, 1978.

Chelladurai, P. (1980). Leadership in sports organizations. *Canadian Journal of Applied Sport Sciences, 5,* 226–231.

Chelladurai, P. (1984). Discrepancy between preferences and perceptions of leadership behavior and satisfaction of athletes in varying sports. *Journal of Sport Psychology, 6,* 27–41.

Chelladurai, P. (1993). Leadership. In R. N. Singer, M. Murphey, & L. K. Tennant (Eds.), *Handbook of research in sport psychology* (pp. 647–671). New York: Macmillan.

Chelladurai, P., Imamura, H., Yamaguchi, Y., Oinuma, Y., & Miyauchi, T. (1988). Sport leadership in a cross-national setting. The case of Japanese and Canadian university athletes. *Journal of Sport and Exercise Psychology, 10,* 347–389.

Chelladurai, P., & Saleh, S. D. (1978). Preferred leadership in sports. *Canadian Journal of Applied Sport Sciences, 3,* 85–92.

Chelladurai, P., & Saleh, S. D. (1980). Dimensions of leader behavior in sports: Development of a leadership scale. *Journal of Sport Psychology, 2,* 34–45.

Coakley, J. J. (1990). *Sport in Society: Issues and Controversies.* Toronto: Times Mirror/Mosby.

Côté, J. "Identification and conceptualization of high performance expert gymnastic coaches' knowledge." Ph.D. diss., University of Ottawa, Ottawa, Ontario, Canada, 1993.

Côté, J., & Salmela, J. H. (1996). The organizational tasks of high-performance gymnastic coaches. *The Sport Psychologist, 10,* 247–260.

Côté, J., Salmela, J. H., & Russell, S. J. (1995). The knowledge of high-performance gymnastic coaches: Competition and training considerations. *The Sport Psychologist, 6,* 76–95.

Côté, J., Salmela, J. H., Trudel, P., Baria, A., & Russell, S. J. (1995). The coaching model: A grounded assessment of expert gymnastic coaches' knowledge. *Journal of Sport & Exercise Psychology, 17,* 1–17.

Cox, R. H. (1994). *Sport psychology: Concepts and applications,* 3rd ed. Dubuque, IA: WCB Brown & Benchmark.

Danielson, R. R., Zelhart, P. F., & Drake, C. J. (1975). Multidimensional scaling and factor analysis of coaching behavior as perceived by high school hockey players. *Research Quarterly, 46,* 323–334.

Douge, B., & Hastie, P. (1993). Coach effectiveness. *Sport Science Review, 2,* 14–29.

Dwyer, J. M., & Fischer, D. G. (1990). Wrestlers' perceptions of coaches' leadership as predictors of satisfaction with leadership. *Perceptual and Motor Skills, 71,* 511–517.

Gould, D., Giannini, J., Krane, V., & Hodge, K. (1990). Educational needs of elite U.S. National Team, Pan American and Olympic coaches. *Journal of Teaching in Physical Education, 9,* 332–344.

Gould, D., Hodge, K., Peterson, K., & Giannini, J. (1989). An exploratory examination of strategies used by elite coaches to enhance self-efficacy in athletes. *Journal of Sport & Exercise Psychology, 11,* 128–140.

Gould, D., Hodge, K., Peterson, K., & Petlichkoff, L. (1987). Psychological foundations of coaching: Similarities and differences among intercollegiate wrestling coaches. *The Sport Psychologist, 1,* 293–308.

Jackson, P., & Delehanty, H. (1995). *Sacred hoops: Spiritual lessons of a hardwood warrior.* New York: Hyperion.

Lacy, A. C., & Darst, P. W. (1985). Systematic observation of behaviors of winning high school head football coaches. *Journal of Teaching in Physical Education, 4,* 256–270.

Lacy, A. C., & Goldston, P. D. (1990). Behavior analysis of male and female coaches in high school girls' basketball. *Journal of Sport Behavior, 13,* 29–39.

Martens, R. (1986). Youth sport in the USA. In M. R. Weiss & D. Gould (Eds.), *Sport for children and youth: 1984 Olympic Scientific Congress Proceedings,* Vol. 10 (pp. 27–33). Champaign, IL: Human Kinetics.

Martens, R. (1987). *Coaches guide to sport psychology.* Champaign, IL: Human Kinetics.

Martens, R. (1990). *Successful coaching.* Champaign, IL: Leisure.

Michener, J. (1980). *Sports in America.* New York: Random House.

Miller, P. S., Bloom, G. A., & Salmela, J. H. (1996). The roots of success: From athletic leaders to expert coaches. *Coaches Report, 2* (4), 18–20.

Moraes, L. C. C. D. A. "Influence in the development of beliefs of Canadian expert judo coaches and their impact on action." Ph.D. diss., University of Ottawa, Ottawa, Ontario, Canada, 1998.

Salmela, J. H., (Ed.), *Great job coach! Getting the edge from proven winners.* Ottawa, ON: Potentium, 1996.

Schinke, R. J., Bloom, G. A., & Salmela, J. H. (1995). The career stages of elite Canadian basketball coaches. *Avante, 1,* 48–62.

Schriesheim, C. A., & Stodgill, R. M. (1975). Differences in factor structure across the three versions of the Ohio State leadership scales. *Personnel Psychology, 28,* 189–206.

Sherman, S. J., & Fazio, R. H. (1983). Parallels between attitudes and traits as predictors of behavior. *Journal of Personality, 51,* 308–339.

Smith, R. E., & Smoll, F. L. (1990). Self-esteem and children's reactions to youth sport coaching behaviors: A field study of self enhancement processes. *Developmental Psychology, 26,* 987–993.

Smith, R. E., Smoll, R. L., & Barnett, N. P. (1995). Reduction of children's sport anxiety through social support and stress-reduction training for coaches. *Journal of Applied Developmental Psychology, 16,* 125–142.

Smith, R. E., Smoll, R. L., & Curtis, B. (1978). Coaching behaviors in little league baseball. In F. L. Smoll & R. E. Smith (Eds.), *Psychological perspectives on youth sports* (pp. 173–201). Washington, DC: Hemisphere.

Smith, R. E., Smoll, R. L., & Curtis, B. (1979). Coach effectiveness training: A cognitive behavioral approach to enhancing relationship skills in youth sport coaches. *Journal of Sport Psychology, 1,* 59–75.

Smith, R. E., Smoll, R. L., & Hunt, E. B. (1977). A system for the behavioral assessment of athletic coaches. *Research Quarterly, 48,* 401–407.

Smith, R. E., Zane, N. S., Smoll, F. L., & Coppel, D. B. (1983). Behavioral assessment in youth sports: Coaching behaviors and children's attitudes. *Medicine and Science in Sports and Exercise, 15,* 208–214.

Snyder, C. J. (1990). The effects of leader behavior and organizational climate on intercollegiate coaches' job satisfaction. *Journal of Sport Management, 4,* 59–70.

Stodgill, R. M. (1948). Personal factors associated with leadership: Survey of literature. *Journal of Psychology, 25,* 35–71.

Tharp, R. G., & Gallimore, R. (1976). What a coach can teach a teacher. *Psychology Today, 9,* 75–78.

Walton, G. (1992). *Beyond winning: The timeless wisdom of great philosopher coaches.* Champaign, IL: Human Kinetics.

Weiss, M. R., & Friedrichs, W. D. (1986). The influence of leader behaviors, coach attributes, and institutional variables on performance and satisfaction of collegiate basketball teams. *Journal of Sport Psychology, 8,* 332–346.

Wooden, J. (1988). *They call me coach.* New York: Contemporary.

23

Role of the Elite Coach in the Development of Talent

Gordon Bloom

McGill University

- The stages of development of an individual require coaches to assume different roles. Whether introducing a child to a sport and fostering interest in that sport or developing a more rigorous practice routine, the elite coach will be encouraging, challenging, and understanding with the athletes.
- Talent development can occur only through deliberate practice. The elite coach understands how to stimulate athletes to participate in deliberate practice.
- In competition, the coach must maintain emotional control, develop a positive relationship with officials, and use time-outs and intermissions strategically.
- There is documented support by coaches for the use of sport psychologists either directly or indirectly; in actuality, however, the prevalence of sport psychologists involved in athletics remains uncertain.

Life to him [John Wooden] is a one-room schoolhouse. A pedagogue is all he ever wanted to be. (Tharp & Gallimore, 1976, p. 78)

Vince Lombardi's success, I am convinced, lay not only in his inspirational personality but also in his ability to teach. He was a teacher. He could communicate an idea to his players, explain it so they understood it—not only how to execute it but why! He taught, right to the heart of the matter, without frills or gimmicks. You had to be smart to play for Lombardi. In a split second a lineman had to read and react to the move of his opponent, and react correctly—so for all players, both offense and defense. Of course the physical talent was there, but all teams in professional football have that. The ability of his teams to do the right thing—cut the right way, block the right man, read the key correctly—these are the reasons for championships. (Flynn, 1973, foreword)

The philosophy of a coach should contain room for developing the abilities of all the participants, not only those few who have proven their talents. You do not have to sacrifice the rest of the team to develop the exceptional few. Don't let yourself get caught in the trap illustrated by the remark of one swimmer's parent, "In a race there is one winner; he's the champ, the rest are chumps." (Counsilman, 1977, pp. 258–259)

See you at the top! Highly specialized skills often require meticulous coaching over an extended period of time.

After an Olympic athlete wins a gold medal or a football team wins the Super Bowl, the media and public are quick to praise the expert athletes. Most athletes deserve this recognition because they have sacrificed countless hours training for their event. Many individuals, however, fail to consider the role that the coach, teacher, or mentor plays in helping the athlete achieve a high level of success. This chapter will examine research on elite performers, including the importance and necessity of having a highly qualified coach or teacher. In particular, the work of Bloom (1985), Csikszentmihalyi, Rathunde, and Whalen (1993), Ericsson and colleagues (Ericsson & Charness, 1994; Ericsson, Krampe, & Tesch-Römer, 1993), and Partington (1995) will be discussed, with an emphasis on the coaches and teachers who helped performers excel in their fields. This chapter also will explore the role of the coach in competition as well as the coaches' thoughts and feelings about the role of sport psychology.

Bloom's Research on Developing Talent in Young People

Benjamin Bloom's (1985) work focused on the talent development of world-class performers in the art, science, and sport domains. Bloom, who spent 4 years directing this project with a group of researchers from the University of Chicago, was interested in the process of talent development in young people, beginning with their early years and ending with their rise to prominence. The data was gathered by interviewing 120 young men and women from different parts of the United States after they had completed their careers. Although Bloom felt that no two individuals would have identical developmental experiences, he believed that a number of similarities would emerge across individuals and different disciplines.

Bloom's (1985) research identified three phases of talent development of expert performers and provided important insights on how Olympic swimmers, world-class tennis players, concert pianists, sculptors, research mathematicians, and research neurologists reached the top level of expertise in their domains. The stages of talent development were labeled as the early years, the middle developmental years, and the final years of perfecting the skills. Central to the development of the expert performer at each stage was the teacher, coach, or mentor.

Bloom's Stages of Development

Early Years.   Bloom (1985) found the first phase began when individuals were introduced to activities in their sport. It involved instruction from a local coach/teacher who was caring, thoughtful, and well-respected in the community, and, most importantly, who was situated close to where the child lived. The coach/teacher provided the performer with considerable amounts of positive feedback and approval and allowed the children to play and explore all aspects of their sport. Rewards were garnered for effort rather than for achievement, and rarely was the coach critical of the children. The role of the coach also involved monitoring the children's practice activities by helping them set and achieve reasonable goals.

Bloom (1985, p. 143) also found that parents played a large role by providing their children with encouragement and motivation. (For a more detailed examination of the role of parents in talent development, please refer to Chapter 25 of this textbook.) Many parents attended practices with their children and tried to instill habits of discipline and practice while still focusing on the playful activities and inherent enjoyment of the sport. The following quote typifies what many of these parents said to their children: "You can do anything you set your mind to, if you want to do it." In addition to this support, the children relied on the guidance of their coach or teacher to help them perform well. Whether or not it was related to their exceptional performance, sixteen of the twenty-one expert swimmers reported that the quality of their coach and the caliber of their team were most affected by the proximity to where the outstanding performer lived. About two-thirds of these swimmers lived close to coaches who trained or were training at least one nationally ranked swimmer. The young swimmers obviously improved through their exposure to a positive learning environment. Furthermore, many of their early coaches regarded the athletes as special learners, and gave them extra attention. This form of motivation may have encouraged the children to work and train harder. Also, "many of the teachers kept records of the child's progress (especially in piano and swimming), and this typically helped prove to the children that they were progressing and that if they kept at it, they would make even more progress" (Bloom, 1985, p. 516).

Middle Developmental Years. In the second phase or middle years, typically between the ages of 10 and 13, individuals became fully committed to their performance goals. For the tennis players, the sport became more than a "game;" it became "real business." As one player described it: "I was now eating, sleeping and breathing tennis" (Bloom, 1985, p. 236). During this period, players began receiving acclaim and rewards in the form of articles and pictures in newspapers and recognition by important people in their sport. Bloom reported that most athletes and their parents began to feel that a new and more advanced type of coaching was needed, so they carefully sought out a talented coach, one with a proven record of training outstanding athletes.

In the early years of development, the coaches had been good at getting the athletes interested in and excited about their sport. In the middle years, however, the athletes and their parents felt they needed someone to teach them precision and technique as well as strategy. They also needed to tailor their skills to emphasize their own personal strengths and to compensate for any weaknesses they might have.

The coach during the middle years was more advanced and regarded as one of the best within a larger geographical area. These coaches usually worked with selected individuals who they felt had lots of potential; their athletes often viewed the coaches as perfectionists. The cultivation of talent now became a top priority for the performer. Coaches demanded more hard work, commitment, and discipline from their athletes. The athletes' training regimens became more intense and advanced as coaches introduced them to more strenuous and strategic areas of their sport. For example, the talented swimmers now were expected to devote more hours to their training schedules, usually between three to five hours a day. While the tennis players focused on ball placement, overcoming personal weaknesses, and improving their competitive skills, the swimmers worked on perfecting their strokes and learning how to maximize their stamina. The coaches also helped the athletes set short- and long-term goals.

Later Years. Athletes who achieved high levels of success auditioned for the opportunity to work with yet another coach, an individual widely recognized as a master teacher or expert in the domain. Bloom (1985) noted that there were only a small number of individuals in the whole country considered "expert coaches," perhaps only eight to ten. Those athletes who were fortunate enough to reach this stage were totally committed to their chosen activity and would do whatever was necessary to excel. The progression to the third stage involved a number of sacrifices for both performers and their families, such as greater expenses and often moving to a new city.

For many of the swimmers and tennis players, the later years involved relocating to a specially chosen college where their coach became an important influence. The relationship between athlete and expert coach evolved into one of mutual respect and collegiality with both parties focusing less on instructional methods and more on tactical refinement and the development of the individual's style. This reorientation in the coach–athlete relationship is noted in the following quote: "It was just a new philosophy. Rather than hitting every ball as hard as I could, to try and play the percentages a little bit more. I improved" (Bloom, 1985, p. 260). These coaches challenged their proteges to excel beyond their perceived human capabilities. "This was especially true of the Olympic swimmers, who were expected to exceed records beyond that ever previously accomplished by any human being. So, too, was it true of the mathematicians, who were expected to solve problems that had never been solved before" (Bloom, 1985, p. 525). These coaches expected a high level of mental and physical dedication from their athletes so they could help them reach the highest possible levels in their fields.

In sum, Bloom's (1985) study of top performers revealed important information relating to the development of expertise. Through the use of retrospective interviews with individuals from vastly different domains, a three-stage process of development for talented performers emerged, including the important roles of the coaches who influenced them.

Csikszentmihalyi's Work on Talented Adolescents

Csikszentmihalyi, Rathunde, and Whalen (1993) conducted a longitudinal study that examined the development of talent in five areas—art, athletics, mathematics, music, and science. Over 200 talented high school students were studied over a period of approximately 4 years. The purpose of their research was to determine which factors contributed to the development of talent in some individuals and which contributed to the eventual lack of success in others. This section will review this research with particular emphasis on the role played by the coaches or teachers towards the development of talent.

Data Gathering Techniques

The method of gathering data employed by these researchers was unique and extensive. The first phase of their research used questionnaires to help focus on the adolescents' different biographical and demographic information. The subject's talent-related preferences and accomplishments, family functioning, stressful events, and physical motivation were assessed as well. The core of data, however, was gathered from interviews and the Experience Sampling Method (ESM). In the ESM or "beeper method," subjects carried with them an electronic pager for seven consecutive days, receiving seven to nine random signals per day. After receiving a signal, they filled out a sampling form designed to record their current thoughts, activities, and feelings. The final phase of the study involved more objective measures such as grades and teacher ratings. These measures provided additional support to data gathered earlier in the study. An open-ended interview of each student took place at the end of the data gathering period as well.

The Importance of Motivation and "Flow"

One of the key factors accountable for talent development was motivation. The students who had the highest levels of intrinsic motivation to learn, as well as external rewards like recognition and praise from significant others, had greater chances of succeeding.

> Threats and blandishments may move an adolescent to study math or practice the piano up to a point. He or she may even become proficient and become a respectable professional. But to reach exceptional levels of performance requires a single-minded dedication that will not occur unless one enjoys what one is doing. All the talented students in our study perceived intrinsic rewards to be more important than extrinsic ones in keeping them involved in their domains. (Csikszentmihalyi, Rathunde, & Whalen, 1993, p. 148)

Additionally, Csikszentmihalyi and colleagues found that "flow experiences" contributed to talent development. A **flow experience** is "the state in which people are so involved in an activity that nothing else seems to matter" (Csikszentmihalyi, 1990, p. 4). Csikszentmihalyi (1991) noted that flow experiences take place when the challenges equal the skill level and when one knows what to do, has clear goals, deep concentration, a sense of being in control, and loses a sense of time. Teenagers were unable to develop their talent unless they enjoyed it. Part of this enjoyment was the atmosphere and environment created by the teacher or coach. These young adolescent subjects required constant stimulation and challenges to their skills to avoid boredom and losing interest in their activity. Csikszentmihalyi and colleagues found that two of the main reasons students did not fulfill their potential were that they either gave up from having to work alone or that they did not like the competition or heightened atmosphere.

A comparison of some of the methodological and practical similarities between the research of Csikszentmihalyi, Rathunde, and Whalen (1993) and Bloom (1985) provides a more in-depth understanding of the early stages of talent development, and, more importantly, of those who facilitate this process. All the subjects in Csikszentmihalyi's study had reached the first or second stage of development postulated by Bloom. From a methodological perspective, the use of vivid quotations from the subjects allowed the reader to get a true feeling for what the talented performers were feeling and doing. From a practical standpoint, those who enjoyed emotional and material support from their families tended to have an easier time developing and honing their skills. In fact, Csikszentmihalyi, Rathunde, and Whalen noted that most talented students came from households consisting of two parents. As in Bloom's study, the need for a qualified and experienced master teacher or coach also emerged. According to Csikszentmihalyi, Rathunde, & Whalen (1993, p. 38):

> Whether a young person gifted with outstanding skills will grow into a talented performer depends on many unrelated factors.... There are also the personal qualities that contribute to the realization of talent. A person has no control over some of these: genetic contributions to intelligence, to special skills, and to temperament, for example. But there are also traits

where the individual can make some difference. We cannot increase the inborn gifts of our children, and as individuals we can do little to alter the cultural and societal parameters that affect the unfolding of talent. But if we understood better those elements of the equation over which we have some measure of control, we might be able to protect and nurture the unique human potentials that young people in our families, schools, and communities possess.

Some of the elements which individuals can control include the quality of the home experience, the quality of the school chosen, and more importantly, the teachers/coaches who are working with these children. The logical question thus becomes: What are the crucial characteristics of the coach or teacher?

Characteristics of Successful Coaches and Teachers

Csikszentmihalyi, Rathunde, and Whalen (1993) found three common characteristics of coaches/teachers who helped cultivate the talent of their students. For one, coaches were effective because they enjoyed what they were doing and encouraged their athletes to excel beyond their current level of talent. They were remembered for their "genuine" love and devotion toward their field of study. Second, coaches created optimal learning conditions so that athletes were not bored or overly frustrated, enabling them to maximize their levels of concentration, self-esteem, potency, and involvement. Finally, a third characteristic of distinguished coaches was their ability to understand the needs of athletes. They were recalled for their "reassuring kindness" as well as their genuine concern for the overall development of the student both inside and outside of school.

Increasing Flow Experiences

Although the three characteristics noted previously must firmly be in place, talent development is enhanced when the teachers are able to intensify optimal "flow" learning conditions for their students (Csikszentmihalyi, Rathunde, & Whalen, 1993). The chance of reaching a flow experience was increased in a number of ways. First, the teachers nurtured or bettered their own talent by partaking in activities within their domain outside of the work setting. As a result, "they seemed determined to help students experience the same rewards that they found in the continuing exploration of their domain" (Csikszentmihalyi, Rathunde, & Whalen 1993, p. 191). Second, teachers tried to eliminate external rewards such as grades, competition, and bureaucratic pressures, instead encouraging the inherent satisfaction of learning something new and challenging. The authors suggested that teachers developed crucial ways of providing feedback to students by avoiding the trap that many others fell into whereby they "divert attention away from the activity at hand and toward the new game of winning prizes, avoiding punishments, and ingratiating oneself with those who mete them out. In the process, students cease to cultivate sources of self-reward that yield only undivided concentration and sustained immersion in a challenging task" (Csikszentmihalyi, Rathunde, & Whalen, 1993, p. 192). Finally, teachers were concerned with the shifting needs of learners that allowed the flow experience to take effect. Thus, they praised and reprimanded performers at appropriate moments and allowed the students the freedom, whenever possible, to control the pace of the learning process. They also provided the students with emotional support as they strived for success.

In short, Csikszentmihalyi's research highlighted many important points of expert coaching and teaching. The authors concluded that athletes and students will learn only if they are placed in enjoyable learning environments with individuals who know how to provide information in a manner that is both challenging and gratifying.

Info Box

Children often are motivated to participate in sport solely by enjoyment. Coaches can learn from children and provide developing athletes of all ages an enjoyable learning environment. If athletes enjoy learning, they attend directly to learning the skill and become more proficient at that skill.

Ericsson's View of Deliberate Practice

The issue of expertise development was advanced even further in the mid-1990s. Ericsson and associates (Ericsson & Charness, 1994; Ericsson, Krampe, & Tesch-Römer, 1993; Ericsson & Lehmann, 1996) have taken the understanding of expertise to new levels by discounting the popular notion that outstanding achievement is innate or genetically inborn. Ericsson and colleagues have shown how many human characteristics, such as size of the heart, number of capillaries supplying blood to muscles, and metabolic properties of fast and slow twitch muscles, are changeable with intense practice. Ericsson's research has ramifications for the role of expert coaches and, most notably, how expert athletes require a top coach to oversee their long hours of training. Without a competent coach, it would be difficult for most expert performers to maximize their potential.

Highest Level—Eminence

Ericsson, Krampe, and Tesch-Römer's (1993, p. 370) research extended Bloom's (1985) framework to include a fourth developmental phase entitled **eminence:** "The criteria for eminent performance goes beyond expert mastery of available knowledge and skills and requires an important and innovative contribution to the domain." Examples of eminent sport performers are Kareem Abdul Jabbar and his patented basketball "hook shot," Wayne Gretzky's incredible passing skills in ice hockey, and Martina Navratilova's aggressive net play in women's tennis. Examples of coaching eminence include Bill Walsh's "West Coast Offense" in football and Phil Jackson's use of the "Triangle Offense" in basketball. All of these individuals reached the pinnacle of their sport by making significant advances in skill and knowledge.

Deliberate Practice

Ericsson and colleagues argued that reaching a level of eminence involved more than innate abilities; it was a result of effortful, sustained activities designed to optimize improvement, a process that was labeled **deliberate practice.** Ericsson, Krampe, and Tesch-Römer's (1993,

Talented athletes understand that each competition is a logical extension of practice.

p. 368) fundamental view is best summarized as follows: "In contrast to play, deliberate practice is a highly structured activity, the explicit goal of which is to improve performance. Specific tasks are invented to overcome weaknesses, and performance is carefully monitored to provide cues for ways to improve it further…the amount of time an individual is engaged in deliberate practice is monotonically [linearly] related to that individual's acquired performance." Resources, including time, energy, access to competent teachers, training materials, and training facilities, as well as effort and motivation, were identified as possible constraints inhibiting the process of deliberate practice. In addition to resources, effort, and motivational constraints, Ericsson and colleagues also found that the age at which individuals began their deliberate practice affected their rise to prominence. In particular, individuals who started deliberate practice at a younger age had a better chance of reaching high levels of success. Durand-Bush and Salmela (1996, p. 90) further elaborated on this issue when they noted: "It has been shown that it is impossible for an individual with less accumulated practice at some age to catch up with the best individuals who started deliberate practice earlier and maintained optimal levels of practice that did not lead either to exhaustion or burnout."

A time frame also was forwarded for the development of expertise that follows Simon and Chase's (1973) "10 year rule." In their research on international chess masters, Simon and Chase found that a minimum of 10 years or more of full-time dedication was required to achieve the highest performance level in chess from the first time an individual learned the rules. This time frame was extended to 16.5 years if the person began playing chess before the age of 11. The following quotations, although anecdotal, appear to offer support towards the importance of deliberate practice:

> I'm gifted, but I've worked for everything I've gotten. Gordie Howe and Bobby Orr worked hard too. Like them, I didn't say, "I'm gifted. I don't have to work anymore."
> —Wayne Gretzky, former professional hockey player

> The dictionary is the only place success comes before work. Hard work is the price we must all pay for success. I think we can accomplish almost anything if we are willing to pay the price. The price of success is hard work, dedication to the job at hand, and the determination that whether we win or lose, we have applied the best of ourselves to the task at hand.
> —Vince Lombardi, Hall of Fame football coach

> Genius is one percent inspiration and 99 percent perspiration. I never did anything worth doing by accident, nor did any of my inventions come by accident; they came by work.
> —Thomas Edison, American inventor

> I learned to fight. I worked and studied it. If I got beat up or did something sloppy in the gym, I'd go home and work on it until I got it right. Man, it was hard work but I didn't want to just be good. I wanted to be the best.   —Thomas Hearns, former boxer

Coach and Deliberate Practice

Although deliberate practice is an extremely important precursor to reaching levels of success, it is not sufficient in and of itself. Ericsson and colleagues (1993, 1994, 1996) alluded to the importance of the coach or teacher in facilitating the process of deliberate practice. For example, Ericsson and associates found that coaches and teachers played an important role in setting an appropriate environment for athletes to engage in the 10 years or 10,000 hours of deliberate practice required to reach high levels of expertise. The importance of this task should not go unnoticed. In fact, it was revealed that musicians who reached the highest levels of their profession deliberately practiced for 24.3 hours per week compared to 9.3 hours per week for less accomplished musicians. One could hypothesize that athletes expecting to reach the same levels of success in their sports need to first put in the required hours of deliberate practice. The question then becomes: What effect does the coach have in motivating the athlete and perpetuating deliberate practice?

Another important role of the coach relates to the quality of practice time experienced by the athletes. In the absence of coaches or teachers, subjects usually played rather than practiced. In addition, feedback was crucial, and expert performers needed to be taught and corrected when errors occurred:

> To assume effective learning, subjects ideally should be given explicit instructions about the best method and be supervised by a teacher to allow individualized diagnosis of errors, informative feedback, and remedial part training. The instructor has to organize the sequence of appropriate training tasks and monitor improvement to decide when transitions to more complex and challenging tasks are appropriate (Ericsson, Krampe, & Tesch-Römer 1993, p. 367).

The thoughts of many great athletes and coaches appear to support what Ericsson and colleagues (1993, 1994, 1996) are alluding to with respect to the quality of practice and the role of the coach in ensuring this takes place.

> Practice does not make the athlete. It is the quality and intensity of practice that makes the athlete, not just repeated practicing.   —Ray Meyer, college basketball coach

> When fans watch me hit, they think the game must have been easy for me. But it wasn't. I worked very hard to get where I am. For four years, I came to the parks early and worked with our batting coach, Charley Lau. There were a lot of things I could've done, and probably would have rather done, but I knew that if I was going to become successful in baseball, I had to do it; I had to work on it.   —George Brett, Hall of Fame baseball player

> Our approach for getting ready for a football game is a seven-day process. All that fired-up emotion is good, but if a team lines up in a formation that we're not prepared for, then all that emotion doesn't do us much good. We believe a highly motivated team is a team that is basically very soundly prepared.   —Tom Osborne, former college football coach

In summary, the groundbreaking research of Ericsson and colleagues (1993, 1994, 1996) offers some new insights into the field of expertise including the importance of quality coaching. It needs to be stated, however, that the research of Bloom, Csikszentmihalyi and colleagues, and Ericsson and associates was primarily carried out with middle- and upper-class subjects. One should exhibit caution when comparing these results to other populations.

Partington's Research on Elite Music Performers

Partington (1995) examined the careers of 21 expert principal players in symphony orchestras through the use of semi-structured interviews. Like Bloom, Csikszentmihalyi, and Ericsson before him, Partington used subjects who had attained a high level of expertise in their domain. The subjects were asked to describe their background and career development up to its present stage. Partington (1995, p. 4) specifically chose certain musicians whose roles affected the play of others.

> I decided to target principal players because of the multiple roles each must play within the orchestra. These roles make enormous demands, especially on the player's attentional focus. For example, as part of the ensemble, principals need to be team players, intimately tuned in to what is going on around them in the orchestra; simultaneously, they have to provide leadership to guide others in their section; finally, principals must be ready to step forward as soloists when designated in the score.

Importance of Deliberate Practice

Partington presented his results in a manner analogous to Bloom (1985), identifying personal, pedagogical, and experiential factors conducive to a performer's rise to the top. Many similarities can be found in Partington's work compared to those listed earlier in this chapter. For example, he found that expert musicians possessed certain characteristics such as commitment, passion, creativity, and an ability to communicate and express their emotions in a certain way. Of particular interest was the finding that deliberate practice seemed more important than innate talent in the development of expert music performers. As Partington (1995, p. 61) stated:

> The first highlight for me was that background experiences, interest, and effort were more often cited than innate talent as necessary for a career in music. Informal opportunities in the family home, such as hearing and singing a variety of music, being taken to concerts, and receiving encouragement for playing from at least one caring adult, usually a mother, appear to be necessary foundations for the development of most of the predisposing tendencies associated with a successful career performing music. Important music-related characteristics include interest in, curiosity about, openness to, and love for the sounds of music and how they are made. Coupled with these learnings is a prodigious readiness and capacity to work hard in order to achieve self-imposed high standards, based on a conscious decision and commitment to master the necessary skills in order to become the best performer possible.

Physical and Emotional Development of Students

Partington (1995) also examined the devoted teachers who helped performers reach such a high level of expertise. He noted that having a highly qualified teacher was sometimes the difference between very good and expert performers. Essentially, three separate areas of the teachers were discussed. First was the description of the performers' most effective and memorable teachers. Those teachers, at the early stages of learning, made it a positive experience for the young musicians by providing feedback in a constructive and upbeat manner and by teaching them how to practice intelligently. Second was the methods of teaching and how teachers inspired their students to excel beyond perceived capabilities. These teachers made studying music enjoyable so that the expert performers were encouraged to maintain effortful practice. Third, Partington explained how expert performers dealt with the problems and conflicts they experienced with their master teachers. The teachers acted as friends and confidants, and also as disciplinarians when required. It can be concluded that the teachers in Partington's study were mentors, playing vital roles in the physical and emotional development of expertise.

Mental Development of Students

Partington found that in addition to nurturing their students' physical and emotional development, the teacher played a critical role in their mental development. For some teachers it was important for the musicians to adhere to a mental training program geared for playing their instrument. For other teachers, mentally training their pupils meant ensuring they acted independently and sought answers to their own questions. Problems arose when teachers emphasized skill perfection and winning at competitions at the expense of fun. According to Partington (1995, p. 40) deliberate practice could only be attained if musicians derived some enjoyment from their activity, a conclusion that differed from Ericsson and his colleagues:

> A lot of teachers make their students work on one piece all year. That is my criticism of the festivals. Some teachers make you prepare a whole year for one piece so that you can be the winner at the festival. That approach doesn't create a love for music, but it takes its toll. Once the kids get beyond a certain age, when their parents can't make them, then they just pack it in.

Summary on Talent Development

An important finding from Bloom's (1985), Csikszentmihalyi and colleagues', Ericsson and associates', and Partington's research was that talent development requires tremendous amounts of practice and training, and central to this was the teacher or coach. Perhaps, Salmela (1994, p. 25) best summarized the issue of talent development when he stated: "For the moment, it is clear in our minds that talent development appears to have a much greater environmentally determined stimulus, specifically in terms of how expert coaches can facilitate the development of expert performance rather than the genetically based viewpoint of innate gifts or talent that we considered a decade ago."

Info Box

Athletes are not born with talent; they must develop it by engaging in deliberate practice. Effective coaches inspire athletes to practice and ensure that the quality of the practice is high.

Role of the Coach in Competition

Up to this point, the chapter has explored the role of the coach prior to competition. It seems logical to proceed with an exploration of the role of the elite coach during competition. Probably one of the greatest differences between coaches of individual and team sports occurs during competition. Although coaches of divers, weight lifters, ice skaters, and cyclists often nervously and passively watch their athletes compete, the same cannot be said of ice hockey, baseball, or football coaches. In fact, sometimes these team sport coaches receive more television coverage than many of their athletes. This does not imply that team sport coaches are more important to the overall development and success of their athletes. What it does suggest, however, is that the role of the coach in competition is far more important in team sports than it is in individual sports. Up to this point, Bloom (1996) has provided one of the few accounts of team sport coaches' roles during competition. Four areas receiving considerable attention were emotional control, officials, time-outs, and intermissions. These areas all will be briefly discussed.

Emotional Control

Legendary head coaches like Earl Weaver and Billy Martin in baseball, Bobby Knight in college basketball, and John Madden in football were well-known for their emotional outbursts during athletic competitions, especially toward officials. Bloom (1996), however, noted that many of the past and present Olympic coaches interviewed in his research stated that although inwardly they felt emotionally unsettled during competitions, they were cognizant of outwardly projecting a demeanor that made them appear calm and in control. These coaches feared that losing their composure might cause their players to behave in a similar manner and also might cause the players to lose the coaches' respect. On the other hand, these coaches also noted that a preplanned emotional outburst often can fire up their team. These views are best summarized in the following quote:

> I think every coach has to be prepared to show some true emotions. I think if you want to lose it a little bit, you lose it by design. I don't mean it in the wrong way. It's not phony. You really feel it but you say this is the right time to get emotional. But to me, if you lose it involuntarily, then you're not doing yourself any favors. You're taking yourself out of the rational thought process. (Bloom, 1996, p. 164)

Officials

Bloom (1996) noted that coaches believed interactions with referees and other sport officials also was an important dimension of the coaches' role during competition. It was, therefore, no surprise to find that coaches put a great deal of time and effort into their interactions with referees. They studied and learned just how far they could push a referee before their team would be penalized. Also, many of the expert coaches who were interviewed said that as they matured, they began to treat officials more as allies and learned to not embarrass or belittle them in front of spectators or athletes.

Time-Outs

Bloom (1996) stated that time-outs (as well as substitutions) were viewed as important strategies by team sport coaches. The coaches realized that their team could gain momentum and, thus, a possible edge over their opponent if they used these strategies properly. A few suggestions offered by these coaches during time-outs were as follows: (1) everybody needs to listen, not just those in the game at that time, (2) prepare what you are going to say to your athletes ahead of time, (3) don't overload your athletes with too much information—one or two points is enough, (4) use time-outs to regroup your athletes, stop the other team's momentum, and modify team strategies.

Intermissions

The coaches interviewed in Bloom's (1996) research strongly endorsed the importance of the intermission. This was the only time when head coaches were able to speak with assistant coaches, analyze the effectiveness of the game plan, and personally regroup. According to these coaches, every minute of time was crucial. Intermissions often began with a short meeting with their assistant coaches because they wanted to give their players about five minutes to cool off. During this meeting time with their assistants, they tried to detect any errors or flaws in the game plan. If changes were needed, they were sure to only refine a few selected points of the game plan rather than attempt a complete overhaul. After this, they met with their athletes for 5 to 7 minutes to relay two or three of the important points. Players then had a few minutes to themselves before heading back to the contest.

Coaches' Perceptions on the Role of Sport Psychology

The last section of this chapter on the role of expert coaches in developing talent will assess their perceptions on the importance of sport psychology. Coaches, like athletes, have different views about the benefits and uses of sport psychology techniques. An example of this can be seen in the two different types of approaches used in team building studies; either an indirect (e.g., Prapavessis, Carron, & Spink, 1996) or a direct (e.g., Cogan & Petrie, 1995) approach. According to the **indirect approach,** the sport psychologist facilitates team effectiveness through coach education. In the **direct approach,** the sport psychologist assumes an active role in the intervention process by working closely with athletes and coaches. Thus, some coaches will request the services of a sport psychologist and let that individual work directly with their team. Other coaches will use a sport psychologist, but prefer to personally administer all mental training techniques. Finally, there are some coaches who do not use a sport psychologist in any capacity.

Silva (1984) conducted a study that examined general and specific areas of sport psychology deemed important by coaches including how coaches would like to integrate sport psychology practices into their programs. The sample consisted of over 200 high school and college coaches across various regions of the United States. An important finding was that over 90 percent of the coaches who responded to the survey indicated that sport psychology could be of assistance in their sport and in the development of their athletes' potential. Despite these positive responses, it is interesting to note that 80 percent of the coaches responded that they never had a sport psychologist work with their team.

Why don't more coaches utilize sport psychologists? Hardy, Jones, and Gould (1996, p. 294) offer one reason when they note that many people are initially skeptical of sport psychologists, especially elite athletes.

> Elite athletes and coaches are often skeptical of new people because they are so often approached by individuals who want to know them for their celebrity status or because they want something from them. Hence, even when proven consulting techniques for establishing rapport are used it takes time to develop trust, so effective sport psychology consultants must be patient.

Despite the initial skepticism forwarded by many coaches and athletes, it is becoming increasingly more common to hear coaches embrace the use of sport psychology techniques. One example comes from college football coach Gary Barnett (Barnett & Gregorian, 1996, p. 27), who offered the following words to describe his team's sport psychologist:

> Beginning in my second season, 1993, I enlisted Steve Musseau, who was 71 at the time, to come to Camp Kenosha every year. He has the peaceful, inspiring presence of Gandhi, and he immediately became a significant part of our program. What Steve does is teach how the mind works. How we think, how we learn, how we store things. His greatest lesson is that vividly imagined events and activities actually can be more productive than physically practiced ones, because anything vividly imagined becomes the truth to your mind.

Another example of a head coach who espouses the virtues of mental training is Phil Jackson, the former head basketball coach of the NBA's Chicago Bulls. In his book, Jackson discusses the importance of mental preparation as a coach by alluding to experiences from his playing career.

> I had been a center in college and, by instinct, focused on following the ball and protecting the basket. But Bradley was such a great player off the ball, I had to learn how to attach myself to him without being distracted and losing track of what was happening on the rest of the floor. To train myself to be relaxed and fully alert, I began practicing visualization. I would sit quietly for fifteen or twenty minutes before the game in a secluded part of the stadium—my favorite place was the New York Rangers' locker room—and create a moving picture in my mind of what was about to happen. (Jackson & Delahanty, 1995, p. 38)

Yet another example comes from the Washington State Cougars football team (Walters, 1997). After losing a teammate in a car crash, it was reported that the team relied heavily on Jim Bauman, its sport psychologist, to help sort out their thoughts and feelings. The unfortunate part of this story is that it took a tragic event to highlight the beneficial work of a trained sport psychology consultant. Still, this demonstrates that some sport psychologists play many roles, including that of counselor.

Durand-Bush (1996) provides a comprehensive summary of coaches' perceptions of sport psychology. The data was acquired by interviewing 22 past and present Canadian Olympic team coaches. Durand-Bush concluded that all the coaches supported sport psychology training with their team, but some preferred to do it themselves while others recruited a trained sport psychologist. Durand-Bush aptly summarized the state of sport psychology in the following way: "Coaches and sport psychologists must develop a symbiotic relationship and work together to develop suitable programs for the team" (Durand-Bush, 1996, p. 124).

In summary, it has been shown that many coaches believe in the positive benefits of sport psychology techniques. Still, the prevalence or absence of sport psychologists is not really known because we don't often hear about the behind-the-scenes work of a sport psychologist unless a tragedy or some other exceptional situation has occurred. The bottom line is that the field of sport psychology must continue to move forward and educate everyone, especially coaches, about its benefits.

Info Box

Sport psychologists contribute to the development of effective coaching by suggesting applications that are supported by sport psychology research. However, given that coaches believe strongly in practical experience over academia, many have not yet fully accepted the role of sport psychology in athletics. In addition, sport psychologists may threaten coaches. As coach education evolves, coaches should learn the beneficial role that sport psychologists can assume in developing athletes and producing successful performances.

Conclusion

This chapter began by reviewing some of the leading bodies of research in the field of talent development. It can be seen that for athletes to reach the top of their sport, they need a qualified coach instructing, guiding, and pushing them to excel. We also examined the role of the coach in competition as well as coaches' perceptions about the role of sport psychology. During competition, team sport coaches have a number of important roles that can help their team gain an advantage over their opponent. These include dealing with officials, calling time-outs, and maximizing time during intermissions. While it appears that most coaches support and understand the positive aspects of sport psychology training, not all of them are allowing sport psychologists to work with their teams. Hopefully, with time, this will begin to change. Listed below are a number of key recommendations highlighted from this chapter:

1. Coaches should treat elite athletes with mutual respect and collegiality.
2. Coaches should stimulate and motivate athletes to excel beyond their perceived capabilities.
3. Coaches should create innovative, enjoyable, and informative training sessions.
4. Coaches must understand and respect their athletes' goals and aspirations, both inside and outside of sport.
5. Coaches must understand that athletes need to enjoy their sport if they are to perform well.
6. Effective coaches know how to set learning conditions that enhance the chances of their athletes achieving "flow" experiences.
7. Top coaches should have a genuine love and devotion for what they are doing.
8. Research on talent development discounts the popular notion that outstanding achievement is innate or genetically inborn.
9. Coaches of team sports play an important role during competition.
10. Elite coaches know how to maintain emotional control during sporting contests.
11. Elite coaches understand the importance of incorporating mental training techniques into their athletes regimens.

Key Terms (in order of appearance) _____

Bloom's Stages of Development	eminence	indirect approach
flow experience	deliberate practice	direct approach

References

Barnett, G., & Gregorian, V. (1996). *High hopes: Taking the purple to Pasadena.* New York: Warner.

Bloom, B. S., (Ed.). (1985). *Developing talent in young people.* New York: Ballantine.

Bloom, G. A. (1996). Competition: Preparing for and operating in competition. In J. H. Salmela (Ed.), *Great job coach! Getting the edge from proven winners* (pp. 138–178). Ottawa, ON: Potentium.

Cogan, K. D., & Petrie, T. A. (1995). Sport consultation: An evaluation of a season-long intervention with female collegiate gymnasts. *The Sport Psychologist, 9,* 282–296.

Csikszentmihalyi, M. (1990). *Flow: The psychology of optimal experience.* New York: Harper & Row.

Csikszentmihalyi, M. "Talent and enjoyment: Findings from a longitudinal study." Keynote address at the annual meeting of the Association for the Advancement of Applied Sport Psychology (AAASP), Savannah, GA, 1991.

Csikszentmihalyi, M., Rathunde, K., & Whalen, S. (1993). *Talented teenagers: The roots of success and failure.* New York: Cambridge.

Counsilman, J. E. (1977). *Competitive swimming manual for coaches and swimmers.* Bloomington, IN: Counsilman.

Durand-Bush, N. (1996). Training: Blood, sweat, and tears. In J. H. Salmela (Ed.), *Great job coach! Getting the edge from proven winners* (pp. 102–137). Ottawa, ON: Potentium.

Durand-Bush, N., & Salmela, J. H. (1996). Nature over nurture: A new twist to the development of expertise. *Avante, 2,* 87–109.

Ericsson, K. A., & Charness, N. (1994). Expert performers. *American Psychologist, 49,* 725–747.

Ericsson, K. A., Krampe, R. T., & Tesch-Römer, C. (1993). The role of deliberate practice in the acquisition of expert performance. *Psychological Review, 100,* 363–406.

Ericsson, K. A., & Lehmann, A. C. (1996). Expert and exceptional performance: Evidence of maximal adaptation to test constraints. *Annual Review of Psychology, 47,* 273–305.

Flynn, G., (Ed.). (1973). *Vince Lombardi on football.* New York: New York Graphics Society.

Hardy, L., Jones, G., & Gould, D. (1996). *Understanding psychological preparation for sport.* Chichester: Wiley.

Jackson, P., & Delahanty, H. (1995). *Sacred hoops: Spiritual lessons of a hardwood warrior.* New York: Hyperion.

Partington, J. T. (1995). *Making music.* Ottawa, ON: Carleton Univ. Press.

Prapavessis, H., Carron, A. V., & Spink, K. S. (1996). Team building in sport. *International Journal of Sport Psychology, 27,* 269–285.

Salmela, J. H. "How expert coaches develop sport talent through deliberate practice." Keynote address to the Goodwill Games Scientific Congress, St. Petersburg, Russia, 1994.

Simon, H., & Chase, W. (1973). Skill in chess. *American Scientist, 61,* 394–403.

Silva, J. M. (1984). The status of sport psychology. *Journal of Physical Education, Recreation, and Dance, 55,* 46–49.

Tharp, R. G., & Gallimore, R. (1976). What a coach can teach a teacher. *Psychology Today, 9,* 75–78.

Walters, J. (1997, Octoboer 6). "The long way back." *Sports Illustrated, 87*(14), 50, 52, 57.

24

Children's Involvement in Sport: A Developmental Perspective

Jean Côté
Queen's University

John Hay
Brock University

- Organized sport is one of many institutions, such as family, education, or religion, that provides for the socialization of children.
- The sampling years consist of an introduction to a variety of sports, and sport psychologists are most interested in how enjoyment of sport motivates children.
- Children settle into a few sports during the specializing years. During this time, adults should help to develop skills and adherence to rules in a manner that emphasizes enjoyment rather than competition.
- As children develop into the investment years, many activities are sacrificed to expend all resources, such as time and effort, on the competitive sport.
- Most children eventually will develop into a period of recreational years when enjoyment and health are of primary importance.

Sport is one of the most popular activities among youth all over the world (De Knop, Engström, & Skirstad, 1996). In the United States it is estimated that 20–35 million children between the ages of 5 to 18 are involved in nonschool sports (Ewing & Seefeldt, 1996). Another 10 million are estimated to be involved in school-sponsored sport programs for children between the ages of 14 and 18 (Seefeldt, Ewing, & Walk, 1992). A survey in England found that 88 percent of children between the ages of 9 and 15 reported participating in exercise outside of school (White & Rowe, 1996). Engström (1996) showed that almost 85 percent of boys and 70 percent of girls were regularly active in Sweden. Studies from two different states in Australia (Clough & Traill, 1992; Sale, 1991) indicated that the percentage of participation rates for 7- to 12-year-olds was 55 to 60 percent. A survey conducted in

Coaches and parents play a crucial role in a child's ability to understand the meaning of competition.

Japan showed that 55.4 percent of Japanese children were involved in sport other than the physical education classes offered in school (Yamaguchi, 1996). In Canada, Wankel and Mummery (1996) recently indicated that approximately 40 percent of children between the ages of 10 and 14 participated in sport at least once a week. The comparable participation rates for 15- to 19-year-olds is approximately 35 percent. Because these statistics were taken using different survey instruments, assessed "sport participation" differently, and were collected at different periods in time, comparing participation rates between countries should be done with caution. However, the above statistics establish the pervasiveness of sport participation among youth in countries all over the world.

In a discussion of the worldwide trends in youth sport, De Knop, Engström, and Skirstad (1996) provided important characteristics in the development of youth sport. Essentially, in most countries:

1. More boys than girls participate in sport.
2. The most common sports are soccer among boys and swimming among boys and girls.
3. The most common reasons for participating in sport are enjoyment and social interactions.
4. Sport has become institutionalized; that is, they are not played spontaneously to the same extent as before.
5. The starting age of organized sport participation has lowered. Children start to play sports around the age of seven or even younger.

6. The number of dropouts reaches a peak in the adolescent years.
7. The most important reasons for not playing sport are "not having enough time," "no interest anymore," and "other leisure activities."

These general trends have raised concerns regarding sport participation among youth. Effort has been made, and continues to be made through both research and applied work, to make sport more equitable among genders (Greendorfer, Lewko, & Rosengren, 1996). Many sport organizations around the world have made a commitment to address the dropout problems among teenagers (De Knop, Engström, & Skirstad, 1996). Another problem is how adults' norms and values have influenced youth sport structure. Negative experience with adult leaders, such as coaches and parents, is an important factor that helps explain the decrease in sport participation as children age (Gould, 1987). For instance, when children evolve through their socialization in sport, increased adult expectations for personal performance, physical excellence, and achievement begin (Carlson, 1997; Wankel & Mummery, 1996). Thus, children begin to specialize earlier in one sport, increase their training intensity, and neglect the enjoyment, well-being, and health aspects of sport participation. The emphasis on performance may influence children's motivation for participation to the extent that they simply drop out of organized sport (Petlichkoff, 1993). Whether children remain in sport and become involved in regular physical activity depends on personal experiences, which are heavily influenced by their social environment.

Socialization into Sport

Socialization is a lifelong process through which individuals develop their self-concept, identity, attitudes, dispositions, and behaviors. Much of the socialization that takes place in a society occurs in the context of social organizations, such as in families and schools. The explicit goals of these organizations are to influence people's values, beliefs, and attitudes (Gecas, 1981). **Socialization** refers to a process by which individuals develop their conceptions of who they are and how they relate to each other through their social interactions. Coakley (1998) emphasized three important aspects in the socialization process:

1. Socialization occurs through social interactions with others.
2. Socialization is an active process of learning and social development that involves more than "a simple one way process of learning." For instance, children may first be introduced to sport through their parents. On the other hand, as a child continues to participate in sport, the direction of influence may be reversed; that is, children may become factors in socializing their parents by promoting parental involvement or parental adjustments in lifestyle.
3. The socialization process is never complete because people never stop developing, extending, and modifying their conceptions of who they are and how they relate to others.

The social context favorable to young children's participation in sport consists of the child, the coach, and the family environment (Scanlan & Lewthwaite, 1988). Accordingly, several studies have investigated children's motives for sport participation and withdrawal

(Gill, Gross, & Huddleston, 1983; Gould & Petlichkoff, 1988, Weiss & Petlichkoff, 1989) and the learning conditions offered by coaches (Salmela, 1996; Trudel & Côté, 1994). Just as important is the question of how parents socialize their child to turn away from many potential distractions within the social milieu such as television, video games, and computer networks (Brustad, 1988). To sustain participation or reach a high level of performance in sport, individuals need to overcome a number of constraints and maintain motivation over a long period of time.

Three Stages of Sport Participation from Early Childhood to Late Adolescence

Côté and colleagues (Abernethy, Côté, & Baker, 1999; Beamer, Côté, & Ericsson, 1999; Côté, 1999) recently investigated the career development of elite Canadian and Australian athletes in rowing, gymnastics, basketball, netball, and field hockey. These investigations identified three stages of sport participation from early childhood to late adolescence: the sampling years, the specializing years, and the investment years/recreational years. In the **sampling years,** parents were responsible for initially getting their children interested in sport. Children were given the chance to sample a wide range of different sports and develop fundamental motor skills such as running, jumping, and throwing. The main emphasis was to experience fun and excitement through sport. In the **specializing years,** the child focused on one or two specific sporting activities. Although fun and excitement remained central elements of the sporting experience, sport-specific skill development emerged in the sampling years as an important characteristic of the child's involvement in sport. Critical incidents that made a child pursue one activity over others were: positive experiences with a coach, encouragement from an older sibling, success, and/or simple enjoyment of the activity. Finally, the child moved into either the investment years or the recreational years.In the **investment years,** the child was committed to achieving an elite level of performance in a single activity. The strategic, competitive, and skill development characteristics of sport emerged as being the most important elements of the investment years. Children who chose not to invest in a single activity but remained in sport entered the recreational years. In the **recreational years,** the child participated regularly in sports without aspiring to reach an elite level of performance. The health and enjoyment characteristics of sport and physical activity were the most important characteristics of the recreational years.

Figure 24.1, on page 488, outlines the three levels of sport participation and shows that at each level, children have the potential to either move on to the next level or drop out of sport.

In terms of progression from the sampling years, children can move in three different directions: they can become more serious about their involvement and focus on one or two sports in the specializing years; they can chose to stay involved in sport as a leisure activity in the recreational years; or they can simply end their participation by dropping out of sport. From the specializing years, individuals also have three potential directions: the recreational years; dropping out; or the investment years where they commit to reach a high level of excellence in one sport. In terms of progression from the investment years, individuals can either drop out of sport or move into the recreational years. Finally, during the recreational

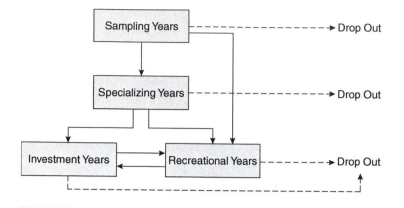

FIGURE 24.1   *Stages of Sport Participation from Early Childhood to Late Adolescence.*

years, some individuals may have an opportunity to move or return to the investment years or end their participation in sport. Skill development and enjoyment are considered to be two important determinants for keeping children involved in sport and progressing from one stage to another. In the discussion that follows, each developmental stage will be addressed individually by outlining how the socialization process affects children's skill development and enjoyment of their sport.

Sampling Years

Although the socialization process occurs over the course of life, socialization into sport takes place mostly during childhood and adolescence (McPherson, 1982). Thus, the family is an important socializing agent in the sampling years. Indeed, a large number of studies on sport socialization point out the importance of parental influence on children's early involvement in sport (e.g., Brustad, 1993; Greendorfer & Lewko, 1978; Greendorfer, Lewko, & Rosengren, 1996; Hellstedt, 1995; Lewko & Greendorfer, 1988; McCullagh et al., 1993; Scanlan & Lewthwaite, 1988; VanYperen, 1995). It is in the sampling years that the child develops basic identities, motivations, values, and beliefs about sport and physical activity. The focus of the sampling years is for the child to sample a wide range of activities without specializing in one specific sport. The main emphasis is to experience fun and excitement through organized play and games.

Children's Motivation to Participate in Sport.   In response to questions about why they play sports, children commonly say, "Because it's fun" (Brustad, 1993; Gill, Gross, & Huddleston, 1983; Gould & Petlichkoff, 1988; Petlichkoff, 1993). Motives mentioned by children for dropping out of sport include more diverse reasons such as interest in other activities, lack of fun, lack of playing time, too little success, loss of motivation, dislike of the coach, overemphasis on competition and performance, and hard physical training (Burton & Martens, 1986; Gould, 1983, 1987; Gould et al., 1982; Klint & Weiss, 1986; Orlick, 1973; Orlick & Botterill, 1975; Pooley, 1980).

Children are often motivated to engage in sport to have fun.

Motives to participate or drop out of sport were conceptualized through the **Sport Commitment Model** (Scanlan et al., 1993). The model consists of five constructs that have the potential to increase or decrease sport commitment. The first construct, which positively affects sport commitment, is "sport enjoyment" or the pleasure resulting from sport participation. The second construct, which negatively affects sport involvement, is "involvement alternatives," defined as the opportunity to engage in other activities instead of participating in the sport. The third construct, which positively affects sport involvement, is "personal investments," defined as personal resources invested in the sport such as time, effort and money. "Social constraints," the fourth construct, addresses the social pressure put on an athlete to participate. This construct is described as positively affecting sport commitment. Finally, "involvement opportunities," such as the chance to improve skills, be with friends, or stay fit, is described as positively influencing sport commitment. These constructs can be seen in the following illustration: If a child is given the opportunity to participate in a sport and enjoys it, most likely the child will chose to pursue that sport. With time, if the enjoyment and opportunity remain, the child will continue participation. Thus, if children have enough confidence to attempt an activity that they think will be enjoyable, they will attempt it when given the opportunity. If they find that the attempt is enjoyable or otherwise rewarding, they will continue in that activity if the opportunity remains or until some other more attractive alternative appears. This analysis can be used to explain why children watch television, play video games, read, play musical instruments, develop hobbies, and play games and sports. In the marketplace of children's lives during the sampling years, a competition for the time of children (and the money of parents) exists. Physical activity and sport are part of this competition, and epidemiological evidence would suggest that they are losing to competitors who have paid better attention to the simple equation (Burton, 1988; Sapp & Haubenstricker, 1978). Even when sport is seen as "cool" by kids, it is more often the look than the activity that is emulated.

The difficulty in understanding sampling behavior, particularly for sport psychologists, comes when attempting to understand what constitutes confidence and enjoyment. Competence motivation theory (Harter, 1978, 1981), achievement goal theory (Maehr & Nicholls, 1980; Nicholls, 1984), and social exchange theory (Thibault and Kelly, 1959) are prominent examples of theories that have undergone substantial investigation to explain why children participate in sport. From a **competence motivation theory,** perpective children are thought to possess an inherent desire to demonstrate competence in sport and therefore attempt to master sport skills (Brustad, 1988). In **achievement goal orientation theory,** children are viewed as being motivated primarily by ability, task, or social approval orientations. In **social exchange theory,** children attempt to maximize positive experiences and minimize negative experiences.

Weiss and Chaumonton (1992), who propose an **integrated theory of sport motivation,** reviewed each of the previously described theoretical viewpoints. They suggest that the areas of greatest concern to sport psychologists are the effects that changes in motivation have on sport choices, effort, and persistence. Motivational orientations differ between individuals, and motivated behavior results from the influence of a wide range of mediating variables. Weiss and Chaumonton suggest that affect or emotion is the final influence on motivated behavior. Positive emotions, such as enjoyment, excitement, and pleasure, increase future motivation participation, whereas negative emotions, such as anxiety, sadness, and disappointment, decrease motivation. They concluded that affect or emotion has received the least attention in sport psychology even though it "holds unlimited potential as a possible mediator of the self-perceptions-motivation link" (Weiss & Chaumonton, 1992, p. 92).

Creating Enjoyment in the Sampling Years.   Kleiber (1981) suggested that the "fun" of sports for young children lies in its play qualities. Although sports have become more organized and institutionalized in the last few years, children's first experiences in sport are still connected with experimenting with new or different means of doing things rather than attaining a goal. Sosniak (1985, p. 411) discusses the importance of play in the early years of expert pianists:

> The early years of learning were playful and filled with immediate rewards. "Tinkering around" at the piano, "tapping out melodies" was "fun." Musical activities were games that could be played over and over again.

Play is an activity that can contribute to improved performance outcomes in areas such as motor development, cognitive development, linguistic development and affective–social development (Cratty, 1986; Garvey, 1990). Play is behavior engaged in by an individual with an experimentation perspective that does not necessarily demand efficiency. Individuals involved in play try out new or different combinations of behaviors that eventually enable them to reach their goals but not essentially in the most efficient or direct manner (Miller, 1973).

Denzin (1975) distinguished between three forms of play: (1) playing at play, (2) playing at a game, and (3) playing a game. **Playing at play** describes the free-floating activities of young children from birth to about age three. **Playing at a game** describes children being involved in games without knowing the specific rules of the game, such as kicking a soccer ball around yet having no knowledge of how soccer is played. Young children from approximately age three to seven are involved in this type of play. Finally, **playing a game** describes activities with specific rules in which matters of skill and chance are more controlled.

Participation in organized sport, usually introduced at around age seven, is an example of playing a game. "Playing a game" or participating in organized sport in the sampling years involves the child's active participation, is voluntary and pleasurable, provides immediate gratification, and includes intrinsic motivation. Because of these characteristics, "playing a game" or being involved in organized sport could be defined as a type of play that is intentional or deliberate. **"Deliberate play"** is distinguished from "playing at play" or "playing at a game" because deliberate play, like "playing a game," involves an implicit or explicit set of rules. Children or adults, however, often modify the rules of existing games. Ice hockey and basketball rules, for example, are regularly changed to suit the needs of children playing in the street or in youth sport leagues. Children typically modify the rules of the sport (as they perceive them) to find a point where it most resembles the sport and yet allows them to play it at their level. Thus, when sports are not working out, when they are perceived as boring and not enjoyable by children, the parameters of the sport could be changed and adjusted to better meet the children's needs and demands. These activities would still be categorized as deliberate play.

Passer (1996, p. 84) recommended that children younger than age seven or eight should not be involved in competitive sport because they may not have sufficient cognitive abilities to understand the competition process. He indicated that "the competitive emphasis of sport should be phased in gradually as children get older...." Often, adults who reward behaviors such as excessive competition, physical aggression against others, and cheating distort early participation in organized sport. Kleiber (1981) argued that to keep sport enjoyable, adults should pay attention to the following factors, which have since received additional empirical support (e.g., Passer, 1996; Shields & Bredemeier, 1995; Strean, 1995).

1. The balance for competition: intense competition at an early age will undermine the potential enjoyment of sports.
2. The potential for player involvement: every child should be given a chance to play.
3. The influence of spectators: there is less potential for enjoyment in sport if children are concerned with what coaches, parents, friends, or spectators may be thinking or saying.
4. The relationship of performance outcomes to future achievement: enjoyment will decrease if too much emphasis is put on the relationship between performance outcomes, such as winning, or finishing first, and future achievement in sport.
5. The locus of control: to enhance enjoyment, children should always have a sense that they have control over the rules and conditions of the sport. For instance, children can make decisions about practice drills or the type of training they do.

In summary, adults' concerns in the sampling years should be on creating games that allow children to have fun, helping them develop and maintain a positive attitude towards sport, and helping them acquire fundamental motor skills such as running, throwing, and jumping. Adults who are involved in children's early participation in organized sport should be careful not to reward a child's negative behaviors such as excessive competition, physical aggression against others, and cheating. A greater focus on play and enjoyment in the sampling years is in line with results of studies that investigate the motives for a child's participation in sport (Brustad, 1993; Gill, Gross, & Huddleston, 1983; Gould & Petlichkoff, 1988; Petlichkoff, 1993). Another line of research that advocates the important role of play and enjoyment in the sampling years comes from studies that have analyzed the socialization process of elite performers, a topic that will be explored next.

Early Development of Elite Performers.   What is the pattern of development of individuals who eventually commit to achieving a high level of excellence? Several studies have focused on elite performers, using a retrospective approach in which the athletes were asked about their early involvement in sport (Bloom, 1985; Carlson, 1988; Csikszentmihalyi, Rathunde, & Whalen, 1993; Kenyon & McPherson, 1973; Scanlan, Stein, & Ravizza, 1989, 1991; Stevenson, 1990). These studies showed that even for those who go on to be elite performers, the sampling years were an important stage of development in which the youngsters experienced play and enjoyment of several activities.

Carlson (1988, 1997) analyzed the process of socialization of elite tennis players in Sweden. His findings showed that elite tennis players, on average, were involved in more than one sport before the age of 14. He indicates that early specialization and "professional-like training" in tennis did not favor the development of elite players. An all-around sport engagement was more important before adolescence. Bloom and colleagues (1985) interviewed 120 individuals at the top of their respective professions in science, art, and athletics. Their study underscores the major influence of the family at the different stages of talent development, specifically in the early years. In the early years of a child's involvement in an activity, parents tended to be supportive, allowing their children freedom to decide whether to practice formally or not.

In the families of elite performers studied by Côté (1999), "deliberate play" was an important experience of early childhood. Parents of children in the sampling years were responsible for initially getting their children interested in sport and allowing their children to sample a wide range of enjoyable activities without focusing on intense training. The main emphasis was to experience fun and excitement through sport. The choice of the sport, however, was not an important issue to the parents. Therefore, children sampled and experienced a variety of different sports in early childhood (generally between ages 7 and 12), as illustrated by this mother of a Canadian junior national rower:

> He's been rowing for two years. He was involved in a lot of sport before that, mostly soccer and then high school basketball and volleyball; hockey a little bit but not a lot. (Côté, 1999)

The notion of "play" was more predominant than the notion of training or practice in the sampling years. During this period, parents kept a positive perspective about their child's participation by putting the emphasis on fun rather than competition. The parents also perceived their child's involvement in youth sport as being an important activity for the development of fundamental motor skills, such as running and throwing, and other life skills.

Kalinowski (1985, p. 145) found the same kind of parental perspective in the development of Olympic swimmers, as illustrated by this mother of a swimmer:

> It was important to have some kind of athletic thing. If you have an athletic child who is very energetic, you always look to some kind of sports. It helps to keep them in shape…it helps to condition them psychologically as well as physically.

In general, the previous investigations of elite performers provide support for children's participation and experimentation in a wide spectrum of activities early in their development. Thus, an important element of the sampling years is to facilitate involvement in activities that are pleasurable and that are cherished by children. Studies of children in sport have shown that play and enjoyment were crucial elements in the early years of a child's participation in sport and in the child's progression to the recreational or specializing years.

Info Box

To facilitate further growth into either the specializing years or the recreational years, children must enjoy being active. Children that are forced to adhere to rules or engage in competition in these years may be discouraged from sport in general.

Specializing Years

In the specializing years, the child focuses on one or two specific sports. For example, children who have been involved in swimming, soccer, basketball, baseball, and ice hockey in the sampling years may choose to focus their energy on baseball in the summer and ice hockey in the winter. Critical incidents that make a child choose to specialize in one activity over another include: positive experiences with a coach, encouragement from an older sibling, success, or simple enjoyment of the sport. Children usually choose to specialize in middle childhood or around age 13 (Bloom, 1985; Carlson, 1988; Côté, 1999). While fun and excitement through play remain central elements of the sporting experience, sport-specific skill development through practice emerges in the specializing years as an important characteristic of the child's involvement.

Practice and Play in the Specializing Years. Fundamental skill development such as running, throwing, jumping, and kicking must be attained before entering the specializing years. These fundamental skills were the product of maturation and development in the sampling years when children experimented and sampled a variety of activities, mainly through play. In middle childhood, or the specializing years, practice becomes a more powerful factor in skill development (French & Thomas, 1987; Kuhlman & Beitel, 1988; Seefeldt, 1988; Thomas & French, 1985; Thomas et al., 1988). Although adolescents may become more committed and serious about their sport involvement by increasing the amount of practice, play and enjoyment remain central elements of the specializing years (Bloom, 1985; Carlson, 1988, 1997; Côté, 1999).

Ericsson, Krampe, and Tesch-Römer (1993) provided a framework for examining the different variables related to the acquisition of expert performance. They suggested that the most effective learning occurs through involvement in a highly structured activity defined as **deliberate practice.** Deliberate practice activities: (1) require effort, (2) are not inherently enjoyable, and (3) are specifically designed to improve the current level of performance. To achieve expert performance, deliberate practice has to be sustained over a period of at least 10 years. According to Ericsson and colleagues, maximization of deliberate practice involves operating within three types of constraints: motivational, effort, and resource constraints. First, because engagement in deliberate practice is not inherently motivating, it requires involved commitment from the performers. Second, deliberate practice may be a strenuous activity that cannot be sustained for a long period of time without leading to mental and/or physical exhaustion; thus, individuals must limit practice to optimize concentration and effort. Finally, deliberate practice requires resources such as access to coaches, training material, and training facilities. In other words, improvement of sport specific skills is not guaranteed by participation alone.

Any activity can be rated in terms of enjoyment, effort, and relevance to one's overall performance. Ericsson, Krampe, and Tesch-Römer (1993) found that less accomplished musicians spent more time playing music for fun (deliberate play) than did accomplished musicians. Musicians gave "practice alone" and "taking lessons" higher ratings for relevance and effort, and low ratings for enjoyment. Similarly, Starkes and associates (1996) showed that figure skaters and wrestlers rated activities that were relevant for improvement of performance (deliberate practice) less enjoyable than other types of activities. In an indepth analysis of 64 talented athletes in their specializing years (14 and 15 years old), Csikszentmihalyi, Rathunde, and Whalen (1993) found that talented teens generally reported less positive emotional states overall in comparison with average peers, a finding somewhat consistent with the notion of deliberate practice. On the other hand, the athletes studied by Csikszentmihalyi and associates reported that the two top reasons they were engaged in sport were "I enjoy it," and " I get satisfaction from getting better or from learning." The activity most likely to create enjoyment in sport is deliberate play; however, the activity most likely to create improvement in performance is deliberate practice.

The two concepts of deliberate practice and deliberate play could be placed opposite each other on a continuum. Behaviors could be located along the continuum from those primarily motivated with a process-experimentation perspective (deliberate play) such as having fun, to those motivated by a goal-directed perspective (deliberate practice) such as learning or improving skills. When individuals are involved in deliberate play, they experiment with new or different combinations of behaviors but not necessarily in the most efficient way to improve performance. On the other hand, when individuals are involved in deliberate practice, they exhibit behavior focused on improving performance by the most efficient means available. For example, the backhand shot in tennis could be learned and improved over time by playing matches or by creating fun situations in practices that would allow a player to practice this specific shot. However, players could maximally improve their level of performance of their backhand shots if they were to practice using drills that might be considered less enjoyable. While the drills used in deliberate practice might not be the most enjoyable, they might be the most relevant activity to improve performance.

Csikszentmihalyi, Rathunde, and Whalen (1993, p. 148) reported that many teenagers drop out of a domain because they never had the chance to enjoy using their talent. These authors stated that "no teenager will develop talent unless he or she enjoys working in the talent area." The wrestlers and figure skaters in the Starkes and associates' (1996) study rated some practice activities as highly relevant and very enjoyable, a finding consistent with the notion of deliberate play. Therefore, the overall quality of the experience in the specializing years should be positive to ensure that teenagers stay involved in sport. Unless individuals are motivated to learn, deliberate practice is useless. To motivate people in the specializing years, it is necessary to provide a certain number of enjoyable activities through deliberate play. Because children in their middle childhood "need to perceive sport as challenging yet fun" (Starkes et al., 1996, p. 354; Gallagher et al., 1996), a balance of both deliberate practice and deliberate play seems appropriate in the specializing years.

Info Box

The specializing years involve the focusing of a child's scope to include one or two sports. For most children, enjoyment is still of primary importance; however, those that develop to the elite status tend to engage in deliberate practice rather than deliberate play during these years.

Investment Years/Recreational Years

After the specializing years, the child may enter either the investment years, by committing to the pursuit of an elite level of performance in one or two sports, or the recreational years, by regularly participating in sport or physical activity for enjoyment and/or health reasons.

Investment Years.   The investment years are, in essence, an extension of the specializing years. The investment years are distinguished from the specializing years mainly by the extreme intensity of the athlete's commitment to the sport and the tremendous amount of practice. The age at which children attain the investment years is typically around age 17 but can vary greatly depending upon the sport or activity they choose. For example, the investment of training time, money, and other resources needs to be made earlier in sports such as gymnastics and figure skating. Although the age at which children typically enter the investment years can vary, the characteristics of this stage of sport participation are very similar across sports (Abernethy, Côté, & Baker, 1999; Beamer, Côté, & Ericsson, 1999; Bloom, 1985; Carlson, 1988; Côté, 1999). In the investment years, parents make a commitment of time and money to support their children's involvement in sport, as illustrated by the father of a Canadian junior national rower:

> It started back when they were younger, buying their first set of weights. Instead of going on vacations, we put the money into buying rowing ergometers. [My son] and I also share a single shell. We put some of our spending money or savings into training equipment and then said, "To heck with going to Whistler to go skiing." We feel that it has paid off. (Côté, 1999)

Consistent with parental investment, the children make a commitment to achieve a high level of excellence in their sport. Deliberate play is now largely replaced by an enormous amount of deliberate practice. Ericsson, Krampe, and Tesch-Römer (1993) showed that individual differences in the amount of deliberate practice were related to the level of performance attained by musicians. An analysis of expert musicians' daily patterns of practice shows that they could sustain about 4 hours of practice a day without leading to exhaustion and burnout. This amount of daily practice is consistent with findings from interviews with athletes currently in their investment years (Côté, 1999; Richter, 1997; Sloane, 1985).

> Right now, in the fall season, training is not quite as intense. I train about one and a half to two hours a day, and then when spring starts we start our serious training. It's probably between

three to three and a half hours a day of training; it has been like this for the last year and a half. (Côté, 1999)

In addition to supportive families and master coaches (Salmela, 1996), what allows athletes to achieve a high level of performance in the investment years is their willingness to "pay the price" to be great. Intensive engagement in deliberate practice does not bring the immediate pleasure and gratification common to deliberate play in the sampling years.

Figure 24.2 shows the relationship between deliberate practice and deliberate play throughout the sampling, specializing, and investment years. In general, the sampling years (typically between ages 7 and 12) are characterized by a low frequency of deliberate practice and a high frequency of deliberate play. The specializing years (typically between ages 13 and 16) are marked by an equal amount of deliberate play and deliberate practice. Finally, a high frequency of deliberate practice and a low frequency of deliberate play characterize the investment years. Athletes and families who choose not to, or are unable to put the tremendous amount of resources into the investment years, can move into the recreational years.

Recreational Years.   Individuals can move into the recreational years either from the sampling years, the specializing years, or the investment years. In the recreational years, individuals find themselves engaged in a pursuit that has the potential to enhance their health and personal growth. The goal of the recreational years is to experience enjoyment and maintain a healthy lifestyle. Deliberate play and deliberate practice both can be ele-

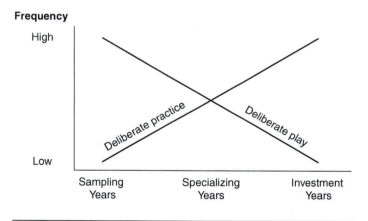

FIGURE 24.2   *The Relationship between Deliberate Play, Deliberate Practice, and the Three Levels of Sport Participation.* Deliberate practice includes activities that (1) require effort, (2) are not inherently enjoyable, and (3) are specifically designed to improve the current level of performance (Ericsson, Krampe, & Tesch-Römer, 1993). Deliberate practice involves delayed gratification. On the other hand, deliberate play are organized activities which (1) require active and pleasurable participation, (2) are inherently enjoyable, and (3) are designed to provide enjoyment. Deliberate play involves immediate gratification and is intrinsically motivating.

ments of the recreational years to different degrees. For children, the recreational years are very similar to what was experienced in the sampling years. Children in the recreational years should have the opportunity to play, have fun, and enhance basic sport skills.

Governmental programs around the world have been instituted to foster children's involvement in sport and physical activity. "Sport For All" programs promote the value of sport and physical activity and encourage more widespread involvement in sport (Wankel, 1988). Examples of these programs established in the 1970s include "Life—Be In It" in Australia and "Participation" in Canada (Wankel, 1988). More recently, "Quality Daily Physical Education" program was founded in Canada to promote Active Living as a positive and healthy way of life for children. This program includes:

1. Recreational/competitive participation opportunities.
2. Competition, fair play, enjoyment, success, and social awareness outcomes.
3. The ability to meet the diverse needs, abilities, and interests of all students by incorporating a wide range of experiences.

Similarly, in the United States, the National Association for Sport and Physical Education's Youth Sports Task Force prepared a set of guidelines to help adults provide quality youth sport programs (Martens & Seefeldt, 1979). In the form of a **Bill of Rights for Young Athletes,** they offered a set of guidelines that adults should acknowledge and implement as leaders of youth sport programs. The ten rights include:

1. The right to participate in sport.
2. The right to participate at a level commensurate with each child's maturity and ability.
3. The right to have qualified adult leadership.
4. The right to play as a child and not as an adult.
5. The right of children to share in the leadership and decision making of their sport participation.
6. The right to participate in safe and healthy environments.
7. The right to proper preparation for participation in sport.
8. The right to have an equal opportunity to strive for success.
9. The right to be treated with dignity.
10. The right to have fun.

Although these guidelines and programs should be considered in the sampling, specializing, and investment years, they become of primary importance in the recreational years because they help maintain an environment conducive to children remaining active in sport.

Children in the recreational years have needs that differ from children in the sampling, specializing, or investment years. Ewing and Seefeldt (1996) suggested that non-school sport programs for youth 12 to 18 years of age (which would include several children involved in the recreational years) should reduce the emphasis on elite competitors and focus more on an adult recreation philosophy. Because children in the recreational years are looking for different things, they will gain enjoyment from different sport programs. Sport programs in the recreational years should be flexible enough to adapt to individual interests.

Info Box

A child who is in the sampling years, specializing years, or recreational years has fun simply participating in the activities. Although the same may be true for a child in the investment years, in general, most children in this stage obtain enjoyment from some later payoff such as successful performances or winning.

Conclusion

The stages of sport participation outlined in this chapter show that different themes are important at each phase of a child's involvement in sport. The sampling years are dominated by deliberate play, enjoyment, and immediate rewards. It is a period when children develop interest and become involved in various sports. The ability to play, explore, and experiment in various movement situations is crucial for the development of fundamental motor skills during the sampling years. The specializing years is a period where children begin to focus on one or two sporting activities. Children are motivated to work harder and more seriously. The investment years are a period of dedication to the pursuit of excellence in a single sport. High-level performance and competition are dominant themes of the investment years. Finally, the recreational years comprise an important period that keeps children and youth involved in sport. It is a period when individuals have the potential to experience sport in a less competitive environment. Recreational sport programs for children, just like those for adults, should be adaptable and offer a wide range of choices in levels of skill, competition, and demands. The developmental perspective proposed in this chapter has the following implications for children's involvement in organized sport.

1. For most children in the sampling years (ages 7 to 12), sport programs should emphasize deliberate play and fun.
2. Overemphasis on competition and/or intense training during the sampling years will undermine children's enjoyment of sport.
3. While fun remains a central element of the specializing years (ages 13–16), sport-specific skill development through practice should be a priority of most sport programs.
4. The overall quality of the sporting experience in the specializing years should be positive to ensure that teenagers stay involved in sport and physical activity.
5. In the investment years (ages 17 and up), because children make a commitment to achieve a high level of performance, the primary focus of sport programs should be on skill and performance development through deliberate practice.
6. In the recreational years, sport programs should emphasize children's enjoyment and health.
7. Sport programs in the recreational years should be flexible to meet the wide spectrum of needs and desires of different children.

Although the stages of sport participation described in this chapter demonstrate a systematic pattern in the process of developing sport motivation and abilities in children, the same pattern of stages may not be universal and applicable to all sporting situations or to specific individuals. However, this model describing the process of development in sport may be more useful than any nonsport-specific theory of child development. The stages of sport participation form a useful framework for researchers studying youth sport. Additionally, practitioners can use these stages as guidelines to help develop programs to encourage children to maintain a commitment to sport and exercise activities. With a clear understanding of the stages that children pass through in their development in sport, the next two chapters will focus on three major influences on this developmental process: family, coaches, and peers.

Acknowledgements.   Preparation of this chapter was supported by standard research grants from the Social Sciences and Humanities Research Council of Canada (SSHRC Grant #410-97-0241 and #410-99-0525). The authors are grateful to Kristin Côté for her helpful comments in the preparation of this chapter.

Key Terms (in order of appearance)

socialization	achievement goal orientation	playing at a game
sampling years	theory	playing a game
specializing years	social exchange theory	deliberate play
investment years	integrated theory of sport	deliberate practice
recreational years	motivation	Bill of Rights for Young Athletes
Sport Commitment Model	play	
competence motivation theory	playing at play	

References

Abernethy, B., Côté, J., & Baker, J. (1999). *Expert decision-making in sport.* Canberra, Australian Institute of Sport Publication.

Beamer, M., Côté, J., & Ericsson, K. A. "A comparison between international and provincial level gymnasts in their pursuit of sport expertise." *Proceedings of the Tenth European Congress of Sport Psychology.* Prague, Czech Republic, 1999.

Bloom, B. S. (Ed.). (1985). *Developing talent in young people.* New York: Ballantine.

Brustad, R. J. (1988). Affective outcomes in competitive youth sport: The influence of intrapersonal and socialization factors. *Journal of Sport & Exercise Psychology, 10,* 307–321.

Brustad, R. J. (1993). Youth in sport: Psychological considerations. In R. N. Singer, M. Murphey & L. K. Tennant (Eds.), *Handbook of research in sport psychology* (pp. 695–718). New York: Macmillan.

Burton, D. (1988). The dropout dilemma in youth sports: Documenting the problem and identifying solutions. In R. M. Martens (Ed.), *Young athletes: Biological, psychological, and educational perspectives* (pp. 245–266). Champaign, IL: Human Kinetics.

Burton, D., & Martens, R. (1986). Pinned by their own goals: An exploratory investigation into why kids drop out of wrestling. *Journal of Sport Psychology, 8,* 183–197.

Carlson, R. C. (1988). The socialization of elite tennis players in Sweden: An analysis of the players' backgrounds and development. *Sociology of Sport Journal, 5,* 241–256.

Carlson, R. C. (1997). In search of the expert sport performer. *Science in the Olympic Sport, 1,* 1–13.

Clough, J., & Traill, R. (1992). *A mapping of participation rates in junior sport in the Australian Capital Territory.* Canberra, Australia: ACT Government.

Coakley, J. (1998). *Sport in society: Issues and controversies,* 6th ed. Boston: McGraw-Hill.

Côté, J. (1999). The influence of the family in the development of talent in sport. *The Sport Psychologist, 13,* 395–417.

Cratty, B. J. (1986). *Perceptual motor development in infants and children,* 3rd ed. Englewood Cliffs, NJ: Prentice Hall.

Csikszentmihalyi, M., Rathunde, K., & Whalen, S. (1993). *Talented teenagers: The roots of success and failure.* New York: Cambridge.

Denzin, N. K. (1975). Play, games and interaction: The contexts of childhood socialization. *The Sociological Quarterly, 16,* 458–478.

De Knop, P., Engström, L. -M., & Skirstad, B. (1996). Worldwide trends in youth sport. In P. De Knop, L. -M. Engström, B. Skirstad, & M. R. Weiss (Eds.), *Worldwide trends in youth sport* (pp. 276–281). Champaign, IL: Human Kinetics.

Engström, L. -M. (1996). Sweden. In P. De Knop, L. -M. Engström, B. Skirstad & M. R. Weiss (Eds.), *Worldwide trends in youth sport* (pp. 231–243). Champaign, IL: Human Kinetics.

Ericsson, K. A., Krampe, R. T., & Tesch-Römer, C. (1993). The role of deliberate practice in the acquisition of expert performance. *Psychological Review, 3,* 363–406.

Ewing, M. E., & Seefeldt, V. (1996). Patterns of participation and attrition in American agency-sponsored youth sports. In F. L. Smoll & R. E. Smith (Eds.), *Children and youth in sport: A biopsychosocial perspective* (pp. 31–45). Indianapolis: Brown & Benchmark.

French, K. E., & Thomas, J. R. (1987). The relation of knowledge development to children's basketball performance. *Journal of Sport Psychology, 9,* 15–32.

Gallagher, J. D., French, K. E., Thomas, K. T., & Thomas, J. R. (1996). Expertise in youth sport: Relations between knowledge and skill. In F. L. Smoll & R. E. Smith (Eds.), *Children and youth in sport: A biopsychosocial perspective* (pp. 338–358). Indianapolis: Brown & Benchmark.

Garvey, K. (1990). *Play.* Cambridge, MA: Harvard Univ. Press.

Gecas, V. (1981). Contexts of socialization. In M. Rosenberg, & R. Turner (Eds.), *Social psychology: Sociological perspectives* (pp. 165–199). New York: Basic.

Gill, D. L., Gross, J. B., & Huddleston, S. (1983). Participation motivation in youth sports. *International Journal of Sport Psychology, 14,* 1–14.

Gould, D. (1983). Future directions in youth sports participation motivation research. In L. Wankel & R. Wilberg (Eds.), *Psychology of sport and motor behavior: Research and practice* (pp. 1–18). Edmonton: University of Alberta.

Gould, D. (1987). Understanding attrition in children's sport. In D. Gould & M. R. Weiss (Eds.), *Advances in pediatric sport sciences* (pp. 61–85). Champaign, IL: Human Kinetics.

Gould, D., Feltz, D., Horn, T., & Weiss, M. R. (1982). Reasons for discontinuing involvement in competitive youth swimming. *Journal of Sport Behavior, 5,* 155–165.

Gould, D., & Petlichkoff, L. (1988). Participation motivation and attrition in young athletes. In F. L. Smoll, R. J. Magill, & M. J. Ash (Eds.), *Children in sport* (pp. 161–178). Champaign, IL: Human Kinetics.

Greendorfer, S., & Lewko, J. (1978). Role of family members in sport socialization of children. *Research Quarterly, 49,* 146–152.

Greendorfer, S. L., Lewko, J. H., & Rosengren, K. S. (1996). Family and gender-based influences in sport socialization of children and adolescents. In F. L. Smoll & R. E. Smith (Eds.), *Children and youth in sport: A biopsychosocial perspective* (pp. 89–111). Indianapolis: Brown & Benchmark.

Harter. S. (1978). Effectance motivation reconsidered. *Human Development, 21,* 34–64.

Harter, S. (1981). The development of competence motivation in the mastery of cognitive and physical skills a place of joy? In G. C. Roberts & D. M. Landers (Eds.), *Psychology of motor behavior and sport* (pp. 3–29). Champaign, IL: Human Kinetics.

Hellstedt, J. C. (1995). Invisible players: A family systems model. In S. H. Murphy (Eds.), *Sport psychology interventions.* Champaign, IL: Human Kinetics.

Kalinowski, A. G. (1985). The development of Olympic swimmers. In B. S. Bloom (Ed.), *Developing talent in young people* (pp. 139–192). New York: Ballantine.

Kenyon, G. S., & McPherson, B. D. (1973). Becoming involved in physical activity and sport: A process of socialization. In G. L. Ratrick (Ed.), *Physical activity: Human growth and development.* (pp. 303–332). New York: Academic.

Kleiber, D. A. (1981). Searching for enjoyment in children's sports. *Physical Educator, 38*(2), 77–84.

Klint, K., & Weiss, M. R. (1986). Dropping in and dropping out: Participation motives of current and former youth gymnasts. *Canadian Journal of Applied Sport Sciences, 11,* 106–114.

Kuhlman, J., & Beitel, P. "Interrelationships among age, sex, and depth of sport experience on a complex motor task by 4-year old children." Paper presented at the annual conference of the North American Society for the Psychology of Sport and Physical Activity, Knoxville, TN, 1988.

Lewko, J. H., & Greendorfer, S. L. (1988). Family influence in sport socialization of children and adolescents. In F. L. Smoll, R. A. Magill, & M. J. Ash (Eds.), *Children in sport* (pp. 288–300). Champaign, IL: Human Kinetics.

Maehr, M. L., & Nicholls, J. G. (1980). Culture and achievement motivation: A second look. In N. Warren (Ed.), *Studies in cross-cultural psychology,* Vol. 3 (pp. 221–267). New York: Academic.

Martens, R., & Seefeldt, V. (1979). *Guidelines for children's sports.* Washington, DC: American Alliance for Health, Physical Education, Recreation and Dance.

McCullagh, P., Matzkanin, K. T., Shaw, S. D., & Maldonado, M. (1993). Motivation for participation in physical activity: A comparison of parent-child perceived competences and participation motives. *Pediatric Exercise Science, 5,* 224–233.

McPherson, B. D. (1982). The child in competitive sport: Influence of the social milieu. In R. Magill, M. Ash, & F. Smoll (Eds.), *Children in sport* (pp. 247–268). Champaign, IL: Human Kinetics.

Miller, S. (1973). Ends, means, and galumphing: Some leitmotifs of play. *American Anthropologist, 75,* 87–98.

Nicholls, J. G. (1984). Achievement motivation: Conceptions of ability, subjective experience, task choice, and performance. *Psychological Review, 91,* 328–346.

Orlick, T. (1973). Children's sport: A revolution is coming. *Canadian Association for Health, Physical Education and Recreation Journal, 39,* 12–14.

Orlick, T., & Botterill, C. (1975). *Every kid can win.* Chicago: Nelson Hall.

Passer, M. W. (1996). At what age are children ready to compete? Some psychological considerations. In F. L. Smoll & R. E. Smith (Eds.), *Children and youth in sport: A biopsychosocial perspective* (pp. 73–86). Toronto: Brown & Benchmark.

Petlichkoff, L. M. (1993). Coaching children: Understanding the motivational process. *Sport Science Review, 2,* 48–61.

Pooley, J. C. (1980). Dropouts. *Coaching Review, 3,* 36–38.

Richter, M. "A case study of a family of three elite swimmers." Unpublished ms., Brock University, St. Catharines, Ontario, 1997.

Sale, B. (1991). *Junior sport in South Australia.* Adelaide, Australia: South Australian Sports Institute.

Salmela, J. H. (Ed.). (1996). *Great job coach: Getting the edge from proven winners.* Ottawa: Potentium.

Sapp, M., & Haubenstricker, J. "Motivation for joining and reasons for not continuing in youth sport programs in Michigan." Paper presented at the meeting of the American Alliance for Health, Physical Education, Recreation and Dance, Kansas City, MO, 1978.

Scanlan, T. K., & Lewthwaite, R. (1986). Social psychological aspects of competition for male youth participants: Predictors of enjoyment. *Journal of Sport Psychology, 8,* 25–35.

Scanlan, T. K., & Lewthwaite, R. (1988). From stress to enjoyment: Parental and coach influences on young participants. In E. W. Brown & C. F. Branta (Eds.), *Competitive sports for children and youth: An overview of research and issues* (pp. 47–58). Champaign, IL: Human Kinetics.

Scanlan, T. K., Simons, J. P., Carpenter, P. J., Schmidt, G. W., & Keeler, B. (1993). The sport commitment model: Measurement development for the youth-sport domain. *Journal of Sport & Exercise Psychology, 15,* 16–38.

Scanlan, T. K., Stein, G. L., & Ravizza, K. (1989). An in-depth study of former elite figure skaters: Sources of enjoyment. *Journal of Sport & Exercise Psychology, 11,* 65–83.

Scanlan, T. K., Stein, G. L., & Ravizza, K. (1991). An in-depth study of former elite skaters: III. Sources of stress. *Journal of Sport and Exercise Psychology, 13,* 103–120.

Seefeldt, V. (1988). The concept of readiness applied to motor skill acquisition. In F. L. Smoll, R. A. Magill, & M. J. Ash (Eds.), *Children in sport,* 3rd ed. (pp. 45–52). Champaign, IL: Human Kinetics.

Seefeldt, V., Ewing, M. E., & Walk, S. (1992). *Overview of youth sport programs in the United States.* Washington, DC: Carnegie Council on Adolescent Development.

Shields, D. L., & Bredemeier, B. J. L. (1995). *Character development and physical activity.* Champaign, IL: Human Kinetics.

Sloane, K. D. (1985). Home influences on talent development. In B. S. Bloom (Ed.), *Developing talent in young people* (pp. 439–476). New York: Ballantine.

Sosniak, L. A. (1985). Learning to be a concert pianist. In B. S. Bloom (Ed.), *Developing talent in young people* (pp. 19–67). New York: Ballantine.

Starkes, J. L., Deakin, J. M., Allard, F., Hodges, N. J., & Hayes, A. (1996). Deliberate practice in sports: What is it anyway?. In K. A. Ericsson (Ed.), *The road to excellence: The acquisition of expert performance in the arts and sciences, sports and games* (pp. 81–106). Mahwah, NJ: Lawrence Erlbaum.

Stevenson, G. L. (1990). The early careers of international athletes. *Sociology of Sport Journal, 7,* 238–253.

Strean, W. B. (1995). Youth sport contexts: Coaches' perceptions and implications for intervention. *Journal of Applied Sport Psychology, 7,* 23–37.

Thibault, J. W., & Kelley, H. H. (1959). *The social psychology of groups.* New York: Wiley.

Thomas, J. R., & French, K. E. (1985). Gender differences across age in motor performance: A meta-analysis. *Psychological Bulletin, 98,* 260–282.

Thomas, J. R., French, K. E., Thomas, K. T., & Gallagher, J. D. (1988). Children's knowledge development and sport performance. In F. L. Smoll, R. A. Magill, & M. J. Ash (Eds.), *Children in sport* (pp. 179–202). Champaign, IL: Human Kinetics.

Trudel, P. & Côté, J. (1994). Pédagogie sportive et conditions d'apprentissage. *Enfance, 2,* 285–297.

VanYperen, N. W. (1995). Interpersonal stress, performance level, and parental support: A longitudinal study among highly skilled young soccer players. *The Sport Psychologist, 9,* 225–241.

Wankel, L. M. (1988). Exercise adherence and leisure activity: Patterns of involvement and interventions to facilitate regular activity. In R. K. Dishman (Ed.), *Exercise adherence* (pp. 369–396). Champaign, IL: Human Kinetics.

Wankel, L. M., & Mummery, W. K. (1996). Canada. In P. De Knop, L. -M. Engstöm, B. Skirstad, & M. R. Weiss (Eds.), *Worldwide trends in youth sport* (pp. 27–42). Champaign, IL: Human Kinetics.

Weiss, M. R., & Chaumeton, N. (1992). Motivational orientations in sport. In T. Horn (Ed.), *Advances in sport psychology* (pp. 61–99). Champaign, IL: Human Kinetics.

Weiss, M. R., & Petlichkoff, L. M. (1989). Children's motivation for participation in and withdrawal from sport: Identifying the missing links. *Pediatric Exercise Science, 1,* 195–211.

White, A., & Rowe, N. (1996). England. In P. De Knop, L. M. Engström, B. Skirstad, & M. R. Weiss (Eds.), *Worldwide trends in sport* (pp. 115–125). Champaign, IL: Human Kinetics.

Yamaguchi, Y. (1996). Japan. In P. De Knop, L. -M. Engström, B. Skirstad, & M. R. Weiss (Eds.), *Worldwide trends in youth sport* (pp. 67–75). Champaign, IL: Human Kinetics.

25

Family Influences on Youth Sport Performance and Participation

Jean Côté

Queen's University

John Hay

Brock University

- The parenting style displayed in a family can have powerful positive or negative effects on children such as providing support or adding stress, respectively.
- Parental support can be demonstrated in four ways in athletics: emotional, informational, tangible, and companionship.
- Parental expectations can help to motivate children to participate in sport; however, in excess they can cause pressure that may result in dropout or burnout.
- Siblings also may influence the sport participation of a child, either positively or negatively.

Stories about parental involvement in sport are common topics of discussion on television and radio shows, in newspapers and magazines, and in electronic discussion groups. Tiger Woods in golf, Wayne Gretzky and Eric Lindros in ice hockey, Mary Pierce and Stefi Graf in tennis, and David Robinson in basketball are well-known examples of athletes who had major parental influences in their careers. Parents' behaviors can be a source of either support or stress to young athletes. One of the main arguments underlying this chapter is that participation in sport, when properly nurtured by parents, can provide a unique arena for learning about oneself and about life. Lessons learned from sport participation, including proper perspectives on winning or losing, help prepare young people for life's challenges.

The social milieu of young children greatly affects early and lifelong participation in sport. This social milieu comprises the immediate and extended family, the neighborhood and community, the school, peers, and peer groups such as teams and includes electronic dimensions such as television, video games, and computer networks. Conflict, too little support, or neglect by their family can still reduce the sport participation of committed children who have the support of an effective coach. Csikszentmihalyi, Rathunde, and Whalen (1993, p. 175) recently suggested that "a home environment in which one is secure enough to feel cheerful and energetic, and challenged enough to become more goal-directed, increases teenagers' chances of progressively refining their talents." Whether children become involved and decide to remain in sport and physical activity depends on personal experiences, which are heavily influenced by their family environment.

A large number of studies on sport socialization point out the importance of parental influence on children's involvement in sport (e.g. Green & Chalip, 1997; Greendorfer & Lewko, 1978; Lewko & Greendorfer, 1988; McCullagh et al., 1993; Scanlan & Lewthwaite, 1984; VanYperen, 1995). As children get older, the importance of parental support diminishes as they turn to close friends for listening support, emotional support, and emotional challenge (Rosenfeld, Richman, & Hardy, 1989). Previous reviews have focused on family, peer, gender, and school influences on the sport socialization of children and adolescents (Lewko & Greendorfer, 1988; Greendorfer, Lewko, & Rosengren, 1996), children and the sport socialization process (Coakley, 1987, 1997), and family and peer influences on children's psychological development (Brustad, 1993, 1996b). The present chapter will borrow from each of the previous areas to describe how the family can create a foundation that nurtures a child's lifelong participation and success in sport.

Characteristics of Families

It is essential to recognize that the **family** is a social group that may appear in diverse forms. Families appear in various settings, have a unique set of experiences, and are in constant development (Hellstedt, 1995). Different types of families include parents and their biological or adoptive children, single parent families, extended families, families centered around committed homosexual relationships, and unmarried couples who have made a life commitment to each other. Klein and White (1996) identified four distinguishing features of families:

1. *Families last for a considerably longer period of time than most other social groups.* Although members of families are added and subtracted regularly and some relationships in families may break down, we think of families as lasting a lifetime. Belonging to a family also is involuntary in the sense that children don't choose their parents.
2. *Families are intergenerational.* Families include people who are related as parents and children. Generally, family members have relatives of both younger and older generations.
3. *Families contain both biological and/or legal relationships between members.* Family members are tied by biological links or by legal links such as adoption. Family members have rights that are codified in laws, informal agreements, or formal agreements such as marriage.
4. *The biological and legal aspects of families link them to a larger kinship organization.* Although everybody at some point stops counting distant relatives as family members, they create the potential for family relationships that could be quite extensive.

These properties defining families underline the distinctiveness of family groups that may be involved in sport. With an idea of the meaning of family, it is possible to envision how a family provides the social setting in which children can develop and maintain an identity, self-esteem, and motivation for sport participation and performance.

Parenting Style

Csikszentmihalyi, Rathunde, and Whalen (1993) used questionnaires and various other psychometric instruments to study over 200 talented teenagers and their parents. Talented teenagers were identified using a combination of standardized measures of student ability and teacher assessments of short- and long-term potential. Csikszentmihalyi, Rathunde, and Whalen (1993, pp. 155, 164) introduced the concept of complex families to describe families who were found to be the best stimulus to a child's talent development. **Complex families** were defined as both integrated and differentiated. Integration referred to a stable condition between family members so that the child felt a sense of support and consistency. Differentiation referred to the notion that members of the family were "encouraged to develop their individuality by seeking out new challenges and opportunities." Complex families appear to "encourage experiences that combine spontaneity with goal-directedness and enjoyment with seriousness." Compared to families that are not integrated and differentiated, children from complex families showed more "efficient" patterns of time use, spending more time on homework and less time on home routines (eating, dressing, picking things up, chores at home, etc.). Children from complex families also reported more

Teammates often serve as an extended family particularly in youth sport participation.

positive experiences, happiness, and excitement at home. In conclusion, Csikszentmihalyi, Rathunde, and Whalen (1993) suggested that the complex family context helps children to enjoy serious and challenging activities such as studying. Csikszentmihalyi and colleagues' notion of a complex family is conceptually attractive in explaining the parents' role in children's motivation to participate in sport.

Parenting style affects how roles, values, and beliefs are transmitted from parents to children. Baumrind (1973) proposed a typology of parenting style as: (1) authoritarian, (2) authoritative, or (3) permissive. The **authoritarian** parent believes in strongly restricting the child's autonomy and limiting the child's input in family decisions. The **authoritative** parent sets clear objectives for prosocial and responsible behavior and uses reason, power, and reinforcement to achieve those objectives. Authoritative parents are firm when responding to children's needs but also will show affection and understanding. Finally, the **permissive** parent provides freedom but does not set clear objectives or guidelines for their child's prosocial and responsible behavior. In a review of the vast literature on child socialization, Maccoby (1992) suggested that the authoritative parenting style (as opposed to authoritarian or permissive) was the most conducive to develop a child's self-esteem, sense of competence, and high achievement motivation.

In sport, parents' involvement in their children's participation can be conceptualized on a continuum from underinvolved, to moderate, to overinvolved (Hellstedt, 1987). **Underinvolved** parents show "a relative lack of emotional, financial, or functional investment" (Hellstedt, 1987, p. 153). Parents that are **moderately involved** are characterized "by firm parental direction, but with enough flexibility so that the young athlete is allowed significant involvement in decision-making" (Hellstedt, 1987, p. 153). Finally, **overinvolved** parents "have an excessive amount of involvement in the athletic success of their children" (Hellstedt, 1987, p. 154). Frequent behaviors of overinvolved parents include yelling during competitions, disagreement with coach about their child's amount of playing time, consistently asking their child to try harder, and "unsolicited coaching" (Hellstedt, 1987). Hellstedt's moderate level of parental involvement and Baumrind's (1973) authoritative parenting style are similar in the sense that parents promote the best interest of the child, even if this means sacrificing personal interests.

Although a typology of parental involvement in sport such as the one presented by Hellstedt (1987) is useful, it provides few insights into the specific types of parental behaviors that have the most favorable socialization effects on a child's participation in sport. Woolger and Power (1993) recently reviewed the literature on parents and sport socialization and identified dimensions of parenting that could be associated with children's socialization, motivation, and behavior in sport. Three dimensions of parental behaviors will be discussed below: (1) support, (2) modeling, and (3) expectations.

Info Box

Parents must attend to their involvement in their child's athletic experience. Parents who allow their child some room to be involved in the decision-making process, yet set and adhere to solid boundaries, will see their child benefit athletically and socially.

Support

Parents' psychosocial support is an essential element in the development of children's self-esteem, competence, and achievement. Parents' support is positively correlated with a child's enjoyment and enthusiasm in swimming (Power & Woolger, 1994). For instance, parents of committed athletes are usually willing and happy to attend any special lessons outside school and often are present at practice sessions (Csikszentmihalyi, Rathunde, & Whalen, 1993; Monsaas, 1985; Sloboda & Howe, 1991). VanYperen (1995) reported that parental support acted as a buffer to alleviate performance stress and was not related to parents' marital status (married or divorced) or ethnic background.

Cauce and colleagues (1990) provided a categorization of the psychosocial support needs most frequently described by children. Table 25.1 provides an adaptation of their categories to sporting family situations. This table presents four different kinds of psychosocial needs of young athletes: (1) emotional support, (2) information support, (3) tangible support, and (4) companionship. We will discuss these in terms of how parents can provide support for their child's sport involvement.

Emotional Support. **Emotional support** includes four dimensions (Table 25.1): (1) support during negative events and experiences, (2) support during positive experiences,

TABLE 25.1 *Examples of Psychosocial Support Needs of Young Athletes*

I. Emotional Support
    A. Support for negative events and experiences (e.g., bad news and negative feelings a child shares)
- getting cut from a team
- dealing with an injury

    B. Support for positive experiences (e.g., good news and positive experiences a child shares)
- playing well in a game
- friendships/positive rapport with coach and teammates

    C. Support for understanding self (e.g., letting a child know he or she is understood)
- helping child to understand potentially confusing sport situations
- listening to child's stories of practice/game/competition

    D. Enhancement of self-worth (e.g., making the child feel good about who he or she is)
- telling the child they are loved, regardless of sport outcome
- positive body language when child is performing (e.g., clapping)

II. Information Support
- explaining the rules of the game
- instructing new sport techniques and/or strategies

III. Tangible Support
- transportation to and/or attendance at practices/games/tournaments
- financial assistance

IV. Companionship
- watching favorite sports figures on TV, or in person
- playing "pick-up" games

(3) support for understanding self, and (4) enhancement of self-worth. Specific sport situations for which emotional support can be provided by parents are outlined for each dimension in Table 25.1. Generally, emotional support represents the ability to turn to others for comfort and security during times of stress and anxiety. It provides for the strengthening of a child's sense of competence or self-esteem by other people (Cutrona & Russell, 1990). Giving children positive feedback on their abilities or expressing belief that children are capable of coping with difficult situations will likely lead children to believe that they are cared for by others. These supportive efforts and gestures also may enhance children's levels of self-esteem.

Self-esteem refers to a global evaluation and personal judgment of self. Harter (1988) showed that children with high self-esteem receive a high level of emotional support from parents. In sport, studies showed that specific coaching behaviors, such as giving encouragement or using reinforcement, can positively influence children's self-esteem (Black & Weiss, 1993; Horn, 1985; Smith & Smoll, 1990; Smoll et al., 1993). On the other hand, parental influence on children's self-esteem in sport has received little attention from researchers (Brustad, 1996b). Weiss (1993, p. 46) summarized the state of our knowledge of sport and self-esteem by expressing surprise at the present lack of understanding and called for "considerably more quality research on self-esteem effects of youth sport participation." There is a need to separate cause from effect. Does playing sport increase self-esteem, or do children with high self-esteem play sport? Attention must continue to be focused on those elements of parenting that lead to increased self-esteem among young sport participants. For parents of young children in sport, the words of Rainer Martens still resonate:

> If a child lives with criticism, he learns to condemn. If a child lives with hostility she learns to fight. If a child lives with fear he learns to be apprehensive. If a child lives with encouragement she learns to be confident. If a child lives with praise, he learns to be appreciative. If a child lives with approval she learns to like herself. If a child lives with recognition he learns to have a goal. If a child lives with honesty she learns to trust. (Martens, 1980, p. 175)

The experience of sport affects many facets of a child's life. Children need to believe that what they do with their time, energy, and talent in sport is meaningful to themselves and others. They need to know, through their parents' emotional support, that they are cared for and accepted.

Informational Support.   In the context of sport, **informational support** refers to the provision of advice or guidance about possible solutions to a problematic situation. For example, parents can provide specific instructions to a child on how to learn a certain technique or general information on how to choose a suitable sport program.

Hess and colleagues (Hess et al., 1984; Hess & McDevitt, 1984) showed that parents who provide numerous directions and criticisms to their children at home decrease their readiness for school and, later, for achievement in school. In sport, Power and Woolger (1994) demonstrated that too much or too little direction from parents was associated with children's decreased level of enjoyment in sport. Power and Woolger defined "directiveness" as parents who tell their child what to do whether the child asks for advice or not.

Recent studies show that parents of junior elite athletes are usually involved in a range of "indirect" roles that facilitate their child's participation in sport (Côté, 1999; Kirk et al., 1997). Parents' roles range from "fitness consultant" to "career advisor" and consist mainly of general helping duties. Côté showed that during the specializing and investment years (age 13 and up), parents provide directions and guidance in personal life decisions as opposed to sport-specific information. More research is needed to determine the amount and type of informational support that positively and negatively affect children's sport participation at different stages of their development.

Tangible Support. **Tangible support** refers to concrete assistance. A child in a stressful situation is given necessary resources to cope with the event. Examples include providing financial assistance and time for lessons, equipment, and travel costs associated with sport participation.

Parents of young athletes have numerous opportunities to provide tangible support. The amount of financial support provided by family to young athletes varies according to the sport and the representative level of the participant. In Australia, Kirk and colleagues (1997) examined the socioeconomic impact for 222 families of junior athletes involved in tennis, gymnastics, netball, field hockey, cricket, and Australian football. They found that over half the parents of gymnasts and tennis players spent more than $1,000 annually so that their children could participate in their sport. Most of the parents of children involved in netball, field hockey, cricket, and Australian football spent between $500 and $1,000 annually. Coakley (1997) noted that parents of young hockey players in the United States spend between $5,000 and $16,000 per year for fees, equipment, travel, and other expenses related to their children's ice hockey participation. In Canada, Côté, Wimmer, and Beamer (1998) reported that parents of promising elite figure skaters spend between $10,000 and $20,000 a year for their children's participation. The cost of registration, equipment, supplies, and travel expenses could run into thousands of dollars a year for many youth sports, particularly at the elite level. Time commitment is another form of tangible support provided by parents that can facilitate a child's participation in sport. Studies of junior athletes in Australia (Kirk et al., 1997) and Canada (Côté, 1999) show that parents are usually heavily involved in spectating and transporting their child to practices, tournaments, and competitions.

Although tangible support is an important aspect of sport participation in youth, results of studies on socioeconomic status and children's participation in sport are not conclusive. Overman and Rao (1981) demonstrated that youth sport involvement and motivation were not associated with parents' socioeconomic status. However, socioeconomic status was positively associated with children's level of physical activity in a number of studies (Gottlieb & Chen, 1985; Shephard & Godin, 1986; Sunnegardh, Bratteby, & Sjolin, 1985). It appears that families who are committed to their child's involvement in sport will somehow find the financial resources necessary. This is highlighted by this statement of a tennis player:

> My clothes were made by my grandmother. All my tennis equipment was given to me free by the companies. So we had travel expenses. I had some friends of my grandmother who gave…$400 or $500 over a couple of summers. And my grandparents gave me money. My dad and mom gave me a minimum, because they couldn't afford it. (Monsaas, 1985)

Although a child can sometimes find tangible support outside of the immediate family, youth sport participation can impose significant burdens on family resources. Tangible support can certainly become a constraint to a child's participation and talent development in many sports.

Companionship.   **Companionship** or "network support" reflects casual relationships that enable an individual to engage in various forms of social and recreational activities (Cutrona & Russell, 1990). Parents can be involved in various kinds of companionships related to their child's participation in sport. For instance, parents can attend sporting events with their child, collect sports cards, or play "pick up games." Côté and Sedgwick (1996) found that companionship was a dominant type of support in the development of a tennis player: "This summer we went to tournaments every weekend; he [father] came with me. He watched me play but he was just like a friend, it was great."

Info Box

Children need to feel the support of their parents despite the form in which it may come. Some may need emotional support for the ups and downs that accompany competition although others may need little bits of information that they can use to enhance their performances. Today, parents may show support simply by contributing money so a child can participate or by being a companion and watching a game on television with their kid.

Modeling

Some authors have reported that there is no relationship between the level of involvement of the parents in a specific domain and the child's level of performance in that domain (Kulieke & Olszewski-Kubilius, 1989; Sloboda & Howe, 1991; Walker, 1990). In sport, Gregson and Colley (1986) found that parents may serve as role models for the sport participation of girls (ages 15 to 16) but that parental modeling may not be as relevant to the sport participation of boys. Power and Woolger (1994) found that maternal modeling was related to both boys' and girls' (ages 8 to 14) enthusiasm for swimming, whereas paternal modeling was negatively associated with boys' enthusiasm for swimming. In sum, it is certainly possible that a child who does not come from a "sporting" family background can still be motivated to participate in sport and achieve a high level of performance. To encourage their child's participation in sport, parents do not necessarily need to be a "sport model" of participation and performance. Nevertheless, parents of committed individuals tend to espouse values related to the importance of achievement, hard work, success, and being active and persistent (Csikszentmihalyi, Rashunde, & Whalen, 1993; Monsaas, 1985; Sloane, 1985; Sloboda & Howe, 1991; Sosniak, 1985). Howe (1990) suggested that parents and family members who transmit their own values toward achievements that depend on learning and practice open up new opportunities for a young person.

Bandura's (1977) self-efficacy theory provides theoretical support to the importance of parental modeling for a child's acquisition of positive values, attitudes, and behaviors toward sport and physical activity. **Self-efficacy** denotes the degree of certainty possessed by individuals that they are capable of successfully completing tasks. Perceptions of self-efficacy develop from past experience (behaviors in the home environment), vicarious reinforcement (seeing parents or family members involved in sport or physical activity), social or verbal encouragement (having parents recognize and support continued practice in sport), and physiological state (child's increased levels of activation when success occurs in sport).

The majority of research investigating the relationship between self-efficacy and sport participation or performance has involved adolescent or adult populations and has shown that past experiences are the strongest influences on self-efficacy (Feltz & Mungo, 1983; Hogan & Santomeier, 1984; McAuley, 1985; Weiss, Wiese, & Klint, 1989). Self-efficacy is difficult to measure, and attempts to measure this construct among children are limited. Hay (1992, p. 192) extended the concept of self-efficacy to the entire domain of sport and physical activity among children and referred to this concept as "adequacy." **Adequacy** was defined as the "perception of being able to achieve some acceptable standard of success, that standard being influenced by self, parents, peers, teachers and society's expectations." Adequacy was found to be a strong predictor of participation in organized sport among children with significant correlations between adequacy and extent of sport participation increasing gradually from grade four to grade nine students.

Therefore, exposing young children to a lifestyle in which sport activities are enjoyed can be demonstrated in the home environment. At the same time, offering opportunities to witness the successful outcomes of sustained efforts in learning new skills can provide a motivational advantage to most children. The mother of a Canadian junior national rower illustrates this concept:

> When I was [marathon] racing a lot, he [my son] would come to my races. I don't know whether that had anything to do with it. I don't know whether that influenced him, seeing that kind of competition. I did a couple of marathons and he saw the training that went into it and how you had to follow a schedule in order to meet your goals. This was at an impressionable age. (Côté & Sedgwick, 1996)

Family members can engage in a variety of behaviors that children can model and transfer to their sport involvement. Such behaviors include family members' past and present involvement in sport and physical activity as well as effort and achievement in school, work, home, and/or leisure activities.

Expectations

Several studies have shown a positive relationship between **parental expectations** and children's success/enjoyment of sport (McElroy & Kirkendall, 1980, Scanlan & Lewthwaite, 1985). On the other hand, parental expectations can become a source of pressure and stress that can interfere with a child's participation in sport (Brustad, 1988). Power and Woolger (1994) found a curvilinear relationship between parental expectations and children's enthusiasm for swimming. High and low parental expectations were associated with less enthusiasm from children while an intermediate level of expectation was associated with children's highest level of enthusiasm for swimming. Parental expectation, therefore, requires a very delicate balance that can have a positive or negative impact on children's involvement in sport, as illustrated by this junior tennis player:

> If they had been over-bearing and had put pressure on me maybe I would have fizzled and not wanted to play because there was all that pressure there. They just said, "Well, if you don't make it that's okay. That's fine as long as you feel you give everything you have." (Côté & Sedgwick, 1996)

The relationship between parental expectations and a child's motivation, attitudes, and behaviors toward sport and physical activity is complex. Kimiecik, Horn, and Shurin (1996) suggested a model that predicts children's level of participation in physical activity. Central to the model is the home environment. The home environment consists of parents'/siblings' beliefs, parents'/sibling' behavior, and family functioning and interaction. These variables are related to a child's belief and behavior regarding physical activity. Kimiecik and colleagues' model was derived from the **expectancy theory of motivation** (Vroom, 1964) and Eccles and Harold's (1991) **expectancy-value model** for understanding gender differences in sport participation.

The expectancy theory of motivation (Vroom, 1964) suggests that motivation is the result of three different types of beliefs: (1) *expectancy*—the belief that one's effort will result in effective performance, (2) *instrumentality*—the belief that one's performance will be rewarded, and (3) *valence*—the perceived value of the rewards to the individual. Sometimes, children putting forth a great deal of effort in sporting activities expect that their effort will translate into good performance. In other cases, children do not expect that their efforts will have much effect on how well they do. For example, children who never receive reinforcement when executing sport skills may have very low *expectancy* levels that their efforts will lead to high levels of performance. Naturally, children working under such conditions probably would not continue to exert much effort. Even if a child works hard and performs well, motivation may falter if that performance is not suitably rewarded—that is, if the performance is not perceived as *instrumental* in bringing about the rewards. For example, children who are extremely skilled may be poorly motivated to improve performance if they have already reached the top level in their age group category. Finally, even if children believe that hard work will lead to good performance and that they will be rewarded commensurate with their performance and participation, they still may be poorly motivated if the rewards offered have low *valence* to them. In other words, if children do not care about the rewards, they will not be motivated to attain them. A powerful valence for children is the acceptance and esteem of a parent.

In sport, Eccles and Harold (1991) proposed that parental expectations influence the decision to engage in particular activities, the intensity of effort expended, and a child's actual performance level. This hypothesis is supported by research that indicates that children's actual levels of participation in physical activity are related to parents' expectations and beliefs regarding children's physical competence (Brustad, 1996a; Dempsey, Kimiecik, & Horn, 1993; Kimiecik, Horn, & Shurin, 1996). Expectancy theory (Vroom, 1964) and Eccles and Harold's (1991) model have direct parental implications for motivating children to participate in sport and physical activity. These implications can be grouped into two suggestions for action. First, parents during the sampling years should determine which sporting activities their child values most. During the transition from the sampling years to the specializing years or recreational years, parents' roles should be to facilitate and provide opportunities for their children to make appropriate choices about their sport involvement. Second, parents should ensure that their expectations are reasonable and congruent with their child's performance or level of participation. Parents with inflated expectations can become a source of stress and anxiety for their children (Gould, Eklund, Petlichkoff, Peterson, & Bump, 1991; Scanlan, Stein, & Ravizza, 1991; Weiss, Wiese, & Klint, 1989).

In sum, how children feel about themselves is largely related to how they are seen and treated by others, particularly their parents. Parents need to be constantly aware of their child's desire, motivation, and attitude toward sport so that they can modify and adjust their own expectations. In addition to the influence of parents, the relationships between siblings constitute a major aspect of the socialization process within a family.

Info Box

Moderate parental expectations can help to motivate children to participate in athletics, yet low expectations can be translated into lack of concern and high expectations can add pressure. Parents should pay attention to how their expectations are affecting their children.

Sibling Relationships

Sibling relationships have unique characteristics. Cicirelli (1995) describes five ways that sibling relationships are different from other interpersonal relationships. First, the longest relationships that individuals experience during their lifetimes are often with siblings. Second, sibling relationships are not learned but ascribed. For instance, brotherhood or sisterhood is a status obtained by birth or by legal action, as in adoptive and step-siblings. Third, the sibling relationship is more intimate in childhood and adolescence than in adulthood. Within the home, children and adolescents have intimate daily contact with siblings; however, in adulthood contact between siblings often is maintained at a distance by telephone, electronic mail, letters, or visits. Fourth, the relationship between brothers and sisters often is perceived as one of "egalitarism." Differences in power and status, however, often exist between siblings. Finally, siblings have a long history of shared and nonshared experiences. These personal experiences contribute to both similarities and differences between siblings.

Although many studies on family influences have focused on the parent–child relationship in sport psychology, few have examined the sibling relationship and its socialization. This missing focus may be attributed to the complexity of studying the whole family environment. To enhance our understanding of children's involvement in sport, research within the context of the complete family (parent–child and sibling–sibling relationships) is necessary. Siblings have a major impact on one another's behavior and development. This impact is influenced by mutual socialization, especially in childhood and adolescence. Sibling relationships, therefore, may have an important influence on a child's participation and achievement in sport. Sibling relationships constitute a major subsystem of the family that can affect the entire climate of a family. Without examining sibling relationships, we will never be able to fully comprehend the influence of the family on a child in sport.

Impact of Sibling Relationships on Sport Participation and Performance

Côté and colleagues (Côté, 1997; Côté, 1999; Côté & Sedgwick, 1996; Richter, 1997) conducted a series of case studies on families of elite performers. Differences between families were found in the nature of the relationships between siblings and the siblings' levels of sport participation and performance. In general, siblings were found to be both competitive and cooperative.

Competition among Siblings.   Competition refers to an interdependency between two individuals so that the attainment of rewards by one individual constrains the attainment of rewards by the other. A serious commitment in sport by one child in the family often creates an uneven distribution of resources within the family, frequently resulting in tension, bitterness, or jealousy between family members. An **ecological theory of the family** could explain sibling bitterness or jealousy (Klein & White, 1996; Sulloway, 1996, p. 85). According to Sulloway, "siblings are different because they exemplify Darwin's principle of divergence." This principle suggests that in the animal world, two species cannot coexist in the same habitat if their ecological requirements are identical. Evolutionary diversification between animals is necessary to minimize competition and to make coexistence possible. In the same line of thought, as children of the same family mature, they undergo adaptation and diversification in their efforts to establish their individual niche. By pursuing different interests and abilities, siblings minimize direct competition. Differences between siblings are common in families (Côté, 1999; Sulloway, 1996). Differences appear because siblings find a distinct niche within the family. For instance, when one sibling excels in a particular sport, other siblings carefully ponder their chances of measuring up to these achievements. Younger siblings, or siblings who have not yet established their niche within the family, are especially susceptible to negative comparison with their siblings. A family with only one child represents a special case in which the only child maximizes parental investment by not having to compete with siblings (Sulloway, 1996).

According to Sulloway (1996), niches are determined not only by birth order but also by the niches already occupied by other family members. Younger siblings, or siblings who have not yet established their niche within the family, will often pursue interests and activities in which they have a good probability of achieving competitive superiority. They may be motivated to explore unoccupied niches because they will not have to compete with other siblings for parental resources. Siblings seeking a niche will tend to develop skills and cultivate a niche not already occupied by other family members. This process could create bitterness and jealousy among family members when these new skills are compared with the achievement of siblings who have already received parental approval and support (Sulloway, 1996). These ecological explanations of human behavior could explain findings that show only one child per family is considered "special" or talented (Albert & Runco, 1986; Kalinowski, 1985; Monsaas, 1985; Sosniak, 1985). Although it is likely that all siblings engage in competitive behaviors at one time or another, they also exhibit cooperative behaviors.

Cooperation among Siblings.   Cooperation and sharing appear to be both antecedents and outcomes of sibling relationships. Siblings often have to coordinate interaction within a family in order to reach a common goal. Cooperation between siblings may, in some instances, create an environment favorable for the development of sport skills. For instance, Richter (1997) recently interviewed a father, mother, and their three children, all nationally ranked swimmers in their age group. The children were a 19-year-old boy, a 17-year-old boy, and a 14-year-old girl. Richter (1997) described the family as a "swimming unit" in which every member operated together while maintaining a viable relationship with each other. The family structure resembled an interdependent, cohesive unit that eliminated the children's desire to seek out a distinct niche for individual recognition. One important variable that explained the cohesiveness of this particular family was that the parents were able to recognize each child's uniqueness within the unit and encourage cooperation rather than competition.

It is important, therefore, that parents either allow children to cultivate niches in which they feel appreciated and challenged or allocate sufficient resources to one niche so that it can be shared by more than one child. If a firstborn excels in sport, a support system is necessary within the family to assure that later siblings are not turned away from exercise and physical activity. Although sibling relationships have not been frequently studied, when they have been, it is often because they are assumed to be inherently conflictual. This is unfortunate. Cooperation between siblings and parental behaviors that encourage cooperation are certainly areas that need further investigation in sport psychology.

Info Box

Parents should foster cooperation among siblings to promote athletic participation in each of their children. Cooperation can be enhanced to reduce competition by spreading resources (e.g., finances, time, etc.) to cover each child in the family.

Conclusion

The purpose of this chapter was to provide insights into how families can create environments that nurture children's participation and performance in sport. The literature indicates that families can influence children in sport in many ways. Parents exert direct influence through their different parenting styles and specific behaviors such as support, expectations, and modeling. Practical implications that can be drawn from this chapter include the following:

1. Emotional support is one of the most important forms of family support for young children involved in sport.
2. Emotional support can be demonstrated by family members' specific behaviors: (1) support during negative events and experiences, (2) support for positive experiences, (3) support for understanding self, and (4) enhancement of self-worth.
3. As children get older, family members' tangible support, companionship, and informational support become increasingly important, although emotional support always remains a fundamental psychosocial need for young athletes.

4. A home environment in which sport activities are enjoyed and in which family members reflect the successful outcomes of sustained efforts in both sport and nonsport activities can provide a motivational advantage to children.

5. Parents' inflated performance expectations can become a source of stress and anxiety for their children.

Because most of the research on family influences in sport has examined only the parent–child relationship, a critical step in further study is to investigate the family as an interactive system throughout the life span. In addition to the influence of parents on their children, relationships between siblings constitute a major socialization process that directly influences the siblings involved in sport and indirectly influences the parent–child relationship. It is essential that future studies obtain a better understanding about the influences of both parent–child and sibling–sibling relationships on family dynamics. In addition, the complete family environment needs to be studied at each stage of a child's development. The potential influence of each member of the nuclear family must be considered. The stages of development in sport presented in the previous chapter can serve as a framework from which further studies can be conducted.

The role of the family in children's sport involvement is a complex phenomenon because of the diversity of the family context. The study of families in sport needs to be expanded to include various types of families, such as single parent or homosexual relationships. Examining the nature of a family's influence at different stages of a child's development in various types of families will greatly increase our understanding of children's participation in sport. While the family is an important socializing agent in a child's development in sport, other influences come into play as well. The next chapter will examine coaches and peers' influence in youth sport.

Acknowledgments.   Preparation of this chapter was supported by standard research grants from the Social Sciences and Humanities Research Council of Canada (SSHRC Grant #410-97-0241 and #410-99-0525). The authors are grateful to Kristin Côté for her helpful comments in the preparation of this chapter.

Key Terms (in order of appearance)

family	overinvolved	adequacy
complex family	emotional support	parental expectation
authoritarian	self-esteem	expectancy theory of motivation
authoritative	informational support	expectancy-value model
permissive	tangible support	ecological theory of the family
underinvolved	companionship	
moderately involved	self-efficacy	

References

Albert, R. S., & Runco, M. A. (1986). The achievement of eminence: A model of exceptionally gifted boys and their families. In R. J. Sternberg & J. E. Davidson (Eds.), *Conceptions of giftedness* (pp. 332–360). New York: Cambridge Univ. Press.

Bandura, A. (1977). Self-efficacy: Toward a unifying theory of behavioral change. *Psychological Review, 84,* 191–215.

Baumrind, D. (1973). The development of instrumental competence through socialization. In A. D. Pick (Ed.), *Minnesota symposium on child psychology,* Vol. 7 (pp. 3–46). Minneapolis: Univ. of Minnesota Press.

Black, S. J., & Weiss, M. R. (1992). The relationship among perceived coaching behaviors, perceptions of ability and motivation in competitive age-group swimmers. *Journal of Sport and Exercise Psychology, 14,* 309–325.

Brustad, R. J. (1988). Affective outcomes in competitive youth sport: The influence of intrapersonal and socialization factors. *Journal of Sport & Exercise Psychology, 10,* 307–321.

Brustad, R. J. (1993). Youth in sport: Psychological considerations. In R. N. Singer, M. Murphey, & L. K. Tennant (Eds.), *Handbook of research in sport psychology* (pp. 695–718). New York: Macmillan.

Brustad, R. J. (1996a). Attraction to physical activity in urban schoolchildren: Parental socialization and gender influences. *Research Quarterly for Exercise and Sport, 67,* 316–323.

Brustad, R. J. (1996b). Parental and peer influence on children's psychological development through sport. In F. L. Smoll & R. E. Smith (Eds.), *Children and youth sport: A biopsychosocial perspective* (pp. 112–124). Indianapolis: Brown & Benchmark.

Cauce, A. M., Reid, M., Landesman, S., & Gonzales, N. (1990). Social support in young children: Measurement, structure, and behavioral impact. In B. R. Sarason, I. G. Sarason, & G. R. Pierce (Eds.), *Social Support: An interactional view* (pp. 64–94). New York: J. Wiley & Sons.

Cicirelli, V. G. (1995). *Sibling relationships across the life span.* New York: Plenum Press.

Coakley, J. J. (1987). Children and the sport socialization process. In D. Gould & M. R. Weiss (Eds.), *Advances in pediatric sport sciences, Vol. 2: Behavioral issues* (pp. 43–60). Champaign, IL: Human Kinetics.

Coakley, J. J. (1997). *Sport in society: Issues & controversies.* New York: McGraw-Hill.

Côté, J. (1997). A family perspective on talent development. *Journal of Applied Sport Psychology, 9,* S37 (Abstracts).

Côté, J. (1999). The influence of the family in the development of talent in sport. *The Sport Psychologist, 13,* 395–417.

Côté, J., & Sedgwick, W. "Family dynamics of talented adolescents." Paper presented at the meeting of the Association for the Advancement of Applied Sport Psychology, Williamsburg, Virginia, October 1996.

Côté, J., Wimmer, C., & Beamer, M. "The role of the family in developing talent in figure skating." Report presented to the Canadian Figure Skating Association, Ottawa, Ontario, 1998.

Csikszentmihalyi, M., Rathunde, K., & Whalen, S. (1993). *Talented teenagers: The roots of success and failure.* New York: Cambridge.

Cutrona, C. E., & Russell, D. W. (1990). Type of social support and specific stress: Toward a theory of optimal matching. In B. R. Sarason, I. G. Sarason & G. R. Pierce (Eds.), *Social support: An interactional view* (pp. 319–366). New York: Wiley.

Dempsey, J., Kimiecik, J., & Horn, T. (1993). Parental influence on children's moderate-to-vigorous physical activity: An expectancy-value approach. *Pediatric Exercise Science, 5,* 151–167.

Eccles, J. S., & Harold, R. D. (1991). Gender differences in sport involvement: Applying the Eccles Expectancy-Value Model. *Journal of Applied Sport Psychology, 3,* 7–35.

Feltz, D. L., & Mungo, D. A. (1983). A replication of the path analysis of the causal elements in Bandura's theory of self-efficacy and the influence on autonomic perception. *Journal of Sports Psychology, 5,* 263–277.

Gottlieb, N. H., & Chen, M. S. (1985). Sociocultural correlates of childhood sporting activities: Their implication for heart health. *Social Science Medicine, 21,* 533–539.

Gould, D., Eklund, R. C., Petlichkoff, L., Peterson, K., & Bump, L. (1991). Psychological predictors of state anxiety and performance in age-group wrestlers. *Pediatric Exercise Science, 3,* 198–208.

Green, B. C., & Chalip, L. (1997). Enduring involvement in youth soccer: The socialization of parent and child. *Journal of Leisure Research, 29,* 61–77.

Greendorfer, S., & Lewko, J. (1978). Role of family members in sport socialization of children. *Research Quarterly, 49,* 146–152.

Greendorfer, S. L., Lewko, J. H., & Rosengren, K. S. (1996). Family and gender-based influences in sport socialization of children and adolescents. In F. L. Smoll & R. E. Smith (Eds.), *Children and youth in sport: A biopsychosocial perspective* (pp. 89–111). Indianapolis: Brown & Benchmark.

Gregson, J. F., & Colley, A. (1986). Concomitants of sport participation in male and female adolescents. *International Journal of Sport Psychology, 17,* 10–22.

Harter, S. (1988). Causes, correlates and the functional role of global self worth: A life-span perspective. In J. Kolligan & R. Sternberg (Eds.), *Perceptions of competence and incompetence across the lifespan.* New Haven, CT: Yale Univ. Press.

Hay, J. A. (1992). Adequacy in and predilection for physical activity in children. *Clinical Journal of Sports Medicine, 2,* 192–201.

Hellstedt, J. C. (1987). The coach/parent/athlete relationship. *The Sport Psychologist, 1,* 151–160.

Hellstedt, J. C. (1995). Invisible players: A family systems model. In S. H. Murphy (Ed.), *Sport psychology interventions.* Champaign, IL: Human Kinetics.

Hess, R. D., Holloway, S. D., Dickson, W. P., & Price, G. G. (1984). Maternal variables as predictors of children's school readiness and later achievement in vocabulary and mathematics in sixth grade. *Child Development, 55,* 1902–1912.

Hess, R. D., & McDevitt, T. M. (1984). Some cognitive consequences of maternal intervention techniques: A longitudinal study. *Child development, 55,* 2017–2030.

Hogan, P. I., & Santomeier, J. P. (1984). Effects of mastering swim skills on older adults' self efficacy. *Research Quarterly for Exercise and Sport, 56,* 284–296.

Horn, T. S. (1985). Coaches' feedback and changes in children's perceptions of their psychological competence. *Journal of Educational Psychology, 77,* 174–186.

Howe, M. J. A. (1990). *The origins of exceptional abilities.* Cambridge, MA: Basil Blackwell.

Kalinowski, A. G. (1985). The development of Olympic swimmers. In B. S. Bloom (Ed.), *Developing talent in young people* (pp. 139–192). New York: Ballantine.

Kimiecik, J. C., Horn, T. S., & Shurin, C. S. (1996). Relationships among children's beliefs, perceptions of their parents' beliefs, and their moderate-to-vigorous physical activity. *Research Quarterly for Exercise and Sport, 67,* 324–336.

Kirk, D., Carlson, T., O'Connor, A., Burke, P., Davis, K., & Glover, S. (1997). The economic impact on families of children's participation in junior sport. *The Australian Journal of Science and Medicine in Sport, 29*(2), 27–33.

Kirk, D., O'Connor, A., Carlson, T., Burke, P., Davis, K., & Glover, S. (1997). Time commitments in junior sport: Social consequences for participants and their families. *European Journal of Physical Education, 2,* 51–73.

Klein, D. M., & White, J. M. (Eds.), *Family theories: An introduction.* Thousand Oaks, CA: Sage, 1996.

Kulieke, M. J., Olszewski-Kubilius, P. (1989). The influence of family values and climate on the development of talent. In J. L. VanTassel-Baska & P. Olszewski-Kubilius (Eds.), *Patterns of influence on gifted learners: The home, the self, and the school* (pp. 40–59). New York: Teachers College.

Lewko, J. H., & Greendorfer, S. L. (1988). Family influence in sport socialization of children and adolescents. In F. L. Smoll, R. A. Magill, & M. J. Ash (Eds.), *Children in sport* (pp. 288–300). Champaign, IL: Human Kinetics.

Maccoby, E. E. (1992). The role of parents in the socialization of children: An historical overview. *Developmental Psychology, 28,* 1006–1017.

Martens, R. (1980). Kids sport: A den of iniquity or a land of promise? In R. M. Swim (Ed.), *Psychology in sports: Methods and applications* (pp. 169–175). Minneapolis: Burgess.

McAuley, E. (1985). Success and causality in sport: The influence of perception. *Journal of Sports Psychology, 5,* 283–295.

McCullagh, P., Matzkanin, K. T., Shaw, S. D., & Maldonado, M. (1993). Motivation for participation in physical activity: A comparison of parent-child perceived competences and participation motives. *Pediatric Exercise Science, 5,* 224–233.

McElroy, M. A., & Kirkendall, D. R. (1980). Significant others and the professional sport attitudes. *Research Quarterly for Exercise and Sport, 51,* 645–653.

Monsaas, J. A. (1985). Learning to be a world-class tennis player. In B. S. Bloom (Ed.), *Developing talent in young people* (pp. 211–269). New York: Ballantine.

Overman, S., & Rao, V. (1981). Motivation for and extent of participation in organized sports by high school seniors. *Research Quarterly, 52,* 228–237.

Power, T. G., & Woolger, C. (1994). Parenting practices and age group swimming: A correlational study. *Research Quarterly for Exercise and Sport, 65,* 59–66.

Richter, M. "The case study of a family of three elite swimmers." Undergraduate thesis, Brock University, St. Catharines, Ontario, Canada, 1997.

Rosenfeld, L. B., Richman, J. M., & Hardy, C. J. (1989). Examining social support networks among athletes: Description and relationship to stress. *The Sport Psychologist, 3,* 23–33.

Scanlan, T. K., & Lewthwaite, R. (1984). Social psychological aspects of competition for male youth sport participants: I. Predictors of competitive stress. *Journal of Sport Psychology, 6,* 208–226.

Scanlan, T. K., & Lewthwaite, R. (1985). Social psychological aspects of competition for male youth sport participants: III. Determinants of personal performance expectancies. *Journal of Sport Psychology, 7,* 389–399.

Scanlan, T. K., Stein, G. L., & Ravizza, K. (1991). An in-depth study of former elite skaters: III. Sources of stress. *Journal of Sport and Exercise Psychology, 13,* 103–120.

Shephard, R. J., & Godin, G. (1986). Behavioral intentions and activity of children. In J. Rutenfranz, R. Mocellin, & F. Klimt (Eds.), *Children and exercise XII: Vol. 17, International series on sport sciences* (pp. 103–109). Champaign, IL: Human Kinetics.

Sloane, K. D. (1985). Home influences on talent development. In B. S. Bloom (Ed.), *Developing talent in young people* (pp. 439–476). New York: Ballantine.

Sloboda, J. A., & Howe, M. J. A. (1991). Biographical precursors of musical excellence: An interview study. *Psychology of Music, 19,* 3–21.

Smith, R. E., & Smoll, F. (1990). Self-esteem and children's reactions to youth sport coaching behaviors: A field study of self-enhancement processes. *Developmental Psychology, 26,* 987–993.

Smoll, F., Smith, R. E., Barnett, N. P., & Everett, J. J. (1993). Enhancement of children's self-esteem through social support training for youth sport coaches. *Journal of Applied Psychology, 78,* 602–610.

Sosniak, L. A. (1985). Learning to be a concert pianist. In B. S. Bloom (Ed.), *Developing talent in young people* (pp. 19–67). New York: Ballantine.

Sulloway, F. (1996). *Born to rebel.* New York: Pantheon.

Sunnegardh, J., Bratteby, L. E., & Sjolin, S. (1985). Physical activity and sports involvement in 8- and 13-year old children in Sweden. *Acta Paediatrica Scandinavia, 74,* 904–912.

VanYperen, N. W. (1995). Interpersonal stress, performance level, and parental support: A longitudinal study among highly skilled young soccer players. *The Sport Psychologist, 9,* 225–241.

Vroom, V. H. (1964). *Work and Motivation.* New York: Wiley.

Walker, W. J. (1990). Development of creative talent: Portrait of an artist as a middle-aged man. *Psychological Reports, 66,* 483–493.

Weiss, M. R. (1993). Psychological effects of intensive sport participation on children and youth: Self-esteem and motivation. In B. R. Cahill & A. J. Pearl (Eds.), *Intensive participation in children's sports* (pp. 39–69). Champaign, IL: Human Kinetics.

Weiss, M. R., Wiese, D. M., & Klint, K. A. (1989). Head over heels with success: The relationship between self-efficacy and performance in competitive youth gymnastics. *Journal of Sport and Exercise Psychology, 11,* 444–451.

Woolger, C., & Power, T. G. (1993). Parent and sport socialization: Views from the achievement literature. *Journal of Sport Behavior, 16,* 171–189.

26

Coach and Peer Influence on Children's Development through Sport

Jean Côté

Queen's University

- Coaches can positively influence a child's psychological development by using appropriate reinforcement and encouragement as well as instruction, specifically of mental skills.
- The physical skill development of athletes is enhanced through instruction primarily in functional time; however, engaged time also provides for less efficient development.
- Sport competition provides a unique educational environment where young athletes can learn social values. Coaches can instruct children on sportsmanship but must also model the desired behaviors consistently.
- Peers are often the catalysts for sport participation by youth. Peers have been found to influence athletes in many positive and negative ways.

As demonstrated in the previous chapter, families play important roles in shaping children's development through sport. With increased age and maturity, however, children involved in sport spend relatively more time in the company of peers and coaches. This chapter is devoted to the influence of coaches and peers on children's participation and performance in sport. The coach's influence will be analyzed from three perspectives: (1) the coach's influence upon children's psychological development, (2) the coach's influence upon children's physical development, and (3) the coach's role in children's development of social values. The influence of peers will be discussed in terms of how it may affect youngsters' motivation to participate in sport.

An understanding coach can be a positive influence on a young athlete in both the good times and the bad times.

Coaches' Influence on Children's Psychological Development

Organized sport programs in industrial societies exist mainly because of the support and involvement of volunteer coaches (Gould & Martens, 1979; Spallanzani, 1988). These volunteer coaches are willing to devote their time to help children practice, enjoy, and learn a sport. Coaching youth sport involves not only teaching physical skills but also instilling integrity and providing guidance to help youngsters become confident and self-reliant adults (Horn, 1987; Martens, 1988). Sport can be a tremendous vehicle for children to develop a realistic and positive self-image. Involvement in sport also can contribute to the development of mental skills, such as coping with stress and maintaining a positive focus, which can be used throughout life. Thus, through their influence, coaches have unique opportunities to affect children's psychological growth and development.

Smith, Smoll and colleagues (Smith & Smoll, 1990, 1995, 1996a, 1996b, 1997; Smith, Smoll, & Barnett, 1995; Smith, Smoll, & Curtis, 1978; Smith, Smoll, and Hunt, 1977; Smith et al., 1983; Smoll & Smith, 1996; Smoll et al., 1993) have conducted major studies examining the coach's influence on a child's psychological growth. Their research took place in two phases and was centered on the development and assessment of a program aimed at improving the ability of coaches to interact more effectively with their young athletes. The first phase of their research was aimed at relating coaching behaviors (e.g., reinforcement, punishment, and general encouragement) to players' attitudes toward their coach, teammates, themselves, and other aspects of their sport involvement. Generally, it was found that players who had a positive attitude toward their coach, teammates, and themselves had coaches who frequently exhibited the following behaviors: (1) reinforced effort as well as results, (2) used a positive approach when correcting mistakes, (3) maintained order and discipline, and (4) taught sport skills effectively.

The second phase of their research involved the development of an intervention program with coaches called **Coach Effectiveness Training** (CET). The core of CET consists of a series of behavioral guidelines that emphasize the desirability of increasing four specific behaviors: reinforcement, mistake-contingent encouragement, corrective instruction, and technical instruction. In the intervention program, coaches were divided into two groups. One group of coaches received training on how to communicate effectively with children. The second group of coaches did not receive any training and formed a control group. The results showed that, in general, the trained coaches were more supportive, giving reinforcement and encouragement, and were less punitive than the nontrained coaches. Additionally, players who played for the trained coaches exhibited a significant increase in self-esteem and a decrease in anxiety compared with players from the control group. Finally, players who played for the trained coaches evaluated their coaches more favorably and got along better with team members despite the fact that the average win–loss records of the two groups of coaches were similar. More recently, Smith and Smoll (1997) demonstrated that the CET program also helped to create a positive and cohesive team atmosphere in youth sport.

In another study, Black and Weiss (1992) assessed athletes' perceptions of their coaches' behaviors. Three hundred twelve competitive swimmers between the ages of 10 and 15 were assessed. In essence, the coaches who gave encouragement, positive reinforcement, instruction and less criticism, as perceived by the swimmers, had athletes with higher levels of self-esteem who enjoyed swimming more. While the frequency of reinforcement and encouragement is obvious and important, they are not the only variables that affect children's perceptions of their abilities and motivation. Horn (1985) compared coaching behaviors in practice and competition settings with changes in female softball players' perceptions of self-competence. Her results indicated that the primary contributor to positive changes in self-perception did not come from the coach directly but from the player's own skill improvement. Nevertheless, behaviors of coaches in practice also contributed significantly to the players' perceptions of their competencies. Players who received high frequencies of positive reinforcement or praise from the coach following successful performances manifested lower perceptions of competence than players receiving high frequencies of criticism in response to unsuccessful performances. Horn indicated that a coach's use of inappropriate praise might establish lower expectations for a player's performance by inducing negative self-perceptions. In discussing these results, Brustad (1993) pointed out that children who received more frequent but less specific feedback, such as "Good job, Jane," were likely to infer low ability because the coach did not praise others who performed at a similar level on the task. Therefore, the quality and appropriateness of praise provided by coaches is crucial in influencing children's self-perception of their abilities. Nakamura (1996, p. 86) reinforced this fact:

> When praise doesn't match the athlete's self-evaluation of performance or behavior, the player loses respect for the coach's integrity and honesty. More important, when praise

doesn't match an athlete's self-evaluation, it denies the athlete's feelings. It tells the athlete that the coach doesn't really understand him or her. Praise in this instance becomes a barrier to further communication.

The coach–athlete relationship also can ultimately influence the athletes' sport enjoyment and their decision to continue participating in the sport. Barnett, Smoll, and Smith (1992) examined the relationship between coach behavior and youth sport attrition. They indicated that when coaches were trained to increase coach–player interaction and intrateam cohesion and to promote participation in sport as an opportunity for achievement rather than for failure, their players dropped out significantly less than when coaches did not receive training.

In sum, studies examined in this section have shown that coaching behavior has a significant influence on a child's psychological development, affecting such characteristics as self-esteem, satisfaction, and enjoyment. Thus, coaches' behaviors most likely to positively influence children's psychological growth are: (1) appropriate reinforcement and praise, (2) encouragement after mistakes, and (3) instruction.

Coach's Influence on Children's Development of Mental Skills

Another important area of coaches' influence on children's psychological growth is in developing mental skills (Ballinger & Heine, 1991; Davis, 1991; Edwards & Hofmeier, 1991; Orlick, 1993, 1995; Smith & Smoll, 1996a, 1996b; Weiss, 1995). Teaching mental skills to children will educate them about stress and relaxation and give them various strategies to enhance performance. Smith and Smoll (1996a) and Weiss (1991) suggested guidelines for youth sport coaches on how to (1) implement a systematic goal setting program, (2) counteract stress and teach mental toughness, and (3) improve performance through the use of imagery. These three mental skill areas and their implications for youth sport coaches will be discussed.

Goal Setting.   According to Weiss (1991), the first step in effective goal setting for youngsters is teaching them to use effective goal setting guidelines. Smith and Smoll (1996) suggested goal setting guidelines for youngsters that are very similar to those employed by older athletes (e.g., Gould, 1998; Locke & Latham, 1985). According to Smith and Smoll (1996), coaches should teach young athletes to do the following with respect to goals:

1. Set specific goals in terms that can be measured.
2. Set difficult but realistic goals.
3. Set short-term as well as long-term goals.
4. Set performance goals as opposed to outcome goals.
5. Express goals in positive rather than negative terms.
6. Set goals for both practices and competitions.
7. Identify specific goal achievement strategies.
8. Record goals, achievement strategies, and target dates for attaining goals.
9. Set up a performance feedback or goal evaluation system.

Once these goal setting principles are well understood by young athletes, the coach's role is to monitor and reinforce children's efforts. Crucial to the success of effective goal setting with children is to have enough time to teach the technique and take the athlete through the program in a systematic manner (Weiss, 1991).

Stress and Mental Toughness.   A number of studies have shown that relaxation techniques with children are beneficial for quieting them down, increasing learning, and enhancing their ability to deal with stress (Ballinger & Heine, 1991; Davis, 1991; Edwards & Hofmeier, 1991). According to Smith and Smoll (1996a, p. 66), **mental toughness** for children includes "the ability to keep physical arousal within manageable limits." Mentally tough athletes are able to keep their emotions in control and are calm and relaxed under pressure situations.

Smith and Smoll (1996a) suggested four elements that youth sport coaches can use to reduce stress and enhance mental toughness. First, it is important for youth sport coaches to change aspects of situations that place unnecessary stress on young athletes. Strean (1995) discussed three contextual factors that can be considered by coaches for alleviating tension that may exist in youth sport: (1) parents, (2) spectator location, and (3) rules. For instance, because the quality of the relationship between the coach and the parents will affect the quality of the experience that the child has in sport, coaches should pay attention and entertain good relationships with the parents. Having spectators separated from the coach and the child may help athletes to focus their attention during practices and games. This can reduce stress by preventing potential negative interactions between spectators and children. Finally, changing the rules of the game to adapt to children's developmental level may reduce stress and enhance fun. Additionally, the positive coaching behaviors (reinforcement, praise, encouragement, and instruction) outlined in the previous section have been found to help coaches create an environment in which children enjoy themselves and develop skills (Smith & Smoll, 1996a).

A second approach to reduce stress in youth sport is increasing children's resources for dealing with pressure situations. Resources include personal characteristics of the youngsters that enhance their capacity to cope with the demands of a situation and the people in the social environment who provide help and support (Smith & Smoll, 1996b) Children's resources can be increased by teaching proper skill progressions and providing appropriate instructions when teaching technical and physical skills. In doing so, coaches provide children the confidence necessary to execute skills and perform under pressure situations. Enhancing the amount of social support that children receive from coaches, teammates, and parents also can increase children's resources.

A third approach to reduce stress and enhance children's mental toughness is helping them develop a positive attitude toward competition. Because there is no way to completely eliminate pressure situations in sport, children should be taught early in their sport involvement that stress and anxiety are not produced solely by a situation but rather by the way one interprets that situation. In their conceptual model of athletic stress, Smoll and Smith (1996) view the "cognitive appraisal" of a situation as one of the most important variables affecting the stress response. "Through their own thought processes, people create the psychological reality to which they respond" (Smoll & Smith, 1996, p. 361). Ravizza and Hanson (1995, p. 32) outlined two fundamental ideas that form the basis of being in control and staying mentally tough in stressful situations: "(1) you can't control what happens around you, but you can control how you choose to respond; and (2) you must be in control of yourself before you can control your performance." Discussing these two ideas with children, using sport-specific examples, can help them to focus their energies on what they can control, resulting in fewer concerns and less anxiety. If children can avoid defining themselves in terms of their performance or the approval of others, then stress will be reduced and mental toughness will be enhanced.

Finally, a fourth approach to reduce stress is to teach children specific relaxation skills. **Relaxation training scripts** have been specifically developed for use with children (Ballinger & Heine, 1991; Orlick, 1993). The language used in these relaxation scripts is adapted with images, words, phrases, and examples that youngsters can relate to. Examples of these scripts will be presented later when discussing a comprehensive mental training program specifically designed for school children.

Imagery.   Imagery in youth sport can be used for learning or improving a skill, preparing for competition or practice, or recovering from an injury. Guidelines and specific exercises have been provided to help sport psychologists and coaches introduce the concept of imagery to older athletes (e.g., Vealey & Walter, 1993). Most of the exercises designed for adults can be adapted for use with children.

One key point when introducing mental imagery to children is to keep the session short and use concepts and images with which children can identify. When using mental imagery, coaches need to be sensitive to the shorter attention span of children and to the motivational capabilities of young athletes.

Mental Training Programs for School Children.   Goal setting, relaxation, and imagery are mental skills that have been included in comprehensive mental training programs specifically designed for children (Orlick, 1993; Solin, 1991). These programs have been successfully implemented in school systems in Canada and Sweden. The main objective is to increase children's awareness of their capacity to control their bodies, focus, and anxiety. Although designed for teachers, these programs have practical implications for youth sport coaches.

The most "child-friendly" program that could be used by coaches in youth sport was designed and implemented by Orlick (1993, 1995). The program suggests activities that teach children important mental skills such as positive thinking, visualization, relaxation, goal setting, focusing and refocusing. For youth sport coaches, the most appealing characteristic of Orlick's program is its child-centered approach. As was the case with Orlick's earlier work with cooperative games for children (Orlick, 1981), the activities suggested are enjoyable and reinforce the application of the mental skills not only in sport but also in real life situations. Table 26.1, on page 526, taken from Orlick's program (Cox & Orlick, 1996; Orlick, 1993), gives examples of activities that can help elementary schoolchildren acquire the mental skills necessary to maintain a positive focus, cope with stress, channel their concentration, and feel good about themselves and their abilities. These exercises have been adapted to show how coaches could make use of them.

Youth sport coaches are in a position to influence children's psychological development through sport. By developing children's mental skills through early experiences in sport, children will develop a positive attitude toward physical activity, sport, and life.

TABLE 26.1   *Mental Skills Activities for Coaches to Use with Elementary-School-Age Children.*

Activity	Description
Spaghetti Toes	Before a competition when children are tense about winning or performing well, ask them to relax by wiggling and relaxing each body part, making it feel like warm, soft spaghetti.
Tree it	During a game ask children to find a place (tree, floor, bench) to put worries or mistakes away and replace them with positive self-enhancing thoughts.
Changing channels	During training or competition when children feel negative, tense or sad suggest to them that they switch to a more positive, relaxed or happy channel.
Reminders for feeling	Ask children to write some reminders down on a card about how to be positive with themselves and their teammates. Before training or competition, allow time for the children to read their card as reminder.
Goal cards	Ask children to write their personal goal for a specific practice on a card along with a concrete action that will help them achieve that goal. At the end of the practice ask children to reflect upon what they did to achieve their goals.
Guided imitation	Provide children with a model of a skilled performer and ask them to imitate their action in order to learn or execute a skill.

Info Box

Coaches can help to develop self-esteem and enjoyment for sport by providing appropriate feedback, encouragement, and instruction. In addition, they can teach mental skills that have already been shown to be effective in sport psychology intervention.

Coaches' Influence on Children's Physical Skill Development

Besides developing children's psychological characteristics, teaching physical skills is another goal of the youth sport coach (Horn, 1987; McKenzie & King, 1982). The variables most likely to affect children's learning of physical skills are the time spent engaged in physical activity and the coaches' instructional behaviors.

Time Spent in Physical Activity

The learning context of players in practices has been investigated using the **Academic Learning Time—Physical Education (ALT-PE)** instrument. Siedentop (1991, p. 41) defined the ALT-PE as a unit of time "when a student is engaged in lessons or activities in such a way that success is likely to occur." On the other hand, **"engaged time"** refers to time when athletes are engaged in physical activity, no matter what the nature of that involvement. For example, a young basketball player may be involved physically in a practice but not necessarily learning basketball skills.

In a review article dealing with the issue of time in sport pedagogy, Meltzer (1989) reported a moderate to strong correlation between **"functional time,"** such as the ALT-PE, and learning. Accordingly, the "functional time" rates of players in practices has been investigated in various sports such as volleyball (Brunelle et al., 1989; McKenzie, 1986; Wuest et al., 1986), ice hockey (Trudel & Brunelle, 1985), soccer (Boudreau & Tousignant, 1991), and Taekwon-do (Brunelle et al., 1989). In general, these authors reported that players' "functional time" rates varied between 25 percent and 54 percent of the total practice time. Naturally, athletes cannot be physically active 100 percent of the time during practices. Coaches need to accomplish managerial chores such as setting up equipment, providing instructions, and moving from place to place. However, one would expect that during practices young athletes would be engaged in motor activities more than 25 percent of the time.

Figure 26.1, adapted from Siedentop (1991), shows the relationship between the time allocated by coaches in practice, the engaged time of players, and the functional time. Coaches often allocate a certain amount of time for players to be engaged in activities during a practice. They expect that most of that engaged time will be functional for their learning of skills. However, the time allocated by a coach for an activity does not always translate into functional learning time for the players. This can be seen in the three kinds of time described in Figure 26.1 and how time is lost in what Metzler (1989) calls the "funneling effect." What is important for player learning is the amount of time at the bottom of

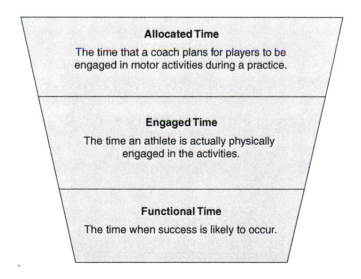

FIGURE 26.1 *The Funnel Effect in Engaged Time (adapted from Siedentop, 1991)*

Hanin also proposes that three other dimensions called temporal, context, and form are part of the model. There has been, however, little work or elaboration on these dimensions.

this funnel. When engaged time is far less than allocated time, it usually indicates that a coach has a problem managing and organizing players. When functional time is far less than engaged time, the coach most likely has problems designing activities in which players can experience success.

Therefore, planning practices becomes a very important job for youth sport coaches in order to increase athletes' functional time during practices. By planning, a coach can effectively control the number of variables that must be handled in a practice. Variables to consider when planning for a specific practice are the number of athletes, the number of pieces of equipment, and the number of skills to be learned and performed. Effective planning will reduce coaches' organizational tasks, increase athletes' functional time, and allow coaches to optimally engage in instructional behaviors during practice.

Coaches' Instructional Behaviors

In line with studies examining players' functional time, systematic observation of successful and less successful coaches has been widely used to obtain information about coaches' teaching roles. In a pioneer study, Tharp and Gallimore (1976) devised a 10-category system to observe John Wooden, a highly successful basketball coach at the University of California at Los Angeles, during fifteen practices. Their results revealed that 50 percent of Wooden's behavior was in the instructional category. The authors further reported that at least 75 percent of Wooden's behavior observed in training carried information. For example, the behavior "scolds" (6.9 percent of all behaviors) was almost always followed by specific instructions.

A modified version of Tharp and Gallimore's (1976) instrument was used to observe youth coaches in football (Lacy & Darst, 1985; Segrave & Cianco, 1990), basketball (Lacy & Goldston, 1990), and soccer (Wandzilak, Ansorge, & Potter, 1988). In each of these studies, the most frequently observed category of behavior was "instruction," and it varied between 33.7 percent and 49.6 percent of all coaches' behaviors. These results are consistent and show that the predominant behavior of a youth sport coach in training is to provide instruction.

Jones and colleagues (1993) suggested guidelines that can help youth sport coaches to provide effective instruction in practice:

1. Introduce the skill: Define it and relate its importance to individual and team success.
2. Teach logically and sequentially; move from the simple to the complex. Provide only essential details. Keep the discussion short.
3. Demonstrate the desired action. Have a coach or skilled players illustrate the correct way (modeling). Direct the players' attention to the most relevant aspects of the action.
4. Use simple and accurate language.

The National Coaching Certification Program of Canada (NCCP, 1988) suggests that coaches' instruction for a specific skill should last approximately 60–70 seconds and not more than 3 minutes. In sum, instruction should be the most dominant behavior of coaches in practices and it should be brief, simple, and clear.

An important aspect of providing instruction is giving **appropriate feedback.** The learning of motor skills can be affected by the kind, quantity, and timing of feedback

(Chamberlin & Lee, 1993; Magill, 1993; Vallerand, 1983). Studies focusing on coaches' feedback in natural settings have shown that the feedback most frequently used by successful coaches is auditory, immediate, and corrective and that players of more successful coaches receive significantly more feedback than players of less successful coaches (Markland & Martinek, 1988). Youth sport coaches, on the other hand, have been observed to give poor quality feedback and provide little specific information useful for improving performance (McKenzie & King, 1982). To improve teaching behaviors, Mancini, Clark, and Wuest (1987) implemented an intervention strategy to improve the quality of feedback given by a field hockey coach to her players. The coach was first observed during practices to gather data on her behavior in training. Based on this data, the coach was provided with systematic supervisory feedback from a qualified instructor to change inadequate teaching behaviors. Following the supervisory feedback, the coach changed her manner of giving feedback. Her feedback to the players became more varied and the type of directions she gave were less ordering and directive. Observation of the same coach in practices a year later indicated that the changes in her teaching behavior were maintained. Thus, training coaches to improve the way they provide feedback can help children develop their physical skills. To maximize the acquisition of physical skills, coaches' feedback should be specific, constructive, informative, concise, and clear (Saffici, 1996).

The studies reviewed in this section highlight the important role of the coach in teaching physical skills. The National Coaching Certification Program of Canada (NCCP 1998, p. 65) regards the teaching of skills as a chain of events containing four main links, as presented in Table 26.2.

Because coaching is a form of teaching, it is important for youth sport coaches to help children acquire knowledge and learn physical skills in a positive and optimal environment.

Info Box

Coaches who maximize their athletes' functional time will see a greater development in athletes' physical skills. Organization can help reduce allocated time that could potentially be wasted on setting up equipment or on other managerial things. The increase of functional time will help to optimize instruction.

TABLE 26.2 *Teaching Physical Skills to Young Athletes.*

Link 1	Choosing the skill you are going to teach—identifying what you want participants to learn.
Link 2	Planning the explanation and demonstration—deciding what to say and how to present it.
Link 3	Planning how participants will practice the skill—deciding how to organize participants to practice the skill.
Link 4	Providing feedback during practice—making appropriate, informative, and constructive remarks about performance.

Coaches' Role in Developing Children's Social Values

Youth sport coaches are in a prime position to increase the child's prosocial behaviors such as cooperating, and decrease antisocial behaviors such as cheating and aggression (Brustad, 1993; Coakley, 1993; Greendorfer, 1992). Gresham and Elliot (1990) documented the development and daily use of children's social skills in five basic domains: cooperation, assertion, responsibility, empathy, and self-control. These five social skills are key elements of sportsmanship. Gresham and Elliot used the acronym of **CARES** to facilitate memory of these five domains of behavior that can be characterized in the sport arena as follows:

1. **Cooperation:** Behaviors such as helping others, sharing materials and equipment with teammates, and complying with rules.
2. **Assertion:** Initiating behaviors such as asking coaches, teammates, or parents for information. Assertive behavior in sport also is related to increased intensity of physical behaviors, such as hitting harder in a collision sport. However, assertive behavior, as opposed to aggressive behavior, is exhibited with no intent to harm and does not violate the rules of the sport being played (Husman & Silva, 1984).
3. **Responsibility:** Behaviors that demonstrate the ability to communicate with coaches, parents, and other adults about one's conduct. For example, if players violate team rules, they are ready to assume and discuss the consequences of their behavior with the coach.
4. **Empathy:** Behaviors that show concern for opponents', teammates', or adults' feelings.
5. **Self-control:** Behaviors that emerge in conflict situations, such as responding appropriately to a penalty during a game, corrective feedback from an adult, or teasing from an opponent.

Many would say that sport builds character through the development of social skills such as those listed above; however, this assumption may not always be true. For instance, some studies have shown that participation in sport decreases behaviors such as sharing and helping and increases behaviors such as aggression and the legitimization of potentially injurious rule-violating behavior (Dubois, 1986; Kleiber & Roberts, 1981; Silva, 1983). Studies observing coaches in real situations have indicated that youth sport coach behavior can be in conflict with a child's development of "appropriate" social behaviors. For example, several authors have reported that youth sport coach behavior during games is mostly directed towards winning instead of focusing on players' actions or on the development of social skills (Chaumeton & Duda, 1988; Hastie & Saunders, 1992; Strong, 1992).

The environment of youth sport participants needs to be specifically structured to teach moral and sportsmanshiplike values to children (Bredemeier et al., 1986; Romance, Weiss, & Bockovan, 1986). Accordingly, coaches have a central position for creating this positive environment (Bredemeier, 1988; Martens, 1987, 1990; Weiss, 1991). In a retrospective portrait of six outstanding coaches, Walton (1992) revealed that great coaches do not simply master their sport but also are champions of wisdom and understanding. The coaches examined by Walton not only produced excellent athletes but also educated and contributed to the human development of these athletes. For instance, all of the coaches were committed to the athletes' integrity, values, and personal growth and were profound thinkers who saw themselves as educators of social values, not just trainers of physical skills.

In a series of studies on aggression/assertion in sport, Trudel and colleagues examined ice hockey coaches' behavior during games to see if their actions could be related to players' aggressive acts. In a first study, Trudel and associates (1991) used an observation form designed to code seven different coach behaviors during games. The seven behaviors were regrouped into three categories: coach behaviors toward the referee, coach behaviors that encouraged players' physical contact, and coach behaviors that encouraged players' respect or violations of rules. They observed eleven different coaches over twenty-seven games with hockey players between the ages of 14 and 15. Their findings showed that the coaches observed did not directly ask players to be aggressive. However, coaches did shout their disagreement at the referee and asked for more intensity from their players. Considering the fine line between the definition of aggression and assertion (Husman & Silva, 1984), Trudel and colleagues (1991) argued that asking for more intensity could be interpreted by players in certain situations as asking for more aggression.

Consequently, a second study (Côté et al., 1993), using the same observation instrument, analyzed the relationship between coach behavior and game score differential. The purpose was to verify if coach's behavior was changed by either winning or losing. Twenty-three coaches from twenty teams were observed in sixty-five different games. The results indicated that, when losing, coaches "disagreed with the referee" significantly more than when winning and simultaneously asked their players to be more assertive. In discussing these results, the authors suggested that because disagreeing with the referee was exhibited in a context where the coaches were hostile and because of the fine line existing between assertion and aggression, the coach behavior exhibited when losing could have easily been interpreted by the players as "Be more aggressive." Similarly, Dubois (1981) found that 14 youth soccer and football coaches showed twice as many negative behaviors toward their players when losing as compared to winning.

Although adults and coaches value social skills in sport, most youth coaches do not explicitly teach players these behaviors. Furthermore, youth sport coaches often set poor examples of sportsmanship. Although it is the parents or guardians who have the central role in their children's moral upbringing, sport involvement gives the child an ideal setting in which to practice and refine many social skills. Thus, the coach has a responsibility to create a context favorable to the development of children's responsible and prosocial behaviors.

Studies have shown that when a coach uses specific instructional strategies such as modeling, giving appropriate reinforcement, and discussing inappropriate sport behavior, the child's prosocial behaviors increase (Bredemeier et al., 1986; Romance, Weiss, & Bockovan, 1986). Elliot and Gresham (1991) suggested that teaching social skills involves many of the same methods used to teach other types of skills. Basically, effective teachers or coaches: (1) model the correct behavior, (2) elicit an imitative response from the child, (3) provide feedback, and (4) arrange for opportunities to practice the new skills. For example, coaches who want to teach a player to control their anger should: (1) control themselves and not get angry in pressure situations, (2) show examples of players that stay in control, and ask the child to imitate such a player, (3) direct some role-playing situations in which the child gets feedback on new behaviors, and (4) periodically review and practice steps in performing self-controlled behavior.

In the realm of youth sports, coaches have a crucial role in enabling young athletes to become self-controlled and constructive members of a team. For many individuals, sports stimulates a change in social values and moral reasoning patterns (Bredemeier & Shields, 1996, p. 396). Youth sport coaches should not "use language or techniques that might encourage participants to separate their sport experiences from 'real life.'" Rather, youth sport should be seen as a medium by which social values are learned and transferred to real life situations.

Info Box

Social values can be learned through sport competition. Often, coaches attempt to teach morals and sportsmanship in practice but fail to exhibit these values in the heat of a game. Coaches must remember that young athletes learn well from modeling and should make sure to demonstrate the values in all situations.

Peer Influences

Generally, peers are defined as individuals who are similar in age and/or developmental level and who do not share kinship or reside within the same family (Bukowski & Hoza, 1989). The influence of peers on children's participation and performance in sport can take different forms. Peers can provide encouragement and discouragement both verbally and nonverbally. Peers also can act as models of involvement or noninvolvement in sport.

The sport socialization literature consistently reports positive influence from peers on children and adolescent's participation in sport. For instance, Brown (1985) indicated that social support, not just from parents but from friends and teammates as well, was related to maintaining participation in competitive sports. Similarly, Greendorfer and Lewko (1978) found that father and peers were the most important socializing agents for children in sport. Reviews of the youth sport motivation literature also have shown that affiliation with others, including peers, has always been listed as one of the main reasons that children participate in sport (Weiss & Chaumeton, 1992; Weiss & Petlichkoff, 1989). Overall, there has been substantial discussion regarding children's socialization into sport (e.g. Brustad, 1988; Greendorfer, 1992; McPherson, 1982). In these discussions, peers consistently have been found to play a key role.

Despite the well-known importance of peers in the children sport socialization process, few studies have been conducted to examine the specific nature of peer relationship in the sport domain (Brustad, 1996; Weiss, Smith, & Theeboom, 1996). In other words, how do peers influence a child's participation in sport? It has been shown that children who receive more encouragement and relative support from peers usually demonstrate a higher rate of participation and enjoyment in sport than children who receive less positive influences from peers (Andersen & Wold, 1992; Brown, Frankel, & Fennell, 1989; Kunesh, Hasbrook, & Lewthwaite, 1992). Weiss and Duncan (1992) indicated that a child's actual and perceived physical competence is strongly associated with peer acceptance in sport. Similarly, Page and colleagues (1992) showed that less active children reported stronger feelings of loneliness than more physically active children.

Peer Relationships in the Sport Context

To gain a better understanding of how peers influence children in sport, Weiss, Smith, and Theeboom (1996) conducted in-depth interviews with thirty-eight participants aged from 8 to 16. The investigation focused on the nature of participant's peer relationships within the social context of sport. Interviews with children and adolescents allowed the researchers to identify 12 positive and 4 negative dimensions of peer relationships. The twelve positive dimensions are:

1. **Companionship.** This dimension is defined as "hanging out together," "spending time together," and "doing things together." Because youth sport is usually embedded in a social context, it provides an opportunity for children to interact and experience companionship with other children such as teammates.

2. **Pleasant/Play Association.** This dimension is different from the companionship dimension in terms of a positive value associated with being together. Involvement in sport allows children to develop relationships with certain individuals that may be more affectionate, enjoyable, and positive than a simple companionship relationship.

3. **Self-Esteem Enhancement.** This dimension is characterized as saying or doing things to reinforce another child's feeling of competence and self-worth. The sport context, therefore, provides opportunities for children to enhance each other's self-esteem through praise, and positive behaviors.

4. **Help and Guidance.** This dimension includes instrumental assistance and tangible support as important characteristics of friendship. Sport presents unique opportunities for children to help each other in areas such as learning a new strategy or executing a skill.

5. **Prosocial Behavior.** This dimension emphasizes the cooperative aspects of sport. Friendship in sport can be enhanced when children share resources instead of competing for them and behave in ways that conform to social expectations.

6. **Intimacy.** This dimension invokes the extent to which participants are prepared to reveal aspects of themselves to each other. Through intimacy, each child acquires knowledge of the other as a total person. Sport can be a medium by which children develop and maintain intimate friendships.

7. **Loyalty.** This dimension is present when individuals share a sense of commitment toward one another. Commitment in friendship requires acceptance of the bad with the good and provides sharing that affords mutual support. Many circumstances in sport allow children to direct their behavior toward insuring the loyalty of a friendship.

8. **Things in Common.** This dimension is present when individuals share similarities in terms of interests, activities, and values inside and outside of the sport context. Having things in common will assure a balanced relationship among friends.

9. **Attractive Personal Qualities.** This dimension includes both physical and psychological qualities. It refers to how each individual in a friendship sees the other. Certain personal qualities, such as athletic ability, may facilitate friendship in a sport context.

10. **Emotional Support.** This dimension was defined as "feelings or expressions of concern for one another" (p. 367). Many situations in sport offer opportunities for young athletes to demonstrate emotional support toward someone else.

11. **Absence of Conflict.** This dimension reflects the absence of fights, arguments, and judgmental attitudes. In the sport context, the absence of conflict will greatly enhance friendship between individuals.

12. **Conflict Resolution.** This dimension is characterized by the constructive resolution of arguments, fights, or conflicts. Sport has the potential to create various kind of conflicts between individuals. Children have to learn at a young age that conflict and friendship are not incompatible.

Along with these positive friendship dimensions, Weiss, Smith, and Theeboom (1996) identified the following four negative friendship dimensions:

1. **Conflict.** This dimensions is characterized by negative behaviors that cause "disagreement," "disrespect," or "dissension" between friends. Examples of negative behaviors that create conflict in sport include: verbal insults, arguing, negative competitiveness, and physical aggression.
2. **Unattractive Personal Qualities.** This dimension is defined as undesirable psychological or physical qualities. Examples of unattractive qualities include being "self-centered," "immature," "indecisive," and "egotistical."
3. **Betrayal.** This dimension encompasses those behaviors that are characterized by disloyalty or insensitivity towards others. Paying more attention to certain friends or ignoring others are examples of betrayal that can take place in the context of youth sport.
4. **Inaccessible.** This dimension is defined as infrequent opportunities to interact together. Friendship can be reduced if a child frequently is away from practices or games or has more interest in other activities than sport.

These dimensions of positive and negative peer relationships in sport add to our understanding of social influences and children's motivation to participate in sport. Weiss, Smith, and Theeboom (1996) have provided emergent qualities of relationships that are most critical for understanding and predicting the effects of relationships on children's development in sport. For instance, the dimensions proposed by Weiss and colleagues can be used to examine the effects of children's friendships on their self-concepts or enjoyment. The dimensions of peer relationships in sport described earlier thus provide opportunities to design studies and programs that could help improve the learning and development of children in sport.

At the heart of young athletes' social and psychological needs lies the urge for harmonious relationships with others. The manner in which young athletes form relationships, with whom they form relationships, and the nature of the relationships help to determine the atmosphere in which youth sport is practiced. Even though there are important gaps in our understanding of peer relationships in youth sport, research has established that peer relationships play a significant role in the development of children and adolescents in sport. Friendship patterns in youth sport constitute an important aspect of a young person's social life and development. Continuing research on the processes and outcomes of peer relationships should be high priorities for researchers in youth sport.

Conclusion

The first priority of sport education is to empower children to reach their full psychological, physical, and social potential through participation in sport. Practical implications that can be drawn from this chapter include the following:

1. Appropriate reinforcement and praise, encouragement after mistakes, and instruction are coaching behaviors most likely to influence children's psychological growth in sport.
2. By teaching mental skills at an early age, coaches can help children develop a positive attitude toward sport, physical activity, and life.
3. Planning of practice, effective instruction, and appropriate use of feedback are essential coaching behaviors when teaching motor skills to young athletes.
4. Through their behaviors and intervention with children, youth sport coaches are in a prime position to increase children's prosocial behaviors and decrease antisocial behaviors.
5. Encouragement and support from peers have a positive influence on youngsters' participation in sport.

In sum, coaches face the same challenges as sport educators with a substantial need to advance their profession through continued research. To improve the knowledge and skill of youth sport coaches, coaches must have goals, feedback, and the opportunity to improve. This implies that research data needs to be collected to provide feedback to coach educators. The main method used to collect data about youth sport coach behaviors has been through systematic observation (Trudel & Côté, 1994; Trudel, Côté, & Donohue, 1993; Trudel & Gilbert, 1995). Systematic observation of coaches has led to important knowledge about the nature of effective coaching behaviors in training and competition. Systematic observation, however, has not provided much insight into aspects of youth sport coaches' organizational work, such as relationships with parents, planning training and competition, and dealing with children's personal concerns. Furthermore, the present state of knowledge about youth sport coaches provides a very superficial understanding of the cognitive processes underlying their behaviors. Although limited in number, qualitative studies with youth sport coaches have provided valuable information on the behaviors and context in which youth sport coaches work (Hastie & Saunders, 1992; Strean, 1995; Strong, 1992). Further use of qualitative methodologies, with coaches, parents, and children, however, is needed to provide a wider knowledge base specific to youth sport settings.

Simply putting youths together on a team will not necessarily produce positive relationships. Coaches need to make sure that children and adolescents interact with each other in a positive context. Literature on peer relationships in the context of youth sport show that peer relationships: (1) influence children's motivation to participate in sport, (2) contribute to the socialization into sport by promoting the acquisition of social attitudes and values towards sport, and (3) predict psychological outcomes such as perceived physical competence. Weiss, Smith, and Theeboom (1996) identified dimensions of relationships that lead to positive and negative friendship among children in sport. These dimensions should be used to design studies and develop educational strategies that will ultimately enhance youth sport participation. In sum, coaches and peers, through their behaviors and interaction, play key roles in shaping children's and adolescents' experiences in sports.

Acknowledgments. Preparation of this chapter was supported by a standard research grant from the Social Sciences and Humanities Research Council of Canada (SSHRC Grant #410-97-0241). The author is grateful to Kristin Côté for her helpful comments in the preparation of this chapter.

Key Terms *(in order of appearance)*

Coach Effectiveness
  Training (CET)
mental toughness
relaxation training script
Academic Learning Time—
  Physical Education (ALT-PE)
engaged time
functional time
appropriate feedback
CARES
cooperation

assertion
responsibility
empathy
self-concept
companionship
pleasant/play association
self-esteem enhancement
help and guidance
prosocial behavior
intimacy
loyalty

things in common
attractive personal quality
emotional support
absence of conflict
conflict resolution
conflict
unattractive personal quality
betrayal
inaccessible

References

Andersen, N., & Wold, B. (1992). Parental and peer influences on leisure-time physical activity in young adolescents. *Research Quarterly for Exercise and Sport, 63,* 341–348.

Ballinger, D. A., & Heine, P. L. (1991). Relaxation training for children—A script. *Journal of Physical Education, Recreation and Dance, 62,* 67–69.

Barnett, N. P., Smoll, F. L., & Smith, R. E. (1992). Effects of enhancing coach–athlete relationships on youth sport attrition. *The Sport Psychologist, 2,* 111–127.

Black, S. J., & Weiss, M. R. (1992). The relationship among perceived coaching behaviors, perceptions of ability and motivation in competitive age-group swimmers. *Journal of Sport and Exercise Psychology, 14,* 309–325.

Boudreau, P., & Tousignant, M. (1991). L'efficacité de l'intervention d'entraîneurs bénévoles en formation. *Canadian Journal of Sport Sciences, 16,* 134–141.

Bredemeier, B. J. (1988). The moral of the youth sport story. In E. W. Brown & C. F. Branta (Eds.), *Competitive sports for children and youth* (pp. 587–599). Champaign, IL: Human Kinetics.

Bredemeier, B. J. L., & Shields, D. L. L. (1996). Moral development and children's sport. In F. L. Smoll & R. E. Smith (Eds.), *Children and youth sport: A biopsychosocial perspective* (pp. 381–404). Chicago, IL: Brown & Benchmark.

Bredemeier, B. J., Weiss, M. R., Shields, D. L., & Shewchuk, R. (1986). Promoting moral growth in a summer sport camp: The implementation of theoretically grounded instructional strategies. *Journal of Moral Education, 15,* 212–220.

Brown, B. A. (1985). Factors influencing the process of withdrawal by female adolescents from the role of competitive age group swimmer. *Sociology of Sport Journal, 2,* 111, 129.

Brown, B. A., Frankel, B. G., & Fennell, M. P. (1989). Hugs or shrugs: Parental and peer influence on continuity of involvement in sport by female adolescents. *Sex Roles, 20,* 397–409.

Brunelle, J., Spallanzani, C., Tousignant, M., Martel, D., & Gagnon, J. (1989). Effets d'une stratégie d'auto-supervision sur les composantes du temps d'apprentissage dans l'enseignement de deux sports. *Revue Canadienne de l'Education, 14,* 189–201.

Brustad, R. J. (1988). Affective outcomes in competitive youth sport: The influence of intrapersonal and socialization factors. *Journal of Sport and Exercise Psychology, 14,* 309–325.

Brustad, R. J. (1993). Youth in sport: Psychological considerations. In R. N. Singer, M. Murphey, & L. K. Tennant (Eds.), *Handbook of research in sport psychology* (pp. 695–718). New York: Macmillan.

Brustad, R. J. (1996). Parental and peer influence on children's psychological development through sport. In F. L. Smoll & R. E. Smith (Eds.), *Children and youth in sport: A biopsychosocial perspective* (pp. 112–124). Indianapolis: Brown & Benchmark.

Bukowski, W. M., & Hoza, B. (1989). Popularity and friendship: Issues in theory, measurement, and outcome. In T. J. Berndt & G. W. Ladd (Eds.), *Peer relationships in child development* (pp. 15–45). New York: Wiley.

Campbell, S. (1993). Coaching education around the world. *Sport Science Review, 2,* 62–74.

Chamberlin, C., & Lee, T. D. (1993). Arranging practice conditions and designing instruction. In R. N. Singer, M. Murphey, & L. K. Tennant (Eds.), *Handbook of research in sport psychology* (pp. 213–242). New York: Macmillan.

Chaumeton, N. R., & Duda, J. (1988). Is it how you play the game or whether you win or lose?: The effect of competitive level and situation on coaching behaviors. *Journal of Sport Behavior, 11,* 157–174.

Coakley, J. (1993). Socialization and sport. In R. N. Singer, M. Murphey, & L. K. Tennant (Eds.), *Handbook of research in sport psychology* (pp. 571–587). New York: Macmillan.

Cohn, D. A., Patterson, C. J., & Christopoulos, C. (1991). The family and children's peer relations. *Journal of Social and Personal Relationships, 8,* 315–346.

Côté, J., Trudel, P., Bernard, D., Boileau, R., & Marcotte, G. (1993). Observation of coach behaviors during different game score differentials. In C. R. Castaldi, P. J. Bishop, & E. F. Hoerner (Eds.), *Safety in ice hockey: Second Volume ASTM STP 1212* (pp. 78–87). Philadelphia: American Society for Testing and Materials.

Cox, J., & Orlick, T. (1996). Feeling great!: Teaching life skills to children. *Journal of Performance Education, 1,* 100–115.

Davis, R. (1991). Teaching stress management in an elementary classroom. *Journal of Physical Education, Recreation and Dance, 62,* 65–66, 70.

Dubois, P. E. (1981). The youth sport coach as an agent of socialization: An exploratory study. *Journal of Sport Behavior, 4,* 95–107.

Dubois, P. E. (1986). The effects of participation in sports and occupational attainment: A comparative study. *Sociology of Sport Journal, 3,* 29–42.

Edwards, V., & Hofmeier, J. (1991). A stress management program for elementary and special population children. *Journal of Physical Education, Recreation and Dance, 62,* 61–64.

Elliot, S. N., & Gresham, F. M. (1991). *Social skills investigation guide.* Circle Pines, MN: AGS.

Evans, J., & Roberts, G. C. (1987). Physical competence and the development of children's peer relations. *Quest, 39,* 23–35.

Gould, D., & Martens, R. (1979). Attitudes of volunteer coaches toward significant youth sport issues. *Research Quarterly, 3,* 369–380.

Gould, D. (1998). Goal setting for peak performance. In J. M. Williams (Eds.), *Applied sport psychology: Personal growth to peak performance* (pp. 182–196). Mountain View, CA: Mayfield.

Green, B. C., & Chalip, L. (1997). Enduring involvement in youth soccer: The socialization of parent and child. *Journal of Leisure Research, 29,* 61–77.

Greendorfer, S. L. (1992). Sport socialization. In T. S. Horn (Ed.), *Advances in sport psychology* (pp. 201–218). Champaign, IL: Human Kinetics.

Greendorfer, S. L., & Lewko, J. H. (1978). Role of family members in sport socialization of children. *Research Quarterly, 49,* 146–152.

Gresham, F. M., & Elliott, S. N. (1990). *Social skills rating system.* Circle Pines, MN: AGS.

Hastie, P. A., & Saunders, J. E. (1992). A study of task systems and accountability in an elite junior sports setting. *Journal of Teaching in Physical Education, 11,* 376–388.

Horn, T. S. (1985). Coaches' feedback and changes in children's perceptions of their physical competence. *Journal of Educational Psychology, 77,* 174–186.

Horn, T. S. (1987). The influence of teacher–coach behavior on the psychological development of children. In D. Gould & M. R. Weiss (Eds.), *Advances in pediatric sport sciences, vol. 2: Behavioral issues* (pp. 121–142). Champaign, IL: Human Kinetics.

Husman, B. F., & Silva, J. M. (1984). Aggression in sport: Definitional and theoretical considerations. In J. M. Silva & R. S. Weinberg (Eds.), *Psychological foundations of sport* (pp. 246–260). Champaign, IL: Human Kinetics.

Jones, B. J., Wells, L. J., Peters, R. E., & Johnson, D. J. (1993). *Guide to effective coaching: Principles and practice,* 3rd ed. Indianapolis, IN: Brown & Benchmark.

Kleiber, D., & Roberts, G. (1981). The effects of sport experience in the development of social character: An exploratory investigation. *Journal of Sport Psychology, 3,* 114–122.

Kunesh, M. A., & Hasbrook, C. A., & Lewthwaite, R. (1992). Physical activity socialization: Peer interactions and affective responses among a sample of sixth grade girls. *Sociology of Sport Journal, 9,* 385–396.

Lacy, A. C., & Darst, P. W. (1985). Systematic observation of behaviors of winning high school head football coaches. *Journal of Teaching in Physical Education, 4,* 256–270.

Lacy, A. C., & Goldston, P. D. (1990). Behavior analysis of male and female coaches in high school girls' basketball. *Journal of Sport Behavior, 13,* 29–39.

Locke, E. A., & Latham, G. P. (1985). The application of goal setting to sports. *Journal of Sport Psychology, 7,* 205–222.

Magill, R. (1993). Augmented feedback in skill acquisition. In R. N. Singer, M. Murphey & L. K. Tennant (Eds.), *Handbook of research in sport psychology* (pp. 193–212). New York: Macmillan.

Mancini, V. H., Clark, E. K., & Wuest, D. A. (1987). Short- and long-term effects of supervisory feedback on the interaction patterns of an intercollegiate field hockey coach. *Journal of Teaching in Physical Education, 6,* 404–410.

Markland, R., & Martinek, T. J. (1988). Descriptive analysis of coach augmented feedback given to high school varsity female volleyball players. *Journal of Teaching in Physical Education, 4,* 289–301.

Martens, R. (1986). Youth sport in the U.S.A. In M. R. Weiss & D. Gould (Eds.), *Sport for children and youths* (pp. 27–31). Champaign, IL: Human Kinetics.

Martens, R. (1987). *Coaches guide to sport psychology.* Champaign, IL: Human Kinetics.

Martens, R. (1988). Helping children become independent, responsible, adults through sports. In E. W. Brown & C. F. Branta (Eds.), *Competitive sports for children and youth* (pp. 297–308). Champaign, IL: Human Kinetics.

Martens, R. (1990). *Successful coaching.* Champaign IL: Human Kinetics.

McKenzie, T. L. (1986). Analysis of the practice behavior of elite athletes. In M. Piéron & G. Graham (Eds.), *The 1984 Olympic scientific congress proceedings (vol. 6): Sport pedagogy* (pp. 117–121). Champaign, IL: Human Kinetics.

McKenzie, T. L., & King, H. A. (1982). Analysis of feedback provided by youth baseball coaches. *Education and Treatment of Children, 2,* 179–188.

McPherson, B. D. (1982). The child in competitive sport: Influence of the social milieu. In R. Magill, M. Ash, & F. Smoll (Eds.), *Children in sport.* (pp. 247–268). Champaign, IL: Human Kinetics.

Meltzer, M. (1989). A review of research on time in sport pedagogy. *Journal of Teaching in Physical Education, 8,* 87–103.

Nakamura, R. M. (1996). *The power of positive coaching.* Sudbury, MA: Jones and Bartlett.

National Coaching Certification Program. (1988). *Coaching theory level 1.* Gloucester, Ontario: The Coaching Association of Canada.

Orlick, T. (1981). Positive socialization via cooperative games. *Developmental Psychology, 17*(4), 426–429.

Orlick, T. (1993). *Free to feel great: Teaching children to excel at living.* Carp, Ontario: Creative Bound.

Orlick, T. (1995). *Nice on my feelings: Nurturing the best in children and parents.* Carp, Ontario: Creative Bound.

Page, R. M., Frey, J., Talbert, R., & Falk, C. (1992). Children's feelings of loneliness and social dissatisfaction: Relationship to measures of physical fitness and activity. *Journal of Teaching in Physical Education, 11,* 211–219.

Ravizza, K., & Hanson, T. (1995). *Heads-up baseball.* Indianapolis, IN: Masters.

Robertson, I. (1986). Youth sport in the U.S.A. In M. R. Weiss & D. Gould (Eds.), *Sport for children and youths* (pp. 5–10). Champaign, IL: Human Kinetics.

Romance, T., Weiss, M., & Bockovan, J. (1986). A program to promote moral development through elementary school physical education. *Journal of Teachers of Physical Education, 5,* 126–136.

Saffici, C. L. (1996). Coaches: Listening to your players. *The Physical Educator, 53,* 164–168.

Segrave, J. O., & Cianco, C. A. (1990). An observational study of a successful Pop Warner football coach. *Journal of Teaching in Physical Education, 9,* 294–306.

Siedentop, D. (1991). *Developing teaching skills in physical education.* Mountain View, CA: Mayfield.

Silva, J. M. (1983). The perceived legitimacy of rule violating behavior in sport. *Journal of Sport Psychology, 5,* 438–448.

Smith, R. E., & Smoll, F. L. (1990). Self esteem and children's reactions to youth sport coaching behaviors: A field study of self-enhancement processes. *Developmental Psychology, 26,* 987–993.

Smith, R. E., & Smoll, F. L. (1995). Educating youth sport coaches: An applied sport psychology perspective. In J. M. Williams (Eds.), *Applied sport psychology: Personal growth to peak performance,* Mountain View, CA: Mayfield.

Smith, R. E., & Smoll, F. L. (1996a). *Way to go, coach.* Portola Valley, CA: Warde.

Smith, R. E., & Smoll, F. L. (1996b). The coach as a focus of research and intervention in youth sport. In F. L. Smoll & R. E. Smith (Eds.), *Children and youth in sport: A biopsychosocial perspective.* (pp. 125–141). Dubuque, IA: Brown & Benchmark.

Smith, R. E., & Smoll, F. L. (1997). Coach-mediated team building in youth sports. *Journal of Applied Sport Psychology, 9,* 114–132.

Smith, R. E., Smoll, F. L., & Barnett, N. P. (1995). Reduction of children's sport performance anxiety through social support and stress-reduction training for coaches. *Journal of Applied Developmental Psychology, 16,* 125–142

Smith, R. E., Smoll, F. L., & Curtis, B. (1978). Coaching behaviors in little league baseball. In F. L. Smoll & R. E. Smith (Eds.), *Psychological perspectives in youth sports* (pp. 273–201). Washington, DC: Hemisphere.

Smith, R. E., Smoll, F. L., & Hunt, B. (1977). A system for the behavioral assessment of athletic coaches. *The Research Quarterly, 48,* 401–407.

Smith, R. E, Zane, N. W. S., Smoll, F. L., & Coppel, D. B. (1983). Behavioral assessment in youth sport: Coaching behaviors and children's attitudes. *Medicine and Science in Sports and Exercise, 15,* 208–214.

Smoll, F. L., & Smith, R. E. (1996). Competitive anxiety: Sources, consequences, and intervention strategies. In F. L. Smoll & R. E. Smith (Eds.), *Children and youth in sport: A biopsychosocial perspective.* (pp. 359–380). Toronto: Brown & Benchmark.

Smoll, F. L., Smith, R. E., Barnett, N. P., & Everett, J. J. (1993). Enhancement of children's self-esteem through social support training for youth sport coaches. *Journal of Applied Psychology, 78,* 602–610.

Solin, E. "Mental training in the Swedish school systems." Paper presented at the First World Congress on Mental Training, University of Orebro, Sweden, 1991.

Spallanzani, C. (1988). Profil d'entraîneur en hockey mineur et motifs de participation et de démission. *Canadian Journal of Sport Science, 13,* 157–165.

Strean, W. B. (1995). Youth sport contexts: Coaches' perceptions and implications for intervention. *Journal of Applied Sport Psychology, 7,* 23–37.

Strong, J. M. (1992). A dysfunctional and yet winning youth football team. *Journal of Sport Behavior, 15,* 319–326.

Tharp, R. G., & Gallimore, R. (1976). What a coach can teach a teacher. *Psychology Today, 9,* 75–78.

Trudel, P., & Brunelle, J. (1985). Les situations d'apprentissage offertes aux joueurs inscrits dans des ligues de hockey mineur. *L'Association Canadienne pour la Santé, l'Education Physique et le Loisir, 51,* 18–25.

Trudel, P., & Côté, J., (1994). Pédagogie sportive et conditions d'apprentissage. *Enfance, 2–3,* 285–298.

Trudel, P., Côté, J., & Donohue, J. (1993). Direct observation of coaches' behaviors during training and competition: A literature review. In S. Serpa, J. Alves, V. Ferreira, & A. Paula-Brito (Eds.), *Sport psychology: An integrated approach* (pp. 316–320). Lisbon, Portugal: Eighth World Congress of Sport Psychology.

Trudel, P., & Gilbert, W. (1995). Research on coaches' behaviors: Looking beyond the refereed journals. *Avante, 1,* 94–106.

Trudel, P., Guertin, D., Bernard, D., Boileau, R., & Marcotte, G. (1991). Analyse des comportements de l'entraîneur par rapport à la violence au hockey mineur. *Canadian Journal of Sport Science, 16,* 103–109.

Vallerand, R. J. (1983). The effect of differential amounts of positive feedback on the intrinsic motivation of male hockey players. *Journal of Sport Psychology, 5,* 100–107.

Vealey, R. S., & Walter, S. M. (1993). Imagery training for performance enhancement and personal development. In J. M. Williams (Ed.), *Applied sport psychology* (pp. 200–224). Mountain View, CA: Mayfield.

Walton, G. M. (1992). *Beyond winning: The timeless wisdom of great philosopher coaches.* Champaign, IL: Human Kinetics.

Wandzilak, T., Ansorge, C. J., & Potter, G. (1988). Comparison between selected practice and game behaviors of youth sport soccer coaches. *Journal of Sport Behavior, 2,* 78–88.

Weiss, M. R. (1991) Psychological skill development in children and adolescents. *The Sport Psychologist, 5,* 335–354.

Weiss, M. R. (1995). Children in sport: An educational model. In S. M. Murphy (Ed.), *Sport psychology interventions.* Champaign, IL.: Human Kinetics.

Weiss, M. R., & Chaumeton, N. (1992). Motivational orientations in sport. In T. S. Horn (Ed.), *Advances in sport psychology* (pp. 61–99). Champaign, IL: Human Kinetics.

Weiss, M. R., & Duncan, S. C. (1992). The relationship between physical competence and peer acceptance in the context of children's sport participation. *Journal of Sport and Exercise Psychology, 14,* 177–191.

Weiss, M. R., & Petlichkoff, L. M. (1989). Children's motivation for participation in and withdrawal from sport: Identifying the missing links. *Pediatric Exercise Science, 1,* 195–211.

Weiss, M. R., Smith, A. L., & Theeboom, M. (1996). "That's what friends are for": Children's and teenagers perceptions of peer relationships in the sport domain. *Journal of Sport and Exercise Psychology, 18,* 347–379.

Wuest, D. A., Mancini, V. H., Van der Mars, H., & Terrilion, K. (1986). The Academic Learning Time-Physical Education of high-, average-, and low-skilled female intercollegiate volleyball players. In M. Piéron & G. Graham (Eds.), *The 1984 Olympic scientific congress proceedings (vol. 6): Sport pedagogy.* (pp. 123–129). Champaign, IL: Human Kinetics.

Index

Note: Page numbers followed by *f* indicate figures; those followed by *t* indicate tables.